The El
Law Primer for
Corporations

Fifth Edition

Jan Witold Baran

The materials contained herein represent the opinions of the authors and editors and should not be construed to be the action of either the American Bar Association or the Section of Business Law unless adopted pursuant to the bylaws of the Association.

Nothing contained in this book is to be considered as the rendering of legal advice for specific cases, and readers are responsible for obtaining such advice from their own legal counsel. This book and any forms and agreements herein are intended for educational and informational purposes only.

Printed in the United States of America.

10 Digit ISBN: 1-59031-742-4
13 Digit ISBN: 978-1-59031-742-6

Library of Congress Cataloging-in-Publication Data

Baran, Jan W.
    The election law primer for corporations / Jan Baran.—5th ed.
       p.   cm.
    Includes bibliographical references and index.
    ISBN 978-1-59031-742-6
    1. Election law—United States.   2. Corporations—Political activity—
    Law and legislation—United States.   I. Title.

    KF4886.B37 2008
    342.73'07—dc22   2008015410

Discounts are available for books ordered in bulk. Special consideration is given to state and local bars, CLE programs, and other bar-related organizations. Inquire at ABA Publishing, American Bar Association, 321 North Clark Street, Chicago, Illinois 60610.

For a complete list of ABA publications, visit www.ababooks.org.

12 11 10 09 08   5 4 3 2 1

Table of Contents

Preface

In my preface to the last edition of *The Election Law Primer for Corporations,* I noted the expansion of lobbying and political activities in recent decades. The growth in the number of lobbyists, campaign contributors, and political and public-policy campaigns has been accompanied by corresponding growth in regulation. Politics and lobbying, I said, have become full-time, regulated industries.

This fifth edition of *The Primer* reflects the continued expansion of political activity, lobbying, and regulation. The 2008 campaigns for president of the United States are breaking records in terms of the number of candidates, the amounts of money raised and spent, and the number of Americans contributing. The Internet has revolutionized fundraising, and has granted citizens instantaneous access to information.

Similarly, lobbying at all levels of government continues unabated. Legislators and other government officials are incessantly confronted by representatives of every segment of society. When they are perceived as unwelcome nuisances, citizen representatives are pejoratively called lobbyists for special interests. When perceived as helpful, organizations are described as grassroots supporters. In either case, the basic act of lobbying implicates an oft-ignored civil liberty preserved in the First Amendment to the constitution—the right to petition government for the redress of grievances. In 2007, Congress passed, and the president signed, the most far-reaching lobbying law in history, but still attempted to respect constitutional safeguards.

What Is Different in this Edition

The fifth edition of *The Primer* continues its longstanding format. The first portion of the book contains narrative chapters on various topics. Each chapter is supported by end notes that enable the reader to look up sources. The chapters are further supported by the appendix, which contains extensive reference material.

The major additions and revisions in this edition include the following:

1. The chapters pertaining to campaign finance regulation now include explanations that should prove helpful to incorporated trade associations and membership organizations. This is most evident in chapter 2 and the discussion about PACs.
2. A discussion of the effect of the Supreme Court's 2007 decision in *Wisconsin Right to Life v. Federal Election Commission* has been added in chapter 4.
3. The Honest Leadership and Open Government Act of 2007 (HLOGA) has affected chapter 5. The chapter has been reorganized and rewritten to address the new requirements pertaining to federal lobbying disclosure, gifts to House and Senate

officials, and disclosure of lobbyists and organizations that "bundle" campaign contributions.

4. Numerous new and updated forms are included in the appendix. They include the Federal Election Commission disclosure forms, Internal Revenue Service forms, and Lobbying Disclosure Act forms, except LD 203 which was not available at the time of print. Also included are new forms required by the House and Senate Ethics Committees for any travel by congressional officials that will be paid by private entities.

5. The appendix also includes updated resource material, such as lobbying disclosure guidelines, IRS publications, charts on contribution limits, and state-contribution law and enforcement agency Web sites.

Acknowledgments

As with all editions of *The Primer,* I am indebted to others for their assistance. In particular, this book benefits from the contributions of my partners, Caleb Burns and Mark Renaud, who have assisted in updating appendices and making editorial suggestions. I also am grateful for the blue booking assistance of Ryan Schmazle. Finally, I thank Pam Ferrell, the successor to my long-time assistant, Robin Barbee, who retired this past year. Like Robin, Pam was indispensable in the preparation of the manuscript. While I acknowledge the role of these individuals and that of the capable staff of the Business Law Section of the American Bar Association, any shortcomings in this publication are mine.

Jan Witold Baran
Washington, DC
March 2008

1. Introduction

Contents

1.1 USING THE PRIMER

The *Election Law Primer for Corporations* is what its name suggests. It is an introduction to a subject and a summary of basic principles. The original *Primer* was devoted exclusively to the basic principles of federal campaign finance laws that regulated political activity by corporations, executives, employees, and stockholders. Over the years, the *Primer* expanded to related legal areas and now includes explanations about the regulation of lobbying activities, ethics rules, and tax laws.

    The *Primer* consists of nine explanatory chapters (including this introduction) and nine appendices. The extensive materials in the appendices are meant to augment the explanatory chapters and serve as useful reference tools. For example, the FEC forms in appendix A include detailed instructions that further explain what needs to be disclosed by a political action committee, as described in chapter 2. Similarly, the lobbying forms and guidance in appendix D contain extensive information in addition to that found in section 5.4. The same is true of the tax forms in appendix H, which supplement chapter 8. For convenience, the appendix items are printed on the back cover of this book and correlate to black tabs on pages that are visible when the edge of the book faces the reader.

    The *Primer* commences with a discussion about campaign finance rules, political action committees, and campaign communications and activities by and at the corporation. The remaining chapters address lobbying laws, tax considerations, and enforcement. We begin now with campaign finance.

1.2 GENERAL RULE ABOUT CORPORATE POLITICAL ACTIVITY

Under the Federal Election Campaign Act (FECA), all corporations, including incorporated trade associations and not-for-profit membership corporations, are barred from making contributions to—and expenditures on behalf of—candidates for federal office.[1] This broad prohibition applies to the use of corporate funds in connection with conventions, as well as primary, special, and general elections at which candidates for senator, U.S.

representative, or president are either nominated or elected.[2] The Federal Election Commission (FEC) construes the law as barring the use of corporate funds and resources for the direct or indirect benefit of any federal candidate or any political organization that supports federal candidates.[3]

The concept of contributions encompasses more than just direct money payments. A contribution is something of value used in connection with a federal election. For example, the use of corporate facilities and personnel for campaign purposes, the reimbursement of corporate personnel for political contributions, or the payment of continued health and retirement benefits for an employee who takes unearned leave to campaign on behalf of a candidate generally constitute illegal corporate contributions. A corporate loan of funds to, or for the use of, political parties or candidates is illegal (unless made by certain lending institutions).

Other corporate resources, including aircraft, automobiles, offices, equipment, phones, credit cards, administrative services, and trade marks, are "something of value," and may not be given to candidates, political parties, or political committees unless paid for at fair market value. Reimbursing employees for political contributions generally is illegal, and particularly is illegal when corporate money is used.

TEST

To determine whether a disbursement or activity is governed by federal law, ask the following questions:

- Is something of value being given or made available to a federal candidate or political committee by the corporation?
- Is the activity or disbursement related to an election to federal office?

If the answer to either question is yes, then the corporate disbursement probably is barred or in some way regulated by federal election laws.

1.3   EXCEPTIONS

The law and the FEC provide many exceptions to the general rule that corporate political contributions are illegal. These exceptions allow significant, direct corporate political action through the use of a corporation's funds and resources. The exceptions permit: the establishment, administration, and solicitation of contributions to a separate segregated fund (commonly referred to as a political action committee, or PAC);[4] any type of communication to a corporation's stockholders and executive or administrative personnel and their families, as well as certain nonpartisan communication, registration, and get-out-the-vote campaigns aimed at employees and the general public;[5] and the use of corporate facilities and property, subject to conditions set forth in FEC regulations.[6]

These general exceptions are discussed in detail later in this *Primer*. In addition, there are other very specific activities that may be financed with corporate dollars. These activities include:

- **Political activity in connection with state and local elections** (unless regulated by state law—see chapter 7), except that foreign corporations, national banks, and federally chartered corporations are barred from financing any elections, whether federal, state, or local.[7]

- **Payment of legal or accounting services** rendered to or on behalf of a political party or a candidate's authorized committee or any other political committee, but only if the services are performed by the company's regularly employed personnel. The services must be solely for the purpose of ensuring compliance with the federal election laws,[8] and may not be attributable to activities that directly further the election of candidates for federal office.[9] A corporation is not allowed, however, to provide personal computers to selected candidates for use in doing the accounting necessary to comply with federal campaign laws.[10]
- **Anything of value given to a state committee of a political party to defray any cost incurred in the construction or purchase of any office facility** that is not acquired for the purpose of influencing the election of any candidate for federal office (the political parties often refer to this exception as the "building fund" exception).[11] State law dictates whether and how much corporations may contribute. This exception became unavailable to national committees of political parties beginning on November 6, 2002.[12]
- **The sale of food or beverages at a charge** at least equal to the corporate vendor's cost up to $1,000 for each candidate per election, and up to $2,000 in a calendar year as to all committees of each political party.[13]
- **Commercial transactions**, unless a political aspect dominates the commercial aspect of the transaction.[14] Generally, a corporation may provide services at the usual and normal charge to a political committee.[15]
- **Unreimbursed volunteer personal services,**[16] such as stuffing envelopes, canvassing, entertainment at fund-raising events,[17] or radio commercials by corporate officers.[18]
- **Loans** by state banks or federally chartered institutions or federally insured depository institutions made in the ordinary course of business, in accordance with applicable banking law and under several other conditions.[19]
- **Extension of credit** to candidates or political committees in connection with a federal election if:
  - the credit is extended in the ordinary course of the corporation's business; and
  - the terms are substantially similar to extensions of credit under similar circumstances to nonpolitical debtors.[20]

  Such debts may be forgiven if the corporation has treated the outstanding debt in a commercially reasonable manner in accordance with federal regulations, or the amount forgiven is exempted from the definition of "contribution."[21]
- **News stories,** if they are bona fide news accounts in a publication, or a broadcast or other medium not owned by a political party or candidate.[22]
- **The cost of providing the use of residential premises** and community meeting rooms.[23]
- **Unreimbursed transportation expenses of a volunteer worker** up to $1,000 on behalf of a candidate per election, and $2,000 on behalf of all political committees of each political party per year.[24]
- **Unreimbursed living expenses** of a volunteer in connection with volunteer services.[25]
- **Hospitality suites** at national political party conventions.[26]
- **National political party convention** "host committees" may accept donations from businesses.[27] Corporations may provide goods and services without charge, in exchange for promotional consideration, to national party convention committees.[28]

- **"Levin Money"** contributions by corporations can be made to state and local political parties to finance political activity, as long as: the activity does not refer to a clearly identified candidate for federal office; the activity is not broadcast, unless it refers solely to a state or local candidate; the contributions are paid in accordance with state law, but not in excess of $10,000 per year; and the contributions are raised by that particular state or local party and are not provided by any other national, state, or local party.[29]

NOTES

1. 2 U.S.C. § 441b(a) (2000). For the definition of what the terms "contribution" and "expenditure" do and do not include, *see* 2 U.S.C. §§ 431(8)-(9) (2000 & Supp. III 2003); 11 C.F.R. § 114.1(a) (2006).
2. 2 U.S.C. § 441b(a) (2000).
3. 11 C.F.R. § 114.2(a) (2006).
4. 2 U.S.C. § 441b(b)(2)(C) (Supp. III 2003); 11 C.F.R. § 114.1(a)(2)(iii) (2006).
5. 2 U.S.C. §§ 441b(b)(2)(A)-(B) (Supp. III 2003); 11 C.F.R. §§ 114.1(a)(2)(i)-(ii), 114.4(c) (2006).
6. 11 C.F.R. § 114.9 (2006).
7. 2 U.S.C. § 441b(a) (2000); 11 C.F.R. § 114.2(a) (2006).
8. 2 U.S.C. § 431(8)(B)(viii) (2000 & Supp. III 2003); 11 C.F.R. § 114.1(a)(2)(vii) (2006).
9. 11 C.F.R. § 114.1(a)(2)(vi) (2006).
10. FEC Advisory Opinion 1989-13, Fed. Election Camp. Fin. Guide (CCH) ¶ 5963 (1989).
11. 2 U.S.C. § 453(b) (Supp. III 2003).
12. 11 C.F.R. § 114.1(a)(2)(ix) (2006).
13. 2 U.S.C. § 431(8)(B)(iii) (2000); 11 C.F.R. §§ 100.78, 114.1(a)(2)(v) (2006).
14. *See, e.g.*, FEC Advisory Opinion 1976-50, Fed. Election Camp. Fin. Guide (CCH) ¶ 5214 (1976) (corporation may not produce T-shirts with candidate's name on them and provide campaign committee with a commission for each shirt sold).
15. FEC Advisory Opinion 1990-1, Fed. Election Camp. Fin. Guide (CCH) ¶ 5980 (1990) (corporation may provide a "900" line phone service to candidates and committees for fundraising purposes); FEC Advisory Opinion 1996-2, Fed. Election Camp. Fin. Guide (CCH) ¶ 6188 (1996) (Internet service provider not permitted to provide free service to candidate).
16. 2 U.S.C. § 431(8)(B)(i) (2000); 11 C.F.R. § 100.74 (2006).
17. FEC Advisory Opinion 1975-97, Fed. Election Camp. Fin. Guide (CCH) ¶ 5150 (1975).
18. FEC Advisory Opinion 1978-77, Fed. Election Camp. Fin. Guide (CCH) ¶ 5365 (1978).
19. 2 U.S.C. § 431(8)(B)(vii) (2000); 11 C.F.R. § 114.1(a)(1) (2006).
20. 11 C.F.R. § 116.3(b) (2006).
21. 11 C.F.R. § 116.4(b) (2006).
22. 2 U.S.C. § 431(9)(B)(i) (2000); 11 C.F.R. §§ 100.73, 100.132 (2006); *see also* FEC Advisory Opinion 1980-90, Fed. Election Camp. Fin. Guide (CCH) ¶ 5538 (1980); Reader's Digest Ass'n v. FEC, 509 F. Supp. 1210 (S.D.N.Y. 1981).
23. 11 C.F.R. §§ 100.75, 100.76, 100.135, 100.136 (2006).
24. 2 U.S.C. § 431(8)(B)(iv) (2000); 11 C.F.R. §§ 100.79, 100.139 (2006).
25. 11 C.F.R. §§ 100.79, 100.139 (2006).
26. FEC Advisory Opinion 1983-23, Fed. Election Camp. Fin. Guide (CCH) ¶ 5728 (1983); Public Financing of Presidential Candidate and Nominating Conventions, 68 Fed. Reg. 47,386, 47,405 (Aug. 8, 2003).
27. 11 C.F.R. § 9008.52 (2006).
28. 11 C.F.R. § 9008.9 (2006).
29. 2 U.S.C. §§ 441i(b)(2)(B)(i)-(iv) (Supp. III 2003).

2. Political Action Committees

Contents

2.1   INTRODUCTION

A corporation may spend corporate funds to establish, administer, and solicit contributions to its political action committee (PAC) and use the PAC for political purposes.[1] For example, a corporation may pay for the costs associated with sponsoring a PAC fundraiser, including printing invitations, renting a room, and supplying food.[2] A corporation's executive or administrative personnel, its stockholders, and the families of these groups may be solicited for voluntary, political contributions.[3] A corporation also may solicit contributions from the executive and administrative personnel (and their families) of its subsidiaries, branches, divisions, and affiliates.[4] A corporation may solicit other employees with some restrictions.[5] The solicitation rules are discussed in section 2.8.

The income, expenditures, solicitations, and political direction of the PAC are completely under the control of the corporation, although the funds must be "separate" and "segregated" from corporate funds.[6] For this reason, the FECA statute and FEC regulations refer to corporate PACs as "separate segregated funds." In essence, the PAC is a vehicle for combining individual contributions to candidates whose views toward business and government are in accord with those of the corporation.

2.2   REGISTRATION

A PAC must register with the FEC.[7] To register, a PAC must file a Statement of Organization on FEC Form 1 (see appendix A) within ten days after the date of organization.[8] A PAC generally is held to be established and registration requirements for it are triggered by:

- a vote by the board of directors or comparable governing body to create a PAC;
- selection of initial PAC officers; or
- a payment by the corporation of the initial operating expenses of the PAC.[9]

The statement of organization, all FEC disclosure reports, and any required disclaimers must include the full name of the PAC, and that name must incorporate the full, official name of the sponsoring corporation, including such abbreviations as "Inc." and "Corp."[10] An acronym or abbreviation may be used at other times if it is one that is commonly known or clearly recognized. To determine whether specific names meet this requirement, the FEC has considered various factors, such as the use of the term in the company trademark or service mark, stock exchange identification, financial reference sources and directories, the corporate Web site, and the corporate annual report.[11] Therefore, "ANR" was not an acceptable acronym for "American Natural Resources, Inc." because it was not "clearly recognized outside of the company."[12] On the other hand, "EQUI-PAC" was an acceptable acronym for "Equitable Life Assurance PAC" because the company had registered "EQUI" as a trademark.[13]

In addition to the name of the PAC, the statement of organization must also disclose the following:

- address and type of committee;
- name, address, relationship, and type of any connected organization or affiliated committee;
- name, address, and position of the custodian of books and accounts of the committee;

- name and address of the treasurer of the committee;
- whether the committee is authorized by a candidate; and
- a listing of all banks, safety deposit boxes, or other depositories used by the committee.[14]

Once registered, the PAC must notify the FEC of any change to the information in the statement within ten days of the change.[15] For example, an amendment to the FEC Form 1 would have to be filed if the corporation changed its name or address or if there were a new PAC treasurer. Corporate mergers often will require amendments to reveal newly affiliated PACs. When the PAC attains the status of a "multicandidate committee" (see section 2.10), it must file a Form 1M notifying the FEC of that fact.[16] A copy of Form 1M can be found in appendix A. If the PAC decides to disband, it must file a termination report with the FEC stating that it will no longer receive any contributions nor make any expenditures, that it has no outstanding debts or obligations and—after filing a final report of receipts and disbursements—how any residual funds will be used.[17]

2.3 STRUCTURE AND OFFICERS

In most respects, a PAC is like any other political committee. Accordingly, the only officer required by law is a treasurer.[18] The treasurer is responsible for recordkeeping and reporting obligations.[19] Other officers or organizational documents are not required. However, because no contribution can be accepted—nor expenditure made—when the treasurer's office is vacant,[20] an assistant treasurer should be named to serve in the treasurer's absence.[21]

A PAC need not adopt governing documents, such as articles and bylaws, unless the PAC becomes incorporated, at which point the law of the state of incorporation governs these issues. The treasurer of an incorporated PAC remains personally responsible for carrying out his or her respective duties under FECA whether the PAC incorporates or not.[22] Governing documents may be useful, however, both to organize PAC activities and to provide guidance to PAC officers. Such bylaws, if adopted, should set forth:

- the name of the PAC;
- the PAC's purpose;
- a description of the PAC's officers and committees, their powers and responsibilities, and the method of appointing them;
- the means of amending the bylaws;
- criteria for the selection of recipients of PAC contributions; and
- disposition of funds upon dissolution of the PAC.

Sample by-laws are included in appendix B.

2.4 DEPOSITORY

A PAC must have an account with a bank or other depository that is separate from the funds of the sponsoring corporation. Although the sponsoring corporation may use its funds to pay for the cost of the PAC's establishment, administration, and solicitation of political contributions, such funds must be segregated from PAC contributions collected under federal election laws. PAC funds cannot be commingled with personal or corporate funds.[23]

2.5   ADMINISTRATIVE EXPENSES AND CONTROL

A corporation that sponsors a PAC may pay the cost of establishing, administering, and soliciting contributions to the PAC. Permissible expenses include the cost of office space, phones, salaries, utilities, supplies, travel to PAC meetings and other fundraising events (including fundraising events sponsored by political parties),[24] legal and accounting fees, and other costs incurred in setting up and running a PAC.[25] A corporation, under certain conditions, may pay insurance premiums for liability insurance for PAC officers and members[26] and for indemnification of PAC officers or employees for fines, judgments, or settlements resulting from PAC activities.[27] A corporation may make matching charitable donations on behalf of PAC donors.[28]

A corporation also may pay for gifts to PAC contributors if it follows the "one-third rule." Under the one-third rule, a corporation may pay no more than one-third of the funds raised for raffle prizes, entertainment, or other fundraising devices (for example, a $50 pen and pencil set to contributors of $1,000 is permissible because the gift set costs the corporation less than $333).[29] On the other hand, PAC income taxes on interest and investment income are not administrative costs "incurred in the pursuit of voluntary contributions, the maintenance of those contributions, or the utilization of those contributions for political purposes," and may not be paid by the corporation.[30]

The sponsoring corporation may exercise complete control over its PAC.[31] The corporation's board of directors, its managers, or any other designated group may determine which candidates receive PAC contributions.

2.6   REPORTING

The PAC's treasurer must maintain the PAC's records[32] and submit regular reports to the FEC.[33] All receipts and disbursements of the PAC must be recorded and reported. The treasurer is personally responsible for the timely and complete filing of any required report and for the accuracy of any information provided. However, if the treasurer can show that "best efforts" have been used to complete these reports, he or she shall be deemed in compliance and not strictly liable for omissions or inaccuracies.[34]

The FEC requires a PAC to file electronically when either its total contributions or total expenditures exceed, or are expected to exceed, $50,000 in a calendar year.[35] PACs otherwise may file electronically or on paper forms. All electronic reports will be checked against the FEC's validation program before the reports will be accepted, in order to confirm that they are in the correct electronic format. All amendments to electronically filed reports also must be filed electronically. The PAC's treasurer shall verify the report by submitting a signed certification on paper that is submitted with the computerized media or by submitting a digitized copy of the signed certification as a separate file in the electronic submission. Finally, a machine-readable copy of the report, as well as an original signed version of all electronic documents, must be maintained.[36]

Several software vendors have programs for FEC filings. The FEC also provides a program for electronic filing, which can be found at www.fec.gov. In order to file electronically, the treasurer must obtain a password from the FEC, so advance preparation is necessary. Copies of all reports, registrations, and amendments are available to the public at the FEC and on the agency's Web site.

Filing Frequency for Reports

A PAC may elect one of two reporting cycles. One schedule requires monthly reporting; the other requires quarterly reporting in an election year and semiannual reporting in a nonelection year. The latter schedule, however, requires preelection reports with respect to each primary election in which the PAC has contributed to a candidate.[37] Monthly filers, however, do not have to file pre-primary election reports or pre-special election reports. These reports easily can outnumber the frequency of monthly reports. For that reason, PACs that contribute to candidates in numerous and different primary elections ordinarily elect monthly reporting, particularly during an election year, to reduce reporting frequency. Reporting cycles may be changed once a year.[38]

In an election year, PACs on a monthly reporting schedule must file as follows:

- on the twentieth day of each month, covering the previous month's activity, except for November and December;
- a year-end report by January 31 of the following year;
- a preelection report twelve days before the November general election; and
- a postelection report thirty days after the November general election.[39]

PACs on quarterly reporting schedule must file in an election year as follows:

- on the fifteenth day of April, July, and October;
- a year-end report by January 31 of the following year;
- a preelection report twelve days preceding each primary election in which a candidate has received support and twelve days preceding each general election in which a candidate has received support; and
- a postelection report thirty days after each general election in which a candidate has received support. (No post-primary report is required.)[40]

In a nonelection year, a PAC that has chosen to file on a quarterly cycle must file semiannual reports covering January 1 through June 30 by July 31, and covering July 1 through December 31 by January 31,[41] or monthly reports due on the twentieth day of each month.[42] Contributions to candidates in special elections held to fill vacancies will trigger additional reports.

There is no such thing as an "extension" to file a report. A report is due on the exact date specified—even if the day falls on a Saturday, Sunday, or holiday. The FEC does not entertain or grant requests for additional time within which to file a report.

If PAC reports are filed late or not at all, the FEC may impose a fine under its administrative fines program, rather than choosing to resort to its traditional procedures of filing suit or negotiating a conciliation agreement.[43] The size of the monetary fine will be based on multiple factors, including the amount of money that was received and disbursed by the PAC, the number of days the report is filed beyond the deadline, and the number of previous violations.[44]

Contents of Reports

Each report must include:

- the amount of cash on hand at the beginning of the reporting period;[45]
- itemized contributions from donors aggregating over $200 in the calendar year;[46]

- the total of unitemized contributions;
- transfers from affiliated committees;[47]
- loans;[48]
- rebates, refunds, and other offsets to operating expenditures;[49] and
- dividends, interest, and other receipts.[50]

Each report must contain the name, address, occupation, and name of employer for: each individual that contributes in excess of $200 annually,[51] each individual that provides rebates, refunds, or other offsets to operating expenditures over $200 in a calendar year,[52] sources of dividends or interest in excess of $200 annually,[53] and any other sources of receipts totaling over $200 in a calendar year. The report also must include all disbursements for, and the identities and addresses of, those who receive:

- committee operating expenses (except for those paid by the corporation);[54]
- transfers to affiliated committees;[55]
- repayment of loans or any loans made to others;[56]
- independent expenditures;[57]
- contributions to candidates or other political committees;[58] and
- any other disbursements.

The amount and nature of outstanding debts and obligations owed to or by the PAC, and debts settled for less than their reported amount or value also must be reported.[59] Regulations under the federal election laws should be consulted for more specific categories of receipts and disbursements that must be reported by a PAC. All PAC reports are filed on FEC Form 3X: Report of Receipts and Disbursements (a copy of Form 3X and its instructions can be found in appendix A). PACs also must send a copy of the report to the secretary of state in each state or territory in which the PAC has made a contribution or expenditure with respect to a House or Senate candidate.[60] However, if the FEC certifies that a state provides adequate public access to online FEC reports, this requirement will be waived.[61] To date, all fifty states, as well as American Samoa and the Virgin Islands, have received FEC certification. Puerto Rico and Guam are the only jurisdictions that have not.

For reporting purposes, a PAC describes the things of value it receives as "contributions" and the disbursements it makes to candidates and other committees as "expenditures." Anything of value provided by the PAC, such as direct or indirect payments, gifts, subscriptions, loans, advances, or services—made for the purpose of influencing a federal election—must be reported.

In-kind contributions, such as donated goods or services, must be reported at their "usual and normal," or fair-market, value.[62] Common stock or art objects are reported as a memo entry when they are received, and as cash contributions after their sale. The memo entry must identify the contributor and, if the fair market value of the contribution exceeds $200, the contributor's occupation and name of employer. After the sale of an item for more than $200, the contributor and the purchaser must be identified along with their occupations and names of employers.[63]

For all other contributions, the treasurer must record the name and address of individuals contributing more than $50 in the aggregate. For contributions exceeding $200, the contributor's occupation and name of employer also must be identified. In reporting information about contributors, the PAC's treasurer is deemed to have exercised his or her "best efforts" if each PAC solicitation contains a clear request for the information and makes at least one additional attempt (by phone or mail) to obtain the information after the contribution is received.[64]

Internal Controls

Because PACs can raise and spend large sums of money, this has led to instances of embezzlement. For years, the FEC declined to take any enforcement action after the embezzler had been referred to criminal law enforcement and/or made restitution to the victimized committee. However, the frequency of embezzlements prompted the FEC to start seeking penalties and corrective actions against the committees. The FEC concluded that embezzlement causes inaccurate and false reports to be filed with it, and such inaccurate reports are the result of insufficient internal controls.

In 2007, the FEC issued a statement of policy that it would not take action against a defrauded committee if it could demonstrate that the embezzlement occurred notwithstanding the presence of, and adherence to, specific internal controls.[65] This "safe harbor" policy is contained in appendix I, and includes additional guidance from the FEC audit staff on internal controls and best practices.

2.7   RECORDKEEPING

Records and accounts of all contributions and expenditures, and copies of all reports, must be preserved by the treasurer for three years.[66] During this time, the FEC or its authorized representative may audit, inspect, or examine the records.

The records must include:

- all contributions received by or on behalf of the PAC;
- the name and address of any individual whose contribution is in excess of $50, with the date and amount of the contribution;
- the identification of any contributor of more than $200 during the calendar year, with the date and amount of the contribution;
- the identification of any political committee making a contribution, with the date and amount; and
- the name and address of every person to whom a disbursement is made; the date, amount, and purpose of the disbursement; the name and office sought of any candidate for whom the disbursement is made; and a receipt, invoice, or cancelled check for each disbursement in excess of $200.[67]

All contributions exceeding $50 must be deposited within ten days of receipt and all other contributions must be deposited within thirty days.[68]

2.8   FUNDRAISING AND THE "RESTRICTED CLASS"

Federal election laws restrict the class of persons to whom solicitations may be directed, and broadly define the term "solicitation." Solicitations of persons other than those permitted by law are illegal. It is important, therefore, to understand what constitutes a solicitation and who may be solicited.

What Is a Solicitation?

A request for a contribution to a PAC is the most obvious example of a solicitation. This includes asking persons to buy tickets to a fund-raising event[69] or a raffle,[70] or operating a fund-raising booth at a trade association convention.[71] An announcement of the PAC's establishment is not a solicitation unless recipients are encouraged to contribute, praised for their contributions, or given information about how to contribute.[72] Factual, historical, or statistical information about a PAC may be disseminated without being construed as a solicitation.[73]

Who May Be Solicited? The "Restricted Class"

Generally, a corporation or its PAC is barred from soliciting contributions from anyone other than its stockholders and its executive or administrative personnel and their respective families.[74] The FEC calls this group the "restricted class," a term that will be used throughout this discussion and in the later sections on corporate political communication. The corporation may solicit its own restricted class and the executive or administrative personnel and families of the corporation's subsidiaries, branches, and affiliates.[75] PACs of affiliated corporations, parents, and subsidiaries may solicit the others' executive or administrative personnel.[76] Franchisers may solicit the administrative or executive personnel of a franchisee.[77] Similarly, if a corporation has a sufficient degree of control over the operations of its licensees, its PAC may solicit the employees of the licensees.[78] In addition, the PAC of a corporation may solicit the members of the partnership that controls the corporation.[79]

In general, whether members of the restricted class of another corporation can be solicited depends upon whether that corporation is "affiliated" with the PAC's connected corporation. A corporation and its subsidiaries are *per se* affiliated, and other entities may be affiliated if facts indicate that one entity was established, financed, maintained, or controlled by another.[80]

Employees who are neither stockholders nor executive or administrative personnel are not in the restricted class. A corporation or PAC may address only two written solicitations during the calendar year to nonrestricted-class employees, subject to certain restrictions.[81]

The restricted class is slightly larger for nonbusiness corporations. Although such entities may have executive or administrative personnel, they often will have no stockholders to solicit. Instead, other persons are part of the restricted class. For example, an incorporated membership organization may solicit its individual members and their families in addition to any executive or administrative personnel and their families.[82] A trade association may solicit the executive or administrative personnel and stockholders of any of its member corporations, provided that the trade group first receives written permission to do so from its corporate members.[83] Trade association PACs may not, however, solicit the individual members of unincorporated member associations.[84] For more information about PACs formed by nonstock corporations, see section 2.13.

Accidental or inadvertent solicitations of nonmembers of the restricted class do not violate the law if "best efforts" at compliance and immediate correction after discovery are undertaken.[85] The PAC may accept unsolicited contributions from persons outside the restricted class, provided that the donation is not otherwise barred by law.[86] Under no circumstances may a corporation or its PAC solicit the general public or other unaffiliated PACs for contributions.

Stockholders. Stockholders are those individuals who have a vested interest in stock, the power to direct how that stock shall be voted, and the right to receive dividends.[87] Under certain conditions, participation in an employee stock plan is sufficient criteria for legal solicitation as a stockholder.[88] Bondholders or holders of any interest classified as a debt are not stockholders under the law.[89] Although the regulations make clear that a corporation may solicit its subsidiaries' and affiliates' executive or administrative personnel,[90] the regulations do not provide for solicitation of those organizations' stockholders. The FEC, however, has allowed wholly owned subsidiaries to solicit the stockholders of their parent corporations as well as the stockholders of any other affiliated subsidiaries.[91]

Executive or administrative personnel. Individuals who are paid a salary—rather than an hourly wage—and who have policymaking, managerial, professional, or supervisory responsibilities are considered executive or administrative personnel.[92] This includes corporate officers and executives; plant, division, and section managers;[93] and professionals such as lawyers and engineers.[94] Corporate directors may be solicited only if they are stockholders or receive a regular salary or fee from the corporation.[95] Professionals represented by labor unions,[96] salaried lower-level supervisors of hourly employees, former or retired personnel, or consultants not subject to withholding taxes[97] are not executive or administrative personnel. However, if such individuals qualify as stockholders, they may be solicited.

Manner of Solicitation

Federal election laws are specific about the permissible means of making solicitations.

How often: Members of the restricted class may be solicited as often as the PAC desires. Other employees who are not stockholders may be solicited only twice annually and under a restrictive program.

Voluntariness: It is unlawful to obtain contributions by use or threat of physical force, job discrimination, or financial reprisal. PAC contributions cannot be a condition of employment.[98] A superior, however, may solicit a subordinate.[99]

Notices: At the time of solicitation, an employee must be informed of the political purpose of the PAC and of his or her right to refuse to contribute without fear of reprisal.[100]

Suggested contribution amount and additional notices: Contribution amounts may be suggested to employees by a corporation or its PAC, as long as it is made clear that the guidelines: are only suggestions; will not be enforced; and that the individual can contribute in whatever amount he or she desires without reprisal.[101] A PAC cannot set minimum or maximum limits for acceptable contributions.

Reverse check-off systems or payroll deduction plans whereby amounts are automatically deducted unless the employee requests otherwise are illegal.[102]

Payroll deduction plans may be used to collect contributions from the restricted class unless they constitute a reverse check-off.[103]

Contributions by credit card may be solicited by a PAC to be made through advance authorization of credit card charges.[104]

Secretaries/Assistants: Solicitations directed to a member of the restricted class may be routed through that person's secretary or assistant, even though the secretary or assistant is not a solicitable person.[105]

Electronic signatures by computer may be used by the restricted class to authorize payroll deductions.[106]

Nonexecutive employees: Employees who are not within the restricted class may be solicited by the corporation only twice per year for contributions to its PAC.[107] This is a very limited privilege. These twice-yearly solicitations must be made:

- in writing (a videotaped solicitation may be included with the written solicitation, as long as it meets all other requirements);[108]
- by mailing them to employees at their residences and not making solicitations at work;
- by providing that contributions be returned to a third-party custodian who will preserve the anonymity of those contributors donating under $50 and those employees who choose not to contribute; and
- by limiting the mailing to solicitation purposes.

The corporation may not use a payroll deduction plan or check-off system in order to facilitate collection of contributions by nonmembers of the restricted class. The recipient must be informed: of the third-party custodial arrangement set up by the corporation; of the fact that the corporation or its PAC cannot be told who does not contribute; of the political nature of the PAC; and that an employee may refuse to contribute without reprisal.

2.9   AVAILABILITY OF CORPORATE PAC SOLICITATION METHODS TO UNIONS

The methods used by a corporation to solicit or facilitate the making of voluntary contributions to its PAC, such as through payroll deductions, must be made available upon written request to any labor organization representing anyone working for the corporation or its subsidiaries, branches, or affiliates.[109] The corporation itself need not solicit union members for the labor union, but it must make all means it uses available to the union. For example, if the corporation uses a computer, it must make that computer available to the union and do any necessary reprogramming.[110] The union, however, must pay sufficient reimbursement to cover expenses incurred by the corporation.[111]

A corporation must make available to a union, upon written request, any payroll deduction plan or check-off system being used to collect funds from the corporation's restricted class. The payroll deduction can then be used by the union to collect contributions to the union PAC from its restricted class—the union members. Again, the union must reimburse the corporation for expenses.[112]

A corporation that makes a twice-yearly solicitation of employees must make its methods available to a labor union representing any members working for the corporation or its subsidiaries, branches, or affiliates.[113] This reciprocal right permits unions to solicit nonunion employees for PAC contributions under the twice-yearly solicitation procedure described above. The corporation must notify the union of its intent to make any twice-yearly solicitation. It must also inform the union of the method it will use. This notification must be done within a reasonable time prior to the solicitation to enable the union to make a similar solicitation.[114]

2.10   RESTRICTIONS ON CONTRIBUTIONS TO A PAC

Dollar Limits on Contributions to the PAC

On January 1, 2003, the Bipartisan Campaign Reform Act (BCRA) increased certain limitations on contributions. Prior to 2003, federal law limited an individual to

$5,000 in annual contributions to any one political committee[115] and $25,000 annually in the aggregate to all candidates, committees, and other recipients.[116] The BCRA did not change the amount that a PAC may receive from another PAC ($5,000 per year), but because other PACs are not within the restricted class, the contributions may not be solicited.[117]

The BCRA did not change the annual limit on individual contributions to any one PAC, and the limit remained $5,000. However, aggregate contributions to all candidates, committees, and other recipients increased from $25,000 annually[118] to $95,000 for any two-year election cycle. In establishing new aggregate limits on individuals, the BCRA also provided for adjustments every election cycle to reflect increases in the inflation rate. Therefore, the limits from the 2003-04 election were increased for the 2005-06 election, and those limits were increased again for 2007-08. Charts reflecting the contribution limits for each of these election cycles appear in appendix C. Charts for the 2009-10 election cycle will be available on the FEC Web site in early 2009.

The overall biennial limit on all contributions by an individual during the 2007-2008 election cycle is $108,200. In calculating this limit, the following special rules apply:

- of this $108,200, a maximum of $42,700 may be contributed to candidates;
- of this $108,200, a maximum of $65,500 may be contributed to all other political committees; and
- of the $65,500 allowed to be contributed to political committees, a maximum of $42,700 may be contributed to PACs, state party committees, and other political committees that are not national party committees.[119]

There are no limits on transfers between affiliated political committees of funds raised through joint fundraising efforts.[120] As discussed, affiliated committees are committees that are established, financed, maintained, or controlled by the same group of people.[121] PACs set up by a single corporation and/or its subsidiaries are treated as affiliated committees.[122]

The charts in appendix C depict all federal contribution limits post-BCRA. Limits will be adjusted for inflation in future election cycles.

Prohibited Contributions

The PAC may not accept illegal contributions, and PAC officers are prohibited from knowingly accepting any contribution that is barred by the election laws.[123] It is the treasurer's responsibility to prevent acceptance of such contributions by maintaining adequate records. Illegal contributions include the following:

- contributions in excess of the contribution limits described above;
- contributions from other corporations,[124] national banks,[125] or federal government contractors;[126]
- contributions from noncitizens of the United States who have not been admitted for permanent residence;[127]
- contributions made in the name of another person; and[128]
- cash contributions exceeding $100 per contributor per year.[129]

Although the BCRA prohibited children under the age of eighteen from contributing to candidates and political parties, it did not similarly prohibit minors from contributing to PACs.[130] Regardless, the Supreme Court declared the ban on certain contributions by minors unconstitutional, and minors are again permitted to contribute under certain conditions set forth in FEC regulations.[131]

A loan from a corporation—including the PAC's sponsor—should not be used for contributions or expenditures on behalf of candidates because that would be an illegal contribution. Corporate funds should be used for establishment, administration, and solicitation purposes only. A corporation's funds cannot be used for voluntary contributions via bonuses, expense accounts, or other compensation to contributors as reimbursement for their contributions to the PAC.[132] Not only does this constitute an illegal corporate contribution, it also may be construed as a subtle form of coercion and even money laundering.[133]

Interest from the PAC's savings and other income-producing accounts may be deposited into the PAC's account.[134] The PAC must pay tax on interest exceeding $100 annually (see chapter 8).

2.11   RESTRICTIONS ON CONTRIBUTIONS AND EXPENDITURES BY THE PAC

Although FECA uses similar language to define the terms "contributions" and "expenditures,"[135] the Supreme Court has drawn a constitutional distinction between the terms.[136] Contributions are things of value received by a committee and are subject to a $5,000 annual limit per donor.[137] In contrast, PACs may make unlimited expenditures if they are "independent" expenditures.[138] Coordinated—or "nonindependent"—expenditures, however, are deemed contributions and therefore are subject to contribution limits.

Dollar Limits on Contributions by the PAC

How much a PAC may contribute to a candidate depends upon whether the PAC qualifies as a "multicandidate committee." A multicandidate committee is a political committee that has: been registered for at least six months; received contributions from more than fifty persons; and made contributions to five or more candidates for federal office.[139] The PAC must file Form 1M when it attains "multicandidate committee" status.[140] (See appendix C for post-BCRA contribution limits.) PAC contribution limits are not adjusted for inflation. Other limits are adjusted every election cycle.

Multicandidate nonparty committees are subject to the following contribution limits:

- $5,000 per candidate—or the candidate's authorized political committees—per election (i.e., $5,000 per primary, general, and special election);
- $15,000 to national party committees per calendar year; and
- $5,000 to any other political committee per year.[141]

Contributions by a PAC that is not a multicandidate committee used to be limited to the following amounts:

- $1,000 per candidate—or the candidate's authorized committees—per election;
- $20,000 to national party committees per calendar year; and
- $5,000 to any other political committee per year.[142]

The BCRA increased the non-multicandidate committee limits, which for the 2007-08 cycle are:

- $2,300 per candidate or the candidate's authorized committees per election; and
- $28,500 to national party committees per calendar year.[143]

Affiliated Committees

PACs that are established, financed, maintained, or controlled by the same group of people are deemed "affiliated" and are treated as one committee.[144] Contributions by two or more affiliated committees to a particular candidate are subject to a single contribution limit, as though the donations were only from a single committee. Hence, all PACs established by a corporation and its subsidiaries are subject to one contribution limit.[145] Corporations cannot circumvent contribution limits by establishing a number of PACs among subsidiaries, with each able to contribute the maximum allowable amount.

There are some benefits to affiliation. For example, the multicandidate status of one committee—and its corresponding higher candidate contribution ceiling—applies to its affiliates. In addition, transfers of PAC funds among affiliated PACs are not limited.[146]

Independent Expenditures and Electioneering Communications

PACs, but not corporations, may make "independent expenditures." Independent expenditures are expenditures for communications that expressly advocate the election or defeat of a clearly identified candidate and that are made without the cooperation, consent, request, or suggestion of—or in consultation or concert with—a candidate or the candidate's authorized committee.[147] (See section 4.6 for a discussion of what constitutes "express advocacy.") "Electioneering communications" are certain advertisements conducted thirty or sixty days before elections. (See section 4.6). Independent expenditures and electioneering communications, unlike in-kind contributions, must be made without involvement by the candidate. (See section 4.7 for a discussion of what constitutes "coordination.") They are subject to special reporting requirements and are not limited in the amount spent.

A candidate's involvement in an expenditure potentially transforms the expenditure into a contribution subject to contribution limitations. PAC expenditures that are made without the candidate's participation and that do not refer to a clearly identified candidate are not independent expenditures, electioneering communications, or contributions and—subject to regular reporting requirements—can be made without limit.

Because they are not limited, independent expenditures, electioneering communications, and other types of ads that mention candidates are controversial and may attract critical attention from the press and public. Extreme caution must be exercised in order to preserve the independence of the effort. The special independent expenditure reporting requirements, which include the treasurer's sworn statement that the expenditure was made independently, must be observed.

Broadcasts, letters or flyers, billboards, or lawn signs paid for by independent expenditures must contain a notice stating that the candidate did not authorize the communication and must identify both the PAC that paid for the message and its sponsoring corporation.[148] An expenditure that is not independent is a contribution in-kind to, and an expenditure by, the candidate.[149]

One activity is a *per se* contribution in-kind. A PAC must report as contributions expenditures to distribute, disseminate, or republish materials from the candidate or the candidate's committee, regardless of whether the expense is made in coordination or consultation with, with the prior consent of, or at the suggestion or request of the candidate or the candidate's committee.[150] Such activity is thus subject to the PAC's contribution limits. In addition, if the candidate has authorized, consented to, requested, or suggested such activity, he or she must report it as an in-kind contribution and expenditure.[151]

2.12   BUNDLING

"Bundling" is a term used to identify the practice of soliciting individual earmarked contributions, then delivering them *en masse* to a recipient candidate or political committee. Bundling sometimes refers to what the FEC regulations call "facilitation." When PACs participate in bundling, special rules apply.

If the PAC solicits earmarked contributions for a candidate, the "money expended" by the PAC to solicit the contributions must come from PAC funds raised under FECA restrictions, and that expense is treated as an in-kind contribution to the candidate.[152] Accordingly, if the PAC has already given the maximum legal contribution to the candidate, it can no longer solicit earmarked funds.[153] In any instance, the accounting issues raised by ensuring that the money expended by the PAC for the solicitation comes from PAC funds (and not corporate funds) may create some practical difficulty.

If a corporate director or officer solicits the contribution, and the PAC or company receives the check and forwards it to the candidate, the contribution must be reported as if made both to the PAC (by the contributor) and by the PAC (to the candidate). Otherwise, transmittal of the contribution to the candidate may be considered illegal corporate "facilitation" of federal contributions (see section 4.2). The PAC must report the original source and the intended recipient of such earmarked contributions to the FEC and to the recipient.[154] A corporation may urge the restricted class to send contributions directly to candidates and not to the PAC. This procedure will avoid extra reporting by the PAC and will not constitute corporate facilitation.

Individuals collecting and forwarding contributions to federal candidates who are not acting as expressly authorized agents for the candidate or the PAC are required to file conduit reports for the contributions.[155]

The Honest Leadership and Open Government Act of 2007 initiated a disclosure requirement for certain "bundled" contributions. Specifically, campaigns, political parties, and so-called leadership PACs will have to report semiannually to the FEC the names of lobbyists who raised more than $15,000 in contributions to the reporting entity. See section 5.4 for further details.

2.13   ASSOCIATION PACS

General

Like a business corporation, an incorporated association also may establish a PAC. However, the absence of stockholders changes the "restricted class" that may be solicited for voluntary contributions. Nonstock corporations generally will be composed of individual members, organizational members, or both.[156]

In order to determine the "restricted class" of an association, the organization first must establish that it is a "membership organization." The FEC has established regulations that define a membership organization.[157] In summary, the organization must be composed of "members," and must state the qualifications and requirements for membership in its articles, bylaws, or other formal organizational documents.[158] The association must have members. Members must have either a significant financial attachment to the association, pay predetermined dues on at least an annual basis, or have a significant organizational attachment such as a right to vote on association governance or policy.[159]

Membership organizations include trade associations and cooperatives. Trade associations are chambers of commerce or associations of corporations engaged in a similar or related line of commerce.[160] Cooperatives have special rules that govern the manner in which they may establish PACs and solicit voluntary contributions from individual cooperative members.[161]

The Association's "Restricted Class"

The restricted class of an association may include any or all of the following persons:

- Individuals who qualify as "members" of the association;[162]
- Executive or administrative personnel of the association;[163] and/or
- Executive or administrative personnel and stockholders of member corporations.[164]

An association may solicit people in the first two of these categories in the same fashion and under the same rules as business corporations may solicit their restricted class personnel. With respect to the third category, however, associations must first obtain "prior approval" from the member corporation before undertaking any solicitation.[165]

Prior Approval

Before an association may solicit executives of a member company for the association PAC, the member corporation must give the trade association prior approval in writing, which must be separate and specific.[166] Approval must be provided for each calendar year, and applies only through that calendar year.[167] The trade association may request prior approval for several calendar years at one time, but the corporation must approve each year separately and specifically (i.e., by providing a separate signature space for each year on the document or form).[168] The association also may indicate in its request that it intends to solicit only a portion of the restricted class.[169] The member corporation may condition its approval by limiting who may be solicited within the restricted class, or by limiting the number of solicitations the association may make during the calendar year.[170]

A member corporation can give prior approval to only one trade association PAC in each calendar year.[171] Granting approval to a trade association to solicit contributions to the association PAC does not affect or alter the right of the member corporation to solicit donations for its own PAC.[172]

The member company's representative to the association may provide the prior approval.[173] The association's request for approval may contain a copy of the solicitation materials that will be used if approval is granted, but the mailing must indicate that approval must be granted prior to any solicitation and that the member corporation has not approved a solicitation by any other association PAC for the same calendar year.[174]

If a corporation is a member of an association and has provided prior approval, but its subsidiary corporation is not a member of the association, the association may solicit contributions only from the parent/member corporation's restricted class and not from individuals employed by the subsidiary.[175] Conversely, if a subsidiary is a member of an association and has provided prior approval, but the parent is not a member, the trade association may solicit only the subsidiary's restricted class.[176] Separate corporate entities, even if wholly owned, are treated as separate "members" of an association. Accordingly, a parent company may grant approval to association A, while a subsidiary company may grant approval to association B with respect to the same calendar year.

Soliciting and Collecting Contributions to Association PACs

Once written approval is granted, there are no limits on the association's methods of soliciting voluntary contributions or of facilitating the making of voluntary contributions.[177] Upon written request by the association, a member corporation may provide various incidental services, such as payroll deduction or check-off systems to collect contributions from eligible employees and stockholders.[178] If the corporation does so, it and its subsidiaries, branches, divisions, and affiliates must make those same services available to a labor union representing any members working for the corporation or its subsidiaries, branches, divisions, or affiliates, upon written request of the union and at a cost sufficient only to reimburse the expenses incurred.[179] Otherwise, the PAC and the member corporation are free to engage in solicitations including direct mail, e-mail, one-on-one solicitations, special fundraising events, and small group solicitations.

With respect to executive or administrative personnel of the association, those individuals may be solicited under the same rules as those that pertain to fundraising by a business corporation.[180] All contributions must be voluntary, and they may be made by payroll deduction.

Application of Other PAC Rules

In all other respects, an association's PAC must comply with the restrictions on all separate segregated funds including: voluntary contributions, solicitation notices, soliciting only eligible persons, the one-third rule, contribution limits, affiliation rules, registration, recordkeeping, and reporting.

NOTES

1. 2 U.S.C. § 441b(b)(2)(C) (Supp. III 2003); 11 C.F.R. §§ 114.5(b) (2006), 114.11. For historical background on PACs, *see:*

Judicial: United States v. Congress of Indus. Orgs., 335 U.S. 106 (1948); United States v. UAW, 352 U.S. 567 (1957); Pipefitters Local Union No. 562 v. United States, 407 U.S. 385 (1972); Buckley v. Valeo, 424 U.S. 1 (1976); First Nat'l Bank of Boston v. Bellotti, 435 U.S. 765 (1978); Citizens Against Rent Control/Coal. for Fair Housing v. City of Berkeley, 454 U.S. 290 (1981); Cal. Med. Ass'n v. FEC, 453 U.S. 182 (1981); FEC v. Lance, 635 F.2d 1132 (5th Cir.) (en banc), *cert. denied*, 453 U.S. 917 (1981); Austin v. Mich. Chamber of Commerce, 494 U.S. 652 (1990); McConnell v. FEC, 540 U.S. 93 (2003).

Legislative: Hansen Amendment (part of FECA of 1971), Pub. L. No. 92-225, § 205, 86 Stat. 3; FECA Amendments of 1976, Pub. L. No. 94-283, § 112, 90 Stat. 490 (amended former 18 U.S.C. § 610 and recodified as 2 U.S.C. § 441b).

Administrative: FEC Advisory Opinion 1975-23, Fed. Election Camp. Fin. Guide (CCH) ¶ 5151 (1975) (permitting solicitation of all corporate employees but revised by 1976 amendments to FECA to permit solicitation only of restricted class).

2. FEC Advisory Opinion 1995-17, Fed. Election Camp. Fin. Guide (CCH) ¶ 6154 (1995); FEC Advisory Opinion 1988-27, Fed. Election Camp. Fin. Guide (CCH) ¶ 5934 (1988).

3. 2 U.S.C. §§ 441b(b)(4)(A)(i), (b)(7) (2000); 11 C.F.R. § 114.5(g)(1) (2006).

4. *Id.*

5. 2 U.S.C. § 441b(b)(4)(B) (2000); 11 C.F.R. § 114.6 (2006).

6. 11 C.F.R. § 114.5(d) (2006).

7. *See* 2 U.S.C. § 433 (2000) (registration of political committees); FEC Advisory Opinion 1984-18, Fed. Election Camp. Fin. Guide (CCH) ¶ 5762 (1984) (partnership acting merely as a screening committee need not register); FEC Advisory Opinion 1986-4 Fed. Election Camp. Fin. Guide (CCH) ¶ 5846 (1986) (corporation making recommendations on candidates, and then distributing contributions, must register).

8. 2 U.S.C. § 433(a) (2000); 11 C.F.R. § 102.1(c) (2006).

9. *Id.*

10. 2 U.S.C. § 432(e)(5) (2000); FEC Advisory Opinion 1993-7, Fed. Election Camp. Fin. Guide (CCH) ¶ 6088 (1993) (PAC must change name to match current name of corporate sponsor); FEC Advisory Opinion 1988-42, Fed. Election Camp. Fin. Guide (CCH) ¶ 5942 (1988); FEC Advisory Opinion 1980-10, Fed. Election Camp. Fin. Guide (CCH) ¶ 5467 (1980).

11. FEC Advisory Opinion 2002-4, Fed. Election Camp. Fin. Guide (CCH) ¶ 6377 (2002).

12. FEC Advisory Opinion 1980-86, Fed. Election Camp. Fin. Guide (CCH) ¶ 5534 (1980).

13. FEC Advisory Opinion 1999-20, Fed. Election Camp. Fin. Guide (CCH) ¶ 6299 (1999).

14. 2 U.S.C. § 433(b) (2000).

15. 2 U.S.C. § 433(c) (2000).

16. 11 C.F.R. § 102.2(a)(3) (2006).

17. 2 U.S.C. § 433(d)(1) (2000).

18. 2 U.S.C. § 432(a) (2000).

19. 2 U.S.C. §§ 432(c)-(d), 434 (2000 & Supp. III 2003).

20. 2 U.S.C. § 432(a) (2000); 11 C.F.R. § 102.7(b) (2006).

21. 11 C.F.R. § 102.7(a) (2006).

22. 11 C.F.R. § 114.12(a) (2006).

23. 2 U.S.C. § 432(b)(3) (2000); 11 C.F.R. § 102.15 (2006). FEC Advisory Opinion 1991-36, Fed. Election Camp. Fin. Guide (CCH) ¶ 6039 (1992).

24. FEC Advisory Opinion 1991-36, Fed. Election Camp. Fin. Guide (CCH) ¶ 6039 (1992).

25. 11 C.F.R. §§ 114.1(b), 114.5(b) (2006); *See also* FEC Advisory Opinion 1991-36, Fed. Election Camp. Fin. Guide (CCH) ¶ 6039 (1991).

26. FEC Advisory Opinion 1979-42, Fed. Election Camp. Fin. Guide (CCH) ¶ 5428 (1979).

27. FEC Advisory Opinion 1980-135, Fed. Election Camp. Fin. Guide (CCH) ¶ 5580 (1980).

28. FEC Advisory Opinion 1994-6, Fed. Election Camp. Fin. Guide (CCH) ¶ 6110 (1994).

29. FEC Advisory Opinion 1995-17, Fed. Election Camp. Fin. Guide (CCH) ¶ 6154 (1995); FEC Advisory Opinion 1981-40, Fed. Election Camp. Fin. Guide (CCH) ¶ 5622 (1981); FEC Advisory Opinion 1980-50, Fed. Election Camp. Fin. Guide (CCH) ¶ 5522 (1980) (travel, breakfast, and luncheon costs).

30. FEC Advisory Opinion 1977-19, Fed. Election Camp. Fin. Guide (CCH) ¶ 5252 (1977).

31. 11 C.F.R. § 114.5(d) (2006).

32. 2 U.S.C. § 432(c) (2000).

33. 2 U.S.C. § 434(a) (2000 & Supp. III 2003); 11 C.F.R. § 104.14(d) (2006).

34. 11 C.F.R. §§ 102.9(d), 104.7 (2006).

35. 2 U.S.C. § 434(a)(11) (2000 & Supp. III 2003), 11 C.F.R. § 104.18(a)(3)(A) (2006).

36. 11 C.F.R. § 104.18 (2006).

37. 11 C.F.R. § 104.5(c)(1)(ii) (2006).

38. 2 U.S.C. § 434(a)(4)(B) (2000); 11 C.F.R. § 104.5(c) (2006).

39. 2 U.S.C. § 434(a)(4)(B) (2000); 11 C.F.R. § 104.5(c)(3) (2006).

40. 2 U.S.C. § 434(a)(4)(A) (2000); 11 C.F.R. § 104.5(c)(1) (2006).

41. 2 U.S.C. § 434(a)(4)(A)(iv) (2000); 11 C.F.R. § 104.5(c)(2) (2006).

42. 2 U.S.C. § 434(a)(4)(B) (2000); 11 C.F.R. § 104.5(c)(3) (2006).

43. 2 U.S.C. § 437g(a) (2000 & Supp. III 2003).

44. 11 C.F.R. § 111.43 (2006).

45. 2 U.S.C. § 434(b)(1).

46. 2 U.S.C. § 434(b)(3)(A) (2000).

47. 2 U.S.C. § 434(b)(2)(F) (2000).

48. 2 U.S.C. § 434(b)(2)(H) (2000).

49. 2 U.S.C. § 434(b)(2)(I) (2000).

50. 2 U.S.C. § 434(b)(2)(J) (2000).

51. 2 U.S.C. § 434(b)(3)(A) (2000); 11 C.F.R. § 104.8(a) (2006).

52. 2 U.S.C. § 434(b)(3)(F) (2000).

53. 2 U.S.C. § 434(b)(3)(G) (2000).

54. 2 U.S.C. § 434(b)(4)(A) (2000).

55. 2 U.S.C. § 434(b)(4)(C) (2000).

56. 2 U.S.C. §§ 434(b)(4)(E), (H)(ii) (2000).

57. 2 U.S.C. § 434(b)(4)(H)(iii) (2000).

58. 2 U.S.C. § 434(b)(4)(H)(i). (2000)

59. 2 U.S.C. § 434(b)(8) (2000).

60. 2 U.S.C. § 439(a) (2000). The PAC need file only the portions of the report applicable to candidates in that state.

61. 2 U.S.C. § 439(c) (2000).

62. 11 C.F.R. § 104.13(a)(1) (2006). The use by the PAC of an in-kind contribution is reported as an expenditure. 11 C.F.R. § 104.13(a)(2) (2006).

63. 11 C.F.R. § 104.13(b) (2006).

64. 11 C.F.R. § 104.7(b) (2006); Republican Nat'l Comm. v. FEC, 76 F.3d 400 (D.C. Cir. 1996), *cert. denied*, 519 U.S. 1055 (1997).

65. Safe Harbor for Misreporting Due to Embezzlement, 72 Fed. Reg. 16695 (April 5, 2007) (to be codified at 11 C.F.R. pt 104).

66. 2 U.S.C. § 432(d) (2000).

67. 2 U.S.C. §§ 432(c)(1)-(5) (2000).

68. 11 C.F.R. § 102.8(b) (2006).

69. FEC Advisory Opinion 1976-27, Fed. Election Camp. Fin. Guide (CCH) ¶ 5213 (1976).

70. FEC Advisory Opinion 1992-9, Fed. Election Camp. Fin. Guide (CCH) ¶ 6052 (1992).

71. FEC Advisory Opinion 1995-14, Fed. Election Camp. Fin. Guide (CCH) ¶ 6150 (1995); FEC Advisory Opinion 1978-17, Fed. Election Camp. Fin. Guide (CCH) ¶ 5307 (1978).

72. FEC Advisory Opinion 1991-3, Fed. Election Camp. Fin. Guide (CCH) ¶ 6012 (1991) (a PAC newsletter is not a solicitation if the newsletter does not indicate PAC support for candidates, encourage contributions or impart information on how to contribute); FEC Advisory Opinion 1984-57, Fed. Election Camp. Fin. Guide (CCH) ¶ 5799 (1984) (encouraging support of particular legislation in the corporate newsletter is not a solicitation); FEC Advisory Opinion 1979-66, Fed. Election Camp. Fin. Guide (CCH) ¶ 5455 (1980) (providing certain information about PAC activity is not a solicitation).

73. FEC Advisory Opinion 1983-38, Fed. Election Camp. Fin. Guide (CCH) ¶ 5741 (1983); FEC Advisory Opinion 1982-65, Fed. Election Camp. Fin. Guide (CCH) ¶ 5701 (1983) (Annual Report announcement).

74. 2 U.S.C. § 441b(b)(4)(A)(i) (2000); 11 C.F.R. § 114.5(g)(1) (2006). The FEC has determined that families include the children and parents of the restricted class member residing in the same household. FEC Advisory Opinion 1980-102, Fed. Election Camp. Fin. Guide (CCH) ¶ 5552 (1980).

75. 11 C.F.R. § 114.5(g)(1) (2006).

76. FEC Advisory Opinion 1994-11, Fed. Election Camp. Fin. Guide (CCH) ¶ 6115 (1994); FEC Advisory Opinion 1987-34, Fed. Election Camp. Fin. Guide (CCH) ¶ 5920 (1988); FEC Advisory Opinion 1982-45, Fed. Election Camp. Fin. Guide (CCH) ¶ 5688 (1982); FEC Advisory Opinion 1979-44, Fed. Election Camp. Fin. Guide (CCH) ¶ 5429 (1979).

77. FEC Advisory Opinion 1979-38, Fed. Election Camp. Fin. Guide (CCH) ¶ 5422 (1979).

78. FEC Advisory Opinion 1988-46, Fed. Election Camp. Fin. Guide (CCH) ¶ 5948 (1988).

79. FEC Advisory Opinion 1992-17, Fed. Election Camp. Fin. Guide (CCH) ¶ 6060 (1992); FEC Advisory Opinion 1989-8, Fed. Election Camp. Fin. Guide (CCH) ¶ 5959 (1989).

80. 11 C.F.R. §§ 100.5(g)(3)-(4), 110.3(a)(2)-(3), 114.5(g)(1) (2006); *see also* FEC Advisory Opinion 1994-9, Fed. Election Camp. Fin. Guide (CCH) ¶ 6113 (1994).

81. 2 U.S.C. § 441b(b)(4)(B) (2000); 11 C.F.R. § 114.6(a) (2006).

82. 11 C.F.R. § 114.7 (2006).

83. 11 C.F.R. § 114.8 (2006).

84. FEC Advisory Opinion 1988-3, Fed. Election Camp. Fin. Guide (CCH) ¶ 5923 (1988).

85. 11 C.F.R. § 114.5(h) (2006).

86. 11 C.F.R. § 114.5(j) (2006).

87. 11 C.F.R. § 114.1(h) (2006).

88. FEC Advisory Opinion 1998-12, Fed. Election Camp. Fin. Guide (CCH) ¶ 6265 (1988); FEC Advisory Opinion 1996-10, Fed. Election Camp. Fin. Guide (CCH) ¶ 6192 (1996); FEC Advisory Opinion 1988-36, Fed. Election Camp. Fin. Guide (CCH) ¶ 5937 (1988); FEC Advisory Opinion 1988-19, Fed. Election Camp. Fin. Guide (CCH) ¶ 5927 (1988); FEC Advisory Opinion 1983-35, Fed. Election Camp. Fin. Guide (CCH) ¶ 5739 (1983); FEC Advisory Opinion 1983-17, Fed. Election Camp. Fin. Guide (CCH) ¶ 5723 (1983); FEC Advisory Opinion 1977-49, Fed. Election Camp. Fin. Guide (CCH) ¶ 5298 (1978).

89. Letter from FEC to Jules Metzer in response to O/R No. 697 (Sept. 10, 1976) (on file with FEC).

90. 11 C.F.R. § 114.5(g)(1) (2006).

91. FEC Advisory Opinion 1982-18, Fed. Election Camp. Fin. Guide (CCH) ¶ 5664 (1982); FEC Advisory Opinion 1978-75, Fed. Election Camp. Fin. Guide (CCH) ¶ 5368 (1978).

92. 2 U.S.C. § 441b(b)(7) (2000); 11 C.F.R. § 114.1(c) (2006).

93. 11 C.F.R. § 114.1(c)(1)(i) (2006).

94. 11 C.F.R. § 114.1(c)(1)(ii) (2006). *But see* FEC Advisory Opinion 1984-55, Fed. Election Camp. Fin. Guide (CCH) ¶ 5795 (1984) (concluding that PAC may not solicit members of law firm who are not corporate employees).

95. FEC Advisory Opinion 1985-35, Fed. Election Camp. Fin. Guide (CCH) ¶ 5835 (1985); FEC Advisory Opinion 1977-18, Fed. Election Camp. Fin. Guide (CCH) ¶ 5273 (1977).

96. 11 C.F.R. § 114.1(c)(2)(i) (2006).

97. 11 C.F.R. §§ 114.1(c)(2)(ii)-(iv) (2006).

98. 11 C.F.R. § 114.5(a)(1) (2006).

99. FEC Explanation and Justification of § 114.5(a), Fed. Election Camp. Fin. Guide (CCH) ¶ 923 at 1601-17 (1980).

100. 11 C.F.R. §§ 114.5(a)(3)-(4) (2006).

101. 11 C.F.R. § 114.5(a)(2) (2006).

102. FEC Advisory Opinion 1977-37, Fed. Election Camp. Fin. Guide (CCH) ¶ 5309 (1978).

103. *See* 11 C.F.R. §§ 114.1(f), 114.5(k)(1) (2006).

104. FEC Advisory Opinion 1991-1, Fed. Election Camp. Fin. Guide (CCH) ¶ 6008 (1991).

105. FEC Advisory Opinion 1995-33, Fed. Election Camp. Fin. Guide (CCH) ¶ 6167 (1995) (concluding that receipt of an e-mail solicitation by a secretary is not illegal).

106. FEC Advisory Opinion 2001-04, Fed. Election Camp. Fin. Guide (CCH) ¶ 6360 (2001); FEC Advisory Opinion 1999-3, Fed. Election Camp. Fin. Guide (CCH) ¶ 6283 (1999).

107. 2 U.S.C. § 441b(b)(4)(B) (2000); 11 C.F.R. § 114.6 (2006).

108. FEC Advisory Opinion 1991-28, Fed. Election Camp. Fin. Guide (CCH) ¶ 6031 (1991).

109. 2 U.S.C. § 441b(b)(5) (2000); 11 C.F.R. § 114.5(k) (2006).

110. 11 C.F.R. § 114.5(k)(2) (2006).

111. 11 C.F.R. § 114.5(k) (2006).

112. 11 C.F.R. § 114.5(k)(1) (2006).

113. 11 C.F.R. § 114.6(e)(3) (2006).

114. 11 C.F.R. § 114.6(e)(4) (2006).

115. 2 U.S.C. § 441a(a)(1)(C) (2000).

116. 2 U.S.C. § 441a(a)(3) (2000).

117. 2 U.S.C. § 441a(2)(c) (2000 & Supp. III 2003).

118. 2 U.S.C. § 441a(a)(3) (2000).

119. 2 U.S.C. § 441a(a)(3) (2000 & Supp. III 2003).

120. 2 U.S.C. § 441a(a)(5) (2000).

121. 11 C.F.R. §§ 100.5(g)(2), 110.3(a)(1)(ii) (2006).

122. 11 C.F.R. § 110.3(a)(2)(i) (2006).

123. 2 U.S.C. § 441a(f) (2000).

124. 2 U.S.C. § 441b(a) (2000).

125. *Id.*

126. 2 U.S.C. § 441c (2000).

127. 2 U.S.C. § 441e (2000 & Supp. III 2003).

128. 2 U.S.C. § 441f (2000).

129. 2 U.S.C. § 441g (2000).

130. 2 U.S.C. § 441k.

131. McConnell v. FEC, 540 U.S. 93, 231-32 (2003); *see, e.g.,* 11 C.F.R. 110.19 (2006).

132. 11 C.F.R. § 114.5(b)(1) (2006).

133. 2 U.S.C. § 441f (2000); 11 C.F.R. § 110.4(b) (2006).

134. FEC Advisory Opinion 1977-19, Fed. Election Camp. Fin. Guide (CCH) ¶ 5252 (1977).

135. 2 U.S.C. §§ 431(8)(A), 431(9)(A), 441b(b)(2) (2000 & Supp. III 2003).

136. Buckley v. Valeo, 424 U.S. 1 (1976).

137. 11 C.F.R. § 110.1(d) (2006).

138. *Buckley*, 424 U.S. at 39-51.

139. 2 U.S.C. § 441a(a)(4) (2000).

140. 11 C.F.R. § 102.2(a)(3) (2006).

141. 2 U.S.C. §§ 441a(a)(2)(A)-(C) (2000).

142. 2 U.S.C. §§ 441a(a)(1)(A)-(C) (2000).

143. 2 U.S.C. § 441a(a)(1) (Supp. III 20003).

144. 2 U.S.C. § 441a(a)(5) (2000); 11 C.F.R. §§ 100.5(g)(2), 110.3(a) (2006); *see, e.g.,* FEC Advisory Opinion 1990-10, Fed. Election Camp. Fin. Guide (CCH) ¶ 5995 (1990) (finding that a subsidiary and its parent corporation are affiliated until their relationship is legally severed); FEC Advisory Opinion 2001-18, Fed. Election Camp. Fin. Guide (CCH) ¶ 6372 (2002) (concluding that two companies that have unequal ownership in a joint venture, but maintain equal control, are affiliated); FEC Advisory Opinion 2001-7, Fed. Election Camp. Fin. Guide (CCH) ¶ 6362 (2001) (determining that companies with a 20% interest in a joint venture are not affiliated); FEC Advisory Opinion 2000-36, Fed. Election Camp. Fin. Guide (CCH) ¶ 6351 (2000) (finding of disaffiliation resulting from spin-off of Andersen Consulting from Arthur Andersen); FEC Advisory Opinion 2000-28, Fed. Election Camp. Fin. Guide (CCH) ¶ 6350 (2000) (disaffiliation found despite remaining ties); FEC Advisory Opinion 1999-39, Fed. Election Camp. Fin. Guide (CCH) ¶ 6317 (2000) (finding disaffiliation resulting from reorganization of Blue Cross of California); FEC Advisory Opinion 1988-4, Fed. Election Camp. Fin. Guide (CCH) ¶ 5914 (1988) (concluding that, even though a corporation does not directly control another corporation because of the complicated financing by which the second corporation was acquired, their PACs are nevertheless affiliated).

145. Walther v. FEC, 468 F. Supp. 1235 (D.D.C. 1979).

146. 11 C.F.R. § 110.3(c)(1) (2006).

147. 2 U.S.C. § 431(17) (Supp. III 2003); 11 C.F.R. § 109.1(a) (2006).

148. 11 C.F.R. § 110.11(c) (2006).

149. 11 C.F.R. §§ 109.20(b), 109.21(b)(1) (2006).

150. 11 C.F.R. § 109.23(a) (2006).

151. 11 C.F.R. §§ 109.20(b) (2006), 109.21(b)(2).

152. 11 C.F.R. § 110.6(a) (2006).

153. 11 C.F.R. § 114.2(f)(3) (2006); FEC Advisory Opinion 1980-46, Fed. Election Camp. Fin. Guide (CCH) ¶ 5508 (1980).

154. 11 C.F.R. § 110.6 (2006).

155. 11 C.F.R. § 110.6(c) (2006).

156. 11 C.F.R. §§ 114.7, 114.8 (2006).

157. 11 C.F.R. § 114.1(e)(1) (2006).

158. *Id.*

159. 11 C.F.R. § 114.1(e)(2) (2006).

160. 11 C.F.R. § 114.8(a) (2006).

161. 11 C.F.R. § 114.7(k) (2006).

162. 11 C.F.R. § 114.7(a) (2006).

163. 11 C.F.R. § 114.8(i)(2) (2006).

164. 11 C.F.R. § 114.8(c) (2006).

165. *Id.*

166. 11 C.F.R. § 114.8(d)(1) (2006).

167. 11 C.F.R. § 114.8(d)(4) (2006).

168. *Id.*

169. 11 C.F.R. § 114.8(d)(5) (2006).

170. *Id.*

171. 11 C.F.R. §§ 114 8(c), (d) (2006).

172. 11 C.F.R. § 114.8(e)(2) (2006).
173. 11 C.F.R. § 114.8(c)(3) (2006).
174. 11 C.F.R. § 114.8(d)(3) (2006).
175. 11 C.F.R. § 114.8(f) (2006).
176. *Id.*
177. 11 C.F.R. § 114.8(e)(3) (2006).
178. 11 C.F.R. § 114.8(e)(4) (2006).
179. *Id.*
180. 11 C.F.R. § 114.8(i) (2006).

3. Use of Corporate Facilities for Political Purposes

Contents

3.1 INTRODUCTION

This section addresses the use of corporate resources—such as offices, phones, corporate computing equipment, and Internet services[1]—and employee time by employees, shareholders, candidates, and political committees for election-related activity. A corporation's use of its resources to solicit contributions to its own PAC was discussed in chapter 2, and a corporation's use of its resources to communicate its political views will be addressed in chapter 4.

Uncompensated use of corporate facilities for political activity in most cases is an illegal corporate contribution, whether or not the corporation has authorized the use.[2] The corporation must be alert, therefore, to any use of its facilities by executives, employees, shareholders, and others for political activities.

3.2 CAMPAIGNING BY EMPLOYEES

Any individual may volunteer to work for a candidate or a political party. A corporation, however, may not compensate an employee while he or she is performing such services, unless the employee is merely receiving compensation for bona fide earned vacation or leave time.[3] A corporation may not compensate an employee who is taking unearned leave to work on a federal campaign or for a federal political committee or political party. Furthermore, the corporation may not continue paying the employee's benefits, such as retirement benefits or life and health insurance, unless the corporation has a general policy under which it provides benefits for a period of time after an employee leaves the job.[4] The employee may bear these costs using personal funds, or the corporate PAC may cover the expense and treat it as a contribution to the candidate for whom the employee is working.[5]

These rules also must be followed whenever an employee takes unearned leave or leave without pay in order to run for federal office.[6] An employee who is a candidate may continue receiving compensation and benefits, but only to the extent that the corporation is paying him or her a reasonable amount for services actually performed.

Corporate employees may undertake some campaign work during regular working hours without the employee's compensated time becoming an in-kind contribution. For example, an employee who is expected to work a particular number of hours per week may engage in political activity during what otherwise would be a regular work period if the lost work time is made up "within a reasonable time."[7] If the employee is compensated on a commission or piecework basis, the employee's time is considered his or her own to use as he or she sees fit because the employee is paid only for work actually performed.[8]

3.3   CAMPAIGN USE OF CORPORATE FACILITIES BY EMPLOYEES/ SHAREHOLDERS

The corporation may allow its stockholders and employees to use corporate facilities for their own individual volunteer activity in connection with a federal election, provided that the corporation complies with certain guidelines.[9]

Use of corporate facilities by employees for campaign activities will qualify as "occasional, isolated or incidental" if the activities do not prevent the employee from performing the normal amount of work usually completed in a day.[10] For shareholders, use of corporate resources is occasional, isolated, or incidental if it does not interfere with the corporation's normal activities.[11] In addition, the FEC has provided a safe harbor: The use of corporate facilities will qualify as occasional, isolated, or incidental if it does not exceed one hour per week or four hours per month, regardless of whether the use occurs during or after normal working hours.[12]

The employee or shareholder who occasionally uses corporate facilities for political purposes need only reimburse the corporation for increases in operating costs or overhead.[13] For example, the employee or shareholder must reimburse the corporation for long-distance telephone calls made in connection with a federal election. Reimbursement would not be required for the use of a desk or office if the corporation does not incur any incremental expense for it.

If employees or stockholders make more than "occasional" use of corporate facilities in connection with a federal election (i.e., more than one hour per week or four hours per month), they must reimburse the corporation for the normal and usual rental charge within a commercially reasonable time.[14] The normal and usual charge means the market rental charge at the time of use.[15] In addition, *any person* who uses corporate facilities to generate campaign materials must reimburse the corporation at the usual and normal charge within a commercially reasonable time.[16]

A corporate employee may use support staff to assist in his or her volunteer activities if the staff person agrees, without being coerced, and the corporation receives compensation from the candidate or employee in advance for the fair market value of the employee's services.[17] A payment by the employee would be an in-kind contribution to the candidate or political committee for whom the employee is volunteering. Use of corporate lists of customers, clients, vendors, or other people who are not part of the corporation's restricted class to solicit contributions or distribute invitations to fundraisers requires reimbursement to the corporation *in advance* for the fair market value of all services and lists supplied.[18] Providing catering or other food services by the corporation is forbidden unless the corporation receives *advance payment* for the fair market value of the services.

It is important to emphasize that the exception for "occasional, isolated or incidental" use of corporate resources applies to bona fide volunteer activity by employees and stockholders. Sometimes there can be a question of fact as to whether an individual is volunteering. For example, whether an assistant in the government affairs office of a company is a volunteer may depend on the frequency of the activity and whether such activity is taken into account in personnel evaluations. If so, there will be—at the very least—an appearance that the individual's "volunteer" activity is in fact part of the job. Under such circumstances, the exception will not apply, and both the value of the company's resources and even the services of the assistant may be deemed corporate—and therefore illegal—donations to the beneficiary campaign.

A corporate executive or employee should not solicit contributions to a fundraising event from other executives and business vendors of the corporation by using corporate stationery that identifies his or her position in the corporation. (However, solicitations to the restricted class may be conducted on corporate stationery if they are corporate partisan communications, as discussed in section 4.2.)

A corporation may not facilitate contributions to federal candidates or political committees. A corporate executive may act individually for a candidate. However, executives may not "bundle" contributions (see section 2.10) or direct their subordinates in fundraising activities, use corporate resources (such as customer lists) to facilitate fundraising, or solicit entire classes of corporate executives and employees without properly reimbursing the corporation[19] or except as permitted in communications to the restricted class (see section 4.2).

3.4   CAMPAIGN USE OF CORPORATE FACILITIES BY CANDIDATES AND POLITICAL COMMITTEES

If a candidate or a political committee uses corporate resources, the corporation must be reimbursed in full at the normal and usual rental charge within a commercially reasonable time.[20] A corporation may offer a meeting room to a candidate if the corporation customarily makes the room available to civic or other outside groups, and the corporation makes the room available to any other candidate or committee on request.[21] Alternatively, candidates or political committees may rent the room at the commercial rate from the corporation.

A corporation may not expend treasury funds (including the costs of corporate facilities and salaries) on behalf of candidates and later be reimbursed by the corporation's PAC.[22] Instead, the corporation or sponsoring organization must pay such expenses from funds provided in advance by the PAC or enter into joint employment agreements with salaried personnel.[23]

The fact that a corporation arguably receives "something" of value from the candidate or committee (i.e., publicity) does not change the FEC's view that the transaction is a contribution.[24] Nevertheless, a corporation is not deemed to make a contribution to a candidate if it provides goods or services in the ordinary course of business as a commercial vendor at the usual and normal charge.[25]

3.5   CAMPAIGN USE OF CORPORATE AIRPLANES AND VEHICLES

A candidate, a candidate's agent, or a person traveling on behalf of a candidate must pay market value for use of corporate transportation for travel in connection with a federal election.[26] If the candidate, agent, or person traveling on behalf of the candidate is transported in a private aircraft owned or leased by the corporation—other than one licensed to provide commercial travel services—reimbursement is required.[27] Until 2004, advance reimbursement was required. The FEC, however, amended its rules to permit payment to be made within seven days after the flight.[28] However, advance reimbursement may still be a prudent policy.

For decades, the FEC permitted a candidate or agent to pay first-class airfare for travel on a noncommercial corporate aircraft.[29] This practice was changed by the Honest Leadership and Open Government Act of 2007. Under this statute and the rules of the House of Representatives, neither a congressperson nor any candidate for the House may travel on private noncommercial aircraft, except for government-operated aircraft or aircraft owned or leased by the candidate or the candidate's family.[30] Candidates for the Senate and senators may travel on private aircraft, but must pay "the pro rata share of the fair market value of such flight."[31]

The phrase "candidate's agent" is broadly interpreted so that corporate officers or employees who are engaged in activities on behalf of the candidate in connection with the travel also must pay for airfare. However, if the individual accompanying the candidate pays the airfare out-of-pocket, the first $1,000 may be counted as exempt payments for volunteer travel expenses, and the excess may be counted against applicable contribution limits.

If the candidate, candidate's agent, or person traveling on behalf of the candidate in connection with a federal election uses other means of transportation owned or leased by the corporation, the usual rental charge must be paid.[32] The fee, however, need not be paid in advance. Instead, it must be paid within thirty calendar days after receipt of an invoice for the travel, but no more than sixty days after the date of travel.[33]

3.6   PROVIDING LEGAL AND ACCOUNTING SERVICES TO CANDIDATES AND POLITICAL PARTIES

Corporate employees may furnish legal and accounting services to political committees, party committees, and candidate committees without making an illegal contribution under certain circumstances. Such services may be provided to a political party committee if they do not directly further the election of candidates for federal office.[34] Services performed for an authorized candidate committee, or to any other political committee, may be provided if they are performed solely for the purpose of ensuring compliance with the Federal Election Campaign Act or with the presidential public financing scheme in chapters 95 and 96 of the Internal Revenue Code.[35] In either case, the corporation paying for the services must be the regular employer of the person providing the services. This rule prevents third parties from paying a person to render these services where no relationship "would otherwise exist but for the pendency of the campaign."[36] The exemption will not apply if additional employees are hired to make regular employees available to render the services,[37] nor will it apply to the donation of money to cover a candidate or committee's legal expenses.[38] The candidate or committee benefiting from these services must report their value, so the corporation should provide the recipient with a statement of the cost of the services, the date performed, and the name of the person providing them.[39]

Support services—such as secretarial, paralegal, and photocopying—also are included in the exemption if they are used to furnish legal and accounting services.[40] A candidate also may use his or her employer's computer and software to further compliance with federal election laws without the corporation making an illegal contribution.[41]

NOTES

1. FEC Advisory Opinion 1999-17, Fed. Election Camp. Fin. Guide (CCH) ¶ 6308 (1999).
2. See 11 C.F.R. § 114.9 (2006).
3. 11 C.F.R. § 100.54(c) (2006).
4. 11 C.F.R. §§ 114.12(c)(1)-(2) (2006); FEC Advisory Opinion 1992-3, Fed. Election Camp. Fin. Guide (CCH) ¶ 6047 (1992).
5. 11 C.F.R. § 114.12(c)(1) (2006).
6. See FEC Advisory Opinion 2000-1, Fed. Election Camp. Fin. Guide (CCH) ¶ 6318 (2000); FEC Advisory Opinion 1992-3, Fed. Election Camp. Fin. Guide (CCH) ¶ 6047 (1992); FEC Advisory Opinion 1976-70, Fed. Election Camp. Fin. Guide (CCH) ¶ 5217 (1976).
7. 11 C.F.R. § 100.54(a) (2006).
8. 11 C.F.R. § 100.54(b) (2006).
9. 11 C.F.R. § 114.9(a) (2006).
10. 11 C.F.R. § 114.9(a)(1)(i) (2006).
11. 11 C.F.R. § 114.9(a)(1)(ii) (2006).
12. 11 C.F.R. § 114.9(a)(1)(iii) (2006).
13. 11 C.F.R. § 114.9(a)(1) (2006).
14. 11 C.F.R. § 114.9(a)(2) (2006).
15. 11 C.F.R. § 100.52(d)(2) (2006).
16. 11 C.F.R. § 114.9(c) (2006).
17. 11 C.F.R. § 114.2(f)(2)(i)(A) (2006).
18. 11 C.F.R. § 114.2(f)(2)(i)(C) (2006).
19. See Matter of Prudential Securities, FEC Matter Under Review No. 3540; Matter of General Dynamics Corporation, FEC Matter Under Review No. 4005; 11 C.F.R. § 114.2(f) (2006).
20. 11 C.F.R. §§ 114.2(f)(2)(B), 114.9(d) (2006).
21. 11 C.F.R. § 114.13 (2006).
22. FEC Advisory Opinion 1984-24, Fed. Election Camp. Fin. Guide (CCH) ¶ 5771 (1984).
23. FEC Advisory Opinion 1984-37, Fed. Election Camp. Fin. Guide (CCH) ¶ 5784 (1984).
24. FEC Advisory Opinion 1992-40, Fed. Election Camp. Fin. Guide (CCH) ¶ 6077 (1992).
25. 11 C.F.R. § 114.2(f) (2006).
26. See 11 C.F.R. §§ 100.93(c)-(d) (2006). The Federal Aviation Administration has promulgated regulations authorizing aircraft operators who otherwise are not licensed to carry passengers for compensation to receive payment for the carriage of a federal candidate or a person traveling on behalf of a candidate to allow compliance with FEC regulations. 14 C.F.R. § 91.321 (2006).
27. See generally 11 C.F.R. § 100.93.
28. 11 C.F.R. § 100.93(c) (2006).
29. See Honest Leadership & Open Government Act of 2007, Pub. L. No. 110-81, § 601, 212 Stat. 735 (2007) (codified at 2 U.S.C. § 439a).
30. Id.
31. Id.
32. 11 C.F.R. § 100.93(d).
33. Id.
34. 11 C.F.R. § 114.1(a)(2)(vi) (2006).
35. 11 C.F.R. § 114.1(a)(2)(vii) (2006).
36. FEC Advisory Opinion 1982-31, Fed. Election Camp. Fin. Guide (CCH) ¶ 5675 (1982).

37. 11 C.F.R. §§ 114.1(a)(2)(vi)-(vii) (2006).
38. FEC Advisory Opinion 1990-17, Fed. Election Camp. Fin. Guide (CCH) ¶ 5993 (1990).
39. 11 C.F.R. § 104.3(h) (2006).
40. FEC Advisory Opinion 1979-22, Fed. Election Camp. Fin. Guide (CCH) ¶ 5409 (1979).
41. FEC Advisory Opinion 1980-137, Fed. Election Camp. Fin. Guide (CCH) ¶ 5585 (1981).

4. Political Communications by a Corporation

Contents

4.1   GENERAL RULES

Federal law regulates communications financed by a corporation that are "in connection with" federal election campaigns. While political messages to the restricted class are permitted, public political advertising is highly circumscribed.

The scope of FEC regulations depends on the political content of the message and the audience to whom the message is communicated. If the communication contains "express advocacy" of the election or defeat of a clearly identified candidate, the message may be directed only to the restricted class. Public advertising in some circumstances is prohibited. For example, both "express advocacy" and "electioneering communications" by corporations to the public are illegal. Accordingly, the discussion below addresses the rules that apply when an audience attends a corporate-sponsored political event or receives a corporate-sponsored political message.

Audience and content restrictions apply only to communications funded by the corporation, not to those paid by the PAC. Political communications by the PAC may contain any message and be directed to any person (as long as the message does not solicit contributions to the PAC—see chapter 2 for those rules).[1] PAC communications made to influence the election of a federal candidate may be considered in-kind contributions to the candidate subject to contribution limits, unless the expense is made independent of any candidate or political party. However, the PAC must report such independent expenditures to the FEC.

4.2   COMMUNICATIONS TO THE RESTRICTED CLASS

Candidate and Party Appearances

A corporation may invite a candidate, a candidate's representative, or the representative of a political party to appear on corporate or other premises before the restricted class—i.e., shareholders, executives, administrators, and their families—at a corporate meeting, convention, or other function.[2] A limited number of persons from outside the restricted class also may attend these functions, including employees necessary to administer the meeting, limited guests and observers, and representatives of the news media.[3] In the discussion that follows, references to a "candidate" should also be read to include a candidate's representative or the representative of a political party.

A corporation may coordinate with a candidate on the candidate's plans, projects, or needs when planning an event or communicating with its restricted class. However, the FEC may view this coordination as compromising the independence of later public communications by the corporation or its PAC.[4] The candidate may ask for contributions for his or her campaign or request that contributions to the company's PAC be designated for his or her benefit.[5] The candidate also may collect contributions before, during, or after the event. However, no officer, director, or representative of the corporation may collect such contributions, which would be considered illegal corporate facilitation of the contribution (discussed below).[6]

The corporation may endorse the candidate who appears before the audience and/or limit any appearances before the restricted class to certain candidates or political parties.[7] If the corporation allows the news media to cover one candidate's appearance, however, and later invites another candidate for the same office to address the restricted class, the media must be allowed to cover the other candidate's appearance as well.[8] Additionally, the corporation must allow all media representatives access to cover the event, if some media are allowed to do so.[9]

Partisan Communications and "Facilitation"

In addition to candidate appearances, the corporation—at its own expense—may communicate with the restricted class on any topic, including overtly political subjects.[10] These communications may expressly advocate the election or defeat of a named candidate or party. The communications may solicit contributions, but the corporation may not "facilitate" the making of the contributions. This means that the company or its employees may not physically collect or otherwise assist in the transmittal of contributions. Recipients only can be urged to send their contributions directly to the candidate, whose address can be provided. A stamp or envelope may not be provided. If contributions are collected at the corporate offices, they are subject to the "bundling" rules discussed in section 2.10.

Any materials generated for this purpose must be produced at the company's expense, must express the views of the corporation, and shall not simply constitute the republication or reproduction of materials prepared by a candidate.[11] A corporation may, however, use brief quotations from the candidate's materials.

Partisan Telephone Banks

In addition to printed material, the corporation is permitted to establish and operate telephone banks to contact members of the restricted class for the purpose of urging them to register to vote or to vote for specified candidates.[12] Information and other assistance regarding registering or voting cannot be withheld from a member of the restricted class based on support or opposition to a particular candidate or party.[13]

Transportation to Polls or Registration Site

The corporation also may provide transportation to the polls in conjunction with partisan registration and get-out-the-vote efforts aimed at the restricted class.[14] Transportation to the polls or to the registration site, however, may not be denied to an individual because he or she will not vote for a particular candidate or register with a particular party.[15]

Reporting

The cost of internal corporate communications generally do not need to be reported to the FEC. However, costs directly attributable to communications that are primarily devoted to the express advocacy of the election or defeat of a clearly identified candidate must be reported to the FEC if they exceed $2,000 per election.[16] The $2,000 threshold applies separately to parent and subsidiary corporations.[17] The disclosure is made by filing a completed FEC Form 7, a copy of which can be found in appendix A.[18]

4.3   COMMUNICATIONS TO OTHER EMPLOYEES

A corporation may not finance communications that contain "express advocacy" to other employees (who are not stockholders) or others outside the restricted class. Express advocacy messages unambiguously advocate the election or defeat of a "clearly identified" candidate, using words such as "vote for," "vote against," "elect," "defeat," or "Smith for Congress."[19] Candidates are clearly identified when their names or pictures appear in a communication or when their identities are apparent by unambiguous reference.[20]

Candidate Appearances before All Employees

A corporation may invite a candidate or a political party spokesman to the company's facilities or to any meeting, convention, or other function to address any of its employees, including those outside the restricted class.[21] The candidate may expressly advocate his or her election, but the corporation and the PAC may not make any preference known and may not encourage employees to support or oppose a particular candidate.[22] The candidate may solicit contributions, but the corporation and the PAC may not. Corporate and PAC agents are not permitted to collect contributions for the candidate.[23] In appearances before all employees, even the candidate may not collect contributions, but he or she may leave return envelopes and campaign materials for attendees to use to forward contributions if they choose.[24]

If a corporation permits a candidate to appear before employees outside the restricted class, it must provide (upon request) the same opportunity for all other candidates seeking the same office.[25] The corporation may coordinate with the candidate to determine the structure, format, and timing of the appearance, but may not discuss the candidate's plans, projects, or needs more broadly.[26] Media access rules are the same as those that apply to restricted class appearances.[27]

4.4   CORPORATE COMMUNICATIONS TO THE GENERAL PUBLIC

Candidate Appearances

Corporations may sponsor only "noncampaign" candidate appearances before the general public. A corporation may feature a candidate, for example, in the candidate's capacity as an officeholder or community leader. The candidate may speak about issues of concern to the corporation or industry. The candidate may not discuss the election campaign, solicit contributions, or advocate that people vote for him or her or against his or her opponent.[28]

Registration and Voting Information for the General Public

A corporation may provide to the general public (or any employee) registration and voting information. When such communications—or voter registration or get-out-the-vote drives—are directed beyond the restricted class, no part of them may contain express advocacy.[29] These communications may be made through posters, billboards, broadcasting media, newspapers, newsletters, brochures, or similar means.[30]

The corporation also may distribute registration and voting information prepared by official election administrators, as well as registration-by-mail forms.[31] All forms must be distributed in a manner that does not favor the election or defeat of a particular candidate or party, and they may not be accompanied by any endorsements or appeals by the company that promote registration with a particular party.[32] A corporation also may donate money to state or local election officials to help pay for the cost of printing or distributing registration or voting information or forms.[33]

Corporate registration or get-out-the-vote efforts may not be coordinated with a federal candidate or political party.[34] Any services provided in a registration or get-out-the-vote drive—such as transportation—may not be provided or withheld based on a voter's political preferences. Also individuals working on the drive may not receive compensation based on the number of people registered or transported who support a particular candidate or party. The corporation must notify registrants or voters of these requirements in writing at the time of the registration or get-out-the-vote drive.[35]

Voter Guides

The corporation may prepare and distribute voter guides or brochures to its employees and to the public. Alternatively, a corporation may distribute guides prepared by non-profit organizations.[36] In either case, these materials shall feature at least two candidates and their positions, and may not expressly advocate the election or defeat of one candidate or political party over another.[37] The content and distribution of the voter guide may not be coordinated with candidates, other than by sending written questions and receiving answers from candidates to those questions.[38]

If a corporation produces a voter guide based on written questions submitted to candidates:

- the corporation must direct questions in writing to all candidates for a particular congressional seat and receive responses in writing;
- if questioning candidates for U.S. president, for a primary election, the corporation may direct questions only to candidates of one party; for a general election, the corporation may direct questions to those candidates on a sufficient number of general election ballots to win a majority of the electoral votes cast;
- the corporation may not feature one candidate more prominently than another; and
- the guide shall not contain an "electioneering" message or score the candidates' responses in a way that conveys an electioneering message.[39]

Voting Records

A company may prepare and distribute to the general public, or to all employees, the voting records of members of Congress, provided that the records and all communications distributed with them do not expressly advocate the election or defeat of a particular candidate or political party.[40] Decisions on content and distribution of voting records may not be coordinated with a candidate or political party.[41]

Nonpartisan Candidate Debates

The corporation may provide funds to certain nonprofit organizations for the purpose of defraying the costs associated with staging a candidate debate.[42] The debate must include at least two candidates, meeting face to face, and may not promote one candidate over another.[43] Debate participants must be selected on the basis of established objective criteria.[44]

Internet Communications and Hyperlinks

A corporation cannot post Web pages that contain express advocacy unless access to the pages is limited to the restricted class via user-specific passwords.[45] Internet solicitations of contributions to a corporate PAC similarly must be limited to the corporation's restricted class.[46]

A corporation may provide hyperlinks to candidate Web sites from a publicly available corporate Web site, provided that the corporation does not normally charge similarly situated nonpolitical entities for hyperlinks to their Web sites.[47]

4.5   ISSUE ADVERTISING

Corporations sometimes engage in public advertising on issues that mention political parties or politicians. Companies also finance such advertising through trade associations or coalitions. Of course, the federal election laws prohibit corporations from making contributions or expenditures in connection with any federal election by using funds from their general corporate treasuries.[48] The campaign finance laws regulate only certain expenditures, excluding from regulation those that merely constitute "issue advocacy."[49] The distinction between issue advocacy and regulated advocacy becomes crucial in determining when a corporation may use general treasury funds to speak publicly about issues involving candidates. Also, a company's "coordination" of its advertising with a candidate or political party may affect the legality of the speech.

Since the original FECA, corporations have been barred from financing public advertising that expressly advocates the election or defeat of a clearly identified federal candidate. In addition, under the BCRA, a corporation may not directly or indirectly fund "electioneering communication[s]." Electioneering communications are advertisements via broadcast, cable, or satellite that refer "to a clearly identified candidate for Federal office" and are targeted to the relevant electorate within sixty days of a general, special, or runoff election or within thirty days of a primary election or a convention.[50] The prohibition does not apply to newspaper ads, billboards, direct mail, or other types of communications that are not distributed by broadcast, cable, or satellite. The BCRA also does not prohibit broadcast, cable, or satellite messages outside the sixty- or thirty-day blackout periods. However, all communications must be independent of—that is, not "coordinated" with, any candidate or political party.

The BCRA compels disclosure of electioneering communication activity by any person or entity that is permitted to make electioneering communications. FEC regulations exempt PACs from this reporting requirement.[51] The disclosure requirements include: filing with the FEC within twenty-four hours of disbursing more than $10,000 on such ads; identifying the person making or controlling the disbursements and the custodian of the records; identifying those individuals who have contributed $1,000 or more (if individual contributions are made to a "segregated bank account" from which only disbursements for electioneering communications are made, then only individuals who have contributed $1,000 or more to that account need be disclosed); identifying those to whom disbursements of more than $200 have been made; and identifying the election to which the electioneering communications pertain and the names (if known) of the candidates identified or to be identified.[52]

The BCRA allows 501(c)(4) and 527 organizations to engage in electioneering communications as long as they are paid for exclusively with funds provided directly by individuals. The communications may not be funded directly or indirectly by corporate funds.[53] If the 501(c)(4) organization receives business income or funding from corporations, it must establish a segregated account to pay for electioneering communications, and only individuals may contribute.[54] If the communication is "targeted to the relevant electorate," however, then the exception for these organizations is lost.[55] Thus, if a 501(c)(4) or 527 wishes to engage in electioneering communications, it may do so only in districts where the named federal candidates are not running for office. Unincorporated 527 organizations nonetheless may establish discrete funds to pay for electioneering communications pursuant to FEC regulation §114.14 (d). Corporations may finance certain messages under §114.15 as a result of the Wisconsin right to life decision which is discussed in the next section.

4.6   EXPRESS ADVOCACY AND ELECTIONEERING COMMUNICATIONS

Prior to the enactment of the BCRA, "express advocacy" was the general test for deciding whether federal election laws regulate or prohibit expenditures. The Supreme Court noted in *Buckley* that any government intrusion on political advertising, which is protected by the First Amendment, must be narrowly and clearly drawn to allow room for vital public debate:

> [T]he distinction between discussion of issues and candidates and advocacy of election or defeat of candidates may often dissolve in practical application. Candidates, especially incumbents, are intimately tied to public issues involving legislative proposals and governmental actions. Not only do candidates campaign on the basis of their positions on various public issues, but campaigns themselves generate issues of public interest.[56]

Speech that "expressly advocates" the election or defeat of a federal candidate may be limited or restricted.[57] To be considered such speech, the message must clearly identify a specific candidate and encourage his or her election or defeat with specific words such as "vote for," "elect," "support," "Smith for Congress," or the like.[58] One lower court decision has permitted some reference to outside circumstances when evaluating whether a communication constituted express advocacy. However, the decision—known as *Furgatch*—also required a finding that the only reasonable interpretation of a message is that the reader or listener should vote for or against a particular candidate for a particular office.[59]

In 1995, the FEC adopted new regulations redefining express advocacy. Those rules provide as follows:

> "Expressly advocating" means any communication that—
> (a) uses phrases such as "vote for the President," "re-elect your Congressman," "support the Democratic nominee," "cast your ballot for the Republican challenger for U.S. Senate in Georgia," "Smith for Congress," "Bill McKay in

'94," "vote Pro-Life" or "vote Pro-Choice" accompanied by a listing of clearly identified candidates described as Pro-Life or Pro-Choice, "vote against Old Hickory," "defeat" accompanied by a picture of one or more candidate(s), "reject the incumbent," or communications of campaign slogan(s) or individual word(s), which in context can have no other reasonable meaning than to urge the election or defeat of one or more clearly identified candidate(s), such as posters, bumper stickers, advertisements, etc. which say "Nixon's the One," "Carter '76," "Reagan/Bush" or "Mondale!"; or

(b) when taken as a whole and with limited reference to external events, such as the proximity to the election, could only be interpreted by a reasonable person as containing advocacy of the election or defeat of one or more clearly identified candidate(s) because--

  (1) The electoral portion of the communication is unmistakable, unambiguous, and suggestive of only one meaning; and

  (2) Reasonable minds could not differ as to whether it encourages actions to elect or defeat one or more clearly identified candidate(s) or encourages some other kind of action.[60]

This regulation incorporates, as alternatives, both the *Buckley* test (in subsection (a) of the regulation), and the *Furgatch* language (subsection (b)).[61] Subsection (b) was declared unconstitutional as applied in two federal judicial circuits,[62] and other circuit courts considering the "reasonable minds" approach rejected *Furgatch*.[63] Likewise, many state laws regulating issue advocacy have been struck down.[64]

The BCRA introduced a new and additional type of advertising that is regulated by FECA—an "electioneering communication." This term is used to describe an ad: on television, radio, cable, or satellite; thirty days before a primary election or sixty days before a general election; which refers to a candidate; and can be received by over 50,000 persons in the constituency or potential constituency of the referenced candidate.[65] A reference to a candidate includes mention of the candidate's name, the depiction of the candidate's image, or terms such as "the President" or "your Congressman."[66] The FEC has posted on its Web site a calendar of the thirty- and sixty-day preelection periods for all federal elections. The Federal Communications Commission (FCC) has posted on its site a list of the licensed radio and television broadcast signals that can be received by more than 50,000 persons.

An "electioneering communication" is regulated in two general ways. First, corporations and unions are barred from financing such ads, whether directly or indirectly.[67] Second, individuals who finance such ads must file reports with the FEC within twenty-four hours of spending more than $10,000.[68] Such reports must be on FEC Form 9, (see appendix A). A PAC also may pay the expense of an electioneering communication.[69]

The scope of the ban on corporate electioneering communications is large. For example, a company could not pay for a television ad urging viewers in a state to contact a named senator or "your Congressman" in support of specific legislation if the mentioned official is a candidate in any upcoming election and the ad is broadcast within the thirty- or sixty-day blackout period. The message would have to be conveyed by other means, such as direct mail or billboards, or the reference to the candidate would have to be deleted.

In *McConnell v. FEC*, the Supreme Court upheld the facial constitutionality of BCRA's regulation of electioneering communications.[70] The Supreme Court also concluded that "express advocacy" was not the only type of independent speech that may be regulated. However, the court did not otherwise interpret the meaning of "express advocacy," and therefore did not resolve the differences among lower court interpretations or the FEC's definition.

However, in 2007, the Supreme Court concluded that the electioneering communication ban was unconstitutional as applied to issue ads that did not contain express advocacy or the "functional equivalent" of express advocacy. In *Federal Election Commission v. Wisconsin Right to Life, Inc.* (*WRTL*) the court held that ads urging viewers to contact a senator up for reelection to ask him to stop a filibuster of judicial nominees was protected by the First Amendment and could not be barred by the electioneering communication statute. The court ruled that only ads "susceptible of no reasonable interpretation other than an appeal to vote for or against a specific candidate" were the "functional equivalent of express advocacy," and therefore subject to the ban. Protected ads were those that focused and took a position on a legislative issue, exhorted the public to adopt that position and contact public officials with respect to the matter; did not mention an election, candidacy, political party, or challenges; and took no position on a candidate's character, qualifications, or fitness for office.

The BCRA and the *McConnell* and *WRTL* decisions establish a new regulatory paradigm for public political advertising. In summary, corporations may not finance ads that contain express advocacy or electioneering communications (unless they satisfy the *WRTL* test for issue advocacy). Moreover, other public advertising that refers to candidates or political parties may be subject to FEC coordination rules and, therefore, must be executed independently of those candidates and parties. The important legal concept of coordination is the topic of the next section.

4.7   COORDINATION

An additional legal question may arise if spending by a corporation or PAC is controlled by, or coordinated with, a candidate, political party, or political committee. Such coordination may, in some circumstances, lead to the argument that issue spending should be considered an illegal corporate "contribution" to the candidate.

The Supreme Court in *Buckley* distinguished "independent" advocacy from advocacy coordinated with a candidate in the course of declaring restrictions on independent spending unconstitutional:

> [I]ndependent advocacy. . . does not presently appear to pose dangers of real or apparent corruption comparable to those identified with large campaign contributions. The parties defending [the law] contend that it is necessary to prevent would-be contributors from avoiding the contribution limitations by the simple expedient of paying directly for media advertisements or for other portions of the candidate's campaign activities. They argue that expenditures controlled by or coordinated with the candidate and his campaign might well have virtually the same value to the candidate as a contribution and would pose similar dangers of abuse. *Yet such controlled or coordinated expenditures are treated as contributions rather than expenditures under the Act.* . . The absence of prearrangement and coordination of an expenditure with the candidate or his agent not only undermines the value of the expenditure to the candidate, but also alleviates the danger that expenditures will be given as a quid pro quo for improper commitments from the candidate.[71]

Although this discussion was in the context of independent expenditures containing express advocacy, the FEC and others apply the concept to corporate issue advocacy made at the request of, or in coordination with, a federal candidate or committee.

In *FEC v. Christian Coalition*,[72] the United States District Court for the District of Columbia announced a new standard for coordination. The court's standard allowed campaigns to share information with and talk to outside groups, but once campaigns began "negotiating" with or directing these groups to make specific expenditures, they would be considered coordinated and subject to the applicable contribution restrictions.

In the wake of *Christian Coalition*, the FEC defined "coordination" as applied to corporations and other outside groups through rulemaking. Under the resulting regulations, a corporate expenditure for a political communication to the general public was considered coordinated with a candidate or party committee, and thereby illegal, if the communication:

(1) is paid for by any person other than the candidate, the candidate's authorized committee, or a party committee, and
(2) is created, produced or distributed--
   (i) at the request or suggestion of the candidate, the candidate's authorized committee, a party committee, or the agent of any of the foregoing;
   (ii) after the candidate or the candidate's agent, or a party committee or its agent, has exercised control or decision-making authority over the content, timing, location, mode, intended audience, volume of distribution, or frequency of placement of that communication; or
   (iii) after substantial discussion or negotiation between the creator, producer or distributor of the communication, or the person paying for the communication, and the candidate, the candidate's authorized committee, a party committee, or the agent of such candidate or committee, regarding the content, timing, location, mode, intended audience, volume of distribution or frequency of placement of that communication, the result of which is collaboration or agreement. Substantial discussion or negotiation may be evidenced by one or more meetings, conversations or conferences regarding the value or importance of the communication for a particular election.[73]

The BCRA expanded the definition of coordination to include coordination with federal, state, or local political party committees.[74] Additionally, the BCRA mandated that, if electioneering communications are coordinated with a political party, candidate, or an officer or agent of either, then the communication is a contribution to the candidate supported by the communication or that candidate's political party and is subject to contribution limits and prohibitions, such as the ban on contributions from corporate treasuries.[75]

The BCRA repealed the post-*Christian Coalition* FEC regulations on coordination and mandated that the FEC issue new regulations that do not require agreement or formal collaboration and address: the republication of campaign materials; the use of a common vendor; communications directed or made by a person who previously served as an employee of a candidate or a political party; and communications made by a person after substantial discussion about the communication with a candidate or political party.[76]

In sum, corporations planning public advertisements should avoid discussing their programs with federal candidates and political party committees. Issue ads should not be undertaken at the request of a candidate or political party, and a corporation should not seek their approval of particular proposed communications. These precautions should prevent an otherwise permissible issue advertisement from becoming an illegal in-kind contribution to a federal candidate or party.

4.8 FEC COORDINATION REGULATIONS

On December 5, 2002, and again on April 7, 2006, the FEC adopted final rules on "coordinated and independent expenditures."[77] These rules create a two-part test for coordination: content and conduct. The coordination restrictions cover a potentially wider set of interactions between outside entities and federal candidates (including many members of Congress and the president) than the previous rules. Neither formal collaboration nor agreement is required to fulfill the standard on covered conduct. The new law, however, does attempt to create a safe harbor for inquiries about legislative or policy issues. A full description of the new regulations follows.

4.9 COORDINATED COMMUNICATIONS

The definition of "coordinated communication" forms the heart of the new regulations. If a communication by an entity such as a corporation or PAC, or by an individual, is a coordinated communication, then it cannot be an independent communication and is considered to be an in-kind contribution to the candidate, authorized committee, or political party committee with which it is coordinated.[78] This means that the communication is brought within the prohibitions and limitations of FECA, which, among other things, prohibits corporate contributions and limits contributions by PACs to $5,000 per election per candidate. In other words, coordinated corporate communications under these new regulations are illegal corporate contributions.

A communication is a coordinated communication if it is paid for by a person other than a candidate, his or her authorized committee, a political party committee, or an agent of any of the foregoing, and it satisfies one of the content standards *and* one of the conduct standards described below.[79]

4.10 CONTENT STANDARDS

There are four content standards in the new regulations. If a communication is of a type not described by any one of these four content standards, then an entity (including a corporation) has not made a coordinated communication regardless of any interaction with federal candidates or political parties.[80] Close interaction between entities and candidates may, however, give rise to an agency relationship, which would subject any resulting communications to the prohibitions and limitations of FECA.

Electioneering Communications

The first type of communication covered by the coordination regulation involves electioneering communications, as defined in the electioneering communication rulemaking.[81] An electioneering communication is a broadcast, cable, or satellite communication that refers to a clearly identified federal candidate and is broadcast within thirty days of a primary or sixty days of a general or special election.[82] An electioneering communication must also be capable of being received by 50,000 or more persons in the relevant congressional district or state.

Republication of Campaign Materials

The coordination regulations also cover the redistribution, republication, or dissemination of campaign materials such as flyers, brochures, yard signs, etc.[83]

Express Advocacy

A "public communication" that expressly advocates the election or defeat of a clearly identified federal candidate is subject to the coordination rules.[84] There is no time-based limit applicable to this covered conduct category. Based on pre-BCRA court decisions, express advocacy is limited, in most parts of the country, to communications that include such calls for action as "vote for," "elect," "Smith for Congress," or the like.[85]

Communications within Certain Days of an Election

The commission's regulations also prohibit coordination with respect to "public communications" that refer to a political party or a clearly identified candidate for federal office. In the case of presidential candidates, the prohibition applies to public communications that are distributed within 120 days of an election, convention, or caucus.[86] With respect to references to House and Senate candidates, the period is ninety days. Furthermore, the communication must be directed to voters in the jurisdiction of the clearly identified candidate or a jurisdiction in which the political party has one or more candidates appearing on the ballot. According to the commission's explanation and justification, this "directed to voters" factor focuses on the intended audience of the communication and does not attempt to quantitatively measure the audience as in the case of electioneering communications.[87] A ruling by the U.S. Court of Appeals for the District of Columbia (*Shays v. FEC III*, June 13, 2008) struck down the 90/120 day provision thus likely requiring a new regulation with a longer period.

Exceptions to Republication Content Standard

The commission also has issued several exceptions to the content standard involving the dissemination, distribution, or republication of candidate campaign materials. The content standard does not apply if either of the following is true:

- the campaign material is disseminated, distributed, or republished in a news story, commentary, or editorial; or
- the campaign material used by another person consists of a brief quote or portions of materials that demonstrate a candidate's position as part of the person's expression of its own view.[88]

Important for the ninety-day/120-day category and the express-advocacy category, the restrictions apply only to "public communications." Under regulations promulgated by the FEC in its soft money rulemaking, a public communication is "any broadcast, cable or satellite communication, newspaper, magazine, outdoor advertising facility, mass mailing, or telephone bank to the general public, or any other form of general public political advertising."[89] The definition specifically does not include communications made on the Internet or via electronic mail.[90] The term electioneering communication does not include the Internet or e-mail or any communication other than those broadcast on television, radio, cable, and satellite.[91]

4.11   CONDUCT STANDARDS

Only communications that fit one of the content standards described above are subject to the FEC's coordination restrictions. (These are referred to below as "covered communications.") In order to establish "coordination" under the regulations, the conduct must fulfill one of the five conduct standards elucidated below. Unlike the previous coordination rules, no agreement or formal collaboration need be present for the FEC to find coordination.[92] In addition, "[a] candidate's or a political party committee's response to an inquiry about the candidate's or political party committee's positions on legislative or policy issues, but not including a discussion of campaign plans, projects, activities, or needs, does not satisfy any of the conduct standards."[93]

Definition of "Agent"

For the conduct standards, the definition of agent becomes extremely important because coordination with the agent of a candidate or committee is considered to be the same as coordination with the candidate or party.

For a political party, an agent is any person who has "actual authority, either express or implied": to request or suggest that a communication be created, produced, or distributed; to make or authorize a covered communication; to create, produce, or distribute any communication at the request or suggestion of a candidate; to make a direct communication that is created, produced, or distributed with the use of material or information derived from a substantial discussion about the communication with a candidate; or to be materially involved in discussions regarding a communication's content, intended audience, size, prominence, or duration, the means or mode of communication, the specific media outlet used for a communication, or the timing or frequency of a communication.[94]

A candidate's agent is any person who has "actual authority, either express or implied": to request or suggest that a communication be created, produced, or distributed; to make or authorize a covered communication; to request or suggest that any other person create, produce, or distribute any communication; to provide material or information to assist another person in the creation, production, or distribution of any communication; to make or direct a communication that is created, produced, or distributed with the use of material or information derived from a substantial discussion about the communication with a different candidate; or to be materially involved in decisions regarding a communication's content or intended audience, the means or mode of communication, the specific media outlet used for a communication, the timing or frequency of a communication, or the size, prominence, or duration of a communication.[95]

According to the commission, a principal would not assume liability for agents who act outside the scope of their actual authority, but merely acting contrary to the law does not mean that the action is outside the scope of the agent's actual authority.[96] Also, apparent authority is not enough. The authority must be actual, which includes both express and implied authority.[97]

Request or Suggestion

A covered communication "created, produced, or distributed" at the request or suggestion of a candidate, authorized committee, political party committee, or an agent of any of the foregoing, is coordinated. Also, if the person paying for a covered communication suggests how it is to be created, produced, or distributed, and the candidate, authorized committee, political party committee, or agent of the foregoing assents to the suggestion, then the covered communication is coordinated.[98] "Assent" is used by the commission as a form of a request, meaning "an expression of a desire to some person for something to be granted or done."[99]

The "request or suggestion" conduct standard only covers requests or suggestions made to select audiences and does not cover those requests or suggestions offered to the public generally. As a result, requests posted on a public Web page or contained in a newspaper ad would not be covered, whereas those requests e-mailed to a discrete group of persons, made at an invitation-only dinner, or posted on an intranet site would be covered by the standard.[100]

Material Involvement

A covered communication is considered coordinated if a candidate, authorized committee, political party committee, or agent of any of the foregoing is materially involved in decisions regarding any of the following:

- the content of the communication;
- the intended audience for the communication;
- the means or mode of the communication;
- the specific media outlet used for the communication;
- the timing or frequency of the communication; or
- the size or prominence of a printed communication, or the duration of a communication by means of a broadcast, cable, or satellite transmission.[101]

Substantial Discussion

A covered communication is considered coordinated if it is created, produced, or distributed after one or more substantial discussions about the communication between the person paying for the communication (or its employees or agents) and the candidate who is clearly identified in the communication, his or her authorized committee, his or her opponent or the opponent's authorized committee, a political party committee, or an agent of any of the foregoing. "A discussion is substantial . . . if information about the candidate's or political party committee's campaign plans, projects, activities, or needs is conveyed to a person paying for the communication, and that information is material to the creation, production, or distribution of the communication."[102]

Common Vendor

The "common vendor" conduct standard requires several different factors to be present. Each factor is treated separately below.

First, the common vendor conduct standard applies to any commercial vendor—including any owner, officer, or employee of the commercial vendor—that has provided the following services to the candidate who is clearly identified in the covered communication or his or her authorized committee, or his or her opponent or the opponent's authorized committee, or a political party committee, or an agent of any of the foregoing *in the current election cycle*:[103]

- development of media strategy, including the selection or purchasing of advertising slots;
- selection of audiences;
- polling;
- fundraising;
- developing the content of a public communication;
- producing a public communication;
- identifying voters or developing voter lists, mailing lists, or donor lists;
- selecting personnel, contractors, or subcontractors; or
- consulting or otherwise providing political or media advice.[104]

Media buyers that do not involve themselves in any of the above activities are not covered by the common vendor conduct standard.[105]

Second, the common vendor must use or convey to the person paying for the covered communication: information about the clearly identified candidate's campaign[106] plans, projects, activities, or needs, or his or her opponent's campaign plans, projects, activities, or needs; or information used previously by the common vendor in providing services to the candidate who is clearly identified in the covered communication or his or her authorized committee, opponent or opponent's authorized committee, a political party committee, or agent of any of the foregoing.[107]

Finally, for both of the above types of information conveyed or used by the common vendor, "the information [must be] material to the creation, production, or distribution of the [covered] communication."[108] Because of this last requirement, the commission does not consider the common vendor conduct standard to be a flat prohibition on the use of common vendors.[109]

Former Employee or Independent Contractor

The conduct standard involving former employees also involves a multifaceted analysis, which is described in detail below.

First, the former employee conduct standard applies only to covered communications paid for by a former employee or independent contractor, or the employer of a former employee or independent contractor.[110]

Second, a former employee is one who—during the current election cycle—was an employee or independent contractor of the candidate who is clearly identified in the covered communication, or his or her authorized committee, or his or her opponent or the opponent's authorized committee, or a political party committee, or an agent of any of the foregoing.[111]

Third, the former employee or independent contractor must use or convey to the person making the covered communication: information about the clearly identified candidate's campaign plans, projects, activities, or needs, or his or her opponent's campaign plans, projects, activities, or needs; or information used by the former employee or independent contractor in providing services to the candidate who is clearly identified in the covered communication or his or her authorized committee, or opponent, or opponent's authorized committee, political party committee, or agent of any of the foregoing.[112]

Finally, for both of the above types of information conveyed or used by the former employee/independent contractor, "the information [must be] material to the creation, production, or distribution of the [covered] communication."[113] Because of this last requirement, the commission does not consider the former employee or independent contractor conduct standard to be a flat prohibition on the use of former employees or independent contractors.[114]

Safe Harbor for Publicly Available Information

Except with respect to communications made at the request or suggestion of a candidate, authorized committee, political party committee, or agent of the foregoing, there is a safe harbor for communications made where "information material to the creation, production, or distribution of the communication was obtained from a publicly available source." "To qualify for the safe harbor, the person paying for the communication bears the burden of showing that the information used in creating, producing, or distributing the communication was obtained from a publicly available source."[115]

Safe Harbor for the Use of a Firewall

In its 2006 revisions, the FEC created a safe harbor from the coordination rules for the establishment of a firewall between coordinating and noncoordinating individuals or entities by a commercial vendor, former employee, or political committee. To apply, the firewall should be implemented before coordinated activities begin, and it must be described in a written policy that is distributed to all relevant and affected employees, consultants, and clients.

Most importantly, "[t] the firewall must be designed and implemented to prohibit the flow of information between employees or consultants providing services for the person paying for the communication and those employees or consultants currently or previously providing services to the candidate who is clearly identified in the communication, or the candidate's committee, the candidate's opponent, the opponent's authorized committee, or a political party committee." Note that the safe harbor provision "does not dictate the specific procedures required to prevent the flow of information . . . because a firewall is more effective if established and implemented in light of its specific organization, clients, and personnel."[116]

4.12   COMMUNICATIONS BY ASSOCIATIONS

Communications to the Public

Incorporated associations are subject to the FEC rules that regulate corporate-financed political communications. With respect to public communications, the rules are identical to those that apply to business corporations. Accordingly, an association must abide by the principles discussed in sections 4.4 to 4.11 above. Public advertising paid with association funds must avoid "express advocacy" and comply with the electioneering communications laws, and is subject to the "coordination" regulations. There is a limited exception for incorporated ideological associations that do not raise or accept funds from unions or other corporations.[117]

Communications to the Restricted Class

As noted in section 2.12 with regard to association PACs, because associations lack stockholders, there are occasions when the campaign finance rules apply differently to associations than to business corporations. This is true with respect to communications by an association to the "restricted class." The restricted class for business corporations, as described in section 4.2, is the same as the universe that may be solicited for voluntary PAC contributions—i.e., stockholders and executive or administrative personnel. An association also may direct partisan communications to its executive or administrative personnel.[118] However, in lieu of stockholders, associations may include individuals who qualify as "members" of the association.[119] If the association has corporations as members, the association may include "representatives of the corporation with whom the trade association normally conducts the association's activities."[120] For purposes of partisan communications, the association's "restricted class" consists of executive or administrative personnel, individual members, if any, and the representatives of corporate members, if any, as well as their families. Accordingly, an association may, for example, host a candidate appearance before this restricted class under the same circumstances and conditions described in section 4.2. Note, however, that no PAC solicitation may occur if there are in attendance representatives from member companies that have not granted "prior approval." The association also must comply with the "facilitation" rules whenever it solicits individual contributions for candidates.

Communications to Other Employees

An association may sponsor a candidate appearance before an audience that includes nonexecutive employees. If so, the association must observe the conditions described in section 4.3, which include providing similar opportunities to opposing candidates upon request.

NOTES

1. *See* FEC Advisory Opinion 1991-3, Fed. Election Camp. Fin. Guide (CCH) ¶ 6012 (1991) (concluding that copies of a PAC newsletter may be sent to persons who are ineligible to be solicited for contributions if there is no solicitation in the newsletter and no candidates are endorsed).
2. 11 C.F.R. § 114.3(c)(2) (2006); FEC Advisory Opinion 2000-3, Fed. Election Camp. Fin. Guide (CCH) ¶ 6320 (2000). These rules differ slightly for incorporated trade associations.
3. 11 C.F.R. § 114.3(c)(2) (2006).
4. 11 C.F.R. § 114.2(c) (2006).
5. 11 C.F.R. § 114.3(c)(2)(ii) (2006).
6. 11 C.F.R. §§ 114.3(c)(2)(ii)-(iii) (2006).
7. 11 C.F.R. § 114.3(c)(2)(i) (2006).
8. 11 C.F.R. § 114.3(c)(2)(iv) (2006).
9. *Id.*
10. 2 U.S.C. § 441b(b)(2)(A) (Supp. III 2003); 11 C.F.R. § 114.3(a) (2006).
11. 11 C.F.R. § 114.3(c)(1) (2006).
12. 11 C.F.R. § 114.3(c)(3) (2006).
13. 11 C.F.R. § 114.3(c)(4) (2006).
14. *Id.*

15. *Id.*

16. 2 U.S.C. § 431(9)(B)(iii) (2000).

17. 11 C.F.R. §§ 100.8(b)(4), 100.134(a) (2006).

18. 11 C.F.R. § 104.6(a) (2006).

19. 11 C.F.R. § 109.21 (2006).

20. 11 C.F.R. § 109.21(c) (2006).

21. 11 C.F.R. § 114.4(b) (2006).

22. 11 C.F.R. § 114.4(b)(v) (2006).

23. 11 C.F.R. § 114.4(b)(iv) (2006).

24. *Id.*

25. 11 C.F.R. §§ 114.4(b)(i)-(iii) (2006).

26. 11 C.F.R. § 114.4(b)(vii) (2006).

27. 11 C.F.R.. § 114.4(b)(viii) (2006).

28. FEC Advisory Opinion 1996-11, Fed. Election Camp. Fin. Guide (CCH) ¶ 6194 (1996); FEC Advisory Opinion 1988-27, Fed. Election Camp. Fin. Guide (CCH) ¶ 5934 (1988); FEC Advisory Opinion 1980-22, Fed. Election Camp. Fin. Guide (CCH) ¶ 5479 (1980).

29. 11 C.F.R. §§ 114.4(c)(2), (d)(1) (2006).

30. 11 C.F.R. § 114.4(c)(2) (2006).

31. 11 C.F.R. §§ 114.4(c)(3)(i)-(ii) (2006).

32. 11 C.F.R. § 114.4(c)(3)(iv) (2006).

33. 11 C.F.R. § 114.4(c)(3)(iii) (2006).

34. 11 C.F.R. §§ 114.4(c)(3)(v), (d)(2) (2006).

35. 11 C.F.R. §§ 114.4(d)(3)-(6) (2006).

36. 11 C.F.R. § 114.4(c)(5) (2006).

37. *Id.*

38. 11 C.F.R. § 114.4(c)(5)(ii)(A) (2006). This restriction on contacting candidates was held unconstitutional in Clifton v. FEC, 114 F.3d 1309 (1st Cir. 1997), *cert. denied*, 522 U.S. 1108 (1998).

39. 11 C.F.R. §§ 114.4(c)(5)(ii)(A)-(E) (2006).

40. 11 C.F.R. § 114.4(c)(4) (2006).

41. *Id.*

42. 11 C.F.R. § 114.4(f)(1) (2006).

43. 11 C.F.R. § 110.13(b) (2006).

44. 11 C.F.R. § 110.13(c) (2006).

45. FEC Advisory Opinion 1997-16, Fed. Election Camp. Fin. Guide (CCH) ¶ 6246 (1997).

46. FEC Advisory Opinion 2000-7, Fed. Election Camp. Fin. Guide (CCH) ¶ 6325 (2000).

47. FEC Advisory Opinion 1999-17, Fed. Election Camp. Fin. Guide (CCH) ¶ 6308 (1999).

48. 2 U.S.C. § 441b (2000 & Supp. III 2003).

49. Buckley v. Valeo, 424 U.S. 1, 41-44 (1976); *see also* FEC Advisory Opinion 1996-11, Fed. Election Camp. Fin. Guide (CCH) ¶ 6194 (1996) (holding that a nonprofit membership organization could invite candidates for federal office to speak at its convention on issues of interest to its members without violating federal election laws, provided there was no express advocacy by the organization and its employees and agents, or the candidates themselves and their representatives and agents, of the nomination, election, or defeat of any candidate).

50. 2 U.S.C. § 434(f)(3) (Supp. III 2003).

51. 11 C.F.R. § 104.20(b) (2006).

52. 2 U.S.C. §§ 434(f), 441b(c) (2000 & Supp. III 2003); IIC.F.R. § 104.20 (2006).

53. *Id.*

54. *Id.*

55. 2 U.S.C. § 441b(c)(6) (Supp. III 2003).

56. Buckley v. Valeo, 424 U.S. 1, 42-43 (1976).

57. *See id.; see also* FEC v. Mass. Citizens for Life, Inc. (*MCFL*), 479 U.S. 238, 249 (1986); Faucher v. FEC, 928 F.2d 468, 471-72 (1st Cir.), *cert. denied*, 502 U.S. 820 (1991); FEC v. Furgatch, 807 F.2d 857, 860 (9th Cir.), *cert. denied*, 484 U.S. 850 (1987). *MCFL* adopted its express advocacy standard from the narrow construction given to several portions of FECA in *Buckley*. For example, former § 608(e)(1) of FECA restricted certain expenditures "relative to" a candidate for federal office. *Buckley* interpreted the "relative to" language to encompass only "expenditures for communications that in express terms advocate the election or defeat of a

clearly identified candidate for federal office." *Buckley*, 424 U.S. at 44. Similarly, former § 434(e) and (f) of FECA (now § 434(c)(1)) restricted political "contributions or expenditures" made "for the purpose of. . . influencing" the nomination or election of candidates for federal office. *Id.* at 77. In *MCFL*, the court applied a narrowing construction, holding that this language encompassed only contributions or expenditures for express advocacy. *MCFL*, 479 U.S. at 249.

   58. *Buckley*, 424 U.S. at 44 n.52.

   59. *Furgatch*, 807 F.2d at 864; FEC v. Nat'l Org. for Women (*NOW*), 713 F. Supp. 428 (D.D.C. 1989), applied *Furgatch's* express advocacy test to evaluate speech allegedly calling for the election or defeat of particular persons seeking federal office.. The FEC argued that three mailings contained express advocacy, and therefore contended that NOW had violated FECA. *Id.* at 429-30. The court concluded that the FEC's view was too expansive, and instead held that these letters did not contain express advocacy despite their use of "magic words," identification of specific candidates, and direct references to upcoming elections. *See id.* at 435. The court explained:

Further implementation of *Furgatch* necessarily involves the "reasonable minds could differ" test. Reasonable minds could certainly dispute what NOW's letters urged the readers to do. The letters make numerous appeals: . . . raise the nation's consciousness, . . . , speak out, . . . , and put pressure on the Senate and the President. The letters call for action, but they fail to expressly tell the reader to go to the polls and vote against particular candidates in the 1984 election. Because the letters are suggestive of several plausible meanings, because there are numerous pleas for action, and because the types of action are varied and not entirely clear, NOW's letters fail the express advocacy test proposed by the Ninth Circuit in *Furgatch*. </ext>
Id. at 435 (citations omitted).

   60. 11 C.F.R. § 100.22 (2006).

   61. *See Furgatch*, 807 F.2d at 861-65.

   62. *See* Me. Right to Life Comm. Inc. v. FEC, 98 F.3d 1 (1st Cir. 1996); Va. Soc'y for Human Life, Inc. v. FEC, 263 F.3d 379, 392 (4th Cir. 2001).

   63. *See id.* at 391-92 (finding 11 C.F.R. § 100.22(b) unconstitutionally overbroad because it defined express advocacy as a communication that, when taken as a whole, "could only be interpreted by a reasonable person as containing advocacy of the election or defeat of one or more clearly identified candidate(s). . . . The regulation goes too far because it shifts the determination of what is 'express advocacy' away from the words 'in and of themselves' to 'the unpredictability of audience interpretation.'"); *see also* Iowa Right to Life Comm. Inc. v. Williams, 187 F.3d 963, 969 (8th Cir. 1999) (finding an election regulation defining express advocacy according to "what reasonable people or reasonable minds would understand by the communication" was unconstitutional because the regulation "does not require express words of advocacy."); Chamber of Commerce v. Moore, 288 F.3d 187, 195-96 (5th Cir. 2002) ("We agree that the *Furgatch* test is too vague and reaches too broad an array of speech to be consistent with the First Amendment as interpreted in *Buckley* and *MCFL*. Instead, we iterate that the language of the communication must, by its express terms, exhort the viewer to take a specific electoral action for or against a particular candidate."); FEC v. Christian Action Network, Inc., 894 F. Supp. 946 (W.D. Va. 1995), *aff'd*, 92 F.3d 1178 (4th Cir. 1996) (distinguishing *Furgatch* and rejecting the FEC's invitation to consider not only the words used in a television advertisement but also more nebulous characteristics, such as the ad's use of color, music, tone, and editing in determining whether a message constitutes express advocacy).

   64. *See, e.g.*, Vt. Right to Life Comm., Inc. v. Sorrell, 221 F.3d 376, 387 (2d Cir. 2000) (holding statute that imposed disclosure requirements on "[a]ll political advertisements," which it defined as "any communication . . . which expressly or *implicitly* advocates the success or defeat of a candidate" violated *Buckley* and infringed on free speech) (emphasis added); Perry v. Bartlett, 231 F.3d 155, 165 (4th Cir. 2000) (holding state statute imposing disclosure requirements on speakers whose advertisements named political candidate and who manifested intent to advocate election or defeat of candidate unconstitutionally overbroad under First Amendment because advertisement did not use explicit words of express advocacy); Citizens for Responsible Gov't State Political Action Comm. v. Davidson, 236 F.3d 1174, 1187 (10th Cir. 2000) (holding state election statute unconstitutional as applied because it restricted both issue and express advocacy, in violation of the First Amendment); N.C. Right to Life, Inc. v. Bartlett, 168 F.3d 705, 713 (4th Cir. 1999) (finding a statute unconstitutionally vague and overbroad because it encompassed entities engaging in issue advocacy and did not limit its coverage to entities engaging in express advocacy); Va. Soc'y for Human Life, Inc. v. Caldwell, 152 F.3d 268 (4th Cir. 1998) (accepting the view enunciated in the Virginia Supreme Court's answer to a certified question applying a narrowing construction to the phrase "for the purpose of influencing an election" so as to have no

application to individuals or groups that engage solely in issue advocacy); Kansans for Life, Inc. v. Gaede, 38 F. Supp. 2d 928 (D. Kan. 1999) (finding the following statute to be unconstitutionally vague: "A communication which, when viewed as a whole, leads an ordinary person to believe that he or she is being urged to vote for or against a particular candidate for office"); FEC v. Christian Coalition, 52 F. Supp. 2d 45, 61 (D.D.C. 1999), (holding that, under the "express advocacy" test, the communication "must in effect contain an explicit directive," whose effect "is determined first and foremost by the words used"); Planned Parenthood Affiliates of Mich., Inc. v. Miller, 21 F. Supp. 2d 740, 746 (E.D. Mich. 1998) (finding a state statute prohibiting expenditures made from the general fund for communications that use the name or likeness of a candidate within forty-five days of an election, is "overbroad and will chill the exercise of constitutionally protected 'issue advocacy'"); Right to Life of Mich., Inc. v. Miller, 23 F. Supp. 2d 766 (W.D. Mich. 1998) (same).

65. 2 U.S.C. § 434(f)(3) (Supp. III 2003).
66. 11 C.F.R. § 100.29(b)(2) (2006).
67. 2 U.S.C. § 441b(c) (Supp. III 2003).
68. 2 U.S.C. § 434(f)(1) (Supp. III 2003).
69. 11 C.F.R. § 104.20(b) (2006).
70. McConnell v. FEC, 540 U.S. 93, 209 (2003).
71. Buckley v. Valeo, 424 U.S. 1, 46-47 (1976) (emphasis added).
72. FEC v. Christian Coalition, 52 F. Supp. 2d 45 (D.D.C. 1999).
73. 11 C.F.R. § 100.23(c) (2002).
74. 2 U.S.C. § 441a(a)(7)(B) (2000 & Supp. III 2003).
75. 2 U.S.C. § 441a(a)(7)(C) (Supp. III 2003).
76. BCRA § 214(b).
77. 11 C.F.R. §§ 109.20-.23 (2006).
78. 11 C.F.R. §§ 100.16, 109.20(b) (2006).
79. 11 C.F.R. § 109.21 (2006).
80. *See* 68 Fed. Reg. 421, 426-28 (Jan. 3, 2003) (Explanation and Justification on Coordinated and Independent Expenditures).
81. 11 C.F.R. § 109.21(c)(1) (2006).
82. 11 C.F.R. § 100.29 (2006).
83. 11 C.F.R. § 109.21(c)(2) (2006).
84. 11 C.F.R. § 109.21(c)(3) (2006).
85. *See* Buckley v. Valeo, 424 U.S. 1, 42 n.52 (1976); *see also* Chamber of Commerce v. Moore, 288 F.3d 187 (5th Cir. 2002); Va. Soc'y for Human Life, Inc. v. FEC, 263 F.3d 379 (4th Cir. 2001); Iowa Right to Life Comm., Inc. v. Williams, 187 F.3d 963 (8th Cir. 1999); Me. Right to Life Comm., Inc. v. FEC, 98 F.3d 1 (1st Cir. 1996); *but see* FEC v. Furgatch, 807 F.2d 857 (9th Cir. 1987).
86. 11 C.F.R. § 109.21(c)(4) (2006).
87. *See* 68 Fed. Reg. 421, 431 (Jan. 3, 2003).
88. 11 C.F.R. § 109.23 (2006).
89. 11 C.F.R. § 100.26 (2006).
90. *Id. See also* 68 Fed. Reg. at 430; 67 Fed. Reg. 49,064, 49,071-72 (July 29, 2002) (Explanation and Justification on Prohibited and Excessive Contributions: Non-Federal Funds or Soft Money).
91. *See* 11 C.F.R. § 100.29(c) (2006).
92. 11 C.F.R. § 109.21(e) (2006).
93. 11 C.F.R. § 109.21(f) (2006).
94. 11 C.F.R. § 109.3 (2006).
95. 11 C.F.R. § 109.3(b) (2006).
96. 68 Fed. Reg. 421, 424 (Jan. 3, 2003).
97. *Id.*
98. 11 C.F.R. § 109.21(d)(1) (2006).
99. 68 Fed. Reg. at 432 (quoting the definition of "request" in *Black's Law Dict.* 1304 (6th ed. 1990)).
100. *See* 68 Fed. Reg. at 432.
101. 11 C.F.R. § 109.21(d)(2) (2006).
102. 11 C.F.R. § 109.21(d)(3) (2006).
103. The Code of Federal Regulations defines "election cycle" as the time period between the first day after the previous general election for the office by a candidate and the next general election for that office. 11 C.F.R. 100.3(b) (2006).

104. 11 C.F.R. § 109.21(d)(4)(ii) (2006).
105. *See* 68 Fed. Reg. at 437.
106. According to the commission, the term "campaign" is used in order that the conduct standard might not encompass lobbying activities or information that is not related to a campaign. *See* 68 Fed. Reg. at 437.
107. 11 C.F.R. § 109.21(d)(4)(iii) (2006).
108. *Id.*
109. *See* 68 Fed. Reg. at 436.
110. 11 C.F.R. § 109.21(d)(5)(i) (2006).
111. *Id.*
112. 11 C.F.R. § 109.21(d)(5)(ii) (2006).
113. *Id.*
114. *See* 68 Fed. Reg. at 438.
115. 11 C.F.R. §§ 109.21(d)(2), (3), (5) (2006); 71 Fed. Reg. 33,190, 33,205 (June 8, 2006).
116. 11 C.F.R. § 109.21(h) (2006); 71 Fed. Reg. at 33,206-07.
117. 11 C.F.R. § 114.10.
118. 11 C.F.R. § 114.8(h) (2006).
119. *Id.*
120. 11 C.F.R. § 114.8(h) (2006).

5. Corporate Relations with Government Officials

Contents

5.1   INTRODUCTION

There are two sets of laws and rules that govern gifts and payments by corporations to or on behalf of senators and members of Congress (collectively, "Members"). The first source of restrictions on Members' activities are the rules of conduct adopted by each house of Congress.[1] The second source of governance is federal statutory law, which is applicable to all federal officeholders and provides a broad framework for the more specific rules and regulations.[2] The House and Senate each adopt rules of conduct, which they most recently did in 2007, and those rules apply to Members and congressional staff. The rules impose no civil or criminal penalties and may be enforced only by the Senate and House ethics committees against Members and staff. However, lobbyists and companies that hire them are now required to comply with the gift rules because they are incorporated into the Lobbying Disclosure Act.[3] Members who are also candidates are governed by additional restrictions. Executive branch officials are subject to separate laws and regulations administered by the Office of Government Ethics and other applicable agencies and departments.

Companies that employ lobbyists may trigger registration and reporting obligations under the Lobbying Disclosure Act. The status of an individual as a lobbyist subjects the person to additional restrictions under congressional ethics laws.

5.2   LOBBYING DISCLOSURE

Lobbying is a regulated activity. Those who engage in advocacy on behalf of an organization for compensation are potential lobbyists whose identities and activities must be disclosed. Statutory definitions dictate when someone is a lobbyist and when that person and/or the organization must register and start filing reports with the government.

The Lobbying Disclosure Act (LDA) requires lobbyists, lobbying firms, and entities that employ in-house lobbyists (collectively known as "registrants") to register and report with Congress. Guidance with respect to the LDA comes from the Secretary of the Senate and the Clerk of the House, and the Comptroller General is authorized to audit LDA registrations and reports for compliance.[4] There are civil and criminal penalties for violations of the LDA.[5] Also, the gift rules of the House and Senate are made directly applicable to lobbyists, lobbying firms, and employers of in-house lobbyists through the LDA.

The LDA is triggered by the presence of an individual who meets the statutory definition of a "lobbyist." Once there is a lobbyist, either the employer or the lobbyist must register and thereafter file lobbying reports.

Who Is a Federal Lobbyist?

An individual becomes a "lobbyist," as defined by the LDA, when:

- He or she is employed or retained by a client (including an in-house employer) for compensation for services that include more than one "lobbying contact" (without regard to a time period); and
- "Lobbying activities" constitute 20 percent or more of the services rendered by the individual to that client (employer) over a three-month period (e.g., January 1 to March 31).[6]

What Is a Lobbying Contact?

A "lobbying contact" is defined as "any oral or written communication (including an electronic communication) to a covered executive branch official or a covered legislative branch official that is made on behalf of a client with regard to":

- The formulation, modification, or adoption of federal legislation (including legislative proposals);
- The formulation, modification, or adoption of a federal rule, regulation, executive order, or any other program, policy, or position of the United States government;
- The administration or execution of a federal program or policy (including the negotiation, award, or administration of a federal contract, grant, loan, permit, or license); or
- The nomination or confirmation of a person for a position subject to confirmation by the Senate. [7]

What Are the Exceptions to "Lobbying Contact"?

Listed below are some of the more pertinent exceptions to the definition of "lobbying contact":

- A communication that is a request for a meeting, a request for the status of an action, or any other similar administrative request, if the request does not include an attempt to influence a covered executive or legislative official;
- A communication made in the course of participation in an advisory committee subject to the Federal Advisory Committee Act;
- Testimony given before a committee, subcommittee, or task force of Congress, or submitted for inclusion in the public record of a hearing conducted by such committee, subcommittee, or task force;
- Information provided in writing in response to an oral or written request by a covered executive or legislative branch official for specific information;
- Information required by subpoena, civil investigative demand, or otherwise compelled by statute, regulation, or other action of Congress or an agency;
- Any communication compelled by a federal contract, grant, loan, permit, or license;
- A communication made in response to a notice in the Federal Register or other similar publication soliciting communications from the public directed to the agency official specifically designated in the notice to receive such communications;
- Information not possible to report without disclosing information, the unauthorized disclosure of which is prohibited by law;
- A communication made to an official in an agency with regard to a judicial proceeding or a criminal or civil law enforcement inquiry, investigation, or proceeding or with regard to a filing or proceeding that the government is specifically required by statute or regulation to maintain or conduct on a confidential basis;
- Written comments in a public proceeding made on the record in a public proceeding;
- A written petition for agency action required to be a matter of public record; and
- Grassroots efforts (contacting other parties to contact congressional or agency officials).[8]

What Are Lobbying Activities?

"Lobbying activities" are lobbying contacts and any efforts in support of such contacts, including preparation or planning activities, research and other background work that is intended—at the time of its preparation—for use in contacts and in coordination with the lobbying activities of others.[9] Importantly, activities that are not lobbying contacts because of the many exceptions may, if they support lobbying contacts, be lobbying activities.

Who Are Covered Legislative Branch Officials?

A "covered legislative branch official" means:

- A Member of Congress;
- An elected officer of either house of Congress;
- Any employee of a Member of Congress, a committee of either house of Congress, the leadership staff of either house of Congress, a joint committee of Congress, and a working group or caucus organized to provide legislative services or other assistance to Members of Congress; and
- Those designated in section 109(13) of the Ethics in Government Act as an "officer or employee of the Congress."[10]

Who Are Covered Executive Branch Officials?

A "covered executive branch official" includes:

- The president;
- The vice president;
- Any officer or employee in the Executive Office of the President;
- Any officer or employee serving in a position in Level I-V of the Executive Schedule;
- Any member of the uniformed services whose pay grade is at or above O-7; and
- "Schedule C" employees.[11]

However, if a registrant elects to report its lobbying expenses under the so-called "tax method," the Internal Revenue Service definition of "executive branch" may be used. That definition includes:

- The president;
- The vice president;
- Any officer or employee of the White House Office of the Executive Office of the President, and the two most senior-level officers of each of the other agencies in the Executive Office, and
- Any individual serving in a position in level I of the Executive Schedule under section 5312 of title 5, United States Code; any other individual designated by the president as having cabinet-level status; and any immediate deputy of any of the foregoing individuals.[12]

The IRS definition is much more limited than the LDA definition. For example, so-called Schedule C employees, presidential appointees (other than cabinet secretaries and deputy secretaries) and all military personnel (except for the secretary and deputy secretary of defense) are *not* executive branch officials.[13] Accordingly, employees who communicate with such officials would *not* be engaging in lobbying contacts. This distinction is often important to companies that have frequent contact with the military, such as defense contractors, or with independent regulatory agencies. By electing the tax method of reporting lobbying expenses, such registrants often reduce the universe of potential lobbying contacts with covered executive branch officials, and therefore reduce the potential number of employees who meet the LDA definition of "lobbyist." This election, however, is not available to lobbying firms.

When to Register?

Employers must register electronically, on Form LD-1[14] within forty-five days of an employee becoming a lobbyist. On the other hand, for a corporation or trade association that is already registered under the LDA, the entity simply enters the names of new in-house lobbyists on each applicable "lobbying issues" page of the corporation's next LDA report (Form LD-2).[15]

Registrations—and updates by means of the quarterly lobbying reports—must disclose, among other information, the following:

- *Former covered positions*. The covered executive branch and covered legislative branch positions held by each new lobbyist for the past twenty years;[16]
- *Affiliated organizations*. Any entity that contributes more than $5,000 in a calendar quarter to the registrant or client "to fund the lobbying activities of the registrant" and "actively participates in the planning, supervision, or control of such lobbying activities." There is a limited exception for members of, and donors to, an organization listed as such on the organization's public Web site, and there is a broader exception focused on natural-person members. This disclosure requirement is aimed at coalitions and associations, although its impact is not limited to such groups.[17]
- *Foreign entities*. Any foreign entity that:
  - holds at least 20 percent equitable ownership in the client or an affiliated organization;
  - directly or indirectly, in whole or in major part, plans, supervises, controls, directs, finances, or subsidizes the activities of the client or of an affiliated organization; or
  - is an affiliate of the client or an affiliated organization and has a direct interest in the outcome of the lobbying activity.[18]

When to Report?

Quarterly LDA reports (Forms LD-2) must be filed electronically and are due on the twentieth day following the end of each calendar quarter (or the next business day if the twentieth day falls on a weekend or holiday), covering the preceding calendar quarter.[19] The first quarterly report under the amended LDA was due on April 21, 2008. A corporation or trade association reports for all of its in-house lobbyists in one report.[20] Employees who are lobbyists need not file a quarterly report.[21]

Separate LDA semiannual reports on Form LD 203 also must be filed electronically and are due July 30 and January 30 (or the next business day if a weekend or holiday).[22] These semiannual reports cover the time periods of January 1 to June 30 and July 1 to December 31, respectively. These semiannual reports must be filed separately by the registrant (e.g., the corporation) and by each individual who is a lobbyist.[23]

Electronic filings are made through the web site of the Clerk of the House.

What to Report?

Quarterly LD-2 Reports. The following information must be included in the quarterly LDA reports:

- The total amount spent during the calendar quarter on federal lobbying activities, including: the value of time spent engaged in lobbying activities by employees who are not registered lobbyists; payments to outside lobbyists and lobbying firms; and the federal lobbying portion of any dues or other payments made to trade associations and other 501(c) organizations;
- Specific bills, bill numbers, and issues on which registered lobbyists made lobbying contacts during the calendar quarter; and
- Updates to information provided in the registration, including new in-house registered lobbyists, former covered executive and legislative branch positions, affiliated organizations, and foreign entities.[24]

Semiannual LD 203 Reports. LDA registrants and each registered lobbyist must file LD 203 reports. The following information must be included in the reports:

- The names of all political committees established or controlled by the lobbyist or lobbyist employer;
- Contributions of $200 or more made within the semiannual period to a federal candidate, officeholder, leadership PAC, or political party committee by the lobbyist, lobbyist employer, or a PAC established or controlled by either;
- Contributions of $200 or more made within the semiannual period to a presidential library foundation or presidential inaugural committee made by the lobbyist, lobbyist employer, or a PAC established or controlled by either; and
- Payments—other than those required to be disclosed by the recipient to the FEC— by the lobbyist, lobbyist employer, or a PAC established or controlled by either:
  - for the cost of an event to honor or recognize a covered legislative or executive branch official;
  - to an entity that is named for a covered legislative branch official;
  - to a person or entity in recognition of a covered legislative branch official;
  - to an entity established, financed, maintained, or controlled by a covered legislative or executive branch official;
  - to an entity designated by a covered legislative or executive branch official; and
  - to pay the costs of a meeting, retreat, conference, or other similar event, held by—or in the name of—one or more covered legislative or executive branch officials.[25]

What Certifications Must Be Made?

Lobbyist employers and each registered lobbyist must make the following certifications in their respective semiannual LD 203 reports:

- *Gift certification.* That the lobbyist employer or lobbyist "has not provided, requested, or directed a gift, including travel, to a Member of Congress or an officer or employee of either House of Congress with knowledge that receipt of the gift would violate rule XXXV of the Standing Rules of the Senate or rule XXV of the Rules of the House of Representatives."

- *Rules certification.* That the lobbyist employer or lobbyist "has read and is familiar with those provisions of the Standing Rules of the Senate and the Rules of the House of Representatives relating to the provision of gifts and travel."[26]

Failure to comply with LDA requirements may result in civil fines of up to $200,000 or even criminal sanctions.[27]

5.3   HOUSE AND SENATE GIFT RESTRICTIONS

Both houses of Congress use the same definition of "gift," which is extremely broad:

> For the purpose of this rule, the term "gift" means any gratuity, favor, discount, entertainment, hospitality, loan, forbearance or other item having monetary value. The term includes gifts of services, training, transportation, lodging and meals, whether provided in kind, by purchase of a ticket, payment in advance or reimbursement after the expense has been incurred.[28]

Gift Ban on Lobbyists & Entities That Employ or Retain Lobbyists

Under the rules of the Senate and the House, registered federal lobbyists and persons that employ or retain federal lobbyists may not provide gifts to Members of Congress or congressional staff, unless the items or services fall within one of the enumerated exceptions in the rules.[29]

By virtue of the Honest Leadership and Open Government Act of 2007 (HLOGA),[30] the gift rules of Congress are directly applicable to registered federal lobbyists, lobbying firms, entities that employ in-house lobbyists, and in-house employee-lobbyists. It is a violation of the LDA for any of these persons to give a gift or provide travel to a Member of Congress or congressional staffer "if the person has knowledge that the gift or travel may not be accepted by that covered legislative branch official under the Rules of the House of Representatives or the Standing Rules of the Senate (as the case may be)."[31] Violation of the LDA is subject to civil and criminal penalties.[32]

Further, lobbying firms and employers of in-house lobbyists (collectively known as "registrants") twice per year must certify on LD 203 reports as to the following:

- That they have "not provided, requested, or directed a gift, including travel, to a Member of Congress or an officer or employee of either House of Congress with knowledge that receipt of the gift would violate rule XXXV of the Standing Rules of the Senate or rule XXV of the Rules of the House of Representatives;" and
- That they have "read and [are] familiar with those provisions of the Standing Rules of the Senate and the Rules of the House of Representatives relating to the provision of gifts and travel."[33]

Finally, the House and Senate both ban a Member from participating in an event during a national party convention if such event honors that Member and is directly paid for by a lobbyist or an entity that retains or employs lobbyists.[34]

Gifts from Persons That Are Not Lobbyists or Clients of Lobbyists

With respect to nonlobbyists and persons that do not retain or employ lobbyists, Members and staff may not accept an individual gift valued at $50 or more unless the gift falls within a specific exception provided by that house of Congress.[35] Gifts from any individual or company may not aggregate to $100 or more for a calendar year, but gifts of less than $10 are not aggregated for purposes of the $99.99 calendar-year limit.[36] In addition, gifts from employees of an organization are attributed to both the organization and the individual unless the gifts are based on personal friendship.[37]

A gift to a family member of a Member or other individual based on his or her relationship with a Member will normally be considered a gift to a Member if "it is given with the knowledge and acquiescence of the Member . . . and the Member . . . has reason to believe the gift was given because of his official position."[38] If food is provided to a Member and his or her spouse at the same time, then only the food for the Member is considered a gift.[39] Members and staff may not repeatedly accept small gifts otherwise permitted.[40]

Exceptions to the House & Senate Gift Bans

A gift to a Member or staff is subject to the general gift prohibition or limit outlined above unless it falls within an exception. A gift does not include anything for which a Member has paid market value,[41] but Members and staff are not allowed to buy down the price of a gift (i.e., pay for part of a gift or meal such that the remainder is less than $10 or $50). Covered persons may, however, accept some gifts and decline others in order to come under the gift limits if the items are naturally divisible (e.g., tickets).[42]

The specific enumerated exceptions to the House and Senate gift rules are listed below.

1. *Personal friendship.* Gifts provided to Members or staff that are based on personal friendship or family relationship.[43] This exception usually requires that the friendship is preexisting, that there is a history of exchanging gifts, and that there is no tax deduction taken or reimbursement given for the gift.[44] Acceptance of gifts valued at $250 or more requires the written permission of the Ethics Committee or Conduct Committee.[45]

2. *Widely attended event.* Free attendance and meals at a widely attended event, provided the invitation comes from the sponsor of the event and the attendee determines attendance to be within the scope of his or her official duties is permitted.[46] An event is "widely attended" if the organizer expects twenty-five persons other than Members, officers, and staff of Congress and their spouses, and if the event is open to individuals throughout a given industry or profession or is attended by a range of persons with interest in a given matter.[47] The sponsor of the event is the entity (or entities) primarily responsible for organizing the event and not the mere purchasers of tables at the event.[48]

3. *Informational material* sent to a congressional office (e.g., books and videotapes) by the author, publisher, or producer.[49] This exception does not apply to application, developmental, or entertainment software. The exception does apply to informational software as long as the database is entirely self-contained.[50]

4. *Awards or prizes* given in contests open to the general public.[51]

5. *Home-state products* of nominal value intended for promotional purposes.[52]

6. *Training.*[53] This exception may include food and refreshment integral to the training. The Senate has a broad view of training, and includes any meeting with the presentation of information to twenty-five or more persons from more than one

congressional office. The House does not allow the provision of meals at legislative briefings.[54]

7. *Personal hospitality* of an individual for nonbusiness purposes unless provided by a registered lobbyist or foreign agent (unless the latter two are personal friends of the beneficiary per exception #1).[55] The hospitality must occur in the personal residence of the individual.[56] Costs may not be reimbursed nor deducted for income tax purposes.

8. *Commemorative gifts* (e.g., plaques or trophies) given at in-person presentations.[57] Members and employees may not accept a gift if it has significant utilitarian or artistic value.

9. *Items of nominal or little intrinsic value* (e.g., baseball caps, greeting cards, T-shirts, and items worth less than $10.).[58]

10. Food or refreshments of nominal value not offered as part of a meal (i.e., attendance at receptions.)[59]

11. Benefits and opportunities available to the general public or to a class that includes all federal employees.[60]

12. *Contributions to legal expense funds* (except by registered lobbyists and registered agents of foreign principals).[61] Such contributions are subject to dollar limits.

13. (House only) *Meals or local transportation incident to a visit to a business site* where the meal is offered by the management on the business premises and in a group setting with employees of the business.[62]

14. (Senate only) *Meals at certain constituent events.* Senators and staff may accept a meal of less than $50 at an event in the Member's home state sponsored by constituents of the senator or a group that consists primarily of constituents where at least five constituents attend, no registered lobbyist attends, and the senator or staffer participates in the event as a speaker or panel member or performs an appropriate ceremonial function.[63]

15. Political contributions.[64]

16. Food, refreshment, lodging, transportation and other benefits:
    - from outside business activities;
    - customarily provided by prospective employers; or
    - provided by a political organization in connection with a fundraising or campaign event.[65]

17. Honorary degrees and other prizes (and associated travel, food, refreshments, and entertainment) given in recognition of public service.[66]

18. Anything paid for by the federal, state, or local governments.[67]

19. *Travel, food, and lodging reimbursement* (except from a registered lobbyist or agent of a foreign principal) for a meeting, speaking engagement, fact-finding trip, or similar event "in connection with [the Member's] official duties."[68] Travel may be only of certain duration, and other expenses (e.g., entertainment) are not part of this exception.

The Senate Ethics Committee and the House Standards of Conduct Committee regularly provide written waivers for wedding, baby, and similar gifts when the beneficiary makes prior application. Such gifts may not come from persons seeking official action from the beneficiary or his or her Member of Congress.[69]

Food Provided to Congressional Offices (for nonlobbyists and nonclients only)

A private entity may provide food, such as pizza, to a congressional office for consumption by the staff in the office. However, special rules apply to the provision of such food in each house.[70] Despite these special rules, such gifts are prohibited if from a lobbyist or an entity that employs or retains a lobbyist.[71]

In the Senate, such an office gift is a gift to the senator whose office received the food and the value of the gift is the total fair market value of the food.[72] Therefore, the total value of the food must come within the $49.99/$99.99 limits if provided by a nonlobbyist or company that does not employ or retain lobbyists.

In the House, the rules are different and more liberal. "The value of perishable food sent to an office shall be allocated among the individual recipients and not to the Member . . . ."[73] Staffers, however, should refuse food "if the person offering it has a direct interest in the particular legislation or other official business on which the staff is working at the time."[74]

Charity Events

Both the Senate and the House rules contain an exception that allows Members and staff to participate in charity fundraisers.[75] Under certain circumstances, a Member of the House and Senate or a member of the staff of either house may accept free attendance at a charity fundraiser for himself or herself and for his or her spouse or dependent as well as local transportation, transportation, and/or lodging associated with the charity fundraiser. The different rules are described below.

In 2003, the House Committee on Standards of Official Conduct issued a memorandum describing when House members and staff may accept transportation and lodging in connection with a charity fundraiser.[76] First, all of the net proceeds of the fundraiser must accrue to a charity exempt from taxation under section 501(c)(3) of the Internal Revenue Code. Second, more than one-half of the fees paid by the paying participants must be tax deductible as a charitable donation. Third, the offer of free attendance and correspondence concerning the fundraiser made to Members and staff must come from the benefiting charity and from no other source.[77] Finally, although donors to the fundraising event may request that Members and staff be invited, they may not earmark funds for their participation.[78]

"Free attendance" under the House rules includes "waiver of all or part of a conference or other fee, the provision of local transportation, or the provision of food, refreshment, entertainment, and instructional materials furnished to all attendees as an integral part of the event."[79] "The term does not include entertainment collateral to the event, nor does it include food or refreshments taken other than in a group setting with all or substantially all other attendees."[80] A Member or staff member of the House may also accept transportation and lodging reasonably necessary for the individual to attend the event if the above-described criteria for the fundraising event are fulfilled.[81]

Finally, a Member of the House or a staffer also may accept an invitation to be accompanied at an event by either his or her spouse or a dependent.[82]

The Senate Ethics Committee has stated that senators and staff may accept free attendance at a charity fundraising event only from the sponsor of the event.[83] This is the entity principally organizing the event and not merely a donor to the event.[84]

"Free attendance" in the Senate includes the provision of local transportation, the waiver or all or part of a conference or other fee, and the provision of food, refreshments, entertainment, and instructional materials furnished to all attendees as part of the event.[85] "The term does not include entertainment collateral to the event, nor does it include food or refreshments taken other than in a group setting with all or substantially all other attendees."[86] Senators and Senate staff also may accept travel and lodging in connection with the charity event unless the event is substantially recreational in nature.[87]

A senator and a Senate staffer may accept a sponsor's unsolicited offer of free attendance for an accompanying spouse or dependent at a charity event if others at the event generally will be accompanied, or if such attendance is appropriate to assist in the representation of the Senate.[88]

Special Rules for Lobbyists

In addition to the gift ban discussed above, there are several activities by individual registered lobbyists that Congress prohibits:

- Making a gift to any entity maintained or controlled by a Member or staff member.
- Making a charitable contribution on the basis of designation, recommendation, or specification of a Member or staff member (unless in lieu of honorarium).
- Making a contribution to a legal expense fund.
- Making a financial contribution or expenditure relating to a conference or retreat sponsored by or affiliated with an official congressional organization.[89]

Furthermore, a Member of Congress may not accept travel expense reimbursements from a registered lobbyist, foreign agent, or a lobbying firm.[90]

Finally, as to travel, a registered lobbyist may not accompany a senator, representative, or staffer on any segment of an officially connected one-day trip paid for by a lobbyist client (unless, in the House, the sponsor of the trip is an institution of higher education).[91] The same rule applies in the House for any other type of officially connected trip.[92] For other officially connected trips, a lobbyist may not accompany a senator or Senate staffer "at any point throughout the trip."[93] In both houses, a lobbyist may only to a *de minimis* or negligible extent plan, organize, request, or arrange an officially connected one-day trip paid for by a lobbyist client (unless, in the House, the sponsor of the trip is an institution of higher education).[94] The same rule applies in the Senate to any other officially connected trip,[95] although the House prohibits outright the involvement of registered lobbyists in the planning, organizing, requesting, or arranging of other types of officially connected trips.[96]

Privately Funded Travel

Under certain circumstances, a private organization may defray reasonable travel, food, and lodging expenses of a congressman, senator, or staffer whose travel is "officially-connected" (not campaign related or personal).[97] The House and Senate ethics committees require prior written approval and have instituted formal procedures for review and approval. See appendix D5. Entities that employ or retain lobbyists are subject to special restrictions, including a one-day/one-night limit on the length of the travel, limited involvement by lobbyists, and a ban on lobbyists accompanying the congressional official on the privately paid travel.[98]

Honoraria and Outside Income

Honoraria to federal officials are regulated by the Ethics in Government Act of 1978, as amended. That statute flatly prohibits payment of an honorarium to a member (including a senator), officer, or employee.[99] Nonetheless, the statute allows an honorarium of up to $2,000 if paid to a charitable organization.[100] "Honorarium" is defined by statute as "a payment of money or anything of value for an appearance, speech, or article (including a series of appearances, speeches, or articles if the subject matter is directly related to the individual's official duties or the payment is made because of the individual's status with the government) by a Member, officer, or employee . . . ."[101] The member must provide some service in return for an honorarium. In addition, actual and necessary travel expenses incurred by the member and one relative may also be paid or reimbursed by any other person.[102] The rules set forth in the Ethics in Government Act are quoted in the Senate rules and are consistent with the House rules.[103]

In practice, Members or staff may participate in speaking engagements for a corporation but must direct the company to pay the sum, up to $2,000, directly to a particular charity. The Member may not accept the check for transmittal to the charity. The individual, or a parent, spouse, sibling, child, or dependent relative of the individual, may not receive any financial benefit from the designated charitable organization.[104]

Corporations registered under the Lobbying Disclosure Act are required to disclose information regarding expenditures for honoraria or other dealings with Members on Form LD-203. Members who receive such payments also may be required by the Ethics in Government Act to disclose this outside income.[105] Accordingly, honoraria and travel payments, whether made as a reimbursement or otherwise, will most likely be reported publicly by the corporation, or the Member or staffer, or both.

5.4   EXECUTIVE BRANCH GIFT RESTRICTIONS

Like congressional officials, executive branch employees are subject to restrictions on gifts. An employee of the executive branch may not solicit or accept any gift from a prohibited source that is given because of the employee's official position. The definition of "gift"[106] includes training, travel, and meals, among other things. It does not include the following items:

- Modest items of food or drink, such as soft drinks, coffee, and donuts, offered other than at a meal;
- greeting cards and items with little intrinsic value; and
- opportunities available to a broad class of government employees.[107]

The term "prohibited source" means any person who: is seeking official action by the employee's agency; does business or seeks to do business with the employee's agency; conducts activities regulated by the employee's agency; or has interests that may be affected substantially by the performance or nonperformance of the employee's official duties.[108] If the majority of an organization's members fall within the four categories, then the organization itself is a prohibited source.[109]

There are selected exceptions to the general executive branch gift rules. However, even where one or more of the exceptions are applicable, a federal government employee still may not: accept a gift in return for being influenced in the performance of an official act; solicit or coerce the offering of a gift; or accept gifts from the same or different sources on a basis so frequent that a reasonable person would be led to believe the employee is using his or her public office for private gain.[110] Some specific exceptions include:

- *Gifts under $20.* An employee may accept gifts of $20 or less from any source, including a prohibited source. The aggregate of all gifts from any one source must not exceed $50 for the calendar year. An employee may decline some distinct and separate tangible items (e.g., tickets) offered on a single occasion and accept others. An employee may not buy down the price of the gift (i.e., pay for part of a gift or meal such that the remainder is less than $20).[111]
- *Personal relationships.* An employee may accept gifts given based on a personal relationship.[112]
- *Conference participants.* An employee may accept free attendance—including food, refreshment, and entertainment furnished as an integral part of the event—from the event sponsor at a conference or event where he or she is asked to participate as a speaker or panel participant on behalf of the agency.[113]
- *Widely attended gatherings.* Where it is determined that attendance will further agency programs or operations, an employee may accept from the event sponsor free attendance at a widely attended gathering. A gathering is widely attended if it is expected that a large number of persons with a diversity of views or interests, or from throughout an interested industry or profession, will attend. If more than 100 persons are expected, and the value is less than $305, the employee may accept free attendance from a person other than the sponsor.[114]
- *Social invitations.* An employee may accept social invitations from persons other than prohibited sources.[115]

The Office of Government Ethics (OGE) regulations for the executive branch are generally applicable to the Executive Office of the President, and the executive office has no published additional or supplemental gift rules. The executive office, however, may have unpublished policies in relation to certain situations that go beyond the OGE regulations. Also, subunits of the executive office may have their own internal policies, and some subunits, such as the Office of Management and Budget and the National Security Council, extend beyond basic White House employees.

While the above gift rules apply to all executive branch personnel, departments and agencies are permitted to adopt even more restrictive rules. As a result, specific agency rules should always be consulted.

5.5 BRIBERY AND GRATUITIES

The ultimate sanction against improper payments to government officials is the federal bribery and gratuities statute.[116] The bribery portion of the statute is applicable only when there exists clear evidence of an offer of something of monetary value in exchange for a government official's act or omission.[117] The statute provides for criminal penalties against "[w]hoever . . . directly or indirectly . . . offers or promises anything of value to any public official . . . with intent . . . to influence any official act; or . . . to induce such public official . . . to do or omit to do any act in violation of the lawful duty of such official or person."[118] This section requires that, for a violation to occur, there must be a corrupt intent in connection with a specific *quid pro quo*. A violation can result in a fine of up to "three times the monetary equivalent of the thing of value, or imprisonment for not more than fifteen years, or both."[119]

The ban against gratuities does not require a corrupt intent, but it does require a specific link between the giving of a thing of value and a specific "official act."[120] The gratuities section states that "[w]hoever . . . otherwise than as provided by law for the proper discharge of official duty ... directly or indirectly gives, offers, or promises anything of value to any public official, former public official, or person selected to be a public official for or because of any official act performed or to be performed by such public official, former public official, or person selected to be a public official—may be fined or imprisoned for up to two years, or both."[121]

Previously, some courts had found that because no expressed *quid pro quo* was required by this section, a violation could occur if a public official simply accepted anything of value from a person or company that the official could assist or injure in his or her official capacity.[122] The Supreme Court rejected such a broad interpretation in *United States v. Sun-Diamond Growers of California*. The Court found that the statute's "insistence upon an 'official act,' carefully defined, seems pregnant with the requirement that some particular official act be identified and proved."[123] The Court also noted that "the intricate web of regulations" similarly governing gifts to public officials mandated a more tailored interpretation of this provision. Accordingly, the Court held that "the Government must prove a link between a thing of value conferred upon a federal office and a specific 'official act' for or because of which it was given."[124]

The Ethics Reform Act of 1989 is another part of "the intricate web of regulations" governing relationships with public officials.[125] It proclaims that no "employee of the executive, legislative, or judicial branch shall solicit or accept anything of value from a person . . . whose interests may be substantially affected by the performance or nonperformance of the individual's official duties."[126] The Ethics Reform Act also authorizes the promulgation of ethical rules for each branch of the federal government.[127] Pursuant to that authorization, each branch of government regulates the acceptance of gifts by its employees. In summary, gifts—even *de minimus* ones—that convey even the appearance of rewarding a public official for an official act, must be avoided.

5.6   LEADERSHIP PACS

Many Members of Congress have established a political action committee in addition to their campaign committee. This practice was commenced by committee chairmen and members elected to leadership positions in the House or Senate. Hence, these PACs acquired the label of "leadership PACs." Such committees, however, are not limited to senior legislators. In fact, there are more than 100 such committees registered with the FEC.[128] In one instance, a freshman congressman formed a leadership PAC before he was sworn into his first term in office.

A leadership PAC is subject to the same contribution limits as a corporate PAC. They may not accept more than $5,000 per year from an individual or other PAC. They may not contribute more than $5,000 per election to any candidate for federal office.

In the past, leadership PACs formed nonfederal accounts. These accounts accepted "soft money," which included donations from corporations. However, under the BCRA, Members of Congress and their agents may not "solicit, receive, direct, transfer, or spend" soft money.[129] Therefore, since November 6, 2002 (the effective date of BCRA), leadership

PACs have not been permitted to maintain nonfederal accounts because their congressional sponsors are subject to the new restrictions. Furthermore, commencing in 2008, as a result of the Honest Leadership and Open Government Act of 2007, leadership PACS will disclose the names of lobbyists or registrants that "bundle" in excess of $15,000 in contributions to the leadership PAC in a semiannual period.[130]

NOTES

1. Rules of the House of Representatives (110th Congress) [hereinafter House Rule], Rule XXV, *available at* http://www.rules.house.gov/ruleprec/110th.pdf; Standing Rules of the Senate [hereinafter Senate Rule], Rule XXXV, *available at* http://rules.senate.gov/senaterules/Rules091407.pdf.

2. Over the past forty-six years, Congress has passed four prominent pieces of legislation that impose various ethical obligations in government: Act of Oct. 23, 1962, Pub. L. No. 87-849, 76 Stat. 1119 (current version at 18 U.S.C. §§ 201-225); Ethics in Government Act of 1978, Pub. L. No. 95-521, 92 Stat. 1824 (codified as amended in scattered sections of 2, 5, 18, 28, and 39 U.S.C.); Ethics Reform Act of 1989, Pub. L. No. 101-94, 103 Stat. 1716 (codified as amended in scattered sections of 2, 3, 5, 10, 18, 22, 26, 28, 31, 37, 41, 42, and 50 U.S.C.); Honest Leadership and Open Government Act of 2007, Pub. L. No. 110-81 (codified in scattered sections of 2, 5, 18, 22, and 25 U.S.C.).

3. *See infra* appendix D: Lobbying Disclosure Act of 1995.

4. *See infra* appendix D: Guidance on the Lobbying Disclosure Act of 1995.

5. 2 U.S.C. § 1606 (2002).

6. 2 U.S.C. §§ 1602(7)-(8), (10) (2002), *amended by* Honest Leadership and Open Government Act of 2007, Pub. L. No. 110-81, § 201; *see also infra* appendix D: Lobbying Disclosure Act of 1995 §§ 3(7)-(8), (10).

7. 2 U.S.C. § 1602(8)(A) (2002).

8. 2 U.S.C. § 1602(8)(B) (2002); *see also infra* appendix D: Lobbying Disclosure Act of 1995 § 3(8)(B).

9. 2 U.S.C. § 1602(7) (2002); *see also infra* appendix D: Lobbying Disclosure Act of 1995 § 3(7).

10. 2 U.S.C. § 1602(4) (2002); *see also infra* appendix D: Lobbying Disclosure Act of 1995 § 3(4).

11. 2 U.S.C. § 1602(3) (2002); *see also infra* appendix D: Lobbying Disclosure Act of 1995 § 3(3).

12. IRC § 162(e)(6) (2007).

13. *Id.*

14. *See infra* appendix D: Form LD-1.

15. *See infra* appendix D: Guidance on the Lobbying Disclosure Act of 1995, at 19; appendix D: Form LD-2.

16. 2 U.S.C. § 1603(b)(6) (2002), *amended by* Honest Leadership and Open Government Act of 2007, Pub. L. No. 110-81, § 208; *see also infra* appendix D: Lobbying Disclosure Act of 1995 § 4(b)(6).

17. 2 U.S.C. § 1603(b)(3) (2002), *amended by* Honest Leadership and Open Government Act of 2007, Pub. L. No. 110-81, § 201; *see also infra* appendix D: Lobbying Disclosure Act of 1995 § 4(b)(3).

18. 2 U.S.C. § 1603(b)(4) (2002), *amended by* Honest Leadership and Open Government Act of 2007, Pub. L. No. 110-81, § 201; *see also infra* appendix D: Lobbying Disclosure Act of 1995 § 4(b)(4).

19. Honest Leadership and Open Government Act of 2007, Pub. L. No. 110-81, § 201; *see also infra* appendix D: Lobbying Disclosure Act of 1995 § 5(a).

20. *See infra* appendix D: Guidance on the Lobbying Disclosure Act of 1995, at 15.

21. *See id.*

22. Honest Leadership and Open Government Act of 2007, Pub. L. No. 110-81, § 203; *see also infra* appendix D: Lobbying Disclosure Act of 1995 § 5(d)(1).

23. Honest Leadership and Open Government Act of 2007, Pub. L. No. 110-81, § 203; *see also infra* appendix D: Lobbying Disclosure Act of 1995 § 5(d)(1).

24. Honest Leadership and Open Government Act of 2007, Pub. L. No. 110-81, § 201; *see also infra* appendix D: Lobbying Disclosure Act of 1995 § 5(b) (2002).

25. Honest Leadership and Open Government Act of 2007, Pub. L. No. 110-81, § 203; *see also infra* appendix D: Lobbying Disclosure Act of 1995 § 5(d)(1).

26. Honest Leadership and Open Government Act of 2007, Pub. L. No. 110-81, § 203; *see also infra* appendix D: Lobbying Disclosure Act of 1995 § 5(d)(1)(G).

27. 2 U.S.C. § 1606(a)(2) (2002), *amended by* Honest Leadership and Open Government Act of 2007, Pub. L. No. 110-81, § 210; *see also infra* appendix D: Lobbying Disclosure Act of 1995 § 7(a)(2).

28. Senate Rule XXXV, cl. 1(b)(1); *see also* House Rule XXV, cl. 5(a)(2)(A) (stating the rule with substantially similar language).

29. House Rule XXV, cl. 5(a)(1)(A)(ii); Senate Rule XXXV, cl. 1(a)(2)(B).

30. Honest Leadership and Open Government Act of 2007, Pub. L. No. 110-81.

31. Honest Leadership and Open Government Act of 2007, Pub. L. No. 110-81, § 206.

32. 2 U.S.C. § 1606 (2002), *amended by* Honest Leadership and Open Government Act of 2007, Pub. L. No. 110-81, § 210; *see also infra* appendix D: Lobbying Disclosure Act of 1995 § 7.

33. Honest Leadership and Open Government Act of 2007, Pub. L. No. 110-81, § 203; *see also infra* appendix D: Lobbying Disclosure Act of 1995 § 5(d)(1)(G).

34. House Rule XXV, cl. 8; Senate Rule XXXV, cl. 1(d)(5).

35. House Rule XXV, cl. 5(a)(1)(B); Senate Rule XXXV, cl. 1(a)(2); *see also* House Committee on Standards of Official Conduct, *Gift Rule Amendments at the Beginning of the 110th Congress* (June 14, 2007), *available at* http://www.house.gov/ethics/m_gift_rule_amendments_revised_06_07.htm.

36. House Rule XXV, cl. 5(a)(1)(B); Senate Rule XXXV, cl. 1(a)(2).

37. Select Committee on Ethics, *Senate Ethics Manual* 55 (2003), *available at* http://ethics.senate.gov/downloads/pdffiles/manual.pdf; *House Gifts & Travel Booklet, available at* http://www.house.gov/ethics/Gifts_and_Travel_Chapter.htm.

38. House Rule XXV, cl. 5(a)(2)(B)(i); *see also* Senate Rule XXXV, cl. 1(b)(2)(A) (using substantially similar language).

39. House Rule XXV, cl. 5(a)(2)(B)(ii); Senate Rule XXXV, cl. 1(b)(2)(B).

40. *See House Gifts & Travel Booklet, supra* note 36.

41. House Rule XXV, cl. 5(a)(3)(A); Senate Rule XXXV, cl. 1(c)(1).

42. *House Gifts & Travel Booklet, supra* note 36.

43. House Rule XXV, cls. 5(a)(3)(C)-(D); Senate Rule XXXV, cl. 1(c)(3)(4).

44. House Rule XXV, cl. 5(a)(3)(D)(ii); Senate Rule XXXV, cl. 1(c)(4)(B).

45. House Rule XXV, cl. (a)(5); Senate Rule XXXV, cl. 1(e).

46. House Rule XXV, cl. (a)(4)(A); Senate Rule XXXV, cl. 1(d).

47. *House Gifts & Travel Booklet, supra* note 36; *Senate Ethics Manual, supra* note 36, at 38.

48. *House Gifts & Travel Booklet, supra* note 36; *Senate Ethics Manual, supra* note 36, at 38.

49. House Rule XXV, cl. 5(a)(3)(I); Senate Rule XXXV, cl. 1(c)(9).

50. *House Gifts & Travel Booklet, supra* note 36.

51. House Rule XXV, cl. 5(a)(3)(J); Senate Rule XXXV, cl. 1(c)(10).

52. House Rule XXV, cl. 5(a)(3)(V); Senate Rule XXXV, cl. 1(c)(12).

53. House Rule XXV, cl. 5(a)(3)(L); Senate Rule XXXV, cl. 1(c)(13).

54. *House Gifts & Travel Booklet, supra* note 36.

55. House Rule XXV, cl. 5(a)(3)(P); Senate Rule XXXV. cl. 1(c)(4).

56. *House Gifts & Travel Booklet, supra* note 36.

57. House Rule XXV, cl. 5(a)(3)(S); Senate Rule XXXV, cl. 1(c)(20).

58. House Rule XXV, cl. 5(a)(3)(W); Senate Rule XXXV, cl. 1(c)(23).

59. House Rule XXV, cl. 5(a)(3)(U); Senate Rule XXXV, cl. 1(c)(22).

60. House Rule XXV, cl. 5(a)(3)(R)(i); Senate Rule XXXV, cl. 1(c)(19)(A).

61. House Rule XXV, cl. 5(a)(3)(E); Senate Rule XXXV, cl. 1(c)(5).

62. *House Gifts & Travel Booklet, supra* note 36.

63. Senate Rule XXXV, cl. 1(g)(1)(A).

64. House Rule XXV, cl. 5(a)(3)(B); Senate Rule XXXV, cl. 1(c)(2).

65. House Rule XXV, cl. 5(a)(3)(G); Senate Rule XXXV, cl. 1(c)(7).

66. House Rule XXV, cl. 5(a)(3)(K); Senate Rule XXXV, cl. 1(c)(11).

67. House Rule XXV, cl. 5(a)(3)(O); Senate Rule XXXV, cl. 1(c)(16).

68. House Rule XXV, cl. 5(b)(1)(A); Senate Rule XXXV, cl. 2.

69. *House Gifts & Travel Booklet, supra* note 36; *Senate Ethics Manual, supra* note 36, at 41-42. *See also* House Rule XXV, cl. 5(a)(3)(T); Senate Rule XXXV, cl. 1(c)(21).

70. *See Senate Ethics Manual, supra* note 36, at 24-25, 61; *House Gifts & Travel Booklet, supra* note 36.

71. House Rule XXV, cl. 5(a)(1)(A)(ii); Senate Rule XXXV, cl. 1(a)(2)(B).

72. *Senate Ethics Manual, supra* note 36, at 61.

73. House Rule XXV, cl. 5(a)(1)(B).

74. *House Gifts & Travel Booklet, supra* note 36.

75. House Rule XXV, cl. 5(a)(4)(C); Senate Rule XXXV, cl. 1(d)(3).

76. House Committee on Standards and Official Conduct, *Recent Gift Rule Amendments* (April 11, 2003), *available at* http://www.house.gov/ethics/m_gift_rule_amendments.htm.

77. *Id.*

78. *House Gifts & Travel Booklet, supra* note 36.

79. House Rule XXV, cl. 5(a)(4)(D).

80. *Id.*

81. House Rule XXV, cl. 5(a)(4)(C); *Recent Gift Rule Amendments, supra* note 75.

82. *Id.*

83. *Senate Ethics Manual, supra* note 36, at 39.

84. *Id.*

85. Senate Rule XXXV, cl. 1(d)(4).

86. *Id.*

87. *Senate Ethics Manual, supra* note 36, at 39.

88. Senate Rule XXXV, cl. 1(d)(2).

89. House Rule XXV, cl. 5(e); Senate Rule XXXV, cl. 3.

90. House Rule XXV, cl. 5(b)(1)(A); Senate Rule XXXV, cl. 2(a). *See also House Gifts & Travel Booklet, supra* note 36.

91. House Rule XXV, cls. 5(b)-(c); Senate Rule XXXV, cl. 2(d).

92. House Rule XXV, cl. 5(c)(1)(A).

93. Senate Rule XXXV, cl. 2(d)(1)(B)(ii).

94. House Rule XXV, cls. 5(c)(1)-(2); Senate Rule XXXV, cls. 2(d)(1)-(2).

95. Senate Rule XXXV, cl. 2(d)(1)(A).

96. House Rule XXV, cl. 5(c)(3).

97. House Rule XXV, cl. 5(b)(1)(A); Senate Rule XXXV, cl. 2(a)(1).

98. *See infra* appendix D: Travel Guidelines and Regulations, for a memorandum from the House committee that explains the new travel rules and also includes the forms that the sponsor of the trip and the invited official must fill out.

99. Ethics in Government Act of 1978, Pub. L. No. 95-521, § 501(b), *reprinted as amended in* 5 U.S.C. app. (2000).

100. Ethics in Government Act of 1978, Pub. L. No. 95-521, § 501(c), *reprinted as amended in* 5 U.S.C. app. (2000).

101. Ethics in Government Act of 1978, Pub. L. No. 95-521, § 505(3), *reprinted as amended in* 5 U.S.C. app. (2000).

102. *Id.*

103. House Rule XXV cl. 1; Senate Rule XXXVI (quoting 5 U.S.C. app. 7, § 501).

104. *Id.*

105. Ethics in Government Act of 1978, Pub. L. No. 95-521, § 102(a), *reprinted as amended in* 5 U.S.C. app. (2000).

106. 5 C.F.R. § 2635.203(b) (2007).

107. *Id.*

108. 5 C.F.R. § 2635.203(d) (2007).

109. 5 C.F.R. § 2635.203(d)(5) (2007).

110. 5 C.F.R. § 2635.202(c) (2007).

111. 5 C.F.R. § 2635.204(a) (2007).

112. 5 C.F.R. § 2635.204(b) (2007).

113. 5 C.F.R. § 2635.204(g)(1) (2007).

114. 5 C.F.R. §§ 2635.204(g)(2)-(3) (2007).

115. 5 C.F.R. § 2635.204(h) (2007).

116. 18 U.S.C. §§ 201-225 (2000).

117. 18 U.S.C. § 201(b) (2000).

118. 18 U.S.C. § 201(b)(1) (2000).

119. 18 U.S.C. § 201(b) (2000).

120. *See* United States v. Sun-Diamond Growers of Cal., 526 U.S. 398, 404-05 (1999).

121. 18 U.S.C. § 201(c)(1) (emphasis added).

122. *See, e.g.*, United States v. Bustamante, 45 F.3d 933, 940 (5th Cir. 1995).

123. *Sun-Diamond Growers*, 526 U.S. at 406.

124. *Id.* at 414.

125. Ethics Reform Act of 1989, Pub. L. No. 101-194, 103 Stat. 1716 (codified as amended in scattered sections of 2, 3, 5, 10, 18, 22, 26, 28, 31, 37, 41, 42, and 50 U.S.C.).

126. 5 U.S.C. § 7353(a) (2000).

127. 5 U.S.C. § 7353(b)(1) (2000).

128. CQ MoneyLine, *Campaign Finance*, http://moneyline.cq.com/pml/home.do (last visited February 12, 2008).

129. 2 U.S.C. § 441i(e)(1) (2000 & Supp. III 2003).

130   Honest Leadership and Open Government Act of 2007, Pub. L. No. 110-81, § 204.

6. Contributions by Foreign Corporations and Their U.S. Subsidiaries

Contents

6.1 GENERAL RULE

It is unlawful for a foreign national—either directly or indirectly—to make any contribution or donation of money or other thing of value, or to promise to make any such contribution or donation, in connection with an election to any political office or in connection with any primary election, convention, or caucus held to select candidates for any political office. This prohibition includes disbursements for expenditures, independent expenditures, and electioneering communications. Furthermore, a foreign national may not—directly or indirectly—contribute or donate to a political party. It is also illegal for any person to solicit, accept, or receive any such contribution or donation from a foreign national.[1]

A "foreign national" is defined as:

- "an individual who is not a citizen of the United States and who is not lawfully admitted for permanent residence;"[2]
- "a partnership, association, corporation, organization or other combination of persons organized under the laws of or having its principal place of business in a foreign country;"[3]
- a foreign government or political party;[4] and
- an individual or entity "outside of the United States,"[5] except that a U.S. citizen or an entity organized under U.S. law or the law of any place subject to U.S. jurisdiction, and has its principal place of business within the United States, are not foreign nationals.[6]

The BCRA amended this provision. First, it explicitly excluded "a national of the United States" from the definition of foreign national.[7] This is an apparent reference to residents of American Samoa and perhaps other territories and commonwealths that send representatives to Congress.[8] In addition, the BCRA made clear that foreign nationals may not expend funds to influence a federal or nonfederal election—for example, soft money contributions to state and local parties.[9]

Foreign nationals also may not contribute or direct contributions to state party building funds[10] or make disbursements for electioneering communications[11] or independent expenditures.[12] The prohibition on contributions by foreign nationals differs from other provisions of the federal election laws in that it covers all elections at any level of government, rather than only federal elections. The only other class of contributors barred from making contributions or expenditures in campaigns for any political office are national banks and federally chartered corporations.[13] Unlike foreign nationals, these other types of companies may establish PACs. In sum, foreign nationals, including corporations incorporated or headquartered in a foreign country, may not make political donations or disbursements.

Foreign citizens who are lawfully admitted for permanent residence may contribute to U.S. campaigns.[14] The phrase "lawfully admitted for permanent residence" is defined as "the status of having been lawfully accorded the privilege of residing permanently in the United States as an immigrant in accordance with the immigration laws."[15] U.S. Citizenship and Immigration Services (formerly the Immigration and Naturalization Service) uses the designation "lawful permanent resident" (LPR) to identify persons possessing the "status" described in this law. "Green cards" are used by LPRs to prove their status for employment, to obtain drivers' licenses and social security cards, and for government programs such as AFDC and Medicaid. Therefore, the election laws and regulations permitting contributions by permanent resident aliens are usually understood to apply to green card holders.

Not all aliens working in the U.S. have LPR status. For example, an alien may be visiting the U.S. for business.[16] An alien may also work temporarily for a present employer (or a subsidiary or affiliate) in a managerial, executive, or other capacity that requires specialized knowledge.[17] Although these individuals are lawfully in the United States, they are not LPR immigrants, may not contribute to U.S. political parties, candidates, or campaign committees, and they may not participate in the decision-making processes of a PAC.

6.2   PACS AND CONTRIBUTIONS

No foreign corporation or association may itself establish a PAC.[18] United States subsidiaries of foreign corporations may establish a PAC, provided, however, that no foreign national is solicited for contributions or involved in the PAC's decision-making processes.[19] In addition, a joint venture incorporated in the United States and partially owned by a foreign corporation may establish a PAC,[20] as can a U.S.-incorporated trade association whose members include foreign corporations.[21] However, a domestic corporation may not make contributions through its PAC with funds provided or reimbursed by the foreign parent.[22]

Employees of foreign subsidiaries of U.S. corporations, who are not themselves foreign nationals, may be solicited and give through payroll deduction to the PAC of a parent U.S. corporation.[23] Foreign nationals, however, may not direct, dictate, control, or directly or indirectly participate in the PAC or the PAC decision-making process.[24]

A U.S. corporation that is a wholly owned subsidiary of a foreign corporation may contribute in state and local elections if corporate contributions are allowed by state law, if no foreign nationals exercise decision-making authority over the contribution, and if the funds are not provided or reimbursed by the foreign parent.[25]

NOTES

1. 2 U.S.C. § 441e(a) (Supp. III 2003); 11 C.F.R. §§ 110.20(a)(3), (b)-(c) (2006).
2. 11 C.F.R. § 110.20(a)(3)(ii) (2006); *see also* 2 U.S.C. §§ 441e(b)(1)-(2) (2000 & Supp. III 2003).
3. 22 U.S.C. § 611(b) (2000).
4. *Id.*
5. *Id.*
6. *Id.*
7. 2 U.S.C. § 441e(b)(2) (Supp. III 2003).
8. *See* FEC Advisory Opinion 1994-28, Fed. Election Camp. Fin. Guide (CCH) ¶ 6134 (1994); FEC Advisory Opinion 1998-14, Fed. Election Camp. Fin. Guide (CCH) ¶ 6266 (1998).
9. 2 U.S.C. § 441e(a) (Supp. III 2003); 11 C.F.R. § 110.20(b)(c) (2006).
10. 11 C.F.R. § 110.20(d) (2006).
11. 11 C.F.R. § 110.20(e) (2006).
12. 11 C.F.R. § 110.20(f) (2006).
13. *See* 2 U.S.C. § 441b(a) (2000).
14. *See* 2 U.S.C. § 441e (2000 & Supp. III 2003). Permanent residents should be present in the United States at the time of any contribution because 22 U.S.C. § 611(b) specifies that individuals " outside the United States" are " foreign principals" unless they are U.S. citizens.
15. 8 U.S.C. § 1101(a)(20) (2000).
16. 8 U.S.C. § 1101(a)(15)(B) (2000).
17. 8 U.S.C. § 1101(a)(15)(L) (2000).
18. FEC Advisory Opinion 1977-53, Fed. Election Camp. Fin. Guide (CCH) ¶ 5294 (1978).
19. FEC Advisory Opinion 2000-17, Fed. Election Camp. Fin. Guide (CCH) ¶ 6334 (2000); FEC Advisory Opinion 1999-28, Fed. Election Camp. Fin. Guide (CCH) ¶ 6305 (1999); FEC Advisory Opinion 1990-8, Fed. Election Camp. Fin. Guide (CCH) ¶ 5986 (1990); FEC Advisory Opinion 1980-100, Fed. Election Camp. Fin. Guide (CCH) ¶ 5548 (1980); FEC Advisory Opinion 1978-21, Fed. Election Camp. Fin. Guide (CCH) ¶ 5327 (1978); *see* 11 C.F.R. § 110.20(i) (2006) (limiting involvement of foreign nationals).
20. FEC Advisory Opinion 1983-18, Fed. Election Camp. Fin. Guide (CCH) ¶ 5721 (1983).
21. FEC Advisory Opinion 1980-111, Fed. Election Camp. Fin. Guide (CCH) ¶ 5560 (1980).
22. FEC Advisory Opinion 1989-20, Fed. Election Camp. Fin. Guide (CCH) ¶ 5970 (1989).
23. FEC Advisory Opinion 1982-34, Fed. Election Camp. Fin. Guide (CCH) ¶ 5678 (1982).
24. 11 C.F.R. § 110.20(i) (2006).
25. FEC Advisory Opinion 1989-29, Fed. Election Camp. Fin. Guide (CCH) ¶ 5976 (1989); FEC Advisory Opinion 1985-3, Fed. Election Camp. Fin. Guide (CCH) ¶ 5809 (1985); FEC Advisory Opinion 1983-31, Fed. Election Camp. Fin. Guide (CCH) ¶ 5735 (1983); FEC Advisory Opinion 1982-10, Fed. Election Camp. Fin. Guide (CCH) ¶ 5651 (1982).

7. State and Local Elections and Soft Money

Contents

7.1   OVERVIEW

This *Primer* focuses on corporate participation in federal elections, federal lobbying, and the federal election laws. As discussed in chapter 6, foreign corporations, national banks, and federally chartered corporations may not make contributions in any federal, state, or local election. State and local jurisdictions, however, often permit all other corporations to participate in elections, pursuant to regulations that vary from state to state. This chapter addresses state and local election laws as well as so-called soft money.

7.2   STATE CONTRIBUTION LIMITS FOR CORPORATIONS AND PACS

A summary of state contribution limits for corporations and PACs can be found in appendix E. This summary is included only as a guide. State election laws are constantly changing, and it is crucial to verify current laws in any jurisdiction—state or local—in which a corporation becomes politically active. Reporting obligations and deadlines also vary among the states and should be independently confirmed.

The summary briefly lists the state campaign finance laws of the fifty states and the District of Columbia. In general, there are five categories of state laws that may apply to corporate contributions in state and local elections:

- unlimited direct corporate contributions are allowed;
- limited direct corporate contributions are allowed;

- no direct corporate contributions are allowed, but PAC contributions are permitted and the corporation may pay the PAC's administrative expenses;
- no direct corporate contributions are allowed, but PAC contributions are permitted—provided that the PAC reimburses the corporation for all administrative costs; and
- no direct corporate contributions and no PAC contributions are allowed.

The summary is not intended to describe the myriad nuances of each state's laws in detail, but rather to provide an overview. The following legal checklist identifies issues that should be resolved in a given state.

Permissible contributors. The summary identifies whether corporations or PACs may contribute, but does not list other individuals and entities that often are prohibited from making contributions or are more heavily regulated—such as public utilities, gaming operators, lobbyists and their employers, and government contractors.

Dollar limits. The summary identifies how much corporations and PACs may contribute, but time periods vary. For example, some states have contribution limits per election (primary and general are separate), whereas others have contribution limits per election cycle (primary and general are counted together).

Registration and reporting. Most states have registration and reporting requirements for federal and state PACs, but often those requirements are not triggered until a PAC reaches a certain minimum dollar threshold. Many states allow federal PACs to make contributions to state and local candidates with no or minimal additional reporting burdens. Some states require separate reporting by corporations that make direct political contributions.

Aggregation of contributions. States differ as to whether related companies—i.e., subsidiaries and affiliates—must aggregate their contributions in terms of complying with contribution limits.

Fundraising blackout periods. Some states have time periods during which contributions may not be made, such as while the legislature is in session or more than a year in advance of an election.

Political parties and PACs. Some states limit the amount that can be given to state party committees and PACs.

PAC requirements. Some states place additional requirements on out-of-state or federal PACs, such as requiring an out-of-state PAC to designate a resident of that state as the PAC treasurer with respect to contributions made in that state.

Individual contributions. Most states have individual contribution limits.

Laundered contributions. All states prohibit laundered contributions (i.e., contributions made in the name of an individual or entity that is not actually making the contribution).

Additional laws. Certain local jurisdictions, including counties, cities, and special districts such as transit authorities, have their own separate campaign finance laws in addition to the applicable state laws.

Electioneering communications. In the wake of BCRA, several states have enacted provisions that either prohibit or require public reporting of preelection day advertising. The laws vary greatly as to timing and scope.

Referenda. The summary does not identify any limits or other regulations involving referenda contributions.

Federal prohibited contributions. Foreign nationals, national banks, and federally chartered corporations are prohibited by federal law from making any contributions—including soft money contributions—at the state or local level.

7.3   SOFT MONEY

"Soft money" is not a legal term. It usually refers to money contributed for "political" purposes that need not comply with the contribution limits and restrictions of federal election law. Soft money donations from a corporation's general treasury—prior to the effective date of the BCRA—were most commonly donated to the nonfederal accounts of national political parties, including the congressional and senatorial campaign committees. In contrast, donations subject to all the federal restrictions and prohibitions (e.g., PAC donations within contribution limits) are often referred to as "hard money."

The BCRA, effective November 6, 2002, bans certain previously permissible soft money donations and uses. Those provisions include: a ban on soft money contributions to national political party committees; restrictions on the use of soft money funds by state and local parties; and a ban on soft money "building funds" of national political party committees.[1] The BCRA also bars national party officials and federal candidates—including members of Congress—and their "agents" from soliciting soft money donations to state and local parties. Nonetheless, corporate donations to state and local political party committees are legal under BCRA if they are legal under state laws.

In addition to a complete ban on corporate donations to national party committees, the BCRA also bans state and local political parties from using soft money for "federal election activity."[2] Federal election activity includes: voter registration activities within 120 days of a regularly scheduled federal election; voter identification conducted in connection with an election for a federal office; and "issue advertising" that refers to and "promotes, supports, attacks or opposes" a clearly identified candidate for federal office.[3]

Levin Money

The BCRA created an exception to the general rule that state and local political parties must pay for federal election activities with only hard money. This exception is known as the "Levin Amendment."[4] It allows state and local parties to pay for political activity with soft money as long as: the activity does not refer to a clearly identified candidate for federal office; the activity is not broadcast, unless it refers solely to a state or local candidate;[5] the contributions used to pay for these activities are hard money or soft money permitted under state law, but do not exceed $10,000 per year; and the contributions are raised by that particular state or local party and are not provided by any other national, state, or local party.[6] Accordingly, a corporation may contribute Levin money up to $10,000 per year per state or local party committee if permitted by applicable state law. The committee may then use those proceeds and its hard money to finance the excepted activities.

Building Funds

Building funds—monies donated to construct or purchase party office buildings—are subject to restrictions under the BCRA. The BCRA forbids corporations from contributing to the building funds of national party committees. State and local parties, however, remain free to receive such donations, subject to state law.[7]

Tax-Exempt Organizations

Certain tax-exempt organizations, such as § 501(c)(4) social welfare organizations or § 501(c)(6) trade associations, may be engaged in political activities and may still receive soft money donations under the BCRA.[8] Nonparty organizations, including certain committees qualified under section 527 of the Internal Revenue Code (527 organizations), may accept and spend soft money. However, national party officials will not be permitted to solicit such funds.[9] Federal candidates, congressmen, senators, and their respective staffs are also subject to solicitation restrictions.[10]

Inaugural Committees

There are many festivities attendant to the swearing in of a new or reelected president. The actual swearing-in ceremony is controlled by a joint congressional committee and is funded through government appropriations. However, there are other social events, such as parades, balls, receptions, and entertainment. These functions are sponsored by and paid for by the president-elect's inaugural committee.

Historically, an inaugural committee was not regulated by the FEC. The BCRA, however, for the first time required an inaugural committee to file a public financial disclosure report with the FEC. The report must be filed ninety days after the inaugural ceremony and must reveal the name, address, amount, and date of receipt of any donation equal to or greater than $200.[11]

Notwithstanding the new disclosure requirement, an inaugural committee may continue to accept donations from any source, except a foreign national.[12] Accordingly, nonforeign national corporations may donate to such an entity, although donations over $200 must be publicly disclosed by the committee.

Finally, corporations and other entities registered under the Lobbying Disclosure Act must disclose donations to inaugural committees on the Form LD-203 report.

NOTES

1. 2 U.S.C. § 441i (Supp. III 2003).
2. 2 U.S.C. § 441i(b)(1) (Supp. III 2003).
3. 2 U.S.C. § 431(20) (Supp. III 2003).
4. 2 U.S.C. § 441i(b)(2)(B) (Supp. III 2003).
5. *Id.* It is important to note that, if the broadcast communication refers to anything that the BCRA would otherwise treat as federal election activity (voter registration, voter identification, etc.) it may remove the communication from the Levin Amendment exception.
6. 2 U.S.C. §§ 441i(b)(2)(B)(i)-(iv) (Supp. III 2003).
7. 2 U.S.C. § 453(b) (2000 & Supp. III 2003); 11 C.F.R. § 114.1(a)(2)(ix) (2006).
8. 2 U.S.C. § 441i(d) (Supp. III 2003).
9. 2 U.S.C. § 441i(a)(2) (Supp. III 2003).
10. 2 U.S.C. § 441i(e) (Supp. III 2003).
11. 36 U.S.C. § 510 (Supp. III 2003).
12. 36 U.S.C. § 510(c) (Supp. III 2003).

8. Tax Considerations

Contents

8.1 INTRODUCTION

PACs have long been treated as tax-exempt "political organizations" pursuant to section 527 of the Internal Revenue Code. They have been required to pay federal income taxes on income from certain sources such as interest and dividends from investments, income from ancillary commercial activities, and gains from sales of appreciated property. To report such income and pay such taxes, PACs earning more than $100 in such income had to file an annual tax return, Form 1120-POL. Until July 2000, PACs were not subject to any additional registration or reporting requirements with the IRS.

Public Law No. 106-230—enacted in 2000 and later amended in 2002 by Public Law No. 107-276—required most state PACS to register with the IRS on Form 8871. In addition, certain state PACs that are not registered with the FEC or a state campaign finance agency may have to file periodic reports with the IRS on Form 8872, after initially registering with the IRS. These two forms are made available by the IRS on its Web site.[1] Some state PACs also must file annual informational returns on Form 990, and those having taxable income of more than $100 must file Form 1120-POL. All these forms appear in appendix H.

This is an appropriate place to explain the popular term "527 organization." Commentators and journalists sometimes refer to these groups in press accounts. Of course, any political group that claims exempt status under section 527 of the Internal Revenue Code arguably is a 527 organization. Yet this nonlegal term seems most often to refer to a certain subcategory of all such groups. Specifically, 527 organization is a label that usually describes political organizations that are not subject to campaign finance laws and, therefore, are not registered with either the FEC or any state election agency. These types of committees, like others, must register with the IRS. Unlike most other committees, they also are required to report their financial activity with the IRS on Form 8872. Because the 527 organization is not a political committee under campaign finance laws, it may raise and spend soft money, including donations from corporations and unions. Thus, 527 organizations are a vehicle to avoid contribution restrictions and limits. They engage primarily in public advertising, registration, and voter turnout activities.

In the course of the 2004 election campaign, several large 527 organizations were created. Many were subject to complaints with the FEC alleging that the organizations should be treated as "political committees" under the Federal Election Campaign Act. While refusing to pass regulations to provide guidance on when an entity under section 527 becomes a political committee under FECA, the FEC nonetheless conducted several investigations that resulted in negotiated civil penalties of up to $750,000. The resulting uncertainty and lack of clear guidance has reduced the number of 527 organizations that engage in political activity connected to federal elections.

A description of the filing requirements applicable to federal PACs follows. Next is a discussion of the periodic reports required for PACs not reporting to the FEC—mostly state PACs. Section 8.7 gives an explanation of the deductibility or nondeductibility of lobbying expenses for corporations. Finally, section 8.8 provides a brief overview of the taxation of 501(c) organizations that make political expenditures.

8.2   IRS EMPLOYER IDENTIFICATION NUMBER

As stated above, the IRS considers a PAC to be a tax-exempt organization under section 527 of the Internal Revenue Code. Accordingly, the PAC is an entity separate from its connected corporation and must obtain its own employer identification number (EIN) from the IRS. To do this, the PAC needs to submit Form SS-4 by fax to the IRS, or call the IRS and then submit Form SS-4. The appropriate phone numbers and fax numbers can be found on the official instructions to Form SS-4. Both Form SS-4 and its instructions can be found on the IRS Web site.

8.3   PAC FEDERAL INCOME TAX

A PAC is taxed as a political organization under section 527 of the Internal Revenue Code.[2] It is not taxed on its "exempt function income"—income from contributions of money or other property, membership dues, fees or assessments, proceeds from political fund-raising or entertainment events, or the sale of political campaign materials, or bingo games.[3] To retain tax-exempt status, exempt function income should be used for the "exempt function" of the PAC, which includes all activities directly related to or in support of the process of influencing or attempting to influence the selection, nomination, election, or appointment of any individual to office.[4] According to the IRS, as long as they comprise an incidental amount of the PAC's expenditures, only those nonexempt function expenditures that are either illegal or provide an economic benefit to the political organization need to be included in the PAC's taxable income.[5] A PAC is allowed a deduction of $100 on other income.[6]

Income that is taxable to the PAC arises from such sources as interest and dividends from investments, income from ancillary commercial activities, and gains from sales of appreciated property. Against this income, the PAC may deduct expenses, depreciation, and similar items, but only to the extent they are "directly connected with" the production of such income (this does not include exempt function income). Fundraising expenses incurred in the production of exempt function income are not deductible. If a deductible expense is attributable to the production of both taxable and exempt income, it must be allocated between the two types of income on a reasonable and consistent basis.[7] Only the part allocated to the production of taxable income is deductible.

There are three modifications to the general rule of allowable deductions:

- A PAC is allowed a specific deduction of $100;
- No net operating loss deduction under section 172 of the Internal Revenue Code is allowed; and
- None of the Internal Revenue Code's special deductions for corporations, such as the deductions for dividends received under section 243 and for organizational expenses under section 248, are allowed.[8] PACs are taxed at the maximum corporate rate.[9] A PAC files its tax return on IRS Form 1120-POL on or before March 15 of the year following the calendar year in which taxable income is received, if the PAC is a calendar-year tax filer.

Briefly, the following steps should be taken in computing a PAC's taxable income:

(1) Compute total income;
(2) Delete exempt function income, unless it was used for illegal purposes or for the economic benefit of the organization;
(3) Deduct $100;
(4) Deduct expenditures for expenses, depreciation, and similar items that qualify under chapter 1 of the Code and are directly connected with the production of income other than exempt function income;
(5) Do not take a net operating loss deduction or the special corporate deductions allowed under the Code; and
(6) Apply the maximum corporate rate.

Corporate Administrative Expenses

Corporations may not deduct expenses incurred in the formation and administration of a PAC.[10] The IRS also requires a corporation to allocate that part of its officers' and employees' time devoted to PAC operations to determine the portion of their salaries attributable to PAC work. This portion is not deductible as a business expense.[11]

Deductions cannot be taken for political convention program advertising or for the purchase of tickets to campaign events, fundraising dinners, or inaugural balls and festivities.[12]

A corporation cannot pay the income taxes owed by its PAC. A PAC's tax liability is not an administrative cost under the election laws.[13] Therefore, corporate payments for the PAC's taxes would constitute prohibited "contributions" by the corporation to its own PAC.

Contributors and Tax Credits

Contributions to a PAC do not qualify for any federal tax credit or deduction.

PAC Raffles

In 1998, the IRS issued a technical advice memorandum that categorized proceeds from a PAC raffle as not exempt function income and, therefore, taxable.[14] However, the agency subsequently clarified that raffles in connection with PAC fundraising or entertainment events may generate nontaxable exempt function income.[15]

Annual Tax Return (Form 1120-POL)

All political organizations, including PACs, that have more than $100 in taxable income (e.g., income from interest and dividends) must file an annual tax return, Form 1120-POL.[16] Prior law required a return from PACs that had gross receipts—whether taxable or not—of $25,000 or more. PACs are no longer required to make Form 1120-POL available for public inspection.[17]

Form 1120-POL is due on the fifteenth day of the third month following the end of the taxpayer's fiscal year.[18] This is March 15 for calendar-year taxpayers. A PAC may request an automatic six-month extension by filing Form 7004 by the due date for the 1120-POL. (A copy of Form 1120-POL can be found in appendix H.)

Annual Information Return (Form 990)

PACs registered with the Federal Election Commission are not required to file IRS Form 990.[19] This change is a result of Public Law No. 107-276.

8.4   STATE PACS AND IRS FILINGS

If a corporation elects to establish a state PAC—that is, a PAC that supports only non-federal candidates—in any of the states or in the District of Columbia, the PAC will be a political organization exempt from taxation under section 527 of the Internal Revenue Code. As a 527 organization that is not registered with the FEC, it may have to file two annual tax returns as well as register with the IRS and file periodic reports. PACs registered with the FEC do not have to register with the IRS or file the periodic IRS financial disclosure reports.

Initial Notice of Section 527 Status (Form 8871)

All corporate state PACs, except those PACs that reasonably anticipate that their annual gross receipts will always be less than $25,000, must file Form 8871 to inform the IRS of their tax-exempt status. Form 8871 must be filed within twenty-four hours after the date on which the organization was established. An employer identification number (EIN) (*see* section 8.2) must be obtained in order to complete Form 8871.

A newly established political organization is not required to file Form 8871 if it reasonably anticipates that its annual gross receipts will be less than $25,000 for its first six taxable years. However, if an organization, in fact, does have annual gross receipts of $25,000 or more for any taxable year, it is required to file Form 8871 within thirty days of receiving $25,000.[20] State PACs need only file Form 8871 in electronic form.[21] A state PAC must note on Form 8871 whether it qualifies for an exemption from the requirements to file Forms 8872 and 990, both of which are discussed below.

State PACs also must amend Form 8871 within thirty days of any material change in the information contained therein, including termination.[22] Any material changes existing at the time of or after the enactment of Public Law No. 107-276, which was November 2, 2002, must be noted in an amendment to Form 8871 within thirty days after the material change or within forty-five days after the enactment of the new law, whichever is later.

Periodic Reports of Contributions and Expenditures (Form 8872)

Federal law also requires state PACs that are not "qualified State or local political organizations," and that have annual gross receipts in excess of $25,000, to file periodic reports of contributions and expenditures with the IRS.

A "qualified State or local political organization" is exempt from the Form 8872 periodic filing requirement.[23] Political organizations exempt from filing Form 8872 must indicate this exemption on their Form 8871.[24] A "qualified State or local political organization" is defined as a political organization that: focuses all of its exempt function (i.e., political) activity on state and/or local offices; *and* is required under state law to report the type of information about contributions and expenditures that it would have to report to the IRS, provided, further, that the political organization makes its reports available for public inspection per IRS rules, and the state agency makes the reports filed by the organization available to the public.[25] A qualified political organization may claim the IRS reporting exemption even if the applicable state disclosure law does not exactly replicate the IRS's reporting requirements. For example, a political organization may still qualify if the state's minimum threshold for reporting contributions or expenditures is within $300 of the IRS itemization requirement ($200 for contributions and $500 for expenditures). Similarly, a state law that does not require the reporting of the employer or occupation of contributors or recipients of expenditures, the date of contributions or expenditures, or the purpose of expenditures will not disqualify a political organization from this reporting exemption.[26]

A political organization will not qualify for the reporting exemption if a federal candidate or officeholder: "controls or materially participates in the direction of the organization;" solicits contributions to the organization; or directs, in whole or in part, disbursements by the organization.[27]

Nonexempt state PACs, which often are referred to as "527 organizations," must file Form 8872, either monthly or quarterly/semiannually, beginning with the first month or quarter in which they accept contributions or make expenditures. Like Form 8871, Form 8872 is posted by the IRS on its public Web site, and a copy can be found in appendix H.[28] Nonexempt state PACs that expect to receive contributions or make expenditures of more than $50,000 during the year must file Form 8872 electronically, beginning with reports due on or after June 30, 2003.[29]

The reports on Form 8872 must include the name, address (and occupation and employer of an individual), and amount contributed of any person who contributes more than $200 to the PAC in a calendar year. It also must contain the same information for any person to whom expenditures are made that aggregate $500 or more during a calendar year. A PAC, however, is not required to report separately independent expenditures to the IRS. In addition, Form 8872 must include the date and purpose of each disbursement and the date of each contribution.[30] On or after June 30, 2003, the IRS had to make Form 8872 filed by PACs available to the public within forty-eight hours of filing.[31] The IRS also was ordered to make the data contained in these filings searchable electronically by the public.[32]

The IRS Web site provides the filing schedule for Form 8872 in both election and non-election years. Please note that monthly and quarterly/semiannual filing schedules are not purely monthly or quarterly/semiannually. Rather, these schedules include various preelection and postelection reports as well.

Annual Tax Return (Form 1120-POL)

Form 1120-POL, the annual tax return, must be filed if a state PAC has taxable income—income from interest and dividends or from trade or business—in excess of $100.[33] Form 1120-POL, if necessary, must be filed by March 15 of each year for calendar-year taxpayers (*see* section 8.3, *supra,* for information on tax liability calculation for Form 1120-POL; *see* appendix H for Form 1120-POL).

Annual Information Return (Form 990)

"[Q]ualified State and local political organizations" are required to file Form 990 if their taxable-year gross receipts exceed $100,000.[34] Other, nonexempt state PACs (so-called 527 organizations) must file Form 990 if they have gross receipts of $25,000 or more.[35] If a state PAC has gross receipts of less than $100,000 and assets of less than $250,000, it may file Form 990-EZ.[36] Form 990 is subject to public disclosure, including salaries of certain state PAC officers and directors. (See appendix H for Form 990.) State PACs exempt from filing Form 990 must indicate this exemption on their Form 8871.[37] This requirement applies to Forms 8871 that are due more than thirty days after the enactment of the new law.

8.5   STATE TAXES

A PAC also may be subject to corporate income or franchise tax in the state in which it is domiciled. Such taxes usually are imposed on interest and dividends from investments, income from ancillary commercial activities, and gains from sales of appreciated property. Applicable state tax law should be consulted.

8.6   IRS DISCLAIMER REQUIREMENT

Political organizations that anticipate raising $100,000 or more in a year must inform contributors that "contributions [to the PAC] are not deductible as charitable contributions for federal income tax purposes."[38]

8.7   DEDUCTIBILITY OF LOBBYING EXPENSES

As mentioned above, corporations may not deduct PAC administrative costs as ordinary and necessary business expenses. In addition, corporations are prohibited from taking a business deduction for any expenses incurred for lobbying. This prohibition extends to expenses for: influencing or attempting to influence state or federal legislation; participating in or intervening in any political campaign in support of or in opposition to any candidate for public office; attempting to influence the general public with respect to elections, state or federal legislation, or referenda; and attempting to influence certain high-level executive officials.[39] "Legislation" does not include local legislation.[40] Lobbying is defined differently under tax law than under the Lobbying Disclosure Act.

In addition, a corporation may not deduct dues paid to a nonprofit organization to the extent that such dues are used for the above four activities.[41] The nonprofit organization is required to inform the taxpayer of the allocation of dues between deductible and nondeductible expenses, unless the nonprofit organization pays the tax on its lobbying expenditures.[42]

8.8   TAXATION OF POLITICAL EXPENDITURES OF 501(C) ORGANIZATIONS

A 501(c) organization, such as a trade association or social welfare organization, is subject to a tax under section 527(f) of the Internal Revenue Code if it makes an expenditure for an "exempt function." Exempt function means:

> influencing or attempting to influence the selection, nomination, election, or appointment of any individual to any Federal, state, or local public office or office in a political organization, or the election of Presidential or Vice Presidential electors, whether or not such individual or electors are selected, nominated, elected, or appointed.[43]

If a 501(c) organization makes an expenditure for an exempt function, then it must pay the highest corporate tax (35%) on the lesser of the amount it expended for exempt functions or its net investment income.[44]

Such a tax may apply to certain contributions by 501(c) organizations to national and state parties, state and local candidates (where allowed by state law), and state PACs (where allowed by state law). The payment by a 501(c) organization of the administrative expenses of its own PAC is not taxed.[45] Similarly, the payment by a 501(c) organization of the expenses necessary to communicate with its own membership does not trigger any tax liability under section 527(f).[46]

If a 501(c) organization owes a tax under section 527(f), then it must file Form 1120-POL in order to pay the tax.

NOTES

1. See, www.irs.gov/polorgs.
2. I.R.C. § 527(e)(1) (2000); Treas. Reg. § 1.527-2(a)(1) (2006).
3. I.R.C. §§ 527(c)(3)(A)-(D) (2000).
4. I.R.C. § 527(e)(2) (2000); Treas. Reg. § 1.527-2(c) (2006).
5. Tech. Adv. Mem. 94-09-003 (Mar. 4, 1994).
6. I.R.C. § 527(c)(2)(A) (2000).
7. Treas. Reg. § 1.527-4(c)(3) (2006).
8. I.R.C. §§ 527(c)(2)(A)-(C) (2000).
9. I.R.C. § 527(b)(1) (2000).
10. Tech. Adv. Mem. 82-02-019 (Sept. 30, 1981).
11. Id.

12. I.R.C. § 276 (2000).
13. FEC Advisory Opinion 1977-19, Fed. Election Camp. Fin. Guide (CCH) ¶ 5252 (1
14. Tech. Adv. Mem. 98-47-006 (Aug. 11, 1998).
15. IRS Field Memorandum from Director, Exempt Organizations Division, to Regional Chompliance Officers (December 1, 1999).
16. I.R.C. §§ 527(c)(1)-(2), 6012(a)(6) (2000 & Supp. III 2003).
17. I.R.C. § 6012(a)(6) (Supp. III 2003).
18. Rev. Rul. 2000-49, 2000-2 C.B. 430.
19. I.R.C. § 6033(g) (2000).
20. Rev. Rul. 2000-49, 2000-2 C.B. 430.
21. I.R.C. §§ 527(i)(1)(A), (5)(C) (Supp. III 2003).
22. I.R.C. § 527(i)(2) (Supp. III 2003).
23. I.R.C. § 527(j)(5) (Supp. III 2003).
24. I.R.C. § 527(i)(3)(E) (Supp. III 2003).
25   I.R.C. § 527(e)(5)(A) (Supp. III 2003).
26. I.R.C. § 527(e)(5)(B)(ii) (Supp. III 2003).
27. I.R.C. § 527(e)(5)(D) (Supp. III 2003).
28. I.R.C. § 527(k) (Supp. III 2003).
29. I.R.C. § 527(j)(7) (Supp. III 2003).
30. I.R.C. §§ 527(j)(3)(A)-(B) (Supp. III 2003).
31. I.R.C. § 527(k)(1) (Supp. III 2003).
32. I.R.C. § 527(k)(2) (Supp. III 2003).
33. I.R.C. §§ 527(c)(1), (e)(5), 6012(a)(5) (2000 & Supp. III 2003).
34. I.R.C. § 6033(g) (Supp. III 2003).
35. Id.
36. Id.
37. I.R.C. § 527(i)(3) (Supp. III 2003).
38. I.R.C. § 6113 (2000).
39. I.R.C. § 162(e) (2000).
40. I.R.C. § 162(e)(2) (2000).
41. I.R.C. § 162(e)(3) (2000).
42. See I.R.C. § 6033(e) (2000).
43. I.R.C. § 527(e)(2) (2000).
44. I.R.C. § 527(f)(1) (2000).
45. See Treas. Reg. § 1.527-2(c)(2) (2006).
46. See Treas. Reg. § 1.527-6(b)(1) (2006).

9. The Federal Election Commission and Enforcement

Contents

9.1　THE FEDERAL ELECTION COMMISSION

The FEC is the federal agency that administers and enforces the rules governing corporate political activity.[1] The commission is composed of six voting commissioners who are appointed by the president. No more than three commissioners may belong to the same political party.[2] An affirmative vote of four commissioners is required to initiate, defend, or appeal a civil action, render an advisory opinion, develop forms, promulgate regulations, or conduct investigations.[3]

The FEC's sole office is located at 999 E Street, N.W., Washington, D.C. 20463, which is where commission meetings are held. It has established a toll-free telephone number for the public, 800-424-9530, and a Web site, www.fec.gov. Upon request, the staff will provide the public with copies of FEC publications, which include FECA, regulations, registration and reporting forms, brochures, and a free subscription to the FEC monthly newsletter, the *FEC Record*. All of these documents also are available on the commission's extensive Web site.

Staff Organization

Although the commissioners are the final arbiters of FEC matters, informal contact with staff is more common. The nonlegal staff is organized by operational divisions, including public information, reports analysis, audit, administration, data services, and public disclosure. The legal office is called the Office of General Counsel.

The Public Information Division contains the Press Office, and provides services to the general public, including distributing free publications and answering general questions about federal election law and the FEC. However, answers obtained by informal means are not binding on the commission and offer no legal protection.[4]

A corporate PAC files its reports with the FEC's Reports Analysis Division (RAD).[5] If RAD detects a problem with a report, it typically sends out a request for additional information (RFAI) as a nonlegal, informal first step. A recipient must respond to an RFAI. A second, more serious step may involve an inquiry signed by the commissioners or the general counsel, which triggers a more formal administrative enforcement process.

Advisory Opinions

The FEC also renders advisory opinions upon written request regarding the application of any provision of the federal election laws or FEC regulations to a specific fact situation.[6] These advisory opinions provide the requesting party and those similarly situated with legal protection from enforcement sanctions for activity approved by the FEC in an advisory opinion.[7]

Advisory opinions must be issued within sixty days after the FEC receives the request and all necessary facts. Draft opinions are discussed and voted on by the commissioners in public meetings. Requests are subject to public comment. All requests, comments, and advisory opinions are posted on the FEC Web site. Opinions are also available in a searchable database.

9.2   FEC INVESTIGATIONS AND CIVIL ENFORCEMENT

The FEC is empowered to enforce compliance with FECA. It has exclusive authority for civil enforcement.[8] Enforcement proceedings, which are called "matters under review," or "MURs," are initiated either by the filing of a signed sworn complaint or at the FEC's own initiative. All enforcement proceedings are confidential, although MURs and certain documents are made public at the conclusion of the investigation. The FEC maintains a searchable enforcement query system (ESQ) database on its Web site, which contains information and documents from closed MURs.

The first stage of the investigative process is called the "reason to believe" (RTB) stage. An RTB finding is made by an affirmative vote of four commissioners concluding that there is reason to believe a violation of the election laws has occurred. An RTB finding allows the Office of General Counsel to move forward in its investigation of the alleged violation, authorizing the collection of more evidence. At this point, the parties may negotiate a settlement of the matter, known as a conciliation agreement.[9]

The second stage of the process is called the "probable cause to believe" (PCTB) stage, when the Office of General Counsel prepares a brief for the commissioners detailing the results of its investigation. The brief will recommend whether the commissioners should find probable cause to believe a violation has been committed. The respondent in the matter is permitted to submit a reply brief. If four of the commissioners vote to find PCTB, then the parties may engage in settlement negotiations. If the negotiations do not result in a signed conciliation agreement, the commissioners may authorize the Office of General Counsel to file suit in United States District Court for recovery of a civil penalty.[10]

The civil penalty, whether negotiated in a conciliation agreement or imposed by a court, may not exceed the greater of $5,000 (adjusted periodically by the FEC for inflation) or an amount equal to any contribution or expenditure involved in the alleged violation. If the violation is knowing and willful, the penalty may not exceed the greater of $10,000 or an amount equal to 200% of the impermissible contribution or expenditure.[11] In the case of a knowing and willful violation of the prohibition against making contributions in the name of another, the BCRA permits a penalty of not less than 300% of the amount involved in the violation, but not more than the greater of $50,000 or 1,000% of the amount involved.[12]

9.3 THE DEPARTMENT OF JUSTICE AND CRIMINAL ENFORCEMENT

Criminal violations of FECA are prosecuted by the Department of Justice through its Public Integrity Section, with the participation of the local U.S. Attorney's office. The Public Integrity Section, as its name suggests, oversees investigations and prosecutions of various alleged violations of federal public corruption, election fraud, and campaign finance statutes. The office has published a handbook, *Federal Prosecution of Election Offenses*. The most recent, seventh edition was published in 2007, and is available from the Government Printing Office.

A criminal violation of FECA is one that is "knowing and willful which means the offender knew what the law required and flouted it not withstanding that knowledge."[13] Such violation had been punished by a fine not greater than $25,000 or 300% of any contribution or expenditure involved in the violation, imprisonment up to one year, or both.[14] These penalty provisions were amended by the BCRA. Violations occurring on or after November 6, 2002, may be punished by up to five years in prison, fines up to $250,000 for individuals and $500,000 for entities, or both.[15] In addition, the BCRA states that criminal violations of the prohibition against making contributions in the name of another may be punished by imprisonment of not more than five years, a fine of not less than 300% of the amount involved in the violation but not more than the greater of $50,000 or 1,000% of the amount involved, or both.[16] The BCRA also increases the statute of limitations for criminal violations from three to five years.[17]

Finally, the BCRA instructed the United States Sentencing Commission to adopt guidelines regarding criminal violations of FECA.[18] Sentencing guidelines for minimum mandatory sentences were adopted on January 25, 2003.[19] The guidelines ensure jail sentences for many criminal violations of FECA and for all violations that aggregate more than $30,000 in illegal contributions or expenditures.

NOTES

1. 2 U.S.C. §§ 431-455 (2000 & Supp. III 2003); 11 C.F.R. §§ 100-116 (2006).
2. 2 U.S.C. § 437c(a)(1) (2000). The statute also references two *ex officio* commission members, but the membership of these commissioners was found unconstitutional. *See* FEC v. NRA Political Victory Fund, 6 F.3d 821 (D.C. Cir. 1993), *cert. dismissed*, 513 U.S. 88 (1994). The commission has since reorganized to satisfy constitutional separation-of-powers requirements.
3. 2 U.S.C. § 437c(c) (2000).
4. 2 U.S.C. § 437f(b) (2000).
5. 2 U.S.C. § 434 (2000 & Supp. III 2003).
6. 2 U.S.C. § 437d(a)(7) (2000).
7. 2 U.S.C. § 437f(c) (2000).
8. 2 U.S.C. § 437d(a)(6) (2000).
9. 2 U.S.C. § 437g(a) (2000 & Supp. III 2003).
10. *Id.*

11. *Id.*
12. *Id.*
13. United States v. Curran, 20 F.3d 560 (3d Cir. 1994).
14. 2 U.S.C. § 437g(d) (2000).
15. 2 U.S.C. § 437g(d)(1)(A) (Supp. III 2003).
16. 2 U.S.C. § 437g(d)(1)(D) (Supp. III 2003).
17. 2 U.S.C. § 455(a) (Supp. III 2003).
18. 28 U.S.C. § 994 (Supp. III 2003).
19. United States Sentencing Commission, *Guidelines Manual,* § 2C1.8 (Nov. 2003).

Appendix A

FEC Forms and Instructions

FEC FORM 1

STATEMENT OF ORGANIZATION

Office Use Only

12FE4M5

1. NAME OF COMMITTEE (in full)

☐ (Check if name is changed)

Example: If typing, type over the lines.

ADDRESS (number and street)

☐ (Check if address is changed)

CITY   STATE   ZIP CODE

COMMITTEE'S E-MAIL ADDRESS

COMMITTEE'S WEB PAGE ADDRESS (URL)

COMMITTEE'S FAX NUMBER

2. DATE   M M / D D / Y Y Y Y

3. FEC IDENTIFICATION NUMBER   C

4. IS THIS STATEMENT ☐ NEW (N)   **OR**   ☐ AMENDED (A)

I certify that I have examined this Statement and to the best of my knowledge and belief it is true, correct and complete.

Type or Print Name of Treasurer _____

Signature of Treasurer _____   Date   M M / D D / Y Y Y Y

NOTE: Submission of false, erroneous, or incomplete information may subject the person signing this Statement to the penalties of 2 U.S.C. §437g.

ANY CHANGE IN INFORMATION SHOULD BE REPORTED WITHIN 10 DAYS.

Office Use Only

For further information contact:
Federal Election Commission
Toll Free 800-424-9530
Local 202-694-1100

FEC FORM 1
(Revised 12/2007)

FE3AN042.PDF

5.   TYPE OF COMMITTEE

Candidate Committee:

(a)   ☐   This committee is a principal campaign committee. (Complete the candidate information below.)

(b)   ☐   This committee is an authorized committee, and is NOT a principal campaign committee. (Complete the candidate information below.)

Name of Candidate   ⌞⎯⎯⎯⎯⎯⎯⎯⎯⎯⎯⎯⎯⎯⎯⎯⎯⎯⎯⎯⎯⎯⎯⎯⎯⎯⎯⎯⎯⎯⎯⎯⌟

Candidate Party Affiliation ▭   Office Sought: ☐ House ☐ Senate ☐ President   State ▭   District ▭

(c)   ☐   This committee supports/opposes only one candidate, and is NOT an authorized committee.

Name of Candidate   ⌞⎯⎯⎯⎯⎯⎯⎯⎯⎯⎯⎯⎯⎯⎯⎯⎯⎯⎯⎯⎯⎯⎯⎯⎯⎯⎯⎯⎯⎯⎯⎯⌟

Party Committee:

(d)   ☐   This committee is a ▭ (National, State or subordinate) committee of the ▭ (Democratic, Republican, etc.) Party.

Political Action Committee (PAC):

(e)   ☐   This committee is a separate segregated fund. (Identify connected organization on line 6.) Its connected organization is a:

☐ Corporation   ☐ Corporation w/o Capital Stock   ☐ Labor Organization

☐ Membership Organization   ☐ Trade Association   ☐ Cooperative

(f)   ☐   This committee supports/opposes more than one Federal candidate, and is NOT a separate segregated fund or party committee. (i.e., nonconnected committee)

☐   In addition, this committee is a Leadership PAC. (Identify sponsor on line 6.)

Joint Fundraising Representative:

(g)   ☐   This committee collects contributions, pays fundraising expenses and disburses net proceeds for two or more political committees/organizations, at least one of which is an authorized committee of a federal candidate.

(h)   ☐   This committee collects contributions, pays fundraising expenses and disburses net proceeds for two or more political committees/organizations, none of which is an authorized committee of a federal candidate.

Committees Participating in Joint Fundraiser

1.   ⌞⎯⎯⎯⎯⎯⎯⎯⎯⎯⎯⎯⎯⎯⎯⌟   FEC ID number C ▭

2.   ⌞⎯⎯⎯⎯⎯⎯⎯⎯⎯⎯⎯⎯⎯⎯⌟   FEC ID number C ▭

3.   ⌞⎯⎯⎯⎯⎯⎯⎯⎯⎯⎯⎯⎯⎯⎯⌟   FEC ID number C ▭

4.   ⌞⎯⎯⎯⎯⎯⎯⎯⎯⎯⎯⎯⎯⎯⎯⌟   FEC ID number C ▭

5.   ⌞⎯⎯⎯⎯⎯⎯⎯⎯⎯⎯⎯⎯⎯⎯⌟   FEC ID number C ▭

Write or Type Committee Name

6. **Name of Any Connected Organization, Affiliated Committee, Leadership PAC Sponsor or Joint Fundraising Representative**

Mailing Address

CITY   STATE   ZIP CODE

Relationship:

☐ Connected Organization   ☐ Affiliated Committee   ☐ Leadership PAC Sponsor   ☐ Joint Fundraising Representative

7. **Custodian of Records:** Identify by name, address (phone number -- optional) and position of the person in possession of committee books and records.

Full Name

Mailing Address

CITY   STATE   ZIP CODE

Title or Position

Telephone number

8. **Treasurer:** List the name and address (phone number -- optional) of the treasurer of the committee; and the name and address of any designated agent (e.g., assistant treasurer).

Full Name
of Treasurer

Mailing Address

CITY   STATE   ZIP CODE

Title or Position

Telephone number

FE3AN042.PDF

FEC Form 1 (Revised 12/2007)   Page **4**

Full Name of
Designated
Agent

Mailing Address

                                                                CITY   STATE   ZIP CODE

Title or Position

                                                                Telephone number

9. **Banks or Other Depositories:** List all banks or other depositories in which the committee deposits funds, holds accounts, rents safety deposit boxes or maintains funds.

Name of Bank, Depository, etc.

Mailing Address

                                                                CITY   STATE   ZIP CODE

Name of Bank, Depository, etc.

Mailing Address

                                                                CITY   STATE   ZIP CODE

FE3AN042.PDF

FEDERAL ELECTION COMMISSION
Instructions for Statement of Organization (FEC FORM 1)

When to File

New political committees must file this form to register the committee once they exceed the applicable threshold, as described below:

- Principal campaign committees must file this form no later than 10 days after the candidate designates the committee on the Statement of Candidacy (FEC FORM 2). Other authorized committees file this form with the principal campaign committee, which in turn must file this form with the appropriate filing offices.
- Committees sponsored by corporations, labor organizations or trade associations (i.e., separate segregated funds) must file this form no later than 10 days after their establishment.
- Local political party committees must file this form no later than 10 days after exceeding one of the following thresholds during a calendar year: (1) receiving contributions in connection with a federal election aggregating in excess of $5,000; (2) making exempt payments under 11 CFR 100.80, 100.87, 100.89, 100.140, 100.147 or 100.149 aggregating in excess of $5,000; or (3) making contributions or expenditures in connection with a federal election aggregating in excess of $1,000.
- All other political committees must file this form no later than 10 days after receiving contributions or making expenditures in connection with a federal election aggregating in excess of $1,000 during a calendar year.

Note: Political committees (except for committees required to file with the Secretary of the Senate) must file reports in an electronic form

under 11 CFR 104.18 if they have either received contributions or made expenditures in excess of $50,000 during a calendar year, or if they have reason to expect that they will exceed either of those thresholds during the calendar year. If your committee has reached this level of activity, you must file this form in an electronic format.

A political committee is considered to have reason to expect it will exceed the electronic filing threshold for the next two calendar years after the calendar year in which it exceeds $50,000 in contributions or expenditures. Exception: This does not apply to an authorized committee with $50,000 or less in net debts outstanding on January 1 of the year following the general election that anticipates terminating prior to January 1 of the next election year, as long as the candidate has not qualified under 2 U.S.C. §432 as a candidate in the next election and does not intend to become a federal candidate in the next election.

A new committee with no previous contributions or expenditures is considered to have reason to expect it will exceed the electronic filing threshold if it exceeds $12,500 in contributions or expenditures during the first calendar quarter of the calendar year, or $25,000 in contributions or expenditures in the first half of the calendar year. Contact the FEC for more information on filing electronically.

Line-by-Line Instructions

LINE 1. Print or type full name and mailing address of the committee. The name of a principal campaign committee or other authorized

committee must include the name of the candidate who authorized the committee. A political committee which is not an authorized committee can not include the name of any candidate in its name, except that a delegate committee must include the word "delegate(s)" in its name and may also include the name of the Presidential candidate which it supports. A political committee established solely to draft an individual or to encourage an individual to become a candidate may include the name of the individual in the name of the committee, provided the committee's name clearly indicates that it is a draft committee. The name of a separate segregated fund must include the full name of its connected organization. Any abbreviation or acronym used by the fund must also be reported. List the Internet address (URL) of the committee's official Web site, if such a Web site exists. If the committee is required to file electronically, or is a principal campaign committee of a candidate for the Senate or House of Representatives, also list an electronic mail address. Finally, if the committee is a principal campaign committee or an authorized committee, list the committee's fax number.

LINE 2. State the date the group or organization became a political committee. If this filing is an amendment, note the date of the change in information.

LINE 3. Only committees that have previously filed a Statement of Organization should fill in this block with the number that was originally assigned to the committee. All new committees will be assigned identification numbers when the completed statement has been received.

LINE 4. All political committees registering for the first time check the box labeled "NEW." Committees that have previously filed FEC FORM 1 and are now submitting changes or corrections check the box labeled "AMENDED." If "AMENDED" is checked, complete Lines 1 through 4. With respect to Lines 5–9 include only the change(s) in information previously submitted. Committees are reminded that any change or correction in the information previously filed in the Statement of Organization shall be reported no later than 10 days following the date of the change or correction. Committees that are required to file electronically are also required to file amendments to the Statement of Organization in an electronic format.

LINE 5. Check and fill out ONE of the eight sections as follows:

(a) All principal campaign committees check (a) and fill in the corresponding information for the candidate under (b).

(b) All other authorized committees check (b) and fill in the corresponding information for the candidate. In the boxes for candidate/party affiliation, list the abbreviation of the party (e.g., for Democratic party, list "DEM," for Republican party, list "REP," for Reform party, list "REF," for Green party, list "GRE" or for Independent, list "IND.") Consult the Commission's Web site at www.fec.gov if unsure of the proper abbreviation to use.

(c) A committee supporting/opposing a single federal candidate which is not authorized by a candidate checks (c), and includes the candidate's name on the line provided. Delegate and draft committees must check (c), and provide the name of the candidate supported.

(d) All national, State and subordinate committees of a political party check (d) and fill in whether the party is the national party (use code NAT), state party (use code STA) or subordinate committee (use code SUB).

In the boxes for candidate/party affiliation, list the abbreviation of the party (e.g., for Democratic party, list "DEM," for Republican party, list "REP," for Reform party, list "REF," for Green party, list "GRE" or for Independent, list "IND.") Consult the Commission's Web site at www.fec.gov if unsure of the proper abbreviation to use.

(e) All separate segregated funds check (e). A separate segregated fund is a political committee established, financed, maintained or controlled by a corporation, labor organization, membership organization, cooperative or trade association. Check the appropriate box to identify the type of connected organization and provide its name and address on line 6.

(f) A committee supporting/opposing more than one federal candidate and which is not a separate segregated fund or a political party committee (i.e., a nonconnected committee) checks box (f). In addition, if the committee is directly or indirectly established, financed, maintained or controlled by a federal candidate or officeholder, but is not an authorized committee or party, it must check the Leadership PAC box and identify its sponsor on line 6.

(g), (h) All joint fundraising representatives must check either (g) or (h). A committee established to act as a joint fundraising representative is a political committee selected or established by joint fundraising participants as the committee responsible for keeping joint fundraising records, allocating proceeds and expenses among participants and reporting the overall financial activity of the fundraiser. If one or more federal candidates are participating in the joint fundraiser, check (g). If not, check (h). List the participating committees and their FEC identifications numbers in the space provided. NOTE: If a participating committee serves as the joint fundraising representative, it must check (g) or (h) *in addition to* the appropriate box above (a-f).

LINE 6. Political committees must list all affiliated committees and connected organizations (defined below) as follows. Do not leave this line blank. If there are no affiliated committees as described below, enter "None" on this line. Examples of affiliated committees include:

• Principal campaign committees list all other committees authorized by the same candidate. Under "Relationship," enter "affiliated."

• Political committees authorized by the same candidate (other than the principal campaign committee) list the principal campaign committee authorized by the same candidate. Under "Relationship," enter "affiliated."

• Political committees which have been established, financed, maintained or controlled by the highest level parent organization (i.e., the corporation, labor organization, membership organization, cooperative or trade association) list:

• The name of the parent organization. Under "Relationship," enter "connected" AND

• The name of any other political committee(s) established, financed, maintained or controlled by the same parent organization or by a subsidiary, branch or State, local, or other subordinate unit of the same parent organization. Under "Relationship," enter "affiliated."

Political committees which have been established, financed, maintained or controlled by a subsidiary, branch or State, local, or other subordinate unit of an organization list:

• The name of the subsidiary, branch or State, local, or other subordinate unit and the name of the parent organization of which it is a part. Under "Relationship," enter "connected" AND

• The name of the highest level political committee sponsored by the parent organization. Under "Relationship," enter "affiliated."

• State party committees list any subordinate committees (i.e., any county, district or local committee) under the

INSTRUCTIONS FOR FEC FORM 1

control or direction of the State committee. Under "Relationship," enter "affiliated." (See 11 CFR 110.3(b).)

- Subordinate State party committees list the State party committee. Under "Relationship," enter "affiliated." (See 11 CFR 110.3(b).)
- Joint fundraising participants list the committee established to act as the joint fundraising representative. Under "Relationship," enter "joint fundraising representative."

Leadership PACs (as defined in item 5(f) above) must identify their sponsoring candidate or officeholder, but should not list that candidate's campaign committee as an affiliated committee.

Separate segregated funds must provide the full name and address of their "connected organization." Note: The term "connected organization" means any organization which is not a political committee but which directly or indirectly establishes, administers or financially supports a political committee. A connected organization may be a corporation (including a corporation without capital stock), a labor organization, a membership organization, a cooperative or a trade association. The definition of "affiliated committee" is contained at 11 CFR 100.5(g).

LINE 7. Enter the name, address and committee position or the title of custodian of the committee's books and records on Line 7. The telephone number is optional, but is helpful in expeditiously resolving potential filing problems. If the treasurer is the custodian of records, the term "treasurer" is sufficient for Line 7.

LINE 8. Enter the name and address of the committee's treasurer on Line 8. The name and address of any designated agent (e.g., assistant treasurer) must also be included on Line 8. Every political committee must have a treasurer and may designate an assistant treasurer who shall assume the duties and responsibilities of the treasurer, in the event the treasurer is unavailable. The Commission recommends that

each political committee designate an assistant treasurer because no contribution or expenditure may be accepted or made by or on behalf of a political committee at a time when there is a vacancy in the office of the treasurer. No expenditure may be made for or on behalf of a political committee without the authorization of its treasurer or another agent authorized orally or in writing by the treasurer.

LINE 9. The committee must provide the name and mailing address of any bank, repository, or depository where the committee holds funds. Each political committee must have a checking account or transaction account at one of its depositories. All receipts of a political committee must be deposited into a designated campaign depository. All disbursements must be made by check or similar drafts drawn on an account at a designated campaign depository, except for expenditures of $100 or less made from a petty cash fund.

Submit any additional information required for any Line on separate continuation sheets appropriately labeled and attached to the Statement of Organization. Indicate in the appropriate section when information is continued on separate page(s).

Treasurer's Responsibilities

The treasurer of the political committee must preserve a copy of the Statement of Organization and each amendment for a period of not less than 3 years after the date of filing. The treasurer of the political committee is personally responsible for the timely and complete filing of this Statement and for the accuracy of any information contained in it.

Where to File

The original Statement of Organization (FEC FORM 1) and all amendments must be filed with the appropriate office as follows:

- The principal campaign committee of a candidate for the House of Representatives and political committees which support or

oppose only candidates for the House file with the Federal Election Commission, 999 E Street, N.W., Washington, DC 20463.

- The principal campaign committee of a candidate for the Senate and political committees which support or oppose only candidates for the Senate file with the Secretary of the Senate, Office of Public Records, 232 Hart Senate Office Building, Washington, DC 20510-7116. Mail addressed to the Secretary of the Senate should read: "Office of Public Records, P.O. Box 5109, Alexandria, VA 22301-0109."
- An authorized committee which is not the principal campaign committee of a candidate files with the principal campaign committee which must forward a copy to the appropriate office listed herein.
- All other committees, including the principal campaign committee of a candidate for the office of President or Vice President, file with the Federal Election Commission, 999 E Street, N.W., Washington, DC 20463.

Principal campaign committees of House and Senate candidates must file a copy of this form with the state in which the office is sought, with the exception of committees of candidates in states that have qualified for the Commission's state filing waiver program. Principal campaign committees of Presidential candidates must file a copy of this form in each state in which they have made expenditures, with the exception of those states that have qualified for the Commission's state filing waiver program. A list of qualified states is available from the Federal Election Commission.

Unauthorized political committees must continue to file copies of this form with the states in which they have their headquarters, with the exception of committees that are located in states that have qualified for the state waiver program.

The Treasurer must sign the Statement of Organization.

NOTIFICATION OF MULTICANDIDATE STATUS

(See reverse side for instructions)
This form should be filed after the Committee qualifies as a multicandidate committee.

1. (a) NAME OF COMMITTEE IN FULL	
(b) Number and Street Address	2. FEC IDENTIFICATION NUMBER
(c) City, State and ZIP Code	3. TYPE OF COMMITTEE (check one) ☐ STATE PARTY ☐ OTHER

I certify that **one** of the following situations is correct (complete line 4 *or* 5):

4. **STATUS BY AFFILIATION:** The committee submitted its Statement of Organization (FEC FORM 1) on _____ and simultaneously qualified as a multicandidate committee through its affiliation with:

Committee Name: _____

FEC Identification Number: _____.

5. **STATUS BY QUALIFICATION:**

(a) **Candidates:** The committee has made contributions to the five (5) federal candidates listed below (ONLY State party committees may leave this blank.):

	Name	Office Sought	State/District	Date
(i)				
(ii)				
(iii)				
(iv)				
(v)				

(b) **Contributors:** The committee received a contribution from its 51st contributor on:_____.

(c) **Registration:** The committee has been registered for at least 6 months. FEC FORM 1 was submitted on: _____.

(d) **Qualification:** The committee met the above requirements on: _____.

I certify that I have examined this Statement and to the best of my knowledge and belief it is true, correct and complete.

TYPE OR PRINT NAME OF TREASURER	SIGNATURE OF TREASURER	DATE

NOTE: Submission of false, erroneous, or incomplete information may subject the person signing this Statement to the penalties of 2 U.S.C. §437g.
ANY CHANGE IN INFORMATION SHOULD BE REPORTED WITHIN 10 DAYS.

				For further information contact: Federal Election Commission, Washington, DC 20463 Toll-free 800-424-9530 Local 202-694-1100	**FEC FORM 1M**

FE1AN048.PDF

(Revised 1/2001)

FEDERAL ELECTION COMMISSION

Instructions for Notification of Multicandidate Status (FEC FORM 1M)

Multicandidate Status Defined

FEC FORM 1M discloses supplemental information that verifies the date on which your committee became a multicandidate committee. To qualify as a multicandidate committee, a political committee must:

a) Be registered for at least 6 months;

b) Receive contributions from more than 50 persons; and

c) Make contributions to at least 5 Federal candidates. (This requirement does not apply to State party committees.) 11 CFR 100.5(e)(3).

Filing Information

Within ten days after satisfying the three requirements, the committee must file the Notification of Multicandidate Status (FEC FORM 1M) with the appropriate office as follows:

*Political committees which support or oppose only Senate candidates file with the Secretary of the Senate, Office of Public Records, 232 Hart Senate Office Building, Washington, DC 20510-7116. Mail addressed to the Secretary of the Senate should read: "Office of Public Records, P.O. Box 5109, Alexandria, VA 22301-0109."

*All other committees file with the Federal Election Commission, 999 E Street, N.W., Washington, DC 20463.

Additionally, committees maintaining headquarters in Montana, Guam or Puerto Rico must file a copy of the Notification in their state or territory. (As of December 2003, those states and territories had not qualified for the Commission's state waiver program.)

Line-By-Line Instructions

LINE 1. Print or type the full name and mailing address of the committee. The name of a separate segregated fund must include the full name of its connected organization, as well as any abbreviation or acronym used by the fund.

LINE 2. Enter the committee's FEC identification number.

LINE 3. Refer to the committee's Statement of Organization (FEC FORM 1) and indicate the committee type on this line. National and local party committees, nonconnected committees, and separate segregated funds should check the "Other" box.

LINE 4. Status By Affiliation. Enter the date on which the committee's Statement of Organization (FEC FORM 1) was submitted. Provide the name and FEC identification number of the affiliated multicandidate committee.

LINE 5. Status by Qualification.

(a) List the Federal candidates who have received contributions from your committee. Disclose the appropriate information regarding the office sought, the candidate's State and/or District and the contribution date. **Disregard this section if your group is a State party committee.**

(b) Enter the date on which the committee received a contribution from its 51st contributor. Each contributor should satisfy the FEC definition of "person" set forth in 11 CFR 100.10.

(c) Enter the date on which the committee's Statement of Organization (FEC FORM 1) was submitted.

(d) Enter the date on which the committee satisfied its final requirement for multicandidate status.

Federal Election Commission (Revised 1/2004)

┌─

| FEC FORM 3X |

REPORT OF RECEIPTS AND DISBURSEMENTS
For Other Than An Authorized Committee

Office Use Only

1. NAME OF COMMITTEE (in full)   TYPE OR PRINT ▼   Example: If typing, type over the lines.

`12FE4M5`

ADDRESS (number and street) ▼

☐ Check if different than previously reported. (ACC)

2. **FEC IDENTIFICATION NUMBER ▼**   CITY ▲   STATE ▲   ZIP CODE ▲

`C`

3. IS THIS REPORT   ☐ NEW (N)   **OR**   ☐ AMENDED (A)

4. **TYPE OF REPORT** (Choose One)

(a) Quarterly Reports:

☐ April 15 Quarterly Report (Q1)

☐ July 15 Quarterly Report (Q2)

☐ October 15 Quarterly Report (Q3)

☐ January 31 Year-End Report (YE)

☐ July 31 Mid-Year Report (Non-election Year Only) (MY)

☐ Termination Report (TER)

(b) Monthly Report Due On:

☐ Feb 20 (M2)   ☐ May 20 (M5)   ☐ Aug 20 (M8)   ☐ Nov 20 (M11) (Non-Election Year Only)

☐ Mar 20 (M3)   ☐ Jun 20 (M6)   ☐ Sep 20 (M9)   ☐ Dec 20 (M12) (Non-Election Year Only)

☐ Apr 20 (M4)   ☐ Jul 20 (M7)   ☐ Oct 20 (M10)   ☐ Jan 31 (YE)

(c) 12-Day **PRE**-Election Report for the:

☐ Primary (12P)   ☐ General (12G)   ☐ Runoff (12R)

☐ Convention (12C)   ☐ Special (12S)

Election on M M / D D / Y Y Y Y Y Y   in the State of

(d) 30-Day **POST**-Election Report for the:

☐ General (30G)   ☐ Runoff (30R)   ☐ Special (30S)

Election on M M / D D / Y Y Y Y Y Y   in the State of

5. Covering Period   M M / D D / Y Y Y Y Y Y   through   M M / D D / Y Y Y Y Y Y

I certify that I have examined this Report and to the best of my knowledge and belief it is true, correct and complete.

Type or Print Name of Treasurer _____

Signature of Treasurer _____   Date   M M / D D / Y Y Y Y Y Y

NOTE: Submission of false, erroneous, or incomplete information may subject the person signing this Report to the penalties of 2 U.S.C. §437g.

Office Use Only						

FEC FORM 3X
Rev. 12/2004

FE6AN026

─┘

SUMMARY PAGE
OF RECEIPTS AND DISBURSEMENTS

FEC **Form 3X** (Rev. 02/2003)   Page **2**

Write or Type Committee Name

Report Covering the Period: From: M M / D D / Y Y Y Y Y Y   To: M M / D D / Y Y Y Y Y Y

	COLUMN A This Period	COLUMN B Calendar Year-to-Date
6. (a) Cash on Hand January 1, [Y Y Y Y Y Y]		
(b) Cash on Hand at Beginning of Reporting Period............		
(c) Total Receipts (from Line 19)		
(d) Subtotal (add Lines 6(b) and 6(c) for Column A and Lines 6(a) and 6(c) for Column B)...............		
7. Total Disbursements (from Line 31)...........		
8. Cash on Hand at Close of Reporting Period (subtract Line 7 from Line 6(d)).................		
9. Debts and Obligations Owed **TO** the Committee (Itemize all on Schedule C and/or Schedule D)		
10. Debts and Obligations Owed **BY** the Committee (Itemize all on Schedule C and/or Schedule D)		

☐ This committee has qualified as a multicandidate committee. (see FEC FORM 1M)

For further information contact:

Federal Election Commission
999 E Street, NW
Washington, DC 20463

Toll Free 800-424-9530
Local 202-694-1100

FE6AN026

DETAILED SUMMARY PAGE
of Receipts

FEC **Form 3X** (Rev. 06/2004)

Page **3**

Write or Type Committee Name

Report Covering the Period: From: M M / D D / Y Y Y Y Y Y   To: M M / D D / Y Y Y Y Y Y

I. Receipts	COLUMN A Total This Period	COLUMN B Calendar Year-to-Date
11. Contributions (other than loans) From: (a) Individuals/Persons Other Than Political Committees (i) Itemized (use Schedule A)............		
(ii) Unitemized .... (iii) TOTAL (add Lines 11(a)(i) and (ii))................ ▶		
(b) Political Party Committees		
(c) Other Political Committees (such as PACs).....................................		
(d) Total Contributions (add Lines 11(a)(iii), (b), and (c)) (Carry Totals to Line 33, page 5) .... ▶		
12. Transfers From Affiliated/Other Party Committees..		
13. All Loans Received		
14. Loan Repayments Received.......................		
15. Offsets To Operating Expenditures (Refunds, Rebates, etc.) (Carry Totals to Line 37, page 5)..............		
16. Refunds of Contributions Made to Federal Candidates and Other Political Committees.....................................		
17. Other Federal Receipts (Dividends, Interest, etc.)...........................		
18. Transfers from Non-Federal and Levin Funds (a) Non-Federal Account (from Schedule H3).............................		
(b) Levin Funds (from Schedule H5)		
(c) Total Transfers (add 18(a) and 18(b))..		
19. Total Receipts (add Lines 11(d), 12, 13, 14, 15, 16, 17, and 18(c)) .... ▶		
20. Total Federal Receipts (subtract Line 18(c) from Line 19) .... ▶		

FE6AN026

DETAILED SUMMARY PAGE
of Disbursements

FEC **Form 3X** (Rev. 02/2003)   Page **4**

II. Disbursements	COLUMN A Total This Period	COLUMN B Calendar Year-to-Date

21. Operating Expenditures:
  (a) Allocated Federal/Non-Federal
       Activity (from Schedule H4)
       (i) Federal Share		

(ii) Non-Federal Share......................		
(b) Other Federal Operating Expenditures		
(c) Total Operating Expenditures (add 21(a)(i), (a)(ii), and (b)) .... ▶		
22. Transfers to Affiliated/Other Party Committees..		

23. Contributions to
     Federal Candidates/Committees
     and Other Political Committees.................		

24. Independent Expenditures (use Schedule E)		

25. Coordinated Party Expenditures
     (2 U.S.C. §441a(d))
     (use Schedule F)...		

26. Loan Repayments Made...........................		
27. Loans Made...		

28. Refunds of Contributions To:
  (a) Individuals/Persons Other
       Than Political Committees		

(b) Political Party Committees		
(c) Other Political Committees (such as PACs)....................................		
(d) Total Contribution Refunds (add Lines 28(a), (b), and (c))........... ▶		
29. Other Disbursements		

30. Federal Election Activity (2 U.S.C. §431(20))
  (a) Allocated Federal Election Activity
       (from Schedule H6)
       (i) Federal Share		

(ii) "Levin" Share.................................		
(b) Federal Election Activity Paid Entirely With Federal Funds		
(c) Total Federal Election Activity (add .. Lines 30(a)(i), 30(a)(ii) and 30(b))....▶		
31. Total Disbursements (add Lines 21(c), 22, 23, 24, 25, 26, 27, 28(d), 29 and 30(c))..		

32. Total Federal Disbursements
     (subtract Line 21(a)(ii) and Line 30(a)(ii)
     from Line 31)... ▶		

DETAILED SUMMARY PAGE
of Disbursements

FEC **Form 3X** (Rev. 02/2003)   Page **5**

III. Net Contributions/Operating Ex-penditures	COLUMN A Total This Period	COLUMN B Calendar Year-to-Date
33. Total Contributions (other than loans) (from Line 11(d), page 3)		
34. Total Contribution Refunds (from Line 28(d))		
35. Net Contributions (other than loans) (subtract Line 34 from Line 33)		
36. Total Federal Operating Expenditures (add Line 21(a)(i) and Line 21(b)) .... ▶		
37. Offsets to Operating Expenditures (from Line 15, page 3).............................		
38. Net Operating Expenditures (subtract Line 37 from Line 36) ....▶		

FE6AN026

SCHEDULE A (FEC Form 3X)
ITEMIZED RECEIPTS

Use separate schedule(s) for each category of the Detailed Summary Page

FOR LINE NUMBER: PAGE OF
(check only one)

| 11a | 11b | 11c | 12 |
| 13 | 14 | 15 | 16 | 17 |

Any information copied from such Reports and Statements may not be sold or used by any person for the purpose of soliciting contributions or for commercial purposes, other than using the name and address of any political committee to solicit contributions from such committee.

NAME OF COMMITTEE (In Full)

A.
Full Name (Last, First, Middle Initial)

Mailing Address

City   State   Zip Code

FEC ID number of contributing federal political committee.   C

Name of Employer   Occupation

Receipt For:
☐ Primary   ☐ General
☐ Other (specify) ▼

Aggregate Year-to-Date ▼

Date of Receipt
M M / D D / Y Y Y Y

Amount of Each Receipt this Period

B.
Full Name (Last, First, Middle Initial)

Mailing Address

City   State   Zip Code

FEC ID number of contributing federal political committee.   C

Name of Employer   Occupation

Receipt For:
☐ Primary   ☐ General
☐ Other (specify) ▼

Aggregate Year-to-Date ▼

Date of Receipt
M M / D D / Y Y Y Y

Amount of Each Receipt this Period

C.
Full Name (Last, First, Middle Initial)

Mailing Address

City   State   Zip Code

FEC ID number of contributing federal political committee.   C

Name of Employer   Occupation

Receipt For:
☐ Primary   ☐ General
☐ Other (specify) ▼

Aggregate Year-to-Date ▼

Date of Receipt
M M / D D / Y Y Y Y

Amount of Each Receipt this Period

SUBTOTAL of Receipts This Page (optional)......................... ▶

TOTAL This Period (last page this line number only)............... ▶

FE6AN026   FEC **Schedule A (Form 3X)** Rev. 02/2003

SCHEDULE B (FEC Form 3X)
ITEMIZED DISBURSEMENTS

Use separate schedule(s) for each category of the Detailed Summary Page

FOR LINE NUMBER: (check only one)

☐ 21b	☐ 22	☐ 23	☐ 24	☐ 25	☐ 26
☐ 27	☐ 28a	☐ 28b	☐ 28c	☐ 29	☐ 30b

PAGE   OF

Any information copied from such Reports and Statements may not be sold or used by any person for the purpose of soliciting contributions or for commercial purposes, other than using the name and address of any political committee to solicit contributions from such committee.

NAME OF COMMITTEE (In Full)

A.

Full Name (Last, First, Middle Initial)

Mailing Address

City   State   Zip Code

Purpose of Disbursement

Candidate Name

Category/ Type

Office Sought: ☐ House
                 ☐ Senate
                 ☐ President
State: District:

Disbursement For:
☐ Primary   ☐ General
☐ Other (specify) ▼

Date of Disbursement

M M / D D / Y Y Y Y

Amount of Each Disbursement this Period

B.

Full Name (Last, First, Middle Initial)

Mailing Address

City   State   Zip Code

Purpose of Disbursement

Candidate Name

Category/ Type

Office Sought: ☐ House
                 ☐ Senate
                 ☐ President
State: District:

Disbursement For:
☐ Primary   ☐ General
☐ Other (specify) ▼

Date of Disbursement

M M / D D / Y Y Y Y

Amount of Each Disbursement this Period

C.

Full Name (Last, First, Middle Initial)

Mailing Address

City   State   Zip Code

Purpose of Disbursement

Candidate Name

Category/ Type

Office Sought: ☐ House
                 ☐ Senate
                 ☐ President
State: District:

Disbursement For:
☐ Primary   ☐ General
☐ Other (specify) ▼

Date of Disbursement

M M / D D / Y Y Y Y

Amount of Each Disbursement this Period

SUBTOTAL of Disbursements This Page (optional).. ▶

TOTAL This Period (last page this line number only).. ▶

FE6AN026

FEC **Schedule B (Form 3X)** Rev. 02/2003

SCHEDULE C   (FEC Form 3X)
LOANS

Use separate schedule(s) for each category of the Detailed Summary Page	PAGE OF
	FOR LINE 13 OF FORM 3X

NAME OF COMMITTEE (In Full)

LOAN SOURCE Full Name (Last, First, Middle Initial)

Election:
☐ Primary
☐ General
☐ Other (specify) ▼

Mailing Address

City   State   ZIP Code

Original Amount of Loan	Cumulative Payment To Date	Balance Outstanding at Close of This Period

TERMS

Date Incurred	Date Due	Interest Rate	Secured:
M M / D D / Y Y Y Y	M M / D D / Y Y Y Y	____ % (apr)	☐ Yes ☐ No

List All Endorsers or Guarantors (if any) to Loan Source

1. Full Name (Last, First, Middle Initial)   Name of Employer

    Mailing Address   Occupation

    City   State   ZIP Code   Amount Guaranteed Outstanding: _____

2. Full Name (Last, First, Middle Initial)   Name of Employer

    Mailing Address   Occupation

    City   State   ZIP Code   Amount Guaranteed Outstanding: _____

3. Full Name (Last, First, Middle Initial)   Name of Employer

    Mailing Address   Occupation

    City   State   ZIP Code   Amount Guaranteed Outstanding: _____

4. Full Name (Last, First, Middle Initial)   Name of Employer

    Mailing Address   Occupation

    City   State   ZIP Code   Amount Guaranteed Outstanding: _____

SUBTOTALS This Period This Page (optional) .... ▶ _____

TOTALS This Period (last page in this line only) .... ▶ _____

Carry outstanding balance only to LINE 3, Schedule D, for this line. If no Schedule D, carry forward to appropriate line of Summary.

SCHEDULE C–1 (FEC Form 3X)
LOANS AND LINES OF CREDIT FROM LENDING INSTITUTIONS
Federal Election Commission, Washington, D.C. 20463

Supplementary for Information found on Page _____ of Schedule C

NAME OF COMMITTEE (In Full)	FEC IDENTIFICATION NUMBER
	C

LENDING INSTITUTION (LENDER) Full Name	Amount of Loan	Interest Rate (APR)
Mailing Address	Date Incurred or Established	M M / D D / Y Y Y Y Y
City State Zip Code	Date Due	M M / D D / Y Y Y Y Y

A. Has loan been restructured? ☐ No ☐ Yes   If yes, date originally incurred   M M / D D / Y Y Y Y Y

B. If line of credit,
   Amount of this Draw: _____   Total Outstanding Balance: _____

C. Are other parties secondarily liable for the debt incurred?
   ☐ No ☐ Yes   (Endorsers and guarantors must be reported on Schedule C.)

D. Are any of the following pledged as collateral for the loan: real estate, personal property, goods, negotiable instruments, certificates of deposit, chattel papers, stocks, accounts receivable, cash on deposit, or other similar traditional collateral?
   ☐ No ☐ Yes   If yes, specify: _____

   What is the value of this collateral? _____

   Does the lender have a perfected security interest in it? ☐ No ☐ Yes

E. Are any future contributions or future receipts of interest income, pledged as collateral for the loan? ☐ No ☐ Yes   If yes, specify: _____

   What is the estimated value? _____

   A depository account must be established pursuant to 11 CFR 100.82(e)(2) and 100.142(e)(2).

   Date account established: M M / D D / Y Y Y Y Y

   Location of account:
   Address:
   City, State, Zip: _____

F. If neither of the types of collateral described above was pledged for this loan, or if the amount pledged does not equal or exceed the loan amount, state the basis upon which this loan was made and the basis on which it assures repayment.

G. COMMITTEE TREASURER
   Typed Name
   Signature

   DATE   M M / D D / Y Y Y Y Y

H.   Attach a signed copy of the loan agreement.

I.   TO BE SIGNED BY THE LENDING INSTITUTION:
   I.   To the best of this institution's knowledge, the terms of the loan and other information regarding the extension of the loan are accurate as stated above.
   II.   The loan was made on terms and conditions (including interest rate) no more favorable at the time than those imposed for similar extensions of credit to other borrowers of comparable credit worthiness.
   III.   This institution is aware of the requirement that a loan must be made on a basis which assures repayment, and has complied with the requirements set forth at 11 CFR 100.82 and 100.142 in making this loan.

AUTHORIZED REPRESENTATIVE
Typed Name
Signature   Title

DATE   M M / D D / Y Y Y Y Y

SCHEDULE D (FEC Form 3X)
DEBTS AND OBLIGATIONS
Excluding Loans

(Use separate schedule(s) for each numbered line)	PAGE OF
	FOR LINE NUMBER: (check only one)

☐ 9
☐ 10

NAME OF COMMITTEE (In Full)

A. Full Name (Last, First, Middle Initial) of Debtor or Creditor

Nature of Debt (Purpose):

Mailing Address

City   State   Zip Code

Outstanding Balance Beginning This Period

Amount Incurred This Period	Payment This Period	Outstanding Balance at Close of This Period

---

B. Full Name (Last, First, Middle Initial) of Debtor or Creditor

Nature of Debt (Purpose):

Mailing Address

City   State   Zip Code

Outstanding Balance Beginning This Period

Amount Incurred This Period	Payment This Period	Outstanding Balance at Close of This Period

---

C. Full Name (Last, First, Middle Initial) of Debtor or Creditor

Nature of Debt (Purpose):

Mailing Address

City   State   Zip Code

Outstanding Balance Beginning This Period

Amount Incurred This Period	Payment This Period	Outstanding Balance at Close of This Period

---

1) **SUBTOTALS** This Period This Page (optional)... ▶

2) **TOTALS** This Period (last page this line number only)... ▶

3) **TOTAL OUTSTANDING LOANS** from Schedule C (last page only) .... ▶

4) **ADD 2)** and **3)** and carry forward to appropriate line of Summary Page (last page only) ▶

SCHEDULE E (FEC Form 3X)
ITEMIZED INDEPENDENT EXPENDITURES

	PAGE OF
	FOR LINE 24 OF FORM 3X

NAME OF COMMITTEE (In Full)

FEC IDENTIFICATION NUMBER ▼

C

Check if ☐ 24-hour notice   ☐ 48-hour notice

Full Name (Last, First, Middle Initial) of Payee

Date   M M / D D / Y Y Y Y Y

Mailing Address

Amount

City   State   Zip Code

Purpose of Expenditure   Category/Type

Office Sought: ☐ House   State: ___
☐ Senate   District: ___
☐ President

Name of Federal Candidate Supported or Opposed by Expenditure:

Check One: ☐ Support   ☐ Oppose

Calendar Year-To-Date Per Election for Office Sought

Disbursement For: ☐ Primary   ☐ General
☐ Other (specify) ▶ ___

Full Name (Last, First, Middle Initial) of Payee

Date   M M / D D / Y Y Y Y Y

Mailing Address

Amount

City   State   Zip Code

Purpose of Expenditure   Category/Type

Office Sought: ☐ House   State: ___
☐ Senate   District: ___
☐ President

Name of Federal Candidate Supported or Opposed by Expenditure:

Check One: ☐ Support   ☐ Oppose

Calendar Year-To-Date Per Election for Office Sought

Disbursement For: ☐ Primary   ☐ General
☐ Other (specify) ▶ ___

(a) SUBTOTAL of Itemized Independent Expenditures .... ▶

(b) SUBTOTAL of Unitemized Independent Expenditures... ▶

(c) TOTAL Independent Expenditures .... ▶

Under penalty of perjury I certify that the independent expenditures reported herein were not made in cooperation, consultation, or concert with, or at the request or suggestion of, any candidate or authorized committee or agent of either, or (if the reporting entity is not a political party committee) any political party committee or its agent.

_____   Date   M M / D D / Y Y Y Y Y
Signature

FE6AN026   FEC **Schedule E (Form 3X)** Rev. 02/2003

SCHEDULE F (FEC Form 3X)
ITEMIZED COORDINATED PARTY EXPENDITURES MADE BY
POLITICAL PARTY COMMITTEES OR DESIGNATED AGENT(S)
ON BEHALF OF CANDIDATES FOR FEDERAL OFFICE
(2 U.S.C. §441a(d))
(To be used only by Political Committees in the General Election)

PAGE	OF

FOR LINE 25 OF FORM 3X

NAME OF COMMITTEE (In Full)

☐ Check if 24-hour notice

Has your committee been designated to make coordinated expenditures by a political party committee?
☐ YES ☐ NO
If YES, name the designating committee:

Full Name of Subordinate Committee

Mailing Address

City   State   ZIP Code

Full Name (Last, First, Middle Initial) of Each Payee

Mailing Address

City   State   Zip Code

Name of Federal Candidate Supported | Office Sought: ☐ House ☐ Senate ☐ Presidential State: ___ District: ___

Aggregate General Election Expenditure for this Candidate ▶

Purpose of Expenditure

Category/Type

Date M M / D D / Y Y Y Y Y

Amount

☐ Limit Raised Due to Opponent's Spending (2 U.S.C. §441a(i)/441a–1)

Full Name (Last, First, Middle Initial) of Each Payee

Mailing Address

City   State   Zip Code

Name of Federal Candidate Supported | Office Sought: ☐ House ☐ Senate ☐ Presidential State: ___ District: ___

Aggregate General Election Expenditure for this Candidate ▶

Purpose of Expenditure

Category/Type

Date M M / D D / Y Y Y Y Y

Amount

☐ Limit Raised Due to Opponent's Spending (2 U.S.C. §441a(i)/441a–1)

Full Name (Last, First, Middle Initial) of Each Payee

Mailing Address

City   State   Zip Code

Name of Federal Candidate Supported | Office Sought: ☐ House ☐ Senate ☐ Presidential State: ___ District: ___

Aggregate General Election Expenditure for this Candidate ▶

Purpose of Expenditure

Category/Type

Date M M / D D / Y Y Y Y Y

Amount

☐ Limit Raised Due to Opponent's Spending (2 U.S.C. §441a(i)/441a–1)

SUBTOTAL of Expenditures This Page (optional)...▶

TOTAL This Period (last page this line number only)...▶

SCHEDULE H1 (FEC Form 3X)

METHOD OF ALLOCATION FOR:

- **ALLOCATED FEDERAL AND NONFEDERAL ADMINISTRATIVE, GENERIC VOTER DRIVE AND EXEMPT ACTIVITY COSTS**
- **ALLOCATED FEDERAL AND LEVIN FUNDS FEDERAL ELECTION ACTIVITY EXPENSES** (State, District and Local Party Committees Only)
- **ALLOCATED PUBLIC COMMUNICATIONS THAT REFER TO ANY POLITICAL PARTY (BUT NOT A CANDIDATE)** (Separate Segregated Funds And Nonconnected Committees Only)

NAME OF COMMITTEE (In Full)

USE ONLY ONE SECTION, A or B

A. State and Local Party Committees

Fixed Percentage (select one)

_____ Presidential-Only Election Year (28% Federal)

_____ Presidential and Senate Election Year (36% Federal)

_____ Senate-Only Election Year (21% Federal)

_____ Non-Presidential and Non-Senate Election Year (15% Federal)

B. Separate Segregated Funds and Nonconnected Committees

Flat Minimum Federal Percentage

If the committee will allocate using the flat minimum percentage of 50% federal funds, check ☐

or

If the committee is spending more than 50% federal funds, indicate ratio below

Federal.. ☐ %

Nonfederal .... ☐ %

This ratio applies to (check all that apply):

Administrative ☐   Generic Voter Drive ☐   Public Communications Referencing Party Only ☐

SCHEDULE H2 (FEC Form 3X)
ALLOCATION RATIOS

PAGE	OF

NAME OF COMMITTEE (In Full)

RATIOS FOR ALLOCABLE FUNDRAISING EVENTS AND DIRECT CANDIDATE SUPPORT ACTIVITIES APPEARING ON THIS REPORT.

Methods of allocation:

I. FUNDRAISING activities are allocated using the "funds received method" where the federal proportion of expenses must equal the federal proportion of monies raised.

II. Shared **DIRECT CANDIDATE SUPPORT** activities are allocated according to benefit expected to be derived, where the federal proportion of disbursements is based on the benefit derived by federal candidates from the activity. **For PACs Only**: Direct candidate support includes public communications or voter drives that refer to both federal and nonfederal candidates, regardless of whether there is a reference to a political party. Such expenses are allocated using a time/space method.

ACTIVITY OR EVENT IDENTIFIER
_____

ACTIVITY IS:
☐ Fundraising   ☐ Direct Candidate Support
CHECK IF THE RATIO IS:
☐ New   ☐ Revised   ☐ Same as Previously Reported

FEDERAL %   ☐ %   NONFEDERAL %   ☐ %

ACTIVITY OR EVENT IDENTIFIER
_____

ACTIVITY IS:
☐ Fundraising   ☐ Direct Candidate Support
CHECK IF THE RATIO IS:
☐ New   ☐ Revised   ☐ Same as Previously Reported

FEDERAL %   ☐ %   NONFEDERAL %   ☐ %

ACTIVITY OR EVENT IDENTIFIER
_____

ACTIVITY IS:
☐ Fundraising   ☐ Direct Candidate Support
CHECK IF THE RATIO IS:
☐ New   ☐ Revised   ☐ Same as Previously Reported

FEDERAL %   ☐ %   NONFEDERAL %   ☐ %

ACTIVITY OR EVENT IDENTIFIER
_____

ACTIVITY IS:
☐ Fundraising   ☐ Direct Candidate Support
CHECK IF THE RATIO IS:
☐ New   ☐ Revised   ☐ Same as Previously Reported

FEDERAL %   ☐ %   NONFEDERAL %   ☐ %

ACTIVITY OR EVENT IDENTIFIER
_____

ACTIVITY IS:
☐ Fundraising   ☐ Direct Candidate Support
CHECK IF THE RATIO IS:
☐ New   ☐ Revised   ☐ Same as Previously Reported

FEDERAL %   ☐ %   NONFEDERAL %   ☐ %

ACTIVITY OR EVENT IDENTIFIER
_____

ACTIVITY IS:
☐ Fundraising   ☐ Direct Candidate Support
CHECK IF THE RATIO IS:
☐ New   ☐ Revised   ☐ Same as Previously Reported

FEDERAL %   ☐ %   NONFEDERAL %   ☐ %

SCHEDULE H3 (FEC Form 3X)
TRANSFERS FROM NONFEDERAL ACCOUNTS FOR
ALLOCATED FEDERAL / NONFEDERAL ACTIVITY

PAGE   OF

FOR LINE 18a OF FORM 3X

NAME OF COMMITTEE (In Full)

NAME OF ACCOUNT	DATE OF RECEIPT	TOTAL AMOUNT TRANSFERRED
	M M / D D / Y Y Y Y	

BREAKDOWN OF TRANSFER RECEIVED

i) **Total Administrative** ....

ii) **Generic Voter Drive** ....

iii) **Exempt Activities**...

iv) **Direct Fundraising** (List Activity or Event Identifier)

a) _____

b) _____

c) Total Amount Transferred For Direct Fundraising ....

v) **Direct Candidate Support** (List Activity or Event Identifier)

a) _____

b) _____

c) Total Amount Transferred For Direct Candidate Support................................

vi) **Public Communications Referring Only to Party** (Made by PAC) ....

TOTALS FOR BREAKDOWN OF TRANSFER RECEIVED

TOTAL This Period (Administrative) ....

TOTAL This Period (Generic Voter Drive) ....

TOTAL This Period (Exempt Activities) ....

TOTAL This Period (Direct Fundraising) ....

TOTAL This Period (Direct Candidate Support) ....

TOTAL This Period (Public Communications Referring Only to Party) ....

TOTAL This Period (Total Amount Transferred)..

FE6AN026

FEC **Schedule H3 (Form 3X)** Rev. 12/2004

SCHEDULE H4 (FEC Form 3X)

DISBURSEMENTS FOR ALLOCATED FEDERAL/NONFEDERAL ACTIVITY

PAGE	OF

FOR LINE 21a OF FORM 3X

NAME OF COMMITTEE (In Full)

A. Full Name (Last, First, Middle Initial)

Allocated Activity or Event:

☐ Administrative ☐ Fundraising ☐ Exempt

Mailing Address

☐ Voter Drive ☐ Direct Candidate Support

City   State   Zip Code

☐ Public Comm (ref to party only) by PAC

Purpose of Disbursement:

Allocated Activity or Event Year-To-Date

Activity or Event Identifier:

Category/Type

Date   M M / D D / Y Y Y Y Y

FEDERAL SHARE	+	NONFEDERAL SHARE	=	TOTAL AMOUNT

B. Full Name (Last, First, Middle Initial)

Allocated Activity or Event:

☐ Administrative ☐ Fundraising ☐ Exempt

Mailing Address

☐ Voter Drive ☐ Direct Candidate Support

City   State   Zip Code

☐ Public Comm (ref to party only) by PAC

Purpose of Disbursement:

Allocated Activity or Event Year-To-Date

Activity or Event Identifier:

Category/Type

Date   M M / D D / Y Y Y Y Y

FEDERAL SHARE	+	NONFEDERAL SHARE	=	TOTAL AMOUNT

C. Full Name (Last, First, Middle Initial)

Allocated Activity or Event:

☐ Administrative ☐ Fundraising ☐ Exempt

Mailing Address

☐ Voter Drive ☐ Direct Candidate Support

City   State   Zip Code

☐ Public Comm (ref to party only) by PAC

Purpose of Disbursement:

Allocated Activity or Event Year-To-Date

Activity or Event Identifier:

Category/Type

Date   M M / D D / Y Y Y Y Y

FEDERAL SHARE	+	NONFEDERAL SHARE	=	TOTAL AMOUNT

SUBTOTAL of Allocated Federal and NonFederal Activity This Page

FEDERAL SHARE	+	NONFEDERAL SHARE	=	TOTAL AMOUNT

TOTAL This Period (last page for each line only)(Federal share to 21(a)(i) and NonFederal share to 21(a)(ii))

FEDERAL SHARE	NONFEDERAL SHARE	TOTAL AMOUNT

SCHEDULE H5   (FEC Form 3X)

TRANSFERS OF LEVIN FUNDS RECEIVED FOR
ALLOCATED FEDERAL ELECTION ACTIVITY
(To be used by State, District and Local Party Committees Only)

PAGE	OF
FOR LINE 18b OF FORM 3X	

NAME OF COMMITTEE (In Full)

NAME OF ACCOUNT	DATE OF RECEIPT	TOTAL AMOUNT TRANSFERRED
	M M / D D / Y Y Y Y Y	

BREAKDOWN OF THIS TRANSFER

i) **Voter Registration**
   Total Amount Transferred for Voter Registration......

VOTER REGISTRATION

ii) **Voter ID**
   Total Amount Transferred for Voter ID ....

VOTER ID

iii) **GOTV**
   Total Amount Transferred for GOTV ....

GOTV

iv) **Generic Campaign Activity**
   Total Amount Transferred for Generic Campaign Activity ....

GENERIC CAMPAIGN ACTIVITY

NAME OF ACCOUNT	DATE OF RECEIPT	TOTAL AMOUNT TRANSFERRED
	M M / D D / Y Y Y Y Y	

BREAKDOWN OF THIS TRANSFER

i) **Voter Registration**
   Total Amount Transferred for Voter Registration......

VOTER REGISTRATION

ii) **Voter ID**
   Total Amount Transferred for Voter ID ....

VOTER ID

iii) **GOTV**
   Total Amount Transferred for GOTV ....

GOTV

iv) **Generic Campaign Activity**
   Total Amount Transferred for Generic Campaign Activity ....

GENERIC CAMPAIGN ACTIVITY

TOTALS FOR BREAKDOWN OF TRANSFER RECEIVED (Last Page Only)

TOTAL This Period (Voter Registration)............................

TOTAL This Period (Voter ID) ....

TOTAL This Period (GOTV)...

TOTAL This Period (Generic Campaign Activity)...

TOTAL This Period (Total Amount of Transfers Received)...

SCHEDULE H6 (FEC Form 3X)
DISBURSEMENTS OF FEDERAL AND LEVIN FUNDS
FOR ALLOCATED FEDERAL ELECTION ACTIVITY
(To be used by State, District and Local Party Committees Only)

PAGE	OF

FOR LINE 30a OF FORM 3X

NAME OF COMMITTEE (In Full)

A. Full Name (Last, First, Middle Initial) / Full Organization Name

Type of Allocated Activity or Event:
- [ ] Voter Registration
- [ ] Voter ID
- [ ] GOTV
- [ ] Generic Campaign

Mailing Address

Allocated Activity or Event Year-To-Date

City   State   Zip Code

Purpose of Disbursement   Category/Type   Date M M / D D / Y Y Y Y

FEDERAL SHARE	+	LEVIN SHARE	=	TOTAL AMOUNT

B. Full Name (Last, First, Middle Initial) / Full Organization Name

Type of Allocated Activity or Event:
- [ ] Voter Registration
- [ ] Voter ID
- [ ] GOTV
- [ ] Generic Campaign

Mailing Address

Allocated Activity or Event Year-To-Date

City   State   Zip Code

Purpose of Disbursement   Category/Type   Date M M / D D / Y Y Y Y

FEDERAL SHARE	+	LEVIN SHARE	=	TOTAL AMOUNT

C. Full Name (Last, First, Middle Initial) / Full Organization Name

Type of Allocated Activity or Event:
- [ ] Voter Registration
- [ ] Voter ID
- [ ] GOTV
- [ ] Generic Campaign

Mailing Address

Allocated Activity or Event Year-To-Date

City   State   Zip Code

Purpose of Disbursement   Category/Type   Date M M / D D / Y Y Y Y

FEDERAL SHARE	+	LEVIN SHARE	=	TOTAL AMOUNT

SUBTOTAL of Shared Federal and Levin Activity This Page

FEDERAL SHARE	+	LEVIN SHARE	=	TOTAL AMOUNT

TOTAL This Period (last page for each line only)(Federal share to 30(a)(i) and Levin share to 30(a)(ii))

FEDERAL SHARE		TOTAL AMOUNT
	LEVIN SHARE	

TOTAL This Period for the Levin Share

FE6AN026

FEC **Schedule H6 (Form 3X)** Rev. 02/2003

SCHEDULE L (FEC Form 3X)
AGGREGATION PAGE: LEVIN FUNDS

NAME OF COMMITTEE (In Full)

NAME OF ACCOUNT

	COLUMN A TOTAL THIS PERIOD	COLUMN B YEAR-TO-DATE
1. RECEIPTS FROM PERSONS (a) Itemized .... (Use Schedule L–A)		
(b) Unitemized		
(c) Total		
2. OTHER RECEIPTS...............................		
3. TOTAL RECEIPTS .... (Add Lines 1c and 2)		
4. TRANSFERS TO FEDERAL OR ALLOCATION ACCOUNT (Use Schedule L–B) (a) Voter Registration		
(b) Voter ID....................................		
(c) GOTV		
(d) Generic Campaign......................		
(e) Total		
5. OTHER DISBURSEMENTS..................		
6. TOTAL DISBURSEMENTS .... (Add Lines 4e and 5)		
7. BEGINNING CASH ON HAND.............. (for Column B, use cash as of January 1st)		
8. RECEIPTS... (from Line 3)		
9. SUBTOTAL .... (Add Lines 7 and 8)		
10. DISBURSEMENTS............................... (From Line 6)		
11. ENDING CASH ON HAND........................ (Subtract Line 10 From Line 9)		

SCHEDULE L–A (FEC Form 3X)
ITEMIZED RECEIPTS OF LEVIN FUNDS

Use separate schedule(s) for each category of the Aggregation Page

| PAGE | OF |
FOR LINE NUMBER: (check only one)   ☐ 1a   ☐ 2

Any information copied from such Reports and Statements may not be sold or used by any person for the purpose of soliciting contributions or for commercial purposes, other than using the name and address of any political committee to solicit contributions from such committee.

NAME OF COMMITTEE (In Full)

A. Full Name (Last, First, Middle Initial) / Full Organization Name

Mailing Address

City   State   Zip Code

Name of Employer or Principal Place of Business

Occupation

Date of Receipt   M M / D D / Y Y Y Y Y

Amount of Each Receipt this Period

Aggregate Year-to-Date

B. Full Name (Last, First, Middle Initial) / Full Organization Name

Mailing Address

City   State   Zip Code

Name of Employer or Principal Place of Business

Occupation

Date of Receipt   M M / D D / Y Y Y Y Y

Amount of Each Receipt this Period

Aggregate Year-to-Date

C. Full Name (Last, First, Middle Initial) / Full Organization Name

Mailing Address

City   State   Zip Code

Name of Employer or Principal Place of Business

Occupation

Date of Receipt   M M / D D / Y Y Y Y Y

Amount of Each Receipt this Period

Aggregate Year-to-Date

D. Full Name (Last, First, Middle Initial) / Full Organization Name

Mailing Address

City   State   Zip Code

Name of Employer or Principal Place of Business

Occupation

Date of Receipt   M M / D D / Y Y Y Y Y

Amount of Each Receipt this Period

Aggregate Year-to-Date

SUBTOTAL of Receipts This Page (optional).. ▶

TOTAL This Period (last page this line number only)............................... ▶

SCHEDULE L–B (FEC Form 3X)
ITEMIZED DISBURSEMENTS
OF LEVIN FUNDS

Use separate schedule(s)
for each category of the
Aggregation Page

FOR LINE NUMBER: PAGE   OF
(check only one)
☐ 4a   ☐ 4c   ☐ 5
☐ 4b   ☐ 4d

Any information copied from such Reports and Statements may not be sold or used by any person for the purpose of soliciting contributions or for commercial purposes, other than using the name and address of any political committee to solicit contributions from such committee.

NAME OF COMMITTEE (In Full)

A. Full Name (Last, First, Middle Initial) / Full Organization Name

Mailing Address

City   State   Zip Code

Purpose of Disbursement

Date of Disbursement
M M / D D / Y Y Y Y Y Y

Amount of Each Disbursement this Period

B. Full Name (Last, First, Middle Initial) / Full Organization Name

Mailing Address

City   State   Zip Code

Purpose of Disbursement

Date of Disbursement
M M / D D / Y Y Y Y Y Y

Amount of Each Disbursement this Period

C. Full Name (Last, First, Middle Initial) / Full Organization Name

Mailing Address

City   State   Zip Code

Purpose of Disbursement

Date of Disbursement
M M / D D / Y Y Y Y Y Y

Amount of Each Disbursement this Period

D. Full Name (Last, First, Middle Initial) / Full Organization Name

Mailing Address

City   State   Zip Code

Purpose of Disbursement

Date of Disbursement
M M / D D / Y Y Y Y Y Y

Amount of Each Disbursement this Period

E. Full Name (Last, First, Middle Initial) / Full Organization Name

Mailing Address

City   State   Zip Code

Purpose of Disbursement

Date of Disbursement
M M / D D / Y Y Y Y Y Y

Amount of Each Disbursement this Period

SUBTOTAL of Disbursements This Page (optional).. ▶

TOTAL This Period (last page this line number only).. ▶

FE6AN026   FEC **Schedule L–B (Form 3X)** Rev. 02/2003

FEDERAL ELECTION COMMISSION
Report of Receipts and Disbursements for Other than an Authorized Committee (FEC FORM 3X)

(Filed by party committees and political action committees (PACs))

Use FEC FORM 3X to file your report. Listed below are the summary pages and schedules of FEC FORM 3X, with an explanation of what each discloses.

FEC FORM 3X: Page 1, Report of Receipts and Disbursements

Identifies the committee, the type of report and the reporting period.

FEC FORM 3X: Page 2, Summary Page

Identifies the committee; discloses the committee's total receipts and disbursements for the reporting period and the calendar year to date.

FEC FORM 3X: Pages 3 – 5, Detailed Summary Page

Summarizes receipts and disbursements by type of activity; shows reporting period and calendar year to date totals for each type of activity.

FEC FORM 3X: Schedules

A: Provides detailed information for each receipt that is required to be itemized. Use a separate Schedule A to support each Line number that appears on the Detailed Summary Page.

B: Provides detailed information for each disbursement that is required to be itemized. Use a separate Schedule B to support each Line number that appears on the Detailed Summary Page.

C: Shows all loans, endorsements and loan guarantees the committee receives or makes.

C-1: Shows all loans and lines of credit made by lending institutions to the committee.

D: Shows debts and obligations owed to or by the committee that are required to be disclosed.

E: Shows all independent expenditures made during the reporting period. Schedule may also be used to separately disclose last-minute independent expenditures of $1,000 or more made between the 20th day and 24 hours before the date of an election.

F: Shows all coordinated party expenditures. (Used by party committees only.)

H1: Shows method of allocation for allocated federal and nonfederal administrative expenses, exempt activity costs and generic voter drive costs, allocated federal/Levin fund "federal election activity" expenses (for State, district and local party committees only) and allocated public communications that refer only to a party (for PACs only).

H2: Shows allocation ratios for other allocated federal and nonfederal activity, including individual fundraising events and direct candidate support appearing on the report.

H3: Shows transfers from nonfederal accounts to federal accounts for the purpose of paying allocable expenses.

H4: Shows disbursements for allocated federal and nonfederal activity.

H5: Shows transfers of Levin funds for allocable federal election activity.

H6: Shows disbursements of federal and Levin funds for allocable federal election activity.

L: Aggregation page for showing receipt and disbursement of Levin funds.

L-A: Memo schedule for itemizing receipts of Levin funds.

L-B: Memo schedule for itemizing disbursements of Levin funds.

Illegible and Non-FEC Forms

Illegible reports and reports submitted on non-FEC forms are not acceptable and must be refiled.

Electronic Filing

Political committees must file reports in an electronic format under 11 CFR 104.18 if they either receive contributions or make expenditures in excess of $50,000 during the calendar year, or if they have reason to expect that they will exceed either of those thresholds. If the committee has reached this level of activity, DO NOT FILE THIS FORM ON PAPER. Instead, you must file this form in an electronic format. See the instructions for more information on filing electronically.

Computerized Format

FEC FORM 3X may be filed by paper filers in a computerized format, but the Commission must approve the computerized format before the report is filed. Submit sample formats to the Reports Analysis Division.

Faxing Forms

Most reports may not be filed by FAX because original signatures are required.

Other Forms and Their Uses

The forms listed below are also available. When ordering, please order by form number.

FEC FORM 1: Statement of Organization

Used by all political committees to register under the federal election law.

FEC FORM 1M: Notification of Multicandidate Status

Used by PACs and party committees to notify the Commission of their status as a multicandidate committee.

FEC FORM 7: Report of Communications Costs by Corporations and Membership Organizations

Used by corporations and labor organizations to disclose internal partisan communication costs that exceed $2,000 for an election.

FEC FORM 8: Debt Settlement Plan

Used by terminating committees to disclose the terms of debt settlements.

These Forms may be duplicated.

To obtain additional forms, call the Information Division at 1-800/424-9530 or 202/694-1100 or visit the FEC's Web site at www.fec.gov.

INSTRUCTIONS FOR FEC FORM 3X AND RELATED SCHEDULES

INSTRUCTIONS FOR SUMMARY PAGE (FEC FORM 3X, PAGES 1–2)

Who Must File

Any political committee which is not an authorized committee is required to file periodic Reports of Receipts and Disbursements on FEC FORM 3X.

Note: Political committees must file reports in an electronic format under 11 CFR 104.18 if they have either received contributions or made expenditures in excess of $50,000, or if they have reason to expect that they will exceed either of those thresholds during the calendar year. If the committee has reached this level of activity, DO NOT FILE THIS FORM ON PAPER. Instead, you must file this form in an electronic format.

A political committee is considered to have reason to expect it will exceed the electronic filing threshold for the next two calendar years after the calendar year in which it exceeds $50,000 in contributions or expenditures. If it is a new committee, it is considered to have reason to expect it will exceed the electronic filing threshold if it exceeds $12,500 in contributions or expenditures during the first calendar quarter of the calendar year, or $25,000 in contributions or expenditures in the first half of the calendar year.

Contact the FEC for more information on filing electronically.

ALL POLITICAL COMMITTEES AUTHORIZED IN WRITING BY A CANDIDATE FOR THE OFFICE OF PRESIDENT OR VICE PRESIDENT MUST FILE ON FEC FORM 3P.

ALL POLITICAL COMMITTEES AUTHORIZED BY A CANDIDATE FOR THE HOUSE OF REPRESENTATIVES OR SENATE MUST FILE ON FEC FORM 3.

When to File

All political committees required to file on FEC FORM 3X must file either: election and non-election year reports as specified in (A) below; or monthly reports as specified in (B) below.

Note: State, district and local committees of political parties that are political committees under the Act must disclose receipts and disbursements for Federal election activity. If the committee's aggregate amount of such receipts and disbursement is less than $5,000 in a calendar year, it must report only receipts and disbursements of Federal funds for Federal election activity. If the aggregate amount of such receipts and disbursements during the calendar year equals or exceeds $5,000, the committee must report all receipts and disbursements for Federal election activity. 2 U.S.C. §434(e)(2). The reporting periods for political party committees disclosing receipts and disbursements for Federal election activity are monthly, except for pre-general and post-general election reports. 2 U.S.C. §434(e)(4) (citing 2 U.S.C. §434(a)(4)(B)). Otherwise, political committees that are State, district and local committees of political parties must file quarterly and pre- and post-election reports in election years and semi-annual reports in non-election years for their other activity. 2 U.S.C. §434(a).

(A) Election Year and Non-Election Year Reports

In any calendar year in which there is a "regular" November general election, the following reports are required:

• Quarterly reports must be filed no later than April 15, July 15, October 15 and January 31 of the following calendar year. Each such report must disclose all transactions from the last report filed through the last day of the calendar quarter. A quarterly report is not required to be filed if a Pre-Election report is required to be filed during the period beginning the 5th day and ending on the 15th day after the close of the calendar quarter.

• Pre-Election reports must be filed no later than the 12th day before any primary or general election in which the committee supports (i.e., makes contributions to or expenditures on behalf of) or opposes a candidate and must include all transactions

from the closing date of the last report filed through the 20th day before the election. A 12-Day Pre-Election Report sent by certified or registered mail must be mailed no later than the 15th day before the election. A Pre-Primary election report is not required where the contribution(s) or expenditure(s) has been disclosed on a previous report.

• All committees must file a 30-Day Post-General Election Report. A 30-Day Post-General Election Report must be filed no later than 30-Days after the general election and include all transactions from the closing date of the last report filed through the 20th day after the general election.

In any other calendar year, the following reports are required:

• A Mid Year Report must be filed no later than July 31 and include transactions beginning January 1 and ending June 30.

• A Year End Report must be filed no later than January 31 of the following calendar year and include transactions beginning July 1 and ending December 31.

(B) Monthly Reports

Monthly reports must be filed no later than 20 days after the last day of the month and must disclose all transactions from the last report filed through the last day of the month. In lieu of the monthly reports due in November and December for a year in which there is a "regular" November general election, a 12-Day Pre-General election report must be filed including all transactions from the closing date of the last report filed through the 20th day before the election and a 30-Day Post-General election report must be filed including all transactions from the closing date of the Pre-Election report through the 20th day after the general election. A Year End Report must be filed no later than January 31 of the following calendar year and include transactions from the closing date of the Post-General Election Report through the last day of the calendar year.

Except for State, district and local party committees required to file monthly under 11 CFR 300.36(c)(1)

INSTRUCTIONS FOR FEC FORM 3X AND RELATED SCHEDULES

(see above) and national party committees required to file monthly under 11 CFR 104.5(c)(4), a political committee may elect to change the frequency of its reporting from quarterly and semi-annually under (A) to monthly under (B) or vice versa. A committee may change its filing frequency only after notifying the Commission in writing of its intention at the time it files a required report under its current filing frequency. The committee will then be required to file the next required report under its new filing frequency. A committee may change its filing frequency no more than once per calendar year.

A document is timely filed upon delivery to the appropriate office (see "Where To File") by the close of the prescribed filing date or upon deposit as registered or certified mail in an established U.S. Post Office and postmarked no later than midnight of the day the report is due, except that Pre-Election Reports so mailed must be postmarked no later than midnight of the 15th day before the date of the election. Reports and statements sent by first class mail must be received by the appropriate office by the close of business of the prescribed filing date to be timely filed. Reports filed electronically are timely filed if the report is received and validated by the Commission's computer system on or before 11:59 p.m. Eastern Standard/Daylight Savings time on the prescribed filing date.

Where to File

An original and any amendments to an original report must be filed as follows:
•Committees which support or oppose only a candidate(s) for the Senate must file with the Secretary of the Senate, Office of Public Records, 232 Hart Senate Office Building, Washington, D.C. 20510-7116. Mail addressed to the Secretary of the Senate should read: "Office of Public Records, P.O. Box 5109, Alexandria, VA 22301-0109."
•All other committees must file with the Federal Election Commission,

999 E Street, N.W., Washington, D.C. 20463.

Political committees filing FEC FORM 3X must file with the appropriate officer in Guam and Puerto Rico a copy of that portion of the report applicable to candidates seeking election in those territories (as of March 2006, those territories had not qualified for the Commission's state filing waiver program).

Report Preparation

•A political committee may use any recordkeeping or accounting system which will enable it to comply with the Act.
•The Commission recommends that the political committee keep a recordkeeping or accounting system that keeps a separate accounting for each of the various categories of receipts and disbursements on pages 3, 4 and 5 (Detailed Summary Page). This separate accounting will help the political committee fill out the reporting forms, since separate reporting schedules are required for each category.
•The reporting schedules should be filled out so that totals can be derived for each category.
•The total figures should be carried forward to pages 3, 4 and 5 (Detailed Summary Page) and then (where appropriate) from the Detailed Summary Page to page 2 (Summary Page).
•Pages 3, 4 and 5 (Detailed Summary Page) should be filled out before completing page 2 (Summary Page).

Treasurer's Responsibilities

A copy of this Report must be preserved by the treasurer of the political committee for a period of not less than three years from the date of filing. The treasurer of the political committee is personally responsible for the timely and complete filing of the report and the accuracy of any information contained in it.

Line-by-Line Instructions for Page 2 (Summary Page)

LINE 1. Enter the complete name and mailing address of your committee.

LINE 2. Enter the FEC Identification Number assigned to the committee.

LINE 3. If this is an original report, check the "NEW" box. If this is an amendment to a previous report, check the "AMENDED" box.

LINE 4. Check the appropriate box for "Type of Report". If the report is a 12-Day Pre-Election or 30-Day Post-General election report, supply the type of election (primary, general, convention, special or run-off), the date of the election, and the State in which the election is held.

LINE 5. Enter the coverage dates for this report. All activity from the ending coverage date of the last report filed must be included.

LINE 6(a). Enter the total amount of cash on hand at the beginning of the calendar year. The term "cash on hand" includes: currency; balance on deposit in banks, savings and loan institutions, and other depository institutions; traveler's checks owned by the committee; certificates of deposit, treasury bills and other committee investments valued at cost.

LINE 6(b). Enter the total amount of cash on hand at the beginning of the reporting period.

LINE 6(c). Transfer the amounts from Column A and Column B of Line 19 to the corresponding Columns on Line 6(c).

LINE 6(d). Add Lines 6(b) and 6(c) to derive the figure for Column A, and add Lines 6(a) and 6(c) to derive the figure for Column B.

LINE 7. Transfer the amounts from Column A and Column B of Line 31 to the corresponding Columns on Line 7.

LINE 8. For both Column A and Column B subtract Line 7 from Line

6(d) to derive the figure (which should be the same for both columns) for cash on hand at the close of the reporting period of Line 8.

LINE 9. Transfer the total amount of debts and obligations owed TO the committee from Schedule C or D.

LINE 10. Transfer the total amount of debts and obligations owed BY the committee from Schedule C or D.

Multicandidate Committee Status

Check box if the political committee has qualified as a "multicandidate committee" and has filed FORM 1M. A committee qualifies as a "multicandidate committee" when it:
(i)   has been registered with the Commission or Secretary of the Senate for at least six months;
(ii) has received contributions for federal elections from more than 50 persons; and
(iii) (except for any State political party organization) has made contributions to five or more federal candidates; or satisfies requirements (i)-(iii) by affiliation with another committee.

INSTRUCTIONS FOR DETAILED SUMMARY PAGE (FEC FORM 3X, PAGES 3, 4 AND 5)

A political committee must report the total amount of receipts and disbursements during the reporting period and during the calendar year for each category of receipts and disbursements on FEC FORM 3X. The committee's full name and the coverage dates of the report must be entered in the appropriate blocks. If there are no receipts or disbursements for a particular category for a reporting period or calendar year, enter "0".

To derive the "Calendar Year-to-Date" figure for each category, the political committee should add the "Calendar Year-to-Date" total from the previous report to the "Total This Period" from Column A for the current report. For the first report filed for a calendar year, the "Calendar Year-to-Date" figure is equal to the "Total This Period" figure.

LINE 11(a)(i). Itemized Contributions from Individuals/Persons Other Than Political Committees. Enter the total amount of contributions (other than loans) from individuals, partnerships, and other persons who are not political committees that are required to be itemized on Schedule A. For each such person who has made one or more contributions during the calendar year aggregating in excess of $200, the committee must itemize on Schedule A and provide the identification (full name, mailing address, occupation and name of employer) of the person, date and amount of each contribution aggregating in excess of $200 and the aggregate year-to-date total.

LINE 11(a)(ii). Unitemized Contributions from Individuals/Persons Other Than Political Committees. Enter the total amount of all contributions from individuals/persons other than political committees not required to be itemized on Schedule A.

LINE 11(a)(iii). Total Contributions from Individuals/Persons Other Than Political Committees. Add Lines 11(a)(i) and 11(a)(ii) to derive the figure for Column A. For the Column B figure, see above instructions on how to calculate the Calendar Year-to-Date figure.

LINE 11(b). Contributions from Political Party Committees. For political committees (other than political party committees), enter the total amount of contributions (other than loans) from political party committees on Line 11(b). These contributions must be itemized on Schedule A, regardless of the amount. For each contribution, provide the identification (full name and address) of the committee, date and amount of the contribution and the aggregate year-to-date total. Political party committees should use Line 12.

LINE 11(c). Contributions from Other Political Committees (such as PACs). Enter the total amount of contributions (other than loans) from other political committees on Line 11(c). These contributions must be itemized on Schedule A, regardless of the amount. For each contribution, provide the identification (full name and address) of the committee, date and amount of the contribution and the aggregate year-to-date total. Do not abbreviate committee names.

LINE 11(d). Total Contributions. For both Column A and Column B add Lines 11(a)(iii), 11(b) and 11(c) to derive the figures for Line 11(d).

LINE 12. Transfers from Affiliated/Other Party Committees. Political party committees must enter the total amount of transfers from other party committees on Line 12. All other political committees must enter the total amount of transfers from other affiliated committees on Line 12. (See also 11 CFR 102.5 and 102.6.) Loans and loan repayments received from other political party committees or affiliated committees (as appropriate) must be included on Line 12, and not on Line 13. These transfers must be itemized on Schedule A, regardless of the amount. For each transfer provide the identification (full name and mailing address) of the committee, date and amount of the transfer and the aggregate year-to-date total.

LINE 13. All Loans Received. Enter the total amount of loans received (other than loans from affiliated/other party committees) on Line 13. All loans received by the committee must be itemized on Schedule A, regardless of the amount. For each loan, provide the identification (full name, mailing address and, where applicable, occupation and name of employer) of the person making the loan, date and amount of the loan and the aggregate year-to-date total. The committee must also provide on Schedule C the identification of any endorser or guarantor and the amount of the endorsement or guarantee. (See also instructions for Schedule C.)

LINE 14. Loan Repayments Received. Enter the total amount of loan repayments received (other than loan repayments from affiliated/other party committees) on Line 14. All loan repayments received by the committee must be itemized on Schedule A, regardless of the amount. For each loan repayment, provide the identification of the person making the loan repayment, date and amount of the loan repayment and the aggregate year-to-date total.

LINE 15. Offsets to Operating Expenditures. Enter the total amount of offsets to operating expenditures (including refunds, rebates, and returns of deposits) on Line 15. For each person who provides rebates, refunds and other offsets to operating expenditures aggregating in excess of $200 for the calendar year, the committee must provide on Schedule A the identification of the person, date and amount of each receipt aggregating in excess of $200 and the aggregate year-to-date total.

LINE 16. Refunds of Contributions Made to Federal Candidates and Other Political Committees. Enter the total amount of refunds of contributions made to federal candidates and other political committees on Line 16. If the original check was passed through the account of the recipient committee and a check for the refund is written on the recipient committee's account, the refund must be itemized as a receipt on Schedule A, regardless of the amount, and the amount of the refund must be included in the total figure for Line 16. For each contribution refund received, provide the full name and address of the federal candidate or political committee, date and amount of the refund and the aggregate year-to-date total. DO NOT use this Line if the original check is returned uncashed. The return must be reported as a negative entry on Schedule B and subtracted from the total amount for Line 23.

LINE 17. Other Federal Receipts. Enter the total amount of other receipts (including dividends and interest) on Line 17. For each person who provides any dividends, interest or other receipts aggregating in excess of $200 for the calendar year, the committee must provide on Schedule A the identification of the person, the date and amount of each receipt aggregating in excess of $200 and the aggregate year-to-date total.

LINE 18(a). Transfers from Nonfederal Account for Allocated Activity. Enter the total of any transfers from nonfederal accounts to the federal account or a separate allocation account in order to pay for allocated federal/ nonfederal activity. Only committees with separate federal and nonfederal accounts who undertake allocated activity affecting both types of campaigns may make transfers among these accounts. The total transfers for this period come from the last page of Schedule H3 which itemizes any such transfers made for allocated activity. See the instructions for Schedule H3 for more information.

LINE 18(b). Transfers from Levin Funds. Enter the total of any transfers from Levin funds brought to the federal account or a separate allocation account in order to pay for allocated federal/Levin "federal election activity." Only committees with separate federal and Levin funds who undertake allocated federal election activity should report transfers from Levin funds or accounts. The total transfers for this period come from the last page of Schedule H5 which itemizes any such transfers made for allocated activity.

LINE 18(c). Total Transfers. For both Column A and Column B add Lines 18(a) and 18(b) to derive the figures for Line 18(c).

LINE 19. Total Receipts. For both Column A and Column B add the totals on Lines 11(d), 12, 13, 14, 15, 16, 17, and 18(c) to derive the figures for Line 19.

LINE 20. Total Federal Receipts. This Line represents the difference between total receipts reported on Line 19 and the sum of any transfers into the federal account by nonfederal account(s) for allocated activity or from Levin funds for allocated federal election activity. The value is equal to Line 19 minus Line 18(c).

LINE 21. **Note:** Line 21(a) is required only for those committees undertaking activity which is allocated among federal and nonfederal accounts. Committees with no nonfederal accounts, or who do not undertake activities which are allocated among federal and nonfederal accounts complete only Lines 21(b) and (c). All operating expenses for those purely federal committees must be included on Line 21(b).

Operating Expenditures: Enter the total amount of operating expenditures and allocated federal/nonfederal activity on the appropriate Line under Line 21. Examples of operating expenditures are: travel, rent and telephones. Committees report only those operating expenditures paid for from committee funds.

LINE 21(a). Allocated Federal/Nonfederal Activity. Enter the federal portion of all operating expenses for allocated federal and nonfederal activity on Line 21(a)(i). This is equal to the federal share value from the bottom of the last page of Schedule H4 for this period. These allocated activities – including allocated disbursements for administrative expenses, generic voter drives, fundraising expenses and direct candidate support – must be itemized on Schedule H4 regardless of amount. Separate segregated funds and nonconnected committees must also include allocated disbursements for public communications that refer only to a party, while party committees must include disbursements for allocable exempt activity. Line 21(a)(ii) contains the sum of the nonfederal share of operating expenses for allocated federal and nonfederal activity. This value also is brought forward from the last page of Schedule H4 for this period. See the instructions for Schedule H4 for more information.

LINE 21(b). Other Federal Operating Expenditures. Enter on Line 21(b) the sum of all other federal operating expenditures, including those itemized on Schedule B as well as any unitemized federal operating expenditures. Separate segregated funds and nonconnected committees must report disbursements for public communications and voter drives that refer to federal candidates (but not nonfederal candidates), or refer to federal candidates and a party (but not nonfederal candidates), on Line 21(b) or Line 23, as appropriate. See the instructions for Schedule B for more information. For each person who receives payments for other federal operating expenditures aggregating in excess of $200 for the calendar year, the committee must provide on Schedule B the full name and mailing address, date and amount of the expenditure.

INSTRUCTIONS FOR FEC FORM 3X AND RELATED SCHEDULES

LINE 21(c). Total Operating Expenditures. Enter the total of the amounts listed on Lines 21(a)(i), 21(a)(ii) and 21(b).

LINE 22. Transfers to Affiliated/ Other Party Committees. Political party committees must enter the total amount of transfers to all other political party committees on Line 22. All other political committees must enter the total amount of transfers to other affiliated committees on Line 22. Loans and loan repayments made to other political party committees or affiliated committees (as appropriate) must be included on Line 22, not on Line 26 or 27. These transfers must be itemized on Schedule B, regardless of the amount. For each transfer, provide the full name and mailing address of the recipient committee, date, amount and state that the purpose of the disbursement is a "transfer."

LINE 23. Contributions to Federal Candidates/Committees and Other Political Committees. Enter the total amount of contributions to federal candidates and other federally-registered political committees on Line 23, including any in-kind contributions made. These contributions must be itemized on Schedule B, regardless of the amount. DO NOT include transfers reported on Line 22 on this Line. Do not enter contributions made to nonfederal candidates or committees on this Line, but on Line 29. For each contribution to a federal candidate or political committee, provide the full name and address of the political committee or candidate, date and amount of the contribution and, in the case of a candidate or authorized committee, the office sought by the candidate. (Include State and congressional district, where applicable.)

LINE 24. Independent Expenditures. Enter the total amount of independent expenditures on Line 24. (See also the instructions for Schedule E.)

LINE 25. Coordinated Party Expenditures. For political party committees, enter the total amount of coordinated party expenditures made by the committee pursuant to 2 U.S.C. §441a(d) on Line 25. **Note:** Political committees which are not political party committees may not make coordinated party expenditures pursuant to the special allowance at 2 U.S.C. §441a(d). (See also the instructions for Schedule F.)

LINE 26. Loan Repayments Made. Enter the total amount of loan repayments made on Line 26. All loan repayments made must be itemized on Schedule B, regardless of the amount. For each person who receives a loan repayment, provide the full name, mailing address, date, amount, and state that the purpose of the disbursement is a "loan repayment."

LINE 27. Loans Made. Enter the total amount of loans made (excluding transfers reported on Line 22) on Line 27. For each loan made by the committee provide the full name and mailing address of the person, date and amount of the loan, and state that the purpose of the disbursement is a "loan."

LINE 28(a). Refunds of Contributions Made to Individuals/Persons Other Than Political Committees. Enter the total amount of contribution refunds to individuals/persons other than political committees on Line 28(a). For each person who receives a refund of a contribution which was previously itemized on Schedule A, the committee must provide on Schedule B the full name, mailing address, date, amount and state that the purpose of the disbursement is a "contribution refund."

LINE 28(b). Refunds of Contributions to Political Party Committees. Enter the total amount of contribution refunds to political party committees on Line 28(b). All such refunds must be itemized on Schedule B, regardless of the amount. For each contribution refund, provide the full name, mailing address, date, amount and state that the purpose of the disbursement is a "contribution refund."

LINE 28(c). Refunds of Contributions to Other Political Committees. Enter the total amount of contribution refunds to other political committees on Line 28(c). (See instructions for Line 28(b) for other reporting requirements.)

LINE 28(d). Total Contribution Refunds. For both Column A and Column B add the totals on Lines 28(a), 28(b) and 28(c) to derive the figures for Line 28(d).

LINE 29. Other Disbursements. Enter the total amount of other disbursements (including contributions to nonfederal candidates) on Line 29. Separate segregated funds and nonconnected committees that use their federal accounts to pay for any portion of a public communication or voter drive that refers to nonfederal candidates (but not federal candidates) or to nonfederal candidates and a party (but not federal candidates) must enter those disbursements on Line 29. See the instructions for Schedule B for more information. For each such person who receives any disbursement(s) not otherwise disclosed where the aggregate amount or value is in excess of $200, the committee must provide the full name and address of each such person, together with the date, amount and purpose of any such disbursement.

    Federal Election Commission (Revised 4/2006)   FE6AN026

LINE 30. Federal Election Activity. Only State, district and local party committees making disbursements for federal election activities as defined by 2 U.S.C. §431(20) and 11 CFR 100.24 must enter figures on Line 30. See the instructions for Schedules B, H1, H5 and H6 for more information. Break out such disbursements as follows:

LINE 30(a). Allocated Federal Election Activity. Enter the total amount of the federal portion of all such disbursements for allocable federal election activity on Line 30(a)(i). This is equal to the federal share value from the bottom of the last page of Schedule H6 for this period. All such disbursements must be itemized regardless of amount on Schedule H6. Enter the total amount of the Levin share of disbursements for allocable federal election activity on Line 30(a)(ii). (See also the instructions for Schedules H1, H5 and H6 for definitions of "allocable federal election activity" and more information.) Note that if the federal election activity is not allocable under 11 CFR 300.33, or if the party committee chooses to pay for allocable federal election activity completely from its federal account, those payments must instead be reported on Line 30(b) below and itemized as required on Schedule B.)

LINE 30(b). Federal Election Activity Paid Entirely With Federal Funds. Enter the total amount of all disbursements made for public communications that qualify as federal election activity under 11 CFR 100.24(b)(3) and the total amount of all disbursements made to pay the salary of any employee of a State, district or local party committee who spends over 25% of his or her compensated time in a given month on federal election activities or on activities in connection with a federal election. See 11 CFR 100.24(b)(4). Itemize all such disbursements of $200 or more on Schedule B for Line 30(b). (See also the instructions for Schedule B.)

LINE 30(c). Total Federal Election Activity. For Column A and Column B, add the totals on Lines 30(a)(i), 30(a)(ii) and 30(b) to derive the figures for Line 30(c).

LINE 31. Total Disbursements. For Column A and Column B add the totals on Lines 21(c), 22, 23, 24, 25, 26, 27, 28(d), 29 and 30(c) to derive the figures for Line 31.

LINE 32. Total Federal Disbursements. Subtract from Line 31 (total disbursements) the total nonfederal share of disbursements from Line 21(a)(ii) and the total Levin share of disbursements from Line 30(a)(ii).

LINES 33-38. Enter the figures requested and complete the calculations as noted.

INSTRUCTIONS FOR FEC FORM 3X AND RELATED SCHEDULES

INSTRUCTIONS FOR SCHEDULE A, ITEMIZED RECEIPTS (FEC FORM 3X)

The Detailed Summary Page is broken down into various categories of receipts. Use Schedule A to list each receipt required to be itemized. DO NOT combine more than one category of receipts on the same Schedule A. Instead, use a separate Schedule A for each category of receipts. The Line number of the Detailed Summary Page to which each Schedule A pertains should be identified in the upper right corner of each Schedule. In addition, the committee's full name must be entered in the appropriate block. For each receipt required to be itemized during the reporting period, the political committee must provide the identification, date and amount of the receipt, and the aggregate year-to-date total. If disclosing a contribution from a federal political committee, the committee should enter the committee's FEC identification number. (This number is readily available from the Commission's Web site or its Public Disclosure Division.)

The term "identification" means, in the case of an individual, his or her full name, including: first name, middle name or initial, if available, and last name; mailing address; occupation; and the name of his or her employer; and, in the case of any other person, the person's full name and address. Do not abbreviate committee names.

The occupation and name of employer is only required to be provided for receipts from individuals. "Occupation" means the principal job title or position of an individual and whether or not self-employed. "Employer" means the organization or person by whom an individual is employed, and not the name of his or her supervisor.

The "receipt for" block does not apply to contributions received by political committees. Only use these blocks for receipts relating to refunds or loan repayments received from federal candidates. The "aggregate year-to-date" total must be given for each receipt and must equal the total amount that

the person has given to the committee for that particular category of receipts for the calendar year. If a receipt is the only receipt from a person during the calendar year, the aggregate year-to-date total must still be entered.

Add the "Total This Period" amount (the last Line on Schedule A) to all other receipts for that category which are not itemized and carry it forward to Column A of the corresponding Line of the Detailed Summary Page.

If a contribution is received from a business entity or is drawn on what is or appears to be a business account, the political committee must determine that the contribution is not from a corporation, government contractor, or other prohibited source. If the contribution is from a prohibited source, the committee must refund it within thirty days of its receipt.

A contribution that appears to be excessive, either on its face or when aggregated with other contributions from the same person, may be reattributed, if either is applicable, or it may be returned or deposited into a committee depository but not used. If deposited, the contributor may be asked if a joint contribution was intended and, if so, to submit a written reattribution of the contribution signed by each contributor. Alternatively, contributions may also be presumptively reattributed to a joint contributor whose name also appears imprinted on the contribution check if the reattribution will not cause the contributor to exceed any contribution limits. If the committee presumptively reattributes the excessive contribution, the committee must notify the contributor of its action, and offer the opportunity to request a refund, within sixty days of its receipt of the original contribution. Written reattributions are to be reported as memo entries on the report covering the period in which the committee receives the reattributions. Indicate how the contribution(s) was reported initially, followed by the reattributed entry(ies). Presumptive reattributions must also be noted as such. See 11 CFR 110.1(k)(3)(ii)(B) for presumptive reattributions, and 11 CFR 104.8 and the Campaign Guide for the reporting of

these types of contributions.

Contributions In-Kind. Contributions in-kind (i.e., goods and services provided to a political committee) are treated as any other contribution and must be reported and itemized under the appropriate category of receipts. For example, itemize a contribution in-kind from an individual on Schedule A and report it under the category for "Contributions From Individuals/Persons Other Than Political Committees." Enter the value of each contribution in-kind in the "Amount of Each Receipt This Period" column. The amount or value of the contribution in-kind is the difference between the usual and normal charge for the goods or services at the time of the contribution and the amount charged the political committee. The "aggregate year-to-date" total must include the total amount of all contributions which the person has contributed to the committee during the calendar year. The item must be labeled "contribution in-kind" and include the nature of the contribution (e.g., consulting, polling, etc.). Each contribution in-kind must also be reported in the same manner as an operating expense on Schedule B and included in the total for "Operating Expenditures." (Note: A political committee that makes a contribution in-kind only reports it as a disbursement and itemizes the transaction on Schedule B with a notation "contribution in-kind." The itemization must include the purpose of the expenditure (e.g., consulting, polling, etc.) and the aggregated year-to-date amount. The committee receiving the contribution in-kind must report it as both a receipt and an expenditure.)

Report contributions of stocks, bonds, art objects, and other similar items to be liquidated as follows:
(1) If the item has not been liquidated at the close of the reporting period, the committee must record as a memo entry (not as cash) on Schedule A the item's fair market value on the date received, including the name and mailing address (and when in excess of $200, the occupation and name of the em-

ployer) of the contributor. Enter the total amount of items to be liquidated under "Total This Period" on the last Line of Schedule A. This amount must NOT be carried forward to the Detailed Summary Page.

(2) When the item is sold, the committee must report the proceeds and include them in the appropriate categories on the Detailed Summary Page. It must also report the (i) name and mailing address (and, where in excess of $200, the occupation and name of employer) of the purchaser on Schedule A, if purchased directly from the committee (the purchaser is considered to have made a contribution to the committee); and (ii) the identification of the original contributor on Schedule A.

Exempt Legal or Accounting Services. Legal or accounting services rendered to or on behalf of any political committee are not contributions or expenditures and are not, therefore, subject to the contribution limitations and prohibitions, if the person paying for the services is the regular employer of the individual rendering the services and if the services are solely to ensure compliance with the Act.

The political committee must itemize as a memo entry on a separate Schedule A each person who provides legal or accounting services to the political committee in an aggregate value or amount in excess of $200 within the calendar year, together with the date of receipt and amount or value of the exempt legal or accounting services, and state that the receipt is for "exempt legal or accounting service." Enter the total amount of exempt legal or accounting services on the Line for "Total This Period" on the bottom of Schedule A, but do not carry it forward to any category or Line number on the Detailed Summary Page.

Earmarked Contributions. For each earmarked contribution received (regardless of the amount), the political committee must report on Schedule A the name and address of the original contributor, the date of receipt, the amount of the contribution and, if the original contributor makes contributions aggregating in excess of $200 to the political committee during the calendar year, the occupation and name of employer. If the contribution passes through the political committee's account and is forwarded to another political committee or federal candidate, the conduit committee must disclose each contribution, regardless of the amount, on both Schedule A and Schedule B and include the amount under the appropriate category of receipts and disbursements. If the contribution was passed on in the form of the contributor's check, the conduit must disclose each contribution on a separate Schedule A attached to the conduit's (intermediary) next report. The amounts of such contributions are not required to be included in the totals for the appropriate categories of receipts and disbursements. If a political committee is not a conduit, but is the intended recipient, report each conduit through which the earmarked contribution passed, including the name and address of the conduit, and whether the contribution was passed on in cash, by the contributor's check, or by the conduit's check. If the conduit exercises direction and control over the contribution, the earmarked contribution must also be attributed to the contribution limitations of the conduit.

Checks Returned Due to Insufficient Funds. If a contributor's check is returned to the political committee due to insufficient funds and the receipt of the check was previously reported, the political committee must report the return under the appropriate category of receipts as a negative entry and net out the amount of the check from the total for that category. If the original receipt of the check was itemized on Schedule A, the return of the check must also be itemized as a negative entry on Schedule A. If the receipt of the check was never reported, do not report the return of the check.

Check Refunded to the Committee. A contribution may be refunded to the committee in one of two ways:
(1) The original check is returned uncashed. If the contribution was reported, report the return as a negative entry on Schedule B, and subtract the amount of the contribution refund from the disbursement totals on the Line of the Detailed Summary Page that it was reported on.
(2) The original check is not returned and the refund is made by a check from the recipient of the contribution. Such a transaction should be reported as a receipt on Schedule A for the appropriate Line of the Detailed Summary Page. This procedure is applicable regardless of whether the amount refunded is a full or only a partial refund of the contribution or whether the contribution was previously reported.

Best Efforts. When the treasurer of a political committee shows that best efforts have been used to obtain, maintain and submit the information required, the committee shall be considered in compliance with the Act.

With regard to reporting the identification of each person whose contribution(s) to the committee and its affiliated committees aggregate in excess of $200 in a calendar year, the treasurer will only be deemed to have exercised best efforts to obtain, maintain and report the required information if all written solicitations for contributions include a clear request for the information (i.e., name, mailing address, occupation, name of employer) and include an accurate statement of federal law regarding the collection and reporting of individual contributor identifications. In addition, for each contribution requiring itemization which lacks contributor information, the treasurer must, within 30-Days of receipt of the contribution, make one effort to obtain the missing information. See 11 CFR 104.7 and the Campaign Guide for more information.

INSTRUCTIONS FOR SCHEDULE B, ITEMIZED DISBURSEMENTS (FEC FORM 3X)

The Detailed Summary Page is broken down into various categories of disbursements. Use Schedule B to list each disbursement required to be itemized. DO NOT combine more than one category of disbursements on the same Schedule B. Instead, use a separate Schedule B for each category of disbursements. The Line number of the Detailed Summary Page to which each Schedule B pertains must be identified in the upper right corner of each Schedule. In addition, the committee's full name must be entered in the appropriate block. After itemizing the required disbursements for each separate line number, add the "Total This Period" amount (the last line on Schedule B for that Line number) to all other disbursements for that category which are not itemized and carry the total forward to Column A of the corresponding Line of the Detailed Summary Page.

Required Information. For each disbursement required to be itemized during the reporting period, the political committee must provide the full name, mailing address, date, amount, and purpose of the disbursement.

Purpose of Disbursement. The term "purpose" means a brief statement or description of why the disbursement was made. Examples of adequate descriptions include the following: dinner expenses, media, salary, polling, travel, party fees, phone banks, travel expenses and catering costs. However, statements or descriptions such as "advance," "election day expenses," "other expenses," "expense reimbursement," "miscellaneous," "outside services," "get-out-the-vote," and "voter registration," would not meet the requirement for reporting the purpose of an expenditure. If the disbursement is a "loan repayment," "contribution refund," or other similar category of disbursement (other than an operating expenditure), the name of the category of disbursement (i.e., "loan repayment," etc.) is sufficient to meet the requirement for reporting the purpose of an expenditure.

Along with reporting the purpose of the expenditure as required above, the committee should also broadly characterize disbursements by providing the code for each category of disbursement. Examples of the types of disbursements that fall within each of the broad categories are listed below. Use only one code for each itemized disbursement. In cases where the disbursement was for several purposes, the political committee should assign one code according to the primary purpose of the disbursement. Note that some of the category titles are not acceptable as the "purpose" of the disbursement and that the categories are not intended to replace or to serve as a substitute for the "purpose of disbursement."

001 Administrative/Salary/Overhead Expenses (e.g., rent, staff salaries, postage, office supplies, equipment, furniture, ballot access fees, petition drives, party fees and legal and accounting expenses)

002 Travel Expenses—including travel reimbursement expenses (e.g., costs of commercial carrier tickets; reimbursements for use of private vehicles; advance payments for use of corporate aircraft; lodging and meal expenses incurred during travel)

003 Solicitation and Fundraising Expenses (e.g., costs for direct mail solicitations and fundraising events including printing, mailing lists, consultant fees, call lists, invitations, catering costs and room rental)

004 Advertising Expenses—including general public political advertising (e.g., purchases of radio/television broadcast/cable time, print advertisements and related production costs)

005 Polling Expenses

006 Campaign Materials (e.g., buttons, bumper stickers, brochures, mass mailings, pens, posters and balloons)

007 Campaign Event Expenses (e.g., costs associated with candidate appearances, campaign rallies, town meetings, phone banks, including catering costs, door to door get-out-the-vote efforts and driving voters to the polls)

008 Transfers (e.g., to other affiliated/party committees)

009 Loans (e.g., loans made or repayments of loans received)

010 Refunds of Contributions (e.g., contribution refunds to individuals/persons, political party committees or other political committees)

011 Political Contributions (e.g., contributions to other federal committees and candidates, and donations to nonfederal candidates and committees)

012 Donations (e.g., donations to charitable or civic organizations)

Contributions to Federal Candidates. For disbursements that are contributions to federal candidates, or authorized committees, list, in the appropriate boxes, the name of the candidate and office sought (including State and congressional district, where applicable).

For each contribution to a federal candidate or authorized committee, indicate in the election check-off box the election for which the contribution was made. Contributions to a candidate or authorized committee that are not designated by the contributor for a specific election must be counted toward the contributor's limitation for the next election after the contribution is made. Contributions may be made for a past election only to the extent that the recipient has net debts outstanding from that particular election. In the event the contribution was made for an election prior to the current election cycle, the "Other" box must be checked and the type of election specified (e.g., "General 2004," "Primary 2004") and debt retirement (if applicable). The election check-off boxes provided for each itemized entry on Schedule B should not be used when itemizing operating expenditures. For in-kind contributions, including coordinated public communications, note "in-kind."

Contributions In-Kind Received

Contributions in-kind received by the committee which are itemized on Schedule A must also be itemized as an operating expenditure on Schedule B. In addition, in the "Purpose of Disbursement" box include the notation "Contribution In-Kind," and the nature of the expenditure (e.g., consulting, polling, etc.).

Disbursements for Federal Election Activities That Are Made Entirely With Federal Funds (State, District and Local Party Committees Only)

Certain federal election activities under 2 U.S.C. §431(20)(A)(iii) and (iv) conducted by State, district or local party committees must be paid for with federal funds only. These activities are:

- Disbursements for public communications that refer to a clearly identified candidate for federal office and that promote, support, attack or oppose any candidate for federal office. Identify the candidate supported or opposed when itemizing such disbursements.
- Disbursements for the salary of any employee who spends more than 25 percent of his or her compensated time in a given month on activities in connection with a federal election.

Disbursements for other federal election activities may be allocated between federal funds and Levin funds. 2 U.S.C. §431(20)(A)(i) and (ii). State, district or local party committees must itemize such allocated disbursements for federal election activity on Schedules H5 and H6; for more information and definitions of "allocable federal election activity," see the instructions for Schedule H1, H5 and H6. However, a State, district or local political party committee may choose to pay for such allocable federal election activities with 100% federal funds (that is, they may choose not to allocate the disbursements even though they could do so).

Use Schedule B to report disbursements of federal funds for federal election activities made entirely with federal funds. This includes disbursements for federal election activities that may not be allocated, and those that may be allocated, but which are not in fact allocated (i.e., that are made with 100% federal funds). Itemize such disbursements of $200 or more on Schedule B for Line 30(b). When itemizing disbursements for public communications, identify the candidate supported or opposed.

Disbursements for Public Communications and Voter Drives (Separate Segregated Funds and Nonconnected Committees Only)

Public Communication/Voter Drive – Federal. A separate segregated fund or nonconnected committee that disburses funds for a public communication or a voter drive that refers only to a federal candidate, or to both a political party and a federal candidate (but not a nonfederal candidate) must pay for such disbursements solely out of its federal account. Voter drives are subject to this requirement only if there is a reference to a clearly identified federal candidate in printed materials, scripted messages or written instructions. Itemize such disbursements as "Other Federal Operating Expenditures" on Schedule B for Line 21b. The committee may identify the federal candidate referred to in the communication or voter drive in the space provided. (Exceptions: (1) If the communication or voter drive has been coordinated with a candidate or political party, the committee must report the disbursement as an in-kind contribution on Schedule B for Line 23 regardless of amount. See "Contributions to Federal Candidates" above for more information. (2) If the communication would otherwise satisfy the definition of an "electioneering communication" under 11 CFR 100.29(a), the committee must report it as an expenditure on Line 21b or 23, and itemize it on a Schedule B for that Line, as appropriate.)

Public Communications/Voter Drives – Nonfederal. A separate segregated fund or nonconnected committee that pays for a public communication or a voter drive that refers only to a nonfederal candidate, or to both a political party and a nonfederal candidate (but not a federal candidate) may pay for such disbursement solely out of its nonfederal account. Voter drives are subject to this requirement only if there is a reference to a clearly identified nonfederal candidate in printed materials, scripted messages or written instructions. If it chooses to use its federal account to pay for a portion of the expense, categorize the disbursement by the federal account as an "other disbursement" on Line 29 and itemize on a Schedule B for Line 29 if necessary.

Public Communications/Voter Drives Referencing Party Only or Both Federal/Nonfederal Candidates. If a separate segregated fund or nonconnected committee chooses to allocate disbursements for public communications or voter drives that refer to both federal and nonfederal candidates, regardless of any reference to a political party, or that refer to a party only, the federal/nonfederal disbursements must be reported accordingly as allocated expenditures. For more information, see the instructions for Schedules H1, H2 and H4. Alternatively, if the committee pays for such expenditures solely with federal funds, or if it does not have a nonfederal account, itemize the disbursements according to the instructions for itemizing "Public Communication/Voter Drive – Federal," above.

INSTRUCTIONS FOR SCHEDULE C, LOANS (FEC FORM 3X)

A loan is a contribution at the time it is made and is a contribution to the extent it remains unpaid. A LOAN WHICH EXCEEDS THE CONTRIBUTION LIMITATIONS IS UNLAWFUL WHETHER OR NOT IT IS REPAID. The aggregate amount loaned to a candidate or committee by another individual or political committee, when added to other contributions from that individual or political committee to that candidate or committee, shall not exceed the contribution limitations. A loan, to the extent it is repaid, is no longer a contribution. All loans to a political committee (regardless of amount) must be disclosed on the first report filed with the Commission after the date the loan is made.

When filling out Schedule C, the committee must enter its full name in the box at the top of the page.

DO NOT combine loans owed TO the committee with those owed BY the committee on the same Schedule C. Instead, use a separate Schedule C. Each loan should be reported separately until extinguished.

Loans Owed By the Committee

When a loan is received by the committee, it must be itemized on Schedule A and must also be disclosed on Schedule C (see also instructions for Schedule A for itemizing loans received by the committee). For each loan owed BY the reporting committee at the close of the reporting period, the committee must report certain basic information on Schedule C in the appropriate boxes: (1) full name, mailing address and zip code of the creditor; (2) if the committee is an authorized committee, the election to which the loan applies (i.e., primary, general or other); (3) the original amount of the loan; (4) the cumulative payment to date on the loan; and (5) the outstanding balance at the close of

the reporting period (i.e., the remaining unpaid portion of the loan).

Certain additional information must be entered on Schedule C in the box entitled TERMS: (1) if an intermediary is reported as the source of the loan, the original source of the loan (which must be disclosed in the first box for endorsers and guarantors with a notation that the person identified is the original source); (2) the date the obligation was incurred; (3) the date the loan is due or the amortization schedule (if there is no due date or amortization schedule, enter "None" on the appropriate Line); (4) the actual rate of interest charged on each loan (if the loan does not bear an interest rate, enter "None" on the appropriate Line); and (5) check the box if the loan has been secured.

In instances where the loan has endorsers or guarantors, the following information must be supplied: (1) the identification of each endorser or guarantor, and (2) the amount of the endorsement or guarantee outstanding at the close of the reporting period. The term "identification" means (a) in the case of an individual, his or her full name, mailing address, occupation, and name of employer; and (b) in the case of any other person, the person's full name and address.

Loans owed BY the committee must continue to be reported on each subsequent report until repaid. When a payment is made to reduce or extinguish the amount of a loan owed BY the committee, the payment must be itemized on Schedule B, reported on the appropriate Line of the Detailed Summary Page, and included in the "Cumulative Payment to Date" column on Schedule C. If any extension for repayment is granted, this should be reported on the first report after the extension is made.

If a loan is settled for less than the reported amount, the reporting committee must include a statement as to the circumstances and conditions under which the debt or obligation was extinguished and the amount paid. A loan owed BY a political committee which is forgiven or settled for less than the amount owed is a contribu-

tion. The total amount of loans owed BY the committee at the close of the reporting period must be entered on the Line for "Total This Period" on the bottom of the last page and transferred to Line 3 of the last page of Schedule D. If no debts or obligations are reported on Schedule D, carry the outstanding balance forward to the Summary Page.

Loans Owed To the Committee

When a loan is made by the committee, it must be itemized on Schedule B and must also be disclosed on Schedule C (see also instructions for Schedule B for itemizing loans made by the committee). For each loan owed TO the committee at the close of the reporting period, the committee must report certain basic information on Schedule C in the appropriate boxes: (1) the full name, mailing address and zip code of each debtor; (2) if the loan was made by a political committee other than an authorized committee and was made to a federal candidate or authorized committee, the election to which the loan applies (i.e., primary, general or other); (3) the original amount of the loan; (4) the cumulative payment to date on the loan; and (5) the outstanding balance at the close of the reporting period (i.e., the remaining unpaid portion of the loan).

Certain additional information must be entered on Schedule C in the box entitled TERMS: (1) the date the obligation was incurred; (2) the date the loan is due or the amortization schedule (if there is no due date or amortization schedule, enter "None" on the appropriate Line; (3) the actual rate of interest charged on the loan (if the loan does not bear an interest rate, enter "None" on the appropriate Line); and (4) check the box if the loan has been secured. Loans owed TO the committee must continue to be reported on each subsequent report until repaid. When a payment is received to reduce or extinguish a loan owed TO the committee, the payment must be itemized on Schedule A, reported on the appropriate Line of the Detailed Summary Page, and included in the "Cumulative Payment to Date" column on Schedule C. If any extension of repayment is granted or made, this should be reported on the first report after the extension is made.

The total amount of loans owed TO the committee at the close of the reporting period must be entered on the Line for "Total This Period" on the bottom of the last page and transferred to Line 3 of the last page of Schedule D. If no debts or obligations are reported on Schedule D, carry the outstanding balance forward to the Summary Page.

Miscellaneous

Loans by Financial Institutions. A loan of money by a State bank, a federally chartered depository institution (including a national bank) or a depository institution whose deposits and accounts are insured by the Federal Deposit Insurance Corporation or the National Credit Union Administration is not a contribution by the lending institution if the loan is made in accordance with applicable banking laws and regulations and is made in the ordinary course of business. A loan will be deemed to be made in the ordinary course of business if it: bears the usual and customary interest rate of the lending institution for the category of loan involved; is made on a basis that assures repayment; is evidenced by a written instrument; and is subject to a due date or an amortization schedule.

Loans by Political Committees. If a political committee makes a loan TO any person, the loan shall be subject to the contribution limitations. Repayment to the political committee of the principal amount of the loan is not a contribution by the debtor to the lender committee. The repayment must be made with funds which are permissible under the Act. The payment of interest to the committee by the debtor is a contribution only to the extent that the interest paid exceeds a commercially reasonable rate prevail-

ing at the time the loan is made. All payments of interest must be made from funds which are permissible under the Act.

Endorsers and Guarantors. A loan is a contribution by each endorser or guarantor. Each endorser or guarantor shall be deemed to have contributed that portion of the total amount of the loan for which he or she agreed to be liable in a written agreement. Any reduction in the unpaid balance of the loan shall reduce proportionately the amount endorsed or guaranteed by each endorser or guarantor in such written agreement. In the event that such agreement does not stipulate the portion of the loan for which each endorser or guarantor is liable, the loan shall be considered a loan by each endorser or guarantor in the same proportion to the unpaid balance that each endorser or guarantor bears to the total number of endorsers or guarantors.

Loan Repayments. Each committee must disclose all loan payments received or made by the committee. When a loan repayment is **received by** a committee, the repayment must be itemized on Schedule A and included in the "Cumulative Payment to Date" column on Schedule C. When a loan repayment is **made by** a committee, the repayment must be itemized on Schedule B and included in the "Cumulative Payment to Date" column on Schedule C. Disclose the total amount of loan repayments received and the total amount of loan repayments made on the appropriate Lines of the Detailed Summary Page.

INSTRUCTIONS FOR SCHEDULE C-1, LOANS AND LINES OF CREDIT FROM LENDING INSTITUTIONS (FEC FORM 3X)

Background: FEC Regulations on Loans from Lending Institutions

Schedule C-1 seeks information on loans—including lines of credit—from lending institutions such as state or federally chartered banks, federally insured savings and loan associations or federally insured credit unions. The purpose of Schedule C-1 is to verify that a loan or line of credit does not result in a prohibited contribution from the lending institution, a violation of the federal campaign finance law.

Under FEC regulations at 11 CFR 100.82 and 100.142, a loan "made in accordance with applicable banking laws" and "in the ordinary course of business" is not considered a contribution if certain conditions are met. One of these conditions is that the loan "is made on a basis which assures repayment." Schedule C-1 documents whether or not the loan complies with these requirements.

Who Must File Schedule C-1

A political committee that obtains a loan or line of credit from a bank or other lending institution must file Schedule C-1.

When to File Schedule C-1

A Schedule C-1 must be filed for each loan and each line of credit obtained from a lending institution. 11 CFR 104.3(d)(1).

Loans. A committee must file a Schedule C-1 with its next report when it first obtains a loan and in succeeding reporting periods each time the terms of the loan are restructured. 11 CFR 104.3(d)(1) and (3). (A restructured loan is considered a new loan.)

Lines of Credit. A committee must file a Schedule C-1 with its next report when a line of credit is established and in succeeding reporting periods each time any draws are made on the line of credit and each time the line of credit is restructured to change the repayment terms. 11 CFR 104.3(d)(1) and (3).

Reporting Loans and Lines of Credit on Schedules A and C

Schedule A. When a committee obtains a loan, the committee must itemize the receipt on a Schedule A for the appropriate Line number. However, a line of credit is itemized on Schedule A only when the committee obtains funds by making a draw on the credit.

Schedule C. As with all loans, loans from lending institutions (including lines of credit) must be continuously disclosed on Schedule C, starting with the first report due after the committee obtains the loan and continuing with each report thereafter until the loan is repaid.

Line-by-Line Instructions

Schedule C Cross-Reference. Enter the Schedule C page number where information on the loan or line of credit appears.

Name of Committee Obtaining Loan. Enter the full name of the reporting committee.

Identification Number. Enter the reporting committee's FEC identification number. If the committee is newly registered and has not yet obtained a number, enter "not yet assigned."

Name/Address of Lender. Enter the full name, address and zip code of the lending institution.

Loan Amount. Enter the amount of the loan or line of credit. If reporting a restructured loan or line of credit, enter the amount under the new terms. 11 CFR 104.3(d)(1)(i) and (3).

Interest Rate. Enter the annual percentage rate (APR) of interest on the loan or each draw on the line of credit. If reporting a restructured loan or line of credit, enter the interest rate under the new terms. 11 CFR 104.3(d)(1)(ii) and (3).

Date Incurred or Established. Enter the date the committee incurred the debt by signing the loan agreement (the original agreement or a restructured agreement, as appropriate). 11 CFR 104.3(d)(1)(i) and (3).

Due Date. Enter the date on which full repayment of the loan or line of credit is due (under the original agreement or a restructured agreement, as appropriate). 11 CFR 104.3(d)(1)(ii) and (3).

A. Restructured Loans. Check yes if the loan or line of credit has been restructured to change the terms; enter the date on which the original loan or line of credit was incurred. 11 CFR 104.3(d)(3).

B. Draws on Line of Credit. If reporting a draw on a line of credit, enter the amount of the draw and the outstanding balance owed on the line of credit (cumulative draws less any repayments made). 11 CFR 104.3(d)(1)(ii).

C. Secondary Sources of Repayment. Check yes if the loan or line of credit was endorsed or guaranteed by secondary parties. 11 CFR 104.3(d)(1)(iii). Information on endorsers and guarantors must be disclosed on Schedule C. (Note that guarantees and endorsements of loans are considered contributions; see Schedule C instructions.)

D. Traditional Collateral. Check yes if the loan or line of credit was obtained using traditional sources of collateral, and list the specific assets that were pledged. Enter the total fair market value of the collateral as of the date of the loan agreement. Indicate whether the lender has a perfected security interest in the collateral. 11 CFR 104.3(d)(1)(iii). (Note that a perfected security interest is a requirement under FEC regulations. 11 CFR 100.82(e)(1)(i) and 100.142(e)(1)(i)).

E. Future Receipts as Collateral. Check yes if the loan or line of credit was obtained using future receipts as collateral; list the types of receipts that were pledged; and enter their estimated amount. 11 CFR 104.3(d)(1)(iii). Enter the date the separate account was established for the deposit of pledged receipts. (A depository account is required under 11 CFR 100.82(e)(2) and 100.142(e)(2).) Provide the full name and address of the depository institution where the account was established.

F. Other Means of Obtaining Loan. Complete this section if "no" was checked in sections C, D, and E or if the amount cosigned and/or pledged for the loan or line of credit is less than the loan amount. If so, state the basis upon which the loan was made and the basis on which it assures repayment. 11 CFR 104.3(d)(1)(iv).

G. Treasurer's Signature and Date. The committee treasurer (or properly designated assistant treasurer) must sign and date the form; the signer's name should be printed or typed beside the signature.

H. Copy of Loan Agreement. Attach a copy of the signed agreement. 11 CFR 104.3(d)(2).

I. Lender Certification. An authorized representative of the lending institution must sign and date the form to certify that the lender has complied with items I through III. 11 CFR 104.3(d)(1)(v). The representative's name should be printed or typed beside his or her signature. The representative's title must also be entered.

INSTRUCTIONS FOR SCHEDULE D, DEBTS AND OBLIGATIONS (FEC FORM 3X)

When filling out Schedule D, the committee must enter its full name in the box at the top of the page.

DO NOT combine debts and obligations owed to the committee with those owed by the committee on the same Schedule D. Instead, use a separate Schedule D.

Debts and Obligations Owed BY the Committee (Other Than Loans)

For debts and obligations owed BY the reporting committee at the close of the reporting period and which are required to be disclosed, the committee must report the full name and mailing address of each creditor, the amount of the debt outstanding at the beginning of the period, the amount of the debt or obligation incurred this period (including any finance charges), the payment(s) this period to retire the debt or obligation, the outstanding balance at the close of the reporting period and the nature or purpose of the debt and obligation. The terms "nature" or "purpose" mean a brief statement or description of why the debt or obligation was incurred (e.g., media, salary, polling, supplies, mailing).

A written contract (including a media contract), promise, or agreement to make an expenditure which has not been paid for by the committee is an expenditure as of the date the contract, promise or obligation is made and is subject to the reporting requirements. Accounts payable and written contracts, promises, or agreements to make expenditures, in amounts of $500 or less, need not be disclosed until outstanding for sixty days or more.

Debts and obligations owed BY the committee must continue to be reported on each subsequent report until extinguished or settled in a manner permitted by Federal Election Commission regulations (see 11 CFR Part 116 for settlement of corporate debts). When a payment is made to reduce or extinguish an obligation owed BY the committee, the payment must be itemized on Schedule B, reported on the appropriate line of the Detailed Summary Page, and included in the "Payment This Period" column on Schedule D. If a debt or obligation is settled for less than the reported amount or value, the reporting committee must include a statement as to the circumstances and conditions under which the debt or obligation was extinguished and the amount paid. A debt owed BY a political committee which is forgiven or settled for less than the amount owed is a contribution unless the debt is forgiven or settled in accordance with 11 CFR Part 116. The extension of credit by any person for a length of time beyond normal business or trade practice is a contribution, unless the creditor has made a commercially reasonable attempt to collect the debt. The total amount of debts and obligations owed BY the committee during the reporting period must be entered at the bottom of the last page under "Total This Period" and added to the total loans owed BY the committee from Schedule C. The total amount of debts and obligations owed BY the committee (including loans) must be carried forward to the Summary Page.

Debts and Obligations Owed TO the Committee (Other Than Loans)

For each debt and obligation owed TO the committee at the close of the reporting period, the committee must report: the full name and mailing address of each debtor, the amount of the debt outstanding at the beginning of the period, the amount of the debt or obligation incurred this period, the payment(s) this period to retire the debt or obligation, the outstanding balance at the close of the reporting period and the nature or purpose of the debt or obligation. The terms "nature" or "purpose" mean a brief statement or description of why the

debt or obligation was incurred (e.g., media, salary, polling, supplies, mailing). Written contracts or agreements (such as signed pledge cards), or oral promises to make contributions are not required to be reported.

Debts and obligations owed TO the committee must continue to be reported on each subsequent report until extinguished. When a payment is received to reduce or extinguish a debt or obligation owed TO the committee, the payment must be itemized on Schedule A, reported on the appropriate line of the Detailed Summary Page, and included in the "Payment This Period" column on Schedule D. The total amount of debts and obligations owed TO the committee during the reporting period must be entered at the bottom of the last page under "Total This Period" and added to the total loans owed TO the committee from Schedule C. The total amount of debts and obligations owed TO the committee (including loans) must be carried forward to the Summary Page.

INSTRUCTIONS FOR SCHEDULE E, ITEMIZED INDEPENDENT EXPENDITURES (FEC FORM 3X)

General

Definition

The term "independent expenditure" means: "an expenditure by a person for a communication expressly advocating the election or defeat of a clearly identified candidate that is not made in cooperation, consultation or concert with, or at the request or suggestion of, a candidate, a candidate's authorized committee or their agents, or a political party committee or its agents.

When to File

Any political committee that makes independent expenditures must report such independent expenditures on Schedule E for the applicable reporting period. Special additional reporting procedures apply to expenditures aggregating $1,000 or more and made within 20 days before an election; these are described below under "24-hour Reports". In addition, special reporting procedures apply to expenditures aggregating $10,000 or more and are described below under "48-hour Reports."

48-hour Reports

Any political committee that makes or contracts to make independent expenditures regarding a particular election (e.g., a particular party's Presidential nomination or a particular Senate general election) aggregating $10,000 or more during the calendar year up to and including the 20th day before an election must ensure that the Commission receives a report of these expenditures no later than 11:59 p.m. Eastern Standard/Daylight Time of the second day following the date on which the independent expenditure meeting the $10,000 threshold is publicly distributed or otherwise publicly

disseminated. See Explanation and Justification for 11 CFR 104.4(f). The committee must continue to file additional 48-hour reports each time subsequent independent expenditures reach the $10,000 threshold with respect to the same election to which the first report related. For purposes of determining whether 48-hour reports must be filed, aggregations of independent expenditures must be calculated as of the first date on which a communication that constitutes an independent expenditure is publicly distributed or otherwise publicly disseminated. See 11 CFR 104.4(f). The report must include all of the information required on Schedule E and be filed with the Federal Election Commission. Committees that are not electronic filers may file 48-hour reports by fax or electronic mail. All filers may submit 48-hour reports online at www.fec.gov.

24-hour Reports

The committee must file a report of any independent expenditures aggregating $1,000 or more made after the 20th day, but more than 24 hours before an election, before 12:01 A.M. of the day of the election. The committee must ensure that the Commission receives the report no later than 11:59 p.m. Eastern Standard/Daylight Time of the day following the date on which the $1,000 threshold is reached during the final 20 days before the election. For purposes of determining whether 24-hour reports must be filed, aggregations of independent expenditures must be calculated as of the first date on which a communication that constitutes an independent expenditure is publicly distributed or otherwise publicly disseminated. See Explanation and Justification for 11 CFR 104.4(f). The report must include all of the information required on Schedule E and be filed with the Federal Election Commission. The committee must file a new 24-hour report each time it makes subsequent independent expenditures relating to the same election and aggregating $1,000 or more. Committees that are

not electronic filers may file 24-hour reports by fax or electronic mail. All filers may submit 24-hour reports online at www.fec.gov.

Line By Line Instructions

For Schedule E, enter the full name of the committee and the FEC Identification Number in the appropriate boxes at the top of the page. Check the box "48-hour Report" or "24-hour Report" if applicable.

For each person who receives a payment or disbursement during the calendar year aggregating in excess of $200 in connection with an independent expenditure, provide on Schedule E the full name, mailing address and zip code of the payee receiving any disbursement, the date and amount of any independent expenditure aggregating in excess of $200, and the purpose of the independent expenditure (e.g., radio, television, newspaper). Also indicate, in the election check-off box, the election for which the independent expenditure was made.

In situations where the committee incurs a reportable obligation for an independent expenditure in one reporting period, and the communication will be publicly disseminated in a future reporting period, report the obligation on Schedule D (Debts and Obligations) in the first period and, in the future reporting period, report the independent expenditure on Schedule E referencing the debt on Schedule D (using a memo entry if actual payment has not been made). Continue to report the debt on Schedule D and itemize payments on it using Schedule E until the debt is extinguished.

In situations where the committee pays in advance for an independent expenditure in one reporting period and the communication will be publicly disseminated in a future reporting period, report the payment on Schedule B as an operating expenditure. When, in a subsequent reporting period, the communication is publicly disseminated, itemize the independent expenditure and its date of dissemination on Schedule E, and itemize the previous expenditure again as a negative entry on Schedule B so that total disbursements are not inflated.

Along with reporting the purpose of the expenditure as required above, the committee should also broadly characterize disbursements by providing the code for each category of disbursement. Examples of the types of disbursements that fall within each of the broad categories are listed below. Use only one code for each itemized disbursement. In cases where the disbursement was for several purposes, assign one of the following codes according to the primary purpose of the disbursement. Note that some of the category titles are not acceptable as the "purpose" of the disbursement and that the categories are not intended to replace or to serve as a substitute for the "purpose of disbursement."

004 Advertising Expenses -including general public political advertising (e.g., purchases of radio/television broadcast/cable time, print advertisements and related production costs)

In addition, provide the name of the candidate, the office sought by the candidate (including State and Congressional District, where applicable), and whether the independent expenditure was in support of, or in opposition to, the candidate. Also, list the total amount expended in the aggregate during the calendar year, per election, per office sought. A subtotal of itemized expenditures must be disclosed on Line (a) of the last Schedule E filed. A subtotal of independent expenditures not required to be itemized must also be disclosed on Line (b) of the last Schedule E filed.

The total of all independent expenditures (Line (c)) is carried forward to the appropriate Line of the Detailed Summary Page.

Certification

The treasurer of the committee must sign Schedule E (for electronically-filed reports, type the name of the treasurer) and certify under penalty of perjury that the expenditure was not in fact made in cooperation, consultation or concert with, or at the request or suggestion of, any candidate or authorized committee or agent thereof. If the committee is not a political party committee, it must also certify that the expenditure was not, in fact, made in cooperation, consultation or concert with, or at the request or suggestion of a political party committee or its agents.

Note: Any other person or entity (other than a political committee) that makes an independent expenditure must file on FEC FORM 5, or, if not required to file electronically, may file by Form 5 or letter.

INSTRUCTIONS FOR SCHEDULE F, ITEMIZED COORDINATED PARTY EXPENDITURES MADE BY POLITICAL PARTIES (FEC FORM 3X)

Definition and Limitations

The Federal Election Campaign Act provides political party committees with special spending limits on behalf of their candidates in the general election (2 U.S.C. §441a(d)). These special spending limits do not apply in primary elections, are not contributions to the candidate and are not contributions in-kind reported on Schedule B. These spending limits are separate from expenditures made by the candidate's authorized committee(s). Expenditures made under 2 U.S.C. §441a(d) are reported by the political party committee or designated agent and not by the candidate or the candidate's authorized committee(s) on whose behalf the expenditure was made.

National party political committees are subject to separate limits for Presidential, Senate and House general elections. State party political committees are subject to separate limits for Senate and House general elections, but may not make any separate expenditures in the Presidential general election, unless designated by the national committee of the political party. Within a State, committees subordinate to a State party political committee (county, city, local, etc.) are included within the State party political committee limits.

The formulas for the party spending limits are as follows:

President: $0.02 times the national Voting Age Population, adjusted to reflect the latest cost-of-living increase.

Senate: The greater of: (a) $0.02 times the state Voting Age Population, adjusted to reflect the latest cost-of-living increase; or (b) $20,000, adjusted to reflect the latest cost-of-living increase.

*House: $10,000 adjusted to reflect the latest cost-of-living increase.

Who Must File

Any political party committee or designated agent that makes coordinated party expenditures must itemize each expenditure on Schedule F. For each coordinated party expenditure; provide the full name and mailing address of the payee, date and amount of the expenditure, the purpose of the expenditure (e.g., polling, campaign consulting, media preparation, etc.) and the name of the office sought by (including State and Congressional district, when applicable) the candidate on whose behalf the expenditure was made. If the limits for an expenditure are modified as described below under "24-hour Notices" (pursuant to 2 U.S.C. §441a(i)(C)(iii)(III) on behalf of a Senate candidate or to 2 U.S.C. §441a-1(a)(1)(C) on behalf of a House candidate) check the box in each block disclosing an expenditure to indicate this fact.

Along with reporting the purpose of the expenditure as required above, the committee should also broadly characterize disbursements by providing the code for each category of disbursement. Examples of the types of disbursements that fall within each of the broad categories are listed below. Use only one code for each itemized disbursement. In cases where the disbursement was for several purposes, the political committee should assign one code according to the primary purpose of the disbursement. Note that some of the category titles are not acceptable as the "purpose" of the disbursement and that the categories are not intended to replace or to serve as a substitute for the "purpose of disbursement."

001 Administrative/Salary/Overhead Expenses (e.g., rent, staff salaries, postage, office supplies, equipment, furniture, ballot access fees, petition drives, party fees and legal and accounting expenses)

002 Travel Expenses—including travel reimbursement expenses (e.g., costs of commercial carrier tickets; reimbursements for use of private vehicles; advance payments for use of corporate aircraft; lodging and meal expenses incurred during travel)

003 Solicitation and Fundraising Expenses (e.g., costs for direct mail solicitations and fundraising events including printing, mailing lists, consultant fees, call lists, invitations, catering costs and room rental)

004 Advertising Expenses—including general public political advertising (e.g., purchases of radio/television broadcast/cable time, print advertisements and related production costs)

005 Polling Expenses

006 Campaign Materials (e.g., buttons, bumper stickers, brochures, mass mailings, pens, posters and balloons)

007 Campaign Event Expenses (e.g., costs associated with candidate appearances, campaign rallies, town meetings, phone banks, including catering costs, door to door get-out-the-vote efforts and driving voters to the polls)

011 Political Contributions (e.g., contributions to other federal committees and candidates, and donations to non-federal candidates and committees)

In addition, the committee must provide the amount of coordinated expenditures made on behalf of each candidate for the general election. Expenditures made on behalf of more than one candidate should be attributed to each candidate in proportion to, and should be reported to reflect, the benefit reasonably expected to be derived.

---

*In the case of a candidate for election to the House of Representatives from a State which is entitled to only one Representative, the Senate party spending limits are applicable.

INSTRUCTIONS FOR FEC FORM 3X AND RELATED SCHEDULES

24-hour Notices

If a candidate qualifies for modified coordinated expenditure limits under 11 CFR 400.40 or 400.41, the campaign must notify the national and State political party within 24 hours using FEC Form 11. Upon receipt of a candidate's FEC Form 11, the party committee, after verifying the information, may make coordinated party expenditures in excess of the limitations set forth in 11 CFR 109.32. However, if the committee does make expenditures in excess of the limitations, it must file a Schedule F disclosing such expenditures by facsimile machine (to 202-219-0174) or by electronic mail (to 2022190174@fec.gov) with the Federal Election Commission within 24 hours of making such expenditures. 11 CFR 400.30(c)(2). The party committee must also simultaneously send a copy via facsimile machine or electronic mail to the candidate (or his or her authorized committee) on whose behalf the expenditure was made. Fax numbers and electronic mail addresses for authorized committees are available from the FEC's web site at www. fec.gov.

Note: When filing a 24-hour notice, check the box at the top of the form to indicate that the filing is a 24-hour notice.

Designated Agents

The national committee of a political party may make coordinated party expenditures for candidates through any designated agent including any State or subordinate party political committees.

The State party political committee may designate as agents any subordinate committee (county, city, local, etc.). The State party political committee shall be responsible for insuring that the expenditures of the entire party organization within the State are within the limitations, including receiving reports from any subordinate committee making expenditures, and filing consolidated reports showing all expenditures in the State. Committees reporting to the Commission for designated agents should use a separate Schedule F for each agent. Expenditures made by designated agents should not be included in the reporting committee's totals on the Detailed Summary Page. The figure carried forward to the Detailed Summary Page should be the amount of coordinated party expenditures made by the reporting committee.

Federal Election Commission (Revised 4/2006)   FE6AN026

INSTRUCTIONS FOR SCHEDULE H1, METHOD OF ALLOCATION FOR ALLOCATED FEDERAL AND NONFEDERAL ADMINISTRATIVE EXPENSES, GENERIC VOTER DRIVE COSTS, EXEMPT ACTIVITY COSTS, ALLOCATED FEDERAL/ LEVIN FUND "FEDERAL ELECTION ACTIVITY" EXPENSES AND ALLOCATED PUBLIC COMMUNICATIONS THAT REFER TO ANY POLITICAL PARTY (BUT NOT A CANDIDATE) (FEC FORM 3X)

Who Must File Schedule H1

Any State, district and local party committee, separate segregated fund or nonconnected committee that chooses to allocate allocable expenses must report the allocation methods and ratios used on Schedule H1 and/or H2 as explained below and in the instructions for Schedule H2.

When Allocation is Permitted

An unauthorized committee that is active in both federal and nonfederal elections, and that has established separate federal and nonfederal accounts, may either make all payments for allocable administrative and generic voter drive expenses and – for party committees – allocable exempt activity costs, with federally permissible funds or make such payments by allocating the expenses between its federal and nonfederal accounts according to specified allocation methods. A State, district or local party committee engaging in allocable federal election activities may pay for such activities entirely with federal funds, or may allocate such payments between its federal account and Levin funds, according to specified allocation methods. A separate segregated fund or

nonconnected committee that makes disbursements for public communications or voter drives that refer only to a political party (not a candidate) may allocate such expenditures, but must report the allocation method and ratio using Schedule H1.

When to Use Schedule H1

State, District and Local Party Committees. State, district and local party committees that choose to allocate allocable expenses must report on Schedule H1 the allocation methods and ratios used for administrative expenses, the costs of generic voter drives, the costs of allocable exempt activities and the costs of allocable "federal election activities" as defined at 11 CFR 100.24. Such committees must use Schedule H2 to report the allocation methods and ratios used for allocable fundraising and the costs of allocable direct candidate support.

Separate Segregated Funds and Nonconnected Committees. Separate segregated funds and nonconnected committees that choose to allocate allocable expenses must report the allocation methods and ratios used on Schedule H1 for administrative expenses, generic voter drives and public communications that refer only to a political party (not a candidate for federal or nonfederal office). (**Note:** A separate segregated fund need not report administrative expenses paid for by the committee's connected organization.) Such committees must use Schedule H2 to report the allocation methods and ratios used for allocable fundraising and the costs of allocable direct candidate support, including public communications or voter drives that refer to both federal and nonfederal candidates, or both federal and nonfederal candidates and a political party. (**Note:** A separate segregated fund need not report fundraising expenses paid for by the committee's connected organization.) See the instructions for Schedule H2 for more information.

Definitions

The term "generic voter drive" means any voter identification, voter registration, or get-out-the-vote drive, or any other activity that urges the general public to register, vote or support candidates of a particular party or associated with a particular issue, without clearly identifying a candidate. (Note that such activity in a special election involving only a federal candidate is treated as if it mentions a specific candidate.)

The term "Nonfederal account" means an account that contains funds to be used in connection with a State or local election or allocable expenses as permitted by 11 CFR 106.7, 300.30 and 300.33. 11 CFR 300.2(j).

The term "Levin funds" means funds that are raised and that are or will be disbursed for specific "federal election activity" pursuant to 11 CFR 300.31 and 300.32. 11 CFR 300.2(i).

The term "allocable Federal election activity" means

• Voter registration activity (i.e. contacting individuals by telephone, in person or by other individualized means, to assist them in registering to vote (see 11 CFR 100.24(a)(2)) during the period that begins on the date that is 120 days before the date that a regularly scheduled federal election is held and that ends on the date of the election; or

Any of the following, when conducted during the period of time beginning on the date of the earliest filing deadline for primary ballot access for federal candidates, or in those States that do not conduct primary elections, on January 1 of each even numbered year through the date of the general election (including any general election runoff). In the case of a special election, the applicable period runs from the date on which the date of the special election is set and ends on the date of the special election. See 11 CFR 100.24(a)(1).

• Voter identification (i.e., acquiring information about potential voters, including but not limited to, obtaining voter lists and creating or enhancing voter lists by verifying or adding information about the likelihood of voting in a specific election or for specific candidates. See 11 CFR 100.24(a)(4));

• Generic campaign activity, (i.e., a public communication that promotes or opposes a political party and does not promote or oppose a clearly identified federal candidate or a nonfederal candidate. See 11 CFR 100.25); or

• Get-out-the-vote activity (i.e., contacting registered voters by telephone, in person or by other individualized means, to assist them in engaging in the act of voting. See 11 CFR 100.24(a)(3)). 11 CFR 100.24(b)(1) and (2).

Line-by-Line Instructions and When To File

Enter the committee's full name in the appropriate block.

State, district and local party committees must allocate their administrative expenses, generic voter drive costs, allocable exempt activity costs and costs for allocable "federal election activity" according to a fixed percentage. (See 11 CFR 106.7(d) and 300.33(b).) Check the appropriate box on Schedule H1, Method of Allocation, to indicate the fixed federal percentage. The percentage is based on whether a Presidential candidate, a Senate candidate, both or neither are expected on the ballot in the next general federal election.

File Schedule H1 with the first FEC Form 3X submitted each year. 11 CFR 104.17(b)(1).

Nonconnected committees and separate segregated funds that choose to allocate must allocate their administrative expenses, generic voter drive costs and costs for public communications that refer only to a political party (not a candidate) according to the flat minimum federal percentage – 50 %. (See 11 CFR 106.6(b).) Committees must use at least 50% federal funds to pay for these expenses. (To indicate that the committee is using an exact 50/50 ratio, check the box indicated.) The committee may choose to spend more than 50% federal funds, but must show the percentage of federal and nonfederal funds used in the boxes provided.

File Schedule H1, Method of Allocation, with each report that discloses an allocated disbursement for the above categories of expenses. 11 CFR 104.10(b)(1). Supply a separate Schedule H1 for each different ratio the committee used during the reporting period. For each ratio disclosed, check the appropriate box(es) to indicate the category(ies) of disbursements to which the ratio applies.

INSTRUCTIONS FOR SCHEDULE H2, ALLOCATION RATIOS

(To Be Used For Allocable Federal and Nonfederal Fundraising and Direct Candidate Support)

Who Must File

Any State, district or local party committee, separate segregated fund or nonconnected committee that is active in both federal and nonfederal elections, and that has established separate federal and nonfederal accounts, may either make all payments for allocable activity with federally permissible funds, or may allocate expenses for its allocable activities between its federal and nonfederal accounts according to specified allocation methods. Committees that choose to allocate expenses for certain allocable activities must report the allocation ratios used for each activity on Schedule H2, Allocation Ratios. The categories of allocable activity referred to on this Schedule include (1) fundraising events through which both federal and nonfederal funds are collected by one committee and (2) activities providing direct candidate support to both specific federal and specific nonfederal candidates. (**For separate segregated funds and nonconnected committees only**, this includes public communications or voter drives that refer to both federal and nonfederal candidates, regardless of any reference to a political party. Party committees may not allocate such expenses between their federal and nonfederal accounts; instead, they must treat them as "federal election activity" and report them accordingly on Line 30. See the instructions for Schedules B, H5 and H6 for more information.)

When To File

Schedule H2, the Allocation Ratios Schedule, must accompany each FEC Form 3X filed by a committee that discloses a disbursement for an allocated federal and nonfederal fundraising event or direct candidate support activity.

Methods of Allocation

(1) Fundraising expenses are to be allocated according to the "funds received method," whereby allocation is based on the ratio of funds received by the committee's federal account as compared to the total funds received by all of the committee's accounts from each allocable fundraising event. Detailed instructions for calculating this ratio are contained in 11 CFR 106.7(d)(4) (for party committees) and 11 CFR 106.6(d) (for nonconnected committees and separate segregated funds).

(2) The costs of direct candidate support activities are to be allocated according to a ratio based on the benefit expected to be derived by each candidate. Detailed instructions for calculating this ratio are contained in 11 CFR 106.1(a) and 11 CFR 106.6(f)(3) (for certain public communications and voter drives by nonconnected committees and separate segregated funds).

Line-by-Line Instructions

Enter the name of each activity or event in the appropriate blocks.

Note: Each individual fundraising event or activity providing direct candidate support must be assigned a unique identifying title or code. The exact title or code must be used consistently throughout a committee's reports when disclosing transactions related to that activity or event.

The committee must enter the percentage of costs allocated to its federal account and its nonfederal account for each individual activity or event. These percentages are to be calculated according to the appropriate allocation method for each category of activity.

For each individual activity or event, the committee must indicate whether it is a fundraising event or an activity providing direct candidate support. If the event represents activity for more than one category, the committee must list each category on a separate Line. The committee must also indicate whether the allocation ratio is new, revised or the same as previously reported for that activity or event.

INSTRUCTIONS FOR SCHEDULE H3, TRANSFERS FROM NONFEDERAL ACCOUNTS FOR ALLOCATED FEDERAL/ NONFEDERAL ACTIVITY

(To Be Used to Show Transfers From Nonfederal Accounts to Federal Accounts For The Purpose of Paying Allocable Expenses)

Who Must File

Any State, district or local party committee, separate segregated fund or nonconnected committee that is active in both federal and nonfederal elections, and that has established separate federal and nonfederal accounts, may either make all payments for allocable activity with federally permissible funds, or may allocate expenses for its allocable activities between its federal and nonfederal accounts according to specified allocation methods. A committee that chooses to allocate allocable expenses must pay the bills for those expenses from either its federal account or from a separate allocation account which is also a federal account subject to the FECA's reporting requirements. The committee may transfer funds from its nonfederal account to either of these federal accounts, solely for the purpose of paying the nonfederal share of allocable expenses. All such transfers must occur not more than 10 days before or 60 days after the payments for which they are intended are made, and must be itemized on Schedule H3. This Schedule is used only in support of Line 18(a) of the Detailed Summary Page. All other federal account receipts should be itemized as required on Schedule A or Schedule H5, as appropriate.

When To File

Schedule H3 must be filed for each reporting period in which any funds are transferred from a nonfederal account to a federal account for the purpose of paying the nonfederal share of a committee's allocable expenses.

Line-by-Line Instructions

Name of Account; Date of Receipt; Total Amount Transferred. The committee must enter its full name, the name of the nonfederal account from which each transfer is made, and the date and total amount of the transfer in the appropriate blocks.

Each transfer from a nonfederal account to a federal account may include funds intended to pay for more than one allocable activity. Therefore, the committee must indicate on Lines i) through vi) the purposes for which each transfer is made, and the amount designated for each such purpose.

Line i) List the total amount used for administrative expenses.

Line ii) List the total amount used for generic voter drive costs.

Line iii) List the amount used for each allocable exempt activity (State, district and local party committees only).

Line iv) List the amount used for allocable direct fundraising activity.

Line v) List the amount used for allocable direct candidate support. For separate segregated funds and nonconnected committees only, this includes amounts used for public communications or voter drives referencing both federal and nonfederal candidates (regardless of any reference to a political party).

Note: In the space provided on Lines iv and v, list the activity or event identifier used on Schedule H2, Allocation Ratios, to identify each separate fundraising event or direct candidate support activity.

Line vi) List the amount used for public communications referring only to a political party (separate segregated funds and nonconnected committees only).

Compute subtotals for each line at the bottom of each page for the transfers itemized on that page. Carry the "Total This Period" for the column "Total Amount Transferred" forward to Line 18(a) of the Detailed Summary Page.

Federal Election Commission (Revised 4/2006)   FE6AN026

INSTRUCTIONS FOR SCHEDULE H4, DISBURSEMENTS FOR ALLOCATED FEDERAL/ NONFEDERAL ACTIVITY (FEC FORM 3X)

(To Be Used For Allocated Federal/ Nonfederal Activity)

Who Must File

Any State, district or local party committee, separate segregated fund or nonconnected committee that is active in both federal and nonfederal elections, and that has established separate federal and nonfederal accounts, may either make all payments for allocable activity with federally permissible funds, or may allocate expenses for its allocable activities between its federal and nonfederal accounts according to specified allocation methods. A committee that chooses to allocate allocable expenses must pay the bills for those expenses from either its federal account or from a separate allocation account which is also a federal account subject to the FECA's reporting requirements. The committee may transfer funds within specified time limits from its nonfederal account to cover the nonfederal share of the allocated expense. The committee must itemize each allocated disbursement for activity allocated between its federal and nonfederal accounts as made from its federal account or separate allocation account on Schedule H4. Only disbursements supporting Line 21(a), Allocated Federal/Nonfederal Activity, of the Detailed Summary Page are reported on Schedule H4. Disbursements supporting Line 21(b), Other Federal Operating Expenditures, of the Detailed Summary Page must be itemized on Schedule B, as required. All other disbursements from the federal account must also be itemized, as required, on Schedules B or E and by State, district and local party committees also on Schedules F or H6, as appropriate.

When to File

Schedule H4 must be filed for each reporting period in which disbursements are made from a committee's federal account or separate allocation account to pay for allocated federal/ nonfederal expenses under 11 CFR 106.6 or 106.7.

Line-by-Line Instructions

Enter the committee's full name in the appropriate block of each page.

For each disbursement itemized during the reporting period, provide the payee's full name and mailing address, the date, and the purpose for which the disbursement was made.

Note: Purpose

(a) **Purpose**. The term "purpose" means a brief statement or description of why the disbursement was made. Examples of adequate descriptions include the following: salary (in the case of a party committee, only allocable when an employee spends 25 percent or less of his or her time in a given month on federal election activity or activity in connection with a federal election), dinner expenses, media, polling, travel, party fees, phone banks, travel expenses and catering costs. However, descriptions such as "advance," "election day expenses," "other expenses," "expense reimbursement," "miscellaneous," "outside services," "get-out-the-vote" and "voter registration," would not meet the requirement for reporting the purpose of a disbursement.

(b) **Category/Type Code.** Along with reporting the purpose of the expenditure as required above, the committee should also broadly characterize disbursements by providing the category/type code for each category of disbursement. Examples of the types of disbursements that fall within each of the broad categories are listed below. Use only one code for each itemized disbursement. In cases where the disbursement was for several purposes, the political committee should assign one code according to the primary purpose of the disburse-

ment. Note that some of the category titles are not acceptable as the "purpose" of the disbursement and that the categories are not intended to replace or to serve as a substitute for the "purpose of disbursement."

001 Administrative/Overhead Expenses (e.g., rent, postage, office supplies, equipment, furniture, ballot access fees, petition drives, party fees and legal and accounting expenses)

002 Travel Expenses—including travel reimbursement expenses (e.g., costs of commercial carrier tickets; reimbursements for use of private vehicles; advance payments for use of corporate aircraft; lodging and meal expenses incurred during travel)

003 Solicitation and Fundraising Expenses (e.g., costs for direct mail solicitations and fundraising events including printing, mailing lists, consultant fees, call lists, invitations, catering costs and room rental)

004 Advertising Expenses—including general public political advertising (e.g., purchases of radio/television broadcast/cable time, print advertisements and related production costs)

005 Polling Expenses

006 Campaign Materials (e.g., buttons, bumper stickers, brochures, mass mailings, pens, posters and balloons)

007 Campaign Event Expenses (e.g., costs associated with candidate appearances, campaign rallies, town meetings, phone banks, including catering costs, door to door get-out-the-vote efforts and driving voters to the polls)

008 Transfers (e.g., to other affiliated/ party committees)

009 Loans (e.g., loans made or repayments of loans received)

010 Refunds of Contributions (e.g., contribution refunds to individuals/persons, political party committees or other political committees)

011 Political Contributions (e.g., contributions to other federal committees and candidates, and donations to nonfederal candidates and committees)

012 Donations (e.g., donations to charitable or civic organizations)

(c)   **Unique Activity or Event Identifier.** If the disbursement was for an allocable fundraising event or allocable direct federal and nonfederal candidate support, the activity or event must be identified by the unique activity or event identifier assigned to it on Schedule H2, Allocation Ratios, in addition to the purpose for which the disbursement was made.

Allocated Activity or Event. Identify the type of "allocated activity or event" for which each disbursement is made by checking the appropriate box. (**Note for separate segregated funds and nonconnected committees only:** For public communications that are made by a nonconnected committee or separate segregated fund and that refer only to a political party, check "Public Comm (ref to Party Only) by PAC." For public communications and voter drives that refer to both federal and nonfederal candidates, regardless of any reference to a political party, check "Direct Candidate Support.") A disbursement representing payment for more than one type of activity is reported as a memo entry followed by a break down of the disbursement by type of activity, with the appropriate boxes checked. The committee must also enter the aggregate amount of all disbursements made year-to-date as of this report for each type of activity or individual event. For fundraising and direct candidate support, a separate aggregate amount must be reported for each individual activity or event. For administrative expenses, generic voter drive activity, allocable exempt activities and allocable public communications that refer only to a party and are made by a separate segregated fund or nonconnected committee, one aggregate amount for all disbursements in that type is sufficient.

Enter the total amount of each disbursement in the appropriate box. For each disbursement for allocated expenses, the committee must enter the total amounts allocated to the federal and nonfederal accounts in the appropriate boxes. For State, district and local party committees disclosing administrative expenses, allocable exempt activities and generic voter drive costs, the federal and nonfederal shares are derived from the fixed percentage stated on Schedule H1, Method of Allocation. For separate segregated funds and nonconnected committees disclosing administrative expenses, generic voter drive costs and public communications that refer only to a party, the federal and nonfederal shares are derived from the flat minimum federal percentage ratio disclosed on Schedule H1 for that type of disbursement. For the costs of fundraising and direct candidate support, these amounts are derived from the percentages stated for each event on Schedule H2, Allocation Ratios. (Note that administrative and fundraising expenses are neither allocated nor disclosed by a separate segregated fund when those costs are paid by its connected organization.)

If an allocated disbursement was made, in whole or in part, for direct candidate support (e.g., an in-kind contribution benefiting both specific federal and specific nonfederal candidates), the federal share of the disbursement must be disclosed on Schedule B, E or F, supporting Line 23, 24 or 25 of the Detailed Summary Page, as appropriate and disclosed as a memo entry in the "Federal Share" box on Schedule H4. The "Federal Share" box on Schedule H4 should contain a reference to Schedule B, E or F and the appropriate Line number of the Detailed Summary Page on which this information is reported. The nonfederal share of the disbursement must be entered in the "Nonfederal Share" box on Schedule H4.

Compute subtotals for each page and totals for the reporting period for the total amount of disbursements, and for the total federal and nonfederal shares. The "Total This Period" for the federal share and the nonfederal share are carried forward to Lines 21(a)(i) and 21(a)(ii), respectively, of the Detailed Summary Page.

INSTRUCTIONS FOR SCHEDULE H5, TRANSFERS OF LEVIN FUNDS RECEIVED (FEC FORM 3X)

(To Be Used to Show Transfers of Levin Funds from Nonfederal Account or Levin Account to Federal Account For The Purpose of Paying Allocable Expenses for Federal Election Activity)

Who Must File

Any State, district or local party committee that is a political committee and engages in allocable federal election activities must file. (Definitions of "allocable federal election activities" appear on the instructions for Schedule H1.)

Reporting committees may either make all payments for that allocable federal election activity with federally permissible funds, or may allocate expenses for it between its federal account and Levin funds, according to the fixed percentage reported on Schedule H1. A party committee that chooses to allocate allocable expenses for "federal election activity" must pay for those expenses from either its federal account or from a separate allocation account which is also a federal account subject to the FECA's reporting requirements. The committee may transfer Levin funds from its Levin account or nonfederal account to either of these federal accounts, solely for the purpose of paying the Levin share of allocable expenses. All such transfers must occur not more than 10 days before or 60 days after the payments for which they are intended are made, and must be itemized as receipts on Schedule H5. This Schedule is used only in support of Line 18(b) of the Detailed Summary Page.

Line-by-Line Instructions

Name of Committee: Enter the committee's full name.

For each transfer made, complete a block as follows:

Account Name: Enter the name of the Levin account or the name of the non-federal account from which a transfer of Levin funds has been made.

Breakdown of Transfer Received:

Note: Each transfer of Levin funds to a federal account may include funds intended to pay for more than one type of allocable federal election activity. Therefore, the committee must indicate in each block on Lines i) through iv) the amount of each transfer for each type of allocable federal election activity.

1. Enter the date and total amount of the transfer in the appropriate blocks.
2. Line i): List the total amount to be used for voter registration costs.
3. Line ii): List the amount to be used for voter identification costs.
4. Line iii): List the amount to be used for get-out-the-vote costs.
5. Line iv): List the amount to be used for the costs of generic campaign activity (i.e., public communications covered by 11 CFR 100.25).

Compute subtotals as indicated at the bottom of each page for the transfers itemized on that page. Carry forward the "Total This Period" for the column "Total Amount Transferred" to Line 18(b) of the Detailed Summary Page.

When To File

File Schedule H5 for each reporting period in which any Levin funds are transferred to a federal account for the purpose of paying the Levin share of a committee's allocable expenses.

INSTRUCTIONS FOR SCHEDULE H6, DISBURSEMENTS OF FEDERAL AND LEVIN FUNDS FOR ALLOCATED FEDERAL ELECTION ACTIVITY (FEC FORM 3X)

(To Be Used For Allocated Federal/Levin Federal Election Activity)

Who Must File

Any State, district or local party committee that engages in allocable federal election activities (see 11 CFR 300.32 and 300.33 and the instructions for Schedule H1), and that has established separate federal and Levin accounts, or that has raised Levin funds, may either make all payments for allocable federal election activity with federally permissible funds, or may allocate expenses for its allocable federal election activity between its federal account and Levin funds according to the fixed percentage reported on Schedule H1. A committee that chooses to allocate federal election activity expenses must pay for those expenses from either its federal account or from a separate allocation account which is also a federal account subject to the FECA's reporting requirements. The committee may transfer Levin funds within specified time limits to cover the Levin share of the allocated expense. The committee must itemize each allocated disbursement made from its federal account or separate allocation account for allocable federal election activity on Schedule H6. Only disbursements supporting Line 30(a), Allocated Federal Election Activity, of the Detailed Summary Page should be reported on Schedule H6. Disbursements supporting Line 30(b), Federal Election Activity Paid Entirely with Federal Funds, should be reported on Schedule B for Line 30(b), as required. Itemize all other disbursements from the federal account, as required, on Schedule B, E, F or H4.

Line-by-Line Instructions

Enter the committee's full name in the appropriate block of each page.

For each disbursement itemized during the reporting period, provide:
1. The payee's full name and mailing address;
2. The date; and
3. The purpose for which the disbursement was made.

Purpose: The term "purpose" means a brief statement or description of why the disbursement was made. Examples of adequate descriptions include the following: dinner expenses, media, polling, travel, party fees, phone banks, travel expenses and catering costs. However, descriptions such as "advance," "election day expenses," "other expenses," "expense reimbursement," "miscellaneous," "outside services," "get-out-the-vote," and "voter registration," would not meet the requirement for reporting the purpose of a disbursement.

Identify the "type of allocated activity" for which each disbursement is made by checking the appropriate box. A disbursement representing payment for more than one category of activity is reported as a memo entry followed by a break down of the disbursement by category of activity, with the appropriate boxes checked. The committee must also enter the aggregate amount of all disbursements made year-to-date for each category of activity or individual event.

The total amount of each disbursement must be entered in the appropriate box. For each disbursement, enter the total amounts allocated to the federal account and Levin funds in the appropriate boxes. The federal and Levin shares are derived from the percentage stated on the Schedule H1, Method of Allocation.

Federal Election Commission (Revised 4/2006)   FE6AN026

INSTRUCTIONS FOR FEC FORM 3X AND RELATED SCHEDULES

INSTRUCTIONS FOR SCHEDULE L, AGGREGATION PAGE, LEVIN FUNDS OF STATE, DISTRICT OR LOCAL PARTY COMMITTEES (FEC FORM 3X)

Who Must File

All State, district or local party committees that are political committees under 11 CFR 100.5 must disclose certain information about Levin funds raised, and transferred or otherwise disbursed by the committee. Every reporting period, each such committee must file an Aggregation Page summarizing the receipts and disbursements of its Levin funds for that reporting period and for the calendar year-to-date. The committee may disclose and itemize under 11 CFR 300.36(b)(2)(iv) its receipt of Levin funds either at the time the receipts are first received and deposited or at a later date when the committee makes Levin disbursements out of Levin-eligible funds. If a committee maintains a separate Levin account, the committee must disclose and itemize the Levin receipts when they are deposited in the Levin account. A separate Aggregation Page must be submitted for each of the committee's accounts that handles Levin funds, whether that account is a dedicated "Levin account" or whether it is another non-federal account. The committee must also attach Schedule L-A and Schedule L-B, itemizing the receipts and disbursements of Levin funds.

Line-by-Line Instructions

Enter the committee's full name and the coverage dates of the report in the appropriate blocks.

To calculate the "Calendar Year-to-Date" figure for each Line, the committee should add the figure from the same Line of its previous report to the "Total This Period" for the current report. For the first report filed in a calendar year, the "Calendar Year-to-Date" figure and the "Total This Period" figure will be the same.

If there were no receipts or disbursements for a particular Line during the reporting period or the calendar year, enter "0" on the appropriate Lines.

Receipts (Schedule L-A)

LINE 1. Enter the total amount of receipts of Levin funds from individuals, committees and other entities. For each individual or entity who has made one or more donations during the calendar year, the committee must disclose in a memo Schedule L-A the following information: the identification of the individual (full name, mailing address, name of employer and occupation) or entity (full name and mailing address), and the date of receipt and amount of each donation aggregating $200 or more. (See also instructions for Schedule A).

LINE 2. Enter the total of any other receipts disclosed in a memo Schedule L-A.

LINE 3. Add the total of Line 1 and Line 2.

Disbursements (Schedule L-B)

LINE 4. Enter the total amount of transfers of Levin funds made to the committee's federal account or allocation account for each category of allocable federal election activity. Itemize each such transfer on a memo Schedule L-B in full. (See also instructions for Schedule B).

LINE 5. Enter the total amount of all other disbursements disclosed on a memo Schedule L-B. All such disbursements must be itemized if they exceed $200 or more.

LINE 6. Add Lines 4(e) and 5 to derive the figure for total disbursements.

Summary

LINE 7. Enter the total amount of cash on hand at the beginning of the reporting period. For Column B ("Calendar Year-to-Date"), enter the total amount of cash on hand as of January 1 of the calendar year.

LINE 8. Enter the "Total This Period" figure from Line 3.

LINE 9. Add Lines 7 and 8 to derive the subtotal for receipts.

LINE 10. Enter the "Total This Period" figure from Line 6.

LINE 11. Subtract Line 10 from Line 9 to derive the figure for Levin funds on hand at the close of the reporting period.

When To File

Submit Schedule L, the Levin Funds Aggregation Page, and supporting memo Schedules L-A and L-B with each report once the committee has combined receipts and disbursements of $5,000 or more in the aggregate for "federal election activity" during the calendar year as defined at 11 CFR 100.24. Note that once this threshold is passed, the committee must file FEC reports on a monthly basis. 11 CFR 300.36(c)(1).

REPORT OF COMMUNICATION COSTS
BY CORPORATIONS AND MEMBERSHIP ORGANIZATIONS

1. (a) NAME OF ORGANIZATION	2. IDENTIFICATION NUMBER (Assigned by FEC)

(b) ADDRESS (Number and Street)	3. TYPE OF ORGANIZATION (Check Appropriate Box)
	☐ Corporation ☐ Trade Association
(c) CITY, STATE AND ZIP CODE	☐ Labor Organization ☐ Cooperative
	☐ Membership Organization ☐ Corporation without capital stock

4. TYPE OF REPORT (Check One):

   (a) ☐ April 15 Quarterly Report   ☐ July 15 Quarterly Report   ☐ October 15 Quarterly Report

     ☐ 12 Day Pre-General Election Report held on _____ in the State of _____.
                                     (date)

     ☐ January 31 Year End Report

   (b) Is this Report an Amendment?   ☐ YES   ☐ NO

5. THIS REPORT COVERS THE PERIOD _____ THROUGH _____

SUMMARY OF COMMUNICATION COSTS

Type of Communication	Class or Category Communicated With	Date(s) of Communication	Check One		Identify Candidate, Office Sought, District and State, and Whether for Primary or General Election	Cost of Communication (Per Candidate)
			Support	Oppose		
☐ Direct Mail ☐ Telephone ☐ Telegram ☐ Other: _____ (Specify) _____	☐ Executive/ Administrative Personnel ☐ Stockholders ☐ Members					
☐ Direct Mail ☐ Telephone ☐ Telegram ☐ Other: _____ (Specify) _____	☐ Executive/ Administrative Personnel ☐ Stockholders ☐ Members					

(NOTE: For additional communications, attach separate sheets containing the same information as above.)

TOTAL COMMUNICATION COSTS FOR THIS PERIOD $ _____

I certify that I have examined this report and, to the best of my knowledge and belief, it is true, correct and complete.

_____   _____   _____
    Type or Print Name   Signature and Title of Person Designated to Sign This Report   Date

NOTE: Submission of false, erroneous, or incomplete information may subject the person signing this report to penalties of 2 U.S.C. §437g.

WHERE TO FILE:
   Federal Election Commission
   999 E Street, N.W.
   Washington, D.C. 20463

FOR FURTHER INFORMATION CONTACT:
   Federal Election Commission
   Toll Free: 800-424-9530
   Local: 202-694-1100

FE1AN069.PDF

FEC FORM 7 (2/2001)

FEDERAL ELECTION COMMISSION
Instructions for Report of Communication Costs By Corporations and Membership Organizations (FEC FORM 7)

2 U.S.C. 441b allows "communications by a corporation to its stockholders and executive or administrative personnel and their families or by a labor organization to its members and their families on any subject," including the express advocacy of the election or defeat of any Federal candidate. Further, 2 U.S.C. 431(9)(B)(iii) requires that the costs of such communications be reported to the Federal Election Commission under certain circumstances. This section states in pertinent part:

"…the costs incurred by a membership organization (including a labor organization) or by a corporation directly attributable to a communication expressly advocating the election or defeat of a clearly identified candidate (other than a communication primarily devoted to subjects other than the express advocacy of the election or defeat of a clearly identified candidate), shall, if those costs exceed $2,000 per election, be reported to the Commission."

For the purpose of interpreting these provisions of law, the Commission's regulations provide the following definitions:

(i) "Labor organization" means an organization of any kind (any local, national, or international union, or any local or State central body of a federation of unions is each considered a separate labor organization for purposes of this section) or any agency or employee representative committee or plan, in which employees participate and which exists for the purpose, in whole or in part, of dealing with employers concerning grievances, labor disputes, wages, rates of pay, hours of employment or conditions of work.

(ii) "Stockholder" means a person who has a vested beneficial interest in stock, has the power to direct how that stock shall be voted, if it is voting stock, and has the right to receive dividends.

(iii) "Executive or administrative personnel" means individuals employed by a corporation who are paid on a salary rather than hourly basis and who have policy-making, managerial, professional or supervisory responsibilities.

(iv) "Members" means all persons who are currently satisfying the requirements for membership in a membership organization, trade association, cooperative or corporation without capital stock and in the case of the labor organization, persons who are currently satisfying the requirements for membership in a local, national or international labor organization. Members of a local union are considered to be members of any national or international union of which the local union is a part and of any federation with which the local, national or international union is affiliated. A person is not considered a member under this definition if the only requirement for membership is a contribution to a separate segregated fund.

(v) "Election" means two separate processes in a calendar year, to each of which the $2,000 threshold described above applies separately. The first process is comprised of all primary elections for Federal office, wherever and whenever held; the second process is comprised of all general elections for Federal office, wherever and whenever held. The term "election" also includes each special election held to fill a vacancy in a Federal office or each run-off election.

(vi) "Corporation" means any separately incorporated entity, whether or not affiliated.

WHO MUST FILE

Every membership organization (including a labor organization) or corporation which makes disbursements for communications pursuant to 11 CFR 100.8(b)(4) and 114.3 of the Commission's regulations shall report to the Federal Election Commission, 999 E Street, N.W., Washington, D.C. 20463 on FEC FORM 7 such costs which are directly attributable to any communication expressly advocating the election or defeat of a clearly identified candidate (other than a communication primarily devoted to subjects other than the election or defeat of a clearly identified candidate), if such costs exceed $2,000 for any election.

WHAT MUST BE REPORTED

Each report filed under 11 CFR 104.6 of the Commission's regulations must include, for each communication:

(1) The type of communication (such as direct mail, telephone or telegram);

(2) The class or category communicated with (Executive/Administrative Personnel, Stockholders, Members);

(3) The date(s) of the communication;

(4) Whether the communication was in support of, or in opposition to, a particular candidate;

(5) The name of the candidate, the office sought (and the district and state of the office, if applicable), and whether the communication was for the primary or general election; and

(6) The cost of the communication.

Generally, the total cost of a communication which advocates the election or defeat of more than one candidate should be allocated to and reported for each candidate in equal proportions. If, however, one or more candidates are emphasized, the cost should be allocated and reported to reflect the benefit reasonably expected to be derived by each candidate.

WHEN TO REPORT

Organizations required to report under 11 CFR 104.6(a) of the Commission's regulations must file such reports during a calendar year in which a regularly scheduled general election is held. Such reports must be filed quarterly and, with respect to any general election, a 12 Day Pre-General Election Report must also be filed. The organization is required to file reports beginning with the first reporting period during which the aggregate cost for such communications exceeds $2,000 per election as defined in 11 CFR 104.6(a)(1) of the Commission's regulations, and for each period thereafter in which the organization makes additional disbursements in connection with the same election.

— Quarterly reports must be filed no later than April 15, July 15, October 15 and January 31 of the following calendar year. Each such report must disclose all transactions from the last report filed through the last day of the calendar quarter.

— A 12 Day Pre-General Election Report must be filed no later than the 12th day before the general election and must include all transactions from the closing date of the last report filed through the 20th day before the election. A 12 Day Pre-General Election Report sent by certified or registered mail must be mailed no later than the 15th day before the election.

A document is timely filed upon delivery to the Federal Election Commission by the close of the prescribed filing date or upon deposit as registered or certified mail in an established U.S. Post Office postmarked no later than midnight of the day the report is due, except that the 12 Day Pre-General Election Report so mailed must be postmarked no later than midnight of the 15th day before the date of the election. Reports sent by first class mail must be received by the Federal Election Commission by the close of business of the prescribed filing date to be timely filed.

FEC FORM 9
24 HOUR NOTICE OF DISBURSEMENTS/OBLIGATIONS FOR ELECTIONEERING COMMUNICATIONS

1. Person Making the Disbursements/Obligations

(a) Name

(b) Address (number and street) ☐ check if different than previously reported

(c) City, State and ZIP Code

(d) Name of Employer or Principal Place of Business   (e) Occupation

2. FEC Identification Number

C _____

3. Is This Statement ☐ **New** or ☐ **Amended**

4. Covering Period   M M / D D / Y Y Y Y   through   M M / D D / Y Y Y Y

5. (a) Date of Public Distribution(s) M M / D D / Y Y Y Y   **(b) Communication Title** _____

6. The filer is a(n): (a) ☐ Individual (b) ☐ Unincorporated Organization (c) ☐ Qualified Nonprofit Corporation (11 CFR 114.10)

(d) ☐ Corporation, Labor Organization or Qualified Nonprofit Corporation making communications under 11 CFR 114.15

(e) ☐ Other, specify: _____

7. If the filer is an individual, unincorporated organization or qualified nonprofit corporation, were the disbursements made exclusively from donations to a segregated bank account? Yes ☐ No ☐

8. Custodian of Records

(a) Name

(b) Address (number and street)

(c) City, State and ZIP Code

(d) Name of Employer or Principal Place of Business   (e) Occupation

9. Total Donations This Statement _____

10. Total Disbursements/Obligations This Statement _____

Under penalty of perjury, I certify that this statement is true, correct and complete.

TYPE OR PRINT NAME OF PERSON COMPLETING FORM _____

SIGNATURE _____   **DATE** _____

NOTE: Submission of false, erroneous or incomplete information may subject the person signing this statement to the penalties of 2 U.S.C. §437g.

FEC FORM 9 (REV. 12/2007)

List of Person(s) Sharing/Exercising Control
(use additional pages as necessary)

PAGE   OF

11. Person(s) Sharing/Exercising Control

A. (a) Name

(b) Address (number and street)

(c) City, State and ZIP Code

(d) Name of Employer or Principal Place of Business   (e) Occupation

B. (a) Name

(b) Address (number and street)

(c) City, State and ZIP Code

(d) Name of Employer or Principal Place of Business   (e) Occupation

C. (a) Name

(b) Address (number and street)

(c) City, State and ZIP Code

(d) Name of Employer or Principal Place of Business   (e) Occupation

D. (a) Name

(b) Address (number and street)

(c) City, State and ZIP Code

(d) Name of Employer or Principal Place of Business   (e) Occupation

E. (a) Name

(b) Address (number and street)

(c) City, State and ZIP Code

(d) Name of Employer or Principal Place of Business   (e) Occupation

SCHEDULE 9-A
Donation(s) Received

PAGE   OF

A. Full Name of Donor

Mailing Address of Donor

City   State   Zip

Date of Receipt

M   M / D   D / Y   Y   Y   Y   Y

Amount

B. Full Name of Donor

Mailing Address of Donor

City   State   Zip

Date of Receipt

M   M / D   D / Y   Y   Y   Y   Y

Amount

C. Full Name of Donor

Mailing Address of Donor

City   State   Zip

Date of Receipt

M   M / D   D / Y   Y   Y   Y   Y

Amount

D. Full Name of Donor

Mailing Address of Donor

City   State   Zip

Date of Receipt

M   M / D   D / Y   Y   Y   Y   Y

Amount

E. Full Name of Donor

Mailing Address of Donor

City   State   Zip

Date of Receipt

M   M / D   D / Y   Y   Y   Y   Y

Amount

SUBTOTAL of Donations This Page (optional) .... ▶

TOTAL This Period (last page this line number only) .... ▶
(carry total from last page to Line 9)

SCHEDULE 9-B
Disbursement(s) Made or Obligation(s)

PAGE   OF

A. Full Name (Last, First, Middle Initial) of Payee

Date of Disbursement or Obligation

M M / D D / Y Y Y Y

Mailing Address of Payee

Amount

City   State   Zip Code

Communication Date

Name of Employer   Occupation

M M / D D / Y Y Y Y

Purpose of Disbursement (Including title(s) of communication(s))

Name of Federal Candidate	Office Sought:	House Senate President	State: _____ District: _____	Disbursement/Obligation For: Primary ☐ General ☐ Other (specify) ▸ _____
Name of Federal Candidate	Office Sought:	House Senate President	State: _____ District: _____	Disbursement/Obligation For: Primary ☐ General ☐ Other (specify) ▸ _____
Name of Federal Candidate	Office Sought:	House Senate President	State: _____ District: _____	Disbursement/Obligation For: Primary ☐ General ☐ Other (specify) ▸ _____

B. Full Name (Last, First, Middle Initial) of Payee

Date of Disbursement or Obligation

M M / D D / Y Y Y Y

Mailing Address of Payee

Amount

City   State   Zip Code

Communication Date

Name of Employer   Occupation

M M / D D / Y Y Y Y

Purpose of Disbursement (Including title(s) of communication(s))

Name of Federal Candidate	Office Sought:	House Senate President	State: _____ District: _____	Disbursement/Obligation For: Primary ☐ General ☐ Other (specify) ▸ _____
Name of Federal Candidate	Office Sought:	House Senate President	State: _____ District: _____	Disbursement/Obligation For: Primary ☐ General ☐ Other (specify) ▸ _____
Name of Federal Candidate	Office Sought:	House Senate President	State: _____ District: _____	Disbursement/Obligation For: Primary ☐ General ☐ Other (specify) ▸ _____

SUBTOTAL of Disbursements/Obligations This Page (optional) .... ▸

TOTAL This Period (last page this line number only) .... ▸
(carry total from last page to Line 10)

FEDERAL ELECTION COMMISSION
Instructions for Preparing FEC FORM 9 (24 Hour Notice of Disbursements for Electioneering Communications)

Who Must File

Every person that makes disbursements for electioneering communications aggregating in excess of $10,000 during a calendar year must report these disbursements by submitting FEC Form 9. For purposes of these notices "disbursements" includes actual disbursements and the execution of contracts creating an obligation to make disbursements for electioneering communications. The Commission must receive the notice by 11:59 p.m. of the day following the date of the first public disclosure of the electioneering communication that triggers the reporting requirement. Each time subsequent disbursements for electioneering communications made by the same person or entity aggregate in excess of $10,000, another notice must be submitted. (Note: Political committees that make disbursements for such communications must report such disbursements on FEC Form 3X as expenditures or independent expenditures, as appropriate.)

By submitting Form 9, Qualified Nonprofit Corporations that make disbursements for or execute contracts obligating them to make disbursements for electioneering communications not permissible under 11 CFR 114.15 certify that they fit the criteria for exemption from the prohibition on corporations making electioneering communications under 11 CFR 114.10.

Definitions

Electioneering Communication means any broadcast, cable or satellite communication that (1) refers to a clearly identified candidate; (2) is publicly distributed; (3) is distributed within 60 days prior to a general election or 30 days prior to a primary election; and (4) can be received by 50,000 or more people in the House District or State that the candidate seeks to represent, or in the case of Presidential primaries, the State holding a Presidential primary within 30 days of the date of public distribution. 11 CFR 100.29.

Public Distribution of an electioneering communication means the airing, broadcast, cablecast or other dissemination of such a communication through the facilities of a television station, radio station, cable television system or satellite system.

Date of Public Distribution refers to the **"Disclosure Date"** under 11 CFR 104.20(a)(l). That regulation defines the date that triggers disclosure of an electioneering communication. The first reportable date of public distribution in a calendar year is the date that an electioneering communication is publicly distributed when the maker of the communication has also surpassed the $10,000 disbursement threshold. Counting toward the $10,000 threshold are disbursements made for the direct costs of producing or airing the communication aired on the first reportable date plus the direct costs of any previously unreported electioneering communications. After the first disclosure date, subsequent disclosure notices must be filed on the day following each date on which an electioneering communication is publicly distributed, provided that the direct costs for any electioneering communications since the last Form 9 was filed aggregate in excess of $10,000.

Direct Costs of Producing or Airing Electioneering Communications means (1) costs charged by a vendor (e.g., studio rental time, staff salaries, costs of video or audio recording media and talent) or (2) costs of airtime on broadcast, cable and satellite radio and television stations, studio time, material costs and the charges for a broker to purchase the airtime. 11 CFR 104.20(a)(2).

Qualified nonprofit corporation is a corporation that either (i) has the following characteristics: **(a)** Its only express purpose is the promotion of political ideas (i.e., issue advocacy, election influencing activity and research, training or educational activity expressly tied to its political goals); **(b)** It cannot engage in business activities; **(c)** It does not have **(1)** shareholders or persons (other than employees and creditors) who are affiliated in a way that could allow them to make a claim on its assets or earnings; or **(2)** persons who receive a benefit that is a disincentive for them to disassociate themselves with the corporation on the basis of the corporation's position on a political issue; **(d)** It was not established by a business corporation or labor organization, does not accept donations from business corporations or labor organizations; and if unable, for good cause, to demonstrate that it has not accepted such donations, has a written policy against accepting donations from business corporations or labor organizations; and **(e)** It is described in 26 U.S.C. § 501(c)(4). (See 11 CFR 114.10); or (ii) has been deemed entitled to qualified nonprofit corporation status by a court in competent jurisdiction in a case in which the same corporation was a party. (See 11 CFR 114.10(e)(l)(i)(B).)

Donation as used on this Form means any gift, subscription, loan, advance or deposit of money or anything of value given to any person that is used to finance an electioneering communication.

INSTRUCTIONS FOR FEC FORM 9 AND RELATED SCHEDULES

Name of Employer means the organization or person by whom an individual is employed, rather than the name of his or her supervisor. Individuals who are self-employed should indicate "self-employed."

Occupation means the principal job title or position of an individual.

Purpose means a brief statement or description of why the disbursement was made.

When to File

The Commission must receive notices of electioneering communications no later than 11:59 p.m. Eastern Standard/Daylight Time of the day following the date on which an electioneering communication is publicly distributed for the first time, provided that the $10,000 threshold has been reached. The Commission must receive notices of subsequent disbursements for additional airings of the same electioneering communication and/or for other electioneering communications by 11:59 p.m. Eastern Standard/Daylight Time of the days that follow the dates of public distribution of later electioneering communications, whenever the costs of such communications bring subsequent aggregate disbursement totals to more than $10,000. These later aggregations must include any previously unreported disbursements for electioneering communications that have been publicly distributed since the most recent notice was filed.

Notices of electioneering communications may be filed by fax to (202)219-0174, by electronic mail to 2022190174@fec.gov or by online webform available on the Commission's web site at http://www.fec.gov/elecfil/online.shtml.

Where To File

File all notices of electioneering communications with the Federal Election Commission, 999 E Street, N.W., Washington, DC 20463.

For notices of electioneering communications referencing a candidate for the House in Guam or Puerto Rico, submit a copy to the territory in which the candidate seeks election. For notices of electioneering communications made in Guam or Puerto Rico referencing a candidate for President or Vice President, submit a copy to the territory in which the expenditure is made. As of March 2006, those territories had not qualified for the Commission's state filing waiver program.

Persons filing notices of electioneering communications must retain copies of their notices for a period of not less than 3 years from the date of filing.

Line By Line Instructions

LINE 1. Person Making the Disbursements/Obligations. Provide the requested information. A "person" may be an individual, unincorporated organization, qualified nonprofit corporation, other corporation or labor organization. Individual filers: provide the name of your employer and your occupation.

LINE 2. FEC Identification Number. First time filers—leave this line blank. Previous filers with an identification number—enter that number.

LINE 3. New or Amended. Check "Amended" if you are filing an amendment to a previous notice. Otherwise, check "New."

LINE 4. Covering Period. Enter the first and last dates of financial activity covered by the statement; these dates should begin with the date of the first related disbursement and end with the date of public distribution.

LINE 5. a) Date of Public Distribution. Enter the public distribution date of the electioneering communication for which disbursements have exceeded $10,000 or whose related costs together with earlier disbursements for electioneering communications have exceeded $10,000,

thereby triggering the 24-hour notice requirement. If this is the first notice filed with regard of a particular electioneering communication by the maker, enter the date that the communication was first publicly distributed. If this is not the first notice filed with regard to a particular electioneering communication by the maker, enter the date on which the previously reported electioneering communication was publicly distributed an additional time, provided that costs related to the additional public distribution have exceeded $10,000 or the costs of the additional distribution plus disbursements related to other electioneering communications aired since the last notice was filed have exceeded $10,000. For subsequent, new electioneering communications, enter the date on which the communication was first aired whenever related and/or aggregated costs exceed $10,000. See the definitions above and under 11 CFR 104.20(a) of "Date of Public Distribution" and "Direct Costs of Producing or Airing Electioneering Communications."

b) Communication title. List the title of the communication as named by the media vendor or producer of the communication. (Titles of individual communications should remain the same throughout their various public distributions unless the content changes.)

LINE 6. The filer is. Check the box that identifies the type of person making the electioneering communication. A Qualified Nonprofit Corporation making electioneering communications permissible under 11 CFR 114.15 must check box (d), rather than box (c).

LINE 7. Account for Donations. Individual, unincorporated organization and qualified nonprofit corporation filers only: Check "Yes" if the disbursements for the electioneering communication were made exclusively from donations to a segregated bank account that was set up

INSTRUCTIONS FOR FEC FORM 9 AND RELATED SCHEDULES

expressly under 11 CFR 114.14(d)(2) for the purpose of financing electioneering communication(s). Otherwise, check "No."

LINE 8. Name of Custodian of Records. Provide the requested information about the individual who controls the books and records that support this filing.

LINE 9. Total Donations This Statement. All filers: Provide the sum total of donations itemized on Schedule 9-A. If you are a corporation, labor organization or Qualified Nonprofit Corporation making communications permissible under 114.15 and you received no donations made specifically for the purpose of funding electioneering communications, enter "0" (zero).

LINE 10. Total Disbursements/Obligations This Statement. Provide the sum total of disbursements itemized on Schedule 9-B.

LINE 11. List of Persons Sharing/Exercising Control. Provide the requested information for each person who shared or exercised control of making the disbursement/obligation for the electioneering communication. This means officers, directors, executive directors or their equivalents, partners, and, in the case of unincorporated organizations, owners of the entity or persons making disbursements for the electioneering communication. The senior staff position in an organization, whatever its title, that functions as an executive director is the equivalent of an executive director.

Verification

FEC Form 9 must be signed by the person making the electioneering communication, who is making a verified certification under penalty of perjury that the statement is correct.

By submitting Form 9, Qualified Nonprofit Corporations making communications not permissible under

11 CFR 114.15 certify that they fit the criteria for Qualified Nonprofit Corporation status under 11 CFR 114.10.

INSTRUCTIONS FOR SCHEDULE 9-A (DONATIONS RECEIVED)

Who Must File Every individual and unincorporated association making electioneering communications –and any Qualified Nonprofit Corporations making electioneering communications not permissible under 11 CFR 114.15—must file Schedule 9A. Corporations, labor organizations and Qualified Nonprofit Corporations making communications permissible under 11 CFR 114.15 must file Schedule 9A only if any part of the amount on Form 9, Line 10 includes donations made for the purpose of paying for electioneering communications.

Donations Made to Segregated Account. If the disbursements for the electioneering communication were made exclusively from donations to a segregated bank account that was set up expressly under 11 CFR 114.14(d)(2) for the purpose of financing electioneering communication(s), provide the requested information for those donors who donated an amount aggregating $1,000 or more since the first day of the preceding calendar year. 11 CFR 104.20(c)(7).

Donations Made to Non-Segregated Account. If the disbursements/obligations for the communication were made from an account that is not segregated as described above, provide the requested information for all donors who donated an amount aggregating $1,000 or more since the first day of the preceding calendar year to the person or entity making the disbursement.

After itemizing the donations, subtotal each Schedule 9-A. (You may use multiple pages.) Add the subtotals

on the last page of Schedule 9-A, and carry the total to Line 9 of Form 9.

INSTRUCTIONS FOR SCHEDULE 9-B (DISBURSEMENT(S) MADE OR OBLIGATIONS)

For each disbursement made or contract executed, including each disbursement made or contract executed prior to exceeding the $10,000 threshold, provide the requested information. If the payee is an individual, list that individual's occupation and employer. Additionally, list each federal candidate clearly identified in the communication, including the office sought and the election that the disbursement/obligation is made for. Along with listing the specific purpose of the disbursement (e.g., radio ad, television ad), list the title of the communication as named by the media vendor or producer of the communication. (Titles of individual communications should remain the same throughout their various public distributions unless the content changes.) Also list the communication date for the electioneering communication. In most instances, this date will be the Date of Public Distribution. If the maker of the electioneering communication is also required to report disbursements related to other electioneering communications (e.g., electioneering communications with costs below the $10,000 threshold), the disbursements listed on Schedule 9-B must indicate the other electioneering communication's title in the purpose line, the date the electioneering communication was publicly distributed and the federal candidate that was clearly identified in the communication.

After itemizing the disbursements/obligations, subtotal each Schedule 9-B. (You may use multiple pages). Add the subtotals on the last page of Schedule 9-B, and carry the total to Line 10 on Form 9.

This form may be duplicated.

Appendix B

Sample PAC Articles of Organization

_____CORPORATION POLITICAL ACTION COMMITTEE ARTICLES OF ORGANIZATION

ARTICLE I: NAME

There is hereby established the _____ Political Action Committee (hereinafter called "_____ PAC").

ARTICLE II: PRINCIPLE OFFICE AND ADDRESS

The principal office and address of _____ PAC shall be:

_____

_____

ARTICLE III: ORGANIZATION

_____ PAC shall be a voluntary, nonprofit, unincorporated political association. _____ PAC shall be independent of any political party, candidate, or organization except that _____ Corp. shall defray all the costs and expenses incurred in the establishment and administration of, and in the solicitation of contributions to _____ PAC, to the extent and in the manner such costs and expenses may be defrayed by _____ Corp. under applicable federal and state law. None of the funds used to defray the establishment, administrative, or solicitation expenses shall come from any foreign entity or source. All other costs and expenses of the PAC shall be paid out of the separate segregated fund as defined in Article VII below.

ARTICLE IV: PURPOSE

The purpose of _____ PAC is to support and encourage the election to federal offices of persons who support the needs of business in a free and healthy economy and to engage in political activities permitted by the federal election campaign laws, regulations promulgated thereunder by the Federal Election Commission, and relevant state law. _____ PAC will also provide programming and activities to educate and involve _____ employees in the political process.

To achieve these purposes, _____ PAC is empowered to solicit and accept voluntary contributions from eligible shareholders, executive, or administrative personnel, and their families. Only United States citizens or individuals who are lawfully admitted for permanent residence in the United States as defined by 8 U.S.C. § 1101(a)(20) may be solicited for contributions, and _____ PAC will not accept contributions from any individual who is not a United States citizen or lawfully admitted for permanent residence in the United States as defined above. See 11 C.F.R. § 110.20. _____ PAC also is empowered to spend such contributions to influence the nomination for election, and the election, of candidates for federal elective public offices who are believed to be in general agreement with the purposes of _____ PAC. In carrying out the forgoing, _____ PAC is empowered to make contributions to the full extent approved by law to federal candidates and committees.

ARTICLE V: MEMBERSHIP

The members of _____ PAC shall consist of all _____ shareholders, employees, and their families who have contributed to the PAC during the current or the preceding calendar year, provided such individuals are United States citizens or lawfully admitted for permanent residence in the United States.

ARTICLE VI: CONTRIBUTIONS

Section 1: All contributions to _____ PAC shall be voluntary, and no contribution to _____ PAC shall be solicited or secured by physical force, job discrimination, or financial reprisal, or by the threat thereof, or as a condition of employment with _____ Corp., or obtained in any commercial transaction.

Section 2: No contribution shall be accepted, and no expenditure shall be made, by or on behalf of _____ PAC at a time when there is a vacancy in the office of Treasurer.

Section 3: No member of _____ PAC, or contributor thereto, shall have a right to share personally in any funds or assets of _____ PAC upon its dissolution, or at any other time.

Section 4: The expenditure of any funds of _____ PAC shall be within the sole discretion of _____ PAC's Steering Committee.

Section 5: Policies with respect to the availability of payroll deduction and its procedures, and regarding expenditures or distribution of all designated and undesignated contributions, shall be within the sole discretion of _____ PAC as permitted by law and in accordance with these Articles of Organization.

Section 6: Contributions shall be in the form of a check or other comparable bank instrument or authorized payroll deduction. No cash contributions shall be accepted.

Section 7: _____ PAC will not make contributions to, or expenditures on behalf of, political parties and/or their committees.

ARTICLE VII: SEPARATE SEGREGATED FUND

All contributions to _____ PAC shall be maintained by the PAC as a separate, segregated fund, and all expenditures by _____ PAC in support of any candidate or political committee shall be made from such fund and from no other source. All books, records, and accounts of _____ PAC shall be separate from those of _____ Corp.

ARTICLE VIII: OFFICERS

Section 1: The officers of _____ PAC shall be a Chairman, two Vice Chairmen, a Secretary, a Treasurer, and an Assistant Treasurer, all of whom must be United States citizens and who shall be designated by the Chief Executive Officer of _____ Corp.

Section 2: The chief executive officer of _____ Corp. shall be Chairman of _____ PAC and shall, subject to the determination of the Steering Committee provided in Article IX hereof, administer the financial affairs of _____ PAC. The Chairman shall preside at meetings of _____ PAC or the Steering Committee.

Section 3: The chief financial officer of _____ Corp. shall be the Treasurer of _____ PAC. The Treasurer shall have general responsibility for all funds collected by _____ PAC and shall cause all funds to be deposited and all books of account to be kept in accordance with the directives of the Steering Committee, and in conformance with all applicable laws and regulations. The Treasurer shall cause an audit to be made of the books of _____ PAC at least once during every two-year election cycle.

Section 4: During the absence or incapacity of the Chairman, the Treasurer shall assume the duties and exercise the powers of the Chairman. The Treasurer shall perform such other duties as may be assigned by these Articles, or by the Chairman.

Section 5: During the absence or incapacity of the Treasurer, or when circumstances prevent the Treasurer from acting, the Assistant Treasurer shall perform the duties, and exercise the powers, of the Treasurer. Both the Treasurer and Assistant Treasurer shall be designated agents of _____ PAC for the purpose of signing all FEC reports and other _____ PAC documents.

Section 6: The Treasurer shall designate an employee of _____ Corp. who is a United States citizen to open an account for _____ PAC contributions. Further, funds deposited in such accounts may be withdrawn by check of the PAC or other orders for the payment of money drawn in the name of the PAC when signed by any two of the Chairman, Vice Chairmen, Secretary, Treasurer, or Assistant Treasurer of the PAC.

ARTICLE IX: STEERING COMMITTEE

Section 1: The financial affairs of _____ PAC, including particularly the making of any contributions to candidates or political committees, shall be supervised and directed by the Steering Committee, which shall consist of no fewer than five members, all of whom shall be designated by the Chief Executive Officer of _____ Corp. All members of the Steering Committee must be United States citizens or lawfully admitted to the United States for permanent residence. The Chairman of _____ PAC shall serve as a member of the Steering Committee and as its Chairman. Other members of the Committee shall be the Secretary, Treasurer, and/or the Assistant Treasurer of _____ PAC.

Section 2: If a vacancy shall occur on the Steering Committee, the Chairman may appoint someone to fill the vacated position in accordance with Section 1 above. A quorum of the Steering Committee for the transaction of business shall consist of a majority of its members.

ARTICLE X: MEETINGS

Section 1: Meetings of the Steering Committee shall be held quarterly at a place and time designated by the Chairman or Treasurer. The Steering Committee shall act by a majority of the members present.

Section 2: A majority of the members of the Steering Committee may call for a meeting of the Steering Committee at any other time when such members deem it necessary or expedient that a question relating to the affairs of _____ PAC be considered. Meetings of the Steering Committee called by a majority of its members must be held within thirty (30) days after the request has been received by the Chairman.

Section 3: Meetings of the Steering Committee may be held through communications equipment if all persons participating can communicate with each other, and such participation shall constitute presence at such a meeting.

ARTICLE XI: REPORTS

The Chairman shall cause to be prepared a written annual report which shall cover the activities of _____ PAC for the preceding calendar year. Such reports shall set forth (a) the total amount of contributions to _____ PAC, (b) the identity of all recipients of political disbursements by _____ PAC, and (c) the amount disbursed to each recipient. This report shall be available for inspection by the Membership of _____ PAC.

ARTICLE XII: AUDIT

An audit of the accounting books of _____ PAC shall be performed at least once during every two-year election cycle to ensure compliance with the Federal Election Campaign Act of 1971, as amended, and its regulations, and all other applicable laws. Such audits shall be initiated within sixty (60) days after the close of each election year.

ARTICLE XIII: INDEMNIFICATION

Subject to the general provisions of the Articles of Incorporation and Bylaws of _____ Corp., and without a view toward limitation of such provisions, in case any person was or is a party, or is threatened to be made a party, to any threatened, pending, or completed action, suit, or proceeding, whether civil, criminal, administrative, or investigative, other than any action by or in the right of _____ Corp., by reason of the fact that he or she is or was an officer of _____ PAC, or is or was serving at the request of _____ Corp. as an officer, employee, or agent of _____ PAC, _____ Corp. shall indemnify such person against expenses, including attorneys' fees, judgments, decrees, fines, penalties, and amounts paid in settlement actually and reasonably incurred by him or her in connection with such action, suit, or proceeding, if he or she acted in good faith and in a manner he or she reasonably believed to be in or not opposed to the best interests of _____ Corp., and with respect to any matter the subject of a criminal action, suit, or proceeding, he or she had no reasonable cause to believe that his or her conduct was unlawful. The termination of any action, suit, or proceeding by judgment, order, settlement, or conviction, or upon a plea of nolo contendere or its equivalent, shall not, itself, create a presumption that the person did not act in good faith and in a manner which he or she reasonably believed to be in or not opposed to the best interests of _____ Corp., and with respect to any matter the subject of a criminal action, suit, or proceeding, that he or she had reasonable cause to believe that his or her conduct was unlawful. And,

Subject to the general provisions of the Articles of Incorporation and Bylaws of _____ Corp., and without a view toward limitation of such provisions, in case any person was or is a party, or is threatened to be made a party, to any threatened, pending, or completed action or suit by or in the right of _____ Corp. to procure a judgment in its favor by reason of the fact that he or she is or was an officer of _____ PAC, or is or was serving at the request of _____ Corp. as an officer, employee, or agent of _____ PAC, _____ Corp. shall indemnify such person against expenses, including attorneys' fees, actually and reasonably incurred by him or her in connection with the defense or settlement of such action or suit if he or she acted in good faith and in a manner he or she reasonably believed to be in or not opposed to the best interests of _____ Corp., except that no indemnification shall be made in respect of any claim, issue, or matter as to which such person shall have been adjudged to be liable for negligence or misconduct in the performance of his or her duty to _____ Corp., unless and only to the extent that the court in which such action or suit was brought shall determine upon application that, despite the adjudication of liability, but in view of all the circumstances of the case, such person is fairly and reasonably entitled to indemnity for such expenses as the court shall deem proper. And,

To the extent that an officer, employee or agent of _____ PAC has been successful on the merits or otherwise in defense of any action, suit, or proceeding referred to above or in defense of any claim, issue, or matter therein, _____ Corp. shall indemnify him or her against expenses, including attorneys' fees, actually and reasonably incurred by him or her in connection therewith.

ARTICLE XIV: ADOPTION AND AMENDMENTS

These Articles shall be effective _____, 20__.

These Articles may be amended from time to time by action of a majority of the Steering Committee.

ARTICLE XV: DISSOLUTION

While the duration of _____ PAC is to be perpetual, _____ PAC may be dissolved at any time by a majority vote of the Steering Committee. In that event, all remaining funds shall be distributed in a manner consistent with Article VI hereof.

Adopted and executed as of this _____ day of _____, 20__, at _____.

_____   _____

Chairman   Treasurer

Sworn and subscribed to before me
this _____ day of _____, 20____

_____

Notary Public

My Commission expires: _____

Appendix C

Federal Contribution Limits

Contribution Limits 2003–2004

	To each candidate or candidate committee per election	To national party committee per calendar year	To state, district & local party committee per calendar year	To any other political committee per calendar year[3]	Special Limits
Individual may give	$2,000*	$25,000*	$10,000 (combined limit)	$5,000	$95,000* overall biennial limit: • $37,500* to all candidates • $57,500* to all PACs and parties[4]
National Party Committee may give	$5,000	No limit	No limit	$5,000	$35,000* to Senate candidate per campaign[5]
State, District & Local Party Committee may give	$5,000 (combined limit)	No limit	No limit	$5,000 (combined limit)	No limit
PAC (multicandidate)[6] may give	$5,000	$15,000	$5,000 (combined limit)	$5,000	No limit
PAC (not multicandidate) may give	$2,000[7]*	$25,000*	$10,000 (combined limit)	$5,000	No limit

* These contribution limits are indexed for inflation.

1. The chart included is reproduced from the Federal Election Commission, Contributions Brochure (available at www.fec.gov/pages/brochures/contrib.htm).

2. These limits became effective January 1, 2003.

3. A contribution earmarked for a candidate through a political committee counts against the original contributor's limit for that candidate. In certain circumstances, the contribution may also count against the contributor's limit to the PAC. 11 CFR 110.6. See also 11 CFR 110.1(h).

4. No more than $37,500 of this amount may be contributed to state and local party committees and PACs.

5. This limit is shared by the national committee and the Senate campaign committee.

6. A multicandidate committee is a political committee with more than 50 contributors which has been registered for at least 6 months and, with the exception of state party committees, has made contributions to 5 or more candidates for federal office. 11 CFR 100.5(e)(3).

7. A federal candidate's authorized committee(s) may contribute no more than $2,000 per election to another federal candidate's authorized committee(s). 11CFR 102.12(c)(2).

CONTRIBUTION LIMITS 2005-2006 (FROM THE FEDERAL ELECTIONCOMMISSION WEBSITE)

DONORS	RECIPIENTS				SPECIAL LIMITS
	Candidate or Candidate Committee per election[1]	**State, District & Local Party Committee per year**[2]	**National Party Committee per year**[3]	**Any other Political Committee per year**[4]	
Individuals	$2,100*	$10,000 combined limit	$26,700*	$5,000	Biennial limit of $101,400* ($40,000 to all candidates and $61,400[5] to all PACs and parties)
State, District & Local Party Committee	$5,000 combined limit	No limit		$5,000 combined limit	
National Party Committee	$5,000	No limit		$5,000	$37,000* to Senate candidate per campaign[6]
PAC Multicandidate[7]	$5,000	$5,000 combined limit	$15,000	$5,000	
PAC Not Multicandidate	$2,100*[8]	$10,000 combined limit	$26,700	$5,000	

* These limits are indexed for inflation in odd-numbered years.

---

[1] Each of the following is considered a separate election with a separate limit: primary election, caucus or convention with the authority to nominate, general election, runoff election and special election.

[2] A state party committee shared its limits with local and district party committees in that state unless a local or district committee's independence can be demonstrated. These limits apply to multicandidate committees only.

[3] A party's national committee, Senate campaign committee and House campaign committee are each considered national party committees, and each have separate limits, except with respect to Senate candidates—see Special Limits column.

[4] These limits apply both to separate segregated funds (SSFs) and political action committees (PACs). Affiliated committees share the same set of limits on contributions made and received.

[5] No more than $40,000 of this amount may be contributed to state and local party committees and PACs.

[6] This limit is shared by the national committee and the Senate campaign committee.

[7] A multicandidate committee is a political committee with more than 50 contributors which has been registered for at least 6 months and, with the exception of state party committees, has made contributions to 5 or more candidates for federal office. 11 C.F.R § 100.5(e)(3).

[8] A federal candidate's authorized committee(s) may contribute no more than $2,000 per election to another federal candidates authorized committee(s). 2 U.S.C. § 432(e)(3)(B).

CONTRIBUTION LIMITS 2007-2008 (FROM THE FEDERAL ELECTIONCOMMISSION WEBSITE)

DONORS	RECIPIENTS				SPECIAL LIMITS
	Candidate or Candidate Committee per election	**State, District & Local Party Committee per year**	**National Party Committee per year**	**Any Other Political Committee per year**[1]	
Individuals	$2,300*	$10,000 combined limit	$28,500	$5,000	Biennial limit of $108,200* ($42,700* to all candidates and $65,500*[2] to all PACs and parties)
State, District & Local Party Committee	$5,000 combined limit	No limit		$5,000 combined limit	
National Party Committee	$5,000	No limit		$5,000	$39,000* to Senate candidate per campaign[3]
PAC Multicandidate[4]	$5,000	$5,000 combined limit	$15,000	$5,000	
PAC Not Multicandidate	$2,300*	$10,000 combined limit	$28,500*	$5,000	
Authorized Campaign Committee	2,000[5]	No limit		$5,000	

* These limits are indexed for inflation in odd-numbered years.

---

[1] A contribution earmarked for a candidate through a political committee counts against the original contributor's limit for that candidate. In certain circumstances, the contribution may also count against the contributor's limit to the PAC. 11 C.F.R § 110.6. See also 11 C.F.R § 110.1(h).

[2] No more than $42,700 of this amount may be contributed to state and local party committees and PACs.

[3] This limit is shared by the national committee and the Senate campaign committee.

[4] A multicandidate committee is a political committee with more than 50 contributors which has been registered for at least 6 months and, with the exception of state party committees, has made contributions to 5 or more candidates for federal office. 11 C.F.R § 100.5(e)(3).

[5] A federal candidate's authorized committee(s) may contribute no more than $2,000 per election to another federal candidate's authorized committee(s). 2 U.S.C. § 432(e)(3)(B).

Appendix D

Lobbying Forms and Guidance

Prev Page   Next Page   Go To Page ▼   Online Help   Page 1 of 3

Clerk of the House of Representatives
Legislative Resource Center
B-106 Cannon Building
Washington, DC 20515
http://lobbyingdisclosure.house.gov

Secretary of the Senate
Office of Public Records
232 Hart Building
Washington, DC 20510
http://www.senate.gov/lobby

Add Additional Update Page -->

LOBBYING REGISTRATION

Lobbying Disclosure Act of 1995 (Section 4)

Check One: ☐ New Registrant ☐ New Client for Existing Registrant ☐ Amendment

1. Effective Date of Registration _____

2. House Identification _____   Senate Identification _____

REGISTRANT   ⊙ Organization/Lobbying Firm   ⊙ Self Employed Individual

3. Registrant   Organization _____

Address _____   Address2 _____

City _____   State ▼   Zip ____ - ____   Country ▼

4. Principal place of business (if different than line 3)

City _____   State ▼   Zip ____ - ____   Country ▼

5. Contact name and telephone number   ☐ International Number

Contact ▼ _____   Telephone ( ) - ____   E-mail _____

6. General description of registrant's business or activities

_____

CLIENT   *A Lobbying Firm is required to file a separate registration for each client. Organizations employing in-house lobbyists should check the box labeled "Self" and proceed to line 10.*   ☐ Self

7. Client name _____

Address _____

City _____   State ▼   Zip ____ - ____   Country ▼

8. Principal place of business (if different than line 7)

City _____   State ▼   Zip ____ - ____   Country ▼

9. General description of client's business or activities _____

LOBBYISTS

10. Name of each individual who has acted or is expected to act as a lobbyist for the client identified on line 7. If any person listed in this section has served as a "covered executive branch official" or "covered legislative branch official" within twenty years of first acting as a lobbyist for the client, *state the executive and/or legislative position(s) in which the person served.*

Name			Covered Official Position (if applicable)
First	Last	Suffix	

v6.0.0b

| Prev. Page | Next Page | Go To Page ▼ | Online Help | Page 2 of 3 |

Registrant _____   Client Name _____

LOBBYING ISSUES

11. General lobbying issue areas (Select all applicable codes)

[▼] [▼] [▼] [▼] [▼] [▼] [▼] [▼] [▼]

12. Specific lobbying issues (current and anticipated)

AFFILIATED ORGANIZATIONS

13. Is there an entity other than the client that contributes more than $5,000 to the lobbying activities of the registrant in a quarterly period and either actively participates in and/or in whole or in major part plans, supervises or controls the registrant's lobbying activities?

☐ No --> Go to line 14.   ☐ Yes --> Complete the rest of this section for each entity matching the criteria above, then proceed to line 14.

Internet Address: _____

Name	Address				Principal Place of Business
	Street				
	City	State/Province	Zip Code	Country	
					City
		▼		▼	State ▼ Country ▼
					City
		▼		▼	State ▼ Country ▼
					City
		▼		▼	State ▼ Country ▼

FOREIGN ENTITIES

14. Is there any foreign entity

    a) holds at least 20% equitable ownership in the client or any organization identified on line 13: or
    b) directly or indirectly, in whole or in major part, plans, supervises, controls, directs, finances or subsidizes activities of the client or any organization identified on line 13, or
    c) is an affiliate of the client or any organization identified on line 13 and has a direct interest in the outcome of the lobbying activity?

☐ No --> Sign and date the registration   ☐ Yes --> Complete the rest of this section for each entity matching the criteria above, then sign the registration.

Name	Address			Principal place of business (city and state or country)	Amount of contribution for lobbying activities	Ownership
	Street					
	City	State/Province	Country			
				City		
		▼	State ▼	Country ▼		%
				City		
		▼	State ▼	Country ▼		%

Signature   [Click here to digitally sign this form with your password] _____   Date _____

Printed Name and Title _____

File with Congress
[Submit]

Prev. Page | Next Page | Go To Page ▼   Online Help   Page 3 of 3
                                                                           Delete Page

Registrant _____   Client Name _____

ADDITIONAL LOBBYISTS

10. Supplemental. List any additional lobbyists for this client not listed on page 1, number 10.

Name			Covered Official Position (if applicable)
First	Last	Suffix	

ADDITIONAL LOBBYING ISSUES

11. Supplemental. General lobbying issue areas. Enter any additional codes for issues not listed on page 2, number 11.

▼   ▼   ▼   ▼   ▼   ▼   ▼   ▼   ▼

ADDITIONAL AFFILIATED ORGANIZATIONS

13. Supplemental. List any other affiliated organization thats meets the criteria specified and is not listed on page 2, number 13.

Name	Address				Principal Place of Business		
	Street						
	City	State/Province	Zip Code	Country	City		
		▼		▼	State	▼ Country	▼
					City		
		▼		▼	State	▼ Country	▼
					City		
		▼		▼	State	▼ Country	▼

ADDITIONAL FOREIGN ENTITIES

14. Supplemental. List any other foreign entity that meets the criteria specified and is not listed on page 2, number 14.

Name	Address			Principal place of business (city and state or country)			Amount of contribution for lobbying activities	Ownership
	Street			City				
	City	State/Province	Country	State	▼ Country	▼		%
		▼	▼	City				
				State	▼ Country	▼		%
		▼	▼	City				
				State	▼ Country	▼		%

Add Additional Update Page -->

v6.0.0b

Form LD-1 Instructions

Form LD-T Registration Information

The Lobbying Disclosure Act of 1995, as amended (2 U.S.C. § 1601 et. seq.), requires lobbying firms and organizations to register and file reports of their lobbying activities with the Secretary of the Senate and the Clerk of the House of Representatives.

Form LD-1 is used for initial registration under Section 4 of the Act (2 U.S.C. § 1603). Form LD-2 is used for complying with the semiannual reporting requirements of Section 5 of the Act (2 U.S.C. § 1604).

WHO MUST REGISTER. LOBBYING FIRMS, i.e., entities with one or more lobbyists, including self-employed individuals who act as lobbyists for outside clients, are required to file a separate registration for each client. ORGANIZATIONS employing in-house lobbyists file a single registration.

A lobbying firm is exempt from registration for a particular client if its total income from that client for lobbying activities does not exceed and is not expected to exceed $5,500 during a semiannual period. An organization employing in-house lobbyists is exempt from registration if its total expenses for lobbying activities do not exceed and are not expected to exceed $22,500 during a semiannual period.

WHEN TO REGISTER. Registration is required no later than 45 days after a lobbyist first makes a lobbying contact or is employed or retained to make a lobbying contact.

WHERE TO REGISTER. Prepare two originals of Form LD-1 and file one with each office listed below:

Secretary of the Senate   Clerk of the House of Representatives
Office of Public Records   Legislative Resource Center
232 Hart Senate Office Building   **AND**   B-106 Cannon House Office Building
Washington, DC 20510   Washington, DC 20515

PUBLIC AVAILABILITY. The Act requires the Secretary of the Senate and the Clerk of the House of Representatives to make all registrations and reports available to the public as soon as practicable after they are received.

ADDENDUM. If the space on Form LD-1 is insufficient for any required information, attach additional pages as needed, clearly stating the name of the registrant and client and identifying the line number(s) to which the information pertains.

AMENDMENTS. A registrant must immediately file an amended Form LD-1: (1) if notified of a defect in the original filing by the Secretary of the Senate or the Clerk of the House of Representatives; or (2) if erroneously reported information is discovered by the registrant. Once registered, updated information (name and address changes, new lobbyists, new issue area codes, etc.) must be disclosed in the registrant's next semiannual report (See Form LD- 2 instructions for details).

TERMINATION. A registrant terminates a registration by submitting a completed LD-2 report, indicating termination, to the Secretary of the Senate (Office of Public Records) and the Clerk of the House of Representatives (Legislative Resource Center).

REVIEW AND COMPLIANCE. The Secretary of the Senate (Office of Public Records) and the Clerk of the House (Legislative Resource Center) must review, verify, and request corrections in writing to ensure the accuracy, completeness, and timelinessof registrations filed under the Act.

PENALTIES. Whoever knowingly fails: (1) to correct a defective filing within 60 days after notice of such a defect by the Secretary of the Senate or the Clerk of the House; or (2) to comply with any other provision of the Act, may be subject to a civil fine of not more than $50,000.

FOR FURTHER INFORMATION. Contact the Senate Office of Public Records, 232 Hart Senate Office Building, Washington, DC 20510, (202) 224-0758, or the House Legislative Resource Center, B-106 Cannon House Office Building, Washington, DC 20515, (202) 226-5200.

Instructions for completing the Form LD-1

Technical Requirements: You need to have the following versions of these browsers or higher—Internet Explorer 5.x or Netscape 4.7 in order to use the new forms. Type the information into each field on the form. When all the information has been entered into that field, press the TAB key to move to the next field. When all of the fields have been completed, press the ENTER key. To print the form, press the PRINT FORM button at the top of the form. This will print the form on the printer designated by your computer.

Line-By-Line Instructions for completing the Form LD-1

LINE 1. EFFECTIVE DATE OF REGISTRATION: Enter the date that the registrant is retained by the client or first makes a lobbying contact, whichever is earlier. If the effective date is prior to the end of a quarterly reporting period, a lobbying report must be filed detailing the activity for that quarterly period.

LINE 2. IDENTIFICATION NUMBER: Leave this line blank if this is an initial registration. The House ID will be assigned by the Legislative Resource Center after the registration is processed and will be unique to each registrant-client relationship. The Senate ID will be assigned by the Office of Public Records and will be unique to each registrant-client relationship. After being notified of this number, use it in all correspondence pertaining to this relationship.

LINE 3. REGISTRANT NAME AND ADDRESS: If the registrant is a lobbying firm or an organization employing in-house lobbyists, enter the full legal name, any trade name, and mailing address. Individual lobbyists do not register unless they are self-employed, in which case they register as firms and **indicate their own names, and any trade** or **business name.** A full address is required to complete the filing.

LINE 4. PRINCIPAL PLACE OF BUSINESS: Indicate the city, state, and country of the registrant's principal place of business, if different from the address on line 3.

LINE 5. TELEPHONE NUMBER, CONTACT NAME AND E-MAIL: Enter the full name of the person to contact for any questions concerning the registration. Enter the telephone number, including area code. Please use the 222-222-2222 format. Enter the contact e-mail address. A telephone number, contact name and e-mail address are required to complete the filing.

LINE 6. GENERAL DESCRIPTION OF REGISTRANT'S BUSINESS OR ACTIVITIES: Provide a general description of the registrant's business or activities, e.g. "manufacturing," "computer software developer," "law firm," "public relations firm," "self-employed public affairs consultant," "social welfare organization," etc. The business description is required to complete the filing.

LINE 7. CLIENT NAME AND ADDRESS: For an organization lobbying on its own behalf, check the box labeled 'SELF'. When 'Self' is checked, the registrant name is inserted automatically in the client name line. For a lobbying firm or self-employed lobbyist lobbying on behalf of a client, DO NOT check "Self". Instead, state the name and address of the client. Lobbying firms must file a separate registration for each client. The client address is required in this case.

LINE 8. CLIENT PRINCIPAL PLACE OF BUSINESS: If 'Self' is not checked, indicate the client's principal place of business (city and state and country), if different from line 7.

LINE 9. GENERAL DESCRIPTION OF CLIENT'S BUSINESS OR ACTIVITIES: If 'Self' is not checked, provide a general description of the business or activities of the client (see instructions to line 6 for examples).

LINE 10. LOBBYISTS: List the name of each individual who acted or is expected to act as a lobbyist for the client identified on line 7. If any person listed in this section has served as a "covered executive branch official" or "covered legislative branch official" within twenty years of first acting as a lobbyist for the client, identify that person as a "covered official" and state the executive and/or legislative position in which the person served. Self-employed lobbyists must restate their names on this line and indicate any covered status as described above.

Note that an individual whose lobbying activities for the client are less than 20% of that individual's total services to the client (as measured by time spent during any three month period) is not considered a lobbyist.

LINE 11. LOBBYING ISSUES: Select categories from the following list that most closely match the client's lobbying issue areas. The form provides a list of descriptions and corresponding codes (for reference only) in a select box above the fields where the codes are to be entered. Select each applicable code from the small select boxes on line 11. Enter as many as necessary to accurately reflect all actual and anticipated lobbying activities.

ACC	Accounting	HCR	Health Issues
ADV	Advertising	HOU	Housing
AER	Aerospace	IMM	Immigration
ACR	Agriculture	IND	Indian/Native American Affairs
ALC	Alcohol & Drug Abuse	INS	Insurance
ANI	Animals	LBR	Labor Issues/Antitrust/Workplace
APP	Apparel/Clothing Industry/Textiles	LAW	Law Enforcement/Crime/Criminal Justice
ART	Arts/Entertainment	MAN	Manufacturing
AUT	Automotive Industry	MAR	Marine/Maritime/Boating/Fisheries
AVI	Aviation/Aircraft/Airlines	MIA	Media (Information/Publishing)
BAN	Banking	MED	Medical/Disease Research/Clinical Labs
BNK	Bankruptcy	MMM	Medicare/Medicaid
BEV	Beverage Industry	MON	Minling/Money/Gold Standard
BUD	Budget/Appropriations	NAT	Natural Resources
CHM	Chemicals/Chemical Industry	PHA	Pharmacy
CIV	Civil Rights/Civil Liberties	POS	Postal
CAW	Clean Air & Water (Quality)	RRR	Railroads
CDT	Commodities (Big Ticket)	RES	Real Estate/Land Use/Conservation
COM	Communications/Broadcasting/Radio/TV	REL	Religion
CPI	Computer Industry	RET	Retirement
CSP	Consumer Issues/Safety/Protection	ROD	Roads/Highway
CON	Constitution	SCI	Science/Technology
CPT	Copyright/Patent/Trademark	SMB	Small Business
DEF	Defense	SPO	Sports/Athletics
DOC	District of Columbia	TAX	Taxation/Internal Revenue Code
DIS	Disaster Planning/Emergencies	TEC	Telecommunications
ECN	Economics/Economic Development	TOB	Tobacco
EDU	Education	TOR	Torts
ENG	Energy/Nuclear	TRD	Trade (Domestic & Foreign)
ENV	Environmental/Superfund	TRA	Transporation
FAM	Family Issues/Abortion/Adoption	TOU	Travel/Tourism
FIR	Firearms/Guns/Ammunition	TRU	Trucking/Shipping
FIN	Financial Institutions/Investments/Securities	URB	Urban development/Municipalities
		UNM	Unemployment
FOO	Food Industry (Safety, Labeling, etc.)	UTI	Utilities
FOR	Foreign Relations	VET	Veterans
FUE	Fuel/Gas/Oil	WAS	Waste (hazardous/solid/interestate/nuclear)
GAM	Gaming/Gambling/Casino		
GOV	Government Issues	WEL	Welfare

LINE 12. SPECIFIC LOBBYING ISSUES: Identify the client's specific issues that have been addressed (as of the date of the registration) or are likely to be addressed in lobbying activities. Include, for example, specific bills before Congress or specific executive branch actions.

BE SPECIFIC, but brief. Bill numbers alone do not satisfy the requirements for reporting on this line and restatement of the general issue code is insufficient. Use the following format to describe legislation: BILL NO, BILL TITLE, AND DESCRIPTION OF THE SPECIFIC SECTION(S) OF INTEREST, i.e.;

"H.R. 3610, Department of Defense Appropriations Act of 1996, Title 2, all provisions relating to environmental restoration."

For specific issues other than legislation, provide detailed descriptions of lobbying efforts. Do not leave line blank. No additional space is available, so please abbreviate and enter the information in paragraph format to maximize space.

LINE 13. AFFILIATED ORGANIZATIONS: Identify the name, address, and principal place of business of any entity other than the client that contributes in excess of $5,000 toward the registrant's lobbying activities in a quarterly period **and** actively participates in the planning, supervision, or control of such activities.

Either 'No' or 'Yes' must be checked for each level of affiliation. The LDA amendments require disclosure of some affiliates that were heretofore undisclosed, and retained the requirement for **listing** those affiliates that contribute in excess of $5,000 **and** in whole or major part (20%) plans, supervises or controls such lobbying activities.

If 'No' is checked, the affiliated organization lines will be 'skipped'. If 'Yes' is checked, at least one affiliated organization name and address is required. If 'No' is checked after information has been entered in the lines, the information will be deleted.

The LDA Amendments state in part: "No disclosure is required under paragraph (3)(B) if the organization that would be identified as affiliated with the client is listed on the client's publicly accessible Internet website as being a member of or contributor to the client unless the organization in whole or in major part plans, supervises or controls such lobbying activities." If a registrant relies upon the preceding sentence, the registrant must disclose the specific Internet address of the web page containing the information relied upon. If the registrant chooses to use the website, it is responsible for ensuring that the web page remains valid and accurate until a new LD-2 is filed with updated information. Please enter the URL underneath the address of any affiliates that apply.

LINE 14. FOREIGN ENTITIES: Identify the name, address, principal place of business, amount of any contribution in excess of $5,000, and the approximate percentage of equitable ownership in the client of any foreign entity that:

- holds at least 20% equitable ownership in the client or any organization identified on line 13; or;

- directly or indirectly, in whole or in major part, plans, supervises, controls, directs, finances, or subsidizes activities of the client or any organization identified on line 13; or;

- is an affiliate of the client or any organization identified on line 13 and has direct interest in the outcome of the lobbying activity.

Either 'No' or 'Yes' must be checked. If 'No' is checked, the foreign entity lines will be 'skipped'. If 'Yes' is checked, at least one foreign entity name, address, principal place of business, contribution amount and percentage of ownership is required. If no contribution was made and no ownership exists, enter zero in those fields. If 'No' is checked after information has been entered in the lines, the information will be deleted.

PRINTED NAME AND TITLE: Enter the name and title of the person who will sign the filing. The signer must be the officer or employee of the registrant who is responsible for the accuracy of the information contained in the registration.

GENERAL LOBBYING ISSUE AREAS: Select those from the following list that most closely match the client's lobbying issue areas. Enter the corresponding codes on line 11.

ACC	Accounting	HOM	Homeland Security
ADV	Advertising	HOU	Housing
AER	Aerospace	IMM	Immigration
AGR	Agriculture	IND	Indian/Native American Affairs
ALC	Alcohol & Drug Abuse	INS	Insurance
AMI	Animals	LBR	Labor Issues/Antitrust/Workplace
APP	Apparel/Clothing Industry/Textiles	LAW	Law Enforcement/Crime/Criminal Justice
ART	Arts/Entertainment	MAN	Manufacturing
AUT	Automotive Industry	MAR	Marine/Maritime/Boating/Fisheries
AVI	Aviation/Aircraft/Airlines	MIA	Media (Information/Publishing)
BAN	Banking	MED	Medical/Disease Research/Clinical Labs
BNK	Bankruptcy	MMM	Medicare/Medicaid
BEV	Beverage Industry	MON	Minting/Money/Gold Standard
BUD	Budget/Appropriations	NAT	Natural Resources
CHM	Chemicals/Chemical Industry	PHA	Pharmacy
CIV	Civil Rights/Civil Liberties	POS	Postal
CAW	Clean Air & Water (Quality)	RRR	Railroads
CDT	Commodities (Big Ticket)	RES	Real Estate/Land Use/Conservation
COM	Communications/Broadcasting/Radio/TV	REL	Religion
CPI	Computer Industry	RET	Retirement
CSP	Consumer Issues/Safety/Protection	ROD	Roads/Highway
CON	Constitution	SCI	Science/Technology
CPT	Copyright/Patent/Trademark	SMB	Small Business
DEF	Defense	SPO	Sports/Athletics
DOC	District of Columbia	TAX	Taxation/Internal Revenue Code
DIS	Disaster Planning/Emergencies	TEC	Telecommunications
ECN	Economics/Economic Development	TOB	Tobacco
EDU	Education	TOR	Torts
ENG	Energy/Nuclear	TRD	Trade (Domestic & Foreign)
ENV	Environmental/Superfund	TRA	Transportation
FAM	Family Issues/Abortion/Adoption	TOU	Travel/Tourism
FIR	Firearms/Guns/Ammunilion	TRU	Trucking/Shipping
FIN	Financial Insutitutions/Investments/Securities	URB	Urban Development/Municipalities
FOO	Food Industry (Safety, Labeling, etc.)	UNM	Unemployment
FOR	Foreign Relations	UTI	Utilities
FUE	Fuel/Gas/Oil	VET	Veterans
GAM	Gaming/Gambling/Casino	WAS	Waste (hazardous/solid/interstate/nuclear)
GOV	Government Issues	WEL	Welfare
HCR	Health Issues		

| Prev. Page | Next Page | Go To Page ▼ | | Online Help | | Page 2 of 5 |

Registrant _____   Client Name _____

LOBBYING ACTIVITY. Select as many codes as necessary to reflect the general issue areas in which the registrant engaged in lobbying on behalf of the client during the reporting period. Using a separate page for each code, provide information as requested. Add additional page(s) as needed.

15. General issue area code   [Select] ▼ [_____]   (one per page)

16. Specific lobbying issues   [Add page to continue specific issues description for this issue ...]

[   ]

17. House(s) of Congress and Federal agencies   ❑ Check if None

Complete List of Agencies: Selected Agencies:

U.S. HOUSE OF REPRESENTATIVES	[Add --->]	
U.S. SENATE		
Administration for Children & Families (ACF)	[<---Remove]	
Administration on Aging		
Advisory Council on Historic Preservation (ACHP)		
African Development Foundation		
Agency for Health Care Policy & Research		
Agency for Toxic Substances & Disease Registry		
Agriculture - Dept of (USDA)		
Air Force - Dept of		
Alcohol & Tobacco Tax & Trade Bureau (TTB)		
Alternative Agricultural Research & Commercialization Center		
American Battle Monuments Commission		

18. Name of each individual who acted as a lobbyist in this issue area   [Add a page to continue adding lobbyists for this issue ...]

First Name	Last Name	Suffix	Covered Official Position (if applicable)	New
				❑
				❑
				❑
				❑
				❑
				❑
				❑
				❑
				❑

19. Interest of each foreign entity in the specific issues listed on line 16 above   ❑ Check if None

[   ]

[Add Additional Issue Page -->]

Registrant _____ Client Name _____

LOBBYING ACTIVITY. Select as many codes as necessary to reflect the general issue areas in which the registrant engaged in lobbying on behalf of the client during the reporting period. Using a separate page for each code, provide information as requested. Add additional page(s) as needed.

15. General issue area code. [Select] ▼ [_____] (one per page)

16. Specific lobbying issues   Add page to continue specific issues description for this issue -->

17. House(s) of Congress and Federal agencies   ❑ Check if None

Complete List of Agencies: Selected Agencies:

U.S. HOUSE OF REPRESENTATIVES
U.S. SENATE
Administration for Children & Families (ACF)
Administration on Aging
Advisory Council on Historic Preservation (ACHP)
African Development Foundation
Agency for Health Care Policy & Research
Agency for Toxic Substances & Disease Registry
Agriculture - Dept of (USDA)
Air Force - Dept of
Alcohol & Tobacco Tax & Trade Bureau (TTB)
Alternative Agricultural Research & Commercialization Center
American Battle Monuments Commission

[Add -->] [<-- Remove]

18. Name of each individual who acted as a lobbyist in this issue area   Add a page to continue adding lobbyists for this issue -->

First Name	Last Name	Suffix	Covered Official Position (if applicable)	New
				❑
				❑
				❑
				❑
				❑
				❑
				❑
				❑
				❑

19. Interest of each foreign entity in the specific issues listed on line 16 above   ❑ Check if None

Add Additional Issue Page -->

Printed Name and Title _____

v6.0.1

Prev. Page	Next Page	Go To Page ▼		Online Help		Page 3 of 5
						Delete Page

ADDENDUM for General Lobbying Issue Area:

Add page to continue specific issues description for this issue

Printed Name and Title

v6.0.1

Prev. Page | Next Page | Go To Page ▼ | Online Help | Page 4 of 5 | Delete Page

Registrant _____ Client Name _____

ADDENDUM for General Lobbying Issue ⎮_____

	Name			Covered Official Position (if applicable)	New
First	Last	Suffix			

Add a page to continue adding lobbyists for this issue ▷

Printed Name and Title _____
v6.0.1

Prev. Page	Next Page	Go To Page ▼		Online Help		Page 5 of 5
						Delete Page

Registrant _____   Client Name _____

Information Update Page - Complete ONLY where registration information has changed.

20. Client new address

Address _____

City _____ State ▼ Zip Code ___-___ Country ▼

21. Client new principal place of business (if different than line 20)

City _____ State ▼ Zip Code ___-___ Country ▼

22. New General description of client's business or activities

_____

LOBBYIST UPDATE

23. Name of each previously reported individual who is no longer expected to act as a lobbyist for the client

First Name	Last Name	Suffix	First Name	Last Name	Suffix
1			3		
2			4		

ISSUE UPDATE

24. General lobbying issue that no longer pertains

▼	▼	▼	▼	▼	▼	▼	▼	▼

AFFILIATED ORGANIZATIONS

25. Add the following affiliated organization(s)

Internet Address: _____

Name	Address		Principal Place of Business (city and state or country)
	Street Address		
	City	State/Province Zip Country	
			City
	▼	▼	State ▼ Country ▼
			City
	▼	▼	State ▼ Country ▼

26. Name of each previously reported organization that is no longer affiliated with the registrant or client

1	2	3

FOREIGN ENTITIES

27. Add the following foreign entities

Name	Address		Principal place of business (city and state or country)	Amount of contribution for lobbying activities	Ownership percentage in client
	Street Address				
	City	State/Province Country			
			City		
	▼	▼	State ▼ Country ▼		%

28. Name of each previously reported foreign entity that no longer owns, or controls, or is affiliated with the registrant, client or affiliated organization

1	3	5
2	4	6

Add Additional Update Page →

Printed Name and Title _____

v6.0.1

GENERAL LOBBYING ISSUE AREAS: Select those from the following list that most closely match the client's lobbying issue areas. Enter the corresponding codes on line 15.

ACC	Accounting	HOM	Homeland Security
ADV	Advertising	HOU	Housing
AER	Aerospace	IMM	Immigration
AGR	Agriculture	IND	Indian/Native American Affairs
ALC	Alcohol & Drug Abuse	INS	Insurance
ANI	Animals	LBR	Labor Issues/Antitrust/Workplace
APP	Apparel/Clothing Industry/Textiles	LAW	Law Enforcement/Crime/Criminal Justice
ART	Arts/Entertainment	MAN	Manufacturing
AUT	Automotive Industry	MAR	Marine/Maritime/Boating/Fisheries
AVI	Aviation/Aircraft/Airlines	MIA	Media (Information/Publishing)
BAN	Banking	MED	Medical/Disease Research/Clinical Labs
BNK	Bankruptcy	MMM	Medicare/Medicaid
BEV	Beverage Industry	MON	Minling/Money/Gold Standard
BUD	Budget/Appropriations	NAT	Natural Resources
CHM	Chemicals/Chemical Industry	PHA	Pharmacy
CIV	Civil Rights/Civil Liberties	POS	Postal
CAW	Clean Air & Water (Quality)	RRR	Railroads
CDT	Commodities (Big Ticket)	RES	Real Estate/Land Use/Conservation
COM	Communications/Broadcasting/Radio/TV	REL	Religion
CPI	Computer Industry	RET	Retirement
CSP	Consumer Issues/Safety/Protection	ROD	Roads/Highway
CON	Constitution	SCI	Science/Technology
CPT	Copyrighl/Patent/Trademark	SMB	Small Business
DBF	Defense	SPO	Sports/Athletics
DOC	District of Columbia	TAX	Taxation/Internal Revenue Code
DIS	Disaster Planning/Emergencies	TEC	Telecommunications
ECN	Economics/Economic Development	TOB	Tobacco
EDU	Education	TOR	Torts
ENG	Energy/Nuclear	TRD	Trade (Domestic & Foreign)
ENV	Environmental/Superfund	TRA	Transportation
FAM	Family Issues/Abortion/Adoption	TOU	Travel/Tourism
FIR	Firearms/Guns/Ammunition	TRU	Trucking/Shipping
FIN	Financial Institutions/Investments/Securities	URB	Urban Development/Municipalities
FOO	Food Industry (Safety, Labeling, etc.)	UNM	Unemployment
FOR	Foreign Relations	UTI	Utilities
FUE	Fuel/Gas/Oil	VET	Veterans
GAM	Garning/Gambling/Casino	WAS	Waste (hazardous/solid/interstate/nuclear)
GOV	Government Issues	WEL	Welfare
HCR	Health Issues		

Form LD-2 Instructions

Form LD-2 Registration Information

The Lobbying Disclosure Act of 1995, as amended (2 U.S.C. § 1601 et. seq.), requires lobbying firms and organizations to register and file reports of their lobbying activities with the Secretary of the Senate and the Clerk of the House of Representatives.

Form LD-2 is used for complying with the semiannual reporting requirements of Section 5 of the Act (2 U.S.C. § 1604). Form LD-1 is used for initial registration under Section 4 of the Act (2 U.S.C. § 1603).

WHO MUST REPORT. A registrant must file a report for the semiannual period for which it initially registered and for each semiannual period thereafter, including the reporting period during which it terminates. **LOBBYING FIRMS,** i.e., entities with one or more lobbyists, including self-employed individuals who act as lobbyists for outside clients, are required to file a separate report for each client covered by a registration. **ORGA-NIZATIONS** employing in-house lobbyists file a single report for each semiannual period.

WHEN TO FILE. The semiannual report is required no later than 45 days after the end of a semiannual period beginning on the first day of January and the first day of July of every year in which a registrant is registered.

WHERE TO FILE. Prepare two originals of Form LD-2 and file one with each office listed below:

Secretary of the Senate   Clerk of the House of Representatives
Office of Public Records   Legislative Resource Center
232 Hart Senate Office Building   **AND**   B-106 Cannon House Office Building
Washington, DC 20510   Washington, DC 20515

PUBLIC AVAILABILITY. The Act requires the Secretary of the Senate and the Clerk of the House of Representatives to make all registrations and reports available to the public as soon as practicable after they are received.

TERMINATION REPORT. A registrant terminates by submitting a completed LD-2 report, indicating termination, no later than 45 days after the end of the reporting period in which it terminates.

REVIEW AND COMPLIANCE. The Secretary of the Senate (Office of Public Records) and the Clerk of the House (Legislative Resource Center) must review, verify, and request corrections in writing to ensure the accuracy, completeness, and timeliness of registrations filed under the Act.

ADDENDUM. If the space on Form LD-2 is insufficient for any required information, attach additional pages as needed, clearly stating the name of the registrant and client and identifying the line number(s) to which the information pertains.

AMENDMENTS. A registrant must immediatelyy file an amended Form LD-2: (1) if notified of a defect in the original filing by the Secretary of the Senate or the Clerk of the House of Representatives; or (2) if erroneously reported information is discovered by the registrant. Once registered, updated information (name and address changes, new lobbyists, new issue area codes, etc.) must be disclosed in the registrant's semiannual report.

PENALTIES. Whoever knowingly fails: (1) to correct a defective filing within 60 days after notice of such a defect by the Secretary of the Senate or the Clerk of the House; or (2) to comply with any other provision of the Act, may be subject to a civil fine of not more than $50,000.

FOR FURTHER INFORMATION. Contact the Senate Office of Public Records, 232 Hart Senate Office Building, Washington, DC 20510, (202) 224-0758, or the House Legislative Resource Center, B-106 Cannon House Office Building, Washington, DC 20515, (202) 226-5200.

Instructions for completing the Form LD-2

Technical Requirements: You need to have the following versions of these browsers or higher—Internet Explorer 5.x or Netscape 4.7 in order to use the new forms.

Type the information into each field on the form. When all the information has been entered into that field, press the TAB key to move to the next field. When all of the fields have been completed, press the ENTER key. To print the form, press the PRINT FORM button at the top of the form. This will print the form on the printer designated by your computer.

Line-By-Line Instructions for completing the Form LD-2

LINE 1. REGISTRANT NAME: Indicate the registrant's full legal name and any trade name. The name must be either the name of the lobbying firm or the name of the organization employing in-house lobbyists. Individual lobbyists do not file reports unless they are self-employed, in which case they file as firms, and indicate their own name and any trade or business names.

If the registrant is a self-employed lobbyist, click 'Individual' to switch to name fields, then select the preferred prefix and enter the first name and last name. If you used a middle name, initial or suffix when you filed, enter a middle name or initial with the first name and the suffix with the last name. For future electronic filing, it is important to enter the name exactly the same each time.

LINE 2. REGISTRANT ADDRESS: Enter the mailing address for correspondence. Mark the box if the address is different than previously reported. A full address is required to complete the filing.

Note: If you enter a new address and you do not check this box, the pre-populated templates will not be updated.

LINE 3. PRINCIPAL PLACE OF BUSINESS: Indicate the city, state and country of the registrant's principal place of business, if different from the address on line 2.

LINE 4. TELEPHONE NUMBER AND CONTACT NAME: Enter the telephone number, including area code. Please use the (222)222-2222 or 222-222-2222 format. A US telephone number is preferred. Select the preferred prefix (Mr., Ms. Mrs.), and enter the full name of the person to contact for any questions concerning the report. Enter the contact e-mail address. A telephone number, contact name and email address in valid format are required to complete the filing.

LINE 5. SENATE IDENTIFICATION NUMBER: This number, assigned by the Office of Public Records, is unique to each registrant-client relationship. Enter the number and use it in all correspondence pertaining to this relationship.

LINE 6. HOUSE IDENTIFICATION NUMBER: This 9 digit number, assigned by the Legislative Resource Center, is unique to each registrant-client relationship. Enter the nine-digit number and use it in all correspondence pertaining to this relationship. This number is required to complete the filing.

LINE 7. CLIENT NAME AND ADDRESS: For an organization lobbying on its own behalf, check the box labeled 'SELF'. When 'Self' is checked, the registrant name is inserted in the client name line.

For a lobbying firm or self-employed lobbyist lobbying on behalf of a client, DO NOT check "Self". Instead, state the name and address of the client. Lobbying firms must file a separate report for each client. The client address is required in this case.

Check the box if client is a state or local government or a department, agency, special district, or other instrumentality controlled by one or more state or local governments.

LINE 8. YEAR: Enter the year and mark the appropriate box to indicate which quarterly reporting period is covered by this report. A separate report is required for each filing period. A valid four-digit year is required to be entered. (Electronic filing is only available for reports and amendments for the year-end 2004 report and later. However, older reports or amendments may be prepared on the form and printed for filing by mail or hand delivery.)

LINE 9. AMENDED REPORT If amending a previously filed version of this report, place a mark in the box. Otherwise, leave blank.

LINE 10. TERMINATION REPORT: If lobbying for the client has ended and the registrant wishes to terminate this registration, mark the box and enter the date that lobbying activities ceased. Enter the date in mm/dd/yyyy format. It is not necessary to put '0' in front of a single digit day or month. The date must be in the filing period you have marked in Line 8. If the date entered is not in that period, an error message will be returned.

LINE 11. NO LOBBYING ISSUE ACTIVITY BOX: If there were no **lobbying issue** activity, check the box. Otherwise, file a complete report (page 2 and addendum pages as necessary) detailing the lobbying activity. If this box is checked, page 2 will no longer be displayed as it does not need to be part of the filing.

Note: You cannot check this box if you have entered information on an issue page. You must delete the entries before you can select No lobbying activity.

INCOME OR EXPENSE SUMMARY (YOU MUST COMPLETE EITHER LINE 12 OR LINE 13 AS INSTRUCTED): The form will only allow the appropriate section to be completed. Any attempt to check a box or enter an amount in the incorrect area will return an error message.

INCOME OR EXPENSE SUMMARY (ANSWER LINE 12 OR LINE 13 AS INSTRUCTED): You must complete Line 12 if lobbying on behalf of a client. You must complete line 13 if you are lobbying on your own behalf.

LINE 12. LOBBYING FIRMS (INCOME): Indicate whether income relating to lobbying activities on behalf of the client identified on line 7 was less than $5,000, or was $5,000 or more, during this reporting period by checking the appropriate box. If income was $5,000 or more, provide a good faith estimate of all lobbying related income from the client (include all payments to the registrant by any other entity for lobbying activities on behalf of the client). Round your estimate to the nearest $10,000. (One selection is required for lobbying firms.) Any amount under $5,000 entered in the line will return an error. (You must check one box or the other.)

LINE 13. ORGANIZATIONS (EXPENSES): Indicate whether expenses related to lobbying activities were less than $5,000, or were $5,000 or more, during the reporting period by checking the appropriate box. If expenses were $5,000 or more, provide a good faith estimate of all lobbying expenses (include all payments to third parties for lobbying activities) and round estimates to the nearest $10,000. (One selection is required for organizations lobbying on their own behalf.)

LINE 14. REPORTING METHODS: Mark the appropriate box to indicate the expense accounting method used to determine expenses. One selection is required if 'Self' is checked.

- Method A. Reporting amounts using LDA definitions only. This method is available to all organizations.

- Method B. Reporting amounts using Internal Revenue Code definitions as defined under Section 4911(d) of the IRC. This method is only available to a NON-PROFIT registrant that is required to report and does report under Section 6033(b)(8) of the IRC. The amount disclosed must pertain to the quarterly period covered by this report.

- Method C. Reporting amounts using Internal Revenue Code definitions of lobbying activities, of which the cost is not deductible pursuant to Section 162(e) of the IRC. This method is available to any registrant that is subject to Section 162(e) of the IRC. The amount disclosed must pertain to the quarterly period covered by this report. Grass-roots and state lobbying expenses **may not be subtracted from this amount.**

FIRST PAGE SIGNATURE: This signature line is used to apply your digital signature using the Senate password. The signer name will appear after you have completed the signing process.

PRINTED NAME AND TITLE: Enter the name and title of the person who will sign the filing. The signer must be the officer or employee of the registrant who is responsible for the accuracy of the information contained in the registration.

LOBBYING ISSUE PAGE: The electronic form includes one lobbying issue page when it is opened. You may add additional issue pages as needed. Each new issue page is inserted at the end of the form and numbered automatically. You may also insert addendum pages for issue descriptions and additional lobbyist names related to each general lobbying issue. Each addendum page is inserted after the issue page you are adding it to and numbered automatically.

LINE 15. GENERAL LOBBYING ISSUE AREA: Select the applicable code(s) from the list below which accurately reflect all general areas in which the registrant engaged in lobbying during the reporting period, whether or not the issue area was previously disclosed. Complete a separate page for each code selected.

The select box lists both the code and description for convenience. The code is required and must be entered before supplementary pages can be added.

ACC	Accounting		HCR	Health Issues
ADV	Advertising		HOU	Housing
AER	Aerospace		IMM	Immigration
AGR	Agriculture		IND	Indian/Native American Affairs
ALC	Alcohol & Drug Abuse		INS	Insurance
ANI	Animals		LBR	Labor Issues/Antitrust/Workplace
APP	Apparel/Clothing Industry/Textiles		LAW	Law Enforcement/Crime/Criminal Justice
ART	Arts/Entertainment		MAN	Manufacturing
AUT	Automotive Industry		MAR	Marine/Maritime/Boating/Fisheries
AVI	Aviation/Aircraft/Airlines		MIA	Media (Information/Publishing)
BAN	Banking		MED	Medical/Disease Research/Clinical Labs
BNK	Bankruptcy		MMM	Medicare/Medicaid
BEV	Beverage Industry		MON	Minting/Money/Gold Standard
BUD	Budget/Appropriations		NAT	Natural Resources
CHM	Chemicals/Chemical Industry		PHA	Pharmacy
CIV	Civil Rights/Civil Liberties		POS	Postal
CAW	Clean Air & Water (Quality)		RRR	Railroads
CDT	Commodities (Big Ticket)		RES	Real Estate/Land Use/Conservation
COM	Communications/Broadcasting/Radio/TV		REL	Religion
CPI	Computer Industry		RET	Retirement
CSP	Consumer Issues/Safety/Protection		ROD	Roads/Highway
CON	Constitution		SCI	Science/Technology
CPT	Copyright/Patent/Trademark		SMB	Small Business
DEF	Defense		SPO	Sports/Athletics
DOC	District of Columbia		TAX	Taxation/Internal Revenue Code
DIS	Disaster Planning/Emergencies		TEC	Telecommunications
ECN	Economics/Economic Development		TOB	Tobacco
EDU	Education		TOR	Torts
ENC	Energy/Nuclear		TRD	Trade (Domestic & Foreign)
ENV	Environmental/Superfund		TRA	Transporation
FAM	Family Issues/Abortion/Adoption		TOU	Travel/Tourism
FIR	Firearms/Guns/Ammunition		TRU	Trucking/Shipping
FIN	Financial Institutions/Investments/Securities		URB	Urban development/Municipalities
FOO	Food Industry (Safety, Labeling, etc.)		UNM	Unemployment
FOR	Foreign Relations		UTI	Utilities
FUE	Fuel/Gas/Oil		VET	Veterans
GAM	Gaming/Gambling/Casino		WAS	Waste (hazardous/solid/interestate/nuclear)
GOV	Government Issues		WEL	Welfare

LINE 16 SPECIFIC LOBBYING ISSUES: For each general lobbying area, list the specific issues which were actually lobbied during the quarterly period. Include, for example, specific bills before Congress or specific executive branch actions. BE SPECIFIC. **Bill numbers alone do not satisfy the requirements for reporting on this line and restatement of the general issue code is insufficient.** Use the following format to describe legislation: BILL NO., BILL TITLE, AND DESCRIPTION OF THE SPECIFIC SECTION(S) OF INTEREST.

i.e., "H.R. 3610, Department of Defense Appropriations Act of 1996, Title 2, all provisions relating to environmental restoration."

For specific issues other than legislation, provide detailed descriptions of lobbying efforts. Do not leave line blank.

To maximize space, use a paragraph format. If needed, you can add addendum pages to enter more descriptions.

LINE 17 CONTACTS: Identify the Houses of Congress and Federal agencies contacted by the registrant in connection with the general issue area during the reporting period. Disclose only the houses or agencies, such as "Senate," "House of Representatives," "Department of Agriculture," or "Executive Office of the President," rather than the individual office. If there were no contacts during the period, mark the box labeled "none." This line is required to complete the filing.

If there were no contacts during the period, mark the box labeled "none." If there were contacts, select the agency names from the list on the left and click the **Add** button. The name will be added to the list on the right. A full formatted list of selected names will be inserted in the text box for line 17 if the form is printed.

LINE 18. LOBBYISTS: List the name of each **lobbyist** who had **any activity** in this general issue area. Enter the first name, last name and suffix in separate fields.

If there are lobbyists not previously disclosed, enter the names of the new lobbyist(s) under each pertinent issue code, and mark the box labeled "New." If any new lobbyist listed in this section has served as a "covered executive branch official" or "covered legislative branch official" within twenty years of first acting as a lobbyist for the client, identify that person as a "covered official," state the executive and/or legislative position in which the person served.

NOTE: The 20% threshold does not apply to this line and is only used for determining who may be considered a "lobbyist" for registration/updating purposes.

You may enter up to 9 lobbyist names on the issue page. If needed, you can add addendum pages to enter more names.

LINE 19. FOREIGN INTEREST: Describe the interest of each foreign entity in the specific issues listed on line 16. **If there are no foreign entity interests in this issue, check the box marked 'None'.** If 'None' is checked after data has been entered in this field, it will be deleted.

LINE 20. CLIENT NEW ADDRESS: Enter complete address of the client if different than previously reported. No address may be entered here if 'Self' is check in the client name box.

LINE 21. CLIENT NEW PRINCIPAL PLACE OF BUSINESS: Indicate the client's new principal place of business (city, state and country), if different from line 20. No address may be entered here if 'Self' is check in the client name box.

LINE 22 NEW DESCRIPTION OF CLIENT'S BUSINESS OR ACTIVITIES: Provide a general description of the new business or activities of the client. No business description may be entered here if 'Self' is check in the client name box.

LINE 23 LOBBYIST DELETE: Enter the name of each individual who **no longer** acts as a lobbyist for the client identified on line 7. Enter the first name, last name and suffix in separate boxes. If there are no names to remove, skip to line 24.

LINE 24 GENERAL ISSUE AREA DELETE: Select the codes from the list on page 3 of the instructions of all previously reported issue areas that no longer apply and enter them on line 24. If there are no codes to be deleted, skip to line 25.

LINE 25. AFFILIATED ENTITY ADD: Identify the name, address, and principal place of business of any entity other than the client that contributes in excess of $5,000 toward the registrant's lobbying activities in a quarterly period **and** actively participates in the planning, supervision, or control of such activities.

The LDA amendments require disclosure of some affiliates that were heretofore undisclosed, and retained the requirement for listing those affiliates that contribute in excess of $5,000 and in whole or major part (20%) plans, supervises or controls such lobbying activities.

The LDA Amendments state in part: "No disclosure is required under paragraph (3)(B) if the organization that would be identified as affiliated with the client is listed on the client's publicly accessible Internet website as being a member of or contributor to the client unless the organization in whole or in major part plans, supervises or controls such lobbying activities." If a registrant relies upon the preceding sentence, the registrant must disclose the specific Internet address of the web page containing the information relied upon. If the registrant chooses to use the website, it is responsible for ensuring that the web page remains valid and accurate until a new LD-2 is filed with updated information. Please enter the URL underneath the address of any affiliates that apply.

LINE 26. AFFILIATED ENTITY DELETE: List the names of all previously reported organizations that no longer meet the disclosure requirement. If there are no organizations to remove, skip to line 27.

LINE 27. FOREIGN ENTITY ADD: Identify the name, address, principal place of business, amount of any contribution in excess of $5,000, and the approximate percentage of equitable ownership in the client of any foreign entity that:

- holds at least 20% equitable ownership in the client or any organization identified on line 13 of the registration or line 25 of this report; **or**

- directly or indirectly, in whole or in major part, plans, supervises, controls, directs, finances, or subsidizes activities of the client or any organization identified on line 13 of the registration or line 25 of this report; **or**

- is an affiliate of the client or any organization identified on line 13 of the registration or line 25 of this report and has direct interest in the outcome of the lobbying activity.

LINE 28. FOREIGN ENTITY DELETE: List the names of all previously reported foreign entities that no longer meet the disclosure requirement. Leave this line blank if there are no deletions.

SIGNATURE: This line is populated automatically if you are signing the form electronically. If you are printing the form and this is the last page of the report, sign and date this page and type or print the signer's name and title. Only the last page of the report need be signed. Form LD-2DS must be signed and dated by the officer or employee of the registrant who is responsible for the accuracy of the information contained in the report.

Form LD-203

Please see http://lobbyingdisclosure.house.gov for form LD-203.

Lobbying Disclosure Act of 1995--Current through October 1, 2007

Note: This compilation includes language from Public Law 104–65, as well as amending language from Public Laws 105–166 and 110–81. These materials are not official evidence of the laws set forth herein. Sections 112 and 204 of title 1 of the United States Code establish the rules governing which text serves as legal evidence of the laws of the United States.

For changes, after the closing date of this publication, to provisions of law in this publication, see the United States Code Classification Tables published by the Office of the Law Revision Counsel of the House of Representatives at http://uscode.house.gov/classification/tables.shtml

LOBBYING DISCLOSURE ACT OF 1995 [1]

[As Amended Through P.L. 110–81, Enacted September 14, 2007]

AN ACT To provide for the disclosure of lobbying activities to influence the Federal Government, and for other purposes.

Be it enacted by the Senate and House of Representatives of the United States of America in Congress assembled,

SECTION 1. [2 U.S.C. 1601 note] SHORT TITLE.

This Act may be cited as the "Lobbying Disclosure Act of 1995".

SEC. 2. [2 U.S.C. 1601] FINDINGS.

The Congress finds that—

(1) responsible representative Government requires public awareness of the efforts of paid lobbyists to influence the public decisionmaking process in both the legislative and executive branches of the Federal Government;

(2) existing lobbying disclosure statutes have been ineffective because of unclear statutory language, weak administrative and enforcement provisions, and an absence of clear guidance as to who is required to register and what they are required to disclose; and

(3) the effective public disclosure of the identity and extent of the efforts of paid lobbyists to influence Federal officials in the conduct of Government actions will increase public confidence in the integrity of Government.

SEC. 3. [2 U.S.C. 1602] DEFINITIONS.

As used in this Act:

(1) AGENCY.—The term "agency" has the meaning given that term in section 551(1) of title 5, United States Code.

(2) CLIENT.—The term "client" means any person or entity that employs or retains another person for financial or other compensation to conduct lobbying activities on behalf of that person or entity. A person or entity whose employees act as lobbyists on its own behalf is both a client and an employer of such employees. In the case of a coalition or association that employs or retains other persons to conduct lobbying activities,

---

[1] Title II of Public Law 110–81 provides for amendments to the Lobby Discolusure Act of 1995. Section 215 of such Public Law provides:

SEC. 215. EFFECTIVE DATE.

Except as otherwise provided in sections 203, 204, 206, 211, 212, and 213, the amendments made by this title shall apply with respect to registrations under the Lobbying Disclosure Act of 1995 having an effective date of January 1, 2008, or later and with respect to quarterly reports under that Act covering calendar quarters beginning on or after January 1, 2008.

the client is the coalition or association and not its individual members.

(3) COVERED EXECUTIVE BRANCH OFFICIAL.—The term "covered executive branch official" means—

 (A) the President;

 (B) the Vice President;

 (C) any officer or employee, or any other individual functioning in the capacity of such an officer or employee, in the Executive Office of the President;

 (D) any officer or employee serving in a position in level I, II, III, IV, or V of the Executive Schedule, as designated by statute or Executive order;

 (E) any member of the uniformed services whose pay grade is at or above O–7 under section 201 of title 37, United States Code; and

 (F) any officer or employee serving in a position of a confidential, policy-determining, policy-making, or policy-advocating character described in section 7511(b)(2)(B) of title 5, United States Code.

(4) COVERED LEGISLATIVE BRANCH OFFICIAL.—The term "covered legislative branch official" means—

 (A) a Member of Congress;

 (B) an elected officer of either House of Congress;

 (C) any employee of, or any other individual functioning in the capacity of an employee of—

  (i) a Member of Congress;

  (ii) a committee of either House of Congress;

  (iii) the leadership staff of the House of Representatives or the leadership staff of the Senate;

  (iv) a joint committee of Congress; and

  (v) a working group or caucus organized to provide legislative services or other assistance to Members of Congress; and

 (D) any other legislative branch employee serving in a position described under section 109(13) of the Ethics in Government Act of 1978 (5 U.S.C. App.).

(5) EMPLOYEE.—The term "employee" means any individual who is an officer, employee, partner, director, or proprietor of a person or entity, but does not include—

 (A) independent contractors; or

 (B) volunteers who receive no financial or other compensation from the person or entity for their services.

(6) FOREIGN ENTITY.—The term "foreign entity" means a foreign principal (as defined in section 1(b) of the Foreign Agents Registration Act of 1938 (22 U.S.C. 611(b)).

(7) LOBBYING ACTIVITIES.—The term "lobbying activities" means lobbying contacts and efforts in support of such contacts, including preparation and planning activities, research and other background work that is intended, at the time it is performed, for use in contacts, and coordination with the lobbying activities of others.

(8) LOBBYING CONTACT.—

 (A) DEFINITION.—The term "lobbying contact" means any oral or written communication (including an electronic communication) to a covered executive branch official or a covered legislative branch official that is made on behalf of a client with regard to—

(i) the formulation, modification, or adoption of Federal legislation (including legislative proposals);

(ii) the formulation, modification, or adoption of a Federal rule, regulation, Executive order, or any other program, policy, or position of the United States Government;

(iii) the administration or execution of a Federal program or policy (including the negotiation, award, or administration of a Federal contract, grant, loan, permit, or license); or

(iv) the nomination or confirmation of a person for a position subject to confirmation by the Senate.

(B) EXCEPTIONS.—The term "lobbying contact" does not include a communication that is—

(i) made by a public official acting in the public official's official capacity;

(ii) made by a representative of a media organization if the purpose of the communication is gathering and disseminating news and information to the public;

(iii) made in a speech, article, publication or other material that is distributed and made available to the public, or through radio, television, cable television, or other medium of mass communication;

(iv) made on behalf of a government of a foreign country or a foreign political party and disclosed under the Foreign Agents Registration Act of 1938 (22 U.S.C. 611 et seq.);

(v) a request for a meeting, a request for the status of an action, or any other similar administrative request, if the request does not include an attempt to influence a covered executive branch official or a covered legislative branch official;

(vi) made in the course of participation in an advisory committee subject to the Federal Advisory Committee Act;

(vii) testimony given before a committee, subcommittee, or task force of the Congress, or submitted for inclusion in the public record of a hearing conducted by such committee, subcommittee, or task force;

(viii) information provided in writing in response to an oral or written request by a covered executive branch official or a covered legislative branch official for specific information;

(ix) required by subpoena, civil investigative demand, or otherwise compelled by statute, regulation, or other action of the Congress or an agency, including any communication compelled by a Federal contract, grant, loan, permit, or license;

(x) made in response to a notice in the Federal Register, Commerce Business Daily, or other similar publication soliciting communications from the public and directed to the agency official specifically designated in the notice to receive such communications;

(xi) not possible to report without disclosing information, the unauthorized disclosure of which is prohibited by law;

(xii) made to an official in an agency with regard to—

(I) a judicial proceeding or a criminal or civil law enforcement inquiry, investigation, or proceeding; or

(II) a filing or proceeding that the Government is specifically required by statute or regulation to maintain or conduct on a confidential basis,

if that agency is charged with responsibility for such proceeding, inquiry, investigation, or filing;

(xiii) made in compliance with written agency procedures regarding an adjudication conducted by the agency under section 554 of title 5, United States Code, or substantially similar provisions;

(xiv) a written comment filed in the course of a public proceeding or any other communication that is made on the record in a public proceeding;

(xv) a petition for agency action made in writing and required to be a matter of public record pursuant to established agency procedures;

(xvi) made on behalf of an individual with regard to that individual's benefits, employment, or other personal matters involving only that individual, except that this clause does not apply to any communication with—

(I) a covered executive branch official, or

(II) a covered legislative branch official (other than the individual's elected Members of Congress or employees who work under such Members' direct supervision),

with respect to the formulation, modification, or adoption of private legislation for the relief of that individual;

(xvii) a disclosure by an individual that is protected under the amendments made by the Whistleblower Protection Act of 1989, under the Inspector General Act of 1978, or under another provision of law;

(xviii) made by—

(I) a church, its integrated auxiliary, or a convention or association of churches that is exempt from filing a Federal income tax return under paragraph 2(A)(i) of section 6033(a) of the Internal Revenue Code of 1986, or

(II) a religious order that is exempt from filing a Federal income tax return under paragraph (2)(A)(iii) of such section 6033(a); and

(xix) between—

(I) officials of a self-regulatory organization (as defined in section 3(a)(26) of the Securities Exchange Act) that is registered with or established by the Securities and Exchange Commission as required by that Act or a similar organization that is designated by or registered with the Commodities Future Trading Commission as provided under the Commodity Exchange Act; and

(II) the Securities and Exchange Commission or the Commodities Future Trading Commission, respectively;

relating to the regulatory responsibilities of such organization under that Act.

(9) LOBBYING FIRM.—The term "lobbying firm" means a person or entity that has 1 or more employees who are lobbyists on behalf of a client other than that person or entity. The term also includes a self-employed individual who is a lobbyist.

(10) LOBBYIST.—The term "lobbyist" means any individual who is employed or retained by a client for financial or other compensation for services that include more than one lobbying contact, other than an individual whose lobbying activities constitute less than 20 percent of the time engaged in the services provided by such individual to that client over a 3-month period.

(11) MEDIA ORGANIZATION.—The term "media organization" means a person or entity engaged in disseminating information to the general public through a newspaper, magazine, other publication, radio, television, cable television, or other medium of mass communication.

(12) MEMBER OF CONGRESS.—The term "Member of Congress" means a Senator or a Representative in, or Delegate or Resident Commissioner to, the Congress.

(13) ORGANIZATION.—The term "organization" means a person or entity other than an individual.

(14) PERSON OR ENTITY.—The term "person or entity" means any individual, corporation, company, foundation, association, labor organization, firm, partnership, society, joint stock company, group of organizations, or State or local government.

(15) PUBLIC OFFICIAL.—The term "public official" means any elected official, appointed official, or employee of—

(A) a Federal, State, or local unit of government in the United States other than—

(i) a college or university;

(ii) a government-sponsored enterprise (as defined in section 3(8) of the Congressional Budget and Impoundment Control Act of 1974);

(iii) a public utility that provides gas, electricity, water, or communications;

(iv) a guaranty agency (as defined in section 435(j) of the Higher Education Act of 1965 (20 U.S.C. 1085(j))), including any affiliate of such an agency; or

(v) an agency of any State functioning as a student loan secondary market pursuant to section 435(d)(1)(F) of the Higher Education Act of 1965 (20 U.S.C. 1085(d)(1)(F));

(B) a Government corporation (as defined in section 9101 of title 31, United States Code);

(C) an organization of State or local elected or appointed officials other than officials of an entity described in clause (i), (ii), (iii), (iv), or (v) of subparagraph (A);

(D) an Indian tribe (as defined in section 4(e) of the Indian Self-Determination and Education Assistance Act (25 U.S.C. 450b(e));

(E) a national or State political party or any organizational unit thereof; or

(F) a national, regional, or local unit of any foreign government, or a group of governments acting together as an international organization.

(16) STATE.—The term "State" means each of the several States, the District of Columbia, and any commonwealth, territory, or possession of the United States.

SEC. 4. [2 U.S.C. 1603] REGISTRATION OF LOBBYISTS.

(a) REGISTRATION.—

(1) GENERAL RULE.—No later than 45 days after a lobbyist first makes a lobbying contact or is employed or retained to make a lobbying contact, whichever is earlier, or on the first business day after such 45th day if the 45th day is not a business day, such lobbyist (or, as provided under paragraph (2), the organization employing such lobbyist), shall register with the Secretary of the Senate and the Clerk of the House of Representatives.

(2) EMPLOYER FILING.—Any organization that has 1 or more employees who are lobbyists shall file a single registration under this section on behalf of such employees for each client on whose behalf the employees act as lobbyists.

(3) EXEMPTION.—

(A) GENERAL RULE.—Notwithstanding paragraphs (1) and (2), a person or entity whose—

(i) total income for matters related to lobbying activities on behalf of a particular client (in the case of a lobbying firm) does not exceed and is not expected to exceed $2,500; or

(ii) total expenses in connection with lobbying activities (in the case of an organization whose employees engage in lobbying activities on its own behalf) do not exceed or are not expected to exceed $10,000, (as estimated under section 5) in the quarterly period described in section 5(a) during which the registration would be made is not required to register under subsection (a) with respect to such client.

(B) ADJUSTMENT.—The dollar amounts in subparagraph (A) shall be adjusted—

(i) on January 1, 1997, to reflect changes in the Consumer Price Index (as determined by the Secretary of Labor) since the date of enactment of this Act; and

(ii) on January 1 of each fourth year occurring after January 1, 1997, to reflect changes in the Consumer Price Index (as determined by the Secretary of Labor) during the preceding 4-year period,

rounded to the nearest $500.

(b) CONTENTS OF REGISTRATION.—Each registration under this section shall contain—

(1) the name, address, business telephone number, and principal place of business of the registrant, and a general description of its business or activities;

(2) the name, address, and principal place of business of the registrant's client, and a general description of its business or activities (if different from paragraph (1));

(3) the name, address, and principal place of business of any organization, other than the client, that—

(A) contributes more than $5,000 to the registrant or the client in the quarterly period to fund the lobbying activities of the registrant; and

(B) actively participates in the planning, supervision, or control of such lobbying activities;

(4) the name, address, principal place of business, amount of any contribution of more than $5,000 to the lobbying activities of the registrant, and approximate percentage of equitable ownership in the client (if any) of any foreign entity that—

(A) holds at least 20 percent equitable ownership in the client or any organization identified under paragraph (3);

(B) directly or indirectly, in whole or in major part, plans, supervises, controls, directs, finances, or subsidizes the activities of the client or any organization identified under paragraph (3); or

(C) is an affiliate of the client or any organization identified under paragraph (3) and has a direct interest in the outcome of the lobbying activity;

(5) a statement of—

(A) the general issue areas in which the registrant expects to engage in lobbying activities on behalf of the client; and

(B) to the extent practicable, specific issues that have (as of the date of the registration) already been addressed or are likely to be addressed in lobbying activities; and

(6) the name of each employee of the registrant who has acted or whom the registrant expects to act as a lobbyist on behalf of the client and, if any such employee has served as a covered executive branch official or a covered legislative branch official in the 20 years before the date on which the employee first acted as a lobbyist on behalf of the client, the position in which such employee served.

No disclosure is required under paragraph (3)(B) if the organization that would be identified as affiliated with the client is listed on the client's publicly accessible Internet website as being a member of or contributor to the client, unless the organization in whole or in major part plans, supervises, or controls such lobbying activities. If a registrant relies upon the preceding sentence, the registrant must disclose the specific Internet address of the web page containing the information relied upon. Nothing in paragraph (3)(B) shall be construed to require the disclosure of any information about individuals who are members of, or donors to, an entity treated as a client by this Act or an organization identified under that paragraph.

 (c) GUIDELINES FOR REGISTRATION.—

  (1) MULTIPLE CLIENTS.—In the case of a registrant making lobbying contacts on behalf of more than 1 client, a separate registration under this section shall be filed for each such client.

  (2) MULTIPLE CONTACTS.—A registrant who makes more than 1 lobbying contact for the same client shall file a single registration covering all such lobbying contacts.

 (d) TERMINATION OF REGISTRATION.—A registrant who after registration—

  (1) is no longer employed or retained by a client to conduct lobbying activities, and

  (2) does not anticipate any additional lobbying activities for such client,

may so notify the Secretary of the Senate and the Clerk of the House of Representatives and terminate its registration.

SEC. 5. [2 U.S.C. 1604] REPORTS BY REGISTERED LOBBYISTS.

 (a) QUARTERLY REPORT.—No later than 20 days after the end of the quarterly period beginning on the first day of January, April, July, and October of each year in which a registrant is registered under section 4, or on the first business day after such 20th day if the 20th day is not a business day, each registrant shall file a report with the Secretary of the Senate and the Clerk of the House of Representatives on its lobbying activities during such quarterly period. A separate report shall be filed for each client of the registrant.

 (b) CONTENTS OF REPORT.—Each quarterly report filed under subsection (a) shall contain—

  (1) the name of the registrant, the name of the client, and any changes or updates to the information provided in the initial registration, including information under section 4(b)(3);

  (2) for each general issue area in which the registrant engaged in lobbying activities on behalf of the client during the quarterly period—

   (A) a list of the specific issues upon which a lobbyist employed by the registrant engaged in lobbying activities, including, to the maximum extent practicable, a list of bill numbers and references to specific executive branch actions;

   (B) a statement of the Houses of Congress and the Federal agencies contacted by lobbyists employed by the registrant on behalf of the client;

   (C) a list of the employees of the registrant who acted as lobbyists on behalf of the client; and

(D) a description of the interest, if any, of any foreign entity identified under section 4(b)(4) in the specific issues listed under subparagraph (A);

(3) in the case of a lobbying firm, a good faith estimate of the total amount of all income from the client (including any payments to the registrant by any other person for lobbying activities on behalf of the client) during the quarterly period, other than income for matters that are unrelated to lobbying activities;

(4) in the case of a registrant engaged in lobbying activities on its own behalf, a good faith estimate of the total expenses that the registrant and its employees incurred in connection with lobbying activities during the quarterly period; and

(5) for each client, immediately after listing the client, an identification of whether the client is a State or local government or a department, agency, special purpose district, or other instrumentality controlled by one or more State or local governments.

(c) ESTIMATES OF INCOME OR EXPENSES.—For purposes of this section, estimates of income or expenses shall be made as follows:

(1) Estimates of amounts in excess of $5,000 shall be rounded to the nearest $10,000.

(2) In the event income or expenses do not exceed $5,000, the registrant shall include a statement that income or expenses totaled less than $5,000 for the reporting period.

(d) SEMIANNUAL REPORTS ON CERTAIN CONTRIBUTIONS.—

(1) IN GENERAL.—Not later than 30 days after the end of the semiannual period beginning on the first day of January and July of each year, or on the first business day after such 30th day if the 30th day is not a business day, each person or organization who is registered or is required to register under paragraph (1) or (2) of section 4(a), and each employee who is or is required to be listed as a lobbyist under section 4(b)(6) or subsection (b)(2)(C) of this section, shall file a report with the Secretary of the Senate and the Clerk of the House of Representatives containing—

(A) the name of the person or organization;

(B) in the case of an employee, his or her employer;

(C) the names of all political committees established or controlled by the person or organization;

(D) the name of each Federal candidate or officeholder, leadership PAC, or political party committee, to whom aggregate contributions equal to or exceeding $200 were made by the person or organization, or a political committee established or controlled by the person or organization within the semiannual period, and the date and amount of each such contribution made within the semiannual period;

(E) the date, recipient, and amount of funds contributed or disbursed during the semiannual period by the person or organization or a political committee established or controlled by the person or organization—

(i) to pay the cost of an event to honor or recognize a covered legislative branch official or covered executive branch official;

(ii) to an entity that is named for a covered legislative branch official, or to a person or entity in recognition of such official;

(iii) to an entity established, financed, maintained, or controlled by a covered legislative branch official or covered executive branch official, or an entity designated by such official; or

(iv) to pay the costs of a meeting, retreat, conference, or other similar event held by, or in the name of, 1 or more covered legislative branch officials or covered executive branch officials,

except that this subparagraph shall not apply if the funds are provided to a person who is required to report the receipt of the funds under section 304 of the Federal Election Campaign Act of 1971 (2 U.S.C. 434);

(F) the name of each Presidential library foundation, and each Presidential inaugural committee, to whom contributions equal to or exceeding $200 were made by the person or organization, or a political committee established or controlled by the person or organization, within the semiannual period, and the date and amount of each such contribution within the semiannual period; and

(G) a certification by the person or organization filing the report that the person or organization—

(i) has read and is familiar with those provisions of the Standing Rules of the Senate and the Rules of the House of Representatives relating to the provision of gifts and travel; and

(ii) has not provided, requested, or directed a gift, including travel, to a Member of Congress or an officer or employee of either House of Congress with knowledge that receipt of the gift would violate rule XXXV of the Standing Rules of the Senate or rule XXV of the Rules of the House of Representatives.

(2) DEFINITION.—In this subsection, the term "leadership PAC" has the meaning given such term in section 304(i)(8)(B) of the Federal Election Campaign Act of 1971.

(e) ELECTRONIC FILING REQUIRED.—A report required to be filed under this section shall be filed in electronic form, in addition to any other form that the Secretary of the Senate or the Clerk of the House of Representatives may require or allow. The Secretary of the Senate and the Clerk of the House of Representatives shall use the same electronic software for receipt and recording of filings under this Act.

SEC. 6. [2 U.S.C. 1605] DISCLOSURE AND ENFORCEMENT.

(a) IN GENERAL.—The Secretary of the Senate and the Clerk of the House of Representatives shall—

(1) provide guidance and assistance on the registration and reporting requirements of this Act and develop common standards, rules, and procedures for compliance with this Act;

(2) review, and, where necessary, verify and inquire to ensure the accuracy, completeness, and timeliness of registration and reports;

(3) develop filing, coding, and cross-indexing systems to carry out the purpose of this Act, including—

(A) a publicly available list of all registered lobbyists, lobbying firms, and their clients; and

(B) computerized systems designed to minimize the burden of filing and maximize public access to materials filed under this Act;

(4) make available for public inspection and copying at reasonable times the registrations and reports filed under this Act and, in the case of a report filed in electronic form under section 5(e), make such report available for public inspection over the Internet as soon as technically practicable after the report is so filed;

(5) retain registrations for a period of at least 6 years after they are terminated and reports for a period of at least 6 years after they are filed;

(6) compile and summarize, with respect to each quarterly period, the information contained in registrations and reports filed with respect to such period in a clear and complete manner;

(7) notify any lobbyist or lobbying firm in writing that may be in noncompliance with this Act;

(8) notify the United States Attorney for the District of Columbia that a lobbyist or lobbying firm may be in noncompliance with this Act, if the registrant has been notified in writing and has failed to provide an appropriate response within 60 days after notice was given under paragraph (7);

(9) maintain all registrations and reports filed under this Act, and make them available to the public over the Internet, without a fee or other access charge, in a searchable, sortable, and downloadable manner, to the extent technically practicable, that—

(A) includes the information contained in the registrations and reports;

(B) is searchable and sortable to the maximum extent practicable, including searchable and sortable by each of the categories of information described in section 4(b) or 5(b); and

(C) provides electronic links or other appropriate mechanisms to allow users to obtain relevant information in the database of the Federal Election Commission;

(10) retain the information contained in a registration or report filed under this Act for a period of 6 years after the registration or report (as the case may be) is filed; and

(11) make publicly available, on a semiannual basis, the aggregate number of registrants referred to the United States Attorney for the District of Columbia for noncompliance as required by paragraph (8).

(b) ENFORCEMENT REPORT.—

(1) REPORT.—The Attorney General shall report to the congressional committees referred to in paragraph (2), after the

end of each semiannual period beginning on January 1 and July 1, the aggregate number of enforcement actions taken by the Department of Justice under this Act during that semiannual period and, by case, any sentences imposed, except that such report shall not include the names of individuals, or personally identifiable information, that is not already a matter of public record.

(2) COMMITTEES.—The congressional committees referred to in paragraph (1) are the Committee on Homeland Security and Governmental Affairs and the Committee on the Judiciary of the Senate and the Committee on the Judiciary of the House of Representatives.

SEC. 7. [2 U.S.C. 1606] PENALTIES.

(a) CIVIL PENALTY.—Whoever knowingly fails to—

(1) remedy a defective filing within 60 days after notice of such a defect by the Secretary of the Senate or the Clerk of the House of Representatives; or

(2) comply with any other provision of this Act;

shall, upon proof of such knowing violation by a preponderance of the evidence, be subject to a civil fine of not more than $200,000, depending on the extent and gravity of the violation.

(b) CRIMINAL PENALTY.—Whoever knowingly and corruptly fails to comply with any provision of this Act shall be imprisoned for not more than 5 years or fined under title 18, United States Code, or both.

SEC. 8. [2 U.S.C. 1607] RULES OF CONSTRUCTION.

(a) CONSTITUTIONAL RIGHTS.—Nothing in this Act shall be construed to prohibit or interfere with—

(1) the right to petition the Government for the redress of grievances;

(2) the right to express a personal opinion; or

(3) the right of association,

protected by the first amendment to the Constitution.

(b) PROHIBITION OF ACTIVITIES.—Nothing in this Act shall be construed to prohibit, or to authorize any court to prohibit, lobbying activities or lobbying contacts by any person or entity, regardless of whether such person or entity is in compliance with the requirements of this Act.

(c) AUDIT AND INVESTIGATIONS.—Nothing in this Act shall be construed to grant general audit or investigative authority to the Secretary of the Senate or the Clerk of the House of Representatives.

SEC. 9. AMENDMENTS TO THE FOREIGN AGENTS REGISTRATION ACT.

[Sec. 9 provides for amendments to the Foreign Agents Registration Act of 1938 (22 U.S.C. 611 et seq.)]

SEC. 10. AMENDMENTS TO THE BYRD AMENDMENT.

[Sec. 10 provides for amendments to section 1352 of title 31, United States Code]

SEC. 11. REPEAL OF CERTAIN LOBBYING PROVISIONS.

(a) REPEAL OF THE FEDERAL REGULATION OF LOBBYING ACT.— [Sec. 11(a) provides for the repeal of the Federal Regulation of Lobbying Act (2 U.S.C. 261 et seq.) in its entirety]

(b) REPEAL OF PROVISIONS RELATING TO HOUSING LOBBYIST ACTIVITIES.—

(1) [Sec. 11(b)(1) provides for the repeal of section 13 of the Department of Housing and Urban Development Act (42 U.S.C. 3537b)]

(2) [Sec. 11(b)(2) provides for the repeal of section 536(d) of the Housing Act of 1949 (42 U.S.C. 1490p(d))]

SEC. 12. CONFORMING AMENDMENTS TO OTHER STATUTES.

(a) AMENDMENT TO COMPETITIVENESS POLICY COUNCIL ACT.— [Sec. 12(a) provides for an amendment to section 5206(e) of the Competitiveness Policy Council Act (15 U.S.C. 4804(e))]

(b) AMENDMENTS TO TITLE 18, UNITED STATES CODE.—[Sec. 12(b) provides for amendments to section 219(a) of title 18, United States Code]

(c) AMENDMENT TO FOREIGN SERVICE ACT OF 1980.—[Sec. 12(c) provides for an amendment to section 602(c) of the Foreign Service Act of 1980 (22 U.S.C. 4002(c))]

SEC. 13. [2 U.S.C. 1608] SEVERABILITY.

If any provision of this Act, or the application thereof, is held invalid, the validity of the remainder of this Act and the application of such provision to other persons and circumstances shall not be affected thereby.

SEC. 14. [2 U.S.C. 1609] IDENTIFICATION OF CLIENTS AND COVERED OFFICIALS.

(a) ORAL LOBBYING CONTACTS.—Any person or entity that makes an oral lobbying contact with a covered legislative branch official or a covered executive branch official shall, on the request of the official at the time of the lobbying contact—

(1) state whether the person or entity is registered under this Act and identify the client on whose behalf the lobbying contact is made; and

(2) state whether such client is a foreign entity and identify any foreign entity required to be disclosed under section 4(b)(4) that has a direct interest in the outcome of the lobbying activity.

(b) WRITTEN LOBBYING CONTACTS.—Any person or entity registered under this Act that makes a written lobbying contact (including an electronic communication) with a covered legislative branch official or a covered executive branch official shall—

(1) if the client on whose behalf the lobbying contact was made is a foreign entity, identify such client, state that the client is considered a foreign entity under this Act, and state whether the person making the lobbying contact is registered on behalf of that client under section 4; and

(2) identify any other foreign entity identified pursuant to section 4(b)(4) that has a direct interest in the outcome of the lobbying activity.

(c) IDENTIFICATION AS COVERED OFFICIAL.—Upon request by a person or entity making a lobbying contact, the individual who is contacted or the office employing that individual shall indicate whether or not the individual is a covered legislative branch official or a covered executive branch official.

SEC. 15. [2 U.S.C. 1610] ESTIMATES BASED ON TAX REPORTING SYSTEM.

(a) ENTITIES COVERED BY SECTION 6033(b) OF THE INTERNAL REVENUE CODE OF 1986.—A person, other than a lobbying firm, that is required to report and does report lobbying expenditures pursuant to section 6033(b)(8) of the Internal Revenue Code of 1986 may—

(1) make a good faith estimate (by category of dollar value) of applicable amounts that would be required to be disclosed under such section for the appropriate quarterly period to meet the requirements of sections 4(a)(3) and 5(b)(4); and

(2) for all other purposes consider as lobbying contacts and lobbying activities only—

(A) lobbying contacts with covered legislative branch officials (as defined in section 3(4)) and lobbying activities in support of such contacts; and

(B) lobbying of Federal executive branch officials to the extent that such activities are influencing legislation as defined in section 4911(d) of the Internal Revenue Code of 1986.

(b) ENTITIES COVERED BY SECTION 162(e) OF THE INTERNAL REVENUE CODE OF 1986.—A person, other than a lobbying firm, who is required to account and does account for lobbying expenditures pursuant to section 162(e) of the Internal Revenue Code of 1986 may—

(1) make a good faith estimate (by category of dollar value) of applicable amounts that would not be deductible pursuant to such section for the appropriate quarterly period to meet the requirements of sections 4(a)(3) and 5(b)(4); and

(2) for all other purposes consider as lobbying contacts and lobbying activities only—

(A) lobbying contacts with covered legislative branch officials (as defined in section 3(4)) and lobbying activities in support of such contacts; and

(B) lobbying of Federal executive branch officials to the extent that amounts paid or costs incurred in connection with such activities are not deductible pursuant to section 162(e) of the Internal Revenue Code of 1986.

(c) DISCLOSURE OF ESTIMATE.—Any registrant that elects to make estimates required by this Act under the procedures authorized by subsection (a) or (b) for reporting or threshold purposes shall—

(1) inform the Secretary of the Senate and the Clerk of the House of Representatives that the registrant has elected to make its estimates under such procedures; and

(2) make all such estimates, in a given calendar year, under such procedures.

(d) STUDY.—Not later than March 31, 1997, the Comptroller General of the United States shall review reporting by registrants under subsections (a) and (b) and report to the Congress—

(1) the differences between the definition of "lobbying activities" in section 3(7) and the definitions of "lobbying expenditures", "influencing legislation", and related terms in

sections 162(e) and 4911 of the Internal Revenue Code of 1986, as each are implemented by regulations;

(2) the impact that any such differences may have on filing and reporting under this Act pursuant to this subsection; and

(3) any changes to this Act or to the appropriate sections of the Internal Revenue Code of 1986 that the Comptroller General may recommend to harmonize the definitions.

SEC. 16. REPEAL OF THE RAMSPECK ACT.

(a) REPEAL.—Subsection (c) of section 3304 of title 5, United States Code, is repealed.

(b) REDESIGNATION.—Subsection (d) of section 3304 of title 5, United States Code, is redesignated as subsection (c).

(c) EFFECTIVE DATE.—The repeal and amendment made by this section shall take effect 2 years after the date of the enactment of this Act.

SEC. 17. EXCEPTED SERVICE AND OTHER EXPERIENCE CONSIDERATIONS FOR COMPETITIVE SERVICE APPOINTMENTS.

(a) IN GENERAL.—Section 3304 of title 5, United States Code (as amended by section 2 of this Act) is further amended by adding at the end thereof the following new subsection:

"(d) The Office of Personnel Management shall promulgate regulations on the manner and extent that experience of an individual in a position other than the competitive service, such as the excepted service (as defined under section 2103) in the legislative or judicial branch, or in any private or nonprofit enterprise, may be considered in making appointments to a position in the competitive service (as defined under section 2102). In promulgating such regulations OPM shall not grant any preference based on the fact of service in the legislative or judicial branch. The regulations shall be consistent with the principles of equitable competition and merit based appointments.".

(b) EFFECTIVE DATE.—The amendment made by this section shall take effect 2 years after the date of the enactment of this Act, except the Office of Personnel Management shall—

(1) conduct a study on excepted service considerations for competitive service appointments relating to such amendment; and

(2) take all necessary actions for the regulations described under such amendment to take effect as final regulations on the effective date of this section.

SEC. 18. [2 U.S.C. 1611] EXEMPT ORGANIZATIONS.

An organization described in section 501(c)(4) of the Internal Revenue Code of 1986 which engages in lobbying activities shall not be eligible for the receipt of Federal funds constituting an award, grant, or loan.

SEC. 19. AMENDMENT TO THE FOREIGN AGENTS REGISTRATION ACT (P.L. 75–583).

[Sec. 19 provides for an amendment to strike and insert section 11 of the Foreign Agents Registration Act of 1938]

SEC. 20. DISCLOSURE OF THE VALUE OF ASSETS UNDER THE ETHICS IN GOVERNMENT ACT OF 1978.

[Sec. 20 provides for amendments to section 102 of the Ethics in Government Act of 1978]

SEC. 21. BAN ON TRADE REPRESENTATIVE REPRESENTING OR ADVISING FOREIGN ENTITIES.

(a) REPRESENTING AFTER SERVICE.—[Sec. 21(a) provides for amendments to section 207(f)(2) of title 18, United States Code]

(b) LIMITATION ON APPOINTMENT AS UNITED STATES TRADE REPRESENTATIVE AND DEPUTY UNITED STATES TRADE REPRESENTATIVE.—[Sec. 21(b) provides for an amendment to section 141(b) of the Trade Act of 1974 (19 U.S.C. 2171(b))]

(c) EFFECTIVE DATE.—The amendments made by this section shall apply with respect to an individual appointed as United States Trade Representative or as a Deputy United States Trade Representative on or after the date of enactment of this Act.

SEC. 22. FINANCIAL DISCLOSURE OF INTEREST IN QUALIFIED BLIND TRUST.

(a) IN GENERAL.—[Sec. 22(a) and (b) provides for amendments to section 102 of the Ethics in Government Act of 1978]

(c) EFFECTIVE DATE.—The amendment made by this section shall apply with respect to reports filed under title I of the Ethics in Government Act of 1978 for calendar year 1996 and thereafter.

SEC. 23. [2 U.S.C. 1612] SENSE OF THE SENATE THAT LOBBYING EXPENSES SHOULD REMAIN NONDEDUCTIBLE.

(a) FINDINGS.—The Senate finds that ordinary Americans generally are not allowed to deduct the costs of communicating with their elected representatives.

(b) SENSE OF THE SENATE.—It is the sense of the Senate that lobbying expenses should not be tax deductible.

SEC. 24. [2 U.S.C. 1601 note] EFFECTIVE DATES.

(a) Except as otherwise provided in this section, this Act and the amendments made by this Act shall take effect on January 1, 1996.

(b) The repeals and amendments made under sections 9, 10, 11, and 12 shall take effect as provided under subsection (a), except that such repeals and amendments—

(1) shall not affect any proceeding or suit commenced before the effective date under subsection (a), and in all such proceedings or suits, proceedings shall be had, appeals taken, and judgments rendered in the same manner and with the same effect as if this Act had not been enacted; and

(2) shall not affect the requirements of Federal agencies to compile, publish, and retain information filed or received before the effective date of such repeals and amendments.

SEC. 25. [2 U.S.C. 1613] PROHIBITION ON PROVISION OF GIFTS OR TRAVEL BY REGISTERED LOBBYISTS TO MEMBERS OF CONGRESS AND TO CONGRESSIONAL EMPLOYEES.

(a) PROHIBITION.—Any person described in subsection (b) may not make a gift or provide travel to a covered legislative branch official if the person has knowledge that the gift or travel may not be accepted by that covered legislative branch official under the

Rules of the House of Representatives or the Standing Rules of the Senate (as the case may be).

(b) PERSONS SUBJECT TO PROHIBITION.—The persons subject to the prohibition under subsection (a) are any lobbyist that is registered or is required to register under section 4(a)(1), any organization that employs 1 or more lobbyists and is registered or is required to register under section 4(a)(2), and any employee listed or required to be listed as a lobbyist by a registrant under section 4(b)(6) or 5(b)(2)(C).

SEC. 26. [2 U.S.C. 1614] ANNUAL AUDITS AND REPORTS BY COMPTROLLER GENERAL.

(a) AUDIT.—On an annual basis, the Comptroller General shall audit the extent of compliance or noncompliance with the requirements of this Act by lobbyists, lobbying firms, and registrants through a random sampling of publicly available lobbying registrations and reports filed under this Act during each calendar year.

(b) REPORTS TO CONGRESS.—

(1) ANNUAL REPORTS.—Not later than April 1 of each year, the Comptroller General shall submit to the Congress a report on the review required by subsection (a) for the preceding calendar year. The report shall include the Comptroller General's assessment of the matters required to be emphasized by that subsection and any recommendations of the Comptroller General to—

(A) improve the compliance by lobbyists, lobbying firms, and registrants with the requirements of this Act; and

(B) provide the Department of Justice with the resources and authorities needed for the effective enforcement of this Act.

(2) ASSESSMENT OF COMPLIANCE.—The annual report under paragraph (1) shall include an assessment of compliance by registrants with the requirements of section 4(b)(3).

(c) ACCESS TO INFORMATION.—The Comptroller General may, in carrying out this section, request information from and access to any relevant documents from any person registered under paragraph (1) or (2) of section 4(a) and each employee who is listed as a lobbyist under section 4(b)(6) or section 5(b)(2)(C) if the material requested relates to the purposes of this section. The Comptroller General may request such person to submit in writing such information as the Comptroller General may prescribe. The Comptroller General may notify the Congress in writing if a person from whom information has been requested under this subsection refuses to comply with the request within 45 days after the request is made.

LOBBYING DISCLOSURE ACT GUIDANCE

Effective January 1, 2008
(Revised May 29, 2008[1])

Table of Contents

---

[1] The most recent revision reflects changes intended to provide additional guidance to clarify LDA reporting requirements under section 203 (see section 7) and minor technical and stylistic changes to other parts of the Guidance.

Lobbying Disclosure Act Guidance
Revised May 29, 2008

Section 1 – Introduction

Section 6 of the Lobbying Disclosure Act (LDA), 2 U.S.C. §1605, provides that: The Secretary of the Senate and the Clerk of the House of Representatives shall (1) provide guidance and assistance on the registration and reporting requirements of this Act and develop common standards, rules and procedures for compliance with this Act; [and] (2) review, and, where necessary, verify and inquire to ensure the accuracy, completeness and timeliness of registrations and reports.

The LDA does not provide the Secretary or the Clerk with the authority to write substantive regulations or issue definitive opinions on the interpretation of the law. The Secretary and Clerk have, from time to time, jointly issued written guidance on the registration and reporting requirements. This document is both a compilation of previously issued guidance documents and our interpretation of the changes that were made to the LDA as a result of the Honest Leadership and Open Government Act of 2007 (HLOGA).

This compilation supersedes all previous guidance documents. This combined guidance document does not have the force of law, nor does it have any binding effect on the United States Attorney for the District of Columbia or any other part of the Executive Branch. To the extent that the guidance relates to the accuracy, completeness and timeliness of registration and reports, it will serve to inform the public as to how the Secretary and Clerk intend to carry out their responsibilities under the LDA.

Section 2 – What's New

Honest Leadership and Open Government Act of 2007

The HLOGA, enacted on September 14, 2007 (P.L. 110-81), amends the Lobbying Disclosure Act of 1995 in the following eight areas.

Quarterly Filing of Lobbying Reports

The HLOGA changed the filing schedule of LD-2 reports from semiannual to quarterly. The filing dates for quarterly reports are April 20th, July 20th, October 20th, and January 20th, or the next business day should the filing date occur on a weekend or holiday. The coverage periods are January 1 through March 31, April 1 through June 30, July 1 through September 30, and October 1 through December 31 for the April Quarterly (Q1), July Quarterly (Q2), October Quarterly (Q3), and January Quarterly (Q4) reports respectively.

Registration and Reporting Thresholds

Section 4 of the LDA was amended so that the financial threshold for registration for the new quarterly reporting periods is $2,500 in lobbying income for a lobbying firm and $10,000 in lobbying expenses for organizations that employ in-house lobbyists. The threshold as of January 1, 2008 will be as stated above. The Consumer Price Index (CPI) will be used to adjust these figures after January 1, 2009.

The Section 5(c) rounding rules for income or expenses were also amended to require amounts in excess of $5,000 to be rounded to the nearest $10,000. Amounts less than $5,000 do not have to be rounded; and the checkbox for reporting this information on Form LD-2 has been retained.

Additional Disclosure of a Client as a State or Local Government or Instrumentality

Section 5 of the LDA was amended to require additional disclosure regarding whether the client is a state or local government or department, agency, special purpose district, or other instrumentality controlled by one or more state or local governments. A checkbox has been added to Line 7 of LD-2 to accomplish this disclosure.

Lobbying Disclosure Act Guidance
Revised May 29, 2008

Semiannual Reports of Certain Contributions

Section 5 of the LDA was amended by mandating an additional filing requirement. Form LD-203 is required to be filed semiannually by July 30th and January 30th (or the next business day should either of those days fall on a weekend or holiday) covering the first and second calendar halves of the year. Registrants **and each of their lobbyists (who were active for the entire or part of the semi-annual period)** must file separate reports which detail various expenses including FECA contributions, honorary contributions, presidential library contributions, and payments for event costs. In addition, the filer must certify that the filer has read and understands the Rules of the House and Senate relating to gifts and travel and has not provided, requested, or directed a gift with knowledge that it would violate either House or Senate Rules. (See discussion in Section 7 below.)

Revised Definition of Affiliation

Section 4 of the LDA was amended to expand disclosure in regard to previously undisclosed affiliated entities that contribute more than $5,000 toward the registrant's lobbying activities (either directly to the registrant or indirectly through the client) in a quarterly period **and** actively participate in the planning, supervision, or control of such lobbying activities. The revised section includes exceptions to narrow the scope of additional disclosure to make clear that an individual member or donor who only is a member of, or only contributes to, the client or other affiliate does not have to be disclosed.

Additional Disclosure of Past Governmental Employment

Section 4 of the LDA was amended to lengthen the covered period for disclosure of previous government service. The law now requires disclosure regarding whether a lobbyist served as a covered Executive Branch official or a covered Legislative Branch official in the 20 years before the date on which the individual first acted as a lobbyist on behalf of the client. This requirement applies to registrations having an effective date of 01/01/2008 or later. For any new registrant/client relationship requiring a registration which has an effective date of January 1, 2008 or later, government employment information going back 20 years is required. Registrants do not have to amend their pre-2008 registration information to reflect this additional disclosure requirement in reference to lobbyists listed in those reports.

Mandatory Electronic Filing of LDA Documents

Section 5 of the LDA was amended to require the mandatory electronic filing of all documents required by the LDA. The only exception to mandatory electronic filing is for the purpose of amending reports in the format previously filed, or for compliance with the Americans with Disabilities Act. Each electronic lobbying disclosure form provides usability for people with vision impairments who have the appropriate software and hardware. If you have questions regarding additional ADA accommodations, please contact the Senate Office of Public Records at 202, 224-0758.

Increased Civil and Criminal Penalties

Whoever knowingly fails: (1) to correct a defective filing within 60 days after notice of such a defect by the Secretary of the Senate or the Clerk of the House; or (2) to comply with any other provision of the Act, may be subject to a civil fine of not more than $200,000. Whoever knowingly and corruptly fails to comply with any provision of this Act shall be imprisoned for not more than five years or fined under title 18, United States Code, or both.

Revised Forms, Instructions and Format

LD-1, the registration form, and LD-2, the reporting form, have been revised. Previous editions of these forms are obsolete. Additionally, all LDA documents must be filed electronically (with the ADA exception noted above) Instructions for both LD-1 and LD-2 have been updated to correspond with the new forms.

Lobbying Disclosure Act Guidance
Revised May 29, 2008

LD-1 Changes

The revised LD-1 (11/07) closely resembles the obsolete LD-1. The changed content is discussed below.

1. The disclosure of previous governmental service has been changed from 2 to 20 years on Line 10.
2. The definition of an affiliate has been expanded on Line 13. Please note that Line 13 may only accommodate sixty (60) total listings. Those affiliates that "in whole or major part" participate in the planning, control, or supervision of the lobbying activities of the client or affiliate must be listed first, as it is mandated that they be disclosed in the filing and not through other means. The remaining active participants must be listed following the ones described above. For disclosure of more than 60 organizations, it is strongly recommended that you either (i) complete the Internet Address field instead and list the additional affiliated organizations on your web site (as the electronic form only accommodates up to 60 listings) or (ii) file an amendment(s) to your filing disclosing the other additional affiliated organizations.

LD-2 Changes

The revised LD-2 (11/07) closely resembles the obsolete LD-2. Specific refinements to LD-2 are discussed below.

1. Line 7 has a checkbox for disclosing whether the client is a state or local government or instrumentality.
2. The reporting thresholds on Lines 12 and 13 have been changed to a quarterly basis.
3. The disclosure of previous governmental service has been changed from 2 to 20 years on Line 18.

The definition of an affiliate has been expanded on Line 25. Please note that Line 25 may only accommodate forty (40) total listings. Those affiliates that "in whole or major part" participate in the planning, control, or supervision of the lobbying activities of the client or affiliate must be listed first and so identified as "in whole or in major part ...", as it is mandated that they be disclosed in the filing and not through other means. The remaining active participants must be listed following the ones described above. For disclosure of more than 40 organizations, it is strongly recommended that you either (i) complete the Internet Address field instead and list the additional affiliated organizations on your web site (as the electronic form only accommodates up to 40 listings) or (ii) file an amendment(s) to your filing disclosing the other additional affiliated organizations.

Section 3 – Definitions

"Actively Participates": An organization "actively participates" in the planning, supervision, or control of lobbying activities of a client or registrant when that organization (or an employee of the organization in his or her capacity as an employee) engages directly in planning, supervising, or controlling at least some of the lobbying activities of the client or registrant. Examples of activities constituting active participation would include participating in decisions about selecting or retaining lobbyists, formulating priorities among legislative issues, designing lobbying strategies, performing a leadership role in forming an ad hoc coalition, and other similarly substantive planning or managerial roles, such as serving on a committee with responsibility over lobbying decisions.

Organizations that, though members of or affiliated with a client, have only a passive role in the lobbying activities of the client (or of the registrant on behalf of the client), are not considered active participants in the planning, supervision, or control of such lobbying activities. Examples of activities constituting only a passive role would include merely donating or paying dues to the client or registrant, receiving information or reports on legislative matters, occasionally responding to requests for technical expertise or other information in support of the lobbying activities, attending a general meeting of the association or coalition client, or expressing a position with regard to legislative goals in a manner open to, and on a par with that of, all members of a coalition or association – such as through an annual meeting, a questionnaire, or similar vehicle. Mere occasional participation, such as offering an ad hoc informal comment regarding lobbying strategy to the client or registrant, in the absence of any formal or regular supervision or direction of lobbying activities, does not constitute active participation if neither the organization nor its employee has the authority to direct the client or the registrant on lobbying matters <u>and</u> the participation does not otherwise exceed a de minimis role.

Affiliated Organization: An affiliated organization is any entity other than the client that contributes in excess of $5,000 toward the registrant's lobbying activities in a quarterly period, and actively participates in the planning, supervision, or control of such lobbying activities. The amendments did not change the way in which Pre-HLOGA identified affiliates (i.e., those that in whole or in major part plan, supervise, or control such lobbying activities) are to be disclosed on LD-1 and LD-2.

Reports of Certain Contributions: Form LD-203 is required to be filed semiannually by July 30th and January 30th (or next business day should either of those days fall on a weekend or holiday) covering the first and second calendar halves of the year. Registrants and active lobbyists (who are not terminated for all clients) must file separate reports which detail FECA contributions, honorary contributions, presidential library contributions, and payments for event costs. (See discussion in Section 7 below.)

Client: Any person or entity that employs or retains another person for financial or other compensation to conduct lobbying activities on behalf of the person or entity. An organization employing its own lobbyists is considered its own client for reporting purposes.

Covered Executive Branch Official: The application of coverage of Section 3(3) (F) of the LDA (who is a covered Executive Branch official) was intended for Schedule C employees only. Senior Executive Service employees are not covered Executive Branch officials as defined in the Act unless they fall within one of the categories below. Covered Executive Branch officials are:

1. The President
2. The Vice President
3. Officers and employees of the Executive Office of the President
4. Any official serving in an Executive Level I through V position
5. Any member of the uniformed services serving at grade 0 7 or above
6. Schedule C employees.

Lobbying Disclosure Act Guidance
Revised May 29, 2008

Covered Legislative Branch Official: Covered Legislative Branch officials are:

1. A Member of Congress
2. An elected Officer of either the House or the Senate
3. An employee, or any other individual functioning in the capacity of an employee, who works for a Member, committee, leadership staff of either the Senate or House, a joint committee of Congress, a working group or caucus organized to provide services to Members, and any other Legislative Branch employee serving in a position described under section 109(13) of the Ethics in Government Act of 1978.

In whole or major part: The term "in major part" means in substantial part. It is not necessary that an organization or foreign entity exercise majority control or supervision in order to fall within Sections 4(b) (3) (B) and 4(b)(4)(B). In general, 20 percent control or supervision should be considered "substantial" for purposes of these sections.

Lobbying Activities: Lobbying contacts and any efforts in support of such contacts, including preparation or planning activities, research and other background work that is intended, at the time of its preparation, for use in contacts and coordination with the lobbying activities of others.

Lobbying Contact: Any oral, written or electronic communication to a covered official that is made on behalf of a client with regard to the enumerated subjects at 2 U.S.C. §1602(8)(A). Note the exceptions to the definition at 2 U.S.C. ' 1602(8)(B). See Discussion at Section 5 below.

Lobbying Firm: A lobbying firm is a person or entity consisting of one or more individuals who meet the definition of a lobbyist with respect to a client other than that person or entity. The definition includes a self-employed lobbyist.

Lobbying Registration: An initial registration on Form LD-1 filed pursuant to Section 4 of the Act (2 U.S.C. §1603).

Lobbying Report: A quarterly report on Form LD-2 filed pursuant to Section 5 of the Act (2 U.S.C. §1604).

Lobbyist: Any individual (1) who is either employed or retained by a client for financial or other compensation (2) whose services include more than one lobbying contact; and (3) whose lobbying activities constitute 20 percent or more of his or her services' time on behalf of that client during any three-month period.

Person or Entity: Any individual, corporation, company, foundation, association, labor organization, firm, partnership, society, joint stock company, group of organizations, or state or local government.

Public Official: A public official includes an elected or appointed official, or an employee of a Federal, state or local government in the United States. There are five exceptions to this definition, including a college or university, a government–sponsored enterprise, a public utility, guaranty agency or an agency of any state functioning as a student loan secondary market. The 1998 amendments to the LDA expanded the definition of a public official in Section 3(15)(F) to add a group of governments acting together as an international organization. Its purpose was to ensure those international organizations, such as the World Bank, would be treated in the same manner as the governments that comprise them.

Registrant: A lobbying firm or an organization employing in-house lobbyists that files a registration pursuant to Section 4 of the Act.

Section 4 - Lobbying Registration

Who Must Register and When

Lobbying firms are required to file a separate registration for each client. A lobbying firm is exempt from registration for a particular client if its total income from that client for lobbying activities does not exceed and is not expected to exceed $2,500 during a quarterly period.

Note: A lobbyist is not the registrant unless he/she is self-employed. In that case, the self-employed lobbyist is treated as a lobbying firm.

Organizations employing in-house lobbyists file a single registration. An organization is exempt from registration if its total expenses for lobbying activities do not exceed and are not expected to exceed $10,000 during a quarterly period.

The registration requirement is triggered at the earlier of the date a lobbyist is employed or retained to make one lobbying contact on behalf of a client, or the date a lobbyist in fact makes a second lobbying contact. In either case, registration is required within 45 days.

Example 1: Lobbying firm "A" is retained on May 1, 2008 by Client "B" to make a lobbying contact.. Assuming that "B" continues to want "A" to make lobbying contacts for B, "A" files an LD-1 on behalf of "B" with an effective date of registration of May 1, 2008.

Example 2: Corporation "C" does not employ an individual who meets the definition of "lobbyist." Employee "X" is told by her supervisor to contact the Congressman representing the district in which Corporation "C" is headquartered. "X" makes a lobbying contact on June 1, 2008. "X" does not anticipate making any further lobbying contacts, but spends 25% of her time on this legislative issue. No registration is required at this point. In August 2008, "X" is instructed to follow up with the Congressman again. "C" registers and discloses August 5, 2008 as the effective date of registration (the date that "X" contacted the Congressman for the second time and thereby meets the definition of a lobbyist.

Preparing to File a Registration - Threshold Requirements

In order to determine the applicability of the LDA, one must first look at the definition of "lobbyist" under Section 3(10). Under this definition, an individual is a "lobbyist" with respect to a particular client if he or she makes more than one lobbying contact **and** his or her "lobbying activities" (as defined in Section 3(7)) constitute at least 20 percent of the individual's time in services for **that** client over any three-month period. Note that a registration would not be required for pro bono clients since the monetary thresholds of Section 4(a)(3)(A)(i) in the case of a lobbying firm, or of Section 4(a)(3)(A)(ii) in the case of an organization employing in-house lobbyists, would not be met. Keep in mind that the obligation to report under the LDA arises from active status as a registrant. Therefore if a registration has been filed for a pro bono client, reports would be expected to be filed until the registration is validly terminated.

More than One Lobbying Contact

"More than one lobbying contact" means more than one communication to a covered official. Note that an individual falls within the definition of "lobbyist" by making more than one lobbying contact over the course of services provided for a particular client (even if the second contact occurs in a later quarterly period).

Example 1: Lobbyist "A" telephones Covered Official "B" in the morning to discuss proposed legislation. In the afternoon she telephones Covered Official "C" to discuss the same legislation. Lobbyist "A" has made more than one lobbying contact.

Example 2: Under some circumstances a series of discussions with a particular official might be considered a single communication, such as when a telephone call is interrupted and continued at a later time. Discussions taking place on more than one day with the same covered official, however, should be presumed to be more than one lobbying contact.

Clarification of an Exception to Lobbying Contact

Section 3(8)(B)(ix) excepts from the definition of "lobbying contact" communications "required by subpoena, civil investigative demand, or otherwise compelled by statute, regulation, or other action of the Congress or an agency." The amendments in 1998 clarified that communications that are compelled by the action of a Federal agency would include communications that are required by a Federal agency contract, grant, loan, permit, or license.

Example: Contractor "A" has a contract to provide technical assistance to Agency "B" on an ongoing basis. Technical communications between Contractor "A's" personnel and covered officials at Agency "B" would be required by the contract and therefore would not constitute "lobbying contacts."

Note, however, that this exception would not encompass an attempt by "A" to influence covered officials regarding either matters of policy, or an award of a new contract, since such communications would not be required by the existing contract.

Do Lobbying Activities Constitute 20% Or More of an Individual's Time?

Lobbying activity is defined in Section 3(7) as "lobbying contacts and efforts in support of such contacts, including . . . background work that is intended, at the time it is performed, for use in contacts, and coordination with the lobbying activities of others." If the intent of the work is to support ongoing and future lobbying, then it would fall within the definition of lobbying activities. Timing of the work performed, as well as the status of the issue, is also pivotal. Generally, if work such as reporting or monitoring occurs at a time when future lobbying contacts are contemplated, such reporting and monitoring should be considered as a part of planning or coordinating of lobbying contacts, and therefore included as "lobbying activity." If, on the other hand, a person reports back to the relevant committee or officer regarding the status of a completed effort, that activity would probably not be included as a lobbying activity, if reports are not being used to prepare a lobbying strategy the next time the issue is considered.

Communications excepted from the definition of "lobbying contact" under Section 3(8)(B) of the LDA may be considered "lobbying activities" under some circumstances. Communications excepted by Section 3(8)(B) will constitute "lobbying activities" if they are in support of other communications which constitute "lobbying contacts."

Example: Under Section 3(8)(B)(v), the term "lobbying contact" does not include "a request for a meeting, a request for the status of an action, or any other similar administrative request, if the request does not include an attempt to influence a covered Executive Branch official or a covered legislative branch official." However, a status request would constitute "lobbying activity" if it were in support of a subsequent lobbying contact.

Please note that the 20% of time threshold applies to registration and not to the reporting section.

Lobbying Disclosure Act Guidance
Revised May 29, 2008

Is it Lobbying Contact/Lobbying Activity?

If a communication is limited to routine information-gathering questions and there is not an attempt to influence a covered official, the exception of Section 3(8)(B)(v) for "any other similar administrative request" would normally apply. In determining whether there is an attempt to influence a covered official, the identity of the person asking the questions and her relationship to the covered official obviously will be important factors.

Example 1: Lobbyist "A", a former chief of staff in a congressional office, is now a partner in the law firm retained to lobby for Client "B." After waiting one year to comply with post-employment restrictions on lobbying, Lobbyist "A" telephones the Member on whose staff she served. She asks about the status of legislation affecting Client "B's" interests. Presumably "B" will expect the call to have been part of an effort to influence the Member, even though only routine matters were raised at that particular time.

Example 2: Company "Z" offers temporary employment to recent college graduates. The graduates are hired to conduct surveys of congressional staff by reading prepared questions and recording the answers. The questions seek only information. These communications do not amount to lobbying contacts.

Lobbying Contacts and Activities Using Section 15 Election (Alternate Reporting Methods)

Section 15 of the LDA permits those organizations that are required to file and do file under Sections 6033(b)(8) of the Internal Revenue Code and organizations that are subject to Section 162(e) of the IRC to use the tax law definitions of lobbying in lieu of the LDA definitions for determining "contacts" and "lobbying activities" for Executive Branch lobbying. Registrants should note that the tax definition of lobbying is broader with respect to the type of activities reported, while it is narrower with respect to the universe of Executive Branch officials who qualify as covered Executive Branch employees.

Under the 1998 amendments to the LDA, registrants making a Section 15 election must use the Internal Revenue Code definition for Executive Branch lobbying, and the LDA definition for Legislative Branch lobbying. Because there are fewer Executive Branch officials under the IRC definitions than under the LDA definitions, this may result in fewer individuals being listed as lobbyists and fewer lobbying contacts reflected on the LD-2.

Also note that definitions under the tax code include "grass-roots," "state" and "local" lobbying, while the LDA excludes those types of lobbying from the definition of "lobbying activities." The LDA does not permit modification of the tax code definition to exclude such expenditures when reporting lobbying expenses.

Relationship Between 20% of Time and Monetary Threshold

If the definition of "lobbyist" is satisfied with respect to at least one individual for a particular client, the potential registrant (either a lobbying firm or an organization employing the lobbyist, or a self-employed individual lobbyist) is **not** required to register if it does not meet the monetary thresholds of Section 4(a)(3)(A)(i), in the case of a "lobbying firm," or of Section 4(a)(3)(A)(ii), in the case of an organization employing in-house lobbyists. Note that the monetary exemption is computed based on the lobbying activities of the potential registrant as a whole for the particular client in question, not simply on the lobbying activities of those individuals who are "lobbyists."

Example 1: A law firm has two lawyers who perform services for a particular client. Lawyer "A" spends 15 percent of the time she works for that client on lobbying activities, including some lobbying contacts. Lawyer "B" spends 25 percent of the time he works for the client on lobbying activities, but makes no lobbying contacts. Neither lawyer falls within the definition of "lobbyist," and therefore the law firm is not required to register for that client, even if the income it receives for lobbying activities on behalf of the client exceeds $2,500.

Example 2: Employee "A" of a trade association is a "lobbyist" who spends 25 percent of his time on lobbying activities on behalf of the association. There are $6,000 of expenses related to Employee "A's" lobbying activities. Employee "B" is not a "lobbyist" but engages in lobbying activities in support of lobbying contacts made by Employee "A." There are $6,000 of additional expenses related to the lobbying activities of Employee "B." The trade association is required to register because it employs a "lobbyist" and its total expenses in connection with lobbying activities on its own behalf exceed $10,000.

Lobbying Disclosure Act Guidance
Revised May 29, 2008

Example 3: Same as Example 2, except the expenses related to the lobbying activities of Employees "A" and "B" total only $9,000, but the trade association also pays $5,000 to an outside firm for lobbying activities. Registration is still required because payments to outside contractors (including lobbying firms that may be separately registered under the LDA) must be included in the total expenses of an organization employing lobbyists on its own behalf.

Timing

The registration requirement is triggered at the earlier of the date a lobbyist is employed or retained to make more than one lobbying contact on behalf of the client, or the date a lobbyist in fact makes a second lobbying contact. In either case, registration is required within 45 days.

Example: Lobbying Firm "A" is retained to monitor an issue, but whether or not lobbying contacts will be made depends on future legislative developments. In another case, Corporation "B," which employs an in-house lobbyist, knows that its lobbyist will make contacts but reasonably expects its lobbying expenditures will not amount to $10,000 in a quarterly period. However, issues of interest to "B" turn out to be more controversial than expected, and the $10,000 threshold is in fact met a month later.

Lobbying firm "A" has no registration requirement at the present time. The requirement to register is triggered if and when the firm makes contacts, or reasonably expects that it will make contacts. Corporation "B's" registration requirement arose as soon as it knew, or reasonably expected, that its lobbying expenditures will exceed $10,000. "B" needs to register immediately.

Lobbying Disclosure Act Guidance
Revised May 29, 2008

Section 5 - Special Registration Circumstances

Elaboration on the Definition of Client

In some cases a registrant is retained as part of a larger lobbying effort that encompasses more than one lobbying firm on behalf of a third party. Generally, the entity that is paying the registrant is listed as the client. The third party, who is paying the intermediary (client) is listed on Line 13 as an affiliate.

> *Example: Client "P" retains lobbying firm "F" for general lobbying purposes, but has a new interest in obtaining an outcome in an area new to "P." "F" realizes that a boutique lobbying firm "L" has an excellent track record for obtaining the type of outcome "P" is seeking, and talks to "P" about subcontracting. "P" agrees with "F's" strategy. "F" contacts "L" to retain the latter to do the project. "F" is responsible for paying "L." Within 45 days, "L" registers disclosing "F" as the client, and "P" as the affiliate.*

Lobbying Firms Retained Under A Contingent Fee

Law other than the LDA governs whether a firm may be retained on a contingent-fee basis. There is, for example, a general prohibition on the payment of contingent fees in connection with the award of government contracts. Assuming, however, that the agreement is not contrary to law or public policy, an agreement to make lobbying contacts for a contingent fee, like other fee arrangements triggers a registration requirement at inception. The fee is disclosed on LD-2 for the quarterly period that the registrant becomes entitled to it.

> *Example 1: On January 1, 2008, Lobbying Firm "G" agrees to lobby for Client "H" for a fee contingent on a certain result, **and the agreement is permitted under other applicable law**. Lobbying activities begin. "G" is required to register by February 14, 2008. The result is not obtained and "G" is not entitled to any fee during the first quarterly period. "G" must report its lobbying activities for the first quarterly period; the income reported is "Less than $5,000." The desired result does occur in the second quarterly period of 2008. In the report for that period, "G" discloses its lobbying activities for that period and the total contingent fee.*

> *Example 2: Lobbying Firm "J" discusses an arrangement to accept stock options worth $4,500 from Client "M" in lieu of payment of a contingency fee. After determining that acceptance of a success fee is not a violation of another statute, "J" signs a contract with "M," and registers. Late in the first quarter of the lobbying activities, it appeared "J" achieved the result. "J's" initial quarterly lobbying report disclosed lobbying income of less than $5,000. "M's" stock value increased shortly thereafter to be valued at $6,000, so "J" exercised its options. "J" amended the previously filed quarterly report to reflect income of "$5,000 or more," and rounding the amount to $10,000.*

Lobbying Disclosure Act Guidance
Revised May 29, 2008

Registration for Entities with Subsidiaries or State and Local Affiliates

Assuming a parent entity or national association and its subsidiary or subordinate are separate legal entities, the parent makes a determination whether it meets the registration threshold based upon its own activities, and does not include subordinate units' lobbying activities in its assessment. Each subordinate must make its own assessment as to whether any of its own employees meet the definition of a lobbyist, and then determine if it meets the registration threshold with respect to lobbying expenses.

Example: Lobbyist "Z" is an employee of Company "A," which is a wholly-owned subsidiary of Company "B." "Z's" lobbying activities advance the interests of both. Which company is responsible for registering and reporting under the LDA?

The registration and reporting requirements apply to the organization of which Lobbyist "Z" is an employee. Therefore, Company "A" would register and file the quarterly reports.

If Company "B" contributes $5,000 or more to "Z's" lobbying activities during a quarterly period and actively participates in the planning, supervision, or control of the lobbying activities, Company "B" must be listed on Company "A's" Form LD-1, Line 13. A contribution may take any form, and may be direct or indirect. For example, if Company "B" established Company "A" with an initial capital contribution of $1,000,000, which "A" draws upon for employee salaries, including "Z's," and to pay for office space used by "Z," a $5,000 contribution probably has been made.

If Company "B" is a foreign entity, and the facts are otherwise the same as above, "B" would be listed on Line 14 of the Form LD-1 filed by Company "A." "B's" interests in specific lobbying issues would also be disclosed on Line 19 of Form LD-2.

The LDA does not make any express provision for combined or consolidated filings. A single filing by a parent corporation may be appropriate in some cases, especially when there are multiple subsidiaries and the lobbyists address the same issues for all and act under the close control of the parent. In this regard, note that the LDA does not contain any specific definition of "employee" (there is only the general definition of Section 3(5)), and the policy of the LDA is to promote disclosure of real parties in interest.

In circumstances in which multiple subsidiaries each have only a fraction of the lobbyist's time and little control over his work, the parent which in fact exercises actual control can be regarded as the "employer" for LDA purposes. In such cases, the parent may file a single registration, provided that Line 10 of Form LD-1 discloses that the listed lobbyists are employees of subsidiaries and the subsidiaries are identified as affiliated organizations on Line 13.

Effect of Mergers and Acquisitions on Registrations

The following examples serve to illustrate hypothetical situations regarding mergers and acquisitions:

Example 1: Corporation "C" registered under the LDA during 2008. Effective upon close of business on December 31, 2008, "C" merged with Corporation "D." "D," the surviving corporation, had no lobbyist-employees before the merger and is not registered. How and when should this information be reported? Assuming that "D" retains at least one of "C's" lobbyist-employees and will incur lobbying expenses of at least $10,000 during the January-March quarterly period, Corporation "D" is required to register. The 45-day period in which its initial registration must be filed begins to run on December 31, 2008, the date "D" first had lobbyist-employees, and the registration is due by February 14, 2009. On the other hand, if "D" will not be lobbying after the merger, it is not required to register. In pre-merger discussions, Corporation "C" might have agreed to terminate its registration and file its final lobbying report before ceasing its corporate existence. If, however, "C" did not do so, Corporation "D" should terminate the registration and file the outstanding lobbying report in "C's" name. "D" may simply annotate the signature block on Form LD-2 to indicate that it is filing as successor-in-interest to "C."

Lobbying Disclosure Act Guidance
Revised May 29, 2008

Example 2: Lobbying Firm "O" is a registrant under the LDA. It merges with Lobbying Firm "P," which is also a registrant. The new entity will be known as Lobbying Firm "T." How and when should this information be reported? The answer depends on the particular facts. If Lobbying Firm "T" is a newly created legal entity, it should file a new registration within 45 days. The registrations of both "O" and "P" should be terminated, and separate final lobbying reports filed for each. But if "T" is simply the new name adopted by "O" following the merger with "P," with "P" going out of existence, "O" should report its new name and other updated information (such as the names of lobbyist-employees of "P" who are retained or hired by "T" on Form LD-2, with a cover note explaining the nature of the change. "P's" registration should be terminated, and a final report for "P" only should be filed.

Example 3: Corporation "J," a registrant, acquired Corporation "K," a non-registrant. At the time of the acquisition, "J" changed its name to "J & K." How and when should this information be reported? For LDA purposes, this is simply a change in the name of the registrant. The change should be reported on Line 1 of the next quarterly report (LD-2).

Associations or Coalitions

The LDA provides that "[i]n the case of a coalition or association that employs or retains other persons to conduct lobbying activities, the client is the coalition or association and not its individual members" (Section 3(2)). A bona fide coalition that employs or retains lobbyists on behalf of the coalition may be the client for LDA purposes, even if the coalition is not a legal entity or has no formal name. A registrant lobbying for an unnamed informal coalition needs to adopt some type of identifier for Line 7 of Form LD-1, and indicate "(Informal Coalition)" or another applicable description. For all coalitions and associations, formal or informal, the LDA requires further disclosures, e.g., of organizations other than the client which contribute more than $5,000 toward the lobbying activities of the registrant in the quarterly period, **and** actively participate in the planning, supervision or control of the lobbying activities (Section 4(b)(3)). Such organizations are identified on Line 13 of Form LD-1.

Example 1: Association "A" has 20 organizational members who each pay $20,000 as a portion of their annual dues to fund "A's" lobbying activities. "E" is an employee of Organization "O", which is a member of "A." "E" serves as a member of "A's" board, as a representative of "O." While "A" carries out various functions, a substantial part of its mission is lobbying on issues of interest to its member organizations. "E's" board membership constitutes active participation by "O" in the lobbying activities of "A," and thus "O" would need to be listed as an affiliated organization of "A.".

Example 2: Another association "A" has 1000 organizational members who each pay $20,000 as a portion of their annual dues to fund A's lobbying activities. "E" is an employee of Organization "O," which is a member of "A." "E" serves as a member of "A's" board, as a representative of "O." "A" performs numerous functions, only a modest portion of which is lobbying. With regard to "A's" lobbying activities, "A's" board is only involved in approving an overall budget for such activities, but otherwise leaves supervision, direction, and control of such matters to a separate committee of member organizations. "E's" board membership in this case does not constitute active participation by "O" in the lobbying activities of "A."

Example 3: Another association "A" has 1000 organizational members who each pay $1,000 a month in annual dues to "A." "E" is an employee of Organization "O,", which is a member of "A." "E" serves as a member of "A's" lobbying oversight group as a representative of "O." The lobbying oversight group plans and supervises lobbying strategy for "A." While "E's" activities in "A" would constitute active participation, because "O" does not contribute $5,000 in the reporting quarter to the lobbying activities of "A," "O" would not need to be listed as an affiliate of "A."

Example 4: Another association "A" has 100 organizational members who each pay $30,000 a month as a portion of their annual dues to fund "A's" lobbying activities. "E" is an employee of Organization "O,", and attends "A's" annual meeting/conference, informally provides "O's" list of legislative priorities to "A," and also facilitates responses from "O" to occasional requests for information by "A's" lobbyists. These activities would not make "O" an active participant in the lobbying activities of "A."

Example 5: Organization "O" joins with a group of nine other organizations to form Coalition "C" to lobby on an issue of interest to it. Each contributes $50,000 to "C's" budget. " O's" vice president for government relations is part of the informal group that directs the lobbying strategy for" C". "O" would be considered an active participant in "C's" lobbying activities and would have to be disclosed.

Note that a coalition with a foreign entity as a member must identify the foreign entity on line 14 of LD-1 if the foreign entity meets the test of either Section 4(b)(3) or 4(b)(4).

Churches, Integrated Auxiliaries, Conventions or Association of Churches and Religious Orders - Hiring of Outside Firms.

Although the definition of a lobbying contact does not include a communication made by a church, its integrated auxiliary, a convention or association of churches and religious orders (Section 3(8)(B)(xviii)), if a church (its integrated auxiliary, a convention or association of churches, and religious orders) hires an outside firm that conducts lobbying activity on its behalf, the outside firm must register if registration is otherwise required.

Registration of Professional Associations of Elected Officials

The Section 3(15) definition of "public official" includes a professional association of elected officials who are exempt from registration. If the association retains an outside firm to lobby, the lobbying firm must register if otherwise required to do so, i.e., the firm employs a lobbyist as defined in Section 3(10) and lobbying income exceeds $2,500 in a quarterly period.

Lobbying Disclosure Act Guidance
Revised May 29, 2008

Section 6 - Quarterly Reporting of Lobbying Activities

When and Why a Report is Needed

Each registrant must file a quarterly report on Form LD-2 no later than 20 days (or on the first business day after such 20th day if the 20th day is not a business day) after the end of the quarterly period beginning on the first day of January, April, July and October **of each year** in which a registrant is registered. Lobbying firms file separate reports for each client for each quarterly reporting period, while organizations employing in-house lobbyists file one report covering their in-house lobbying activities for each quarterly reporting period. All reports must be filed electronically (with exceptions as noted previously). **The Secretary and Clerk do not have the authority under the LDA to grant extensions to registrants.**

The obligation to report under the LDA arises from active status as a registrant (i.e., a registration on file that has not been validly terminated). Section 5(a) of the LDA requires a registrant to file a report for the quarterly period **in which it incurred its registration requirement**, and for each quarterly period thereafter, through and including the reporting period encompassing the date of registration termination. A timely report using Form LD-2 is required even though the registration was in effect for only part of the reporting period. So long as a registration is on file and has not been terminated, a registrant must report its lobbying activities even if those activities during a particular quarterly period would not trigger a registration requirement in the first instance (e.g., a lobbying firm's income from a client amounted to less than $2,500 during a particular quarterly period). A registrant with no lobbying activity during a quarterly period completes and files the first page (only) of Form LD-2.

> *Example 1: "A" is the only lobbyist of Lobbying Firm "Z" listed in the registration filed for Client "Y" on February 14, 2008. During January-March 2008, "A" lobbied for "Y" nearly full-time. During the April - June period in 2008, however, "A" made only one lobbying contact for "Y" in April, but lobbying fees for the quarter were $10,000. For the April – June quarterly period, even though "A" had minimal lobbying activities, Lobbying Firm "Z" must report "A's" lobbying activities (due to "A's" being listed as a lobbyist) and must report the $10,000 lobbying fees.*

> *Example 2: Lobbying Firm "Z" is retained by Client "X" on June 1, 2008 for thirty days to lobby on a particular issue that is on the legislative calendar and the issue is settled prior to the departure of House and Senate Members for the July 4th recess. Firm "Z" must file its registration by July 15, file its Q2 Report by July 20, and, if it chooses to terminate, file its termination report by October 20.*

Disclosing that a Client is a State or Local Government or Instrumentality

If the client is a state or local government or instrumentality, check the box on Line 7 of LD-1 and LD-2.

Mandatory Electronic Filing

Section 5 of the LDA was amended to require the mandatory electronic filing of all documents required by the LDA. The only exception to mandatory electronic filing is for the purpose of amending reports in the format previously filed, or for compliance with the Americans with Disabilities Act. Each electronic lobbying disclosure form provides usability for people with vision impairments who have the appropriate software and hardware. If you have questions regarding additional ADA accommodations, please contact the Senate Office of Public Records at 202, 224-0758.

Preparing to File the Quarterly Report - Income or Expense Recording

The LDA does not contain any special record keeping provisions, but requires, in the case of an outside lobbying firm (including self-employed individuals), a good faith estimate of all income received from the client, other than payments for matters unrelated to lobbying activities. In the case of an organization employing in-house lobbyists, the LDA requires a good faith estimate of the total expenses of its lobbying activities. As long as the registrant has a reasonable system in place and complies in good faith with that system, the requirement of reporting expenses or income would be met. Since Section 6(a)(5) requires the Secretary and Clerk to "retain registrations for a period of at least 6 years after they are terminated and reports for a period of at least 6 years after they are filed," we recommend registrants retain copies of their filings and supporting documentation for the same length of time.

Lobbying Firm Income

Lobbying firms report income earned or accrued from lobbying activities during a quarterly period, even though the client may not be billed or make payment until a later time. For a lobbying firm, gross income from the client for lobbying activities is reportable, including reimbursable expenses costs or disbursements that are in addition to fees and separately invoiced. Line 12 of LD-2 provides boxes for a lobbying firm to report income of less than $5,000, or of $5,000 or more. If lobbying income is $5,000 or more, a lobbying firm must provide a good faith estimate of the actual dollar amount **rounded to the nearest $10,000.**

Organization Expenses using LDA Expense Reporting Method

Organizations that employ in-house lobbyists may incur lobbying-related expenses in the form of employee compensation, office overhead, or payments to vendors which may include lobbying firms. Organizations must report expenses as they are incurred, though payment may be made later. Line 13 of LD-2 provides for an organization to report lobbying expenses of less than $5,000, or $5,000 or more. If lobbying expenses are $5,000 or more, the organization must provide a good faith estimate of the actual dollar amount **rounded to the nearest $10,000.** Organizations using the LDA expense reporting method mark the "Method A" box on Line 14.

To ensure complete reporting, the Secretary and Clerk have consistently interpreted Section 5(b)(4) to require such organizations to report all of their expenses incurred in connection with lobbying activities, including all payments to retained lobby firms or outside entities, without considering whether any particular payee has a separate obligation to register and report under the LDA. Logically, if an organization employing in-house lobbyists also retains a lobbying firm, the expense reported by the organization should be greater than the fees reported by the lobbying firm of which the organization is a client. All employee time spent in lobbying activities must be included in determining the organization's lobbying expenses, even if the employee does not meet the statutory definition of a "lobbyist."

> *Example: The CEO of a registrant, "Defense Contractor," travels to Washington to meet with a covered DOD official regarding the renewal of a government contract. "Defense Contractor" has already determined that its CEO is not a "lobbyist," because he does not spend 20 percent of his time on "lobbying activities" during a quarterly period. Nonetheless, the expenses reasonably allocable to the CEO's lobbying activities (e.g., plane ticket to Washington, salary and benefit costs, etc.) will be reportable.*

Similarly, all expenses of lobbying activities incurred during a quarterly period are reportable. The Section 3(7) definition of lobbying activities is not limited to lobbying contacts.

> *Example: A research assistant in the Washington office of the registrant, "Defense Contractor" (described in the example above) researches and prepares the talking points for the CEO's lobbying contact with the covered DOD official. Likewise, the expenses reasonably allocable to the research assistant's lobbying activities will be included in "Defense Contractor's" expense estimate for the quarterly period.*

The examples below are intended to be illustrative of the possibilities of LDA expense reporting, and are not intended to require detailed accounting rules.

Example 1: An organization employing in-house lobbyists might choose to estimate lobbying expenses by asking each professional staffer to track his/her percentages of time devoted to lobbying activities. These percentages could be averaged to compute the percentage of the organization's total effort (and budget) that is devoted to lobbying activities. Under this example the organization would include salary costs (including a percentage of support staff salaries), overhead, and expenses, including any third-party costs attributable to lobbying.

Example 2: Another organization, which lobbies out of its Washington office, might avoid the need for detailed breakdowns by including the entire budget or expenses (whichever, the organization believes in good faith is closer to the actual amount) of its Washington office.

Organizations Reporting Expenses under Section 15 (Optional IRC Reporting Methods)

Section 15(a) of the LDA allows entities that are required to report and do report lobbying expenditures under section 6033(b)(8) of the Internal Revenue Code ("IRC") to use IRC definitions for purposes of LDA Sections (4)(a)(3) and 5(b)(4). Charitable organizations, as described in IRC Section 501(c)(3), are required to report to the Internal Revenue Service their lobbying expenditures in conformity with Section 6033(b)(8) of the IRC. They may treat as LDA expenses the amounts they treat for "influencing legislation" under the IRC.

Section 15(b) of the LDA allows entities that are subject to section 162(e) of the IRC to use IRC definitions for purposes of LDA Sections (4)(a)(3) and 5(b)(4). The eligible entities include for-profit organizations (other than lobbying firms) and tax-exempt organizations such as trade associations that calculate their lobbying expenses for IRC purposes with reference to Section 162(e) rules. We believe that this reporting option is available to include also a small number of trade association registrants not required by the IRC to report non-deductible lobbying expenses to their members (i.e., those whose members are tax-exempt).

If an eligible organization elects to report under Section 15, it must do so consistently for all reports covering a calendar year. The electing organization also must report **all expenses that fall within the applicable Internal Revenue Code definition.** The total that is ultimately reportable to the Internal Revenue Service is the figure that would be used for Line 13 reporting. Line 13 of LD-2 would require any organization to report if the amount of lobbying expenses were less than $5,000, or $5,000 or more. If the expense amount is $5,000 or more, it should be **rounded to the nearest $10,000.** Line 14 of LD-2 requires the electing organization to mark as applicable, either the "Method B" box (IRC Section 6033(b)(8)) or the "Method C" box (IRC Section 162(e)). The Secretary and Clerk are aware that the IRC and LDA are not harmonized in terms of expense reporting, and registrants are advised that backing out grass roots and state and local lobbying expenses out of the LDA expenses, thereby altering the IRS reportable total, is not permitted.

Quarterly Reporting of Lobbying Activities - Contents of Report

The two core disclosures required by Section 5(b) and 5(c) of the LDA and incorporated into Form LD-2 are: (1) lobbying income or expenses; and (2) lobbying issues. LD-2 has been designed to allow registrants the greatest flexibility in terms of document length to correspond with the varying amounts of information relating to the core disclosures. The following examples illustrate how the nature of the core disclosures builds the form.

Example 1: Registrant "A" represents Client "B" to monitor an issue of interest to B and make occasional lobbying contacts as necessary. During the Q1 2008 reporting period, "A" received $3,000 from "B," but had no lobbying activity because "B's" issue was dormant. "A" would complete the top portion of page 1 of LD-2, mark the boxes labeled "No Lobbying Activity" and "Less than $5,000," and file the report.

Example 2: Same circumstances as above, except that "A" has two lobbyists who make lobbying contacts on a single lobbying issue with the Senate and the House. In this case, the second page of LD-2 also would have to be completed, then "A" would file the report.

Example 3: Same circumstances as example 2, but one of the lobbyists retires during the reporting period. In this case, an update page of LD-2 would be required, as well as the first two completed pages, reflecting the removal of the lobbyist's name (his/her retirement) from A's registration and reports.

Section 5(b) requires specific information on the nature of the lobbying activities. Page 2 of Form LD-2 requires the registrant to:

1. Disclose the general lobbying issue area code (list 1 code per page).
2. Identify the specific issues on which the lobbyist(s) engaged in lobbying activities.
3. Identify the Houses of Congress and Federal Agencies contacted.
4. Disclose the lobbyists who had any activity in the general issue area.
5. Describe the interest of a foreign entity if applicable.

When reporting specific lobbying issues, some registrants have listed only House or Senate bill numbers on the issues page without further indication of their clients' specific lobbying issues. Such disclosures are not adequate, for several reasons. First, Section 5(b)(2)(A) of the LDA requires disclosure of "specific issues upon which a lobbyist employed by the registrant engaged in lobbying activities, including ... bill numbers[.]" As we read the law, a bill number is a required disclosure when the lobbying activities concern a bill, but is not in itself a complete disclosure. Further, in many cases, a bill number standing alone does not inform the public of the client's specific issue. Many bills are lengthy and complex, or may contain various provisions that are not always directly related to the main subject or title. If a registrant's client is interested in only one or a few specific provisions of a much larger bill, a lobbying report containing a mere bill number will not disclose the specific lobbying issue. Even if a bill concerns only one specific subject, a lobbying report disclosing only a bill number is still inadequate, because a member of the public would need access to information outside of the filing to ascertain that subject. In our view, the LDA contemplates disclosures that are adequate to inform the public of the lobbying client's specific issues from a review of the LD-2, without independent familiarity with bill numbers or the client's interest in specific subject matters within larger bills. The disclosures on Line 16 must include bill numbers, where applicable, but must always contain information that is adequate, standing alone, to inform the public of the specific lobbying issues.

Example: Client "A's" general lobbying issue area is "Environment." During the first quarter of 2008, lobbyists for "A" made contacts concerning the Department of Defense appropriations for environmental restoration. For fiscal 2009, the Department of Defense Appropriations Act was part of the Omnibus Consolidated Appropriations Act for 2009, H.R. 3610, a lengthy and complex bill that did not have numbered sections throughout. Title II contained separate but unnumbered provisions making appropriations for "Environmental Restoration, Army," "Environmental Restoration, Navy," "Environmental Restoration, Air Force," "Environmental Restoration, Defense-Wide," and "Environmental Restoration, Formerly Used Defense Sites." Lobbying contacts for Client "A" addressed all environmental restoration funding within the Defense Department bill. An appropriate disclosure of the specific lobbying issue would read as follows: H.R. 3610, Department of Defense Appropriations Act for 2009, Title II, all provisions relating to environmental restoration.

The Houses of Congress and Federal agencies contacted **by lobbyists** during the reporting period must be disclosed on Line 17 of Form LD-2, picking from the list of government entities provided on the form. If the list does not display the government entity contacted, then select the department in which the entity is housed. **In the event that no lobbying contacts were made, the registrant must mark the "Check if None" box.**

Previously identified lobbyists and new lobbyists for this reporting period must be listed on Line 18 of LD-2 if they had any lobbying activities during the reporting period, whether or not they made lobbying contacts. The issue page is only intended to reflect lobbying activity by lobbyists, and not activity of those who are not lobbyists. **Once an individual has met the definition of a lobbyist and has been disclosed or identified as such, he or she does not need to meet that standard every reporting period in order to trigger the required disclosure of his or her lobbying activities.** The registrant does not report the names of individuals who may perform some lobbying activities, but who do not and are not expected to meet the LDA definition of a lobbyist.

Lobbying Disclosure Act Guidance
Revised May 29, 2008

Example: Lobbying Firm "A" filed its initial registration for Client "B" on February 14, listing Lobbyists "X," "Y" and "Z." From January through March, Lobbyists "W" (hired in February) and "X" and "Y" made contacts for "B," while Lobbyist "Z" was assigned work for other clients. Lobbyist "Z" is expected, however, to be active on behalf of Client "B" after Spring Recess until adjournment. In its Q1 report for Client "B," filed on or before April 20, Lobbying Firm "A" lists "W," "X" and "Y" on Line 18. "W" is also identified as "new," and Firm "A" would disclose if "W" occupied a covered position within the last twenty years. "Z" is not listed on the Form LD-2 filed for Client "B" for the January - March quarterly period, but because of the current expectation that he will lobby during the April – June quarterly period, his name is not deleted as a lobbyist for "B."

New lobbyists should be disclosed on the appropriate issue(s) page(s) for the reporting period in which the individual first meets the definition of lobbyist. Filers must also disclose whether a new lobbyist has served as a "covered executive or legislative branch official" within twenty (20) years of first acting as a lobbyist for the client and state the executive and/or legislative position in which the person served.

We are aware that there will be situations in which a registrant expects an individual to become a lobbyist and wishes to disclose the name of that individual as a matter of public record. Section 5 of the LDA, however, provides that updated registration information is contained in the registrant's next quarterly report. Therefore, there may be a period of time in which an individual is legitimately making lobbying contacts but is not identified on the public record until the next quarterly report is filed. In such cases, the registrant reports updated information as the LDA requires.

A foreign entity is reported on Line 19 if both of two circumstances apply: 1) the foreign entity must be an entity that is required to be identified on Form LD-1 or on the registration information update page. That, in turn, depends on whether the entity meets one of the three conditions of Section 4(b)(4) of the LDA; and 2) the entity must have an interest in the specific lobbying issues listed on Line 16. If a foreign entity has an interest in the specific issues, Line 19 requires a description of that interest. For the sake of clarity the registrant should indicate whether the foreign entity(s) is/are the same as identified on the registration.

Example: "[Name of foreign entity], identified on LD-1, exports [type of product] to United States and would benefit from [specific desired outcome]."

Lobbying Disclosure Act Guidance
Revised May 29, 2008

Section 7 – Semiannual Reporting of Certain Contributions

When and Why a Report is Needed

Active registrants and individuals who have been listed as active lobbyists by their employer-registrant on Forms LD-1 and LD-2, must file a semiannual report on Form LD-203 by July 30 and January 30 (or on the next business day should either day occur on a weekend or holiday) for each semiannual period in which a registrant or lobbyist remains active. The coverage periods for the semiannual reports are January 1 through June 30, and July 1 through December 31. In the case of a registrant, "active" means not having filed a valid termination report for all clients. In the case of a lobbyist, "active" is an employee listed on any registrant's LD-1 or LD-2 and who has not been terminated **by the Registrant through their listing of the lobbyist** on Line 23 of LD-2 as being removed. If a lobbyist is active for any part of or for all of a semi-annual period, he or she must file a LD-203 Report (see Section 8). **The Secretary and the Clerk do not have the authority under the LDA to grant extensions for filing LDA documents.**

Mandatory Electronic Filing

Section 5 of the LDA was amended to require the mandatory electronic filing of all documents required by the LDA. The only exception to mandatory electronic filing is for the purpose of amending reports in the format previously filed, or for compliance with the Americans with Disabilities Act. Each electronic lobbying disclosure form provides usability for people with vision impairments who have the appropriate software and hardware. If you have questions regarding additional ADA accommodations, please contact the Senate Office of Public Records at 202, 224-0758.

It will be necessary for each active lobbyist to obtain his/her individual user identification number and password in order to file semiannual LD-203 reports electronically with the Secretary and Clerk.

Semiannual Reporting of Certain Contributions – Contents of Report

The core information required by Section 5(d) of the LDA and incorporated into Form LD-203 are: (1) certain contributions that are not disclosed in the LD-2; and (2) a certification that the filer has read and understands the gift and travel provisions in the Rules of both the House and the Senate, and that the filer has not knowingly violated the aforementioned Rules.

The beginning part of Form LD-203 contains identifying information. Section 5(d) requires specific information regarding certain contributions and payments made by the filer (i.e. each active registrant and active lobbyist), as well as any political committee established or controlled by the filer. In many cases, a political committee established or controlled by a registrant would be a separate segregated fund. In some cases, a political committee established or controlled by a lobbyist would be a leadership PAC.

The middle part of Form LD-203 requires the filer to disclose for itself, and for any political committee the filer establishes or controls:

1. The date, recipient, and amount of funds contributed to any Federal candidate or officeholder, leadership PAC, or political party committee, if the aggregate during the period to that recipient equals or exceeds $200.
2. The date, the name of honoree and or honorees, the payee(s) and amount of funds paid for an event to honor or recognize a covered Legislative Branch or covered Executive Branch official.
3. The date, the name of honoree and or honorees, the payee(s) and amount of funds paid to an entity or person that is named for a covered Legislative Branch official, or to an entity or person in recognition of such official (except for information required to be disclosed by another entity under 2 U.S.C §434).
4. The date, recipient, the name of the covered official, the payee(s) and amount of funds paid to an entity established, financed, maintained, or controlled by a covered Legislative or Executive Branch official or to an entity designated by such official (except for information required to be disclosed by another entity under 2 U.S.C §434).

5. The date, the name of honoree and or honorees, the payee(s) and amount of funds paid for a meeting, retreat, conference, or other similar event held by, or in the name of, one or more covered Legislative Branch or covered Executive Branch officials (except for information required to be disclosed by another entity under 2 U.S.C §434).

6. The date, the name of honoree, the payee(s) and amount of funds equal to or exceeding $200 paid to each Presidential library foundation and each Presidential inaugural committee.

This section of the LDA has been written broadly, and, in light of other provisions in P.L. 110-81, it would be prudent to consult with the appropriate Ethics Committee, as well as the Office of Government Ethics, in order to determine if any event listed above is otherwise prohibited under law, Senate or House Rules, or Executive Branch regulations. For some events, it may be prudent to consult with the Federal Election Commission as well. Please note that HLOGA and the Federal Election Campaign Act are not harmonized to contributions of exactly $200.

Example 1: In State "A," a group of constituents involved in widget manufacturing decide to honor Senator "Y" and Representative "T" with the "Widget Manufacturing Legislative Leaders of 2008" plaques. Registrant "B" is aware that "Y" has checked with the Senate Select Committee on Ethics regarding her ability to accept the award and attend the coffee, and "T" has checked with the House Committee on Standards of Official Conduct. "B" pays caterer "Z" $500 and Hotel "H" $200 to partially fund the event. "B" would report that it paid $500 to "Z" and $200 to "H" on November 20, 2008 for the purpose of an event to honor or recognize "Y" and "T" with the plaques.

Example 2: Senator "Y" and Representative "T" are honorary co-hosts of an event sponsored by Registrant "R" to promote "Widget Awareness." "R" would disclose the date, amount, recipient(s) of funds and "Y" and "T" since "Y" and "T" are being honored and or recognized.

Example 3: Registrant "R" sponsors an event. Senator "Y" is listed on the invitation as an attendee. Representative "T" is listed on the invitation as a speaker. "R" would disclose the date, amount, recipient(s) of funds, and "Y" and "T" as being recognized.

Example 4: After checking to discover if the activity is permissible, Lobbyist "C," contributes $300 on June 1, 2008 to Any State University towards the endowment of a chair named for Senator "Y". "C" would report the information above noting that the payment was made to Any State for the endowment of "Y's" chair.

Example 5: Senator "Y" has been asked to speak at a conference held in Washington, DC, sponsored by a professional association of which Registrant "B" is a member. "B" makes a donation of $100 to Charity "X" in lieu of honoraria. "B" would disclose a contribution of $100 on July 15, 2008, with the notation that "Y" was the speaker and the contribution was made in lieu of honoraria."

Example 6: In State "A," there is a large regional conference on "Saving Our River," sponsored by three 501c(3) organizations. Senator "Y" and Representatives "T" and "R" are invited to appear as honored guests. Registrant "B" contributes $3,000 to the event, paying one of the sponsors. "B" would disclose a payment of $3,000 on August 1, 2008 payable to the sponsor with the notation that "Y," "T," and "R" are honored guests.

Example 7: Registrant "B" is a large organization with 50 state offices in which its employees are assigned to handle state and local government affairs issues. A separate local organization hosts an event that honors primarily local officials, but also includes Representative "T," as an honoree. "B" pays for its employees' lunches at the honoring event. Accordingly, "B" would report that it paid the local organization $200 for lunch to honor "T."

Example 8: Lobbyists "C" and "D" serve on the board of an unaffiliated PAC as member and treasurer respectively. As board members, they are in positions that controls direction of the PAC's contributions. Since both are controlling to whom the PAC's contributions are given, they must disclose applicable contributions and payments on their semi-annual reports.

The final part of the form is a certification that the filer has read and is familiar with those provisions of the

Lobbying Disclosure Act Guidance
Revised May 29, 2008

Standing Rules of the Senate and the Rules of the House of Representatives relating to the provisions of gifts and travel and has not provided, requested or directed a gift, including travel, with knowledge that receipt of the gift would violate either Chamber's Rules. The form contains a check box for the certification, and the user ID and password process will verify the filer identity. Please note that in the case of a registrant, a signatory is an individual who is responsible for the accuracy of the information contained in the filing. Under section 6 of the LDA, the Secretary and Clerk refer the names of registrants and lobbyists who fail to provide an appropriate response within sixty (60) days to either officer's written communication rather than the name of the signatory.

Each registrant and active lobbyist, regardless of any contribution activity or any lack thereof, must file Form LD-203 semiannually due to the certification provision.

Lobbying Disclosure Act Guidance
Revised May 29, 2008

Section 8 -- Termination of a Lobbyist/ Termination of a Registrant

Termination of a Lobbyist

The LDA is not specific as to how far into the future the registrant should project an expectation that an individual will act as a lobbyist. It seems neither realistic nor necessary to expect registrants to make such projections beyond the next succeeding quarterly reporting period. Accordingly, if a registrant reasonably expects an individual to meet the definition of lobbyist in either the current or next quarterly period, the lobbyist should remain in an "active" status. If a registrant does not believe this to be the case, the lobbyist can be removed from the list of lobbyists for the registrant. Line 23 of LD-2 is used to delete names of employees who are no longer expected to act as lobbyists for the client, due to changed job duties, assignments, or employment status.

> *Example 1: Lobbying Firm "Y" registers for Client "Z" on March 15, 2008, listing employees "A," "B," "C," and "D" on line 10 of Form LD-1. For the first quarterly reporting period in 2008, "Y" will list "A," "B" and "C" on Line 18 of LD-2. "D" has no lobbying activities for that quarterly period, so he would not be listed. During the second quarter of 2008, "D" leaves firm "Y" to start his own lobbying business. For the second quarterly period, "Y" will report that "D" no longer meets the definition of "lobbyist" for Client "Z" on Line 23 of LD-2.*

> *Example 2: Lobbying Firm "Y" registers for Client "Z" as above listing the aforementioned "A," "B," "C," and "D" as lobbyists on March 15, 2008. One month after registration, "C" and "D," who engaged in lobbying activities for "Z" as partners of "Y," decide to leave the partnership effective June 1, 2008. On the Q2 Report for 2008, "Y" would report any lobbying activity for "C" and "D" on Line 18 of LD-2. "Y" would also reflect "C" and "D's" departure by listing them on Line 23 of LD-2 in the same filing.*

After January 1, 2008, lobbyists who have been terminated by their registrant/employer for every client they were registered to lobby on behalf of, do not have to file form LD-203 for any filing period subsequent to the one in which they were removed for the last remaining active client. The obligation to file LD-203 arises from being listed as meeting the statutory test of "lobbyist" - and not being terminated - by the registrant/employer. Thus, if a lobbyist has not been removed from the list of lobbyists on Line 23 of the LD-2 for every client for which the lobbyist was listed, the Secretary and Clerk will expect to receive a semi-annual report from him/her.

> *Example: Registrant "A" employs Lobbyist "C" who has lobbying activity on behalf of Client "R" in January and February 2008. In March Lobbyist "C" no longer expects to engage in lobbying activities for "R" or any other client in the firm, although "C" will continue to do non-lobbying consultation for numerous clients. "A" removes Lobbyist "C" as an active lobbyist by listing "C" on line 23 of the LD-2 form for the Q1 reporting period and not listed on subsequent quarterly LD-2 reports. However in July, Lobbyist "C" is required to file an LD-203 report due July 30 disclosing his activity from January 1 through the date of his termination.*

Termination of a registrant/client relationship

Under Section 4(d) of the LDA, a lobbying firm may terminate a registration for a particular client when it is no longer employed or retained by that client to conduct lobbying activities and anticipates no further lobbying activities for that client. An organization employing in-house lobbyists may terminate its registration when in-house lobbying activities have ceased and are not expected to resume. Similarly, in situations in which a registration is filed in anticipation of meeting the registration threshold that subsequently is not met, a registrant also has the option of termination. Just as we have been interpreting that the obligation to report quarterly under the LDA arises from active status as a registrant, we believe that a report disclosing the final lobbying activity of a registrant is mandatory. In order to terminate the registration, the registrant must file Form LD-2 by the next quarterly filing date, checking the "Termination Report" box, and supplying the date that the lobbying activity terminated. A valid termination report discloses lobbying income or expenses **and** any lobbying activity by lobbyists during the period up to and including the termination date.

Lobbying Disclosure Act Guidance
Revised May 29, 2008

Example 1: Lobbying Firm "A" accepted a contract with Client "B" on January 1, 2008, began lobbying activities, and timely registered on or before February 14. On March 31, the contract with "B" ended. Lobbying Firm "A" must file Form LD-2 by April 20, 2008, disclosing the lobbying income from and lobbying activity for Client "B" that took place during the period January 1 through March 31. The firm will check the "Q1" box on Line 8, the "Termination Report" box on Line 10, and fill in "3/31/2008" in the TerminationDate space (also on Line 10).

Example 2: Corporation "C" filed its registration on February 14, 2008, listing employee "E" as its only lobbyist. Through March 31, "E" spends less than 20 percent of her total time in lobbying activities. "C" would not have filed a registration if it had foreseen that its lobbying activities would be so limited, and there is no expectation that "E" or any other employee of "C" will meet the Section 3(10) definition of "lobbyist" for the April – June quarterly period nor that lobbying expenses will exceed $10,000. While Corporation "C" as a registrant must file a report for January - March 2008, "C" will check the "Termination Report" box on Form LD-2, write in 3/31/08, disclose the amount of expenses for the reporting period, and "E's" lobbying activity for the reporting period.

Section 9 - Relationship of LDA to Other Statutes

LDA and FARA

The technical amendments to the LDA made in 1998 reflected a determination that the Foreign Agents Registration Act (FARA) standards are appropriate for lobbying on behalf of foreign governments and political parties, but that LDA disclosure standards should apply to other foreign lobbying. An agent of a foreign commercial entity is exempt under FARA if the agent has engaged in lobbying activities and registers under the LDA. An agent of a foreign commercial entity not required to register under the LDA (such as those not meeting the de minimis registration thresholds) may voluntarily register under the LDA. The amendments reaffirm the bright line distinction between governmental and non-governmental representations, and are not meant to shroud foreign government enterprises. Questions relating to the Foreign Agents Registration Act must be directed to the Department of Justice Foreign Agent Registration Unit at (202) 514-1231.

LDA and IRC

Restrictions on lobbying by tax-exempt organizations are governed by the definitions in the IRC, not those of the LDA. The LDA and the IRC intersect in three different ways.

First, Section 15 of the LDA defines which registrants are eligible for the "safe harbor." Section 15 allows entities that are required to report and do report lobbying expenditures under section 6033(b)(8) of the IRC to use IRC definitions for purposes of LDA Sections 4(a)(3) and 5(b)(4). Section 15(b) of the LDA allows entities that are subject to section 162(e) of the IRC to use IRC definitions for purposes of LDA Sections 4(a)(3) and 5(b)(4).

Second, Section 15 advises registrants regarding how they should use IRC definitions. Prior to the technical amendments, the statute was not clear as to the extent to which eligible organizations could use IRC definitions for other (i.e., non-expense) reporting and disclosure requirements of the LDA. As a result of the amendments, registrants who make the Section 15 expense election must use for other reporting the IRC definitions (including the IRC definition of a covered Executive Branch official) for Executive Branch lobbying, and the LDA definitions for Legislative Branch lobbying.

Third, Section 15 allows electing registrants to plug in the amount that is ultimately reportable to the Internal Revenue Service for LDA quarterly reports.

Lobbying Disclosure Act Guidance
Revised May 29, 2008

LDA and False Statements Accountability Act of 1996

The False Statements Accountability Act of 1996, amending 18 U.S.C. § 1001, makes it a crime knowingly and willfully: (1) to falsify, conceal or cover up a material fact by trick, scheme or device; (2) to make any materially false, fictitious, or fraudulent statement or representation; or (3) to make or use any false writing or document knowing it to contain any materially false, fictitious, or fraudulent statement or entry; with respect to matters within the jurisdiction of the Legislative, Executive, or Judicial branch. The False Statements Accountability Act does not assign any responsibilities to the Clerk and Secretary.

LDA and Prohibitions on the Use of Federal Funds for Lobbying

The LDA does not itself regulate lobbying by federal grantees, or contractors, though other laws, as well as contractual prohibitions, may apply. Questions concerning lobbying activities of federal grantees or contractors should be directed to the appropriate agency or office administrating the contract or grant.

Note, however, that Section 18 of the LDA prohibits 501(c)(4) organizations who engage in lobbying activities from receiving federal funds through an award, grant or loan.

Section 10 - Public Availability

The Act requires the Secretary of the Senate and the Clerk of the House of Representatives to make all registrations and reports available for public inspection over the Internet as soon as technically practicable after the report is filed.

Section 11 - Review and Compliance

The Secretary of the Senate (Office of Public Records) and the Clerk of the House (Legislative Resource Center) must review, verify, and request corrections in writing to ensure the accuracy, completeness, and timeliness of registrations and reports filed under the Act.

Section 12 - Penalties

Whoever knowingly fails: (1) to correct a defective filing within 60 days after notice of such a defect by the Secretary of the Senate or the Clerk of the House; or (2) to comply with any other provision of the Act, may be subject to a civil fine of not more than $200,000, and whoever knowingly and corruptly fails to comply with any provision of this Act may be imprisoned for not more than 5 years or fined under title 18, United States Code, or both.

For Further Information

Senate Office of Public Records
232 Hart Senate Office Building
Washington, DC 20510
(202) 224-0758

Legislative Resource Center
B-106 Cannon House Office Building
Washington, DC 20515
(202) 226-5200

𝔘.𝔖. 𝔥𝔬𝔲𝔰𝔢 𝔬𝔣 𝔯𝔢𝔭𝔯𝔢𝔰𝔢𝔫𝔱𝔞𝔱𝔦𝔳𝔢𝔰

COMMITTEE ON STANDARDS OF
OFFICIAL CONDUCT

𝔚𝔞𝔰𝔥𝔦𝔫𝔤𝔱𝔬𝔫, 𝔇𝔠 20515

TRAVEL GUIDELINES AND REGULATIONS

MEMORANDUM TO ALL MEMBERS, OFFICERS, AND EMPLOYEESS

From: **Committee on Standards of Official Conduct**
              Stephanie Tubbs Jones, Chairwoman
              Doc Hastings, Ranking Republican Member

Date: February 20, 2007

The new travel rules that were passed at the beginning of the 110th Congress require the Committee to issue guidelines concerning the reasonableness of travel expenses and the types of information that must be submitted to the Committee in order to obtain prior approval of privately-sponsored, officially-connected travel.[1] The rules also direct the Committee to issue regulations describing when a two-night stay will be permitted in order for a Member, officer, or employee to participate in a one-day event sponsored by a private entity that retains or employs a lobbyist, and the circumstances under which a lobbyist is permitted to have *de minimis* involvement in planning, organizing, requesting, or arranging a trip.[2]

The Committee hereby issues guidelines and regulations concerning the new travel restrictions and requirements. In many significant areas, the regulations and guidelines set forth below are new restrictions and requirements that *supersede* the Committee's policies under the travel rules that existed in previous congresses, and *they take effect on March 1, 2007*.

Travel Guidelines and Regulations[3]

A. Connection between Trip and Official Duties

A Member, officer, or employee seeking approval for travel must demonstrate that the activities on the trip are related to the individual's official responsibilities or matters arising from his or her official duties. In evaluating a request for approval to

---

[1] House Rule 25, cl. 5(i).

[2] House Rule 25, cl. 5(b)(1)(C). For brevity's sake, references in the text to the term "lobbyist" also include agents of a foreign principal.

[3] These provisions address both the acceptance of in-kind transportation, lodging, and meals as well as reimbursement of travel expenses.

2

travel at private expense, the Committee will evaluate the individual's responsibilities, and/or whether the purpose of the trip relates to matters within the general legislative or policy interests of the Congress.   Travel will not be approved if it does not include sufficient officially-connected activities, or if it includes excessive amounts of unscheduled time or opportunities for recreational activities during the official itinerary, even if such activities are engaged in at personal expense.

B. Reasonableness of Travel Expenses

(1) *Transportation to the Event*:   Members, officers, and employees may accept up to business-class transportation on commercial air carriers or trains to participate in Committee-approved, privately-sponsored travel.   Other transportation (including first-class airfare or train fare, charter travel, or travel on private aircraft) may *only* be accepted if:

(a) it is demonstrated that the cost of such travel does not exceed the cost of available business-class transportation (or if the traveler uses the traveler's own frequent flyer or similar benefits to upgrade to first class);

(b) such travel is necessary to accommodate a disability or other special need as substantiated in writing by a competent medical authority;

(c) genuine security circumstances require such travel;

(d) the scheduled flight time, including stopovers and change of planes, is in excess of 14 hours; or

(e) the Committee permits such travel based on *exceptional* circumstances.

(2) *Local Transportation*:   Local area transportation expenses during a trip must be reasonable and unrelated to personal or recreational activities.

(3) *Lodging*:

(a) For travel to events arranged or organized *without regard* to congressional participation (for example, annual meetings of business or trade associations or other membership organizations), Members, officers, and employees may accept lodging accommodations at a pre-arranged location for event attendees commensurate with those customarily provided to or purchased by other event attendees. The quality or location of the accommodations may not be enhanced because of the official position of the Member, officer, or employee.

(b) For travel to events arranged or organized *specifically with regard* to congressional participation (for example, fact-finding trips, site visits, educational conferences, and other trips designed for congressional attendance), Members, officers, and employees may accept reasonable lodging expenses at an appropriate facility. Among the factors to be considered in judging the reasonableness of expenses for a lodging facility are the cost of the facility, the location of the facility and its proximity to

3

the site(s) being visited, the quality of its conference facilities, any security concerns, and whether the facility may accommodate the number of attendees at the event.

(4) *Food*:

(a) For travel to events arranged or organized *without regard* to congressional participation (for example, annual meetings of business or trade associations or other membership organizations), Members, officers, and employees may accept meals related to the event that are similar to those provided to or purchased by other event attendees.

(b) For privately-sponsored travel to events arranged or organized *specifically with regard* to congressional participation (for example, fact-finding trips, site visits, educational conferences, and other trips designed for congressional attendance), Members, officers, and employees may accept reasonable meal expenses at an appropriate facility. The factors to be considered in judging the reasonableness of a meal expense include the maximum *per diem* rates for meals for official Government travel published by the General Services Administration or, for international travel, the maximum *per diem* rate for meals published by the State Department.

(5) *Other Travel Expenses*: Members, officers, and employees may accept reasonable miscellaneous travel expenses, such as transportation to and from airports, security costs, interpreter fees, visa application fees, and similar expenses that are necessary for the officially-connected purpose of the trip.

C. Relationship Between an Event and the Officially-Connected Purpose of the Trip

The location of events arranged or organized *without regard* to congressional participation (for example, annual meetings of business or trade associations) is presumptively reasonable. The location of *other* events must be necessary to the purpose of the event, or if more than one possible location may be relevant to the event, then the location selected must be a reasonable one in relation to the alternatives. If there is no specific location necessary or relevant to the purpose of the event, the location selected must be a reasonable one in light of the nature of the event and its participants, and should not create the appearance that the Member, officer, or employee attending the event is using his or her public office for personal gain.

D. Direct and Immediate Relationship between Source of Funding and an Event

Expenses may only be accepted from an entity or entities that have a significant role in organizing and conducting a trip, and that also have a clear and defined organizational interest in the purpose of the trip or location being visited. Expenses may not be accepted from a source that has merely donated monetary or in-kind support to the trip but does not have a significant role in organizing and conducting the trip.

4

E.   One-day Event Trips Sponsored by a Private Entity that Retains or Employs a Lobbyist

The Committee will authorize a Member, officer, or employee to accept a second night's lodging and meal expenses in order for the individual to participate in a one-day event when it determines that such expenses are necessary due to availability of transportation to or from the event, or in those circumstances when an additional night's stay is practically required in order to facilitate the individual's full participation in the event.   The Member, officer, or employee seeking approval for a two-night stay *must request approval from the Committee.*

In determining whether to permit a second night's stay, the Committee will consider the following factors:

(1) the availability of transportation to and from the location of the one-day event;

(2) whether the trip is outside the continental United States or involves travel across two or more time zones;

(3) whether the Member or staff person is participating in a full-day's worth of officially-connected activities (*e.g.*, is the individual giving a speech, taking part in fact-finding, observing presentations, or participating in a panel discussion); or

(4) any other *exceptional* circumstances that are described in detail by the traveler.

F.   *De Minimis* Lobbyist Involvement in Planning, Organizing, Requesting, or Arranging a Trip

Member and staff participation in officially-connected travel that is in any way planned, organized, requested, or arranged by a lobbyist is *prohibited*, except as provided below:

(1) when the travel is sponsored by an institution of higher education within the meaning of section 101 of the Higher Education Act of 1965; or

(2) when the travel is for a one-day event trip *and* the involvement of a lobbyist in planning, organizing, requesting, or arranging the trip is *de minimis*, meaning only negligible or otherwise inconsequential in terms of time and expense to the overall planning and purpose of the trip.

5

G. Information that must be Submitted to the Standards Committee for Purposes of Receiving Prior Approval of Privately-Sponsored Travel

A private sponsor offering officially-connected travel to a Member, officer, or employ must complete and sign a Private Sponsor Certification Form, and provide a copy of that form to the invitee(s). The sponsor should not submit that form directly to the Committee. Private sponsors are strongly urged to submit the form to the invitee(s) at least 30 days before the travel is scheduled to begin.

A Member, officer, or employee must submit to the Committee a completed and signed Privately Sponsored Travel Approval Form that attaches or includes the Private Sponsor Certification Form and, for staff travel, a copy of the Advance Authorization of Employee Travel Form.

U.S. House of Representatives
Committee on Standards of Official Conduct

PRIVATE SPONSOR TRAVEL CERTIFICATION FORM
(provide directly to invitee)

This form should be completed by private entities offering to provide travel or reimbursement for travel to House Members, officers or employees under House Rule XXV, clause 5. A completed copy of the form should be provided to each invited House Member, officer or employee, who will then forward the form to the Committee. The trip sponsor should NOT submit the form directly to the Committee.

Private sponsors are urged to submit this form to the invitee at least 30 days before travel is scheduled to begin. The failure to provide the Committee with adequate time to review the form and attachments may result in the invitee not receiving approval for the trip. The submission of an incomplete form will delay the review process. Before completing this form, sponsors are also urged to *carefully review* the Committee's private travel regulations, guidelines and advisory memoranda detailing the rules and restrictions for private travel, and to call the Committee with any questions. *Please type form.*

1.   Sponsor(s) (who will be paying for the trip): _____

_____

2.   I represent that the trip will not be financed (in whole or in part) by a federally-registered lobbyist or a registered foreign agent (*signify "yes" by checking box*): ☐

3.   I represent that the trip sponsor(s) has not accepted from any other source funds earmarked directly or indirectly to finance any aspect of the trip (*signify "yes" by checking box*): ☐

4.   Is travel being offered to an accompanying family member of the House invitee(s)? ☐ Yes   ☐ No

5.   Provide names and titles of House invitees; for each invitee, provide explanation of why the individual was invited (include additional pages if necessary): _____

_____

_____

6.   Dates of travel: _____

7.   If travel is for participation in a one-day event, check one of the following:
a. One-night's lodging and meals are being offered: ☐ <u>or</u>
b. Two-nights' lodging and meals are being offered: ☐
If "b" is checked, please indicate the circumstances under which the second night is warranted: ___

_____

8.   Cities of departure – destination – return: _____

_____

9.   Reason for selecting the location of the event or trip: _____

_____

_____

10. Attached is a detailed agenda of the activities taking place during the travel (*i.e.*, an hourly description of planned activities) (*signify "yes" by checking box*): ☐

11. I represent that (*check as applicable*):

    a. The sponsor of the trip does not retain or employ a federally registered lobbyist or registered foreign agent: ☐ <u>or</u>

    b. The sponsor of the trip is an institution of higher education within the meaning of section 101 of the Higher Education Act of 1965: ☐ <u>or</u>

    c. The trip is for attendance at a one-day event *and* lobbyist involvement in planning, organizing, requesting, or arranging the trip was *de minimis* under the Committee's travel regulations. ☐

12. If the trip is not sponsored by an institution of higher education, I represent that a federally-registered lobbyist or foreign agent will not accompany House Members or employees on any segment of the trip (*signify "yes" by checking box*): ☐

13. Private sponsors must have a direct and immediate relationship with to the purpose of the trip or location being visited. Please describe the role of the sponsor(s) in organizing and conducting the trip:

_____

_____

14. Describe the sponsor's organizational interest in the purpose of the trip: _____

_____

_____

15. Describe the type and class of the transportation being provided. Indicate whether coach, business-class or first-class transportation will be provided. In addition, for travel via aircraft, please indicate if travel is being offered on a commercial flight, chartered flight or on an aircraft operated or paid for by a carrier not licensed by the Federal Aviation Administration to operate for compensation or hire (*i.e.,* a private aircraft). If first-class fare is being provided, or if travel is via chartered or private aircraft, please provide an explanation describing why such travel is warranted: _____

_____

_____

16. I represent that the expenditures related to local area travel during the trip will be unrelated to personal or recreational activities of the invitee(s) (*signify "yes" by checking box*): ☐

17. Name of hotel or other lodging facility: _____

18. Cost per night of hotel or other lodging facility (approximate cost may be provided): _____

_____

19. Reason(s) for selecting hotel or other lodging facility: _____

_____

_____

20. I represent that either (*check one of the following*):

    a. The trip involves an event that is arranged or organized *without regard* to congressional participation and that meals provided to congressional participants are similar to those provided to or purchased by other event attendees: ☐ <u>or</u>

    b. The trip involves events that are arranged or organized *specifically with regard* to congressional participation: ☐

    If "b" is checked, detail the cost per day of meals (approximate cost may be provided): _____

_____

2

21.   TOTAL EXPENSES FOR EACH PARTICIPANT:

☐ actual amounts ☐ good faith estimates	Total *Transportation* Expenses per Participant	Total *Lodging* Expenses per Participant	Total *Meal* Expenses per Participant
For each Member, Officer, or employee			
For each accompanying family member			

	Other Expenses (dollar amount)	Identify Specific Nature of "Other" Expenses (*e.g.*, taxi, parking, registration fee, *etc.*)
For each Member, Officer, or employee		
For each accompanying family member		

22. I represent that reimbursement for miscellaneous travel expenses for the trip, such as travel to and from airports, security costs, interpreter fees, visa application fees, and similar expenses, will be for actual costs incurred and are necessary for the purpose of the trip (*signify "yes" by checking box*): ☐

23. I certify that the information contained in this form is true, complete, and correct to the best of my knowledge.

    Signature: _____

    Name and title: _____

    Organization: _____

    Address: _____

    Telephone number: _____

    Fax number: _____

    Email Address: _____

    The Committee staff may contact the above individual above if additional information is required.

If there are any questions regarding this form please contact the Committee at the following address:

    Committee on Standards of Official Conduct
    U.S. House of Representatives
    HT-2, The Capitol
    Washington, DC 20515
    (202) 225-7103 (phone)
    (202) 225-7392 (general fax)
    (202) 226-7172 (fax for travel approvals)

Version date 2/2007 by Committee on Standards of Official Conduct

3

**U.S. House of Representatives
Committee on Standards of Official Conduct**

**PRIVATELY-SPONSORED TRAVEL APPROVAL FORM
For Members, Officers and Employees
(submit directly to the Committee)**

This form should be completed by House Members, officers or employees seeking Committee approval of privately-sponsored travel or reimbursement for travel under House Rule XXV, clause 5. The completed form should be submitted directly to the Committee by each invited House Member, officer or employee, together with the completed and signed Private Sponsor Travel Certification Form.

Members, officers and employees seeking approval for travel are urged to submit all forms to the Committee at least 30 days before travel is scheduled to begin. The failure to provide the Committee with adequate time to review the form and attachments may result in the invitee not receiving approval for the trip. The submission of an incomplete form will delay the review process. A copy of this form will be made available for public inspection. *Please type form.* ***Form (and any attachments) may be faxed to the Committee at (202) 226-7172.***

1. Name of Member, officer or employee (traveler): _____

2. Sponsor(s) (who will be paying for the trip): _____

    _____

3. Is travel being offered to an accompanying family member? ☐ Yes   ☐ No

4. Dates of travel: _____

5. If travel is for participation a one-day event, check one of the following:
    a. Approval for one-night's lodging and meals is being requested: ☐ <u>or</u>
    b. Approval for two-nights' lodging and meals is being requested: ☐
       If "b" is checked, please indicate the circumstances under which the second night is warranted: ____

    _____

6. Travel destination(s): _____

7. Purpose of the trip: _____

    _____

8. Provide explanation of why participation in the trip is connected to your official or representational
    duties: _____

    _____

    _____

9. Private Sponsor Travel Certification Form is attached (*signify "yes" by checking box*): ☐

10. For staff, Advance Authorization of Employee Travel Form is attached (*signify "yes" by checking*

11. I certify that the information contained in this form is true, complete, and correct to the best of my knowledge.

Signature: _____

Office address: _____

Phone number: _____

Email address: _____

Committee staff may contact you if additional information is required.

If there are any questions regarding this form please contact the Committee:

Committee on Standards of Official Conduct
U.S. House of Representatives
HT-2, The Capitol
Washington, DC 20515
(202) 225-7103 (phone)
(202) 225-7392 (general fax)
(202) 226-7172 (fax for travel approvals)

Version date 2/2007 by Committee on Standards of Official Conduct

2

Senate Select Committee on Ethics'
Regulations and Guidelines for Privately-Sponsored Travel

Introduction

The Honest Leadership and Open Government Act, which was signed into law on September 14, 2007, made significant changes to the Senate Rules governing privately-sponsored travel for Senators and staff members, and gave the Ethics Committee the authority to issue regulations and guidelines to implement these changes. The new law did not affect travel sponsored by federal, state, and local governments or by foreign governments under the Foreign Gifts and Decorations Act or the Mutual Educational and Cultural Exchange Act.

The Committee hereby issues the guidelines and regulations for the new rules on privately-sponsored travel, which supersede any prior Committee guidance, including the Senate Ethics Manual. Please see the glossary for more detailed explanations of the terms and concepts discussed below.

Travel Review Process and Required Public Filings

Because of these new requirements, sponsors of privately-funded travel should begin the invitation process as early as possible. Senate Members, Officers, and employees **must** submit a completed travel package to the Ethics Committee **no later than 30 days prior to the departure dates of a proposed privately-sponsored trip**. These materials must include:

- *A copy* of the invitation from the sponsor.
- *A copy* of the signed and *completed "Private Sponsor Travel Certification Form"* with any attachments.
- For Senate employees, *a copy* of the *"Employee Advance Travel Authorization and Disclosure Form"* with Part I completed and signed by the employee and the supervising Member or Officer.

After receiving the complete travel package, the Ethics Committee will review it as quickly as possible, contact the travel sponsor and/or Senate invitee with any additional questions if necessary, and issue a letter to the Senate invitee after the review is complete.

Within 30 Days of returning from the privately-funded travel, the following original documents must be filed with the Office of Public Records in Hart 232:

- Members and Officers must complete, sign and file the *Senators and Officers:*

Disclosure of Travel Expenses form and the completed *Private Sponsor Travel Certification Form* with any attachments.

- Senate Employees must complete and file the signed *Employee Advance Travel Authorization and Disclosure Form* (Parts 1 and 2) and must file the completed *Private Sponsor Travel Certification Form* with any attachments.

- Senate offices should retain copies of all relevant travel forms and documents for their records.

For additional detail regarding the travel review process, please see the Committee's *Privately-Sponsored Travel Checklist* which is available on the Ethics Committee Web site (www.ethics.senate.gov) or can be picked up at the Ethics Committee office in Hart 220.

Privately-Sponsored Travel Must Be Connected To the Senate Invitee's Official Duties

Senate invitees must demonstrate that any proposed privately-sponsored travel relates to their official duties and will not create the appearance that they are using their public office for private gain.

On a case-by-case basis, Members and Senate officers may be required to explain in writing to the Committee how attendance on a given trip relates to their official and representational duties.

Employees must have their supervising Members or Officers certify in advance (on the *Employee Advance Travel Authorization and Disclosure Form*) that the travel relates to the invitees' official duties. The Committee will give this determination great weight and will consider a number of factors in determining whether to approve the travel request, including:

- The Senate invitee's official responsibilities and whether there is an adequate connection between a trip and the official duties of the invitee;
- Whether the trip relates to matters within the legislative or policy interests of the Senate;
- Whether the trip's length and itinerary is consistent with its official purpose;
- The stated mission of the organization(s) sponsoring the trip and whether there is a direct and immediate relationship between a source of funding and an event;
- The organization's prior history of sponsoring congressional trips, if any;
- Other educational activities performed by the organization besides sponsoring congressional trips, if any;
- Whether any trips previously sponsored by the organization led to an investigation by the Ethics Committee;
- Any other factors the Committee deems relevant.

Who May Be a Sponsor of Privately-Funded Travel

Senate invitees may accept necessary travel expenses only from the sponsors of the event or fact-finding trip. A sponsor is any person or entity that contributes funds or in-kind support for the trip. A sponsor must have a significant role in organizing or conducting the travel and must have a specific organizational interest in the purpose of the trip. The following are permissible sponsors:

- *Non-profit organizations that are designated as 501(c)(3) tax-exempt organizations,* regardless of whether they retain or employ lobbyists or foreign agents, may sponsor 3-day domestic trips or 7-day foreign trips.

- *Private entities that neither employ nor retain lobbyists or foreign agents* may sponsor 3-day domestic trips or 7-day foreign trips.

- *Private entities that retain or employ lobbyists or foreign agents* are only allowed to sponsor 1-day trips.

It is important to note that privately-funded travel may NEVER be accepted from, paid for, or reimbursed by lobbyists or foreign agents, even if they are reimbursed later. For the purposes of this prohibition, a lobbyist is someone required to register under the Lobbying Disclosure Act. An organization employing lobbyists (outside or in-house) to represent only the organization's interests would not be considered a lobbyist. For example, Widget Corporation which employs in-house lobbyists to represent only the Widget Company's interest would not be a "lobbyist." But a lobbying firm that provides lobbying services for that firm's clients would be considered a lobbyist. An agent of a foreign principal is someone required to be registered under the Foreign Agents Registration Act.

A sponsor may not accept any funds or in-kind support from a lobbyist or foreign agent that is earmarked directly or indirectly for a trip. Earmarking would include any direction, agreement, or suggestion--formal or informal--to use donated funds, goods, services or other in-kind contributions.

Lobbyist Involvement in Planning and Organizing Privately-Funded Travel

Senate invitees may not participate in trips planned, organized, arranged, or requested by a lobbyist or foreign agent in more than a de minimis way, which means negligible or inconsequential. It would be considered inconsequential for one or more lobbyists to serve on the board of an organization that is sponsoring travel, as long as the lobbyists are not involved in the trip. It is also permissible for a lobbyist to respond to a trip sponsor's request to identify Senate invitees with interest in a particular issue relevant to a planned trip.

However, a lobbyist is not allowed to solicit or initiate communications with a trip sponsor, have control over which Senate employees are invited on a trip, extend or forward an invitation to a participant, determine the trip itinerary, or be mentioned in the invitation.

Example: A trip sponsor that is a 501(c)(3) non-profit organization asks a lobbyist to recommend staffers who might be most interested in joining a trip to the U.S.-Mexican border. If a lobbyist knows a staffer who has a particular interest in the DEA's activities at the border, then providing that information (in light of the trip sponsor's request), in and of itself, would not exceed a de minimis level of participation, and would be permitted. However, it would not be permissible for the lobbyist to initiate contact with the trip sponsor to suggest that a particular Senate employee be invited or forward an invitation to that staffer.

Time Limits for Privately-Funded Travel

- **Private entities that employ or retain one or more lobbyists or foreign agents MAY sponsor one-day trips with one-overnight stay.**

  When calculating one-day attendance, travel time and the overnight stay are not included. For these one-day trips, neither lobbyists nor foreign agents may accompany a Senate invitee on any segment of the trip, which means any parts of the travel to and from the event (not at the event itself or the location being visited).

- **Private entities that employ or retain one or more lobbyists or foreign agents may be allowed to sponsor one-day trips with two-night stays when practically required.**

  The Senate invitee must request prior written approval from the Committee for two-overnight stays and must explain satisfactorily why the two night stay is practically required. The Committee will examine these requests on a case-by-case basis and consider the following factors when deciding whether a two-night stay may be practically required:

  - Whether the trip destination is outside the contiguous United States, for example, travel to Hawaii or Alaska;
  - Whether the travel is across country, for example travel from Washington, DC to San Diego, CA;
  - The availability of transportation to or from the location of the one-day event;
  - Whether a Senate invitee is participating in a full day's worth of officially-connected activities (without any substantial gaps in the schedule) such that a second night's stay is necessary to accomplish the purpose of the trip; or
  - Any other exceptional circumstances described by the Senate invitee in detailed writing prior to the travel which leads the Committee to find that a two-day stay is practically necessary to achieve the purpose of the trip.

Just as above, neither lobbyists nor foreign agents may accompany a Senate invitee on *any segment* of the trip

- **Entities that do not employ or retain lobbyists or foreign agents and all 501(c)(3) non-profit organizations may sponsor domestic trips for up to three days or foreign trips for seven days.**

  The Committee has determined that the three-day and seven-day time limitations shall be three or seven 24-hour periods, respectively. For these trips, a lobbyist or foreign agent may not accompany a Senate invitee *at any point throughout the trip*, other than in a *de minimis* way. This means lobbyists may not accompany Senate invitees at any point to and from the event, at the event itself, or at the location being visited. This is a broader prohibition than the *at any segment of a trip* standard.

De Minimis Exception to Lobbyist/Foreign Agent Accompaniment Standards

Both lobbyist "accompaniment" prohibitions above include a *de minimis* exemption. *De minimis* means negligible or inconsequential. The mere coincidental presence of a lobbyist or foreign agent at an event would likely be considered *de minimis*. But in making the final determination, the Committee will consider the totality of the circumstances, including the amount of time lobbyists or foreign agents are present at the event; the amount of direct contact they have with Senate invitees; and the amount of control a trip sponsor has over their presence or contact with Senate guests.

For example, if the trip includes attendance at an event considered widely-attended under Rule 35(1)(c)(18), the trip sponsor is unlikely to know all attendees present. Thus, it is likely to be permissible for such widely-attended events to include both a Senate guest and a lobbyist. Similarly, an organization cannot possibly know all the other passengers taking the same flight or other common carrier to a given destination. Accordingly, the sponsor does not need to certify that it knows for certain that no lobbyist or foreign agent will be on such a common carrier.

Necessary Expenses

Necessary expenses are generally limited to reasonable payments for transportation, lodging, conference fees and materials, food and refreshments, and miscellaneous costs (such as fees for interpreters and visas) necessary for the official purpose of the trip.

Family Travel: Travel expenses for a Senate invitee's spouse or child (but not both) may be permissible if the family member has received an unsolicited invitation from the event sponsor and the supervising Member determines in writing that the spouse or child's attendance will assist in representing the Senate.

Transportation: Coach or business class transportation is acceptable. Local transportation provided during a trip must be reasonable and customary for the location--and not related to personal or recreational activities.

First-class travel is generally not permitted except when written prior approval is granted due to exceptional circumstances. Such circumstances could include a disability or security concern, a flight longer than 14 hours, a cost that doesn't exceed business class fare, or travelers using their own frequent flier benefits to upgrade.

Lodging and Food: When possible, the Committee will look to see whether the expenses are generally comparable to the maximum per diem rates for official Federal Government travel published annually by the General Services Administration, the Department of State, and the Department of Defense. However, certain circumstances—such as, for example, when the event was planned without regard to Congressional participation—could legitimately require lodging and meal expenses that exceed the federal government per diem rates.

Prohibited Expenses: Necessary expenses do not include:

Alcoholic beverages
- Private or charter aircraft
- Recreational activities
- Personal expenses such as telephone calls
- Entertainment unless it is provided to all attendees as an integral part of   the event.
- First class transportation without prior written approval by Ethics Committee.

Factors to Determine the Reasonableness of Expenses

The Ethics Committee will give weight to the determination made by a Senator or Officer that the proposed travel will not create the appearance of a Senate invitee using a public office for private gain and will assume that this determination was made after concluding that the expenses are necessary and reasonable. The Ethics Committee will also consider the following factors:

- Whether the trip's length and itinerary is consistent with its official purpose;
- The reasonableness of a sponsor's expenditures for the entire trip and any portion of it;
- Whether the expenditures are consistent with maximum per diem rates for lodging and meals for official Federal Government travel and, if they exceed those rates, whether the specific circumstances legitimately require lodging and meal expenses that exceed these rates;
- Any other factors deemed relevant by the Select Committee on Ethics.

Senate Select Committee on Ethics'
Regulations and Guidelines for Privately-Sponsored Travel

Glossary of Terms

1-Day Trips[1]

Subject to all applicable Senate Rules, one-day trips (attendance or participation for one day at an event) may be sponsored by *private entities that employ or retain one or more lobbyists or foreign agents.* By Senate Rule, "one-day's attendance" is exclusive of travel time and an overnight stay.

2-Night Stay When Practically Required[2]

Subject to all applicable Senate Rules and on a case-by-case basis, the Ethics Committee *may* allow two-overnight stays, for trips sponsored by *private entities that employ or retain one or more lobbyists or foreign agents,* when practically required. The sponsor or sponsors must request prior written approval from the Committee. The Committee may consider the following factors when deciding whether a two-night stay may be practically required to participate in an event.

- Whether the trip destination is outside the continental United States, for example, travel to Hawaii or Alaska;
- Whether the travel is across the country, for example travel from Washington, DC to San Diego, CA;
- The availability of transportation to or from the location of the one-day event;
- Whether a Member, Senate officer, or employee is participating in a full day's worth of officially-connected activities (without any substantial gaps in his or her day's schedule) such that a second night's stay is necessary to accomplish the purpose of the trip; or

---

[1] Senate Rule 35.2(a)(2)(A).

[2] Senate Rule 35.2(a)(2)(B); Cong. Rec. S10712 (Aug. 2, 2007).

-1-

- Any other exceptional circumstances which must be described in writing and in detail prior to the travel by the traveler where the Committee finds that a two-day stay is practically necessary to achieve the purpose of the trip.

3-Days for Domestic Trips/7-Days for Foreign Trips[3]

Subject to all applicable Senate Rules, *entities that do not employ or retain lobbyists or foreign agents* and *501(c)(3) non-profit organizations (*regardless of whether they employ or retain lobbyists s or foreign agents) may sponsor domestic trips for no more than three days or foreign trips for no more than seven days. The Committee has determined that the three-day and seven-day time limitations shall be three or seven 24-hour periods, respectively.

Accompanying Spouse *or* Child[4]

The sponsor of privately-funded travel may pay travel expenses not only for the participating Senator, Senate officer, or employee, but also for the spouse *or* child of the participant, if the Senator, Senate officer or in the case of an employee, the employee's supervising Senator or Senate officer, signs a determination in advance that the attendance of the spouse or child is appropriate to assist in the representation of the Senate. The Committee has concluded that necessary expenses which may be paid by the sponsor of privately-funded travel for a Member, Senate officer, or employee do not include expenses for any individual (aide, fiance, significant other, etc.) who is not either the spouse *or* a child of the Member, officer, or employee.

Alcoholic Beverages[5]

Alcoholic beverages are not considered to be a reasonable expense.

"At Any Point Throughout the Trip"[6]

For all trips other than one-day trips paid for by entities that employ or retain lobbyists or foreign agents, a lobbyist or foreign agent may not accompany a Member, Senate officer, or employee *at any point throughout the trip.* "At any point throughout the trip" means accompaniment in other than a *de minimis* way. Lobbyist accompaniment is forbidden on any parts of the travel to and from the event, as well as at the event itself or the location being

---

[3] Senate Rule 35.2(a)(1) and (2).

[4] Senate Rule 35.2(f)(4). *See Senate Ethics Manual* at pp. 44-45 (2003 ed.).

[5] Honest Leadership and Open Government Act of 2007 (S.1), §544(b) GUIDELINES. *See also* U.S. Senate Handbook, Appendix IV-D: Travel Regulations, Page IV-40.

[6] Senate Rule 35.2(d); Cong. Rec. S10713 (Aug. 2, 2007).

-2-

visited. This standard is a broader prohibition than the "at any segment of a trip" standard (*see* below).

"At Any Segment of the Trip"[7]

For one day trips paid for by entities that employ or retain lobbyists or foreign agents, a lobbyist or foreign agent may not accompany a Member, Senate officer, or employee on *any segment of the trip.* "Any segment of the trip" means any parts of the travel to and from the event, rather than at the event itself or the location being visited.

Coach and Business-Class Fare[8]

Coach or business-class air or train fare (or other mode of transportation) may be accepted.

De Minimis Exception to Lobbyist/Foreign Agent Accompaniment Standards[9]

Both lobbyist "accompaniment" standards for accompaniment "at any point throughout the trip" and "at any segment of the trip" include a *de minimis* exception. The term "*de minimis*" means negligible or inconsequential. Therefore, the mere coincidental presence of a lobbyist or foreign agent at an event would likely be considered *de minimis.* However, the Committee will consider the totality of the circumstances, including, but not limited to, the amount of time a lobbyist or foreign agent is present at the event; the amount of direct contact between the lobbyist or foreign agent and the Members, Senate officers and staff; the level of control by the trip sponsor over lobbyist's or foreign agent's presence and their contact with Members, Senate officers and staff.

For example, if the trip includes attendance at an event that meets the definition of a widely-attended event under Rule 35(1)(c)(18), the trip sponsor is unlikely to know all attendees at the event. Accordingly, a lobbyist's or foreign agent's attendance at a widely-attended event also attended by Senate invitees on the trip would likely be a type of *de minimis* accompaniment. Similarly, an organization cannot possibly know the other passengers that might be on a common carrier used during a trip if the organization has had no contact or coordination with the other passengers. Accordingly, the new rule does not require a sponsor to certify that it knows for certain that no lobbyist or foreign agent will be on such a common carrier.

---

[7] Senate Rule 35.2(d)(1)(B); Cong. Rec. S10712 (Aug. 2, 2007).

[8] Honest Leadership and Open Government Act of 2007 (S.1), §544(b) GUIDELINES.

[9] Senate Rule 35.2(d)(2); Cong. Rec. S10713 (Aug. 2, 2007).

De Minimis Exception to Lobbyist/Foreign Agent Participation, Planning, or Arrangement[10]

Senators, Senate officers, or employees may not participate in trips planned, organized, or arranged by or at the request of a lobbyist or foreign agent in other than a *de minimis* way. The term *de minimis* means negligible or inconsequential. It would be negligible or inconsequential for a lobbyist to respond to a trip sponsor's request that the lobbyist identify Members or staff with a possible interest in a particular issue relevant to a planned trip or to suggest particular aspects of a Member or staffer's interest. Additionally, the mere presence of one or more lobbyists on the board of an organization that is sponsoring travel does not exceed *de minimis* involvement.

If a lobbyist solicits or initiates an exchange of information with a trip sponsor, however, that would go beyond *de minimis* involvement and would not be allowed. Additionally, if the lobbyist has ultimate control over which Members or employees are actually invited on the trip, or determines the trip itinerary, or if a lobbyist actually extends or forwards an invitation to a participant, or if an invitation mentions a referral or suggestion of a lobbyist, this would go beyond *de minimis* involvement and would not be allowed.

For example, if a trip sponsor that is a 501(c)(3) non-profit organization asks a lobbyist which staffers might be most interested in joining a trip to the U.S.-Mexican border and the lobbyist knows that a potential trip participant has a particular interest in the DEA's activities at the border, or in a particular border facility, then the conveyance and receipt of that information (in light of the trip sponsor's request), in and of itself, would not exceed a *de minimis* level of participation and would not be forbidden.

Duty Station[11]

A Member, Senate officer, or employee may not accept reimbursement for necessary expenses of privately-sponsored fact-finding travel connected with the performance of official duties for travel within a thirty-five (35) mile radius of the Member, Senate officer, or employee's local duty station.

A *Senator's duty station* is the metropolitan area of Washington, DC. During adjournment, *sine die*, or the August recess period, the Senator's usual place of residence in the home state is also considered the Senator's duty station. At the beginning of each Congress, a Senator files with the Disbursing Office his "usual place of residence" in the home state.

---

[10] Senate Rule 35.2(d)(2) and (e)(1)(D); Cong. Rec. S10713 (Aug. 2, 2007).

[11] *See Senate Ethics Manual* at pp. 44-45 (2003 ed.). *See also* U.S. Senate Handbook, Appendix IV-D: Travel Regulations, Page IV-49.

A *Senate employees' duty station*, if other than Washington, DC, is designated when an employee is appointed and must be kept up to date in the Disbursing Office.

Earmarking

Earmarking would include any direction, agreement, or suggestion, formal or informal, to use donated funds, goods, or services or other in-kind contributions for a particular trip or a particular purpose.

Extension of Travel for Personal or Official Senate Business Reasons[12]

As a general rule, if Senate Members, Senate officers, or employees extend their stay for personal reasons, they are personally responsible for the cost of any incremental increases in expenses incurred because of their personal travel (including any food, lodging, or incremental increases in airfare or other transportation costs due to the extension of the travel). Similarly, if Senate Members, Senate officers, or employees extend their stay for official Senate business, the Senate office or committee is responsible for the cost of any incremental increases in expenses incurred because of the official travel (including any food, lodging, or incremental increases in airfare or other transportation costs due to the extension of the travel).

In addition, one should consider the length of the personal or official Senate business travel in relation to the length of the privately-sponsored fact-finding travel. If the time spent on personal or official Senate business travel is essentially equal to or greater than the time spent on privately-sponsored fact-finding travel, one should consider that, at a minimum, the appearance may arise that private third-party funds are being used for personal or official Senate purposes. Therefore, in advance of such trip arrangements, a staffer's supervising Senator as well as the Ethics Committee should be made aware of all the circumstances surrounding the trip, including a staffer's intention to undertake personal travel or official Senate business travel in conjunction with the fact-finding travel and the length of the personal or official Senate business travel in relation to the length of the privately-sponsored fact-finding portion of the trip.

First Class Fare[13]

First-class air, train fare or first class fare for any other mode of transportation may be permitted only under the following limited conditions and only with specific prior written approval by the Ethics Committee:

- When the cost of the first class fare does not exceed the cost of business-class transportation;

---

[12] *See Hon*est Leadership and Open Government Act of 2007 (S.1), §544(b) GUIDELINES.

[13] Honest Leadership and Open Government Act of 2007 (S.1), §544(b) GUIDELINES. *See also* U.S. Senate Handbook, Appendix IV-D: Travel Regulations, Page IV-64.

- When the traveler's frequent flyer or similar benefits are used to upgrade to first class;
- When first-class travel is necessary due to a disability of the traveler;
- When there are genuine security concerns such that first-class seating is required;
- When the flight is in excess of 14 hours; or
- When exceptional circumstances are demonstrated in writing by the private sponsor.

Foreign Agent (for Purposes of the Gifts Rule)[14]

A Member, Senate officer, or employee may not accept reimbursement from a foreign agent for privately-sponsored travel. Under the Senate Gifts Rule, an agent of a foreign principal is defined as an agent of a foreign principal registered (or required to be registered) under the Foreign Agents Registration Act.

Lobbyist (for Purposes of the Gifts Rule)[15]

A Member, Senate officer, or employee may not accept reimbursement from a registered lobbyist for privately-sponsored travel. Under the Senate Gifts Rule a "registered lobbyist" is a lobbyist registered (or required to be registered) under the Lobbying Disclosure Act of 1995. Pursuant to the Lobbying Disclosure Act, in addition to individuals who must register, many organizations are required to act as registrants, as, for example, organizations employing in-house lobbyists, and lobbying firms (entities with one or more employees who act as lobbyists for outside clients).

For purposes of applying the special restrictions on lobbyists in the Gifts Rule, an organization employing lobbyists (outside or in-house) to represent solely the interests of the organization or its members will not be considered to be a "lobbyist." Thus, a corporation, trade association, or labor union that employs lobbyists to serve only the interests of the corporation or the members of the trade association or union would not be a "lobbyist" for purposes of the Gifts Rule. On the other hand, a lobbying firm—that is, a firm that provides lobbying services for others—will be considered a lobbyist for purposes of these restrictions. Thus, the law firm that provides lobbying services for the firm's clients through an individual registered (or required to be registered) as a lobbyist will also be considered to be a "lobbyist" for purposes of the Gifts Rule, and may not reimburse for privately-sponsored travel.

---

[14] *See Senate Ethics Manual* at p. 43 (2003 ed.), Senate Rule 35.2.

[15] *See Senate Ethics Manual* at p. 43 (2003 ed.), Senate Rule 35.2.

Local Transportation[16]

Local transportation provided during a trip must be reasonable and customary for the location and must not be related to personal or recreational activities.

Lodging and Food Expenses[17]

As a general and initial matter, the Committee will consider the maximum *per diem* rates for official Federal Government travel published annually by the General Services Administration, the Department of State, and the Department of Defense when judging the reasonableness of food and lodging expenses on privately-sponsored fact-finding travel. The Ethics Committee will consider these rates for general comparative purposes; thus, where feasible and available, trip expenses for lodging and meals should generally be comparable with these government *per diem* rates. The Ethics Committee recognizes, however, that the circumstances of a particular trip may legitimately require lodging and meal expenses that exceed these rates. Such circumstances may include, for example, whether the trip includes attendance at an event organized without regard to congressional participation.

If an *event is organized without regard to congressional participation* (for example, annual meetings, conferences, seminars, and symposiums of trade associations, professional societies, business associations, and other membership organizations), the Committee may, but is not required to, allow greater flexibility when authorizing lodging and food expenses in order for Members and staff to participate in or appear at events that are organized principally for the benefit of non-congressional attendees. The Committee may, but is not required to, allow Members, Senate officers and employees to accept lodging and food that is commensurate with what is customarily provided to or purchased by the non-congressional attendees in similar circumstances. The quality or location of the accommodations or meals may not be enhanced because of the official position of the Member, Senate officer, or employee. The Committee will consider any other factor deemed relevant by the Committee.

If the *event is organized specifically for congressional participation*, the Committee will take into consideration the cost of the facility, the location of the facility, the facility's proximity to any sites' being visited, the quality of the conference facility, any security concerns, the size of the facility in relation to the number of attendees, any special needs of or accommodations required by any invitees, the federal government *per diem* rates for meals, and any other factor deemed relevant by the Committee. The location and lodging selected must be reasonable in light of the nature of the event and should not create the appearance that the Member, Senate officer or employee attending the event is using his or her public office for personal gain, including for purposes of recreation.

---

[16] Honest Leadership and Open Government Act of 2007 (S.1), §544(b) GUIDELINES.

[17] Honest Leadership and Open Government Act of 2007 (S.1), §544(b) GUIDELINES. *See also* U.S. Senate Handbook, Appendix IV-D: Travel Regulations, Page IV-50.

Miscellaneous Expenses[18]

Members, Senate officers, and employees may accept reasonable miscellaneous expenses such as interpreter fees, visa fees, conference fees and similar expenses that are necessary for the officially-connected purpose of the trip. Such expenses may not include personal expenses or recreational expenses (for example, personal telephone calls, sightseeing tours, theater or concert visits).

Necessary Expenses[19]

Necessary expenses are generally limited to reasonable expenditures for transportation, lodging, conference fees and materials, and food and refreshments. Necessary expenses may also include reasonable miscellaneous expenses such as interpreter fees, conference fees, visa fees and similar expenses that are necessary for the officially-connected purpose of the trip. However, necessary expenses do not include expenses for entertainment other than that provided to all attendees as an integral part of the event, and in no event may they include expenditures for recreational activities. Necessary expenses may also include travel expenses for the spouse *or* child of a Member, Senate officer, or employee, if a written determination has been made by the supervising Member that the attendance of the spouse *or* child is appropriate to assist in the representation of the Senate and if the sponsor has issued an unsolicited invitation for a spouse *or* child to accompany the Member, Senate officer, or employee.

Private or Charter Aircraft[20]

Provision of transportation on a private or charter aircraft is not considered to be a reasonable expense. Thus, travel on private or charter aircraft is not permitted for privately-sponsored travel.

Reasonableness of Expenses[21]

As a threshold matter, the Ethics Committee will give weight to the Member's or Senate officer's determination (either for that Member or Senate officer, or for an employee supervised by that Member or Senate officer) that the travel will not create the appearance that the Senate traveler is using his or her public office for private gain. The Committee will consider that this determination by the Member or Senate officer includes the Member's or Senate officer's evaluation that the expenses for the trip are necessary and reasonable. When evaluating a trip

---

[18] Honest Leadership and Open Government Act of 2007 (S.1), §544(b) GUIDELINES.

[19] Senate Rule 35.2(a)(3). *See also Senate Ethics Manual* at pp. 46-47 (2003 ed.)

[20] Senate Ruler 35.2(b)(3).

[21] Honest Leadership and Open Government Act of 2007 (S.1), §544(b) GUIDELINES.

proposal and judging the reasonableness of an expense or expenditure, the Ethics Committee will also consider the following factors:

- the stated mission of the organization sponsoring the trip;
- the organization's prior history of sponsoring congressional trips, if any;
- other educational activities performed by the organization besides sponsoring congressional trips, if any;
- whether any trips previously sponsored by the organization led to an investigation by the Select Committee on Ethics;
- Whether the length of the trip and the itinerary is consistent with the official purpose of the trip:

  > Members and staff must demonstrate that the purpose of the trip relates to their official and representational duties and that the purpose of the trip relates to matters within the legislative or policy interests of the Senate. There must be sufficient officially-related activities for Senate invitees during each day of the trip. As a general matter, the Committee advises that each day contain a minimum of 6 hours of officially-related activities for Senate invitees for each travel day. Therefore, for many trips it may be necessary for the private sponsor to develop an agenda specifically for Senate participants that reflects a sufficient amount of officially-related activities on each day of the trip;

- Whether there is an adequate connection between a trip and the official duties the Senate invitee:

  > Members, Senate officers and employees requesting approval for travel paid for by a private source must demonstrate that the travel is connected to their individual official duties, and would not create the appearance that the individual is using public office for private gain. Members and Senate officers may, on a case-by-case basis, be required to explain in writing to the Committee how attendance on a given trip relates to their official and representational duties. As a general matter, for employee travel, the supervising Member or Senate officer must certify in advance that the travel relates to the employee's official duties. The Committee will give this determination great weight and, as a general matter, this determination may be dispositive of the matter. The Committee will consider a number of factors in determining whether to approve a Member's, Senate officer's, or employee's travel request, including, but not limited to:

- The Member, Senate officer or employee's official responsibilities;
- Whether the trip relates to matters within the legislative or policy interests of the Senate;
- The amount of officially-connected activities scheduled to take place during the trip; and
- Any other factor the Committee deems relevant.

• The reasonableness of an amount spent by a sponsor of the trip, whether for an individual expenditure on a trip or for the trip in its entirety;

• Whether there is a direct and immediate relationship between a source of funding and an event:

> There must be a direct and immediate relationship between the private sponsor or sponsors of the event or trip and the event or trip itself. Expenses may only be accepted from the sponsor or sponsors of an event or trip. A sponsoring entity must have a significant role in organizing and conducting a trip, as well as a specific organizational interest in the purpose of the trip or location being visited. Expenses may not be accepted from a source that has merely donated monetary or in-kind support to the trip, but does not have a significant role in organizing or conducting the trip;

• The maximum *per diem* rates for lodging and meals for official Federal Government travel published annually by the General Services Administration, the Department of State, and the Department of Defense: GSA rates, for example, are published on the internet [*e.g.*, www.gsa.gov]. The Ethics Committee will consider these rates for general comparative purposes; thus, where feasible and available, trip expenses for lodging and meals should generally be comparable with these government *per diem* rates. The Ethics Committee recognizes, however, that the circumstances of a particular trip may legitimately require lodging and meal expenses that exceed these rates. Such circumstances may include, for example, whether the trip includes attendance at an event organized without regard to congressional participation.

• Whether the travel to a location or event is arranged or organized without regard to Congressional participation, or whether it is specifically organized for Congressional staff:

> If an *event is organized without regard to congressional participation* (for example, annual meetings, conferences, seminars, and symposiums of trade associations, professional societies, business associations, and other membership

organizations), the Committee may, but is not required to, allow greater flexibility when authorizing lodging and food expenses in order for Members and staff to participate in or appear at events that are organized principally for the benefit of non-congressional attendees. The Committee may, but is not required to, allow Members, Senate officers and employees to accept lodging and food that is commensurate with what is customarily provided to or purchased by the non-congressional attendees in similar circumstances. The quality or location of the accommodations or meals may not be enhanced because of the official position of the Member, Senate officer, or employee. The Committee will also consider any other factor deemed relevant by the Committee;

If the *event is organized specifically for congressional participation*, the Committee will take into consideration the cost of the facility, the location of the facility, the facility's proximity to any sites' being visited, the quality of the conference facility, any security concerns, the size of the facility in relation to the number of attendees, any special needs of or accommodations required by any invitees, the federal government *per diem* rates for meals, and any other factor deemed relevant by the Committee;

- any other factors deemed relevant by the Select Committee on Ethics.

Sponsor[22]

A sponsor of a trip is any person, organization, or other entity contributing funds or in-kind support for the trip. A sponsor must have a significant role in organizing and conducting a trip and must have a specific organizational interest in the purpose of the trip. If the Member, Senate officer or employee is participating in an event or fact-finding trip in connection with the duties of the Member or employee, he or she may accept necessary travel expenses only from a sponsor of the event or fact-finding trip.

Privately-funded travel may NEVER be accepted from, paid for, or reimbursed by lobbyists or foreign agents (regardless of whether, for example, the lobbyist's client reimburses the lobbyist or foreign agent at a later date for those costs or expenses of privately-funded travel).

---

[22] Honest Leadership and Open Government Act of 2007 (S.1), §544(b) GUIDELINES.

**U.S. House of Representatives
Committee on Standards of Official Conduct**

**PRIVATE SPONSOR TRAVEL CERTIFICATION FORM
(provide directly to each House invitee)**

This form should be completed by private entities offering to provide travel or reimbursement for travel to House Members, officers or employees under House Rule XXV, clause 5. A completed copy of the form (and any attachments) should be provided to each invited House Member, officer or employee, who will then forward it to the Committee. The trip sponsor should NOT submit the form directly to the Committee.

*Private sponsors are urged to submit this form to each House invitee at least **30 days** before travel is scheduled to begin.* The failure to provide the Committee with adequate time to review the form and attachments may result in the invitee not receiving approval for the trip. The submission of an incomplete form will delay the review process. Before completing this form, sponsors are urged to *carefully review* the Committee's private travel guidelines and advisory memoranda detailing the rules and restrictions for private travel, as well as the instructions for completing this form. Sponsors should call the Committee with any questions prior to submitting the form. *Please type form.*

1. Sponsor(s) (who will be paying for the trip): _____

_____

2. I represent that the trip will not be financed (in whole or in part) by a federally-registered lobbyist or a registered foreign agent (*signify "yes" by checking box*): ☐

3. I represent that the trip sponsor(s) has not accepted from any other source funds earmarked directly or indirectly to finance any aspect of the trip (*signify "yes" by checking box*): ☐

4. Is travel being offered to an accompanying family member of the House invitee(s)? ☐ Yes   ☐ No

5. Provide names and titles of ALL House invitees; for each invitee, provide explanation of why the individual was invited (include additional pages if necessary): _____

_____

6. Dates of travel: _____

7. Cities of departure – destination – return: _____

_____

8. Attached is a detailed agenda of the activities taking place during the travel (*i.e.*, an hourly description of planned activities) (*signify "yes" by checking box*): ☐

9. I represent that (*check one of the following*):
   a. The sponsor of the trip is an institution of higher education within the meaning of section 101 of the Higher Education Act of 1965: ☐ or
   b. The sponsor of the trip does not retain or employ a federally registered lobbyist or registered foreign agent: ☐ or
   c. The trip is for attendance at a one-day event *and* lobbyist involvement in planning, organizing, requesting, or arranging the trip was *de minimis* under the Committee's travel regulations. ☐

10. If travel is for participation in a one-day event (*i.e.*, if you checked Question 9(c)), check one of the following:
    a. One-night's lodging and meals are being offered: ☐ or
    b. Two-nights' lodging and meals are being offered: ☐
    If "b" is checked, explain why the second night is warranted: _____

_____

11. If the trip is not sponsored by an institution of higher education, I represent that a federally-registered lobbyist or foreign agent will not accompany House Members or employees on any segment of the trip (*signify "yes" by checking box*): ❑

12. Private sponsors must have a direct and immediate relationship to the purpose of the trip or location being visited. Describe the role of each sponsor in organizing and conducting the trip: _____

_____

_____

13. Describe each sponsor's organizational interest in the purpose of the trip: _____

_____

_____

14. Describe the type and class of the transportation being provided. Indicate whether coach, business-class or first-class transportation will be provided. In addition, for travel via aircraft, please indicate if travel is being offered on a commercial flight, chartered flight or on an aircraft operated or paid for by a carrier not licensed by the Federal Aviation Administration to operate for compensation or hire (*i.e.*, a private aircraft). If first-class fare is being provided, or if travel is via chartered or private aircraft, please provide an explanation describing why such travel is warranted: _____

_____

_____

15. I represent that the expenditures related to local area travel during the trip will be unrelated to personal or recreational activities of the invitee(s). (*signify "yes" by checking box*): ❑

16. I represent that either (*check one of the following*):

a. The trip involves an event that is arranged or organized *without regard* to congressional participation and that meals provided to congressional participants are similar to those provided to or purchased by other event attendees: ❑ or

b. The trip involves events that are arranged or organized *specifically with regard* to congressional participation: ❑

If "b" is checked, detail the cost per day of meals (approximate cost may be provided): _____

_____

17. Reason for selecting the location of the event or trip: _____

_____

18. Name of hotel or other lodging facility: _____

19. Cost per night of hotel or other lodging facility (approximate cost may be provided): _____

_____

20. Reason(s) for selecting hotel or other lodging facility: _____

_____

_____

21. TOTAL EXPENSES FOR EACH PARTICIPANT:

☐ actual amounts ☐ good faith estimates	Total *Transportation* Expenses per Participant	Total *Lodging* Expenses per Participant	Total *Meal* Expenses per Participant
For each Member, Officer, or employee			
For each accompanying family member			

	Other Expenses (dollar amount)	Identify Specific Nature of "Other" Expenses (*e.g.*, taxi, parking, registration fee, *etc.*)
For each Member, Officer, or employee		
For each accompanying family member		

22. I represent that reimbursement for miscellaneous travel expenses for the trip, such as travel to and from airports, security costs, interpreter fees, visa application fees, and similar expenses, will be for actual costs incurred and are necessary for the purpose of the trip (*signify "yes" by checking box*): ☐

23. I certify that the information contained in this form is true, complete, and correct to the best of my knowledge.

Signature: _____

Name and title: _____

Organization: _____

Address: _____

Telephone number: _____

Fax number: _____

Email Address: _____

The Committee staff may contact the above individual above if additional information is required.

If there are any questions regarding this form please contact the Committee at the following address:

Committee on Standards of Official Conduct
U.S. House of Representatives
HT-2, The Capitol
Washington, DC 20515
(202) 225-7103 (phone)
(202) 225-7392 (general fax)
(202) 226-7172 (fax for travel approvals)

Version date 4/2007 by Committee on Standards of Official Conduct

3

PRIVATE SPONSOR TRAVEL CERTIFICATION FORM

This form must be completed by any private entity offering to provide travel or reimbursement for travel to Senate Members, Officers, or employees (Senate Rule 35, clause 2). Each sponsor of a fact-finding trip must sign the completed form. The trip sponsor(s) must provide a copy of the completed form to each invited Senate traveler, who will then forward it to the Ethics Committee with any other required materials. The trip sponsor(s) should NOT submit the form directly to the Committee. Please consult the accompanying instructions for more detailed definitions and other key information.

The Senate Member, Officer or employee MUST also provide a copy of this form, along with the appropriate travel authorization and reimbursement form, to the Office of Public Records (OPR), Room 232 of the Hart Building, within thirty (30) days after the travel is completed.

1.   Sponsor(s) of the trip (please list all sponsors):_____

2.   Description of the trip: _____

3.   Dates of travel: _____

4.   Place of travel:_____

5.   Name and title of Senate invitees:_____

6.   I *certify* that the trip fits one of the following categories:
   ☐   (A) The sponsor(s) are not registered lobbyists or agents of a foreign principal **and** do not retain or employ registered lobbyists or agents of a foreign principal **and** no lobbyist or agents of a foreign principal will accompany the Member, officer, or employee *at any point* throughout the trip.

   OR

   ☐   (B) The sponsor or sponsors are not registered lobbyists or agents of a foreign principal, but retain or employ one or more registered lobbyists or agents of a foreign principal and the trip meets the requirements of Senate Rule 35.2(a)(2)(A)(i) or (ii) *(See Question 9)*.

7.   ☐   I *certify* that the trip will not be financed in any part by a registered lobbyist or agent of a foreign principal.

   AND

   ☐   I *certify* that the sponsor or sponsors will not accept funds or in-kind contributions earmarked directly or indirectly for the purpose of financing this specific trip from a registered lobbyist or agent of a foreign principal or from a private entity that retains or employs one or more registered lobbyists or agents of a foreign principal.

8.   I *certify* that:
   ☐   The trip will not in any part be planned, organized, requested or arranged by a registered lobbyist or agent of a foreign principal except for *de minimis* lobbyist involvement.

   AND

   ☐   The traveler will not be accompanied on the trip by a registered lobbyist or agents of a foreign principal except as provided for by Committee regulations relating to lobbyist accompaniment *(See question 9)*.

9.   **USE ONLY IF YOU CHECKED QUESTION 6(B)**
     I *certify* that if the sponsor or sponsors retain or employ one or more registered lobbyists or agents of a foreign principal, one of the following scenarios applies:

□   (A) The trip is for attendance or participation in a one-day event (exclusive of travel time and **one** overnight stay) and no registered lobbyist or agents of a foreign principal will accompany the Member, officer, or employee *on any segment* of the trip.
OR

□   (B) The trip is for attendance or participation in a one-day event (exclusive of travel time and **two** overnight stays) and no registered lobbyist or agents of a foreign principal will accompany the Member, officer, or employee *on any segment* of the trip (*See Questions 6 and 10*).
OR

□   (C) The trip is being sponsored only by an organization or organizations designated under Section 501(c)(3) of the Internal Revenue Code of 1986 and no registered lobbyist or agents of a foreign principal will accompany the Member, officer, or employee *at any point* throughout the trip.

10. **USE ONLY IF YOU CHECKED QUESTION 9(B)**
     If the trip includes two overnight stays, please explain why the second night is practically required for Senate invitees to participate in the travel: _____
     _____

11. □   An itinerary for the trip is attached to this form. I *certify* that the attached itinerary is a detailed (hour-by-hour), complete, and final itinerary for the trip.

12. Briefly describe the role of each sponsor in organizing and conducting the trip: _____
     _____
     _____

13. Briefly describe the stated mission of each sponsor and how the purpose of the trip relates to that mission:_____
     _____

14. Briefly describe each sponsor's prior history of sponsoring congressional trips: _____
     _____
     _____

15. Briefly describe the educational activities performed by each sponsor (other than sponsoring congressional trips): _____
     _____

16. Total Expenses for Each Participant:

	Transportation Expenses	Lodging Expenses	Meal Expenses	Other Expenses
□ Good Faith estimate □ Actual Amount				

17.   State whether a) the trip involves an event that is arranged or organized *without regard* to congressional participation **or** b) the trip involves events that are arranged or organized *specifically with regard* to congressional participation:_____

18.   Reason for selecting the location of the event or trip: _____

19.   Name and location of hotel or other lodging facility: _____

20.   Reason(s) for selecting hotel or other lodging facility: _____

21.   Describe how the daily expenses for lodging, meals, and other expenses provided to trip participants compares to the maximum *per diem* rates for official Federal Government travel:

22.   Describe the type and class of transportation being provided. Indicate whether coach, business-class or first class transportation will be provided. If first-class fare is being provided, please explain why first-class travel is necessary: _____

23.   ☐   I represent that the travel expenses that will be paid for or reimbursed to Senate invitees do not include expenditures for recreational activities or entertainment (other than entertainment provided to all attendees as an integral part of the event, as permissible under Senate Rule 35)

24.   List any entertainment that will be provided to, paid for, or reimbursed to Senate invitees and explain why the entertainment is an integral part of the event:_____

25.   I hereby *certify* that the information contained herein is true, complete and correct. (You must include the completed signature block below for each travel sponsor):

Signature of Travel Sponsor: _____
Name and Title: _____
Name of Organization: _____
Address: _____
Telephone Number: _____
Fax Number: _____
E-mail Address: _____

Instructions
(Do not file the Instructions with OPR)

General Instructions

- The Senate Select Committee on Ethics ("Ethics Committee") has developed guidelines for evaluating privately-sponsored trips and for judging whether trip expenses are reasonable. Trip sponsors should consult the *Senate Select Committee on Ethics' Regulations and Guidelines for Privately-Sponsored Travel*, including the *Glossary of Terms*, prior to filling out the *Private Sponsor Travel Certification Form* and contact the Ethics Committee at (202)224-2981 with any additional questions. The Ethics Committee will make the final determination as to whether the expenses incurred during a privately-sponsored trip are reasonable.

- If there are multiple sponsors, they should jointly complete one *Private Sponsor Travel Certification Form* for the trip. Each travel sponsor should complete the signature block.

- When evaluating a trip proposal and judging the reasonableness of expenses, the Ethics Committee will consider the following factors:

  a. The stated mission of the organization sponsoring the trip;
  b. The organization's prior history of sponsoring congressional trips, if any;
  c. Other educational activities performed by the organization besides sponsoring congressional trips;
  d. Whether any trips previously sponsored by the organization led to an investigation by the Select Committee on Ethics;
  e. Whether the length of the trip and the itinerary is consistent with the official purpose of the trip;
  f. Whether there is an adequate connection between a trip and official duties;
  g. The reasonableness of the total amount spent by a sponsor of the trip;
  h. Whether there is a direct and immediate relationship between a source of funding and an event;
  i. The maximum per diem rates for official Federal Government travel published annually by the General Services Administration, the Department of State, and the Department of Defense;
  j. Whether travel to a location or event is arranged or organized without regard to congressional participation, or whether it is specifically organized for Congressional staff; and
  k. Any other factor deemed relevant by the Select Committee on Ethics.

  Consult the *Senate Select Committee on Ethics' Regulations and Guidelines for Privately-Sponsored Travel*, including the *Glossary of Terms*, for further discussion of these factors.

- Responses to each question should be brief, consistent with the requirement to provide all relevant information. Attach additional pages, as necessary.

- To allow sufficient time for the Ethics Committee to review requests for privately sponsored travel, the participating Senate Members, officers and employees must submit the completed form to the Ethics Committee at least thirty (30) days before the date of the proposed trip.

Filling out the Private Sponsor Travel Certification Form (Question by Question Instructions)

1. *Sponsor(s) of the trip (please list all sponsors):* A sponsor of a trip is any person, organization, or other entity contributing funds or in-kind support for the trip. A sponsor must have a significant role in organizing and conducting a trip and must have a specific organizational interest in the purpose of the trip. If Members, officers and employees are participating in an event or fact-finding trip in connection with their duties, they may accept necessary travel expenses only from the event or trip sponsor.

2. *Description of the trip:* Provide a brief statement about the purpose of the trip.

3. *Dates of travel:* Provide the dates of departure and return.

4. *Place of travel:* Provide the destination(s) for the trip.

5. *Name and titles of Senate invitees:* Provide the name and title for each Senate Member, officer or employee who is invited on the trip.

6. *I certify that the trip fits one of the following categories:* A Senate Member, officer or employee may accept privately-sponsored travel only from sponsor(s) of a trip that fits one of the categories listed. Consult the instructions for Question 9 to determine if the trip meets the lobbyist accompaniment standard.

7. *Financing of the trip, earmarked funds and in-kind contributions:* Senate Members, officers and staff may not accept privately-sponsored travel funded by a registered lobbyist or foreign agent. Members, officers and staff may not participate in privately-sponsored travel when the sponsors accept funds or in-kind contributions earmarked for this particular trip from a registered lobbyist or agent of a foreign principal or from a private entity that retains or employs one or more registered lobbyists or agent of a foreign principal. Earmarking includes any direction, agreement, or suggestion-- formal or informal--to use donated funds, goods, services or other in-kind contributions for a particular trip or purpose.

8. *Lobbyist/Agent of a Foreign Principal involvement:* Senate invitees may not participate in trips planned, organized, arranged, or requested by a lobbyist or foreign agent in more than a *de minimis* way, which means negligible or inconsequential. It would be considered inconsequential for one or more lobbyists or foreign agent to serve on the board of an organization that is sponsoring travel, as long as the lobbyists or foreign agent are not involved in the trip. It is also permissible for a lobbyist to respond to a trip sponsor's request to identify Senate invitees with interest in a particular issue relevant to a planned trip. However, a lobbyist is not allowed to solicit or initiate communication with a trip sponsor, have control over which Senate employees are invited on a trip, extend or forward an invitation to a participant, determine the trip itinerary, or be mentioned in the invitation.

    Example: A trip sponsor that is a 501(c)(3) non-profit organization asks a lobbyist to recommend staffers who might be most interested in joining a trip to the U.S.-Mexican border. If a lobbyist knows a staffer who has a particular interest in the DEA's activities at the border, then providing that information (in light of the trip sponsor's request), in and of itself, would not exceed a *de minimis* level of participation, and would be permitted. However, it would not be permissible for the lobbyist to initiate contact with the trip sponsor to suggest that a particular Senate employee be invited or forward an invitation to that staffer. Consult the instructions for Question 9 to determine if the trip meets the lobbyist accompaniment standards.

9. *Lobbyist/Agent of a Foreign Principal accompaniment standards:* Senate Members, officers and staff may not accept privately-sponsored travel from an entity that retains or employs one or more federally-registered lobbyists or foreign agents unless one of the listed scenarios applies. *At any segment of the trip* means lobbyists may not accompany the Senate invitee for parts of the travel to and from the event (not at the event itself or the location being visited). *At any point throughout the trip* means lobbyists may not accompany

Senate invitees at any point to and from the event, at the event itself, or at the location being visited, other than in a *de minimis* way. This is a broader prohibition than the *at any segment of a trip* standard.

Both lobbyist/agent of a foreign principal "accompaniment" prohibitions include a *de minimis* exemption. *De minimis* means negligible or inconsequential. The mere coincidental presence of a lobbyist or foreign agent at an event would likely be considered *de minimis*. But in making the final determination, the Committee will consider the totality of the circumstances, including the amount of time lobbyists or foreign agents are present at the event; the amount of direct contact they have with Senate invitees; and the amount of control a trip sponsor has over their presence or contact with Senate guests. For example, if the trip includes attendance at an event considered widely-attended under Rule 35(1)(c)(18), the trip sponsor is unlikely to know all attendees present. Thus, it is likely to be permissible for such widely-attended events to include both a Senate guest and a lobbyist. Similarly, an organization cannot possibly know all the other passengers taking the same flight or other common carrier to a given destination. Accordingly, the sponsor does not need to certify that it knows for certain that no lobbyist or foreign agent will be on such a common carrier.

10. *If travel includes two overnight stays:* The Committee may approve two overnight stays for trips sponsored by an entity that employs or retains one or more lobbyists or foreign agents under certain conditions. Consult Committee regulations for additional information.

11. *An itinerary for the trip is attached to this form:* The Committee will not review the trip request without a detailed (hour-by-hour), complete and final itinerary for the trip. As a general matter, the Committee advises that each travel day contain a minimum of 6 hours of officially-related activities for Senate invitees.

12. *Briefly describe the role of each sponsor in organizing and conducting the trip:* A sponsor must have a significant role in organizing and conducting a trip and must have a specific organizational interest in the purpose of the trip.

13. *Briefly describe the stated mission of each sponsor and how the purpose of the trip relates to that mission:* Provide a brief description of the stated mission of each sponsor and how it relates to the trip.

14. *Briefly describe each sponsor's prior history of sponsoring congressional trips:* Provide a brief discussion of the sponsor's history of sponsoring congressional travel. It is not necessary to list every trip.

15. *Briefly describe the educational activities performed by each sponsor (other than sponsoring congressional trips):* Provide a brief description of the educational activities performed by each sponsor. It is not necessary to list every individual activity; description may be by kind or category of educational activity.

16. *Total expenses for each participant:* Indicate whether the figures provided are actual amounts or good faith estimates by checking the appropriate box. All trip expenses should be included. Expenses other than those for transportation, lodging and meals must be individually listed and specified. Attached additional pages as necessary.

17. *Congressional participation:* For events that are arranged without regard to congressional participation (for example, annual meetings, conferences, seminars, and symposiums of trade associations, professional societies, business associations, and other membership organizations), the Committee may, but is not required to, allow Senate Members, officers and employees to accept lodging and meal expenses that are commensurate with what is customarily provided to non-congressional attendees in similar circumstances. For events specifically arranged around congressional participation, lodging, meal expenses and other expenses must be "reasonable" in accordance with Committee regulations.

18. *Reason for selecting the location of the event or trip:* The location of the trip must be related to its purpose.

19.   *Name and location of hotel or other lodging facility:* Include the exact name and address of the hotel or other lodging facility.

20.   *Reasons for selecting hotel or other lodging facility:* Provide an explanation of the sponsor's rationale for selecting the particular lodging, include information such as proximity to the airport or site to be visited.

21.   *Describe how the daily expenses for lodging, meals, and other expenses provided to trip participant compare to the maximum per diem rates for official Federal Government travel:* Where feasible and available, trip expenses for lodging and meals should generally be comparable to the government *per diem* rates. The circumstances surrounding a particular trip may legitimately require lodging and meal expenses to exceed these rates. Consult the Ethics Committee regulations for additional information.

22.   *Describe the type and class of transportation being provided:* While coach or business-class fare may be accepted, first-class fare for any mode of transportation may be permitted only under limited conditions and only with specific prior written approval by the Ethics Committee. Transportation on a private or charter aircraft is not permitted for privately-sponsored travel under any circumstances.

23.   *Expenses for recreational activity or entertainment:* The only recreational or entertainment activities that will be approved by the Committee are those that are provided to all attendees and are an integral part of an event.

24.   *List any entertainment that will be provided to, paid for or reimbursed to Senate invitees and explain why the entertainment is an integral part of the event:* Entertainment expenses that are not provided to all attendees and deemed an integral part of the event will not be approved by the Committee.

25.   *Certification:* Each sponsor of a trip should sign the form and certify that the information is complete and correct. Attach additional pages with the certification and signature block, as necessary, for each trip sponsor.

U.S. House of Representatives
Committee on Standards of Official Conduct

INSTRUCTIONS FOR FILLING OUT THE PRIVATE SPONSOR TRAVEL
CERTIFICATION FORM

1. *Sponsor(s) (who will be paying for the trip):* Fill in the names of each person, organization, or other entity contributing funds or in-kind support towards the trip.

2. *I represent that the trip will not be financed (in whole or in part) by a federally-registered lobbyist or a registered foreign agent:* House Members and staff may not accept travel funded by a lobbyist or registered foreign agent, even when the lobbyist or foreign agent will be reimbursed by a client or employer.

3. *I represent that the trip sponsor(s) has not accepted from any other source funds earmarked directly or indirectly to finance any aspect of the trip:* All financial contributors to the trip must qualify as sponsors and should be listed as a sponsor in response to question 1.

4. *Is travel being offered to an accompanying family member of the House invitee(s)?* Check yes or no. House Rules permit Members and House staff to accept travel benefits for one accompanying family member if offered by the trip sponsor.

5. *Provide names and titles of ALL House invitees; for each invitee, provide explanation of why the individual was invited:* You must list every House Member and employee who is invited on the trip, together with your reason for inviting that individual. Members and House staff may accept privately sponsored travel only when related to the individual's official duties. The explanation should demonstrate a connection between the trip and each invitee's official duties.

6. *Dates of Travel:* State the dates of departure and return.

7. *Cities of departure – destination – return:* For example, an appropriate entry might read: "DC – Detroit – DC". Include additional destinations if there will be more than one. Do not list the names of airports, times of flights, or cities where travelers will have an airport layover (this information should be included in the attached detailed agenda).

8. *Attached is a detailed agenda of the activities taking place during the travel:* The agenda should be a detailed, hour-by-hour agenda. Include the names of speakers and the subjects of briefings. The agenda should also include information regarding the time spent on travel to and from the destination, as well as local travel. Travel will not be approved if the agenda includes an excessive amount of either unscheduled time and/or opportunities for recreational activities, even if such activities are at the personal expense of the invitees.

9.   *I represent that (check one of the following):*   Check only one box in response to this question.   "Institutions of higher education" generally includes accredited public and private colleges or trade schools located in the U.S. and its territories; such entities should check box "a," regardless of whether they employ or retain a federal lobbyist or foreign agent.   Entities other than institutions of higher education that do not employ or retain a federal lobbyist or foreign agent should check box "b."   Entities other than institutions of higher education that do employ or retain a registered lobbyist or foreign agents may sponsor travel only for one-day events.   For such trips, lobbyist involvement must be *"de minimis"* as defined by Committee regulations (see question 12).

10.   *If travel is for participation in a one-day event, check one of the following:*   Complete this question only if you checked box "c" in response to question 9.   For travel to one-day events sponsored by an entity that retains or employs a lobbyist, lodging and meals generally may be provided only for one night.   However, two nights may be authorized by the Committee in accordance with the factors set forth in Committee regulations.

11.   *If the trip is not sponsored by an institution of higher education, I represent that a federally-registered lobbyist or foreign agent will not accompany House Members or employees on any segment of the trip:*   House Rules prohibit Members and employees from being accompanied by registered lobbyists or foreign agents while traveling.   This rule does not prohibit lobbyist or foreign agent participation in briefings or meetings that occur at the destination.

12.   *Private sponsors must have a direct and immediate relationship to the purpose of the trip or location being visited.   Describe the role of each sponsor in organizing and conducting the trip:*   The sponsor(s) (the entity or entities paying for the trip) should be the entity primarily responsible for organizing the trip.   Travel may not be accepted from an entity that merely contributes money towards the travel and is not otherwise involved in planning or conducting the trip.

13.   *Describe each sponsor's organizational interest in the purpose of the trip:*   Briefly describe the interest or purpose of each sponsor in the trip.

14.   *Describe the type and class of transportation being provided:*   See directions on form.

15.   *I represent that the expenditures related to local area travel during the trip will be unrelated to personal or recreational activities of the invitee(s):*   While Members and staff may accept local transportation necessary in facilitating their participation in officially-connected aspects of a trip, Members and staff may not accept local transportation in connection with recreation or entertainment.

16.   *I represent that either:*   For events that are arranged or organized without regard to congressional participation (*e.g.*, annual meetings of business or trade associations), Members or employees may accept the meals that are provided to all other attendees as part of the event.   For events put on specifically for Members or staff, meal expenses must be "reasonable" in accordance with Committee regulations.

17. *Reason for selecting the location of the event or trip:* The destination of a trip must be related to its purpose. Travel to a location of an event organized without regard to congressional participation (for example, annual meetings of business or trade associations) is presumptively reasonable.

18. *Name of hotel or other lodging facility:* Include the names of all hotels and lodging facilities to be used during the trip.

19. *Cost per night of hotel or other lodging facility:* Self-explanatory. Trip sponsors should not pay for a "package" that includes recreational or entertainment activities. However, Members and staff may generally use a pool or gym facilities that are offered free of charge to all hotel guests.

20. *Reason(s) for selecting hotel or other lodging facility:* For events held without regard to congressional participation (*e.g.*, annual meetings of business or trade associations), an entry such as "location of annual trade association meeting" is sufficient. When the trip is held specifically for Members or staff, include rationale such as proximity to the site to be visited or to the airport.

21. *Total Expenses for Each Participant:* Indicate whether the figures provided are actual amounts or good faith estimates by checking the appropriate box. All trip expenses should be included. Expenses other than those for transportation, lodging and meals must be individually listed and specified.

22. *I represent that reimbursement for miscellaneous travel expenses for the trip, such as travel to and from airports, security costs, interpreter fees, visa application fees, and similar expenses, will be for actual costs incurred and are necessary for the purpose of the trip:* Members and staff may not accept a lump sum based on an estimate of incidental expenses.

23. *Certification Information:* Self-explanatory.

THE TRIP SPONSOR SHOULD PROVIDE A COPY OF THE COMPLETED FORM, INCLUDING ALL ATTACHMENTS, TO EACH HOUSE MEMBER OR EMPLOYEE INVITED ON THE TRIP.

Version date 4/2007 Committee on Standards of Official Conduct

3

Appendix E

Summary of State Contribution Limits for Corporations and PACs

Note: State law should be consulted to determine whether and to what extent federal and state PACs must register and report.

	LIMITS ON CONTRIBUTIONS FROM:		
STATE	CORPORATION	FEDERAL PAC	STATE PAC
Alabama	$500 to any candidate, PAC, or political party per election.	None.	None.
Alaska	Prohibited.	Effectively prohibited.	Alaska-based groups may donate $1,000 per year to a candidate, group, or political party.
Arizona	Prohibited.	Contributions are prohibited if the candidate participates in public funding. If a candidate does not participate in public funding: a certified[1] PAC may contribute $4,008 to statewide candidates, $2,000 to local candidates, and $1,600 to legislative candidates per election; a noncertified PAC may contribute $808 to statewide candidates, $390 to local candidates, and $312 to legislative candidates per election.[2] General and primary elections are counted as one election for contribution limit purposes.[3]	Same as for federal PACs.

	LIMITS ON CONTRIBUTIONS FROM:		
STATE	**CORPORATION**	**FEDERAL PAC**	**STATE PAC**
Arkansas[4]	$2,000 to any candidate, regardless of the office sought; no limit on contributions to PACs or state party committees.	$2,000 to any candidate per election for both small donor PACs[5] and other PACs. PACs may not accept more than $5,000 per year from a person.	$2,000 to any candidate per election for both small donor PACs and other PACs. PACs may not accept more than $5,000 per year from a person.
California	$3,600 per election for legislative candidates; $24,100 per election for governor; $6,000 per election for other statewide offices; $30,200 per year to state party committees. Corporations that contribute $10,000 or more in a calendar year must report to the state.[6]	$3,600 per election for legislative candidates; $24,100 per election for governor; $6,000 per election for other statewide offices; $30,200 per year to state party committees.	$3,600 per election for legislative candidates; $24,100 per election for governor; $6,000 per election for other statewide offices; $30,200 per year to state party committees.
Colorado[7]	Prohibited, except for contributions to political committees that do not exceed $525 per two-year state house of representatives election cycle.	$525 to gubernatorial candidates for a primary election; $525 to governor/lieutenant governor (as joint candidates) for a general election; $525 to secretary of state, treasurer, and attorney general candidates; $200 legislative, district attorney, state board of education, University of Colorado regent candidates.	$525 to gubernatorial candidates for a primary election; $525 to governor/lieutenant governor (as joint candidates) for a general election; $525 to secretary of state, treasurer, attorney general candidates; $200 to legislative, district attorney, state board of education, University of Colorado regent candidates.
Connecticut	Prohibited.	Effectively prohibited.	$5,000 to governor; $3,000 to other statewide candidates; $1,500 to state senator, probate judge, or chief elected official of a municipality candidates; $750 to state representative candidates; $375 to candidates for other municipal office (primary and general elections are treated separately). Contributions may not aggregate to more than $100,000 per election.
Delaware	$1,200 to statewide candidates; $600 to nonstatewide candidates per election; $20,000 to any political party per election.	$1,200 to statewide candidates; $600 to nonstatewide candidates per election period; $20,000 to any political party per election period.[8]	$1,200 to statewide candidates; $600 to nonstatewide candidates per election period; $20,000 to any political party per election period.

	LIMITS ON CONTRIBUTIONS FROM:		
STATE	**CORPORATION**	**FEDERAL PAC**	**STATE PAC**
District of Columbia	$2,000 to mayor; $1,500 to chairperson of city council; $1,000 to at-large councilpersons per election (includes both primary and general elections); $8,500 in aggregate to all candidates and political committees per election; $5,000 per election to any one state party committee. A corporation, its subsidiaries, and all political committees established by it share a single contribution limit.	$2,000 to mayor; $1,500 to chairperson of city council; $1,000 to at-large councilpersons per election (includes both primary and general elections); $8,500 in aggregate to all candidates and political committees per election. $5,000 per election to any one state party committee.	$2,000 to mayor; $1,500 to chairperson of city council; $1,000 to at-large councilpersons per election (includes both primary and general elections); $8,500 in aggregate to all candidates and political committees per election. $5,000 per election to any one state party committee.
Florida[9]	$500 to any candidate for statewide or nonstatewide office per election;[10] no limits to any state party committee.	Effectively prohibited.	$500 to any candidate for statewide or legislative office per election; no limits to any state party committee.
Georgia[11]	$5,700 per election (primary or general) to statewide candidates, $2,300 per election (primary or general) to nonstatewide candidates; unlimited to state party committees. Corporations must register in Georgia before making contributions over $5,000 to more than one candidate, party, or committee.[12]	$5,700 per election (primary or general) to statewide, $2,300 per election (primary or general) to nonstatewide candidates.	$5,700 per election (primary or general) to statewide, $2,300 per election (primary or general) to nonstatewide candidates.
Hawaii	In light of a state court decision overturning the rules regarding corporate contributions (and subject to reversal on appeal), the Hawaii Campaign Spending Commission has advised that corporations may contribute up to $6,000 per election period to candidates for four-year statewide office, $4,000 per election period to candidates for four-year nonstatewide office, $2,000 per election period for candidates for two-year office, and $25,000 to a political party in a two-year election period.	$6,000 per election period to candidates for four-year statewide office, $4,000 per election period to candidates for four-year nonstatewide office, $2,000 per election period for candidates for two-year office, and $25,000 to a political party in a two-year election period.	$6,000 per election period to candidates for four-year statewide office, $4,000 per election period to candidates for four-year nonstatewide office, $2,000 per election period for candidates for two-year office, and $25,000 to a political party in a two-year election period.

	LIMITS ON CONTRIBUTIONS FROM:		
STATE	CORPORATION	FEDERAL PAC	STATE PAC
Idaho	$5,000 to statewide and $1,000 to legislative candidates per election. No limits for contributions to state party committees.	$5,000 to statewide and $1,000 to legislative candidates per election. No limits for contributions to state party committees.	$5,000 to statewide and $1,000 to legislative candidates per election. No limits for contributions to state party committees.
Illinois	None.	None.	None.
Indiana	$5,000 in the aggregate to all statewide candidates; $5,000 in the aggregate to state central political party committees; $2,000 in the aggregate to all state senate candidates; $2,000 in the aggregate to all state representative candidates; $2,000 in the aggregate for noncentral state political party committees; $2,000 in the aggregate to state senate caucuses; $2,000 in the aggregate to state house caucuses; $2,000 in the aggregate to candidates for local offices during a calendar year.	None.	None.
Iowa	Prohibited.	None.	None.
Kansas	$2,000 to statewide, $1,000 to state senate, and $500 to all other candidates per election; $15,000 in the aggregate to a state political party committee, and $5,000 in the aggregate to other party committees per calendar year.	$2,000 to statewide, $1,000 to state senate, and $500 to all other candidates per election; $5,000 in the aggregate to a state political party committee, and $5,000 in the aggregate to other party committees per calendar year.	$2,000 to statewide, $1,000 to state senate, and $500 to all other candidates per election; $5,000 in the aggregate to a state political party committee, and $5,000 in the aggregate to other party committees per calendar year.
Kentucky	Prohibited. PACs must reimburse corporations for administrative expenses.	$1,000 to any statewide or legislative candidate per election; and $1,500 to other state PACs per calendar year in the aggregate.	$1,000 to any statewide or legislative candidate per election; and $1,500 to other state PACs per calendar year in the aggregate.

	LIMITS ON CONTRIBUTIONS FROM:		
STATE	CORPORATION	FEDERAL PAC	STATE PAC
Louisiana	$5,000 to "major office"[13] candidates, $2,500 to legislative candidates; and $1,000 to any other office candidates per election; $100,000 in the aggregate to a PAC or a state party committee over four years. Parents/subsidiaries of a corporation are subject to a single limit.	Big PAC[14] Limits: $10,000 to "major office" candidates, $5,000 to legislative candidates, and $2,000 to any other office candidates per election; from $2,000 to $10,000 to another PAC. Non-Big PAC limits are the same as corporate limits, except for contributions to another PAC: limits range from $1,000 to $5,000 depending on what types of candidates the recipient PAC supports.[15]	Big PAC Limits: $10,000 to "major office" candidates, $5,000 to legislative candidates, and $2,000 to any other office candidates per election; from $2,000 to $10,000 to another PAC. Non-Big PAC limits are the same as corporate limits, except for contributions to another PAC: limits range from $1,000 to $5,000 depending on what types of candidates the recipient PAC supports.
Maine	$500 to any candidate for governor per election; $250 to any other candidate per election. If a candidate participates in public financing,[16] contributions to that candidate are prohibited. Corporate parents and subsidiaries are subject to a single contribution limit. No limits on contributions to state party committees.	$500 to any candidate for governor per election; $250 to any other candidate per election. If a candidate participates in public financing, contributions are prohibited.	$500 to any candidate for governor per election; $250 to any other candidate per election. If a candidate participates in public financing, contributions are prohibited.
Maryland	$4,000 in the aggregate to any campaign account and $10,000 in the aggregate to all campaign accounts over a four-year election cycle. The current cycle began on January 1, 2007. There are special reporting requirements for corporations doing business in the state and those having a registered lobbyist.	$4,000 in the aggregate to any campaign account and $10,000 in the aggregate to all campaign accounts over a four-year election cycle. The current cycle began on January 1, 2007.	$6,000 in the aggregate to any campaign account over a four-year election cycle. The current cycle began on January 1, 2007.
Massachusetts[17]	Prohibited. PACs must reimburse corporations for administrative expenses.	Effectively prohibited.	$500 per year to any statewide or legislative candidate, and $5,000 to state political parties per calendar year.

	LIMITS ON CONTRIBUTIONS FROM:		
STATE	CORPORATION	FEDERAL PAC	STATE PAC
Michigan	Prohibited.	If a federal PAC qualifies as an "independent PAC"[18]: $34,000 to any statewide, $10,000 to any state senate, and $5,000 to any state representative candidate per election cycle (includes primary and general). If not an "independent PAC": $3,400 to any statewide candidate, $1,000 to any state senate candidate, and $500 to any state representative candidate per election cycle. (includes primary and general). Federal PACs are required to treat contributions made by payroll deductions differently from other contributions.	"Independent PAC": $34,000 to any statewide, $10,000 to any state senate, and $5,000 to any state representative candidate per election cycle (includes primary and general). If not an "independent PAC": $3,400 to any statewide candidate, $1,000 to any state senate candidate, and $500 to any state representative candidate per election cycle. (includes primary and general).
Minnesota	Prohibited.	Effectively prohibited.	Prohibited. A corporation may sponsor only an employee "conduit fund."
Mississippi	$1,000 to any statewide or legislative candidate per year (includes primary and general); $1,000 annually to political parties.	Unincorporated federal PACs may contribute without limit to Mississippi campaigns. However, PACs not affiliated with a political party may not contribute in excess of $5,000 to supreme court/court of appeals candidates or $2,500 to other judicial candidates. Incorporated federal PACs are subject to the $1,000 corporate limit.	Generally none. However, PACs not affiliated with a political party may not contribute in excess of $5,000 to supreme court/court of appeals candidates or $2,500 to other judicial candidates.
Missouri[19]	$1,275 to governor, lieutenant governor, secretary of state, state treasurer, state auditor, or attorney general candidates per election; $650 to state senator candidates per election; $325 for state representative candidates per election.[20] No limits on contributions to state party committees	$1,275 to governor, lieutenant governor, secretary of state, state treasurer, state auditor, or attorney general candidates per election; $650 to state senator candidates per election; $325 to state representative candidates per election. Out-of-state PACs (including federal PACs) must make contributions no later than thirty (30) days prior to an election. Separate committee necessary if aggregate contributions exceed $1,499 in a calendar year.	$1,275 to governor, lieutenant governor, secretary of state, state treasurer, state auditor, or attorney general candidates per election; $650 to state senator candidates per election; $325 to state representative candidates per election.

	LIMITS ON CONTRIBUTIONS FROM:		
STATE	**CORPORATION**	**FEDERAL PAC**	**STATE PAC**
Montana	Prohibited.	$500 to any governor/lieutenant governor ticket,[21] $250 to other statewide, and $130 to all other public office candidates per election.[22] Pursuant to a 2007 amendment (2007 Mont. Laws ch. 328 (H.B. 706), these limits will be subject to periodic adjustment for inflation effective October 1, 2007.	$500 to any governor/lieutenant governor ticket, $250 to other statewide, and $130 to all other public office candidates per election. Pursuant to a 2007 amendment (2007 Mont. Laws ch. 328 (H.B. 706), these limits will be subject to periodic adjustment for inflation effective October 1, 2007.
Nebraska[23]	None. Corporations doing business in the state must report contributions of $250 or more during a calendar month. All other corporations must report contributions that exceed $10,000 per year.	None. Unless it wants to register in Nebraska, a federal PAC may not solicit funds explicitly for the purpose of making contributions in Nebraska.	None.
Nevada	$5,000 to any candidate per election; contributions to political parties are unlimited.	$5,000 to any candidate per election; contributions to political parties are unlimited.	$5,000 to any candidate per election; contributions to political parties are unlimited.
New Hampshire	$5,000 per election, provided the candidate has voluntarily agreed to limit his or her own expenditures. Otherwise, $1,000 per election. The limit is $5,000 per year for state party committees.[24]	None, provided the candidate has voluntarily agreed to limit his or her own expenditures. Otherwise, $1,000 per election.	None, provided the candidate has voluntarily agreed to limit his or her own expenditures. Otherwise, $1,000 per election.
New Jersey	Prohibited for certain "regulated" corporations. Nonregulated corporations may contribute up to $3000 for governor; $2,600 to statewide or legislative candidates per election; $25,000 to state political parties; $37,000 to county political parties; $7,200 to municipal political parties per calendar year.	If contributing as an "association" without registration, then the limits are the same as for corporations. If registered as a PAC in New Jersey, then the limits are as follows: $8,200 to statewide or legislative candidates per election; $25,000 to state political parties; $37,000 to county political parties per calendar year.	$8,200 to statewide or legislative candidates per election; $25,000 to state political parties; $37,000 to county political parties per calendar year.
New Mexico[25]	None.	None.	None.

	LIMITS ON CONTRIBUTIONS FROM:		
STATE	CORPORATION	FEDERAL PAC	STATE PAC
New York	$5,000 in the aggregate to all state and local candidates, PACs, and political parties per calendar year. Each affiliated or subsidiary corporation, if a separate legal entity, has its own limit. In addition, lower candidate-specific contribution limits, discussed under the PAC listings, are also applicable. PAC administrative expenses paid by corporations count against the $5,000 corporate limit. There are no limits on contributions to state party "housekeeping" accounts.	No aggregate limit. The total number of enrolled voters in the candidate's party in the state * $0.005 per primary, and $37,800 per general to statewide; $6,000 per primary and $9,500 per general to state senate; and $3,800 per primary and $3,800 per general to state assembly candidates. Federal PACs must have a New York depository in order to register and make contributions of more than $1000.	No aggregate limit. The total number of enrolled voters in the candidate's party in the state * $0.005 per primary, and $37,800 per general to statewide; $6,000 per primary and $9,500 per general to state senate; and $3,800 per primary and $3,800 per general to state assembly candidates.
North Carolina[26]	Prohibited.	$4,000 to any statewide or legislative candidate per election.	$4,000 to any statewide or legislative candidate per election.
North Dakota	Prohibited.	None.	None.
Ohio	Mostly prohibited except for $10,000 per calendar year to a state or county political party's "restricted fund" account from which the party may make certain limited uses.	$10,000 to any statewide or legislative candidate per election cycle (primary and general are separate) and $30,000 to any state political party per calendar year.	$10,000 to any statewide or legislative candidate per election cycle (primary and general are separate) and $30,000 to any state political party per calendar year.
Oklahoma	Prohibited.	$5,000 to any statewide or legislative candidate; $1,000 to any other local office candidate per election cycle (includes primary and general).	$5,000 to any statewide or legislative candidate; $1,000 to any other local office candidate per election cycle (includes primary and general).
Oregon[27]	None.	None.	None.
Pennsylvania	Prohibited.	None.	None.
Rhode Island	Prohibited.[28]	Effectively prohibited.	$1,000 to any statewide or legislative candidate, $10,000 annual aggregate limit on contributions made by an individual, and $25,000 annual aggregate limit on contributions made by PACs. PACs are limited to $1,000 per contributor.

STATE	CORPORATION	FEDERAL PAC	STATE PAC
		LIMITS ON CONTRIBUTIONS FROM:	
South Carolina	$3,500 to statewide, $1,000 to nonstatewide candidates per election; $3,500 to PACs and political parties per calendar year.	$3,500 to statewide, $1,000 to nonstatewide candidates per election; $3,500 to PACs and political parties per calendar year.	$3,500 to statewide, $1,000 to nonstatewide candidates per election; $3,500 to PACs and political parties per calendar year.
South Dakota	Prohibited.	None.[29]	None.
Tennessee	Prohibited. PACs must reimburse corporations for administrative expenses.	$7,500 to any statewide, $7,500 to any state senate, $5,000 to any state representative candidate per election. Candidates are limited as to their total percentage of contributions from PACs.	$7,500 to any statewide, $7,500 to any state senate, $5,000 to any state representative candidate per election. Candidates are limited as to their total percentage of contributions from PACs.
Texas	Prohibited.[30]	None, except for judicial candidates.	None, except for judicial candidates.
Utah	None. Corporations that receive contributions or make expenditures greater than $750 in a calendar year are required to file state financial disclosure reports.	None. PACs that receive contributions or make expenditures greater than $750 in a calendar year are required to file state financial disclosure reports.	None. PACs that receive contributions or make expenditures greater than $750 in a calendar year are required to file state financial disclosure reports.
Vermont[31]	$1000 per election to any state, county, local, or legislative candidate.	$3000 per election to any state, county, local, or legislative candidate.	$3000 per election to any state, county, local, or legislative candidate.
Virginia	None.	None.	None.
Washington	$1,400 to any statewide, $700 to any legislative candidate per election, $3500 per year to state political party committees, provided the corporation does business in the state. Corporations must report contributions to the state if: (1) aggregate contributions exceed $14,500 in a calendar year; or (2) the corporation employs a registered lobbyist.	$1,400 to any statewide, $700 to any legislative candidate per election, $3500 per year to state political party committees.	$1,400 to any statewide, $700 to any legislative candidate per election. $3500 per year to state political party committees.
West Virginia	Prohibited. Corporations that sponsor PACs must report administrative expenses.	$1,000 to any statewide candidate per election. Primary and general elections are considered separate elections.	$1,000 to any statewide candidate per election. Primary and general elections are considered separate elections.

	LIMITS ON CONTRIBUTIONS FROM:		
STATE	**CORPORATION**	**FEDERAL PAC**	**STATE PAC**
Wisconsin	Prohibited.	$43,128 to governor, $12,939 to lieutenant governor, $21,560 to attorney general, $8,625 to treasurer and secretary of state, $1,000 to state senate, $500 to state assembly candidates per election cycle (includes primary and general); and $6,000 in a calendar year to a political party.	$43,128 to governor, $12,939 to lieutenant governor, $21,560 to attorney general, $8,625 to treasurer and secretary of state, $1,000 to state senate, $500 to state assembly candidates per election cycle (includes primary and general); and $6,000 in a calendar year to a political party.
Wyoming	Prohibited.	None.	None.

NOTES

1. Arizona: A PAC may become "certified" by the secretary of state if it receives contributions of $10 or more from 500 or more individuals in the one-year period immediately before certification.

2. Arizona: Limits for Arizona are effective for 2007-2008, and are adjusted every two years.

3. Arizona: A candidate may not accept contributions from all political committees (excluding political parties) combined (general and primary elections together) totaling more than $80,088 for statewide office, more than $10,020 for a nonstatewide office, or more than $8,016 for a legislative office.

4. Arkansas: Previous contribution limits of $300 to statewide candidates, $100 to other candidates, $200 to PACs, and $2,500 by small donor PACs, have been held unconstitutional. Russell v. Burris, 978 F. Supp. 1211 (E.D. Arkansas 1997), *aff'd in part and rev'd in part*, 146 F.3d 563 (8th Cir. 1998), *on remand*, No. LR-C-97-0089 (E.D. Arkansas 1998).

5. Arkansas: A small donor PAC receives contributions of $25 or less per donor in a calendar year from its contributors.

6. California: Limits for California became effective January 1, 2007, and are adjusted January 1 of each odd-numbered year.

7. Colorado: Limits for Colorado became effective April 1, 2007, and are adjusted every four years.

8. Delaware: With respect to PACs, "election period" is defined so as to include both the primary and general elections.

9. Florida: On November 3, 1998, voters approved an amendment to the state constitution providing for public financing of campaigns for statewide candidates who agree to campaign spending limits. Although the constitutional amendment technically took effect January 5, 1999, it requires the enactment of enabling legislation to establish the parameters of the public financing scheme. The Florida legislature has yet to enact such legislation.

10. Florida: Candidates for governor and lieutenant governor on the same ticket are considered a single candidate for purposes of the contribution limit. The first primary, second primary, and general elections count as separate elections, as long as the candidate is opposed.

11. Georgia: Contributions made by a corporation and its PAC will be aggregated in evaluating whether the limits have been reached.

12. Georgia: Limits for Georgia became effective February 27, 2007, and are adjusted every election cycle.

13. Louisiana: "Major office" candidates include candidates for statewide office, supreme court, court of appeals, district court judges in districts comprised of a single parish with a population in excess of 450,000 persons, and candidates for office in districts with a population greater than 250,000.

14. Louisiana: A PAC may be certified as a "Big PAC" if it has more than 250 members who contributed at least $50 each to the PAC during the preceding year. This exception is available only to PACs registered in Louisiana.

15.   Louisiana: Aggregate limits from all PACs combined to candidates for primary and general elections: $80,000 for major office; $60,000 for district office; and $20,000 for any other office.

16.   Maine: Under the Maine Clean Election Act, candidates who voluntarily participate in a public financing scheme are prohibited from accepting contributions from external sources, including corporations and PACs.

17.   Massachusetts: Effective July 1, 2003, the Massachusetts Clean Election Law was repealed. In its place, the Massachusetts legislature reinstituted a system of public financing, which provides limited funds to statewide candidates only and does not impose additional contribution limits.

18.   Michigan: An "independent PAC" must receive contributions from 25 contributors, make contributions to at least three candidates, and be in existence for six months prior to the election.

19.   Missouri: Limits for Missouri were restored after a July 19, 2007, state supreme court decision striking down the legislative repeal of contribution limits. Assuming no legislative changes, the limits will remain in effect, subject to periodic increases for inflation.

20.   Missouri: In Shrink Missouri Government PAC, et al v. Adams, 161 F.3d 519 (8th Cir. 1998), the Eighth Circuit Court of Appeals held Missouri's contribution limits unconstitutional. In 2000, the Supreme Court reversed the decision and held that Mo. Rev. Stat. § 130.032 was constitutional. Nixon v. Shrink Missouri Government PAC, 528 U.S. 377 (2000). In addition, the Eighth Circuit found Missouri's limitations on the amount of cash and in-kind contributions that political parties may give to candidates constitutional in Missouri Republican Party v. Lamb, 270 F.3d 567 (8th Cir. 2001).

21.   Montana: The candidates for governor and lieutenant governor run jointly as a ticket so any contribution to one candidate is a contribution to the candidates combined.

22.   Montana: In addition, state senate candidates are subject to an aggregate limit of $2,150 in contributions from political committees, and an aggregate limit of $1,300 from political committees applies to candidates for the state house of representatives.

23.   Nebraska: Although there are no limits on contributions made by corporations and PACs, the following limits apply to how much certain candidates may accept in the aggregate from corporations and PACs: $1,148,500 for governor, $104,500 for other statewide candidates, $44,500 for state legislature candidates. (See http://nadc.nol.org/pdf/CFLABrochure-LegislatureRevised-2008.pdf; see also http://nadc.nol.org/pdf/2007cfla.pdf)

24.   New Hampshire: See also Letter from Steven M. Houran, Deputy Attorney General, to William M. Gardner, Secretary of State, dated June 6, 2000 (stating the limits for "persons" were applicable to corporations). In 2007, New Hampshire repealed the statutory prohibition against corporate contributions previously held to be unconstitutional. See 2007 NH S.B. 91 (Mar. 22, 2007).

25.   New Mexico: Contributions to Public Regulation Commission (PRC) candidates from regulated corporations are prohibited, and the state limits all other PRC contributions to $500.

26.   North Carolina: North Carolina Right to Life, Inc. v. Bartlett, 168 F.3d 705 (4th Cir. 1999), held that the North Carolina statute provisions prohibiting corporate expenditures or contributions for political purposes, and the provision defining "political committee," were substantially overbroad and unconstitutionally vague. The state has subsequently amended its corporate prohibition so that nonprofits meeting certain criteria are excluded from the ban. Most recently, in North Carolina Right to Life, Inc. v. Leake, 482 F. Supp. 2d 686 (E.D.N.C. 2007), the campaign finance provision providing for a $4,000 dollar limit on individual contributions to political committees and candidates was held unconstitutional as applied to political committees that make only independent expenditures.

27.   Oregon: Measure 9, a campaign finance initiative passed by the voters in 1997, was invalidated by the Oregon Supreme Court. Vannatta v. Keisling, 324 Or. 514, 931 P.2d 770 (1997).

28.   Rhode Island: The state ACLU challenged the application of the statute prohibiting corporate contributions in a recent lawsuit. See R.I. ACLU, Inc. v. Begin, 431 F. Supp. 2d 227 (D.R.I. 2006). The district court declared the statute unconstitutional "to the extent that [it] prohibit[s] corporations or other entities from making contributions from their own funds in support of or opposition to ballot questions." Id. at 244. The court also held that the dollar limits on individual and PAC contributions contained in the statute do not apply to "contributions made in support of or opposition to ballot questions." Id.

29.   South Dakota: While there are no limits on the amounts PACs may contribute to candidates, individuals are subject to a $10,000 limitation on the amount they may contribute to PACs.

30.   Texas: A corporation may make contributions to state party committees to (1) defray normal overhead and administration or operating costs; or (2) administer a primary election or convention held by a party. A corporation may not make a contribution to a party within sixty days of an election for state or county offices.

31.   Vermont: In June 2006, the U.S. Supreme Court struck down portions of Vermont's Campaign Finance Law, most notably spending limits, as unconstitutional. Randall v. Sorrell, 126 S. Ct. 2479 (2006). In response, the Vermont legislature in 2007 passed legislation amending the campaign contribution limits listed in this table. On May 30, 2007, Governor Jim Douglas vetoed this legislation, and the legislature failed to override the veto.

Appendix F

State Campaign Finance
and Ethics/Lobbying Web Sites

NOTE: Electronic links may be accessed at profs.lp.findlaw.com/election/election_9.html.

STATE	ELECTION LAW WEB SITE	ETHICS/LOBBYING WEB SITE
Alabama	www.sos.state.al.us/election/index.aspx	www.ethics.alalinc.net/
Alaska	Elections: www.gov.state.ak.us/ltgov/elections Campaign Finance: www.state.ak.us/apoc/index.htm	Legislative Ethics Committee: http://ethics.legis.state.ak.us/ Public Offices Commission: www.state.ak.us/apoc/index.htm
Arizona	www.azsos.gov/election//	http://www.azsos.gov/election/lobbyist
Arkansas	Elections: www.sosweb.state.ar.us/elections.html Campaign Finance: www.arkansasethics.com/	www.arkansasethics.com/
California	Elections: www.sos.ca.gov/elections/elections.htm Campaign Finance: www.fppc.ca.gov/	www.fppc.ca.gov/
Colorado	www.elections.colorado.gov/DDefault.aspx?/ main.htm	www.elections.colorado.gov/ DDefault.aspx?/main.htm
Connecticut	State Elections Enforcement Division: www.ct.gov/seec/site/default.asp Campaign Finance: www.ct.gov/seec/site/default.asp	www.ct.gov/ethics/site/default.asp
Delaware	http://elections.delaware.gov/	http://depic.delaware.gov/
District of Columbia	Board of Elections and Ethics: www.dcboee.org/ Office of Campaign Finance: http://ocf.dc.gov/ index.shtm	http://ocf.dc.gov/index.shtm
Florida	http://election.dos.state.fl.us/index.html	Legislative Ethics: www.leg.state.fl.us/ Executive Ethics: www.ethics.state.fl.us/
Georgia	Elections: www.sos.state.ga.us/elections/ Campaign Finance: www.ethics.state.ga.us	www.ethics.state.ga.us/

STATE	ELECTION LAW WEB SITE	ETHICS/LOBBYING WEB SITE
Hawaii	Elections: www.hawaii.gov/elections Campaign Finance: www.hawaii.gov/elections	www.hawaii.gov/ethics
Idaho	www.idsos.state.id.us/	www.idsos.state.id.us/
Illinois	www.elections.state.il.us	www.cyberdriveillinois.com/ departments/index/home.html
Indiana	www.in.gov/sos/elections/	Lobby Registration Commission: www.state.in.us/ilrc Ethics Commission: www.in.gov/ig
Iowa	Elections: www.sos.state.ia.us/elections/ Campaign Finance: www.state.ia.us/government/iecdb/index.htm	Lobbyist Information: www.legis.state.ia.us/Lobbyist.html Ethics and Campaign Disclosure Board: www.state.ia.us/government/iecdb/ index.htm
Kansas	Elections: www.kssos.org/elections/elections.html Campaign Finance: www.accesskansas.org/ethics/	www.accesskansas.org/ethics
Kentucky	Elections: http://sos.ky.gov/elections Campaign Finance: http://kref.ky.gov	Executive Branch Ethics Commission: http://ethics.ky.gov/ Legislative Ethics Commission: http://klec.ky.gov
Louisiana	Elections: www.sos.louisiana.gov/ Campaign Finance: www.ethics.state.la.us/cf.htm	www.ethics.state.la.us/lobby.htm
Maine	Elections: www.maine.gov/sos/cec/elec/ Campaign Finance: www.maine.gov/ethics/	www.maine.gov/ethics/
Maryland	www.elections.state.md.us/campaign_finance/ index.html	http://ethics.gov.state.md.us/
Massachusetts	Elections: www.state.ma.us/sec/ele/eleidx.htm Campaign Finance: www.mass.gov/ocpf/	Ethics Commission: www.mass.gov/ethics/ Public Records Division: www.sec.state.ma.us/pre/preidx.htm
Michigan	Elections: www.michigan.gov/sos/0,1607,7-127- 1633—,00.html Campaign Finance: www.michigan.gov/sos/0,1697,7-127-1633_ 8723—,00.html.	www.michigan.gov/sos/0,1607,7-127- 1633---,00.html
Minnesota	Elections: www.sos.state.mn.us/home/index.asp?page=4 Campaign Finance: www.cfboard.state.mn.us	www.cfboard.state.mn.us/
Mississippi	Elections: www.sos.state.ms.us/elections/elections.asp Campaign Finance: www.sos.state.ms.us/elections/CampFinc/ index.asp	Secretary of State www.sos.state.ms.us/elections/ lobbying/ Ethics Commission www.ethics.state.ms.us/ethics/ ethics.nsf

STATE	ELECTION LAW WEB SITE	ETHICS/LOBBYING WEB SITE
Missouri	www.sos.mo.gov/elections/	www.moethics.mo.gov
Montana	Elections: http://sos.mt.gov/ELB/index.asp Campaign Finance: http://politicalpractices.mt.gov/ 5campaignfinance/	http://politicalpractices.mt.gov/3ethics/
Nebraska	Elections: www.sos.state.ne.us/#boxingName Campaign Finance: http://nadc.nol.org	http://nadc.nol.org/
Nevada	http://sos.state.nv.us/elections	Legislative Commission: www.leg.state.nv.us/lcb/admin/ lobbyist.htm Commission on Ethics: http://ethics.nv.gov
New Hampshire	www.sos.nh.gov/electionsnew.htm	Secretary of State: www.sos.nh.gov/electionsnew.htm Legislative Ethics Committee: www.gencourt.state.nh.us/misc/ethics. html
New Jersey	Elections: www.state.nj.us/lps/elections/electionshome. html Campaign Finance: www.elec.state.nj.us/	www.elec.state.nj.us/
New Mexico	General Elections: www.sos.state.nm.us/displayContent. asp?id=17 Campaign Finance: www.sos.state.nm.us/displayContent. asp?id=35	www.sos.state.nm.us/displayContent. asp?id=35
New York	Elections: www.elections.state.ny.us Campaign Finance: www.elections.state.ny.us	Temporary State Commission on Lobbying: www.nylobby.state.ny.us Ethics Commission: www.dos.state.ny.us/ethc/ethics.html
North Carolina	www.app2.sboe.state.nc.us/	www.secretary.state.nc.us/lobbyists/ default.asp
North Dakota	Elections: www.nd.gov/sos/electvote/ Campaign Finance: www.nd.gov/sos/campfinance/	www.nd.gov/sos/lobbylegislate/
Ohio	Elections: www.sos.state.oh.us/sos/ElectionsVoter/ohio- Elections.aspx Campaign Finance: www.sos.state.oh.us/sos/campaignfinance/ campaignFinance.aspx?Section=116	Joint Legislative Ethics Committee: www.jlec-olig.state.oh.us/ Ethics Commission: www.ethics.ohio.gov/
Oklahoma	Elections: www.oklaosf.state.ok.us/~elections Campaign Finance: www.ethics.state.ok.us/	www.ethics.state.ok.us/
Oregon	Elections: www.sos.state.or.us/elections/ Campaign Finance: www.sos.state.or.us/elections/c&e/	www.gspc.state.or.us/
Pennsylvania	www.dos.state.pa.us/bcel/site/default.asp	www.ethics.state.pa.us

STATE	ELECTION LAW WEB SITE	ETHICS/LOBBYING WEB SITE

Rhode Island	Elections:
	www.elections.state.ri.us/default.htm
	Campaign Finance:
	www.elections.state.ri.us/CampFinance/
	   cfmain.htm
		Secretary of State:
		www2.sec.state.ri.us/cpi/Lobby
		   Tracker2004/
		Ethics Commission:
		www.state.ri.us/ethics/

South Carolina	Elections: www.scvotes.org Campaign Finance: http://ethics.sc.gov	http://ethics.sc.gov

South Dakota	Elections:
	www.sdsos.gov/electionsvoteregistration/
	   electionsvoteregistration_overview.shtm
	Campaign Finance:
	www.sdsos.gov/electionsvoteregistration/
	   campaignfinance.shtm
		www.sdsos.gov/adminservices/
		   lobbyistreg.shtm

Tennessee	Elections: state.tn.us/sos/election/index.htm Campaign Finance: www.state.tn.us/tref/	www.state.tn.us/tref
Texas	Elections: www.sos.state.tx.us/elections/index.shtml Campaign Finance: www.ethics.state.tx.us	www.ethics.state.tx.us
Utah	www.elections.utah.gov/	www.elections.utah.gov/lobbyists.html

Vermont	Elections:
	http://vermont-elections.org/soshome.htm
	Campaign Finance:
	http://vermont-elections.org/elections1/
	   campaign_finance.html
		www.commonwealth.virginia.gov/
		   StateGovernment/Lobbyist/
		   lobbyist.cfm

Virginia	www.sbe.virginia.gov/cms/	www.commonwealth.virginia.gov/ Lobbyist/lobbyist.cfm
Washington	Elections: www.secstate.wa.gov/elections/ Campaign Finance: www.pdc.wa.gov/	Public Disclosure Commission: www.pdc.wa.gov/ Executive Ethics Board: http://ethics.wa.gov/ Legislative Ethics Board: www.leg.wa.gov/LEB/
West Virginia	www.wvsos.com/elections/main.htm	www.wvethicscommission.org
Wisconsin	http://elections.state.wi.us/	http://ethics.state.wi.us/
Wyoming	http://soswy.state.wy.us/election/election.htm	http://soswy.state.wy.us/election/ election.htm

Appendix G

Additional Election- and Ethics-Related Web Sites

NAME & WEB SITE	COMMENTS
Business-Industry Political Action Committee (BIPAC) www.bipac.org	An independent, bipartisan organization that works to elect pro-business candidates to Congress.
Campaign Finance Data on the Internet www1.soc.american.edu/campfin/index.cfm	Provides Internet-accessible, database-formatted campaign finance files.
Campaign Finance Information Center www.campaignfinance.org	Primarily intended to help journalists cover campaigns in more depth by following the campaign money trail, but useful and accessible for all. Provides useable state campaign finance data from across the nation.
Center for Responsive Politics (CRP) www.opensecrets.org	A nonpartisan, nonprofit research group that tracks money in politics and its effect on elections and public policy.
Combined Federal/State Disclosure & Election Directory www.fec.gov/pubrec/cfsdd/cfsdd.shtml	Established by the Federal Election Commission (FEC), this Web site provides the addresses of the relevant state officials and links to state Web pages.
Council on Government Ethics Laws (COGEL) www.cogel.org	A national organization of state officials involved in the enforcement of campaign finance and ethics laws.
The Democracy Network (DNet) www.dnet.org	A comprehensive directory of election-related sites in every state and the "premier public interest site for election information."
Democratic National Committee www.democrats.org	Provides issue discussions, voter registration information, opportunities to donate, and information about state and federal party officials.

NAME & WEB SITE	COMMENTS
CQ Money Line (Formerly FECInfo; Public Disclosure, Inc.). http://moneyline.cq.com/pml/home.do	Provides a "place to discover who gave what to which Federal candidates when." Databases include: U.S. House/Senate Campaign Money; U.S. Presidential Candidate Money; PAC and Party Committee Listings; Contributors by Name, Occupation, Employer, or Zip Code; and Soft Money Contributors.
Federal Election Commission www.fec.gov	Provides information on the laws governing federal elections; access to financial and other information of PACs, parties, and candidates; and information on how to contact the FEC and/or use FEC services.
House Committee on Standards of Official Conduct Ethics Manual www.house.gov/ethics	Provides the committee's explanatory memoranda for members, officers, and employees of the U.S. House of Representatives; the *House Ethics Manual*; and other information related to House ethics rules and the committee that has jurisdiction over such matters.
League of Women Voters www.lwv.org	Provides candidate information and access to each of the league's local offices.
Legal Ethics www.legalethics.com	Provides links to articles, rules, and information relating to ethics issues.
National Association of Business Political Action Committees (NABPAC) www.nabpac.org	A national organization "dedicated to promoting, defending, and professionalizing PACs and political action professionals."
National Association of Secretaries of State http://nass.org/index.php?option= com_wrapper&Itemid=209	Provides links to official state government election offices.
Office of Government Ethics (OGE) www.usoge.gov	Provides data about OGE and the services it offers.
Project Vote Smart www.vote-smart.org	Provides a wealth of election/government-related information and links to myriad other election-related Web sites, including links to applicable federal and state sites.
Republican National Committee www.rnc.org	Provides issue discussions, information on registering to vote, access to making a donation, and contact information for state and federal party officials.
Senate Select Committee on Ethics ethics.senate.gov	Provides access to committee members, the *Senate Ethics Manual*, the Public Financial Disclosure form, and related links and information.
Stanford Law School www.law.stanford.edu/publications/ projects/campaignfinance/	Provides case materials filed in connection with *McConnell v. FEC*, the consolidated case challenging the Bipartisan Campaign Reform Act of 2002.
Web White & Blue www.webwhiteblue.org	Provides access to some of the best online election directories and voter information sites.

Appendix H

IRS Forms and Information

Instructions for Form 8871

Department of the Treasury
Internal Revenue Service

(Rev. February 2007)

Political Organization Notice of Section 527 Status

Section references are to the Internal Revenue Code unless otherwise noted.

General Instructions

Purpose of Form

Political organizations must use Form 8871 to notify the IRS that the organization is to be treated as a tax-exempt section 527 organization. The IRS is required to make publicly available on the Internet and at its offices a list of the organizations that file Form 8871 (including the organization's mailing address, email address, custodian of records, and contact person as shown on Form 8871).

Political organizations must also use Form 8871 to notify the IRS of any material change in the information reported on a previously filed Form 8871.

Definitions

Political organization

Political organization means a party, committee, association, fund, or other organization (whether or not incorporated) organized and operated primarily for the purpose of directly or indirectly accepting contributions or making expenditures, or both, for an exempt function.

Exempt function

Exempt function means the function of influencing or attempting to influence the selection, nomination, election, or appointment of any individual to any federal, state, or local public office or office in a political organization, or the election of the Presidential or Vice Presidential electors, whether or not such individual or electors are selected, nominated, elected, or appointed. It also includes expenditures made relating to one of these offices, which if incurred by the individual, would be allowable as a business deduction under section 162(a).

Who Must File

Every political organization that is to be treated as a tax-exempt political organization under the rules of section 527 must file Form 8871, except for:
- An organization that reasonably expects its annual gross receipts to always be less than $25,000,
- A political committee required to report under the Federal Election Campaign Act of 1971 (2 U.S.C. 431 et seq.),
- A political committee of a state or local candidate,
- A state or local committee of a political party, or
- A tax-exempt organization described in section 501(c) that is treated as having political organization taxable income under section 527(f)(1).

When To File

Initial Filing

Form 8871 must be electronically filed within 24 hours of the date on which the organization was established. If the due date falls on a Saturday, Sunday, or legal holiday, the organization may file on the next business day. See Pub. 4216, Political Organization Filing and Disclosure, Filing Process Guide, for more information.

To Report a Material Change

In general, an organization must file an amended Form 8871 within 30 days after the occurrence of the material change being reported. An organization must file a final Form 8871 within 30 days of termination. If the due date falls on a Saturday, Sunday, or legal holiday, the organization may file on the next business day. See Pub. 4216, Political Organization Filing and Disclosure, Filing Process Guide, for more information.

Where and How To File

Section 527(i)(1)(A) requires that the organization file Form 8871 electronically. The paper version of Form 8871 is obsolete. File Form 8871 using the IRS Internet website at: *www.irs.gov/polorgs* (IRS Keyword: political orgs).

A first-time user electronically submitting an initial Form 8871 will be instructed to print, sign, and mail a Form 8453-X, Political Organization Declaration for Electronic Filing of Notice of Section 527 Status, to the IRS. An authorized official must sign and date Form 8453-X. Send the completed Form 8453-X to:

Internal Revenue Service Center
Ogden, UT 84201

Upon receipt of Form 8453-X, the IRS will mail to the organization a username and password that must be used to file an amended or final Form 8871 or to electronically file Form 8872, Political Organization Report of Contributions and Expenditures.

Who Must Sign

Form 8871 must be signed by an official authorized by the organization to sign this notice.

Effect of Failure To File Form 8871

An organization that is required to file Form 8871, but fails to do so on a timely basis, will not be treated as a tax-exempt section 527 organization for any period before the date Form 8871 is filed. In addition, the taxable income of the organization for that period (or, for a material change, where there is a failure to file timely an amended Form 8871, for the period beginning on the date the change occurred and ending on the date on which Form 8871 is filed) will be computed by including its exempt function income (minus any deductions directly connected with the production of that income).

Other Required Reports and Returns

An organization that files Form 8871 may also be required to file the following forms:

Cat. No. 35287H

- Form 8872, Political Organization Report of Contributions and Expenditures (periodic reports are required during the calendar year).
- Form 990, Return of Organization Exempt From Income Tax, or Form 990-EZ, Short Form Return of Organization Exempt From Income Tax (or other designated annual information return).
- Form 1120-POL, U.S. Income Tax Return for Certain Political Organizations (annual income tax return).

Public Inspection of Form 8871 and Related Materials

Form 8871 (including any supporting papers), and any letter or other document the IRS issues with regard to Form 8871, are open to public inspection at the IRS in Washington, DC, and on the IRS Internet website at *www.irs.gov/polorgs* (IRS Keyword: political orgs). In addition, the organization must make available for public inspection a copy of these materials during regular business hours at the organization's principal office and at each of its regional or district offices having at least three paid employees. A penalty of $20 per day will be imposed on any person under a duty to comply with the public inspection requirement for each day a failure to comply continues.

Telephone Assistance

If you have questions or need help completing Form 8871, please call 1-877-829-5500. This toll-free telephone service is available Monday through Friday from 8:30 a.m. to 4:30 p.m. Eastern time.

Specific Instructions

Part I. General Information

Employer Identification Number (EIN)

Enter the EIN in the space provided. If the organization does not have an EIN, it must apply for one on Form SS-4, Application for Employer Identification Number. Form SS-4 can be obtained by downloading it from the IRS Internet website at *www.irs.gov* or by calling 1-800-TAX-FORM (1-800-829-3676). See the Form SS-4 instructions for information about where and how to file, including by telephone, fax, mail, or online.

When electronically filing an amended or final Form 8871, the organization's EIN will be entered by the computer program and may not be changed.

Line 3. Applicable Notice

- Check *Initial notice* if this is the first Form 8871 filed by the organization.
- Check *Amended notice* if the organization is filing an amended notice.
- Check *Final notice* when the organization ceases operations and dissolves as a tax-exempt Section 527 organization or is no longer required to file Form 8871.

Line 4b. Date of Material Change

For an initial notice, the date of material change is not required unless the organization is filing its initial notice because it no longer qualifies for an exception to the filing requirements, such as reasonably anticipating it will always have annual gross receipts of less than $25,000.

In that case, enter the date the organization no longer qualified for the exception. For an amended notice, enter the date of the material change being reported. For a final notice, enter the date the organization terminated.

Lines 6a and 6b. Custodian of Records

Enter the name and address of the person in possession of the organization's books and records.

Lines 7a and 7b. Contact Person

Enter the name and address of the person whom the public may contact for more information about the organization.

Lines 9a and 9b. Election Authority Identification Number

Enter the name of the election authority on line 9a. If the organization has not been assigned any identification number by any election authority, enter "None" on line 9b. Otherwise, provide each identification number assigned and identify the state in which the election authority is located. For a federal identification number, enter "Federal" for the state.

Part II. Notification of Claim of Exemptions From Filing Certain Forms

Lines 10a and 10b. Qualified State or Local Political Organization

Qualified state or local political organizations (defined below) are exempt from filing Form 8872. If you are claiming this exemption for the organization, you must check the "Yes" box on line 10a and enter the state where the organization files its reports on line 10b. If not, check the "No" box.

A qualified state or local political organization is a political organization that meets the following requirements:
- The organization limits its exempt function to the purpose of influencing or attempting to influence the selection, nomination, election, or appointment of any individual to any state or local public office or office in a state or local political organization;
- The organization is required under a state law to report to a state agency (and the organization does so) the information that otherwise would be required to be reported on Form 8872. The organization will meet this requirement even if the state law does not require reporting of the identical information required on the Form 8872, so long as at least the following information is required to be reported under the state law and is reported by the organization:

1. The name and address of every person who contributes $500 or more in the aggregate to the organization during the calendar year and the amount of each contribution, and
2. The name and address of every person to whom the organization makes expenditures aggregating $800 or more during the calendar year, and the amount of each expenditure.

However, if the state law requires the reporting of (if an individual) the occupation or employer of any person to whom such expenditures are made, or the date or purpose of each such expenditure; or, if the state law

requires the reporting of (if an individual) the occupation or employer of any such contributor or the date of each such contribution, the organization will meet this requirement only if it reports that additional information to the state agency;
• The state agency makes the reports filed by the organization publicly available;
• The organization makes the reports filed with the state agency publicly available for public inspection during regular business hours at the organization's principal office (and at each of its regional or district offices having at least three paid employees). Contributor information must be disclosed to the public; and
• No federal candidate or officeholder controls or materially participates in the direction of the organization, solicits contributions to the organization, or directs any of the organization's disbursements.

For additional information, see section 527(e)(5) and Revenue Ruling 2003-49, 2003-20 I.R.B. 903.

Line 11. Caucus or Association

A political organization that is a caucus or association of state or local officials is exempt from filing Form 990. If you are claiming this exemption for the organization, you must check the "Yes" box on line 11. If not, check the "No" box.

Part IV. List of All Related Entities

Line 13.

If there are no related entities, check this box and proceed to the next step.

Lines 14a through 14c. Name, Relationship, and Address of Related Entity

If there is more than one related entity, add each related entity until all related entities are entered and proceed to the next step.

List the name, relationship, and address of all related entities. An entity is a related entity if either 1 or 2 below applies:

1. The organization and that entity have (a) significant common purposes and substantial common membership

or (b) substantial common direction or control (either directly or indirectly).

2. Either the organization or that entity owns (directly or through one or more entities) at least a 50% capital or profits interest in the other. For this purpose, all entities that are defined as related entities under 1 above must be treated as a single entity.

If 1 applies, enter "connected" under relationship. If 2 applies, enter "affiliated" under relationship.

Part V. List of All Officers, Directors, and Highly Compensated Employees

Lines 15a through 15c. Name, Title, and Address

Enter the name, title, and address of all of the organization's officers, members of the board of directors (that is, governing body, regardless of name), and highly compensated employees. *Highly compensated employees* are the five employees (other than officers and directors) who are expected to have the highest annual compensation over $50,000. Compensation includes both cash and noncash amounts, whether paid currently or deferred.

If there is more than one individual required to be listed in Part V, add each officer name until all names are entered and proceed to the next step.

Filing

You will not be able to reach this step until you have provided all required information. Before moving on to this step, please review all information entered to ensure that it is true, correct, and complete. Once you have attested to this by entering your name and using the "Submit Form 8871" button, the information entered will be made available to the public. Form 8453-X is generated when the initial Form 8871 is electronically filed. See *Where and How to File* on page 1.

Paperwork Reduction Act Notice. We ask for the information on this form to carry out the Internal Revenue laws of the United States. If the organization is to be treated as a tax-exempt section 527 organization, you are required to give us the information. We need it to ensure that you are complying with these laws.

You are not required to provide the information requested on a form that is subject to the Paperwork Reduction Act unless the form displays a valid OMB control number. Books or records relating to a form or its instructions must be retained as long as their contents may become material in the administration of any Internal Revenue law. The rules governing the confidentiality of Form 8871 are covered in section 6104.

The time needed to complete and file these forms will vary depending on individual circumstances. The estimated average times are:

Forms	8871	8453-X
Recordkeeping	5 hr., 15 min.	28 min.
Learning about the law or the form	47 min.	6 min.
Preparing and sending the form to the IRS	55 min.	6 min.

If you have comments concerning the accuracy of these time estimates or suggestions for making this form simpler, we would be happy to hear from you. You can write to the Internal Revenue Service, Tax Products Coordinating Committee, SE:W:CAR:MP:T:T:SP, 1111 Constitution Ave. NW, IR-6406, Washington, DC 20224. Do not send Form 8871 to this address. Instead, see *Where and How To File* on page 1.

Form 8872
(November 2002)

Department of the Treasury
Internal Revenue Service

**Political Organization
Report of Contributions and Expenditures**

▶ See Seperate instructions.

OMB No. 1545-1696

A   For the period beginning _____ ,20 _____ and ending _____ , 20 _____

B   Check applicable boxes: ☐ Intial report   ☐ Change of address   ☐ Amended report   ☐ Final report

1   Name of organization | **Employer identification number**

2   Mailing address (P.O. Box or number, street, and room or suite number)

City or town, state, and ZIP code

3   E-mail address of organization | **4**   Date organization was formed

5a   Name of custodian of records | **5b**   Custodian's address

6a   Name of contact person | **6b**   Contact person's address

7   Business address of organization (if different from mailing address shown above). Number, street, and room or suite number

City or town, state, and ZIP code

8   Type of report (check only one box)

a   ☐ First quarterly report (*due by April 15*)

b   ☐ Second quarterly report (*due by July 15*)

c   ☐ Third quarterly report (*due by October 15*)

d   ☐ Year-end report (*due by January 31*)

e   ☐ Mid-year report (*Non-election year only-due by July 31*)

f   ☐ Monthly report for the month of: _____
(*due by the 20th day following the month shown above, except the December report, which is due by January 31*)

g   ☐ Pre-election report (*due by the 12th or 15th day before the election*)
(1) Type of election: _____
(2) Date of election: _____
(3) For the state of: _____

h   ☐ Post-general election report (*due by the 30th day after general election*)
(1) Date of election: _____
(2) For the state of: _____

9   Total amount of reported contributions (total from all attached **Schedules A**).   .   .   .   . | **9**

10   Total amount of reported expenditures (total from all attached **Schedules B**).   .   .   .   .   .   . | **10**

Sign Here

Under penalties of perjury, I declare that I have examined this report, including accompanying schedules and statements, and to the best of my knowledge and belief, it is true, correct, and complete.

▶ _____   ▶ _____
Signature of authorized official   Date

For Paperwork Reduction Act Notice, see separate instructions.   Cat. No. 30406G   Form **8872** (11-2002)

Form 8872 (11-2002)

Schedule A	Itemized Contributions	Schedule A page	of

Name of organization		Employer identification number

Contributor's name, mailing address and ZIP code	Name of contributor's employer	Amount of contribution
	Contributor's occupation	$
	Aggregate contributions year-to-date . . ▶ $	Date of contribution
Contributor's name, mailing address and ZIP code	Name of contributor's employer	Amount of contribution
	Contributor's occupation	$
	Aggregate contributions year-to-date . . ▶ $	Date of contribution
Contributor's name, mailing address and ZIP code	Name of contributor's employer	Amount of contribution
	Contributor's occupation	$
	Aggregate contributions year-to-date . . ▶ $	Date of contribution
Contributor's name, mailing address and ZIP code	Name of contributor's employer	Amount of contribution
	Contributor's occupation	$
	Aggregate contributions year-to-date . . ▶ $	Date of contribution
Contributor's name, mailing address and ZIP code	Name of contributor's employer	Amount of contribution
	Contributor's occupation	$
	Aggregate contributions year-to-date . . ▶ $	Date of contribution
Contributor's name, mailing address and ZIP code	Name of contributor's employer	Amount of contribution
	Contributor's occupation	$
	Aggregate contributions year-to-date . . ▶ $	Date of contribution
Contributor's name, mailing address and ZIP code	Name of contributor's employer	Amount of contribution
	Contributor's occupation	$
	Aggregate contributions year-to-date . . ▶ $	Date of contribution
Contributor's name, mailing address and ZIP code	Name of contributor's employer	Amount of contribution
	Contributor's occupation	$
	Aggregate contributions year-to-date . . ▶ $	Date of contribution
Contributor's name, mailing address and ZIP code	Name of contributor's employer	Amount of contribution
	Contributor's occupation	$
	Aggregate contributions year-to-date . . ▶ $	Date of contribution

Subtotal of contributions reported on this page only. Enter here and also include this amount in the total on line 9 of Form 8872 . . . . ▶ | $

Form **8872** (11-2002)

Form 8872 (11-2002)

Schedule B	Itemized Expenditures	Schedule B page	of
Name of organization		**Employer identification number**	

Recipient's name, mailing address and ZIP code	Name of recipient's employer	Amount of expenditure $
	Recipient's occupation	Date of expenditure

Purpose of expenditure

Recipient's name, mailing address and ZIP code	Name of recipient's employer	Amount of expenditure $
	Recipient's occupation	Date of expenditure

Purpose of expenditure

Recipient's name, mailing address and ZIP code	Name of recipient's employer	Amount of expenditure $
	Recipient's occupation	Date of expenditure

Purpose of expenditure

Recipient's name, mailing address and ZIP code	Name of recipient's employer	Amount of expenditure $
	Recipient's occupation	Date of expenditure

Purpose of expenditure

Recipient's name, mailing address and ZIP code	Name of recipient's employer	Amount of expenditure $
	Recipient's occupation	Date of expenditure

Purpose of expenditure

Recipient's name, mailing address and ZIP code	Name of recipient's employer	Amount of expenditure $
	Recipient's occupation	Date of expenditure

Purpose of expenditure

Subtotal of expenditures reported on this page only. Enter here and also include this amount in the total on line 10 of Form 8872 . . . . ▶ | $

Form **8872** (11-2002)

Instructions for Form 8872

 Department of the Treasury
Internal Revenue Service

(Rev. January 2007)

Use with Form 8872 (Rev. November 2002)

Political Organization
Report of Contributions and Expenditures

Section references are to the Internal Revenue Code unless otherwise noted.

General Instructions

What's New

• You are now required to report aggregate contributions less than $200 on Schedule A. See *Schedule A—Itemized Contributions* for more information.
• If expenditures below the $500 reporting threshold were made to a person, you must now report the aggregate of those expenditures on Schedule B. See *Schedule B—Itemized Expenditures* for more information.

Purpose of Form

Unless an exception applies (see *Who Must File* below), a tax-exempt section 527 political organization must file Form 8872 to report certain contributions received and expenditures made. Generally, an organization that is required to file Form 8872 also must file Form 8871, Political Organization Notice of Section 527 Status, within 24 hours of the organization's formation or within 30 days of any material change to the information reported on Form 8871.

Note. The organization is not required to report contributions accepted or expenditures made after July 1, 2000, if they were received or made under a contract entered into before July 2, 2000.

Who Must File

Every section 527 political organization that accepts a contribution or makes an expenditure for an exempt function during the calendar year must file Form 8872, except:
• A political organization that is not required to file Form 8871,
• A political organization that is subject to tax on its income because it did not file or amend a Form 8871, or
• A qualified state or local political organization.

A qualified state or local political organization is a political organization that meets the following requirements:
• The organization's exempt functions are solely for the purpose of influencing or attempting to influence the selection, nomination, election, or appointment of any individual to any state or local political office or office in a state or local political organization.
• The organization is subject to state law that requires it to report information that is similar to that required on Form 8872.

• The organization files the required reports with the state.
• The state makes such reports public and the organization makes them open to public inspection in the same manner that organizations must make Form 8872 available for public inspection.

For additional information, including the prohibition of involvement in the organization of a federal candidate or office holder, see section 527(e)(5).

When To File

Due dates for Form 8872 vary depending on whether the form is due for a reporting period that occurs during an even-numbered or odd-numbered year.

Note. If any due date falls on a Saturday, Sunday, or legal holiday, the organization may file on the next business day.

Even-Numbered Years

The organization may opt to file its reports on either a quarterly or monthly basis, but it must file on the same basis for the entire calendar year.

Quarterly reports. File the first report for the first quarter of the calendar year in which the organization accepts a contribution or makes an expenditure. Quarterly reports are due by the 15th day after the last day of each calendar quarter, except the year-end report which is due by January 31 of the following year. In addition, the organization may have to file a pre-election report, a post-general election report, or both, as explained below.

Monthly reports. File the first report for the first month of the calendar year in which the organization accepts a contribution or makes an expenditure. Reports are due by the 20th day after the end of the month. This report must reflect all reportable contributions accepted and expenditures made during the month for which the report is being filed. No monthly reports are due for October and November. Instead, the organization must file a pre-general election report and a post-general election report (see *Pre-election report* and *Post-general election report*). In addition, a year-end report must also be filed by January 31 of the following year instead of a monthly report for December.

Pre-election report. This report must be filed before any election for which the organization made a contribution or expenditure. This report must be filed by the:
• 12th day before the election, or
• 15th day before the election, if the organization is posting the report by certified or registered mail.

Cat. No. 30584F

This report must reflect all reportable contributions accepted and expenditures made through the 20th day before the election.

Post-general election report. File by the 30th day after the general election. This report must reflect all reportable contributions accepted and expenditures made through the 20th day after the general election.

Election means:
- A general, special, primary, or runoff election for a federal office,
- A convention or caucus of a political party which has authority to nominate a candidate for federal office,
- A primary election held for the selection of delegates to a national nominating convention of a political party, or
- A primary election held for the expression of a preference for the nomination of individuals for election to the office of President.

General election means:
- An election for a federal office held in even numbered years on the Tuesday following the first Monday in November, or
- An election held to fill a vacancy in a federal office (that is, a special election) that is intended to result in the final selection of a single individual to the office at stake in a general election.

Odd-Numbered Years

The organization may opt to file its reports on either a semiannual or monthly basis, but it must file on the same basis for the entire calendar year.

Semiannual reports. File the mid-year report by July 31 for the period beginning January 1 through June 30. File the year-end report by January 31 of the following year for the period beginning July 1 and ending December 31.

Monthly reports. File the first report for the first month of the calendar year in which the organization accepts a contribution or makes an expenditure. Reports are due by the 20th day after the end of the month, except for the December report, which is due on January 31 of the following year. This report must reflect all reportable contributions accepted and expenditures made during the month for which the report is being filed.

Where and How To File

Form 8872 may be filed either electronically or by mail. Organizations that have, or expect to have, contributions or expenditures exceeding $50,000 are required to file electronically.

To file by mail, send Form 8872 to the:

Internal Revenue Service Center
Ogden, UT 84201

File electronically using the IRS Internet website at *www.irs.gov/polorgs.* A username and a password are required for electronically filing Form 8872. Organizations that have completed the electronic filing of Form 8871 and submitted a completed, signed Form 8453-X, Political Organization Declaration for Electronic Filing of Notice of Section 527 Status, will receive a username and a password in the mail. Organizations that have completed the electronic filing of Form 8871, but have not received their username and password may request them by writing to the following address:

Internal Revenue Service
Attn: Request for 8872
Password Mail Stop 6273
Ogden, UT 84201

If you have forgotten or misplaced the username and password issued to your organization after you filed your initial Form 8871 and Form 8453-X, please send a letter requesting a new username and password to the above address. You may also fax your request to 801-620-3249. It may take 3-6 weeks for your new username and password to arrive, as they will be mailed to the organization. Submit your request now in order to have your username and password available for your next filing.

Who Must Sign

Form 8872 must be signed by an official authorized by the organization to sign this report.

Penalty

A penalty will be imposed if the organization is required to file Form 8872 and it:
- Fails to file the form by the due date, or
- Files the form but fails to report all of the information required or it reports incorrect information.

The penalty is 35% of the total amount of contributions and expenditures to which a failure relates.

Other Required Reports and Returns

An organization that files Form 8872 may also be required to file the following forms.
- Form 990, Return of Organization Exempt From Income Tax, or Form 990-EZ, Short Form Return of Organization Exempt From Income Tax (or other designated annual return).
- Form 1120-POL, U.S. Income Tax Return for Certain Political Organizations (annual return).

Public Inspection of Form 8872

The IRS will make Form 8872 (including Schedules A and B) open to public inspection on the IRS website at *www.irs.gov/polorgs.* In addition, the organization must make available for public inspection a copy of this report during regular business hours at the organization's principal office and at each of its regional or district offices having at least 3 paid employees. A penalty of $20 per day will be imposed on any person under a duty to comply with the public inspection requirement for each day a failure to comply continues. The maximum penalty imposed on all persons for failures relating to one report is $10,000.

Telephone Assistance

If you have questions or need help completing Form 8872, please call 1-877-829-5500. This toll-free telephone service is available Monday through Friday.

Exempt Organizations Update

The IRS has established a new, subscription-based email service for tax professionals and representatives of tax-exempt organizations. Subscribers will receive periodic updates from the IRS regarding exempt organizations tax law and regulations, available services, and other information. To subscribe, visit *www.irs.gov/eo.*

Specific Instructions

Line A

Enter the beginning and ending date for the period to which this report relates. If the organization filed a prior report for the calendar year, the beginning date must be the first day following the ending date shown on the prior report.

Line B

* Check the "Initial report" box if this is the first Form 8872 filed by the organization for this period.
* Check the "Change of address" box if the organization changed its address since it last filed Form 8871, Form 8872, Form 990 (or 990-EZ), or Form 1120-POL.
* Check the "Amended report" box if the organization is filing an amended report.
* Check the "Final report" box if the organization will not be required to file Form 8872 in the future.

Employer Identification Number (EIN)

Enter the correct EIN in the space provided as shown on the Form 8871 the organization filed.

Lines 5a and 5b

Enter the name and address of the person in possession of the organization's books and records.

Lines 6a and 6b

Enter the name and address of the person whom the public may contact for more information about the organization.

Lines 8a through 8h

Check only one box. See *When To File* beginning on page 1 for details on the types of reports and the periods covered.

Line 8f. If the organization is filing on a monthly basis, enter the month for which this report is being filed. During even-numbered years, do not check this box to report October, November, or December activity. Instead, file a pre-general election report, post-general election report, a year-end report, and check the appropriate box on line 8d, 8g, or 8h.

Line 8g. If the organization is filing a pre-election report also indicate the type of election (primary, general, convention, special, or run-off) on line 8g(1), the date of the election on line 8g(2), and the state in which the election is held on line 8g(3).

Line 8h. If the organization is filing a post-general election report, indicate the date of the election on line 8h(1) and the state in which the election was held on line 8h(2).

Line 9

If the organization is required to file Schedule(s) A, enter the total of all subtotals shown on those schedules. If the organization is not required to file Schedule A, enter zero.

Line 10

If the organization is required to file Schedule(s) B, enter the total of all subtotals shown on those schedules. If the organization is not required to file Schedule B, enter zero.

Schedule A—Itemized Contributions

Note. Multiple Schedules A can be filed with any report. Number each schedule in the box in the top right corner of the schedule. Be sure to include both the number of the specific page and the total number of Schedules A (for example, "Schedule A, page 2 of 5").

The organization must list on Schedule A each contributor from whom it accepted contributions during the calendar year if:
* The aggregate amount of the contributions accepted from that person during the calendar year as of the end of this reporting period was at least $200 and
* Any of those contributions were accepted during this reporting period.

Treat contributions as accepted if the contributor has contracted or is otherwise obligated to make the contribution.

In-kind contributions must be included. These contributions may be identified by including "(In-kind)" in the contributor's name field.

As an entry on the last page of Schedule A, enter the total amount of all contributions received from contributors whose aggregate contributions were less than $200 and are not reported elsewhere. Enter "Aggregate below Threshold" instead of the contributor's name. *If filing electronically,* also enter your organization's address and the last day of the reporting period (for example, Jan. 31); and enter "NA" for employer, occupation, and date.

Name of Contributor's Employer

If the contributor is an individual, enter the name of the organization or person by whom the contributor is employed (and not the name of his or her supervisor). If the individual is self-employed, enter "Self-employed." If the individual is not employed, enter "Not employed." If filing electronically and the contributor is not an individual, enter "NA."

Contributor's Occupation

If the contributor is an individual, enter the principal job title or position of that contributor. If the individual is self-employed, enter the principal job title or position of that contributor. If the individual is not employed, enter a descriptive title to explain the individual's status such as "Retired," "Student," "Homemaker," or "Unemployed." If filing electronically and the contributor is not an individual, enter "NA."

Aggregate Year-to-Date Contributions

Enter the total amount of contributions accepted from the contributor during this calendar year as of the end of this reporting period.

Amount of Contribution

If a contributor made more than one contribution in a reporting period, report each contribution separately. If the contribution is an in-kind contribution, report the fair market value of the contribution.

Non-Disclosed Amounts

As the last entry on Schedule A, list the aggregate amount of contributions that are required to be reported on this schedule for which the organization does not disclose all of the information required under section 527(j). Enter "Withheld" as the contributor's name. If filing electronically, enter the organization's address, the date of the report, and "NA" for occupation and employer. This amount is subject to the penalty for the failure to provide all the information required. See *Penalty* on page 2 for details.

Schedule B—Itemized Expenditures

Note. Multiple Schedules B can be filed with any report. Number each schedule in the box in the top right corner of the schedule. Be sure to include both the number of the specific page and the total number of Schedules B (for example, "Schedule B, page 2 of 10").

The organization must list on Schedule B each recipient to whom it made expenditures during the calendar year if:

• The aggregate amount of expenditures made to that person during the calendar year as of the end of this reporting period was at least $500 and

• Any of those expenditures were made during this reporting period.

Treat expenditures as made if the organization has contracted or is otherwise obligated to make the expenditure.

In-kind expenditures must be included. These expenditures may be identified by including "(In-kind)" in the purpose field.

As an entry on the last page of Schedule B, enter the total amount of all expenditures paid to recipients whose aggregate receipts were less than $500 and are not reported elsewhere. Enter "Aggregate below Threshold" instead of the recipient's name. *If filing electronically,* also enter the organization's address and the last day of the reporting period (for example, Jan. 31); and enter "NA" for employer, occupation, and date.

 Do not include any independent expenditures. An independent expenditure means an expenditure by a person for a communication expressly advocating the election or defeat of a clearly identified candidate that is not made with the cooperation or prior consent of, in consultation with, or at the request or suggestion of a candidate or agent or authorized committee of a candidate.

Name of Recipient's Employer

If the recipient is an individual, enter the name of the organization or person by whom the recipient is employed (and not the name of his or her supervisor). If the individual is self-employed, enter "Self-employed." If the individual is not employed, enter "Not employed." If filing electronically and the recipient is not an individual, enter "NA."

Recipient's Occupation

If the recipient is an individual, enter the principal job title or position of that recipient. If the individual is

self-employed, enter the principal job title or position of that recipient. If the individual is not employed, enter a descriptive title to explain the individual's status such as "Volunteer." If filing electronically and the recipient is not an individual, enter "NA."

Amount of Each Expenditure Reported for This Period

Report each separate expenditure made to any person during the calendar year that was not reported in a prior reporting period. If the expenditure is an in-kind expenditure, report the fair market value of the expenditure.

Purpose

Describe the purpose of each separate expenditure.

Non-Disclosed Amounts

As the last entry on Schedule B, list the aggregate amount of expenditures that are required to be reported on this schedule for which the organization does not disclose all of the information required under section 527(j). Enter "Withheld" as the recipient's name and as the purpose. If filing electronically, enter the organization's address, the date of the report, and "NA" for occupation and employer. This amount is subject to the penalty for the failure to provide all the information required. See *Penalty* on page 2 for details.

Paperwork Reduction Act Notice. We ask for the information on this form to carry out the Internal Revenue laws of the United States. If the organization is required to report contributions accepted and expenditures made as required by section 527(j), you are required to give us the information. We need it to ensure that you are complying with these laws.

You are not required to provide the information requested on a form that is subject to the Paperwork Reduction Act unless the form displays a valid OMB control number. Books or records relating to a form or its instructions must be retained as long as their contents may become material in the administration of any Internal Revenue law. The rules governing the confidentiality of Form 8872 are covered in section 6104.

The time needed to complete and file the form will vary depending on individual circumstances. The estimated average time is:

Recordkeeping	9 hr., 48 min.
Learning about the law or the form	24 min.
Preparing and sending the form to the IRS . .	34 min.

If you have comments concerning the accuracy of these time estimates or suggestions for making this form simpler, we would be happy to hear from you. You can write to the Internal Revenue Service, Tax Products Coordinating Committee, SE:W:CAR:MP:T:T:SP, 1111 Constitution Ave. NW, IR-6406, Washington, DC 20224. Do not send Form 8872 to this address. Instead, see *Where and How To File* on page 2.

Form **1120-POL**	**U.S. Income Tax Return for Certain Political Organizations**	OMB No. 1545-0129
Department of the Treasury Internal Revenue Service		2007

For calendar year 2007 or other tax year beginning _____ , 2007, and ending _____ , 20 ____

Check the box if this is a section 501(c) organization . . . . ▶ ☐

Check if:	Name of organization	Employer identification number
☐ Final return		
☐ Name change	Number, street, and room or suite no. (If a P.O. box, see page 5 of instructions.)	**Candidates for U.S. Congress Only**
☐ Address change		If this is a principal campaign committee, and it is the ONLY political committee, check here . . . ☐
☐ Amended return	City or town, state, and ZIP code	If this is a principal campaign committee, but is NOT the only political committee, check here and attach a copy of designation (See instructions on page 2.) . ☐

Income	1	Dividends (attach schedule)	1	
	2	Interest	2	
	3	Gross rents	3	
	4	Gross royalties	4	
	5	Capital gain net income (attach Schedule D (Form 1120))	5	
	6	Net gain or (loss) from Form 4797, Part II, line 17 (attach Form 4797)	6	
	7	Other income and nonexempt function expenditures (see instructions)	7	
	8	**Total income.** Add lines 1 through 7	8	
Deductions	9	Salaries and wages	9	
	10	Repairs and maintenance	10	
	11	Rents	11	
	12	Taxes and licenses	12	
	13	Interest	13	
	14	Depreciation (attach Form 4562)	14	
	15	Other deductions (attach schedule)	15	
	16	**Total deductions.** Add lines 9 through 15	16	
	17	Taxable income before specific deduction of $100 (see instructions). Section 501(c) organizations show:		
	a	Amount of net investment income . . . . ▶ _____		
	b	Aggregate amount expended for an exempt function (attach schedule) . ▶ _____	17c	
	18	Specific deduction of $100 (not allowed for newsletter funds defined under section 527(g)) .	18	
Tax	19	**Taxable income.** Subtract line 18 from line 17c. (If line 19 is zero or less, see the instructions.)	19	
	20	Income tax. (see instructions)	20	
	21	Tax credits. (Attach the applicable credit forms.) (see instructions)	21	
	22	Total tax. Subtract line 21 from line 20	22	
	23	Payments: **a** Tax deposited with Form 7004	23a		
		b Credit for tax paid on undistributed capital gains (attach Form 2439)	23b		
		c Credit for federal tax on fuels (attach Form 4136) .	23c		
		d Total payments. Add lines 23a through 23c	23d	
	24	**Tax due.** Subtract line 23d from line 22. See instructions on page 4 for depository method of payment	24	
	25	**Overpayment.** Subtract line 22 from line 23d	25	

Additional Information	1	At any time during the 2007 calendar year, did the organization have an interest in or a signature or other authority over a financial account (such as a bank account, securities account, or other financial account) in a foreign country? (see instructions) . . . . ☐ Yes ☐ No
		If "Yes," enter the name of the foreign country ▶ _____
	2	During the tax year, did the organization receive a distribution from, or was it the grantor of, or transferor to, a foreign trust? If "Yes," the organization may have to file Form 3520 . . . . ☐ Yes ☐ No
	3	Enter the amount of tax-exempt interest received or accrued during the tax year . ▶ $ _____
	4	Date organization formed ▶ _____
	5a	The books are in care of ▶ _____ **b** Enter name of candidate ▶ _____
	c	The books are located at ▶ _____ **d** Telephone No. ▶ _____

Sign Here	Under penalties of perjury, I declare that I have examined this return, including accompanying schedules and statements, and to the best of my knowledge and belief, it is true, correct, and complete. Declaration of preparer (other than taxpayer) is based on all information of which preparer has any knowledge.
	▶ _____ _____ ▶ _____ ║ May the IRS discuss this return with the preparer shown below (see page 3)? ☐ Yes ☐ No
	Signature of officer Date Title

Paid Preparer's Use Only	Preparer's signature ▶		Date	Check if self-employed ☐	Preparer's SSN or PTIN
	Firm's name (or yours if self-employed), address, and ZIP code ▶		EIN	
			Phone no. ( )

For Privacy Act and Paperwork Reduction Act Notice, see instructions on page 6.   Cat. No. 11523K   Form **1120-POL** (2007)

Photographs of Missing Children

The Internal Revenue Service is a proud partner with the National Center for Missing and Exploited Children. Photographs of missing children selected by the Center may appear in instructions on pages that would otherwise be blank. You can help bring these children home by looking at the photographs and calling 1-800-THE-LOST (1-800-843-5678) if you recognize a child.

IRS E-Services Make Taxes Easier

Now more than ever before, certain political organizations can enjoy the benefits of meeting their federal tax filing and payment responsibilities electronically. Whether you rely on a tax professional or do it yourself, IRS offers you convenient programs to make it easier.

Spend less time and worry on taxes. Use e-file and Electronic Federal Tax Payment System (EFTPS) to your benefit:

● For e-file, visit www.irs.gov/efile for additional information.

● For EFTPS, visit www.eftps.gov or call EFTPS Customer Service at 1-800-555-4477.

Use the electronic options available from IRS and make filing and paying taxes easier.

How To Get Forms and Publications

Internet. You can access the IRS website 24 hours a day, 7 days a week at www.irs.gov to:

● Download forms, instructions, and publications.

● Order IRS products online.

● Research your tax question online.

● Search publications online by topic or keyword.

● View Internal Revenue Bulletins (IRBs) published in the last few years.

● Send us comments or request help by email.

● Sign up to receive local and national tax news by email.

CD for tax products. Order Pub. 1796, IRS Tax Products on CD, and obtain:

● A CD that is released twice so you have the latest products. The first release ships in late December and the final release ships in late February.

● Current year forms, instructions, and publications.

● Prior-year forms, instructions, and publications.

● Bonus: Historical Tax Products DVD - Ships with the final release.

● Tax Map: an electronic research tool and finding aid.

● Tax law frequently asked questions.

● Tax Topics from the IRS telephone response system.

● Fill-in, print, and save features for most tax forms.

● Internal Revenue Bulletins.

● Toll-free and email technical support.

Buy the CD from the National Technical Information Service (NTIS) at www.irs.gov/cdorders for $35 (no handling fee), or call 1-877-CDFORMS (1-877-233-6767) toll free to buy the CD for $35 (plus a $5 handling fee). Price is subject to change.

By phone and in person. You can order forms and publications by calling 1-800-TAX-FORM (1-800-829-3676). You can also get most forms and publications at your local IRS office.

General Instructions

Section references are to the Internal Revenue Code unless otherwise noted.

Purpose of Form

Political organizations and certain exempt organizations file Form 1120-POL to report their political organization taxable income and income tax liability under section 527.

Who Must File

A political organization, whether or not it is tax-exempt, must file Form 1120-POL if it has any political organization taxable income.

An exempt organization that is not a political organization must file Form 1120-POL if it is treated as having political organization taxable income under section 527(f)(1).

Political Organizations

A political organization is a party, committee, association, fund (including a separate segregated fund described in section 527(f)(3) set up by a section 501(c) organization), or other organization, organized and operated primarily for the purpose of accepting contributions or making expenditures, or both, to influence the selection, nomination, election, or appointment of any individual to any public office or office in a political organization, or the election of Presidential or Vice Presidential electors. Political organizations include a:

1. Principal campaign committee, if it is the political committee designated by a candidate for U.S. Congress as his or her principal campaign committee for purposes of section 302(e) of the Federal Election Campaign Act of 1971 and section 527(h).

If a candidate for U.S. Congress elects to make a designation under section 527(h), he or she must designate the principal campaign committee by attaching a copy of the Statement of Candidacy to Form 1120-POL. This can be either the Federal Election Commission's Form 2 or an equivalent statement filed with the Federal Election Commission. The designation may also be made by attaching a signed statement with all of the following information.

● The candidate's name and address,

● The candidate's identifying number,

● The candidate's party affiliation and office sought,

● The district and state in which the office is sought, and

● The name and address of the principal campaign committee.

Note. If the candidate for U.S. Congress has a designation in effect from an earlier year, attach a copy of the earlier year's designation to this year's Form 1120-POL and check the appropriate box on the form. See Regulations section 1.527-9. If a candidate for U.S. Congress has only one political campaign committee, no designation is required. However, be sure to check the appropriate box on Form 1120-POL.

2. Newsletter fund, if it is a fund established and maintained by an individual who holds, has been elected to, or is a candidate (as defined in section 527(g)(3)) for nomination or election to any federal, state, or local elective public office. The fund must be maintained exclusively for the preparation and circulation of the individual's newsletter.

3. Separate segregated fund, if it is maintained by a section 501(c) organization (exempt from tax under section 501(a)). For more information, see section 527(f)(3) and Regulations section 1.527-6(f).

Taxable Income

Political organization taxable income (line 19) is the excess of (a) gross income for the tax year (excluding exempt function income (defined later)) over (b) deductions directly connected with the earning of gross income (excluding exempt function income). Taxable income is figured with the following adjustments.

1. A specific deduction of $100 is allowed (but not for newsletter funds),

2. The net operating loss deduction is not allowed, and

3. The dividends-received deduction and other special deductions for corporations are not allowed. See section 527(c)(2)(C).

Effect of failure to file Form 8871.

Unless excepted (see *Other Reports and Returns That May Be Required*), **every political organization,** in order to be considered a tax-exempt organization, must file Form 8871, Political Organization Notice of Section 527 Status. An organization that is required to file Form 8871, but fails to file it when due, must include in taxable income for the period before Form 8871 is filed, its exempt function income (including contributions received, membership dues, and political fundraising receipts), minus any deductions directly connected with the production of that income. The organization may not deduct its exempt function expenditures because section 162(e) denies a deduction for political campaign expenditures.

Exempt Function and Exempt Function Income

The exempt function of a political organization includes all activities that are related to and support the process of influencing or attempting to influence the selection, nomination, election, or appointment of any individual to any federal, state, or local public office, or office of a political organization, or the election of Presidential or Vice Presidential electors, whether or not the individuals or electors are selected, nominated, elected, or appointed. The term "exempt function" also means the making of expenditures relating to the individual's office, once selected, nominated, elected, or appointed, but only if the expenditures would be deductible by an individual under section 162(a).

Exempt function income is the total of all amounts received from the following sources (to the extent that they are separately segregated only for use for an exempt function):

- Contributions of money and property;
- Membership dues, fees, or assessments paid by a member of a political party;
- Proceeds from a political fundraising or entertainment event, or from the sale of political campaign materials, if those amounts are not received in the active conduct of a trade or business; and
- Proceeds from the conduct of a bingo game, as described in section 513(f)(2).

Specified Taxable Income

Newsletter fund. Taxable income of a newsletter fund is figured in the same manner as taxable income of a political organization except that the specific deduction of $100 is not allowed.

Exempt organization that is not a political organization. Taxable income for an exempt organization described in section 501(c) that is not a political organization is the smaller of:

1. The net investment income of the organization for the tax year, or

2. The amount spent for an exempt function during the tax year either directly or indirectly through another organization.

Net investment income, for this purpose, is the excess of:

1. The gross amount of interest, dividends, rents, and royalties, plus the excess, if any, of gains from the sale or exchange of assets, over the losses from the sale or exchange of assets, over

2. The deductions directly connected with the production of this income.

Taxable income is figured with the adjustments shown in 1, 2, and 3 under *Taxable Income* on page 2.

Who Must Sign

The return must be signed and dated by:
- The president, vice president, treasurer, assistant treasurer, chief accounting officer, or
- Any other officer (such as tax officer) authorized to sign.

Receivers, trustees, and assignees must also sign and date any return filed on behalf of an organization.

If an employee of the organization completes Form 1120-POL, the paid preparer's space should remain blank. In addition, anyone who prepares Form 1120-POL but does not charge the organization should not complete that section. Generally, anyone who is paid to prepare the return must sign it and fill in the *Paid Preparer's Use Only* area.

The paid preparer must complete the required preparer information and:
- Sign the return in the space provided for the preparer's signature.
- Give a copy of the return to the taxpayer.

Note. A paid preparer may sign original or amended returns by rubber stamp, mechanical device, or computer software program.

Paid Preparer Authorization

If the organization wants to allow the IRS to discuss its 2007 tax return with the paid preparer who signed it, check the "Yes" box in the signature area of the return. This authorization applies only to the individual whose signature appears in the *Paid Preparer's Use Only* section of the return. It does not apply to the firm, if any, shown in that section.

If the "Yes" box is checked, the organization is authorizing the IRS to call the paid preparer to answer any questions that may arise during the processing of its return. The organization is also authorizing the paid preparer to:
- Give the IRS any information that is missing from its return,
- Call the IRS for information about the processing of its return or the status of any refund or payment(s), and
- Respond to certain IRS notices that the organization may have shared with the

preparer about math errors, offsets, and return preparation. The notices will not be sent to the preparer.

The organization is not authorizing the paid preparer to receive any refund check, bind the organization to anything (including any additional tax liability), or otherwise represent it before the IRS. If the organization wants to expand the paid preparer's authorization, see Pub. 947, Practice Before the IRS and Power of Attorney.

However, the authorization will automatically end no later than the due date (excluding extensions) for filing the 2008 tax return. If you want to revoke the authorization before it ends, see Pub. 947.

When and Where To File

In general, an organization must file Form 1120-POL by the 15th day of the 3rd month after the end of the tax year.

If the due date falls on a Saturday, Sunday, or legal holiday, the organization may file on the next business day.

File Form 1120-POL with the Department of the Treasury, Internal Revenue Service Center, Ogden, UT 84201.

Private delivery services. In addition to the United States mail, the organization can use certain private delivery services designated by the IRS to meet the "timely mailing as timely filing/payment" rule for tax returns and payments. These private delivery services include only the following.
- DHL Express (DHL): DHL Same Day Service, DHL Next Day 10:30 am, DHL Next Day 12:00 pm, DHL Next Day 3:00 pm, and DHL 2nd Day Service.
- Federal Express (FedEx): FedEx Priority Overnight, FedEx Standard Overnight, FedEx 2Day, FedEx International Priority, and FedEx International First, and
- United Parcel Service (UPS): UPS Next Day Air, UPS Next Day Air Saver, UPS 2nd Day Air, UPS 2nd Day Air A.M., UPS Worldwide Express Plus, and UPS Worldwide Express.

The private delivery service can tell you how to get written proof of the mailing date.

Extension. File Form 7004, Application for Automatic Extension of Time To File Corporation Income Tax Return, to request a 6-month extension of time to file.

Other Reports and Returns That May Be Required

An organization that files Form 1120-POL may also be required to file the following forms:

1. Form 8871, Political Organization Notice of Section 527 Status.

Generally, in order to be tax-exempt, a political organization must file this form within 24 hours of the date it is established and within 30 days of any material change in the organization.

However, do not file this form if the organization is:

• An organization that reasonably expects its annual gross receipts to always be less than $25,000,

• A political committee required to report under the Federal Election Campaign Act of 1971 (2 U.S.C. 431 et seq.),

• A political committee of a state or local candidate,

• A state or local committee of a political party, or

• A tax-exempt organization described in section 501(c) that is treated as having political organization taxable income under section 527(f)(1).

2. Form 8872, Political Organization Report of Contributions and Expenditures (periodic reports are required during the calendar year).

Generally, a political organization that files Form 8871 and accepts a contribution or makes an expenditure for an exempt function during the calendar year must file this form. However, this form is not required to be filed by an organization excepted from filing Form 8871 (see above), or a qualified state or local political organization (QSLPO) (see the instructions for Form 8871 and Rev. Rul. 2003-49, 2003-20 I.R.B. 903, for the definition of a QSLPO).

3. Form 990, Return of Organization Exempt From Income Tax, or Form 990-EZ, Short Form Return of Organization Exempt From Income Tax.

An exempt political organization must also file one of these forms if its annual gross receipts are $25,000 or more ($100,000 or more for a QSLPO).

The following political organizations are not required to file Form 990.

• Any political organization excepted from the requirement to file Form 8871, and

• Any caucus or association of state or local officials.

See the Instructions for Form 990 and Form 990-EZ.

Accounting Methods

Figure taxable income using the method of accounting regularly used in keeping the organization's books and records. Generally, permissible methods include:

• Cash,

• Accrual, or

• Any other method authorized by the Internal Revenue Code.

In all cases, the method used must clearly show taxable income.

Change in accounting method. Generally, the organization may only change the method of accounting used to report taxable income (for income as a whole or for any material item) by getting consent on Form 3115,

Application for Change in Accounting Method. For more information, get Pub. 538, Accounting Periods and Methods.

Accounting Period

The organization must figure its taxable income on the basis of a tax year. The tax year is the annual accounting period the organization uses to keep its records and report its income and expenses if that period is a calendar year or a fiscal year. However, an organization that does not keep books or does not have an annual accounting period must use the calendar year as its tax year. A new organization must adopt its tax year by the due date (not including extensions) of its first income tax return.

Change of tax year. After the organization has adopted a tax year, it must get the consent of the IRS to change its tax year by filing Form 1128, Application To Adopt, Change, or Retain a Tax Year. See Regulations section 1.442-1 and Pub. 538.

Rounding Off to Whole Dollars

The organization may round off cents to whole dollars on the return and accompanying schedules. If the organization does round to whole dollars, it must round all amounts. To round, drop amounts under 50 cents and increase amounts from 50 to 99 cents to the next dollar. For example, $1.39 becomes $1 and $2.50 becomes $3.

If two or more amounts must be added to figure the amount to enter on a line, include cents when adding the amounts and round off only the total.

Depository Method of Tax Payment

The organization must pay the tax due in full no later than the 15th day of the 3rd month after the end of the tax year. The two methods of depositing organization income taxes are discussed below.

Electronic Deposit Requirement

The organization must make electronic deposits of all depository taxes (such as employment tax, excise tax, and corporate income tax) using the Electronic Federal Tax Payment System (EFTPS) in 2008 if:

• The total deposits of such taxes in 2006 were more than $200,000, or

• The organization was required to use EFTPS in 2007.

If the organization is required to use EFTPS and fails to do so, it may be subject to a 10% penalty. If the organization is not required to use EFTPS, it may participate voluntarily. To enroll in or get more information about EFTPS, call 1-800-555-4477.

Depositing on time. For deposits made by EFTPS to be on time, the organization must initiate the transaction at least 1 business day before the date the deposit is due.

Deposits With Form 8109

If the organization does not use EFTPS, deposit organization income tax payments with Form 8109, Federal Tax Deposit Coupon. If you do not have a preprinted Form 8109, use Form 8109-B to make deposits. You can get this form only by calling 1-800-829-4933. Be sure to have your employer identification number (EIN) ready when you call.

Do not send deposits directly to an IRS office; otherwise, the organization may have to pay a penalty. Mail or deliver the completed Form 8109 with the payment to an authorized depositary, that is, a commercial bank or other financial institution authorized to accept federal tax deposits.

Make checks or money orders payable to the depositary. To help ensure proper crediting, write the organization's EIN, the tax period to which the deposit applies, and "Form 1120-POL" on the check or money order. Be sure to darken the "1120" box on the coupon. Records of these deposits will be sent to the IRS.

For more information on deposits, see the instructions in the coupon booklet (Form 8109) and Pub. 583, Starting a Business and Keeping Records.

Caution. If the organization owes tax when it files Form 1120-POL, do not include the payment with the tax return. Instead, mail or deliver the payment with Form 8109 to an authorized depositary or use EFTPS, if applicable.

Interest and Penalties

Interest

Interest is charged on taxes paid late even if an extension of time to file is granted. Interest is also charged on penalties imposed for failure to file, negligence, fraud, gross valuation overstatements, and substantial understatement of tax from the due date (including extensions) to the date of payment. The interest charge is figured at a rate determined under section 6621.

Penalties

Penalties may be imposed if the organization is required to file Form 1120-POL and it fails to file the form by the due date. The following penalties may apply if the organization does not file its tax return by the due date, including extensions.

Late filing of return. The organization may be charged a penalty of 5% of the unpaid tax for each month or part of a month the return is late, up to a maximum of 25% of the unpaid tax. The minimum penalty for a return that is more than 60 days late is the smaller of the tax due or $100. The penalty will not be imposed if the organization can show that the failure to file on time was due to reasonable cause. Organizations that file late must attach a statement explaining the reasonable cause.

Late payment of tax. An organization that does not pay the tax when due generally may have to pay a penalty of ½ of 1% of the unpaid tax for each month or part of a month the tax is not paid, up to a maximum of 25% of the unpaid tax. The penalty will not be imposed if the organization can show that the failure to pay on time was due to reasonable cause.

Other penalties. Other penalties can be imposed for negligence, substantial understatement of tax, and fraud. See sections 6662 and 6663.

Assembling the Return

Attach Form 4136, Credit for Federal Tax Paid on Fuels, after page 1 of Form 1120-POL. Attach schedules in alphabetical order and other forms in numerical order after Form 4136.

Complete every applicable entry space on Form 1120-POL. Do not write "See attached" instead of completing the entry spaces. If you need more space on the forms or schedules, attach separate sheets using the same size and format as on the printed forms. Show the totals on the printed forms. Attach these separate sheets after all the schedules and forms. Be sure to put the organization's name and EIN on each sheet.

Specific Instructions

Period covered. File the 2007 return for calendar year 2007 and fiscal years that begin in 2007 and end in 2008. For a fiscal year, fill in the tax year space at the top of the form.

Note. The 2007 Form 1120-POL may also be used if:

● The organization has a tax year of less than 12 months that begins and ends in 2008, and

● The 2008 Form 1120-POL is not available at the time the organization is required to file its return. The organization must show its 2008 tax year on the 2007 Form 1120-POL and take into account any tax law changes that are effective for tax years beginning after December 31, 2007.

Address. Include the suite, room, or other unit number after the street address. If the Post Office does not deliver mail to the street address and the organization has a P.O. box, show the box number instead of the street address.

Final return, name change, address change, amended return. If the organization ceases to exist, check the "Final return" box.

If the organization has changed its name since it last filed a return, check the "Name change" box.

If the organization has changed its address since it last filed a return, check the "Address change" box.

Note. If a change in address occurs after the return is filed, the organization should use Form 8822, Change of Address, to notify the IRS of the new address.

Amended return. If you are filing an amended Form 1120-POL:

● Check the "Amended return" box,

● Complete the entire return,

● Correct the appropriate lines with the new information, and

● Refigure the tax liability.

Attach a sheet that explains the reason for the amendments and identifies the lines and amounts being changed on the amended return. Generally, the amended return must be filed within 3 years after the date the original return was due or 3 years after the date the organization filed it, whichever is later.

Employer identification number (EIN). Enter the nine-digit EIN assigned to the organization. If the organization does not have an EIN, it must apply for one. An EIN can be applied for:

● Online by clicking the Employer ID Numbers (EINs) link at *www.irs.gov/businesses/small*. The EIN is issued immediately once the application information is validated.

● By telephone at 1-800-829-4933 from 7:00 a.m. to 10:00 p.m. in the employer's local time zone.

The online application process is not yet available for organizations with addresses in foreign countries or Puerto Rico.

If the organization has not received its EIN by the time the return is due, write "Applied for" in the space provided for the EIN. See Pub. 583 for details.

Income and deductions. Campaign contributions and other exempt function income are generally not includible in income; likewise, campaign expenditures and other exempt function expenditures are not deductible. To be deductible in computing political organization taxable income, expenses must be directly connected with the production of political organization taxable income. In those cases where expenses are attributable to the production of both exempt function income and political organization taxable income, the

expenses should be allocated on a reasonable and consistent basis. Only the portion allocable to the production of political organization taxable income may be deducted. No deduction is allowed for general administrative or indirect expenses.

Line 7. Other income and nonexempt function expenditures. Enter the income from other sources, such as:

● Exempt function income that was not properly segregated for exempt functions.

● Income received in the ordinary course of a trade or business.

● Ordinary income from the trade or business activities of a partnership (from Schedule K-1 (Form 1065), box 1).

● Exempt function income (minus any deductions directly connected with the production of that income) taxable under section 527(i)(4) for failure to timely file Form 8871. Include amounts whether or not segregated for use for an exempt function.

Also include on this line:

● Expenditures that were made from exempt function income that were not for an exempt function and resulted in direct or indirect financial benefit to the political organization (see Regulations section 1.527-5 for examples) and

● Illegal expenditures.

Attach a schedule listing all income and expenditures included on line 7.

Line 17. Taxable income before specific deduction of $100. Political organizations, newsletter funds, and separate segregated funds: Subtract line 16 from line 8 and enter the result on line 17(c).

Exempt organizations (section 501(c)) that are not political organizations. Complete lines 17a and 17b if the organization made exempt function expenditures that were not from a separate segregated fund. Enter on line 17c the smaller of line 17a or 17b. See *Exempt organization that is not a political organization* on page 3 for an explanation of the amounts to enter on these lines.

Line 19. Taxable income. If the taxable income on line 19 is zero or less, the Form 1120-POL is not required to be filed, but it may be filed to start the statute of limitations period.

Line 20. Income tax. The rate of tax imposed depends on whether the political organization is a principal campaign committee as defined in section 527(h). The tax rate is lower for a principal campaign committee.

Political organization not a principal campaign committee. An organization that is not a principal campaign committee computes its tax as follows: Multiply line 19 by 35% and enter the result on line 20.

Principal campaign committee (section 527(h)).

A political organization that is a principal campaign committee of a candidate for U.S. Congress computes its tax in the same manner as provided in section 11(b) for corporations. Compute the tax as follows:

1. Enter taxable income (line 19, Form 1120-POL) . . . . _____
2. Enter line 1 or $50,000, whichever is less . . . _____
3. Subtract line 2 from line 1 . _____
4. Enter line 3 or $25,000, whichever is less . . . _____
5. Subtract line 4 from line 3 . _____
6. Enter line 5 or $9,925,000, whichever is less . . . _____
7. Subtract line 6 from line 5 . _____
8. Multiply line 2 by 15% . _____
9. Multiply line 4 by 25% . _____
10. Multiply line 6 by 34% . _____
11. Multiply line 7 by 35% . _____
12. If line 1 is greater than $100,000, enter the smaller of: 5% of taxable income in excess of $100,000, or $11,750 . . . . _____
13. If line 1 is greater than $15 million, enter the smaller of: 3% of taxable income in excess of $15 million or $100,000 . . . . _____
14. Add lines 8 through 13. Enter here and on line 20, Form 1120-POL . . . . _____

Note. Estimated tax and alternative minimum tax do not apply to political organizations.

Line 21. Tax credits. The organization may qualify for the following credits:

● **Foreign tax credit.** See Form 1118, Foreign Tax Credit—Corporations.

● **Qualified electric vehicle credit.** See Form 8834, Qualified Electric Vehicle Credit, and section 30.

● **General business credit** (excluding the Indian employment credit, the work opportunity credit, the welfare-to-work credit, and the empowerment zone and renewal community employment credit). See Form 3800, General Business Credit.

Enter the total amount of qualified credits on line 21 and attach the applicable credit forms.

Line 22. Total tax. If the political organization must recapture any of the qualified electric vehicle credit, include the amount of the recapture in the total for line 22. On the dotted line next to the entry space, write "QEV recapture" and the amount. See Regulations section 1.30-1 for details on how to figure the recapture.

Additional Information

Question 1

Foreign financial accounts. Check the "Yes" box if either 1 or 2 below applies to the organization. Otherwise, check the "No" box.

1. At any time during the 2007 calendar year the organization had an interest in or signature or other authority over a bank, securities, or other financial account in a foreign country; and

● The combined value of the accounts was more than $10,000 at any time during the calendar year; and

● The account was not with a U.S. military banking facility operated by a U.S. financial institution.

2. The organization owns more than 50% of the stock in any corporation that would answer "Yes" to item 1 above.

See Form TD F 90-22.1, Report of Foreign Bank and Financial Accounts, to find out if the organization is considered to have an interest in or signature or other authority over a financial account in a foreign country.

If "Yes" is checked for this question, file Form TD F 90-22.1 by June 30, 2008, with the Department of the Treasury at the address shown on the form. Do not attach it to Form 1120-POL.

You can get Form TD F 90-22.1 by calling 1-800-TAX-FORM (1-800-829-3676) or you can download it from the IRS website at *www.irs.gov*.

Also, if "Yes" is checked for this question, enter the name of the foreign country or countries. Attach a separate sheet if more space is needed.

Question 2

If you checked "Yes," to Question 2, the organization may be required to file Form 3520, Annual Return To Report Transactions With Foreign Trusts and Receipt of Certain Foreign Gifts. For details, see Form 3520.

Note. An owner of a foreign trust must ensure that the trust files an annual information return on Form 3520-A, Annual Information Return of Foreign Trust With a U.S. Owner. For details, see the instructions for Form 3520-A.

Question 3

In the space provided, show any tax-exempt interest income received or accrued. Include any exempt-interest dividends received as a shareholder in a mutual fund or other regulated investment company.

Privacy Act and Paperwork Reduction Act Notice. We ask for the information on this form to carry out the Internal Revenue laws of the United States. You are required to give us the information. We need it to ensure that you are complying with these laws and to allow us to figure and collect the right amount of tax. Section 6109 requires return preparers to provide their identifying numbers on the return.

You are not required to provide the information requested on a form that is subject to the Paperwork Reduction Act unless the form displays a valid OMB control number. Books or records relating to a form or its instructions must be retained as long as their contents may become material in the administration of any Internal Revenue law. Generally, tax returns and return information are confidential, as required by section 6103.

The time needed to complete and file this form will vary depending on individual circumstances. The estimated average time is:

Recordkeeping . . .	17 hr., 13 min.
Learning about the law or the form . . .	5 hr., 15 min.
Preparing the form . .	12 hr., 17 min.
Copying, assembling, and sending the form to the IRS . . .	1 hr., 52 min.

If you have comments concerning the accuracy of these time estimates or suggestions for making this form simpler, we would be happy to hear from you. You can write to the Internal Revenue Service, Tax Products Coordinating Committee, SE:W:CAR:MP:T:T:SP, 1111 Constitution Ave. NW, IR-6526, Washington, DC 20224. Do not send the tax form to this address. Instead, see *When and Where To File* on page 3.

Form **990**	**Return of Organization Exempt From Income Tax**	OMB No. 1545-0047
	Under section 501(c), 527, or 4947(a)(1) of the Internal Revenue Code (except black lung benefit trust or private foundation)	**2007**
Department of the Treasury Internal Revenue Service	▶ The organization may have to use a copy of this return to satisfy state reporting requirements.	**Open to Public Inspection**

A   For the 2007 calendar year, or tax year beginning _____ , 2007, and ending _____ , 20 ____

B Check if applicable:	Please use IRS label or print or type. See Specific Instructions.	**C** Name of organization		**D** Employer identification number
☐ Address change				
☐ Name change		Number and street (or P.O. box if mail is not delivered to street address)	Room/suite	**E** Telephone number
☐ Initial return				( )
☐ Termination		City or town, state or country, and ZIP + 4		**F** Accounting method: ☐ Cash ☐ Accrual
☐ Amended return				☐ Other (specify) ▶
☐ Application pending		● **Section 501(c)(3) organizations and 4947(a)(1) nonexempt charitable trusts must attach a completed Schedule A (Form 990 or 990-EZ).**		**H** and **I** are not applicable to section 527 organizations.

H(a) Is this a group return for affiliates? ☐ Yes ☐ No

G   Website: ▶

H(b) If "Yes," enter number of affiliates ▶ _ _ _ _ _ _ _ _ _ _

H(c) Are all affiliates included? ☐ Yes ☐ No
(If "No," attach a list. See instructions.)

J   **Organization type** (check only one) ▶ ☐ 501(c) (   ) ◀ (insert no.) ☐ 4947(a)(1) or ☐ 527

H(d) Is this a separate return filed by an organization covered by a group ruling? ☐ Yes ☐ No

K   Check here ▶ ☐ if the organization is not a 509(a)(3) supporting organization **and** its gross receipts are normally **not** more than $25,000. A return is not required, but if the organization chooses to file a return, be sure to file a complete return.

I   Group Exemption Number ▶

M   Check ▶ ☐ if the organization is **not** required to attach Sch. B (Form 990, 990-EZ, or 990-PF).

L   Gross receipts: Add lines 6b, 8b, 9b, and 10b to line 12 ▶

Part I   Revenue, Expenses, and Changes in Net Assets or Fund Balances *(See the instructions.)*

1	Contributions, gifts, grants, and similar amounts received:			
a	Contributions to donor advised funds	**1a**		
b	Direct public support (not included on line 1a)	**1b**		
c	Indirect public support (not included on line 1a)	**1c**		
d	Government contributions (grants) (not included on line 1a)	**1d**		
e	**Total** (add lines 1a through 1d) (cash $_____ noncash $_____)		**1e**	
2	Program service revenue including government fees and contracts (from Part VII, line 93)		**2**	
3	Membership dues and assessments		**3**	
4	Interest on savings and temporary cash investments		**4**	
5	Dividends and interest from securities		**5**	
6a	Gross rents	**6a**		
b	Less: rental expenses	**6b**		
c	Net rental income or (loss). Subtract line 6b from line 6a		**6c**	
7	Other investment income (describe ▶ _____)		**7**	
8a	Gross amount from sales of assets other than inventory	(A) Securities ____	(B) Other **8a**	
b	Less: cost or other basis and sales expenses.		**8b**	
c	Gain or (loss) (attach schedule)		**8c**	
d	Net gain or (loss). Combine line 8c, columns (A) and (B)		**8d**	
9	Special events and activities (attach schedule). If any amount is from **gaming**, check here ▶ ☐			
a	Gross revenue (not including $ _____ of contributions reported on line 1b)	**9a**		
b	Less: direct expenses other than fundraising expenses	**9b**		
c	Net income or (loss) from special events. Subtract line 9b from line 9a		**9c**	
10a	Gross sales of inventory, less returns and allowances	**10a**		
b	Less: cost of goods sold	**10b**		
c	Gross profit or (loss) from sales of inventory (attach schedule). Subtract line 10b from line 10a		**10c**	
11	Other revenue (from Part VII, line 103)		**11**	
12	**Total revenue.** Add lines 1e, 2, 3, 4, 5, 6c, 7, 8d, 9c, 10c, and 11		**12**	
13	Program services (from line 44, column (B))		**13**	
14	Management and general (from line 44, column (C))		**14**	
15	Fundraising (from line 44, column (D))		**15**	
16	Payments to affiliates (attach schedule)		**16**	
17	**Total expenses.** Add lines 16 and 44, column (A)		**17**	
18	Excess or (deficit) for the year. Subtract line 17 from line 12		**18**	
19	Net assets or fund balances at beginning of year (from line 73, column (A))		**19**	
20	Other changes in net assets or fund balances (attach explanation)		**20**	
21	Net assets or fund balances at end of year. Combine lines 18, 19, and 20		**21**	

Revenue (left margin label for lines 1-12)
Expenses (left margin label for lines 13-17)
Net Assets (left margin label for lines 18-21)

For Privacy Act and Paperwork Reduction Act Notice, see the separate instructions.   Cat. No. 11282Y   Form **990** (2007)

Part II **Statement of Functional Expenses**   All organizations must complete column (A). Columns (B), (C), and (D) are required for section 501(c)(3) and (4) organizations and section 4947(a)(1) nonexempt charitable trusts but optional for others. *(See the instructions.)*

Do not include amounts reported on line 6b, 8b, 9b, 10b, or 16 of Part I.		**(A)** Total	**(B)** Program services	**(C)** Management and general	**(D)** Fundraising
22a Grants paid from donor advised funds (attach schedule) (cash $ _____ noncash $ _____) If this amount includes foreign grants, check here ▶ ☐	22a				
22b Other grants and allocations (attach schedule) (cash $ _____ noncash $ _____) If this amount includes foreign grants, check here ▶ ☐	22b				
23 Specific assistance to individuals (attach schedule)	23				
24 Benefits paid to or for members (attach schedule)	24				
25a Compensation of current officers, directors, key employees, etc. listed in Part V-A . .	25a				
b Compensation of former officers, directors, key employees, etc. listed in Part V-B . .	25b				
c Compensation and other distributions, not included above, to disqualified persons (as defined under section 4958(f)(1)) and persons described in section 4958(c)(3)(B) . . .	25c				
26 Salaries and wages of employees not included on lines 25a, b, and c	26				
27 Pension plan contributions not included on lines 25a, b, and c	27				
28 Employee benefits not included on lines 25a – 27	28				
29 Payroll taxes	29				
30 Professional fundraising fees	30				
31 Accounting fees	31				
32 Legal fees	32				
33 Supplies	33				
34 Telephone	34				
35 Postage and shipping	35				
36 Occupancy	36				
37 Equipment rental and maintenance . . .	37				
38 Printing and publications	38				
39 Travel	39				
40 Conferences, conventions, and meetings .	40				
41 Interest	41				
42 Depreciation, depletion, etc. (attach schedule)	42				
43 Other expenses not covered above (itemize):					
a _____	43a				
b _____	43b				
c _____	43c				
d _____	43d				
e _____	43e				
f _____	43f				
g _____	43g				
44 **Total functional expenses.** Add lines 22a through 43g. (Organizations completing columns (B)–(D), carry these totals to lines 13–15)	44				

Joint Costs. Check ▶ ☐ if you are following SOP 98-2.

Are any joint costs from a combined educational campaign and fundraising solicitation reported in **(B)** Program services? . ▶ ☐ **Yes** ☐ **No**

If "Yes," enter **(i)** the aggregate amount of these joint costs $_____; **(ii)** the amount allocated to Program services $_____;

(iii) the amount allocated to Management and general $_____ ; and **(iv)** the amount allocated to Fundraising $_____

Part III   **Statement of Program Service Accomplishments** *(See the instructions.)*

Form 990 is available for public inspection and, for some people, serves as the primary or sole source of information about a particular organization. How the public perceives an organization in such cases may be determined by the information presented on its return. Therefore, please make sure the return is complete and accurate and fully describes, in Part III, the organization's programs and accomplishments.

	Program Service Expenses (Required for 501(c)(3) and (4) orgs., and 4947(a)(1) trusts; but optional for others.)
What is the organization's primary exempt purpose? ▶ --	
All organizations must describe their exempt purpose achievements in a clear and concise manner. State the number of clients served, publications issued, etc. Discuss achievements that are not measurable. (Section 501(c)(3) and (4) organizations and 4947(a)(1) nonexempt charitable trusts must also enter the amount of grants and allocations to others.)	

a _____
_____
_____
_____
_____
_____

(Grants and allocations $) If this amount includes foreign grants, check here ▶ ☐

b _____
_____
_____
_____
_____
_____

(Grants and allocations $) If this amount includes foreign grants, check here ▶ ☐

c _____
_____
_____
_____
_____
_____

(Grants and allocations $) If this amount includes foreign grants, check here ▶ ☐

d _____
_____
_____
_____
_____
_____

(Grants and allocations $) If this amount includes foreign grants, check here ▶ ☐

e Other program services (attach schedule)

(Grants and allocations $) If this amount includes foreign grants, check here ▶ ☐

f **Total of Program Service Expenses** (should equal line 44, column (B), Program services).   .   .   ▶

Part IV   Balance Sheets *(See the instructions.)*

Note: *Where required, attached schedules and amounts within the description column should be for end-of-year amounts only.*

			(A) Beginning of year		**(B)** End of year
Assets	45	Cash—non-interest-bearing		45	
	46	Savings and temporary cash investments		46	
	47a	Accounts receivable	47a		
	b	Less: allowance for doubtful accounts .	47b		47c
	48a	Pledges receivable	48a		
	b	Less: allowance for doubtful accounts .	48b		48c
	49	Grants receivable		49	
	50a	Receivables from current and former officers, directors, trustees, and key employees (attach schedule)		50a	
	b	Receivables from other disqualified persons (as defined under section 4958(f)(1)) and persons described in section 4958(c)(3)(B) (attach schedule)		50b	
	51a	Other notes and loans receivable (attach schedule)	51a		
	b	Less: allowance for doubtful accounts .	51b		51c
	52	Inventories for sale or use		52	
	53	Prepaid expenses and deferred charges		53	
	54a	Investments—publicly-traded securities . . ▶ ☐ Cost ☐ FMV		54a	
	b	Investments—other securities (attach schedule) ▶ ☐ Cost ☐ FMV		54b	
	55a	Investments—land, buildings, and equipment: basis	55a		
	b	Less: accumulated depreciation (attach schedule)	55b		55c
	56	Investments—other (attach schedule)		56	
	57a	Land, buildings, and equipment: basis .	57a		
	b	Less: accumulated depreciation (attach schedule)	57b		57c
	58	Other assets, including program-related investments (describe ▶ -------------------------------)		58	
	59	**Total assets** (must equal line 74). Add lines 45 through 58 . .		59	
Liabilities	60	Accounts payable and accrued expenses		60	
	61	Grants payable		61	
	62	Deferred revenue		62	
	63	Loans from officers, directors, trustees, and key employees (attach schedule)		63	
	64a	Tax-exempt bond liabilities (attach schedule)		64a	
	b	Mortgages and other notes payable (attach schedule) . . .		64b	
	65	Other liabilities (describe ▶ -----------------------------)		65	
	66	**Total liabilities.** Add lines 60 through 65		66	
Net Assets or Fund Balances		**Organizations that follow SFAS 117, check here** ▶ ☐ **and complete lines** 67 through 69 and lines 73 and 74.			
	67	Unrestricted		67	
	68	Temporarily restricted		68	
	69	Permanently restricted		69	
		Organizations that do not follow SFAS 117, check here ▶ ☐ **and** complete lines 70 through 74.			
	70	Capital stock, trust principal, or current funds		70	
	71	Paid-in or capital surplus, or land, building, and equipment fund .		71	
	72	Retained earnings, endowment, accumulated income, or other funds		72	
	73	**Total net assets or fund balances.** Add lines 67 through 69 **or** lines 70 through 72. (Column (A) **must** equal line 19 and column (B) **must** equal line 21)		73	
	74	**Total liabilities and net assets/fund balances.** Add lines 66 and 73		74	

Form 990 (2007)   Page **5**

Part IV-A   **Reconciliation of Revenue per Audited Financial Statements With Revenue per Return** *(See the instructions.)*

a	Total revenue, gains, and other support per audited financial statements	**a**	
b	Amounts included on line **a** but not on Part I, line 12:		
1	Net unrealized gains on investments **b1**		
2	Donated services and use of facilities **b2**		
3	Recoveries of prior year grants **b3**		
4	Other (specify): _____		
	_____ **b4**		
	Add lines **b1** through **b4**	**b**	
c	Subtract line **b** from line **a**	**c**	
d	Amounts included on Part I, line 12, but not on line **a**:		
1	Investment expenses not included on Part I, line 6b **d1**		
2	Other (specify): _____		
	_____ **d2**		
	Add lines **d1** and **d2**	**d**	
e	**Total revenue** (Part I, line 12). Add lines **c** and **d** . . . . ▶	**e**	

Part IV-B   **Reconciliation of Expenses per Audited Financial Statements With Expenses per Return**

a	Total expenses and losses per audited financial statements	**a**	
b	Amounts included on line **a** but not on Part I, line 17:		
1	Donated services and use of facilities **b1**		
2	Prior year adjustments reported on Part I, line 20 . . . . . **b2**		
3	Losses reported on Part I, line 20 . . . . **b3**		
4	Other (specify): _____		
	_____ **b4**		
	Add lines **b1** through **b4**	**b**	
c	Subtract line **b** from line **a**	**c**	
d	Amounts included on Part I, line 17, but not on line **a**:		
1	Investment expenses not included on Part I, line 6b **d1**		
2	Other (specify): _____		
	_____ **d2**		
	Add lines **d1** and **d2**	**d**	
e	**Total expenses** (Part I, line 17). Add lines **c** and **d** . . . . ▶	**e**	

Part V-A   **Current Officers, Directors, Trustees, and Key Employees** (List each person who was an officer, director, trustee, or key employee at any time during the year even if they were not compensated.) *(See the instructions.)*

(A) Name and address	(B) Title and average hours per week devoted to position	(C) Compensation (If not paid, enter -0-.)	(D) Contributions to employee benefit plans & deferred compensation plans	(E) Expense account and other allowances
---------------------------------				

Form **990** (2007)

Form 990 (2007)   Page **6**

Part V-A   **Current Officers, Directors, Trustees, and Key Employees** *(continued)* | Yes | No |

75a Enter the total number of officers, directors, and trustees permitted to vote on organization business at board
meetings . . . . ▶ _ _ _ _ _ _ _ _ _ _ _ _ _ _ _ _

  b Are any officers, directors, trustees, or key employees listed in Form 990, Part V-A, or highest compensated
employees listed in Schedule A, Part I, or highest compensated professional and other independent
contractors listed in Schedule A, Part II-A or II-B, related to each other through family or business
relationships? If "Yes," attach a statement that identifies the individuals and explains the relationship(s) .   **75b**

  c Do any officers, directors, trustees, or key employees listed in Form 990, Part V-A, or highest
compensated employees listed in Schedule A, Part I, or highest compensated professional and other
independent contractors listed in Schedule A, Part II-A or II-B, receive compensation from any other
organizations, whether tax exempt or taxable, that are related to the organization? See the instructions for
the definition of "related organization.". . . . . ▶   **75c**
If "Yes," attach a statement that includes the information described in the instructions.

  d Does the organization have a written conflict of interest policy? **75d**

Part V-B   **Former Officers, Directors, Trustees, and Key Employees That Received Compensation or Other Benefits** (If any former
officer, director, trustee, or key employee received compensation or other benefits (described below) during the year, list that
person below and enter the amount of compensation or other benefits in the appropriate column. See the instructions.)

(A) Name and address	**(B)** Loans and Advances	**(C)** Compensation (if not paid, enter -0-)	**(D)** Contributions to employee benefit plans & deferred compensation plans	**(E)** Expense account and other allowances
- -				
- -				
- -				
- -				
- -				
- -				
- -				
- -				
- -				

Part VI   **Other Information** *(See the instructions.)* | Yes | No |

76 Did the organization make a change in its activities or methods of conducting activities? If "Yes," attach a
detailed statement of each change **76**

77 Were any changes made in the organizing or governing documents but not reported to the IRS? . . .   **77**
If "Yes," attach a conformed copy of the changes.

78a Did the organization have unrelated business gross income of $1,000 or more during the year covered by
this return? **78a**

  b If "Yes," has it filed a tax return on **Form 990-T** for this year? **78b**

79 Was there a liquidation, dissolution, termination, or substantial contraction during the year? If "Yes," attach
a statement **79**

80a Is the organization related (other than by association with a statewide or nationwide organization) through
common membership, governing bodies, trustees, officers, etc., to any other exempt or nonexempt
organization? . . . . ▶ . .   **80a**

  b If "Yes," enter the name of the organization ▶ _
_ and check whether it is ☐ exempt **or** ☐ nonexempt

81a Enter direct and indirect political expenditures. (See line 81 instructions.) . | **81a** |

  b Did the organization file **Form 1120-POL** for this year? **81b**

Form **990** (2007)

Form 990 (2007)   Page **7**

Part VI **Other Information** *(continued)* | Yes | No |

82a Did the organization receive donated services or the use of materials, equipment, or facilities at no charge or at substantially less than fair rental value? **82a**

  b If "Yes," you may indicate the value of these items here. Do not include this amount as revenue in Part I or as an expense in Part II. (See instructions in Part III.) **82b**

83a Did the organization comply with the public inspection requirements for returns and exemption applications? **83a**

  b Did the organization comply with the disclosure requirements relating to *quid pro quo* contributions? . . **83b**

84a Did the organization solicit any contributions or gifts that were not tax deductible? **84a**

  b If "Yes," did the organization include with every solicitation an express statement that such contributions or gifts were not tax deductible? **84b**

85a *501(c)(4), (5), or (6).* Were substantially all dues nondeductible by members? **85a**

  b Did the organization make only in-house lobbying expenditures of $2,000 or less? **85b**

   If "Yes" was answered to either 85a or 85b, **do not** complete 85c through 85h below unless the organization received a waiver for proxy tax owed for the prior year.

  c Dues, assessments, and similar amounts from members **85c**

  d Section 162(e) lobbying and political expenditures **85d**

  e Aggregate nondeductible amount of section 6033(e)(1)(A) dues notices . . **85e**

  f Taxable amount of lobbying and political expenditures (line 85d less 85e) . **85f**

  g Does the organization elect to pay the section 6033(e) tax on the amount on line 85f? **85g**

  h If section 6033(e)(1)(A) dues notices were sent, does the organization agree to add the amount on line 85f to its reasonable estimate of dues allocable to nondeductible lobbying and political expenditures for the following tax year? **85h**

86 *501(c)(7) orgs.* Enter: **a** Initiation fees and capital contributions included on line 12 . **86a**

  b Gross receipts, included on line 12, for public use of club facilities . . . **86b**

87 *501(c)(12) orgs.* Enter: **a** Gross income from members or shareholders . . **87a**

  b Gross income from other sources. (Do not net amounts due or paid to other sources against amounts due or received from them.) **87b**

88a At any time during the year, did the organization own a 50% or greater interest in a taxable corporation or partnership, or an entity disregarded as separate from the organization under Regulations sections 301.7701-2 and 301.7701-3? If "Yes," complete Part IX **88a**

  b At any time during the year, did the organization, directly or indirectly, own a controlled entity within the meaning of section 512(b)(13)? If "Yes," complete Part XI . . . . ▶ **88b**

89a *501(c)(3) organizations.* Enter: Amount of tax imposed on the organization during the year under: section 4911 ▶_____; section 4912 ▶_____; section 4955 ▶_____

  b *501(c)(3) and 501(c)(4) orgs.* Did the organization engage in any section 4958 excess benefit transaction during the year or did it become aware of an excess benefit transaction from a prior year? If "Yes," attach a statement explaining each transaction **89b**

  c Enter: Amount of tax imposed on the organization managers or disqualified persons during the year under sections 4912, 4955, and 4958 . . . ▶ _____

  d Enter: Amount of tax on line 89c, above, reimbursed by the organization . ▶ _____

  e *All organizations.* At any time during the tax year, was the organization a party to a prohibited tax shelter transaction? **89e**

  f *All organizations.* Did the organization acquire a direct or indirect interest in any applicable insurance contract? **89f**

  g *For supporting organizations and sponsoring organizations maintaining donor advised funds.* Did the supporting organization, or a fund maintained by a sponsoring organization, have excess business holdings at any time during the year? **89g**

90a List the states with which a copy of this return is filed ▶ ---

  b Number of employees employed in the pay period that includes March 12, 2007 (See Instructions.) **90b**

91a The books are in care of ▶ --------------------------------- Telephone no. ▶ (_____)_____

   Located at ▶ ---------------------------------- ZIP + 4 ▶ ------------------------

  b At any time during the calendar year, did the organization have an interest in or a signature or other authority over a financial account in a foreign country (such as a bank account, securities account, or other financial account)? . . . . | Yes | No | **91b**

   If "Yes," enter the name of the foreign country ▶ ---

   See the instructions for exceptions and filing requirements for **Form TD F 90-22.1,** Report of Foreign Bank and Financial Accounts.

Form **990** (2007)

Part VI Other Information *(continued)*					Yes	No

c At any time during the calendar year, did the organization maintain an office outside of the United States? **91c**
If "Yes," enter the name of the foreign country ▶ ---

92 *Section 4947(a)(1) nonexempt charitable trusts filing Form 990 in lieu of* **Form 1041**—Check here . . . . . ▶ ☐
and enter the amount of tax-exempt interest received or accrued during the tax year . ▶ | **92** |

Part VII Analysis of Income-Producing Activities *(See the instructions.)*

Note: *Enter gross amounts unless otherwise indicated.*

		Unrelated business income		Excluded by section 512, 513, or 514		(E) Related or exempt function income
		(A) Business code	(B) Amount	(C) Exclusion code	(D) Amount	
93	Program service revenue:					
a						
b						
c						
d						
e						
f	Medicare/Medicaid payments . . .					
g	Fees and contracts from government agencies					
94	Membership dues and assessments . .					
95	Interest on savings and temporary cash investments					
96	Dividends and interest from securities .					
97	Net rental income or (loss) from real estate:					
a	debt-financed property					
b	not debt-financed property					
98	Net rental income or (loss) from personal property					
99	Other investment income					
100	Gain or (loss) from sales of assets other than inventory					
101	Net income or (loss) from special events .					
102	Gross profit or (loss) from sales of inventory					
103	Other revenue: **a**					
b						
c						
d						
e						
104	Subtotal (add columns (B), (D), and (E)) .					
105	**Total** (add line 104, columns (B), (D), and (E)) . . . . ▶					

Note: *Line 105 plus line 1e, Part I, should equal the amount on line 12, Part I.*

Part VIII Relationship of Activities to the Accomplishment of Exempt Purposes *(See the instructions.)*

Line No. ▼	Explain how each activity for which income is reported in column (E) of Part VII contributed importantly to the accomplishment of the organization's exempt purposes (other than by providing funds for such purposes).

Part IX Information Regarding Taxable Subsidiaries and Disregarded Entities *(See the instructions.)*

(A) Name, address, and EIN of corporation, partnership, or disregarded entity	(B) Percentage of ownership interest	(C) Nature of activities	(D) Total income	(E) End-of-year assets
	%			
	%			
	%			
	%			

Part X Information Regarding Transfers Associated with Personal Benefit Contracts *(See the instructions.)*

(a) Did the organization, during the year, receive any funds, directly or indirectly, to pay premiums on a personal benefit contract? . ☐ **Yes** ☐ **No**
(b) Did the organization, during the year, pay premiums, directly or indirectly, on a personal benefit contract? ☐ **Yes** ☐ **No**
Note: *If "Yes" to* **(b),** *file Form 8870 and Form 4720 (see instructions).*

Form **990** (2007)

Form 990 (2007)   Page **9**

Part XI   **Information Regarding Transfers To and From Controlled Entities.** *Complete only if the organization is a controlling organization as defined in section 512(b)(13).*

					Yes	No
106	Did the reporting organization **make** any transfers **to** a controlled entity as defined in section 512(b)(13) of the Code? If "Yes," complete the schedule below for each controlled entity.					

	(A) Name, address, of each controlled entity	**(B)** Employer Identification Number	**(C)** Description of transfer	**(D)** Amount of transfer
a				
b				
c				
	Totals			

					Yes	No
107	Did the reporting organization **receive** any transfers **from** a controlled entity as defined in section 512(b)(13) of the Code? If "Yes," complete the schedule below for each controlled entity.					

	(A) Name, address, of each controlled entity	**(B)** Employer Identification Number	**(C)** Description of transfer	**(D)** Amount of transfer
a				
b				
c				
	Totals			

			Yes	No
108	Did the organization have a binding written contract in effect on August 17, 2006, covering the interest, rents, royalties, and annuities described in question 107 above?			

Please Sign Here	Under penalties of perjury, I declare that I have examined this return, including accompanying schedules and statements, and to the best of my knowledge and belief, it is true, correct, and complete. Declaration of preparer (other than officer) is based on all information of which preparer has any knowledge.
	► _____ _____
	Signature of officer Date
	► _____
	Type or print name and title

Paid Preparer's Use Only	Preparer's signature ►		Date	Check if self-employed ► ☐	Preparer's SSN or PTIN (See Gen. Inst. X)
	Firm's name (or yours if self-employed), address, and ZIP + 4 ►			EIN ►	
				Phone no. ► ( )	

Form **990** (2007)

20**07**

Department of the Treasury
Internal Revenue Service

Instructions for Form 990 and Form 990-EZ

Return of Organization Exempt From Income Tax and ..
Short Form Return of Organization Exempt From Income Tax
Under Section 501(c), 527, or 4947(a)(1) of the Internal Revenue Code
(except black lung benefit trust or private foundation)

Caution: Form 990-EZ is for use by organizations other than sponsoring organizations and controlling organizations defined in section 512(b)(13), with gross receipts of less than $100,000 and total assets of less than $250,000 at the end of the year.

Section references are to the Internal Revenue Code unless otherwise noted.

What's New

New annual electronic filing requirement for small tax-exempt organizations. Most small tax-exempt organizations must now file *new* Form 990-N, Electronic Notice (e-Postcard) for Tax-Exempt Organizations Not Required to File Form 990 or 990-EZ. See the IRS website at *www.irs.gov* and click on the Charities & Non-Profits tab for more information.

Purpose of Form

Form 990 and Form 990-EZ are used by tax-exempt organizations, nonexempt charitable trusts, and section 527 political organizations to provide the IRS with the information required by section 6033.

An organization's completed Form 990, Form 990-EZ, and the Form 990-T of 501(c)(3) organizations is available for public inspection as required by section 6104. Schedule B (Form 990, 990-EZ, or 990-PF), Schedule of Contributors, is open for public inspection for section 527 organizations filing Form 990 or Form 990-EZ. For other organizations that file Form 990 or Form 990-EZ, parts of Schedule B may be open to public inspection. See the *Instructions for Schedule B* for more details.

Some members of the public rely on Form 990, or Form 990-EZ, as the primary or sole source of information about a particular organization. How the public perceives an organization in such cases may be determined by the information presented on its return. Therefore, the return must be complete, accurate, and fully describe the organization's programs and accomplishments.

Use Form 990 or Form 990-EZ, to send a required election to the IRS, such as the election to capitalize costs under section 266.

Phone Help

If you have questions and/or need help completing Form 990, or Form 990-EZ, please call 1-877-829-5500. This toll-free telephone service is available Monday through Friday.

Email Subscription

The IRS has established a new subscription-based email service for tax professionals and representatives of tax-exempt organizations. Subscribers

Cat. No. 22386X

will receive periodic updates from the IRS regarding exempt organization tax law and regulations, available services, and other information. To subscribe, visit *www.irs.gov/eo*.

Photographs of Missing Children

The Internal Revenue Service is a proud partner with the National Center for Missing and Exploited Children. Photographs of missing children selected by the Center may appear in instructions on pages that would otherwise be blank. You can help bring these children home by looking at the photographs and calling 1-800-THE-LOST (1-800-843-5678) if you recognize a child.

General Instructions

The *General Instructions* apply to both Form 990 and Form 990-EZ. See also the *Specific Instructions* for each of these forms.

 Certain Form 990 filers must file electronically, see General Instruction H *for who must file electronically.*

A. Who Must File

Filing Tests

Organizations exempt from income tax under Internal Revenue Code section 501(a), which includes sections 501(c), 501(e), 501(f), 501(k), 501(n), and 4947(a)(1) must generally file Form 990 or Form 990-EZ based on their gross receipts for the tax year. (See *General Instruction B* next for exceptions to the filing requirement.) For this purpose, *gross receipts* is the organization's total revenues from all sources during its annual accounting period, without subtracting any costs or expenses.

 However, in addition to the above filing test, 501(c)(15) insurance companies are subject to a separate series of tests to determine whether small insurance companies qualify as tax exempt under section 501(c)(15) for the tax year. These separate tests use a different definition for gross receipts only for purposes of determining whether such insurance companies qualify as tax exempt. See Section 501(c)(15) Organizations *below for additional information.*

If the organization does not meet any of the exceptions listed in *General Instruction B*, and its annual gross receipts are normally more than $25,000, it must file Form 990 or Form

990-EZ. If the organization is a sponsoring organization, or a controlling organization within the meaning of section 512(b)(13), it must file Form 990. However, if the organization is a supporting organization described in section 509(a)(3), it generally must file Form 990 (Form 990-EZ if applicable) even if its gross receipts are normally $25,000, or less. Supporting organizations of religious organizations need not file Form 990 (or Form 990-EZ) if their gross receipts are normally $5,000, or less. See the gross receipts discussion in *General Instruction B*.

If the organization's gross receipts during the year are less than $100,000 and its total assets at the end of the year are less than $250,000, it may file Form 990-EZ instead of Form 990. Even if the organization meets this test, it can still file Form 990.

Organizations required to file Schedule A (Form 990 or 990-EZ), Organization Exempt Under Section 501(c)(3), that do not meet the support tests discussed in the instructions for Part IV of that schedule can contact the IRS at the following address to re-evaluate their determination-of-filing requirements.

Internal Revenue Service
TE/GE EO Determinations
P.O. Box 2508
Cincinnati, OH 45201

Section 501(a), (e), (f), (k), and (n) Organizations

Except for those types of organizations listed in *General Instruction B*, an annual return on Form 990, or Form 990-EZ, is required from every organization exempt from tax under section 501(a), including foreign organizations and cooperative service organizations described in sections 501(e) and (f); child care organizations described in section 501(k); and charitable risk pools described in section 501(n).

Section 501(c)(3), 501(e), (f), (k), and (n) organizations must also attach a completed Schedule A (Form 990 or 990-EZ) to their Form 990 or Form 990-EZ.

 For purposes of these instructions, the term section 501(c)(3) includes organizations exempt under sections 501(e), (f), (k), and (n).

Section 501(c)(15) Organizations

A section 501(c)(15) organization applies the same gross receipts test as other organizations to determine whether they must file the Form 990 or

Form 990-EZ. However, section 501(c)(15) insurance companies are also subject to separate tests to determine whether they qualify as tax-exempt for the tax year. The following tests use a specific definition for gross receipts defined, below only for purposes of the following tests. Insurance companies that do not qualify as tax-exempt must file Form 1120-PC, U.S. Property and Casualty Insurance Company Income Tax Return, or Form 1120, U.S. Corporation Income Tax Return, as taxable entities. See Notice 2006-42, which is on page 878 of the Internal Revenue Bulletin 2006-19 at *www.irs.gov/pub/irs-irbs/irb06-19.pdf*.

Tests for section 501(c)(15) insurance companies to qualify as tax-exempt for the tax year. If any section 501(c)(15) insurance company (other than life insurance) normally has gross receipts of more than $25,000 for the tax year and meets both parts of the following test, then the company can file Form 990 (or Form 990-EZ, if applicable).

1. The company's gross receipts must be equal to or less than $600,000, and

2. The company's premiums must be more than 50% of its gross receipts.

If the company did not meet this test and the company is a mutual insurance company, then it must meet the *Alternate test* to qualify to file Form 990 (or Form 990-EZ, if applicable). Otherwise, the company must file Form 1120 or Form 1120-PC, as appropriate.

Alternate test. If any section 501(c)(15) insurance company (other than life insurance) is a mutual insurance company and it did not meet the above test, then the company must meet both parts of the following alternate test.

1. The company's gross receipts must be equal to or less than $150,000, and

2. The company's premiums must be more than 35% of its gross receipts.

If the company does not meet either test, then it must file Form 1120-PC or Form 1120 (if the company is not entitled to insurance reserves) instead of Form 990 or Form 990-EZ.

 The alternate test does not apply if any employee of the mutual insurance company or a member of the employee's family is an employee of another company that is exempt under section 501(c)(15)(or would be exempt if this provision did not apply).

Gross receipts. To determine whether a section 501(c)(15) organization satisfies either of the above tests, figure gross receipts by adding (1) premiums (including deposits and assessments) without reduction for return premiums or premiums paid for reinsurance; (2) gross investment income of a non-life insurance company (as described in section 834(b)); and (3) other items that are included in the filer's gross income under Subchapter B, Chapter 1, Subtitle A of the Code. This definition does not, however, include contributions to capital. For more information, see *Notice 2006-42*, which is on page 878 of the Internal Revenue Bulletin 2006-19 at *www.irs.gov/pub/irs-irbs/irb06-19.pdf*.

Premiums consist of all amounts received as a result of entering into an insurance contract. For information about the reporting of premiums, see the instructions for Form 990 Part I, line 2.

Anti-abuse rule. The anti-abuse rule, found in section 501(c)(15)(C), explains how gross receipts (including premiums) from all members of a controlled group are aggregated in figuring the above tests.

Political Organizations
Tax-exempt political organizations must file Form 990 or Form 990-EZ (if applicable) unless the organization is excepted from filing under *Exemption 14* or *15* of *General Instruction B.* A qualified state or local political organization (defined below) must file Form 990 (not Form 990-EZ) only if it has gross receipts of $100,000 or more.

Qualified state or local political organizations. A qualified political organization meets all of the following requirements.

1. The organization's exempt functions are solely for the purpose of influencing or attempting to influence the selection, nomination, election, or appointment of any individual to any state or local public office or office in a state or local political organization.
2. The organization is subject to state law that requires it to report the information that is similar to that required on Form 8872.
3. The organization files the required reports with the state.
4. The state makes such reports public and the organization makes them open to public inspection in the same manner that organizations must make Form 8872 available for public inspection.

For additional information, including the prohibition of involvement in the organization of a federal candidate or office holder, see section 527(e)(5).

Disregarded Entities
A disregarded entity, as described in Regulations sections 301.7701-1 through 301.7701-3, is treated as a branch or division of its parent organization for federal tax purposes. Therefore, financial and other information applicable to a disregarded entity must be reported as the parent organization's information.

Section 4947(a)(1) Nonexempt Charitable Trusts
Any nonexempt charitable trust (described in section 4947(a)(1)) not treated as a private foundation is also required to file Form 990, or Form 990-EZ, along with a completed Schedule A (Form 990 or 990-EZ). See the discussion in *General Instruction D* for exceptions to filing Form 1041, U.S. Income Tax Return for Estates and Trusts.

If an Organization's Exemption Application Is Pending
If the organization's application for exemption is pending, check the *Application pending* box in the heading of the return and complete the return.

Organizations That Filed a Return in the Prior Year but Are Not Required To File in the Current Year
Organizations that previously filed Form 990 or Form 990-EZ and meet exemption 15 under *General Instruction B* do not have to file a return.

Exempt organizations that filed Form 990, or Form 990-EZ, but are no longer required to file because they meet a specific exemption (other than exemption 15 in *General Instruction B*) must advise their IRS area office so their filing status can be updated.

Exempt organizations that are not sure of their area office may call the IRS at 1-877-829-5500. Exempt organizations that stop filing Form 990, or Form 990-EZ, without notifying their area office may receive service center correspondence inquiring about their returns. When responding to these inquiries, these organizations must give the specific reason for not filing.

Failure To File and Its Effect on Contributions
Organizations that are eligible to receive tax deductible contributions are listed in Publication 78, Cumulative List of Organizations described in Section 170(c) of the Internal Revenue Code of 1986. An organization may be removed from this listing if our records show that it is required to file Form 990, or Form 990-EZ, but it does not file a return or advises us that it is no longer required to file. However, contributions to such

an organization may continue to be deductible by the general public until the IRS publishes a notice to the contrary in the Internal Revenue Bulletin.

B. Organizations Not Required To File Form 990 or 990-EZ

 Organizations not required to file Form 990, or Form 990-EZ with the IRS may wish to use it to satisfy state reporting requirements. For details, see General Instruction E.

The following types of organizations exempt from tax under section 501(a) (section 527 for political organizations) do not have to file Form 990, or Form 990-EZ, with the IRS. However, if the organization chooses to file a Form 990 or Form 990-EZ, it must also attach the schedules and statements described in the instructions for these forms. In addition, an organization not required to file Form 990 or 990-EZ because it meets exceptions 12, 15, or 16 must file *new* Form 990-N, Electronic Notice (e-Postcard) for Tax-Exempt Organizations Not Required To File Form 990 or 990-EZ.

1. A church, an interchurch organization of local units of a church, a convention or association of churches, an integrated auxiliary of a church (such as a men's or women's organization, religious school, mission society, or youth group).
2. A church-affiliated organization that is exclusively engaged in managing funds or maintaining retirement programs and is described in Rev. Proc. 96-10, 1996-1 C.B. 577.
3. A school below college level affiliated with a church or operated by a religious order.
4. A mission society sponsored by, or affiliated with, one or more churches or church denominations, if more than half of the society's activities are conducted in, or directed at, persons in foreign countries.
5. An exclusively religious activity of any religious order.
6. A state institution whose income is excluded from gross income under section 115.
7. An organization described in section 501(c)(1). A section 501(c)(1) organization is a corporation organized under an Act of Congress that is:
   • An instrumentality of the United States, and
   • Exempt from federal income taxes.
8. A private foundation exempt under section 501(c)(3) and described in section 509(a). Use Form 990-PF, Return of Private Foundation.

9. A black lung benefit trust described in section 501(c)(21). Use Form 990-BL, Information and Initial Excise Tax Return for Black Lung Benefit Trusts and Certain Related Persons.

10. A stock bonus, pension, or profit-sharing trust that qualifies under section 401. Use Form 5500, Annual Return/Report of Employee Benefit Plan.

11. A religious or apostolic organization described in section 501(d). Use Form 1065, U.S. Return of Partnership Income.

12. A foreign organization whose annual gross receipts from sources within the U.S. are normally $25,000 or less (Rev. Proc. 94-17, 1994-1 C.B. 579). See the *$25,000 Gross Receipts Test* below.

13. A governmental unit or affiliate of a governmental unit described in Rev. Proc. 95-48, 1995-2 C.B. 418.

14. A political organization that is:
   - A state or local committee of a political party;
   - A political committee of a state or local candidate;
   - A caucus or association of state or local officials;
   - An authorized committee (as defined in section 301(6) of the Federal Election Campaign Act of 1971) of a candidate for federal office;
   - A national committee (as defined in section 301(14) of the Federal Election Campaign Act of 1971) of a political party;
   - A United States House of Representatives or United States Senate campaign committee of a political party committee;
   - Required to report under the Federal Election Campaign Act of 1971 as a political committee (as defined in section 301(4) of such Act); or
   - An organization described under section 6033(g)(3)(G).

15. Except for supporting organizations described in section 509(a)(3), an organization whose gross receipts are normally $25,000 or less.

16. A section 509(a)(3) supporting organization of a religious organization, if the supporting organization's gross receipts are normally $5,000 or less.

How to Determine If an Organization's Gross Receipts are Normally $25,000 (or $5,000) or Less

To figure whether an organization has to file Form 990-EZ (or Form 990) apply the $25,000 (or $5,000) gross receipts test (below) using the following definition of gross receipts and information in *Figuring Gross Receipts* below.

Gross Receipts

 Do not use the definition of gross receipts described in General Instruction A, *under* Section 501(c)(15) Organizations *to figure gross receipts.*

Gross receipts are the total amounts the organization received from all sources during its annual accounting period, without subtracting any costs or expenses.

Gross receipts when acting as an agent. If a local chapter of a section 501(c)(8) fraternal organization collects insurance premiums for its parent lodge and merely sends those premiums to the parent without asserting any right to use the funds or otherwise deriving any benefit from collecting them, the local chapter does not include the premiums in its gross receipts. The parent lodge reports them instead. The same treatment applies in other situations in which one organization collects funds merely as an agent for another.

Figuring Gross Receipts

Figure gross receipts for Form 990 and Form 990-EZ as follows.

Form 990. Gross receipts are the sum of lines 1e, 2, 3, 4, 5, 6a, 7, 8a (both columns), 9a, 10a, and 11 of Part I. Gross receipts can also be figured by adding back the amounts on lines 6b, 8b (both columns), 9b, and 10b to the total revenue reported on line 12.

Form 990-EZ. Gross receipts are the sum of lines 1, 2, 3, 4, 5a, 6a, 7a, and 8 of Part I. Gross receipts can also be figured by adding back the amounts on lines 5b, 6b, and 7b to the total revenue reported on line 9.

Example. Organization M reported $50,000 as total revenue on line 9 of its Form 990-EZ. M added back the costs and expenses it had deducted on lines 5b ($2,000); 6b ($1,500); and 7b ($500) to its total revenue of $50,000 and determined that its gross receipts for the tax year were $54,000.

$25,000 Gross Receipts Test

To determine if an organization's gross receipts are normally $25,000 or less, apply the following test. An organization's gross receipts normally are considered to be $25,000 or less if the organization is:

1. Up to a year old and has received, or donors have pledged to give, $37,500 or less during its first tax year;

2. Between 1 and 3 years old and averaged $30,000 or less in gross receipts during each of its first 2 tax years; or

3. Three years old or more and averaged $25,000 or less in gross receipts for the immediately preceding 3 tax years (including the year in which the return would be filed).

$5,000 Gross Receipts Test

To determine if an organization's gross receipts are normally $5,000 or less, apply the following test. An organization's gross receipts normally are considered to be $5,000 or less if the organization is:

1. Up to a year old and has received, or donors have pledged to give, $7,500 or less during its first tax year;

2. Between 1 and 3 years old and averaged $6,000 or less in gross receipts during each of its first 2 tax years; or

3. Three years old or more and averaged $5,000 or less in gross receipts for the immediately preceding 3 tax years (including the year in which the return would be filed).

C. Exempt Organization Reference Chart

 To determine how the instructions for Form 990 and Form 990-EZ apply to the organization, you must know the Code section under which the organization is exempt.

Type of Organization	I.R.C. Section
Corporations Organized Under Act of Congress	501(c)(1)
Title Holding Corporations	501(c)(2)
Charitable, Religious, Educational, Scientific, etc., Organizations	501(c)(3)
Civic Leagues and Social Welfare Organizations	501(c)(4)
Labor, Agricultural, and Horticultural Organizations	501(c)(5)
Business Leagues, etc.	501(c)(6)
Social and Recreation Clubs	501(c)(7)
Fraternal Beneficiary and Domestic Fraternal Societies and Associations	501(c)(8) & (10)
Voluntary Employees' Beneficiary Associations	501(c)(9)
Teachers' Retirement Fund Associations	501(c)(11)
Benevolent Life Insurance Associations, Mutual Ditch or Irrigation Companies, Mutual or Cooperative Telephone Companies, etc.	501(c)(12)
Cemetery Companies	501(c)(13)
State Chartered Credit Unions, Mutual Reserve Funds	501(c)(14)
Insurance Companies or Associations Other Than Life	501(c)(15)
Cooperative Organizations To Finance Crop Operations	501(c)(16)
Supplemental Unemployment Benefit Trusts	501(c)(17)
Employee Funded Pension Trusts (created before 6/25/59)	501(c)(18)

D. Forms and Publications

Internet. You can access the IRS website 24 hours a day, 7 days a week, at *www.irs.gov* to:
• Download forms, instructions, and publications.
• Order IRS products online.
• Research your tax questions online.
• Search publications online by topic or keyword.
• View Internal Revenue Bulletins (IRBs) published in the last few years.
• Sign up to receive local and national tax news by email.

CD for tax products. You can order Publication 1796, IRS Tax Products CD, and obtain:
• A CD that is released twice so you have the latest products. The first release ships in late December and the final release ships in late February.
• Current-year forms, instructions, and publications.
• Prior-year forms, instructions, and publications.
• Tax Map: an electronic research tool and finding aid.
• Tax law frequently asked questions (FAQs).
• Tax Topics from the IRS telephone response system.
• Fill-in, print, and save features for most tax forms.
• Internal Revenue Bulletins.
• Toll-free and email technical support.

Buy the CD from National Technical Information Service (NTIS) at *www.irs.gov/cdorders* for $35 (no handling fee) or call 1-877-233-6767 toll free to buy the CD for $35 (plus a $5 handling fee).

By phone and in person. You can order forms and publications by calling 1-800-TAX-FORM (1-800-829-3676). You can also get most forms and publications at your local IRS office.

Other Forms That May Be Required

Schedule A (Form 990 or 990-EZ). Organization Exempt Under Section 501(c)(3) (Except Private Foundation) and Section 501(e), 501(f), 501(k), 501(n), or Section 4947(a)(1), Nonexempt Charitable Trust. An organization is not required to file Schedule A (Form 990 or 990-EZ) if its gross receipts are normally $25,000 or less. See the gross receipts discussion in *General Instruction B.*

Schedule B (Form 990, 990-EZ, or 990-PF). Schedule of Contributors. Schedule B (Form 990, 990-EZ, or 990-PF) provides contributor information for line 1 of Form 990 and 990-EZ. All Form 990 and 990-EZ filers must complete and attach this schedule to their return unless they meet an exception, and check the box in item M of Form 990 (item H on Form 990-EZ).

Forms W-2 and W-3. Wage and Tax Statement; and Transmittal of Wage and Tax Statements.

Form W-9. Request for Taxpayer Identification Number and Certification.

Form 940. Employer's Annual Federal Unemployment (FUTA) Tax Return.

Form 941. Employer's QUARTERLY Federal Tax Return. Used to report social security, Medicare, and income taxes withheld by an employer and social security and Medicare taxes paid by an employer.

Form 943. Employer's Annual Federal Tax Return for Agricultural Employees.

Trust Fund Recovery Penalty. If certain excise, income, social security, and Medicare taxes that must be collected or withheld are not collected or withheld, or these taxes are not paid to the IRS, a Trust Fund Recovery Penalty may apply. The Trust Fund Recovery Penalty may be imposed on all persons (including volunteers) who the IRS determines were responsible for collecting, accounting for, and paying over these taxes, and who acted willfully in not doing so.

This penalty does not apply to volunteer unpaid members of any board of trustees or directors of a tax-exempt organization, if these members are solely serving in an honorary capacity, do not participate in the day-to-day financial activities of the organization, and do not have actual knowledge of the failure to collect, account for, and pay over these taxes. However, the preceding sentence does not apply if it results in no person being liable for the penalty.

The penalty is equal to the unpaid trust fund tax. See Pub. 15 (Circular E), Employer's Tax Guide, for more details,

including the definition of responsible persons.

Form 990-T. Exempt Organization Business Income Tax Return (and proxy tax under section 6033(e)). Filed separately for organizations with gross income of $1,000 or more from business unrelated to the organization's exempt purpose. The Form 990-T is also filed to pay the section 6033(e)(2) proxy tax. For Form 990, see line 85 and its instructions; for Form 990-EZ, see line 35 and its instructions.

Form 990-W. Estimated Tax on Unrelated Business Taxable Income for Tax-Exempt Organizations.

Form 1040. U.S. Individual Income Tax Return.

Form 1041. U.S. Income Tax Return for Estates and Trusts. Required of section 4947(a)(1) nonexempt charitable trusts that also file Form 990 or Form 990-EZ. However, if such a trust does not have any taxable income under Subtitle A of the Code, it can file Form 990, or Form 990-EZ, and does not have to file Form 1041 to meet its section 6012 filing requirement. If this condition is met, complete Form 990, or Form 990-EZ, and do not file Form 1041.

A section 4947(a)(1) nonexempt charitable trust that normally has gross receipts of not more than $25,000 (see the gross receipts discussion in *General Instruction B*) and has no taxable income under Subtitle A must complete line 92 and the signature block on page 9 of the Form 990. On the Form 990-EZ, complete line 43 and the signature block on page 3 of the return. In addition, complete only the following items in the heading of Form 990 or Form 990-EZ:

Item	
A	Tax year (fiscal year or short period, if applicable)
B	Applicable checkboxes
C	Name and address
D	Employer identification number (EIN)
J	Section 4947(a)(1) nonexempt charitable trust box

Form 1096. Annual Summary and Transmittal of U.S. Information Returns.

Form 1098 series. Information returns to report mortgage interest, student loan interest, qualified tuition and related expenses received, and a contribution of a qualified vehicle that has a claimed value of more than $500.

Form 1099 series. Information returns to report acquisitions or abandonments of secured property, proceeds from broker and barter exchange transactions, cancellation of debt, dividends and distributions, certain government and state qualified tuition program payments, taxable distributions from cooperatives, interest payments, payments of long-term care and accelerated death benefits, miscellaneous income payments, distributions from an HSA, Archer MSA or Medicare Advantage MSA, original issue discount, distributions from pensions, annuities, retirement or profit-sharing plans, IRAs, insurance contracts, etc., and proceeds from real estate transactions. Also, use certain of these returns to report amounts that were received as a nominee on behalf of another person.

Form 1120-POL. U.S. Income Tax Return for Certain Political Organizations.

Form 1128. Application To Adopt, Change, or Retain a Tax Year.

Form 3115. Application for Change in Accounting Method.

Form 4506. Request for Copy of Tax Return.

Form 4506-A. Request for Public Inspection or Copy of Exempt or Political Organization IRS Form.

Form 4562. Depreciation and Amortization.

Form 4720. Return of Certain Excise Taxes Under Chapters 41 and 42 of the Internal Revenue Code.

Form 5500. Annual Return/Report of Employee Benefit Plan. Employers who maintain pension, profit-sharing, or other funded deferred compensation plans are generally required to file the Form 5500. This requirement applies whether or not the plan is qualified under the Internal Revenue Code and whether or not a deduction is claimed for the current tax year.

Form 5768. Election/Revocation of Election by an Eligible Section 501(c)(3) Organization To Make Expenditures To Influence Legislation.

Form 8282. Donee Information Return. Required of the donee of charitable deduction property who sells, exchanges, or otherwise disposes of donated property within 3 years after receiving it. The form is also required of any successor donee who disposes of charitable deduction property within 3 years after the date that the donor gave the property to the original donee. It does not matter who gave the property to the successor donee. It may have been the original donee or another successor donee.

Form 8283. Noncash Charitable Contributions.

Form 8300. Report of Cash Payments Over $10,000 Received in a Trade or Business. Used to report cash amounts in excess of $10,000 that were received in a single transaction (or in two or more related transactions) in the course of a trade or business (as defined in section 162).

However, if the organization receives a charitable cash contribution in excess of $10,000, it is not subject to the reporting requirement since the funds were not received in the course of a trade or business.

Form 8822. Change of Address. Used to notify the IRS of a change in mailing address that occurs after the return is filed.

Form 8868. Application for Extension of Time To File an Exempt Organization Return.

Form 8870. Information Return for Transfers Associated With Certain Personal Benefit Contracts. Used to identify those personal benefit contracts for which funds were transferred to the organization, directly or indirectly, as well as the transferors for, and beneficiaries of, those contracts.

Form 8871. Political Organization Notice of Section 527 Status.

Form 8872. Political Organization Report of Contributions and Expenditures.

Form 8886-T. Disclosure by Tax-Exempt Entity Regarding Prohibited Tax Shelter Transaction.

Form 8899. Notice of Income from Donated Intellectual Property. Used to report net income from qualified intellectual property to the IRS and the donor.

Form 8921. Applicable Insurance Contracts Information Return.

Form TD F 90-22.1. Report of Foreign Bank and Financial Accounts.

Helpful Publications

Publication 463. Travel, Entertainment, Gift, and Car Expenses.

Publication 525. Taxable and Nontaxable Income.

Publication 526. Charitable Contributions.

Publication 538. Accounting Periods and Methods.

Publication 598. Tax on Unrelated Business Income of Exempt Organizations.

Publication 910. IRS Guide to Free Tax Services.

Publication 946. How To Depreciate Property.

Publication 1771. Charitable Contributions—Substantiation and Disclosure Requirements.

E. Use of Form 990, or Form 990-EZ, To Satisfy State Reporting Requirements

Some states and local government units will accept a copy of Form 990, or Form 990-EZ, Schedule A (Form 990 or 990-EZ), and Schedule B (Form 990,

990-EZ, or 990-PF) in place of all or part of their own financial report forms. The substitution applies primarily to section 501(c)(3) organizations, but some of the other types of section 501(c) organizations are also affected.

If the organization uses Form 990, or Form 990-EZ, to satisfy state or local filing requirements, such as those under state charitable solicitation acts, note the following discussions.

Determine State Filing Requirements

The organization may consult the appropriate officials of all states and other jurisdictions in which it does business to determine their specific filing requirements. Doing business in a jurisdiction may include any of the following: (a) soliciting contributions or grants by mail or otherwise from individuals, businesses, or other charitable organizations; (b) conducting programs; (c) having employees within that jurisdiction; (d) maintaining a checking account; or (e) owning or renting property there.

Monetary Tests May Differ

Some or all of the dollar limitations applicable to Form 990, or Form 990-EZ, when filed with the IRS may not apply when using Form 990, or Form 990-EZ, in place of state or local report forms. Examples of the IRS dollar limitations that do not meet some state requirements are the $25,000 gross receipts minimum that creates an obligation to file with the IRS (see the gross receipts discussion in *General Instruction B)* and the $50,000 minimum for listing professional fees in Part II-A of Schedule A (Form 990 or 990-EZ).

Additional Information May Be Required

State or local filing requirements may require the organization to attach to Form 990, or Form 990-EZ, one or more of the following: (a) additional financial statements, such as a complete analysis of functional expenses or a statement of changes in net assets; (b) notes to financial statements; (c) additional financial schedules; (d) a report on the financial statements by an independent accountant; and (e) answers to additional questions and other information. Each jurisdiction may require the additional material to be presented on forms they provide. The additional information does not have to be submitted with the Form 990, or Form 990-EZ, filed with the IRS.

Even if the Form 990, or Form 990-EZ, that the organization files with the IRS is accepted by the IRS as complete, a copy of the same return filed with a state will not fully satisfy that state's filing requirement if required information is not provided, including any of the additional information discussed above, or if the state determines that the form was not completed by following the applicable Form 990, or Form 990-EZ, instructions or supplemental state instructions. If so, the organization may be asked to provide the missing information or to submit an amended return.

Use Of Audit Guides May Be Required

To ensure that all organizations report similar transactions uniformly, many states require that contributions, gifts, grants, etc., and functional expenses be reported according to the AICPA industry audit and accounting guide, Not-for-Profit Organizations (New York, NY, AICPA, 2003), supplemented by Standards of Accounting and Financial Reporting for Voluntary Health and Welfare Organizations (Washington, DC, National Health Council, Inc., 1998, 4th edition).

Donated Services and Facilities

Even though reporting donated services and facilities as items of revenue and expense is called for in certain circumstances by the two publications named above, many states and the IRS do not permit the inclusion of those amounts in Parts I and II of Form 990 or Part I of Form 990-EZ. The optional reporting of donated services and facilities is discussed in the instructions for Part III for both Form 990 and Form 990-EZ.

Amended Returns

If the organization submits supplemental information or files an amended Form 990, or Form 990-EZ, with the IRS, it must also send a copy of the information or amended return to any state with which it filed a copy of Form 990, or Form 990-EZ, originally to meet that state's filing requirement.

If a state requires the organization to file an amended Form 990, or Form 990-EZ, to correct conflicts with Form 990, or Form 990-EZ, instructions, it must also file an amended return with the IRS.

Method of Accounting

Most states require that all amounts be reported based on the accrual method of accounting. See also General Instruction G.

Time For Filing May Differ

The deadline for filing Form 990, or Form 990-EZ, with the IRS differs from the time for filing reports with some states.

Public Inspection

The Form 990, or Form 990-EZ, information made available for public inspection by the IRS may differ from that made available by the states. See the discussion of Schedule B (Form 990, 990-EZ, or 990-PF) in General Instruction L.

F. Other Forms as Partial Substitutes for Form 990 or Form 990-EZ

Except as provided below, the Internal Revenue Service will not accept any form as a substitute for one or more parts of Form 990 or Form 990-EZ.

Labor Organizations (Section 501(c)(5))

A labor organization that files Form LM-2, Labor Organization Annual Report, or the shorter Form LM-3, Labor Organization Annual Report, with the U.S. Department of Labor (DOL) can attach a copy of the completed DOL form to Form 990, or Form 990-EZ, to provide some of the information required by Form 990 or Form 990-EZ. This substitution is not permitted if the organization files a DOL report that consolidates its financial statements with those of one or more separate subsidiary organizations.

Employee Benefit Plans (Section 501(c)(9), (17), or (18))

An employee benefit plan may be able to substitute Form 5500 for part of Form 990 or Form 990-EZ. The substitution can be made if the organization filing Form 990, or Form 990-EZ, and the plan filing Form 5500, meet all the following tests:

1. The Form 990, or Form 990-EZ, filer is organized under section 501(c)(9), (17), or (18);
2. The Form 990, or Form 990-EZ, filer and Form 5500 filer are identical for financial reporting purposes and have identical receipts, disbursements, assets, liabilities, and equity accounts;
3. The employee benefit plan does not include more than one section 501(c) organization, and the section 501(c) organization is not a part of more than one employee benefit plan;
4. The organization's accounting year and the employee plan year are the same. If they are not, the organization may want to change its accounting year, as explained in General Instruction G, so it will coincide with the plan year.

Allowable Substitution Areas

Whether an organization files Form 990, or Form 990-EZ, for a labor organization or for an employee benefit plan, the areas of Form 990, or Form

990-EZ, for which other forms can be substituted are the same. These areas are:

Form 990.
● Lines 13 through 15 of Part I (but complete lines 16 through 21);
● Part II; and
● Part IV (but complete lines 59, 66, and 74, columns (A) and (B)).

Form 990-EZ.
● Lines 10 through 16 of Part I (but complete lines 17 through 21).
● Part II (but complete lines 25 through 27, columns (A) and (B)).

If an organization substitutes Form LM-2 or LM-3 for any of the Form 990, or Form 990-EZ, parts or line items mentioned above, it must attach a reconciliation sheet to show the relationship between the amounts on the DOL forms and the amounts on Form 990 or Form 990-EZ. This is particularly true of the relationship of disbursements shown on the DOL forms and the total expenses on line 17, Part I, of both Form 990 and Form 990-EZ. The organization must make this reconciliation because the cash disbursements section of the DOL forms includes nonexpense items. If the organization substitutes Form LM-2, be sure to complete its separate schedule of expenses.

G. Accounting Periods and Methods

 For more information about these topics, see Pub. 538.

Accounting Periods

Calendar year. Use the 2007 Form 990, or Form 990-EZ, to report on the 2007 calendar year accounting period. A calendar year accounting period begins on January 1 and ends on December 31.

Fiscal year. If the organization has established a fiscal year accounting period, use the 2007 Form 990, or Form 990-EZ, to report on the organization's fiscal year that began in 2007 and ended 12 months later. A fiscal year accounting period normally coincides with the natural operating cycle of the organization. Be certain to indicate in the heading of Form 990, or Form 990-EZ, the date the organization's fiscal year began in 2007 and the date the fiscal year ended in 2008.

Short period. A short accounting period is a period of less than 12 months.

If the Form 990, or Form 990-EZ, for the short year is not available until the subsequent year, use the prior year

Form 990, or Form 990-EZ, to meet the organization's filing requirement. Cross out the year on the form and show the short year.

Accounting period change. If the organization changes its accounting period, it must file a return on Form 990, or Form 990-EZ, for the short period resulting from the change. Write "Change of Accounting Period" at the top of this short-period return.

If the organization changed its accounting period within the 10-calendar-year period that includes the beginning of the short period, and it had a Form 990, or Form 990-EZ, filing requirement at any time during that 10-year period, it must also attach a Form 1128 to the short-period return. See Rev. Proc. 85-58, 1985-2 C.B. 740.

Group return. When affiliated organizations authorize their central organization to file a group return for them, the accounting period of the affiliated organizations and the central organization must be the same. See *General Instruction R.*

Accounting Methods

Unless instructed otherwise, the organization should generally use the same accounting method on the return to figure revenue and expenses as it regularly uses to keep its books and records. To be acceptable for Form 990, or Form 990-EZ, reporting purposes, however, the method of accounting used must clearly reflect income.

Generally, the organization must file Form 3115 to change its accounting method. Notice 96-30, 1996-1 C.B. 378, provides relief from filing Form 3115 to section 501(c) organizations that change their method of accounting to comply with the provisions of SFAS 116, Accounting for Contributions Received and Contributions Made. In SFAS 116, the Financial Accounting Standards Board revised certain generally accepted accounting principles relating to contributions received and contributions awarded by not-for-profit organizations.

A not-for-profit organization that changes its method of accounting for federal income tax purposes to conform to the method provided in SFAS 116 must report any adjustment required by section 481(a) on line 20 of Form 990, or Form 990-EZ, as a net asset adjustment made during the year the change is made. The adjustment must be identified as the effect of changing to the method provided in SFAS 116. The beginning of year statement of financial position (balance sheet) should not be restated to reflect any prior period adjustments.

State reporting. If the organization prepares Form 990, or Form 990-EZ, for state reporting purposes, it may file an identical return with the IRS even though the return does not agree with the books of account, unless the way one or more items are reported on the state return conflicts with the instructions for preparing Form 990, or Form 990-EZ, for filing with the IRS.

Example 1. The organization maintains its books on the cash receipts and disbursements method of accounting but prepares a state return based on the accrual method. It could use that return for reporting to the IRS.

Example 2. A state reporting requirement requires the organization to report certain revenue, expense, or balance sheet items differently from the way it normally accounts for them on its books. A Form 990, or Form 990-EZ, prepared for that state is acceptable for the IRS reporting purposes if the state reporting requirement does not conflict with the Form 990, or Form 990-EZ, instructions.

An organization should keep a reconciliation of any differences between its books of account and the Form 990, or Form 990-EZ, that is filed.

Most states that accept Form 990, or Form 990-EZ, in place of their own forms require that all amounts be reported based on the accrual method of accounting. For further information, see *General Instruction E.*

H. When, Where, and How To File

File Form 990, or Form 990-EZ, by the 15th day of the 5th month after the organization's accounting period ends. If the regular due date falls on a Saturday, Sunday, or legal holiday, file on the next business day. A business day is any day that is not a Saturday, Sunday, or legal holiday.

If the organization is liquidated, dissolved, or terminated, file the return by the 15th day of the 5th month after the liquidation, dissolution, or termination.

If the return is not filed by the due date (including any extension granted), attach a statement giving the reasons for not filing on time. Send the return to the:

> Department of the Treasury
> Internal Revenue Service Center
> Ogden, UT 84201-0027

Private delivery services. The organization can use certain private delivery services designated by the IRS to meet the "timely mailing as timely filing/paying" rule for tax returns and payments. These private delivery services include only the following.

• DHL Express (DHL): DHL "Same Day" Service, DHL Next Day 10:30 AM, DHL Next Day 12:00 PM, DHL Next Day 3:00 PM, and DHL 2nd Day Service.
• Federal Express (FedEx): FedEx Priority Overnight, FedEx Standard Overnight, FedEx 2Day, FedEx International Priority, FedEx International First.
• United Parcel Service (UPS): UPS Next Day Air, UPS Next Day Air Saver, UPS 2nd Day Air, UPS 2nd Day Air A.M., UPS Worldwide Express Plus, and UPS Worldwide Express.

The private delivery service can tell you how to get written proof of the mailing date.

Electronic Filing

The organization can file Form 990, or Form 990-EZ, and related forms, schedules, and attachments electronically. However, if an organization files at least 250 returns during the calendar year and has total assets of $10 million or more at the end of the tax year, it must file Form 990 electronically.

To determine if the organization meets the $10 million asset test, use the amount that will be entered on line 59 (total assets), column (B).

If an organization is required to file a return electronically but does not, the organization is considered to have not filed its return. See Temporary Regulations section 301.6033-4T for more information.

For additional information on the electronic filing requirement, visit *www. irs.gov/efile.*

TIP *The IRS may waive the requirements to file electronically in cases of undue hardship. For information on filing a waiver, see Notice 2005-88, which is on page 1060 of the Internal Revenue Bulletin 2005-48 at* www.irs.gov/pub/ irs-irbs/irb05-48.pdf.

I. Extension of Time To File

Use Form 8868 to request an automatic 3-month extension of time to file. Use Form 8868 also to apply for an additional (not automatic) 3-month extension if the original 3 months was not enough time. To obtain this additional extension of time to file, the organization must show reasonable cause for the additional time requested. See the Instructions for Form 8868.

J. Amended Return/Final Return

To change the organization's return for any year, file a new return including any required attachments. Use the revision of Form 990, or Form 990-EZ, applicable to the year being amended. The amended return must provide all the information called for by the form and instructions, not just the new or corrected information. Check the *Amended return* box in the heading of the return.

The organization may file an amended return at any time to change or add to the information reported on a previously filed return for the same period. It must make the amended return available for public inspection for 3 years from the date of filing or 3 years from the date the original return was due, whichever is later.

The organization must also send a copy of the information or amended return to any state with which it filed a copy of Form 990, or Form 990-EZ, originally to meet that state's filing requirement.

Use Form 4506 to obtain a copy of a previously filed return. For information on getting blank tax forms, see *General Instruction D.*

If the return is a final return, see the *Specific Instructions* for Form 990 for line 79, Part VI. For Form 990-EZ, see the *Specific Instructions* for line 36, Part V.

K. Failure to File Penalties

Against the Organization

Under section 6652(c)(1)(A), a penalty of $20 a day, not to exceed the smaller of $10,000 or 5% of the gross receipts of the organization for the year, may be charged when a return is filed late, unless the organization can show that the late filing was due to reasonable cause. Organizations with annual gross receipts exceeding $1 million are subject to a penalty of $100 for each day the failure continues (with a maximum penalty with respect to any one return of $50,000). The penalty begins on the due date for filing the Form 990 or Form 990-EZ.

Use of a paid preparer does not relieve the organization of its responsibility to file a complete and accurate return.

Incomplete return. The penalty may also be charged if the organization files an incomplete return. To avoid having to supply missing information later, be sure to complete all applicable line items; answer "Yes," "No," or "N/A" (not applicable) to each question on the return; make an entry (including a zero when appropriate) on all total lines; and enter "None" or "N/A" if an entire part does not apply.

Incorrect information. This penalty may be imposed if the organization's return contains incorrect information. For example, an organization that reports contributions net of related fundraising expenses may be subject to this penalty.

Against Responsible Person(s)

If the organization does not file a complete return or does not furnish correct information, the IRS will send the organization a letter that includes a fixed time to fulfill these requirements. After that period expires, the person failing to comply will be charged a penalty of $10 a day. The maximum penalty on all persons for failures with respect to any one return shall not exceed $5,000 (section 6652(c)(1)(B)(ii)).

Any person who does not comply with the public inspection requirements, as discussed in *General Instruction M,* will be assessed a penalty of $20 for each day that inspection was not permitted, up to a maximum of $10,000 for each return. The penalties for failure to comply with the public inspection requirements for applications is the same as those for annual returns, except that the $10,000 limitation does not apply (sections 6652(c)(1)(C) and (D)). Any person who willfully fails to comply with the public inspection requirements for annual returns or exemption applications will be subject to an additional penalty of $5,000 (section 6685).

There are also penalties (fines and imprisonment) for willfully not filing returns and for filing fraudulent returns and statements with the IRS (sections 7203, 7206, and 7207). States may impose additional penalties for failure to meet their separate filing requirements. See also the discussion of the *Trust Fund Recovery Penalty*, under *General Instruction D.*

L. Contributions

Schedule B (Form 990, 990-EZ, or 990-PF)

Schedule B (Form 990, 990-EZ, or 990-PF), generally, is a required attachment for the Form 990, 990-EZ, or 990-PF, and is used to report on tax-deductible and non-tax-deductible contributions. See the Instructions for Schedule B for the public inspection rules applicable to that form. See also the Specific Instructions for both Form 990 and Form 990-EZ, under *Completing the Heading . . .* where the instructions are keyed to items in the heading of Form 990 or Form 990-EZ.

Solicitations of Nondeductible Contributions

Any fundraising solicitation by or on behalf of any section 501(c) or 527

organization that is not eligible to receive contributions deductible as charitable contributions for federal income tax purposes must include an explicit statement that contributions or gifts to it are not deductible as charitable contributions. The statement must be in an easily recognizable format whether the solicitation is made in written or printed form, by television or radio, or by telephone. This provision applies only to those organizations whose annual gross receipts are normally more than $100,000 (section 6113 and Notice 88-120, 1988-2 C.B. 454).

Failure to disclose that contributions are not deductible could result in a penalty of $1,000 for each day on which a failure occurs. The maximum penalty for failures by any organization, during any calendar year, shall not exceed $10,000. In cases where the failure to make the disclosure is due to intentional disregard of the law, more severe penalties apply. No penalty will be imposed if the failure is due to reasonable cause (section 6710).

Keeping Fundraising Records for Tax-Deductible Contributions

Section 501(c) organizations that are eligible to receive tax-deductible contributions under section 170(c) of the Code must keep sample copies of their fundraising materials, such as:
- Dues statements,
- Fundraising solicitations,
- Tickets,
- Receipts, or
- Other evidence of payments received in connection with fundraising activities.

IF . . .	THEN . . .
Organizations advertise their fundraising events,	They must keep samples of the advertising copy.
Organizations use radio or television to make their solicitations,	They must keep samples of: • Scripts, • Transcripts, or • Other evidence of on-air solicitations.
Organizations use outside fundraisers,	They must keep samples of the fundraising materials used by the outside fundraisers.

For each fundraising event, organizations must keep records to show the portion of any payment received from patrons that is not deductible; that is, the retail value of the goods or services received by the patrons. See *Disclosure statement for quid pro quo contributions*, later.

Noncash Contributions

See the Instructions for Schedule B (Form 990, 990-EZ, or 990-PF).

If the organization received a partially completed Form 8283 from a donor, complete it and return it so the donor can get a charitable contribution deduction. The organization should keep a copy for its records. See also the reference to Form 8282 in *General Instruction D.*

Qualified intellectual property. An organization described in section 170(c) (except a private foundation) that receives or accrues net income from a qualified intellectual property contribution must file Form 8899. The organization must file the return for any tax year that includes any part of the 10-year period beginning on the date of contribution but not for any tax years in which the legal life of the qualified intellectual property has expired or the property failed to produce net income.

An organization (donee) reports all income from donated qualified intellectual property as income other than contributions (for example, royalty income from a patent). Charities are not required to report as contributions any of the additional deductions claimed by donors under section 170(m)(1). Likewise, these additional deductions are not required to be reported on Schedule B (Form 990, 990-EZ, or 990-PF) and donees are not required to comply with the substantiation requirements of section 170(f)(8) with regard to any donor's additional deductions. See Pub. 526.

Motor vehicles, boats, and airplanes. Special rules apply to charitable contributions of motor vehicles, boats, or airplanes with a claimed value of more than $500. See section 170(f)(12) and the Instructions for Form 1098-C.

Substantiation and Disclosure Requirements for Charitable Contributions

Recordkeeping for cash, check, or other monetary charitable gifts. A donor(s) must maintain a record on any contribution of cash, check, or other monetary gift. This record must be a bank record or a written communication from the donee showing the donee organization's name, date, and amount of the contribution.

Acknowledgment to substantiate charitable contributions. An organization (donee) should be aware that a donor of a charitable contribution of $250 or more cannot take an income tax deduction unless the donor obtains the organization's acknowledgment to substantiate the charitable contribution.

The organization's acknowledgment must:

1. Be written.
2. Be contemporaneous.
3. State the amount of any cash it received.
4. State:
   a. Whether the organization gave the donor any intangible religious benefits (no valuation needed).
   b. Whether or not the organization gave the donor any goods or services in return for the donor's contribution (a *quid pro quo* contribution).
5. Describe goods or services the organization:
   a. Received (no valuation needed).
   b. Gave (good faith estimate needed).

Exception. An organization need not make a good faith estimate of a *quid pro quo* contribution if the goods or services given to a donor are:

• Insubstantial in value.
• Certain membership benefits for $75 or less per year. See *Certain membership benefits,* later.
• Certain goods or services given to the donor's employees or partners.

Disclosure statement for *quid pro quo* contributions. If the organization receives a *quid pro quo* contribution of more than $75, an organization must provide a disclosure statement to the donor. The organization's disclosure statement must:

1. Be written.
2. Estimate in good faith the organization's goods or services given in return for donor's contribution.
3. Describe, but need not value, certain goods or services given donor's employees or partners.
4. Inform the donor that a deductible charitable contribution deduction is limited as follows:

Donor's contribution
Less

Organization's money, and goods or services given in return

Equals

Donor's deductible charitable contribution.

Exception. No disclosure statement is required if the organization gave the following.

1. Goods or services of insubstantial value.
2. Certain membership benefits.
3. An intangible religious benefit.

See Regulations sections 1.170A-1, 1.170A-13, and 1.6115-1.

Certain goods or services disregarded for substantiation and disclosure purposes.

Goods or services with insubstantial value. Generally, under section 170, the deductible amount of a contribution is determined by taking into account the fair market value, not the cost to the charity, of any benefits received in return. However, the cost to the charity may be used in determining whether the benefits are insubstantial. See below.

Cost basis. If a taxpayer makes a payment of $44.50 or more to a charity and receives only token items in return, the items have insubstantial value if they:

• Bear the charity's name or logo, and
• Have an aggregate cost to the charity of $8.90 or less (low-cost article amount of section 513(h)(2)).

Fair market value basis. If a taxpayer makes a payment to a charitable organization in a fundraising campaign and receives only benefits with a fair market value of not more than 2% of the amount of the payment, or $89, whichever is less, the benefits received have insubstantial value in determining the taxpayer's contribution.

 The dollar amounts given above are applicable to tax year 2007 under Rev. Proc. 2006-53 (and other successor documents). They are adjusted annually for inflation.

When a donee organization provides a donor only with goods or services having insubstantial value under Rev. Proc. 2006-53 (and any successor documents), the contemporaneous written acknowledgment may indicate that no goods or services were provided in exchange for the donor's payment.

Certain membership benefits. Other goods or services that are disregarded for substantiation and disclosure purposes are annual membership benefits offered to a taxpayer in exchange for a payment of $75 or less per year that consist of:

1. Any rights or privileges that the taxpayer can exercise frequently during the membership period such as:
   a. Free or discounted admission to the organization's facilities or events,
   b. Free or discounted parking.
2. Admission to events that are:
   a. Open only to members, and are, per person,
   b. Within the low-cost article limitation.

Examples.

1. E offers a basic membership benefits package for $75. The package gives members the right to buy tickets in advance, free parking, and a gift

shop discount of 10%. E's $150 preferred membership benefits package also includes a $20 poster. Both the basic and preferred membership packages are for a 12-month period and include about 50 productions. E offers F, a patron of the arts, the preferred membership benefits in return for a payment of $150 or more. F accepts the preferred membership benefits package for $300. E's written acknowledgment satisfies the substantiation requirement if it describes the poster, gives a good faith estimate of its fair market value ($20), and disregards the remaining membership benefits.

2. If F received only the basic membership package for its $300 payment, E's acknowledgment need state only that no goods or services were provided.

3. G Theater Group performs four plays. Each play is performed twice. Nonmembers can purchase a ticket for $15. For a $60 membership fee, however, members are offered free admission to any of the performances. H makes a payment of $350 and accepts this membership benefit. Because of the limited number of performances, the membership privilege cannot be exercised frequently. Therefore, G's acknowledgment must describe the free admission benefit and estimate its value in good faith.

Certain goods or services provided to donor's employees or partners. Certain goods or services provided to employees or partners of donors may be disregarded for substantiation and disclosure purposes. Describe such goods or services. A good faith estimate is not needed.

Example. Museum J offers a basic membership benefits package for $40. It includes free admission and a 10% gift shop discount. Corporation K makes a $50,000 payment to J and in return, J offers K's employees free admission, a tee shirt with J's logo that costs J $4.50, and a 25% gift shop discount. Because the free admission is offered in both benefit packages and the value of the tee shirts is insubstantial, K's written acknowledgment need not value the free admission benefit or the tee shirts. However, because the 25% gift shop discount to K's employees differs from the 10% discount offered in the basic membership benefits package, K's written acknowledgment must describe the 25% discount, but need not estimate its value.

Definitions.

Substantiation. It is the responsibility of the donor:
• To value a donation, and

• To obtain an organization's written acknowledgment substantiating the donation.

There is no prescribed format for the organization's written acknowledgment of a donation. Letters, postcards, or computer-generated forms may be acceptable. The acknowledgment must, however, provide sufficient information to substantiate the amount of the deductible contribution.

The organization may either:
• Provide separate statements for each contribution of $250 or more, or
• Furnish periodic statements substantiating contributions of $250 or more.

Separate contributions of less than $250 are not subject to the requirements of section 170(f)(8), regardless of whether the sum of the contributions made by a taxpayer to a donee organization during a tax year equals $250 or more.

Contemporaneous. A written acknowledgment is contemporaneous if the donor obtains it on or before the earlier of:
• The date the donor files the original return for the tax year in which the contribution was made, or
• The due date (including extensions) for filing the donor's original return for that year.

Substantiation of payroll contributions. An organization may substantiate a payroll contribution by:
• A pay stub, Form W-2, or other document showing a contribution to a donee organization; and
• A pledge card or other document from the donee organization stating that organization provides no goods or services for any payroll contributions.

The amount withheld from each payment of wages to a taxpayer is treated as a separate contribution.

Substantiation of payments to a college or university for the right to purchase tickets to athletic events. The right to purchase tickets for an athletic event is valued at 20% of the payment.

Example. When a taxpayer pays $312.50 for the right to purchase tickets for an athletic event, the right is valued at $62.50. The remaining $250 is a charitable contribution that the taxpayer must substantiate.

Substantiation of matched payments. If a taxpayer's payment to a donee organization is matched by another payor, and the taxpayer receives goods or services in consideration for its payment and some or all of the matching payment, those goods or services will be treated as provided in consideration for the taxpayer's payment and not in

consideration for the matching payment.

Disclosure statement. An organization must provide a written disclosure statement to donors who make a payment, described as a *quid pro quo* contribution, in excess of $75 (section 6115). This requirement is separate from the written substantiation acknowledgment a donor needs for deductibility purposes. While, in certain circumstances, an organization may be able to meet both requirements with the same written document, an organization must be careful to satisfy the section 6115 written disclosure statement requirement in a timely manner because of the penalties involved.

Quid pro quo *contribution.* A *quid pro quo* contribution is a payment that is given both as a contribution and as a payment for goods or services provided by the donee organization.

Example. A donor gives a charity $100 in consideration for a concert ticket valued at $40 (a *quid pro quo* contribution). In this example, $60 would be deductible. Because the donor's payment exceeds $75, the organization must furnish a disclosure statement even though the taxpayer's deductible amount does not exceed $75. Separate payments of $75 or less made at different times of the year for separate fundraising events will not be aggregated for purposes of the $75 threshold.

Good faith estimate. An organization may use any reasonable method in making a good faith estimate of the value of goods or services provided by an organization in consideration for a taxpayer's payment to that organization. A good faith estimate of the value of goods or services that are not generally available in a commercial transaction may be determined by reference to the fair market value of similar or comparable goods or services. Goods or services may be similar or comparable even though they do not have the unique qualities of the goods or services that are being valued.

Goods or services. Goods or services are:
• Cash,
• Property,
• Services,
• Benefits, and
• Privileges.

In consideration for. A donee organization provides goods or services in consideration for a taxpayer's payment if, at the time the taxpayer makes the payment to the donee organization, the taxpayer receives, or expects to receive, goods or services in exchange for that payment.

Goods or services a donee organization provides in consideration for a payment by a taxpayer include goods or services provided in a year other than the year in which the donor makes the payment to the donee organization.

Intangible religious benefits. Intangible religious benefits must be provided by organizations organized exclusively for religious purposes. Examples include:
• Admission to a religious ceremony, and
• *De minimis* tangible benefits, such as wine, provided in connection with a religious ceremony.

Distributing organization as donee. An organization described in section 170(c), or an organization described as a Principal Combined Fund Organization for purposes of the Combined Federal Campaign, that receives a payment made as a contribution is treated as a donee organization even if the organization distributes the amount received to one or more organizations described in section 170(c).

Penalties. A charity that knowingly provides a false substantiation acknowledgment to a donor may be subject to the penalties under section 6701 for aiding and abetting an understatement of tax liability.

Charities that fail to provide the required disclosure statement for a *quid pro quo* contribution of more than $75 will incur a penalty of $10 per contribution, not to exceed $5,000 per fundraising event or mailing. The charity may avoid the penalty if it can show that the failure was due to reasonable cause (section 6714).

M. Public Inspection of Returns, etc.

Some members of the public rely on Form 990, or Form 990-EZ, as the primary or sole source of information about a particular organization. How the public perceives an organization in such cases may be determined by the information presented on its returns.

An organization's completed Form 990, or Form 990-EZ, is available for public inspection as required by section 6104. Schedule B (Form 990, 990-EZ, or 990-PF) is open for public inspection for section 527 organizations filing Form 990 or Form 990-EZ. For other organizations that file Form 990 or Form 990-EZ, parts of Schedule B may be open to public inspection. Form 990-T filed after August 17, 2006, by a 501(c)(3) organization to report any unrelated business income, is also available for public inspection and disclosure.

Through the IRS
Use Form 4506-A to request:

• A copy of an exempt or political organization's return, report, notice, or exemption application;
• An inspection of a return, report, notice, or exemption application at an IRS office.

The IRS can provide copies of exempt organization returns on a compact disc (CD). Requesters can order the complete set (all Forms 990 and 990-EZ or all Forms 990-PF filed for a year) or a partial set by state or by month. For more information on the cost and how to order CDs, call the TEGE Customer Account Services toll-free number (1-877-829-5500) or write to the IRS in Cincinnati, OH, at the address in *General Instruction A*.

The IRS may not disclose portions of an exemption application relating to any trade secrets, etc. Additionally, the IRS may not disclose the names and addresses of contributors. See the Instructions for Schedule B (Form 990, 990-EZ, or 990-PF) for more information about the disclosure of that schedule.

Forms 990 or 990-EZ can only be requested for section 527 organizations for tax years beginning after June 30, 2000.

A return, report, notice, or exemption application may be inspected at an IRS office free of charge. Copies of these items may also be obtained through the organization as discussed in the following section.

Through the Organization

Public inspection and distribution of certain returns of unrelated business income. Section 501(c)(3) organizations that are required to file Form 990-T after August 17, 2006, must make Form 990-T available for public inspection under section 6104(d)(1)(A)(ii).

Public inspection and distribution of returns and reports for a political organization. Section 527 political organizations required to file Form 990, or Form 990-EZ, must, in general, make their Form 8871, 8872, 990, or 990-EZ available for public inspection in the same manner as annual information returns of section 501(c) organizations and 4947(a)(1) nonexempt charitable trusts are made available. See the public inspection rules for *Tax-exempt organization*, later. Generally, Form 8871 and Form 8872 are available for inspection and printing from the Internet. The website address for both of these forms is */www.irs.gov/charities/political/article/0,,id=109332,00.html*.

 Note that a section 527 political organization (and an organization filing Form 990-PF) must disclose their Schedule B (Form 990, 990-EZ, or 990-PF). See the Instructions for Schedule B.

The penalties discussed in *General Instruction K* also apply to section 527 political organizations (Rev. Rul. 2003-49, 2003-204 I.R.B. 903).

Public inspection and distribution of applications for tax exemption and annual information returns of tax-exempt organizations. Under Regulations sections 301.6104(d)-1 through 301.6104(d)-3, a tax-exempt organization must:
• Make its application for recognition of exemption and its annual information returns available for public inspection without charge at its principal, regional, and district offices during regular business hours.
• Make each annual information return available for a period of 3 years beginning on the date the return is required to be filed (determined with regard to any extension of time for filing) or is actually filed, whichever is later.
• Provide a copy without charge, (for Form 990-T, this requirement only applies to Form 990-T's filed after August 17, 2006) other than a reasonable fee for reproduction and actual postage costs, of all or any part of any application or return required to be made available for public inspection to any individual who makes a request for such copy in person or in writing (except as provided in Regulations sections 301.6104(d)-2 and -3).

Definitions.

Tax-exempt organization is any organization that is described in section 501(c) or (d) and is exempt from taxation under section 501(a). The term tax-exempt organization also includes any section 4947(a)(1) nonexempt charitable trust or nonexempt private foundation that is subject to the reporting requirements of section 6033.

Application for tax exemption includes:
• Any prescribed application form (such as Form 1023 or Form 1024),
• All documents and statements the IRS requires an applicant to file with the form,
• Any statement or other supporting document submitted in support of the application, and
• Any letter or other document issued by the IRS concerning the application.

Application for tax exemption does not include:
• Any application for tax exemption filed before July 15, 1987, unless the organization filing the application had a

copy of the application on July 15, 1987;

• In the case of a tax-exempt organization other than a private foundation, the name and address of any contributor to the organization; or

• Any material that is not available for public inspection under section 6104.

 If there is no prescribed application form, see Regulations section 301.6104(d)-1(b)(4)(i).

Annual information return includes:

• An exact copy of the Form 990, or Form 990-EZ, filed by a tax-exempt organization as required by section 6033.

• Any amended return the organization files with the IRS after the date the original return is filed.

• An exact copy of Form 990-T if one is filed by a 501(c)(3) organization.

The copy must include all information furnished to the IRS on Form 990, Form 990-EZ, or Form 990-T as well as all schedules, attachments, and supporting documents, except for the name and address of any contributor to the organization. See the Instructions for Schedule B (Form 990, 990-EZ, or 990-PF).

Annual returns more than 3 years old. An annual information return does not include any return after the expiration of 3 years from the date the return is required to be filed (including any extension of time that has been granted for filing such return) or is actually filed, whichever is later.

If an organization files an amended return, however, the amended return must be made available for a period of 3 years beginning on the date it is filed with the IRS.

Local or subordinate organizations. For rules relating to annual information returns of local or subordinate organizations, see Regulations section 301.6104(d)-1(f)(2).

Regional or district offices. A regional or district office is any office of a tax-exempt organization, other than its principal office, that has paid employees, whether part-time or full-time, whose aggregate number of paid hours a week are normally at least 120.

A site is not considered a regional or district office, however, if:

• The only services provided at the site further exempt purposes (such as day care, health care, scientific research, or medical research); and

• The site does not serve as an office for management staff, other than managers who are involved solely in

managing the exempt function activities at the site.

Special rules relating to public inspection.

Permissible conditions on public inspection. A tax-exempt organization:

• May have an employee present in the room during an inspection.

• Must allow the individual conducting the inspection to take notes freely during the inspection.

• Must allow the individual to photocopy the document at no charge, if the individual provides photocopying equipment at the place of inspection.

Organizations that do not maintain permanent offices. A tax-exempt organization with no permanent office:

• Must make its application for tax exemption and its annual information returns available for inspection at a reasonable location of its choice.

• Must permit public inspection within a reasonable amount of time after receiving a request for inspection (normally not more than 2 weeks) and at a reasonable time of day.

• May mail, within 2 weeks of receiving the request, a copy of its application for tax exemption and annual information returns to the requester instead of allowing an inspection.

• May charge the requester for copying and actual postage costs only if the requester consents to the charge.

An organization that has a permanent office, but has no office hours, or very limited hours during certain times of the year, must make its documents available during those periods when office hours are limited, or not available, as though it were an organization without a permanent office.

Special rules relating to copies.

Time and place for providing copies in response to requests made in-person. A tax-exempt organization must:

• Provide copies of required documents under section 6104(d) in response to a request made in person at its principal, regional, and district offices during regular business hours.

• Provide such copies to a requester on the day the request is made, except for unusual circumstances (see below).

Unusual circumstances. In the case of an in-person request, where unusual circumstances exist so that fulfilling the request on the same business day causes an unreasonable burden to the tax-exempt organization, the organization must provide the copies no later than the next business

day following the day that the unusual circumstances cease to exist, or the 5th business day after the date of the request, whichever occurs first.

Unusual circumstances include:

• Requests received that exceed the organization's daily capacity to make copies;

• Requests received shortly before the end of regular business hours that require an extensive amount of copying; or

• Requests received on a day when the organization's managerial staff capable of fulfilling the request is conducting special duties, such as student registration or attending an off-site meeting or convention, rather than its regular administrative duties.

Agents for providing copies. For rules relating to use of agents to provide copies, see Regulations sections 301.6104(d)-1(d)(1) and (2).

Request for copies in writing. A tax-exempt organization must honor a written request for a copy of documents (or the requested part) required under section 6104(d) if the request:

1. Is addressed to, and delivered by mail, electronic mail, facsimile, or a private delivery service, as defined in section 7502(f), to a principal, regional, or district office of the organization; and

2. Sets forth the address to which the copy of the documents should be sent.

Time and manner of fulfilling written requests.

IF the organization . .	THEN the organization
Receives a written request for a copy,	Must mail the copy of the requested documents (or the requested parts) within 30 days from the date it receives the request.
Mails the copy of the requested document,	Is deemed to have provided the copy on the postmark date or private delivery mark (if sent by certified or registered mail, the date of registration or the date of the postmark on the sender's receipt).
Requires payment in advance,	Is required to provide the copies within 30 days from the date it receives payment.
Receives a request or payment by mail,	Is deemed to have received it 7 days after the date of the postmark, absent evidence to the contrary.

Receives a request transmitted by electronic mail or facsimile,	Is deemed to have received it the day the request is transmitted successfully.
Receives a written request without payment or with an insufficient payment, when payment in advance is required,	Must notify the requester of the prepayment policy and the amount due within 7 days from the date of the request's receipt.
Receives consent from an individual making a request,	May provide a copy of the requested document exclusively by electronic mail (the material is provided on the date the organization successfully transmits the electronic mail).

Request for a copy of parts of a document. A tax-exempt organization must fulfill a request for a copy of the organization's entire application for tax exemption or annual information return or any specific part or schedule of its application or return. A request for a copy of less than the entire application or less than the entire return must specifically identify the requested part or schedule.

Fees for copies. A tax-exempt organization may charge a reasonable fee for providing copies.

Before the organization provides the documents, it may require that the individual requesting copies of the documents pay the fee. If the organization has provided an individual making a request with notice of the fee, and the individual does not pay the fee within 30 days, or if the individual pays the fee by check and the check does not clear upon deposit, the organization may disregard the request.

Form of payment—(A) Request made in person. If a tax-exempt organization charges a fee for copying, it must accept payment by cash and money order for requests made in person. The organization may accept other forms of payment, such as credit cards and personal checks.

(B) Request made in writing. If a tax-exempt organization charges a fee for copying and postage, it must accept payment by certified check, money order, and either personal check or credit card for requests made in writing. The organization may accept other forms of payment.

Avoidance of unexpected fees. Where a tax-exempt organization does not require prepayment and a requester does not enclose payment with a request, an organization must receive consent from a requester before providing copies for which the fee charged for copying and postage exceeds $20.

Documents to be provided by regional and district offices. Except as otherwise provided, a regional or district office of a tax-exempt organization must satisfy the same rules as the principal office with respect to allowing public inspection and providing copies of its application for tax exemption and annual information returns.

A regional or district office is not required, however, to make its annual information return available for inspection or to provide copies until 30 days after the date the return is required to be filed (including any extension of time that is granted for filing such return) or is actually filed, whichever is later.

Documents to be provided by local and subordinate organizations.

Applications for tax exemption. Except as otherwise provided, a tax-exempt organization that did not file its own application for tax exemption (because it is a local or subordinate organization covered by a group exemption letter) must, upon request, make available for public inspection, or provide copies of, the application submitted to the IRS by the central or parent organization to obtain the group exemption letter and those documents which were submitted by the central or parent organization to include the local or subordinate organization in the group exemption letter.

However, if the central or parent organization submits to the IRS a list or directory of local or subordinate organizations covered by the group exemption letter, the local or subordinate organization is required to provide only the application for the group exemption ruling and the pages of the list or directory that specifically refer to it. The local or subordinate organization must permit public inspection, or comply with a request for copies made in person, within a reasonable amount of time (normally not more than 2 weeks) after receiving a request made in person for public inspection or copies and at a reasonable time of day. See Regulations section 301.6104(d)-1(f) for further information.

Annual information returns. A local or subordinate organization that does not file its own annual information return (because it is affiliated with a central or parent organization that files a group return) must, upon request, make available for public inspection, or provide copies of, the group returns filed by the central or parent organization.

However, if the group return includes separate schedules with respect to

each local or subordinate organization included in the group return, the local or subordinate organization receiving the request may omit any schedules relating only to other organizations included in the group return.

The local or subordinate organization must permit public inspection, or comply with a request for copies made in person, within a reasonable amount of time (normally not more than 2 weeks) after receiving a request made in person for public inspection or copies and at a reasonable time of day.

In a case where the requester seeks inspection, the local or subordinate organization may mail a copy of the applicable documents to the requester within the same time period instead of allowing an inspection. In such a case, the organization may charge the requester for copying and actual postage costs only if the requester consents to the charge.

If the local or subordinate organization receives a written request for a copy of its annual information return, it must fulfill the request by providing a copy of the group return in the time and manner specified in the paragraph earlier, *Request for copies in writing.*

The requester has the option of requesting from the central or parent organization, at its principal office, inspection or copies of group returns filed by the central or parent organization. The central or parent organization must fulfill such requests in the time and manner specified in the paragraphs, *Special rules relating to public inspection* and *Special rules relating to copies* earlier.

Failure to comply. If an organization fails to comply with the requirements specified in this paragraph, the penalty provisions of sections 6652(c)(1)(C), 6652(c)(1)(D), and 6685 apply.

Making applications and returns widely available. A tax-exempt organization is not required to comply with a request for a copy of its application for tax exemption or an annual information return if the organization has made the requested document widely available (see below).

An organization that makes its application for tax exemption and/or annual information return widely available must nevertheless make the document available for public inspection as required under Regulations section 301.6104(d)-1(a).

A tax-exempt organization makes its application for tax exemption and/or an annual information return widely available if the organization complies with the Internet posting requirements and the notice requirements given below.

Internet posting. A tax-exempt organization can make its application for tax exemption and/or an annual information return widely available by posting the document on a World Wide Web page that the tax-exempt organization establishes and maintains or by having the document posted, as part of a database of similar documents of other tax-exempt organizations, on a World Wide Web page established and maintained by another entity. The document will be considered widely available only if:
• The World Wide Web page through which it is available clearly informs readers that the document is available and provides instructions for downloading it;
• The document is posted in a format that, when accessed, downloaded, viewed, and printed in hard copy, exactly reproduces the image of the application for tax exemption or annual information return as it was originally filed with the IRS, except for any information permitted by statute to be withheld from public disclosure; and
• Any individual with access to the Internet can access, download, view, and print the document without special computer hardware or software required for that format (other than software that is readily available to members of the public without payment of any fee) and without payment of a fee to the tax-exempt organization or to another entity maintaining the World Wide Web page.

Reliability and accuracy. In order for the document to be widely available through an Internet posting, the entity maintaining the World Wide Web page must have procedures for ensuring the reliability and accuracy of the document that it posts on the page and must take reasonable precautions to prevent alteration, destruction, or accidental loss of the document when posted on its page. In the event that a posted document is altered, destroyed, or lost, the entity must correct or replace the document.

Notice requirement. If a tax-exempt organization has made its application for tax exemption and/or an annual information return widely available, it must notify any individual requesting a copy where the documents are available (including the address on the World Wide Web, if applicable). If the request is made in person, the organization must provide such notice to the individual immediately. If the request is made in writing, the notice must be provided within 7 days of receiving the request.

Tax-exempt organization subject to harassment campaign. If the Director EO Examination (or designee) determines that the organization is being harassed, a tax-exempt organization is not required to comply with any request for copies that it reasonably believes is part of a harassment campaign.

Whether a group of requests constitutes a harassment campaign depends on the relevant facts and circumstances such as:

A sudden increase in requests; an extraordinary number of requests by form letters or similarly worded correspondence; hostile requests; evidence showing bad faith or deterrence of the organization's exempt purpose; prior provision of the requested documents to the purported harassing group; and a demonstration that the organization routinely provides copies of its documents upon request.

A tax-exempt organization may disregard any request for copies of all or part of any document beyond the first two received within any 30-day period or the first four received within any 1-year period from the same individual or the same address, regardless of whether the Director EO Examination (or designee) has determined that the organization is subject to a harassment campaign.

A tax-exempt organization may apply for a determination that it is the subject of a harassment campaign and that compliance with requests that are part of the campaign would not be in the public interest by submitting a signed application to the Director EO Examination (or designee) for the area where the organization's principal office is located.

In addition, the organization may suspend compliance with any request it reasonably believes to be part of the harassment campaign until it receives a response to its application for a harassment campaign determination. However, if the Director EO Examination (or designee) determines that the organization did not have a reasonable basis for requesting a determination that it was subject to a harassment campaign or reasonable belief that a request was part of the campaign, the officer, director, trustee, employee, or other responsible individual of the organization remains liable for any penalties for not providing the copies in a timely fashion. See Regulations section 301.6104(d)-3.

N. Disclosures Regarding Certain Information and Services Furnished

A section 501(c) organization that offers to sell or solicits money for specific information or for a routine service for any individual that could be obtained by such individual from a federal government agency free or for a nominal charge, must disclose that fact conspicuously when making such offer or solicitation. Any organization that intentionally disregards this requirement will be subject to a penalty for each day on which the offers or solicitations are made. The penalty imposed for a particular day is the greater of $1,000 or 50% of the total cost of the offers and solicitations made on that day that lacked the required disclosure (section 6711).

O. Disclosures Regarding Certain Transactions and Relationships

In their annual returns on Schedule A (Form 990 or 990-EZ), section 501(c)(3) organizations must disclose information regarding their direct or indirect transfers to, and other direct or indirect relationships with, other section 501(c) organizations (except section 501(c)(3) organizations) or section 527 political organizations (section 6033(b)(9)). This provision helps prevent the diversion or expenditure of a section 501(c)(3) organization's funds for purposes not intended by section 501(c)(3). All section 501(c)(3) organizations must maintain records regarding all such transfers, transactions, and relationships. See also *General Instruction K* regarding penalties.

P. Intermediate Sanction Regulations—Excess Benefit Transactions

The intermediate sanction regulations are important to the exempt organization community as a whole, and for ensuring compliance in this area. The rules provide a roadmap by which an organization may steer clear of situations that may give rise to inurement.

Under section 4958, any disqualified person who benefits from an excess benefit transaction with an applicable tax-exempt organization is liable for a 25% tax on the excess benefit. The disqualified person is also liable for a 200% tax on the excess benefit if the excess benefit is not corrected by a certain date. Also, organization managers who participate in an excess benefit transaction knowingly, willfully, and without reasonable cause are liable for a 10% tax on the excess benefit, not to exceed $20,000 for all participating managers on each transaction.

Applicable Tax-Exempt Organization

These rules only apply to certain applicable section 501(c)(3) and 501(c)(4) organizations. An *applicable tax-exempt organization* is a section 501(c)(3) or a section 501(c)(4) organization that is tax-exempt under section 501(a), or was such an organization at any time during a 5-year period ending on the day of the excess benefit transaction.

An applicable tax-exempt organization does not include:
• A private foundation as defined in section 509(a).
• A governmental entity that is exempt from (or not subject to) taxation without regard to section 501(a) or relieved from filing an annual return under Regulations section 1.6033-2(g)(6).
• Certain foreign organizations.

An organization is not treated as a section 501(c)(3) or 501(c)(4) organization for any period covered by a final determination that the organization was not tax-exempt under section 501(a), so long as the determination was not based on private inurement or one or more excess benefit transactions.

Disqualified Person

The vast majority of section 501(c)(3) or 501(c)(4) organization employees and contractors will not be affected by these rules. Only the few influential persons within these organizations are covered by these rules when they receive benefits, such as compensation, fringe benefits, or contract payments. The IRS calls this class of covered individuals disqualified persons.

A *disqualified person*, regarding any transaction, is any person who was in a position to exercise substantial influence over the affairs of the applicable tax-exempt organization at any time during a 5-year period ending on the date of the transaction. Persons who hold certain powers, responsibilities, or interests are among those who are in a position to exercise substantial influence over the affairs of the organization. This would include, for example, voting members of the governing body, and persons holding the power of:
• Presidents, chief executive officers, or chief operating officers.
• Treasurers and chief financial officers.

A *disqualified person* also includes certain family members of a disqualified

person, and 35% controlled entities of a disqualified person.

The following persons are considered disqualified persons along with certain family members and 35% controlled entities associated with them:
• Donors of donor advised funds,
• Investment advisors of sponsoring organizations, and
• The disqualified persons of a section 509(a)(3) supporting organization for the organizations that organization supports.

Substantial contributors to supporting organizations are also considered disqualified persons along with their family members and 35% controlled entities.

See the Instructions for Form 4720, Schedule I for more information regarding these disqualified persons.

Who is not a disqualified person? The rules also clarify which persons are not considered to be in a position to exercise substantial influence over the affairs of an organization. They include:
• An employee who receives benefits that total less than the highly compensated amount ($100,000 in 2007) and who does not hold the executive or voting powers just mentioned; is not a family member of a disqualified person; and is not a substantial contributor;
• Tax-exempt organizations described in section 501(c)(3); and
• Section 501(c)(4) organizations with respect to transactions engaged in with other section 501(c)(4) organizations.

Who else may be considered a disqualified person? Other persons not described above can also be considered disqualified persons, depending on all the relevant facts and circumstances.

Facts and circumstances tending to show substantial influence:
• The person founded the organization.
• The person is a substantial contributor to the organization under the section 507(d)(2)(A) definition, only taking into account contributions to the organization for the past 5 years.
• The person's compensation is primarily based on revenues derived from activities of the organization that the person controls.
• The person has or shares authority to control or determine a substantial portion of the organization's capital expenditures, operating budget, or compensation for employees.
• The person manages a discrete segment or activity of the organization that represents a substantial portion of the activities, assets, income, or expenses of the organization, as compared to the organization as a whole.

• The person owns a controlling interest (measured by either vote or value) in a corporation, partnership, or trust that is a disqualified person.
• The person is a nonstock organization controlled directly or indirectly by one or more disqualified persons.

Facts and circumstances tending to show no substantial influence:
• The person is an independent contractor whose sole relationship to the organization is providing professional advice (without having decision-making authority) with respect to transactions from which the independent contractor will not economically benefit.
• The person has taken a vow of poverty.
• Any preferential treatment the person receives based on the size of the person's donation is also offered to others making comparable widely solicited donations.
• The direct supervisor of the person is not a disqualified person.
• The person does not participate in any management decisions affecting the organization as a whole or a discrete segment of the organization that represents a substantial portion of the activities, assets, income, or expenses of the organization, as compared to the organization as a whole.

What about persons who staff affiliated organizations? In the case of multiple affiliated organizations, the determination of whether a person has substantial influence is made separately for each applicable tax-exempt organization. A person may be a disqualified person with respect to transactions with more than one organization.

Excess Benefit Transaction

An *excess benefit transaction* is a transaction in which an economic benefit is provided by an applicable tax-exempt organization, directly or indirectly, to or for the use of any disqualified person, and the value of the economic benefit provided by the organization exceeds the value of the consideration (including the performance of services) received for providing such benefit. An excess benefit transaction also can occur when a disqualified person embezzles from the exempt organization.

To determine whether an excess benefit transaction has occurred, all consideration and benefits exchanged between a disqualified person and the applicable tax-exempt organization, and all entities it controls, are taken into account.

For purposes of determining the value of economic benefits, the value of property, including the right to use property, is the fair market value. Fair market value is the price at which property, or the right to use property, would change hands between a willing buyer and a willing seller, neither being under any compulsion to buy, sell, or transfer property or the right to use property, and both having reasonable knowledge of relevant facts.

Donor advised funds. For a donor advised fund, an excess benefit transaction includes a grant, loan, compensation, or similar payment from the fund to a:
- Donor or donor advisor,
- Family member of a donor, or donor advisor,
- 35% controlled entity of a donor, or donor advisor, or
- 35% controlled entity of a family member of a donor, or donor advisor.

The excess benefit in this transaction is the amount of the grant, loan, compensation, or similar payment. For additional information see the Instructions for Form 4720.

Supporting organizations. For any supporting organization, defined in section 509(a)(3), an excess benefit transaction includes grants, loans, compensation, or similar payment provided by the supporting organization to a:
- Substantial contributor,
- Family member of a substantial contributor,
- 35% controlled entity of a substantial contributor, or
- 35% controlled entity of a family member of a substantial contributor.

Additionally, an excess benefit transaction includes any loans provided by the supporting organization to a disqualified person (other than an organization described in section 509(a)(1), (2), or (4)).

A substantial contributor is any person who contributed or bequeathed an aggregate of more than $5,000 to the organization, if that amount is more than 2% of the total contributions and bequests received by the organization before the end of the tax year of the organization in which the contribution or bequest is received by the organization from such person. A substantial contributor includes the grantor of a trust.

The excess benefit for substantial contributors and parties related to those contributors includes the amount of the grant, loan, compensation, or similar payment. For additional information see the Instructions for Form 4720.

When does an excess benefit transaction usually occur? An excess benefit transaction occurs on the date the disqualified person receives the economic benefit from the organization for federal income tax purposes. However, when a single contractual arrangement provides for a series of compensation payments or other payments to a disqualified person during the disqualified person's tax year, any excess benefit transaction with respect to these payments occurs on the last day of the taxpayer's tax year.

In the case of the transfer of property subject to a substantial risk of forfeiture, or in the case of rights to future compensation or property, the transaction occurs on the date the property, or the rights to future compensation or property, is not subject to a substantial risk of forfeiture. Where the disqualified person elects to include an amount in gross income in the tax year of transfer under section 83(b), the excess benefit transaction occurs on the date the disqualified person receives the economic benefit for federal income tax purposes.

Section 4958 applies only to post-September 1995 transactions. Section 4958 applies to excess benefit transactions occurring on or after September 14, 1995. Section 4958 does not apply to any transaction occurring pursuant to a written contract that was binding on September 13, 1995, and at all times thereafter before the transaction occurs.

What is reasonable compensation? *Reasonable compensation* is the valuation standard that is used to determine if there is an excess benefit in the exchange of a disqualified person's services for compensation.

Reasonable compensation is the value that would ordinarily be paid for like services by like enterprises under like circumstances. This is the section 162 standard that will apply in determining the reasonableness of compensation. The fact that a bonus or revenue-sharing arrangement is subject to a cap is a relevant factor in determining the reasonableness of compensation.

For determining the reasonableness of compensation, all items of compensation provided by an applicable tax-exempt organization in exchange for the performance of services are taken into account in determining the value of compensation (except for certain economic benefits that are disregarded, as discussed in *What benefits are disregarded?* later). Items of compensation include:
- All forms of cash and noncash compensation, including salary, fees,

bonuses, severance payments, and deferred and noncash compensation.
- The payment of liability insurance premiums for, or the payment or reimbursement by the organization of taxes or certain expenses under section 4958, unless excludable from income as a *de minimis* fringe benefit under section 132(a)(4). (A similar rule applies in the private foundation area.) Inclusion in compensation for purposes of determining reasonableness under section 4958 does not control inclusion in income for income tax purposes.
- All other compensatory benefits, whether or not included in gross income for income tax purposes.
- Taxable and nontaxable fringe benefits, except fringe benefits described in section 132.
- Foregone interest on loans.

Written intent required to treat benefits as compensation. An economic benefit is not treated as consideration for the performance of services unless the organization providing the benefit clearly indicates its intent to treat the benefit as compensation when the benefit is paid.

An applicable tax-exempt organization (or entity that it controls) is treated as clearly indicating its intent to provide an economic benefit as compensation for services only if the organization provides written substantiation that is contemporaneous with the transfer of the economic benefits under consideration. Ways to provide contemporaneous written substantiation of its intent to provide an economic benefit as compensation include:
- The organization produces a signed written employment contract;
- The organization reports the benefit as compensation on an original Form W-2, Form 1099 or Form 990, or on an amended form filed prior to the start of an IRS examination; or
- The disqualified person reports the benefit as income on the person's original Form 1040 or on an amended form filed prior to the start of an IRS examination.

Exception. To the extent the economic benefit is excluded from the disqualified person's gross income for income tax purposes, the applicable tax-exempt organization is not required to indicate its intent to provide an economic benefit as compensation for services. (For example, employer provided health benefits, and contributions to qualified plans under section 401(a).)

What benefits are disregarded? The following economic benefits are disregarded for purposes of section 4958.

• Nontaxable fringe benefits. An economic benefit that is excluded from income under section 132.
• Benefits to volunteer. An economic benefit provided to a volunteer for the organization if the benefit is provided to the general public in exchange for a membership fee or contribution of $75 or less per year.
• Benefits to members or donors. An economic benefit provided to a member of an organization due to the payment of a membership fee, or to a donor as a result of a deductible contribution, if a significant number of nondisqualified persons make similar payments or contributions and are offered a similar economic benefit.
• Benefits to a charitable beneficiary. An economic benefit provided to a person solely as a member of a charitable class that the applicable tax-exempt organization intends to benefit as part of the accomplishment of its exempt purpose.
• Benefits to a governmental unit. A transfer of an economic benefit to or for the use of a governmental unit, as defined in section 170(c)(1), if exclusively for public purposes.

Is there an exception for initial contracts? Section 4958 does not apply to any fixed payment made to a person pursuant to an initial contract. This is a very important exception, since it would potentially apply, for example, to all initial contracts with new, previously unrelated officers and contractors.

An *initial contract* is a binding written contract between an applicable tax-exempt organization and a person who was not a disqualified person immediately prior to entering into the contract.

A *fixed payment* is an amount of cash or other property specified in the contract, or determined by a fixed formula that is specified in the contract, which is to be paid or transferred in exchange for the provision of specified services or property.

A *fixed formula* may, in general, incorporate an amount that depends upon future specified events or contingencies, as long as no one has discretion when calculating the amount of a payment or deciding whether to make a payment (such as a bonus).

Treatment as new contract. A binding written contract providing that it may be terminated or cancelled by the applicable tax-exempt organization without the other party's consent (except as a result of substantial non-performance) and without substantial penalty, is treated as a new contract, as of the earliest date that any termination or cancellation would be effective. Also, a contract in which there

is a material change, which includes an extension or renewal of the contract (except for an extension or renewal resulting from the exercise of an option by the disqualified person), or a more than incidental change to the amount payable under the contract, is treated as a new contract as of the effective date of the material change. Treatment as a new contract may cause the contract to fall outside the initial contract exception, and it thus would be tested under the fair market value standards of section 4958.

Rebuttable Presumption of Reasonableness

Payments under a compensation arrangement are presumed to be reasonable and the transfer of property (or right to use property) is presumed to be at fair market value, if the following three conditions are met.

1. The transaction is approved by an authorized body of the organization (or an entity it controls) which is composed of individuals who do not have a conflict of interest concerning the transaction.

2. Prior to making its determination, the authorized body obtained and relied upon appropriate data as to comparability. There is a special safe harbor for small organizations. If the organization has gross receipts of less than $1 million, appropriate comparability data includes data on compensation paid by three comparable organizations in the same or similar communities for similar services.

3. The authorized body adequately documents the basis for its determination concurrently with making that determination. The documentation should include:

a. The terms of the approved transaction and the date approved;
b. The members of the authorized body who were present during debate on the transaction that was approved and those who voted on it;
c. The comparability data obtained and relied upon by the authorized body and how the data was obtained;
d. Any actions by a member of the authorized body having a conflict of interest; and
e. Documentation of the basis for the determination before the later of the next meeting of the authorized body or 60 days after the final actions of the authorized body are taken, and approval of records as reasonable, accurate and complete within a reasonable time thereafter.

Special rebuttable presumption rule for nonfixed payments. As a general rule, in the case of a nonfixed payment, no rebuttable presumption arises until

the exact amount of the payment is determined, or a fixed formula for calculating the payment is specified, and the three requirements creating the presumption have been satisfied. However, if the authorized body approves an employment contract with a disqualified person that includes a nonfixed payment (for example, discretionary bonus) with a specified cap on the amount, the authorized body may establish a rebuttable presumption as to the nonfixed payment when the employment contract is entered into by, in effect, assuming that the maximum amount payable under the contract will be paid, and satisfying the requirements giving rise to the rebuttable presumption for that maximum amount.

An IRS challenge to the presumption of reasonableness. The Internal Revenue Service may refute the presumption of reasonableness only if it develops sufficient contrary evidence to rebut the probative value of the comparability data relied upon by the authorized body. This provision gives taxpayers added protection if they faithfully find and use contemporaneous persuasive comparability data when they provide the benefits.

Organizations that do not establish a presumption of reasonableness. An organization may still comply with section 4958 even if it did not establish a presumption of reasonableness. In some cases, an organization may find it impossible or impracticable to fully implement each step of the rebuttable presumption process described above. In such cases, the organization should try to implement as many steps as possible, in whole or in part, in order to substantiate the reasonableness of benefits as timely and as well as possible. If an organization does not satisfy the requirements of the rebuttable presumption of reasonableness, a facts and circumstances approach will be followed, using established rules for determining reasonableness of compensation and benefit deductions in a manner similar to the established procedures for section 162 business expenses.

Section 4958 Taxes

Tax on disqualified persons. An excise tax equal to 25% of the excess benefit is imposed on each excess benefit transaction between an applicable tax-exempt organization and a disqualified person. The disqualified person who benefited from the transaction is liable for the tax. If the 25% tax is imposed and the excess benefit transaction is not corrected within the taxable period, an additional excise tax equal to 200% of the excess benefit is imposed.

If a disqualified person makes a payment of less than the full correction amount, the 200% tax is imposed only on the unpaid portion of the correction amount. If more than one disqualified person received an excess benefit from an excess benefit transaction, all such disqualified persons are jointly and severally liable for the taxes.

To avoid the imposition of the 200% tax, a disqualified person must correct the excess benefit transaction during the taxable period. The taxable period begins on the date the transaction occurs and ends on the earlier of the date the statutory notice of deficiency is issued or the section 4958 taxes are assessed. This 200% tax may be abated if the excess benefit transaction subsequently is corrected during a 90-day correction period.

Tax on organization managers. An excise tax equal to 10% of the excess benefit may be imposed on the participation of an organization manager in an excess benefit transaction between an applicable tax-exempt organization and a disqualified person. This tax, which may not exceed $20,000 for any single transaction, is only imposed if the 25% tax is imposed on the disqualified person, the organization manager knowingly participated in the transaction, and the manager's participation was willful and not due to reasonable cause. There is also joint and several liability for this tax. An organization manager may be liable for both the tax on disqualified persons and on organization managers in appropriate circumstances.

An *organization manager* is any officer, director, or trustee of an applicable tax-exempt organization, or any individual having powers or responsibilities similar to officers, directors, or trustees of the organization, regardless of title. An organization manager is not considered to have participated in an excess benefit transaction where the manager has opposed the transaction in a manner consistent with the fulfillment of the manager's responsibilities to the organization. For example, a director who votes against giving an excess benefit would ordinarily not be subject to this tax.

A person participates in a transaction knowingly if the person has actual knowledge of sufficient facts so that, based solely upon such facts, the transaction would be an excess benefit transaction. Knowing does not mean having reason to know. The organization manager ordinarily will not be considered knowing if, after full disclosure of the factual situation to an appropriate professional, the organization manager relied on the professional's reasoned written opinion on matters within the professional's expertise or if the manager relied on the fact that the requirements for the rebuttable presumption of reasonableness have been satisfied. Participation by an organization manager is willful if it is voluntary, conscious, and intentional. An organization manager's participation is due to reasonable cause if the manager has exercised responsibility on behalf of the organization with ordinary business care and prudence.

Correcting an Excess Benefit Transaction

A disqualified person corrects an excess benefit transaction by undoing the excess benefit to the extent possible, and by taking any additional measures necessary to place the organization in a financial position not worse than that in which it would be if the disqualified person were dealing under the highest fiduciary standards. The organization is not required to rescind the underlying agreement; however, the parties may need to modify an ongoing contract with respect to future payments.

A disqualified person corrects an excess benefit by making a payment in cash or cash equivalents equal to the correction amount to the applicable tax-exempt organization. The correction amount equals the excess benefit plus the interest on the excess benefit; the interest rate may be no lower than the applicable Federal rate. There is an anti-abuse rule to prevent the disqualified person from effectively transferring property other than cash or cash equivalents.

Exception. For a correction of an excess benefit transaction described in *Donor advised funds* (discussed earlier), no amount repaid in a manner prescribed by the Secretary may be held in a donor advised fund.

Property. With the agreement of the applicable tax-exempt organization, a disqualified person may make a payment by returning the specific property previously transferred in the excess benefit transaction. The return of the property is considered a payment of cash (or cash equivalent) equal to the lesser of:
• The fair market value of the property on the date the property is returned to the organization, or
• The fair market value of the property on the date the excess benefit transaction occurred.

Insufficient payment. If the payment resulting from the return of the property is less than the correction amount, the disqualified person must make an additional cash payment to the organization equal to the difference.

Excess payment. If the payment resulting from the return of the property exceeds the correction amount described above, the organization may make a cash payment to the disqualified person equal to the difference.

Churches and Section 4958
The regulations make it clear that the IRS will apply the procedures of section 7611 when initiating and conducting any inquiry or examination into whether an excess benefit transaction has occurred between a church and a disqualified person.

Revenue Sharing Transactions
Proposed intermediate sanction regulations were issued in 1998. The proposed regulations had special provisions covering "any transaction in which the amount of any economic benefit provided to or for the use of a disqualified person is determined in whole or in part by the revenues of one or more activities of the organization. . ." — so-called revenue-sharing transactions. Rather than setting forth additional rules on revenue-sharing transactions, the final regulations reserve this section. Consequently, until the Service issues new regulations for this reserved section on revenue-sharing transactions, these transactions will be evaluated under the general rules (for example, the fair market value standards) that apply to all contractual arrangements between applicable tax-exempt organizations and their disqualified persons.

Revocation of Exemption and Section 4958
Section 4958 does not affect the substantive standards for tax exemption under section 501(c)(3) or section 501(c)(4), including the requirements that the organization be organized and operated exclusively for exempt purposes, and that no part of its net earnings inure to the benefit of any private shareholder or individual. The legislative history indicates that in most instances, the imposition of this intermediate sanction will be in lieu of revocation. The IRS has indicated that the following four factors will be considered in determining whether to revoke an applicable tax-exempt organization's exemption status where an excess benefit transaction has occurred:
• Whether the organization has been involved in repeated excess benefit transactions;

• The size and scope of the excess benefit transaction;
• Whether, after concluding that it has been party to an excess benefit transaction, the organization has implemented safeguards to prevent future recurrences; and
• Whether there was compliance with other applicable laws.

Q. Erroneous Backup Withholding

Recipients of dividend or interest payments generally must certify their correct taxpayer identification number to the bank or other payer on Form W-9. If the payer does not get this information, it must withhold part of the payments as backup withholding. If the organization was subject to erroneous backup withholding because the payer did not realize it was an exempt organization and not subject to this withholding, it can claim credit on Form 990-T for the amount withheld. See the Instructions for Form 990-T. Claims for refund must be filed within 3 years after the date the original return was due; 3 years after the date the organization filed it; or 2 years after the date the tax was paid, whichever is later.

R. Group Return

If a parent organization wants to file a group return for two or more of its subsidiaries, it must use Form 990. The parent organization cannot use a Form 990-EZ for the group return.

A central, parent, or like organization can file a group return on Form 990 for two or more local organizations that are:
1. Affiliated with the central organization at the time its annual accounting period ends,
2. Subject to the central organization's general supervision or control,
3. Exempt from tax under a group exemption letter that is still in effect, and
4. Have the same accounting period as the central organization.

If the parent organization is required to file a return for itself, it must file a separate return and may not be included in the group return. See General Instruction B for a list of organizations not required to file.

Every year, each local organization must authorize the central organization in writing to include it in the group return and must declare, under penalty of perjury, that the authorization and the information it submits to be included in the group return are true and complete.

If the central organization prepares a group return for its affiliated organizations, check the "Yes" box in item H(a), in the heading of Form 990, and indicate the number of organizations for which the group return is filed in item H(b).

For item H(c), check "Yes," to indicate that the group return includes all affiliated organizations covered by the group ruling. If the organization answers "No" to H(c), attach a list showing the name, address, and EIN of each affiliated organization included in the group return. If either box in H(a) or H(d) is checked "Yes," enter the four-digit group exemption number (GEN). Do not confuse the four-digit GEN number to be reported for item I with the nine-digit EIN number reported in item D of the form's heading.

The central organization should send the annual information required to maintain a group exemption letter to the:

Department of Treasury
Internal Revenue Service Center
Ogden, UT 84201-0027

An affiliated organization covered by a group ruling may file a separate return instead of being included in the group return. In such case, check the "Yes" box in item H(d), in the heading of Form 990, and enter the GEN number in item I.

Parts IV-A and IV-B of Form 990 do not have to be completed on group returns.

S. Organizations in Foreign Countries and U.S. Possessions

Refer to General Instruction B for the filing exemption for foreign organizations with $25,000 or less in gross receipts from U.S. sources.

Report amounts in U.S. dollars and state what conversion rate the organization uses. Combine amounts from within and outside the United States and report the total for each item. All information must be written in English.

T. Public Interest Law Firms

A public interest law firm exempt under section 501(c)(3) or 501(c)(4) must attach a statement that lists the cases in litigation, or that have been litigated during the year. For each case, describe the matter in dispute and explain how the litigation will benefit the public generally. Also attach a report of all fees sought and recovered in each case. See Rev. Proc. 92-59, 1992-2 C.B. 411.

U. Political Organizations

A political organization subject to section 527 is a party, committee, association, fund, or other organization (whether or not incorporated) organized and operated primarily for the purpose of directly or indirectly accepting contributions or making expenditures, or both, for an exempt function.

The exempt function of a political organization is influencing or attempting to influence the selection, nomination, election or appointment of an individual to a federal, state, or local public office or office in a political organization. A political organization must be organized for the primary purpose of carrying on exempt function activities.

A political organization does not need to be formally chartered or established as a corporation, trust, or association. A separate bank account in which political campaign funds are deposited and disbursed only for political campaign expenses can qualify as a political organization.

V. Information Regarding Transfers Associated With Personal Benefit Contracts

Filers of Form 990 that engaged in activities involving personal benefit contracts must declare in Part X, Information Regarding Transfers Associated With Personal Benefit Contracts, whether or not they:
1. Received any funds, directly or indirectly, to pay premiums on a personal benefit contract.
2. Paid any premiums, directly or indirectly, on a personal benefit contract.

 Filers of Form 990-EZ must make this declaration in a statement attached to their form.

If premiums were paid on a personal benefit contract, the organization must report these payments on Form 8870 and pay an excise tax, equal to premiums paid, with Form 4720.

Section 170(f)(10)(F)(iii) requires a charitable organization to report annually its premium payments on a personal benefit contract with respect to a transferor and to identify the beneficiaries of those contracts. A transfer of funds to a charitable organization receives no charitable contribution deduction if the organization, directly or indirectly, pays, or has previously paid, any premium on a personal benefit contract with respect to the transferor, or there is an understanding or expectation that any person will directly or indirectly pay any premium on a personal benefit contract with respect to the transferor (section 170(f)(10)(A)).

A *personal benefit contract,* generally, is any life insurance, annuity, or endowment contract that benefits, directly or indirectly, the transferor, a member of the transferor's family, or any other person designated by the transferor (other than an organization described in section 170(c)). A charitable organization is an organization described in section 170(c).

Section 170(f)(10)(F)(i) imposes on a charitable organization an excise tax equal to the premiums paid by the organization on any personal benefit contract, if the payment of premiums is in connection with a transfer for which a deduction is not allowed under section 170(f)(10)(A). For purposes of this excise tax, section 170(f)(10)(F)(ii) provides that premium payments made by any other person, pursuant to an understanding or expectation described in section 170(f)(10)(A), are treated as made by the charitable organization.

For more information on the reporting requirements of section 170(f)(10), see Notice 2000-24, 2000-17 I.R.B. 952 (2000-1 C.B. 952) and Announcement 2000-82, 2000-42 I.R.B. 385 (2000-2 C.B. 385).

W. Prohibited Tax Shelter Transactions and Related Disclosure Requirements

New section 4965 imposes an excise tax on:
• Certain tax-exempt entities that are a party to a prohibited tax shelter transaction, and
• Any entity manager who approves or otherwise causes the entity to be a party to a prohibited tax shelter transaction and knows or has reason to know that the transaction is a prohibited tax shelter transaction.

Additionally, section 6033 provides new disclosure requirements on a tax-exempt entity that is a party to a prohibited tax shelter transaction. See Form 8886-T and it's instructions for more information.

Tax-exempt entities. Tax-exempt entities that are subject to section 4965 include:
1. Entities described in section 501(c), including but not limited to the following common types of entities:
    a. Instrumentalities of the United States described in section 501(c)(1);
    b. Churches, hospitals, museums, schools, scientific research

organizations, and other charities described in section 501(c)(3);
    c. Civic leagues, social welfare organizations, and local associations of employees described in section 501(c)(4);
    d. Labor, agricultural, or horticultural organizations described in section 501(c)(5);
    e. Business leagues, chambers of commerce, trade associations, and other organizations described in section 501(c)(6);
    f. Voluntary employees' beneficiary associations (VEBAs) described in section 501(c)(9);
    g. Credit unions described in section 501(c)(14);
    h. Insurance companies described in section 501(c)(15); and
    i. Veterans' organizations described in section 501(c)(19).
2. Religious or apostolic associations or corporations described in section 501(d).
3. Entities described in section 170(c), including states, possessions of the United States, the District of Columbia, political subdivisions of states, and political subdivisions of possessions of the United States (but not including the United States).
4. Indian tribal governments within the meaning of section 7701(a)(40).

Definition of a party to a prohibited tax shelter transaction. A tax-exempt entity is a party to a transaction if it:
• Facilitates the transaction by reason of its tax-exempt, tax-indifferent, or tax-favored status, or
• Enters into a listed transaction and the tax-exempt entity's return (original or amended) reflects a reduction or elimination of liability for applicable federal employment, excise, or unrelated business income taxes that is derived directly or indirectly from tax consequences or tax strategy described in the published guidance that lists the transaction; or
• Is identified in published guidance by type, class, or role as party to a prohibited tax shelter transaction.

Entity manager. An *entity manager* is any person with authority or responsibility similar to that exercised by an officer, director, or trustee, and, for any act, the person that has final authority or responsibility with respect to such act.

Prohibited tax shelter transaction. Generally, a prohibited tax shelter transaction is a transaction that is a listed transaction (including subsequently listed transaction), a confidential transaction, or a transaction with contractual protection. See definitions of these terms later.

Note. In general, if the IRS determines by published guidance that a

transaction will be excluded from the definition of listed transaction, confidential transaction, or transaction with contractual protection, the transaction will not be considered a prohibited tax shelter transaction.

Listed transaction. A listed transaction is a transaction that is the same as or substantially similar to any of the types of transactions that the IRS has determined to be a tax avoidance transaction and are identified by notice, regulation, or other form of published guidance as a listed transaction. For existing guidance see:
• Notice 2004-67, 2004-41 I.R.B. 600;
• Notice 2005-13, 2005-9 I.R.B. 630; and
• Notice 2007-57, 2007-29 I.R.B. 87.

For updates to this list go to the IRS web page at *www.irs.gov/businesses/ corporations* and click on *Abusive Tax Shelters and Transactions.* The IRS may issue new or update the existing notice, regulation, announcement, or other forms of published guidance that identify transactions as listed transactions. You can find a notice or ruling in the Internal Revenue Bulletin at *www.irs.gov/pub/irs-irbs/ irbXX-YY.pdf,* where XX is the two-digit year and YY is the two-digit bulletin number. For example, you can find Notice 2004-67, 2004-41 I.R.B. 600, at *www.irs.gov/pub/irs-irbs/irb04-41.pdf.*

Subsequently listed transaction. A subsequently listed transaction is a transaction that is identified in published guidance as a listed transaction after the tax-exempt entity has entered into the transaction and that was not a confidential transaction or transaction with contractual protection at the time the entity entered into the transaction. See section 4965(e)(2) for more information.

Substantially similar. A transaction is substantially similar to another transaction if it is expected to obtain the same or similar types of tax consequences and is either factually similar or based on the same or similar tax strategy. Receipt of an opinion regarding the tax consequences of the transaction is not relevant to the determination of whether the transaction is the same as or substantially similar to another transaction. Further, the term substantially similar must be broadly construed in favor of disclosure. See Regulations section 1.6011-4(c)(4) for examples.

Confidential transaction. A confidential transaction is a transaction this is offered under conditions of confidentiality and for which a minimum fee (defined below) was paid. A transaction is considered to be offered under conditions of confidentiality if the advisor places a limitation on disclosure of the tax treatment or tax structure of the transaction and the limitation on disclosure protects the confidentiality of the advisor's tax strategies. The transaction is treated as confidential even if the conditions of confidentiality are not legally binding. See Regulations section 1.6011-4(b)(3) for more information.

Minimum fee. For a corporation, or a partnership or trust in which all of the owners or beneficiaries are corporations (looking through any partners or beneficiaries that are themselves partners or trusts), the minimum fee is $250,000. For all others, the minimum fee is $50,000. The minimum fee includes all fees paid directly or indirectly for the tax strategy, advice or analysis of the transaction (whether or not related to the tax consequences of the transaction), implementation and documentation of the transaction, and tax preparation fees to the extent they exceed customary return preparation fees. Fees do not include amounts paid to a person, including an advisor, in that person's capacity as a party to the transaction.

Transaction with contractual protection. A transaction with contractual protection is a transaction for which a participant (or related party as defined under section 267(b) or 707(b)) has the right to a full refund or partial refund of fees if all or part of the intended tax consequences from the transaction are not sustained. It also includes a transaction for which fees are contingent on the realization of tax benefits from the transaction. For exceptions and other details, see Regulations section 1.6011-4(b)(4) and Rev. Proc. 2007-20, 2007-7 I.R.B. 517.

Entity-Level Excise Tax
For Form 990 and 990-EZ filers, section 4965(a)(1) imposes an entity level excise tax for each taxable year that the tax-exempt entity is a party to a prohibited tax shelter transaction and has net income or proceeds attributable to the transaction which are properly allocable to that taxable year. The amount of the excise tax depends on whether the tax-exempt entity knew or had reason to know that the transaction was a prohibited tax shelter transaction at the time it became a party to the transaction.

To figure and report the excise tax imposed on a tax-exempt entity for being a party to a prohibited tax shelter transaction, file Form 4720.

For more information about this excise tax including information about

how it is figured, see the Instructions for Form 4720.

Required Disclosure
Certain tax-exempt entities are required to file disclosure information of:
• Such entity being a party to any prohibited tax shelter transaction, and
• The identity of any other known party to the prohibited tax shelter transaction.

Use Form 8886-T to report the disclosure. Entities that fail to file the required disclosure are subject to a nondisclosure penalty of $100 for each day the failure continues with a maximum penalty for any one disclosure of $50,000.

Also, if the IRS makes a written demand on any entity subject to this penalty, giving the entity a reasonable date to make the disclosure and the entity fails to make disclosure by that date, the entity is subject to a penalty of $100 for each day after the date specified by the IRS until disclosure is made (with a maximum penalty for any one disclosure of $10,000). See Instructions for Form 8886-T for more information.

Excise Tax on Entity Managers
Section 4965(a)(2) imposes an excise tax on any tax-exempt entity manager who approves or otherwise causes the entity to be a party to a prohibited tax shelter transaction and knows (or has reason to know) that the transaction is a prohibited tax shelter transaction. The excise tax, in the amount of $20,000, is assessed for each approval or other act causing the organization to be a party to the prohibited tax shelter transaction. To report this tax, file Form 4720.

X. Requirements for a Properly Completed Form 990 or Form 990-EZ

Public inspection. In general, all information the organization reports on or with its Form 990, or Form 990-EZ, including attachments, will be available for public inspection. Note, however, the public inspection rules for the Schedule B (Form 990, 990-EZ, or 990-PF), a required attachment for organizations that file Form 990 or Form 990-EZ. Make sure the forms and attachments are clear enough to photocopy legibly.

Signature. To make the return complete, an officer of the organization authorized to sign it must sign in the space provided. For a corporation, or association, this officer may be the president, vice president, treasurer, assistant treasurer, chief accounting officer, or other corporate or association officer, such as a tax officer. A receiver, trustee, or assignee must sign any

return he or she files for a corporation or association. For a trust, the authorized trustee(s) must sign.

The paid preparer must:
• Sign the return in the space provided for the preparer's signature.
• Enter the preparer's social security number (SSN), preparer tax identification number (PTIN), or employer identification number (EIN), only if the Form 990, or Form 990-EZ, is for a section 4947(a)(1) nonexempt charitable trust that is not filing Form 1041.
• Complete the required preparer information.
• Give a copy of the return to the organization.

Leave the paid preparer's space blank if the return was prepared by a regular employee of the filing organization.

Recordkeeping. The organization's records should be kept for as long as they may be needed for the administration of any provision of the Internal Revenue Code. Usually, records that support an item of income, deduction, or credit must be kept for 3 years from the date the return is due or filed, whichever is later. Keep records that verify the organization's basis in property for as long as they are needed to figure the basis of the original or replacement property.

The organization should also keep copies of any returns it has filed. They help in preparing future returns and in making computations when filing an amended return.

Rounding off to whole dollars. The organization may round off cents to whole dollars on the return and schedules. If the organization does round to whole dollars, it must round all amounts. To round, drop amounts under 50 cents and increase amounts from 50 to 99 cents to the next dollar. For example, $1.39 becomes $1 and $2.50 becomes $3.

If the organization has to add two or more amounts to figure the amount to enter on a line, include cents when adding the amounts and round off only the total.

Completing all lines. Unless the organization is permitted to use certain DOL forms or Form 5500 as partial substitutes for Form 990, or Form 990-EZ (see *General Instruction F*), do not leave any applicable lines blank or attach any other forms or schedules instead of entering the required information on the appropriate line on Form 990 or Form 990-EZ.

Some parts of the Form 990 (for example, Line 51 or Line 75) require the organization to acquire information from certain persons regarding their relationships with each other and with other organizations. The organization is not required to provide information about such business relationships if it is unable to secure the information after making a reasonable effort to obtain it; in such case, the organization shall (in response to the question) report the efforts undertaken. An example of a reasonable effort is for the Form 990 preparer or an officer eligible to sign the Form 990 to distribute a questionnaire annually to each officer, director, trustee, and key employee listed in Part V-A; each highest compensated employee listed in Schedule A, Part I; and each highest compensated professional and other independent contractor listed in Schedule A, Parts II-A and II-B. The questionnaire should require the name and title, date, and signature of each person reporting this information. The questionnaire should contain the pertinent definitions set out in the instructions.

Assembling Form 990 or Form 990-EZ. Before filing the Form 990, or Form 990-EZ, assemble the package of forms and attachments in the following order:

● Form 990 or Form 990-EZ.

● Schedule A (Form 990 or 990-EZ). The requirement to attach Schedule A (Form 990 or 990-EZ) applies to all section 501(c)(3) organizations and all section 4947(a)(1) nonexempt charitable trusts that file Form 990 or Form 990-EZ.

● Schedule B (Form 990, 990-EZ, or 990-PF).

● Attachments to Form 990 or Form 990-EZ.

● Attachments to Schedule A (Form 990 or 990-EZ).

● Attachments to Schedule B (Form 990, 990-EZ, or 990-PF).

Attachments. Use the schedules on the official form unless more space is

needed. If the organization uses attachments, the attachments must:

1. Show the form number and tax year;

2. Show the organization's name and EIN;

3. Identify clearly the Part or line(s) to which the attachments relate;

4. Include the information required by the form and use the same format as the form;

5. Follow the same Part and line sequence as the form; and

6. Be on the same size paper as the form.

☑ Checklist for a Properly Completed Return

_____ Complete Schedule A (Form 990 or 990-EZ) if the organization is a section 501(c)(3), 501(e), (f), (k), or (n) organization or a section 4947(a)(1) nonexempt charitable trust.

_____ Complete Schedule A (Form 990 or 990-EZ), Part IV-A, _Support Schedule_, if the organization is required to check a box on line 10, 11a, 11b, or 12 of Part IV of Schedule A.

_____ File Form 990 instead of Form 990-EZ if the organization's gross receipts are $100,000 or more or total assets at the end of the year are $250,000 or more, the organization is a sponsoring organization, or controlling organization under section 512(b)(13).

_____ Indicate the correct tax year in the heading of the form.

_____ Have an officer of the organization sign the return.

_____ Complete all Balance Sheet columns (Part IV (and IV-A and IV-B) of Form 990; Part II of Form 990-EZ). Indicate "N/A" if a line, column, or Part does not apply. Indicate too, on the applicable line, if a schedule is attached. Do not substitute another balance sheet instead of completing the Part II Balance Sheet of Form 990-EZ.

_____ Attach all required pages and schedules to the return. Include a list of subordinates if filing a group return.

_____ Double-check the accuracy of the organization's EIN, tax period, and group exemption number (GEN), if applicable.

_____ Indicate the correct 501(c) subsection under which the organization is tax-exempt. If there has been a change, attach a copy of the latest determination letter. If the letter is unavailable, attach a description of the organization's primary exempt purpose.

_____ Be aware that the Form 990, Form 990-EZ, the Schedule A (Form 990 or 990-EZ), and the attachments to be filed with these forms, are publicly disclosable. Note, however, the specific public inspection rules in the Instructions for Schedule B (Form 990, 990-EZ, or 990-PF).

_____ Section 501(c)(3) organizations required to complete lines 26, 27, or 28 of Schedule A (Form 990 or 990-EZ) must prepare lists for their own records to substantiate amounts on those lines. These lists are not to be filed with the return.

_____ Do not check the *Termination* box in the heading of the Form 990 or 990-EZ unless the organization has ceased operations.

Specific Instructions for Form 990

See also the *General Instructions* that apply to both Form 990 and Form 990-EZ.

Contents	Page

Completing the Heading of Form 990

The instructions that follow are keyed to items in the heading for Form 990.

Item A. Accounting Period

File the 2007 return for calendar year 2007 and fiscal years that begin in 2007 and end in 2008. For a fiscal year return, fill in the tax year space at the top of page 1. See *General Instruction G* for additional information on accounting periods and methods.

Item B. Checkboxes

Address change, name change, and initial return. Check the appropriate box if the organization changed its address since it filed its previous return,

or if this is the first time the organization is filing either a Form 990 or a Form 990-EZ.

If the tax-exempt organization has changed its name, attach the following documents:

IF the organization is .	THEN attach . . .
A corporation	Amendments to the articles of incorporation with proof of filing with the state of incorporation.
A trust	Amendments to the trust agreement signed by the trustee.
An association	Amendments to the articles of association, constitution, bylaws, or other organizing document, with the signatures of at least two officers/members.

Final return and Amended return. Organizations should file final returns when they cease to be section 501(a) organizations or section 527 organizations; for example, when they cease operations and dissolve. See the instructions for line 79 that discuss liquidations, dissolutions, terminations, or substantial contractions.

If the return is an amended return, check the box. There are amended return requirements when filing with a state. See *General Instructions E* and *J.*

Application pending. If the organization's application for exemption is pending, check this box and complete the return.

Item C. Name and Address

If the organization operates under a name different from its legal name, give the legal name of the organization but identify its alternate name, after the legal name, by writing "aka" (also known as) and the alternate name of the organization. However, if the organization has changed its name, follow the instructions for *Name change* in *Item B — Checkboxes*.

If the organization receives its mail in care of a third party (such as an accountant or an attorney), enter on the street address line "C/O" followed by

the third party's name and street address or P.O. box.

Include the suite, room, or other unit number after the street address. If the Post Office does not deliver mail to the street address and the organization has a P.O. box, show the box number instead of the street address.

For foreign addresses, enter information in the following order: city, province or state, and the name of the country. Follow the foreign country's practice in placing the postal code in the address. Please do not abbreviate the country name.

If a change in address occurs after the return is filed, use Form 8822 to notify the IRS of the new address.

Item D. Employer Identification Number

The organization should have only one federal employer identification number (EIN). If it has more than one and has not been advised which to use, notify the:

> Department of the Treasury
> Internal Revenue Service Center
> Ogden, UT 84201-0027

State what numbers the organization has, the name and address to which each number was assigned, and the address of its principal office. The IRS will advise the organization which number to use.

- A section 501(c)(9) voluntary employees' beneficiary association must use its own EIN and not the EIN of its sponsor.
- A disregarded entity, as described in Regulations sections 301.7701-1 through 301.7701-3, however, may use the EIN of the organization in Part IX if the disregarded entity does not have its own EIN. See *General Instruction A* and the instructions for Part IX.

Item E. Telephone Number

Enter a telephone number of the organization that members of the public and government regulators may use during normal business hours to obtain information about the organization's finances and activities. If the organization does not have a telephone number, enter the telephone number of an organization official who can provide such information.

Item F. Accounting Method

An organization must indicate the method of accounting used in preparing this return. See *General Instruction G.*

Item G. Website

Show the organization's website address if a website is available. Otherwise, write "N/A" (not applicable). Consider adding the organization's email address to its website.

Item H. Group Return, etc.

See *General Instruction R.* Attach the required list, if applicable, or the organization will be contacted later for the missing information.

Item I. Group Exemption Number

The group exemption number (GEN) is a number assigned by the IRS to the central/parent organization of a group that has a group ruling.

Enter the four-digit group exemption number if "Yes" was checked in item H(a) and H(d). Contact the central/ parent organization if the organization is unsure of the GEN assigned.

Item J. Organization Type

If the organization is exempt under section 501(c), check the applicable box and insert, within the parentheses, the number that identifies the type of section 501(c) organization the filer is. See the chart in *General Instruction C.* The term section 501(c)(3) includes organizations exempt under sections 501(e), (f), (k), and (n). Check the applicable box if the organization is a section 527 political organization. See *General Instruction U.*

If the organization is a section 4947(a)(1) nonexempt charitable trust, check the applicable box. Note also the discussion regarding Schedule A (Form 990 or 990-EZ) and Form 1041 in *General Instruction D* and the instructions to line 92 of Form 990.

Item K. Gross Receipts of $25,000 or Less

Check this box if the organization is not a section 509(a)(3) supporting organization and its gross receipts are normally not more than $25,000, but the organization chooses to file Form 990. If the organization chooses to file Form 990, be sure to file a complete return. For a discussion on gross receipts for this purpose, see *General Instruction B.* Also, see *General Instruction X* for a discussion on a complete return.

 To figure if a section 501(c)(15) organization qualifies for tax exemption for the year, see the definition of gross receipts for section 501(c)(15) purposes under Section

501(c)(15) Organizations *in* General Instruction A. *Do not use the section 501(c)(15) definition of gross receipts to figure if the organization's gross receipts are normally $25,000 or less.*

Item L. Figuring Gross Receipts

The organization's gross receipts are the total amount it received from all sources during its annual accounting period, without subtracting any costs or expenses. See the gross receipts discussion in *General Instruction B.*

 To figure if a section 501(c)(15) organization qualifies for tax exemption for the year, see the definition of gross receipts for section 501(c)(15) purposes under Section 501(c)(15) Organizations *in* General Instruction A. *Do not use the section 501(c)(15) definition of gross receipts to figure the amount to enter here.*

Item M. Schedule B (Form 990, 990-EZ, or 990-PF)

Whether or not the organization enters any amount on line 1e of Form 990, the organization must either check the box in item M or attach Schedule B (Form 990, 990-EZ, or 990-PF). The organization return will be incomplete if it does not either check the box in item M or file Schedule B (Form 990, 990-EZ, or 990-PF). See the Instructions for Schedule B (Form 990, 990-EZ, or 990-PF), for more information.

 Contributor *includes individuals, fiduciaries, partnerships, corporations, associations, trusts, and exempt organizations.*

Guidelines for Meeting the Requirements for Schedule B (Form 990, 990-EZ, or 990-PF)

Section 501(c)(3) org. meeting the 1/3 support test of 170(b)(1)(A)

If . . . . A section 501(c)(3) organization that met the 1/3 support test of the regulations under 509(a)(1)/ 170(b)(1)(A) did not receive a contribution of the greater of $5,000 or 2% of the amount on line 1e of Form 990, from any one contributor,*

Then . . . . The organization should check the box in item M to certify that it is not required to attach Schedule B (Form 990, 990-EZ, or 990-PF).

Otherwise Complete and attach Schedule B (Form 990, 990-EZ, or 990-PF).

Section 501(c)(7), (8), or (10) Organization

If . . . . A section 501(c)(7), (8), or (10) organization did not receive *any* contribution or bequest for use *exclusively* for religious, charitable, scientific, literary, or educational purposes, or the prevention of cruelty to children or animals (and did not receive any noncharitable contributions of $5,000 or more as described below under general rule),

Then . . . . The organization should check the box in item M to certify that it is not required to attach Schedule B (Form 990, 990-EZ, or 990-PF).

Otherwise Complete and attach Schedule B (Form 990, 990-EZ, or 990-PF).

All Other Form 990 or Form 990-EZ Organizations (General rule)

If . . . . The organization did not show as part of line 1e of the Form 990, a contribution of $5,000 or more from any one contributor,*

Then . . . . The organization should check the box in item M to certify that it is not required to attach Schedule B (Form 990, 990-EZ, or 990-PF).

Otherwise Complete and attach Schedule B (Form 990, 990-EZ, or 990-PF).

* Total a contributor's gifts of $1,000 or more to determine if a contributor gave $5,000 or more. Do not include smaller gifts.

Part I. Revenue, Expenses, and Changes in Net Assets or Fund Balances

All organizations filing Form 990 with the IRS or any state must complete Part I. Some states that accept Form 990 in place of their own forms require additional information.

Line 1. In General

Contributions, Gifts, Grants, and Similar Amounts Received

• Report the amount contributed to donor advised funds on line 1a.
• On lines 1b through 1d, report amounts received as voluntary contributions (other than contributions to donor advised funds; that is, payments, or the part of any payment, for which the payer (donor) does not receive full retail value (fair market value) from the recipient (donee) organization.
• Report gross amounts of contributions collected in the charity's name by fundraisers.
• Report all expenses of raising contributions in *Fundraising*, column (D), Part II, and on line 15 of Part I. The organization must show on line 30 professional fundraising fees relating to the gross amounts of contributions collected in the charity's name by fundraisers.

- Report the value of noncash contributions at the time of the donation. For example, report the gross value of a donated car at the time the car was received as a donation.
- For grants, see *Grants That Are Equivalent to Contributions*, on the following page.

Reporting for line 1, in accordance with SFAS 116, is acceptable for Form 990 purposes, but not required by IRS. However, see *General Instruction E*.

An organization that receives a grant to be paid in future years should, according to SFAS 116, report the grant's present value on line 1. Accruals of present value increments to the unpaid grant should also be reported on line 1 in future years.

Contributions Can Arise From Special Events When an Excess Payment Is Received for Items Offered

Fundraising activities relate to soliciting and receiving contributions. However, special fundraising activities such as dinners, door-to-door sales of merchandise, carnivals, and bingo games can produce both contributions and revenue.

If a buyer at such a special event pays more for goods or services than their retail value, report, as a contribution, both on line 1b and on line 9a (within the parentheses), any amount paid in excess of the retail value. This situation usually occurs when organizations seek public support through solicitation programs that are in part special events or activities and are in part solicitations for contributions. The primary purpose of such solicitations is to receive contributions and not to sell the merchandise at its retail value even though this might produce a profit.

Example. An organization announces that anyone who contributes at least $40 to the organization can choose to receive a book worth $16 retail value. A person who gives $40, and who chooses the book, is really purchasing the book for $16 and also making a contribution of $24. The contribution of $24, which is the difference between the buyer's payment and the $16 retail value of the book, would be reported on line 1b and again on line 9a (within the parentheses). The revenue received ($16 retail value of the book) would be reported in the right-hand column on line 9a.

If a contributor gives more than $40, that person would be making a larger contribution, the difference between the book's retail value of $16 and the amount actually given. Rev. Rul.

67-246, 1967-2 C.B. 104, explains this principle in detail. See also the *Lines 9a through 9c* instructions and Pub. 526.

Report the expenses that relate directly to the sale of the book on line 9b. Report the expenses of raising contributions (shown within the parentheses on line 9a and again on line 1b) in *Fundraising*, column (D), Part II, and on line 15 of Part I.

⚠ **CAUTION** *At the time of any solicitation or payment, organizations that are eligible to receive tax-deductible contributions should advise patrons of the amount deductible for federal tax purposes.* See General Instruction L.

Contributions Can Arise From Special Events When Items of Only Nominal Value Are Given or Offered

If an organization offers goods or services of only nominal value through a special event or distributes free, unordered, low-cost items to patrons, report the entire amount received for such benefits as a contribution on line 1b (direct public support). Report all related expenses in *Fundraising*, column (D), Part II. See *General Instruction L* for a definition of benefits that have a nominal or insubstantial value.

Section 501(c)(3) Organizations

Correctly dividing gross receipts from special events into revenue and contributions is especially important for a section 501(c)(3) organization that claims public support as described in section 509(a)(1)/170(b)(1)(A)(vi) or section 509(a)(2). In the public support computations of these Code sections, the revenue portion of gross receipts may be (a) excluded entirely, (b) treated as public support, or (c) if the revenue represents unrelated trade or business income, treated as nonpublic support.

Section 501(c)(3) organizations must separate gross receipts from special events into revenue and contributions when preparing the *Support Schedule* in Part IV-A of Schedule A (Form 990 or 990-EZ).

Section 501(c)(9), (17), and (18) Organizations

These organizations provide participants with life, sickness, accident, welfare, and unemployment insurance, pensions, or similar benefits, or a combination of these benefits. When such an organization receives payments from participants or their employers to provide these benefits, report the payments on line 2 as program service revenue, rather than on line 1 as contributions.

Donations of Services and the Use of Property Are Not Contributions

In Part I, do not include as contributions on line 1 the value of services donated to the organization, or items such as the free use of materials, equipment, or facilities. See the instructions for Part III and for Part VI, line 82, for the optional reporting of such amounts in Parts III and VI.

Any unreimbursed expenses of officers, employees, or volunteers do not belong on the Form 990 or Form 990-EZ. See the discussions for charitable contributions and employee business expenses in Pub. 526 and Pub. 463, respectively.

Grants That Are Equivalent to Contributions

Grants that encourage an organization receiving the grant to carry on programs or activities that further its exempt purposes are grants that are equivalent to contributions. Report them on line 1. The grantor may require that the programs of the grant recipient (grantee) conform to the grantor's own policies and may specify the use of the grant, such as use for the restoration of a historic building or a voter registration drive.

A grant is still equivalent to a contribution if the grant recipient provides a service or makes a product that benefits the grantor incidentally. See *Examples* in the line 1d instructions. However, a grant is a payment for services, and not a contribution, if the grant requires the grant recipient to provide that grantor with a specific service, facility, or product rather than to give a direct benefit primarily to the general public or to that part of the public served by the organization. In general, do not report as contributions any payments for a service, facility, or product that primarily give some economic or physical benefit to the payer (grantor).

Example. A public interest organization described in section 501(c)(4) makes a grant to another organization to conduct a nationwide survey to determine voter attitudes on issues of interest to the grantor. The grantor plans to use the results of the survey to plan its own program for the next 3 years. Under these circumstances, since the survey serves the grantor's direct needs and benefits the grantor more than incidentally, the grant to the organization making the survey is not a contribution. The grant recipient should not report the grant as a contribution but should report it on line 2 as program service revenue.

Treat research to develop products for the payer's use or benefit as directly serving the payer. However, generally, basic research or studies in the physical or social sciences should not be treated as serving the payer's needs.

See Regulations section 1.509(a)-3(g) to determine if a grant is a contribution reportable on line 1b or a revenue item reportable elsewhere on Form 990.

Line 1a. Contributions to Donor Advised Funds

Complete line 1a only if the organization is a sponsoring organization that maintains one or more donor advised funds. Enter the gross amounts of contributions, gifts, grants, and bequests received for all donor advised funds the organization maintains.

A *sponsoring organization* is any organization which:
• Is described in section 170(c), except for governmental entities described in section 170(c)(1),
• Is not a private foundation as defined in section 509(a), and
• Maintains one or more donor advised funds.

In general, a *donor advised fund* is a fund or account:
1. Which is separately identified by reference to contributions of a donor or donors;
2. Which is owned and controlled by a sponsoring organization; and
3. For which the donor (or any person appointed or designated by the donor) has or expects to have advisory privileges concerning the distribution or investment of amounts held in the donor advised funds or accounts because of the donor's status as a donor.

Exception. A *donor advised fund* does not include:
1. Any fund or account that makes distributions only to a single identified organization or governmental entity, or
2. Any fund or account for a person described in **3** above that gives advice about which individuals receive grants for travel, study, or other similar purposes, if:
a. The person's advisory privileges are performed exclusively by such person in their capacity as a committee member of which all of the committee members are appointed by the sponsoring organization.
b. No combination of persons with advisory privileges described in **3** above, or persons related to those in **3** above, directly or indirectly control the committee.

Specific Instructions for Form 990

c. All grants from the fund or account are awarded on an objective and nondiscriminatory basis according to a procedure approved in advance by the board of directors of the sponsoring organization. The procedure must be designed to ensure that all grants meet the requirements of sections 4945(g)(1), (2), or (3).

Line 1b. Direct Public Support

Contributions, gifts, grants, and similar amounts received. Enter the gross amounts of contributions, gifts, grants, and bequests that the organization received directly from the public. Do not include any amounts previously reported on line 1a on this line. Include:
• All donated items. For example, a car is donated to an organization. Immediately after the organization receives the donated car, the organization sells the car. The organization includes the value of the car as of the time of its receipt as a contribution on line 1b and includes it in the total on line 1e as a noncash contribution.
• All funds or the entire value of noncash items raised by an outside fundraiser in a charity's name and not just the amount actually received by the charity. For example, a corporation solicits and sells cars in a charity's name. When a car is received, its entire value is reported as a contribution.
• Amounts received from individuals, trusts, corporations, estates, and foundations, or raised by an outside professional fundraiser.
• Contributions and grants from public charities and other exempt organizations that are neither fundraising organizations nor affiliates of the filing organization.
• See the instructions for line 1c.

Membership dues. Report on line 1b membership dues and assessments that represent contributions from the public rather than payments for benefits received or payments from affiliated organizations. See the instructions for line 3.

Government contributions (grants). Report government grants on line 1d if they represent contributions, or on line 2 (and on line 93(g) of Part VII), if they represent fees for services. See the instructions under the heading, *Grants That Are Equivalent to Contributions*, earlier and the instructions for line 1d later.

Commercial co-venture. Report amounts contributed by a commercial co-venture on line 1b as a contribution received directly from the public. These are amounts received by an organization (donee) for allowing an outside organization (donor) to use the

-27-

donee's name in a sales promotion campaign. In such a campaign, the donor advertises that it will contribute a certain dollar amount to the donee organization for each unit of a particular product or service sold or for each occurrence of a specific type.

Contributions received through special events. Report contributions received through special events on line 1b. See the preceding line 1 instructions and the instructions for *Lines 9a through 9c*.

Line 1c. Indirect Public Support

Enter the total contributions received indirectly from the public through solicitation campaigns conducted by federated fundraising agencies and similar fundraising organizations (such as a United Way organization and certain sectarian federations). These organizations normally conduct fundraising campaigns within a single metropolitan area or some part of a particular state and allocate part of the net proceeds to each participating organization on the basis of the donors' individual designations and other factors.

Include on line 1c amounts contributed by other organizations closely associated with the reporting organization. This includes contributions received from a parent organization, subordinate, or another organization with the same parent. National organizations that share in fundraising campaigns conducted by their local affiliates should report the amount they receive on line 1c.

Do not include any amounts previously reported on line 1a on this line.

Line 1d. Government Contributions (Grants)

The general line 1 instructions, under the heading, *Grants That Are Equivalent to Contributions*, earlier, apply to this item in particular. A grant or other payment from a governmental unit is treated as a contribution if its primary purpose is to enable the donee to provide a service to, or maintain a facility for, the direct benefit of the public rather than to serve the direct and immediate needs of the grantor even if the public pays part of the expense of providing the service or facility.

The following are examples of governmental grants and other payments that are treated as contributions.

Examples.
1. Payments by a governmental unit for the construction or maintenance of library or hospital facilities open to the public.

2. Payments under government programs to nursing homes or homes for the aged in order to provide health care or other services to their residents.

3. Payments to child placement or child guidance organizations under government programs serving children in the community. The general public gets the primary and direct benefit from these payments and any benefit to the governmental unit itself would be indirect and insubstantial as compared to the public benefit.

Do not include any amounts previously reported on line 1a on this line.

Line 1e. Total Contributions, etc.

Enter the total of amounts reported on lines 1a through 1d. In the entry spaces in the description column for line 1e, enter the separate totals for cash and noncash contributions, gifts, grants, and similar amounts received. The total of the two amounts must equal the total on line 1e.

Report as cash contributions, only contributions received in the form of cash, checks, money orders, credit card charges, wire transfers, and other transfers and deposits to a cash account of the organization. If the organization records pledges as contributions, at the time the pledges are made (rather than when the pledges are collected), include as cash contributions, only those pledges actually collected in cash during the year and pledges uncollected at the end of the year that are reasonably expected to be paid in cash in a later year.

Report all other contributions, as noncash contributions in the space provided. Be sure to include as a noncash contribution donated items like cars and clothing valued as of the time of their receipt even if these items were made available for sale immediately after they were received. See *General Instruction L* and Schedule B (Form 990, 990-EZ, or 990-PF), and the instructions for lines 1 and 1b for a discussion of noncash contributions. Noncash contributions do not include donated services, which may be reported on line 82 and in the narrative section of Part III.

Schedule of Contributors. Attach Schedule B (Form 990, 990-EZ, or 990-PF). See *General Instruction L* and the *Specific Instructions for Completing the Heading of Form 990, Item M.*

Lines 2 through 11

 Do not enter any contributions on lines 2 through 11. Enter all contributions on line 1. If the organization enters contributions on lines 2 through 11, it will be unable to complete Part VII correctly. Line 105 (the sum of amounts entered in columns (B), (D), and (E) for lines 93 through 103 of Part VII, Analysis of Income-Producing Activities) should match the total of amounts entered for correlating lines 2 through 11 of Part I. See the instructions for Part VII.

Line 2. Program Service Revenue Including Medicare, Medicaid Payments and Government Fees and Contracts

Enter the total of program service revenue (exempt function income) as reported in Part VII, lines 93(a) through (g), columns (B), (D), and (E). Program services are primarily those that form the basis of an organization's exemption from tax. For a more detailed description of program services, refer to the instructions for Part II, column (B), *Program services.*

Example. A hospital would report on this line all of its charges for medical services (whether to be paid directly by the patients or through Medicare, Medicaid, or other third-party reimbursement), hospital parking lot fees, room charges, laboratory fees for hospital patients, and related charges for services.

Insurance premiums. A section 501(c)(15) organization would report on this line all of its insurance premiums received. The amount reported here for insurance premiums should correlate with the amounts reported on line 93, columns (B), (D), and (E).

Program service revenue. *Program service revenue* includes income earned by the organization for providing a government agency with a service, facility, or product that benefited that government agency directly rather than benefiting the public as a whole. See the line 1d instructions for reporting guidelines when payments are received from a government agency for providing a service, facility, or product for the primary benefit of the general public.

Program service revenue also includes: tuition received by a school; revenue from admissions to a concert or other performing arts event or to a museum; royalties received as author of an educational publication distributed by a commercial publisher; interest income on loans a credit union makes to its members; payments received by a section 501(c)(9) organization from participants, or employers of

participants, for health and welfare benefits coverage; insurance premiums received by a fraternal beneficiary society; and registration fees received in connection with a meeting or convention.

Program-related investments. *Program service revenue* also includes income from program-related investments. These investments are made primarily to accomplish an exempt purpose of the investing organization rather than to produce income. Examples are scholarship loans and low interest loans to charitable organizations, indigents, or victims of a disaster.

Rental income from an exempt function is another example of program-related investment income. When an organization rents to an unaffiliated exempt organization at less than fair rental value for the purpose of aiding that tenant's exempt function, the reporting organization should report such rental income as program service revenue on line 2. See also the instructions for line 6a. For purposes of this return, report all rental income from an affiliated organization on line 2.

Unrelated trade or business activities. Unrelated trade or business activities (not including any special events or activities) that generate fees for services may also be program service activities. A social club, for example, should report as program service revenue the fees it charges both members and nonmembers for the use of its tennis courts and golf course.

Sales of inventory items by hospitals, colleges, and universities. Books and records maintained in accordance with generally accepted accounting principles for hospitals, colleges, and universities are more specialized than books and records maintained according to those accounting principles for other types of organizations that file Form 990. Accordingly, hospitals, colleges, and universities may report, as program service revenue on line 2, sales of inventory items otherwise reportable on line 10a. In that event, show the applicable cost of goods sold as program service expense on line 13 of Part I and in column (B) of Part II. All other organizations, however, should not report sales of inventory items on line 2.

Line 3. Membership Dues and Assessments

Enter members' and affiliates' dues and assessments that are not contributions.

Dues and assessments received that compare reasonably with available benefits. When dues and assessments are received that compare reasonably with membership benefits received, report such dues and assessments on line 3.

Organizations described in section 501(c)(5), (6), or (7) generally provide benefits that have a reasonable relationship to dues, although benefits to members may be indirect.

Dues or assessments received that exceed the value of available membership benefits. Whether or not membership benefits are used, dues received by an organization, to the extent they are more than the monetary value of the membership benefits available to the dues payer, are a contribution that should be reported on line 1b. See Rev. Rul. 54-565, 1954-2 C.B. 95 and Rev. Rul. 68-432, 1968-2 C.B. 104.

Dues received primarily for the organization's support. If a member pays dues mainly to support the organization's activities and not to obtain benefits of more than nominal monetary value, those dues are a contribution to the organization includible on line 1b.

Examples of membership benefits. These include subscriptions to publications, newsletters (other than one about the organization's activities only), free or reduced-rate admissions to events the organization sponsors, the use of its facilities, and discounts on articles or services that both members and nonmembers can buy. In figuring the value of membership benefits, do not include intangible benefits, such as the right to attend meetings, vote or hold office in the organization, and the distinction of being a member of the organization.

Line 4. Interest on Savings and Temporary Cash Investments
Enter the amount of interest income from savings and temporary cash investments reportable on line 46. So-called dividends or earnings received from mutual savings banks, money market funds, etc., are actually interest and should be entered on line 4.

Line 5. Dividends and Interest from Securities
Enter the amount of dividend and interest income from equity and debt securities (stocks and bonds) of the type reportable on line 54. Include amounts received from payments on securities loans, as defined in section 512(a)(5). Do not include any capital gains dividends that are reportable on line 8. See the instructions for line 2 for reporting income from program-related investments.

Line 6a. Gross Rents
Enter on line 6a the rental income received for the year from investment property reportable on line 55. Do not include on line 6a rental income related to the reporting organization's exempt function (program service). Report such income on line 2. For example, an exempt organization whose exempt purpose is to provide low-rental housing to persons with low income would report that rental income as program service revenue on line 2. Rental income received from an unaffiliated exempt organization is generally considered as unrelated to the reporting organization's exempt purpose and reportable on line 6a. However, note an exception given in the instructions for line 2 when the reporting organization aids an unaffiliated organization with its exempt function.

Only for purposes of completing this return, the reporting organization must report any rental income received from an affiliated exempt organization as program service revenue on line 2.

Line 6b. Rental Expenses
Enter the expenses paid or incurred for the income reported on line 6a. Include interest related to rental property and depreciation if it is recorded in the organization's books and records. Report in column (B) of Part II *Program services* any rental expenses allocable to rental income reportable as program service revenue on line 2.

Line 6c. Net Rental Income or (Loss)
Subtract line 6b from line 6a. Show any loss in parentheses.

Line 7. Other Investment Income
Enter the amount of investment income not reportable on lines 4 through 6 and describe the type of income in the space provided or in an attachment. The income should be the gross amount derived from investments reportable on line 56. Include, for example, royalty income from mineral interests owned by the organization. However, do not include income from program-related investments. See the instructions for line 2. Also, do not include unrealized gains and losses on investments carried at market value. See the instructions for line 20.

Lines 8a through 8d. Gains (or Losses) From Sale of Assets Other Than Inventory
Report, on lines 8a through 8c, all sales of securities in column (A). Use column (B) to report sales of all other types of investments (such as real estate, royalty interests, or partnership interests) and all other noninventory

assets (such as program-related investments and fixed assets used by the organization in its related and unrelated activities).

On line 8a, for each column, enter the total gross sales price of all such assets. Total the cost or other basis (less depreciation) and selling expenses and enter the result on line 8b. On line 8c, enter the net gain or loss.

On lines 8a and 8c, also report capital gains dividends, the organization's share of capital gains and losses from a partnership, and capital gains distributions from trusts. Indicate the source on the schedule described later.

Combine the gain and/or loss figures reported on line 8c, columns (A) and (B) and report that total on line 8d. Do not include any unrealized gains or losses on securities carried at market value in the books of account. See the instructions for line 20.

For reporting sales of securities on Form 990, the organization may use the more convenient average cost basis method to figure the organization's gain or loss. When a security is sold, compare its sales price with the average cost basis of the particular security to determine gain or loss. However, generally, for reporting sales of securities on Form 990-T, do not use the average cost basis to determine gain or loss.

Nonpublicly traded securities and noninventory items. Attach a schedule showing the sale or exchange of nonpublicly traded securities and the sale or exchange of other assets that are not inventory items. The schedule should show security transactions separately from the sale of other assets. Show for each of these assets:

- Date acquired and how acquired,
- Date sold and to whom sold,
- Gross sales price,
- Cost, other basis, or if donated, value at time acquired (state which),
- Expense of sale and cost of improvements made after acquisition, and
- If depreciable property, depreciation since acquisition.

Publicly traded securities. On the attached schedule, for sales of publicly traded securities through a broker, total the gross sales price, the cost or other basis, and the expenses of sale on all such securities sold, and report lump-sum figures in place of the detailed reporting required by the above paragraph. Publicly traded securities include common and preferred stocks, bonds (including governmental obligations), and mutual fund shares that are listed and regularly traded in an over-the-counter market or on an established exchange and for which market quotations are published or otherwise readily available.

Lines 9a through 9c. Special Events and Activities

On the appropriate line, enter the gross revenue, expenses, and net income (or loss) from all special events and activities, such as dinners, dances, carnivals, raffles, bingo games, other gaming activities, and door-to-door sales of merchandise.

These activities only incidentally accomplish an exempt purpose. Their sole or primary purpose is to raise funds that are other than contributions to finance the organization's exempt activities. This is done by offering goods or services that have more than a nominal value (compared to the price charged) for a payment that is more than the direct cost of those goods or services.

The gross revenue from gaming activities and other special events must be reported in the right-hand column on line 9a without reduction for cash or noncash prizes, cost of goods sold, compensation, fees, or other expenses. Check the box for gaming if the organization conducted directly, or through a promoter, any amount of gaming during the year.

Gaming includes, but is not limited to: bingo, pull tabs, instant bingo, raffles, scratch-offs, charitable gaming tickets, break-opens, hard cards, banded tickets, jar tickets, pickle cards, Lucky Seven cards, Nevada Club tickets, casino nights, Las Vegas nights, and coin-operated gambling devices. Coin-operated gambling devices include slot machines, electronic video slot or line games, video poker, video blackjack, video keno, video bingo, video pull tab games, etc.

Characterizing any required payment as a donation or contribution on tickets or on advertising or solicitation materials does not affect how such payments should be reported on Form 990 or Form 990-EZ. As discussed in the instructions for line 1, the amount of the contribution is the excess of the amount paid over the retail value of the goods or services received by the payer. See also Pub. 526.

Special events may generate both revenue and contributions. Special events sometimes generate both contributions and revenue. When a buyer pays more than the retail value of the goods or services furnished, enter:
- As gross revenue, on line 9a (in the right-hand column), the retail value of the goods or services,
- As a contribution, on both line 1b and line 9a (within the parentheses), the

amount received that exceeds the retail value of the goods or services given.

Report on line 9b only the expenses directly attributable to the goods or services the buyer receives from a special event. Fundraising expenses attributable to contributions, reported on both line 1b and line 9a (within the parentheses), are reportable in Part II, column (D), *Fundraising*. If the organization includes an expense on line 9b, do not report it again on line 10b or in Part II. Expenses reported on line 10b relate to sales of inventory. Expenses reported in Part II, column (D), relate to contributions raised through fundraising.

Example. At a special event, an organization received $100 in gross receipts for goods valued at $40. The organization entered gross revenue of $40 on line 9a (in the right-hand column) and entered a contribution of $60 on both line 1b and line 9a (within the parentheses). The contribution of $60 was the difference between the gross revenue of $40 and the gross receipts of $100.

The expenses directly relating to the sale of the goods would be reported on line 9b. However, all expenses of raising contributions would be reported in column (D), *Fundraising*, Part II and not on line 9b.

For more details about contributions received through fundraising, and contributions and revenue received through special events, see the line 1 instructions. See also *General Instruction L* and its references.

Sales or gifts of goods or services of only nominal value. If the goods or services given or offered at special events have only nominal value, include all of the receipts as contributions on line 1b and all of the related expenses as fundraising expenses on line 15 and in column (D) of Part II. See *General Instruction L* for a description of nominal or insubstantial benefits.

An activity may generate only contributions. An activity that generates only contributions, such as a solicitation campaign by mail, is not a special event and should not be reported on line 9.

Contributions from such an activity are reportable on line 1, and the related fundraising expenses are reportable in column (D), Part II.

The proceeds of solicitation campaigns in which the names of contributors and other respondents are entered in a drawing for the awarding of prizes (so-called sweepstakes or lotteries) are contributions, reportable on line 1, and the related expenses are fundraising expenses, reportable in column (D) of Part II. However, raffles

and lotteries in which a payment of at least a specified minimum amount is required for each entry are special events, reportable on line 9, unless the prizes awarded have only nominal value. Reporting payments in their entirety as contributions when gifts or services given are nominal in value is discussed above.

Attached schedule. Attach a schedule listing the three largest fundraising events, as measured by gross receipts. If gaming is conducted, treat different types of gaming separately to determine the three largest events. For example, treat bingo and pull tabs as separate fundraising events. Describe each of these events by listing the type of event and the number of occasions that the event occurred and show (for each event):
1. Gross receipts,
2. Contributions included in gross receipts (see *Special events may generate both revenue and contributions,* earlier),
3. Gross revenue (gross receipts less contributions),
4. Direct expenses, and
5. Net income or (loss) (gross revenue less direct expenses).

For gaming, direct expenses include: cash and noncash prizes, compensation to bingo callers and workers, rental of gaming equipment, cost of bingo supplies such as pull tab deals, etc.

Include the same information, in total figures, for all other special events held that were not among the three largest. Indicate the type and number of the events not listed individually (for example, three dances and two raffles).

An example of this schedule of special events might appear in columnar form as follows:

Special Events (and the number of occasions that the event occurred):	(A) #	(B) #	(C) #	All Other	Total
Gross Receipts	$xx	$xx	$xx	$xx	$xx
Less: Contributions	xx	xx	xx	xx	xx
Gross Revenue	xx	xx	xx	xx	xx
Less: Direct Expenses	xx	xx	xx	xx	xx
Net Income or (Loss)	$xx	$xx	$xx	$xx	$xx

If the organization uses the above schedule, report the total for *Contributions* on line 1b of Form 990 and on line 9a (within the parentheses). Report the totals for *Gross Revenue,* in the right-hand column, on line 9a; *Direct Expenses* on line 9b; and *Net Income or (Loss)* on line 9c.

Lines 10a through 10c. Gross Profit or (Loss) from Sales of Inventory

Enter the gross sales (less returns and allowances), cost of goods sold, and gross profit or (loss) from the sale of inventory items. These sales do not include items sold at special events that are reportable on line 9. Sales of inventory items reportable on line 10 are sales of those items the organization makes to sell to others or buys for resale. Sales of investments on which the organization expected to profit by appreciation and sale are not reported here. Report sales of investments on line 8.

On line 10a, report gross sales revenue from sales of inventory items, whether the sales activity is an exempt function of the organization or an unrelated trade or business.

On line 10b, report the cost of goods sold related to the sales of such inventory. The usual items included in cost of goods sold are direct and indirect labor, materials and supplies consumed, freight-in, and a proportion of overhead expenses. Marketing and distribution costs are not included in cost of goods sold but are reported in Part II, column (B), *Program services.*

Attached schedule. In an attached schedule, give a breakdown of items sold; for example, sales of food, souvenirs, electronic equipment, uniforms, or educational publications.

Line 11. Other Revenue

Enter the total amount from Part VII, lines 103(a) through (e) (Other revenue), columns (B), (D), and (E). This figure represents the total income from all sources not covered by lines 1 through 10 of Part I. Examples of income includible on line 11 are interest on notes receivable not held as investments or as program-related investments (defined in the line 2 instructions); interest on loans to officers, directors, trustees, key employees, and other employees; and royalties that are not investment income or program service revenue.

Lines 13 through 15—Program Services, Management and General, and Fundraising Expenses

Section 4947(a)(1) nonexempt charitable trusts and section 501(c)(3) and (4) organizations. Complete Part II and then enter on lines 13 through 15 the appropriate amounts from the totals for columns (B), (C), and (D) reported on line 44, Part II.

All other organizations. All other organizations are not required to complete lines 13 through 15 of the Form 990.

Line 16. Payments to Affiliates

This expense classification is used to report certain types of payments to

organizations affiliated with (closely related to) a reporting agency.

Payments to affiliated state or national organizations. Dues paid by the local charity to its affiliated state or national (parent) organization are usually reported on line 16. Report on this line predetermined quota support and dues (excluding membership dues of the type described below) by local agencies to their state or national organizations for unspecified purposes; that is, general use of funds for the national organization's own program and support services.

Purchases from affiliates. Purchases of goods or services from affiliates are not reported on line 16 but are reported as expenses in the usual manner.

Expenses for providing goods or services to affiliates. In addition to payments made directly to affiliated organizations, expenses incurred in providing goods or services to affiliates may be reported on line 16 if:

1. The goods or services provided are not related to the program services conducted by the organization furnishing them (for example, when a local organization incurs expenses in the production of a solicitation film for the state or national organization); and

2. The costs involved are not connected with the management and general or fundraising functions of the reporting organization. For example, when a local organization gives a copy of its mailing list to the state or national organization, the expense of preparing the copy provided may be reported on line 16, but not expenses of preparing and maintaining the local organization's master list.

Federated fundraising agencies. These agencies (see the instructions for line 1c) should include in their own support the full amount of contributions received in connection with a solicitation campaign they conduct, even though donors designate specific agencies to receive part or all of their individual contributions. These fundraising organizations should report the allocations to participating agencies as grants and allocations (line 22b) and quota support payments to their state or national organization as payments to affiliates (line 16).

Voluntary awards or grants to affiliates. Do not report on line 16 voluntary awards or grants made by the reporting agency to its state or national organization for specified purposes. Report these awards or grants on line 22b, *Other Grants and Allocations.*

Membership dues paid to other organizations. Report membership dues paid to obtain general membership benefits, such as regular

-31-

services, publications, and materials, from other organizations as *Other expenses* on line 43. This is the case, for example, if a charitable organization pays dues to a trade association comprised of otherwise unrelated members.

Attached schedule. Attach a schedule listing the name and address of each affiliate that received payments reported on line 16. Specify the amount and purpose of the payments to each affiliate.

 Properly distinguishing between payments to affiliates and grants and allocations is especially important if the organization uses Form 990 for state reporting purposes. See General Instruction E. If the organization uses Form 990 only for reporting to the IRS, payments to affiliated state or national organizations that do not represent membership dues reportable as Other expenses *on line 43 (see instructions, earlier) may be reported either on line 16 or line 22 and explained in the required attachment.*

Line 17. Total Expenses

Organizations using only column (A) of Part II should enter the total of line 16 and line 44 of column (A), Part II, on line 17. Other organizations should enter the total of lines 13 through 16. Organizations using Form 5500 or an approved DOL form as a partial substitute for Form 990 should enter the total expense figure from Form 5500, or from the required reconciliation schedule if Form LM-2 or LM-3 is used. See *General Instruction F.*

Line 18. Excess or (Deficit) for the Year

Enter the difference between lines 12 and 17. If line 17 is more than line 12, enter the difference in parentheses.

Line 19. Net Assets or Fund Balances, Beginning of Year

Enter the balance at the beginning of the year as reported in column (A) of line 73 (or from Form 5500 or an approved DOL form if *General Instruction F* applies). The balance at the beginning of the year for line 19 was the end of the year balance for line 21 and 73 as reported on the organization's prior year return.

Line 20. Other Changes in Net Assets or Fund Balances

Attach a schedule explaining any changes in net assets or fund balances between the beginning and end of the year that are not accounted for by the amount on line 18. Amounts to report here include adjustments of earlier years' activity; unrealized gains and losses on investments carried at market value; and any difference between fair market value and book value of property given as an award or grant. See *General Instruction G* regarding the reporting of a section 481(a) adjustment to conform to SFAS 116.

Line 21. Net Assets or Fund Balances, End of Year

Enter the total of lines 18, 19, and 20. This total figure must equal the amount reported for the end of the year in column (B) of line 73.

Part II—Statement of Functional Expenses

In General—

Column (A)

All organizations must complete column (A) unless they are using an approved DOL form or Form 5500 as a partial substitute for Form 990. See *General Instruction F.*

Columns (B), (C), and (D)

These columns are optional for all organizations except section 4947(a)(1) nonexempt charitable trusts and section 501(c)(3) and (4) organizations. Section 4947(a)(1) nonexempt charitable trusts and section 501(c)(3) and (4) organizations must complete columns (B), (C), and (D).

In Part II, the organization's expenses are designated by object classification (for example, salaries, legal fees, supplies, etc.) and allocated into three functions: *Program services* (column (B)); *Management and general* (column (C)); and *Fundraising* (column (D)). These functions are explained below in the instructions for the columns. Do not include in Part II any expense items the organization must report on lines 6b, 8b, 9b, 10b, or 16 in Part I.

For reporting to the IRS only, use the organization's normal accounting method to report total expenses in column (A) and to segregate them into functions under columns (B), (C), and (D). However, for state reporting requirements, see *General Instructions E* and *G*. If the accounting system does not provide for this type of segregation, a reasonable method of allocation may be used. The amounts reported should be accurate and the method of allocation documented in the organization's records.

Report, in the appropriate column, expenses that are directly attributable to a particular functional category. In general, allocate expenses that relate to more than one functional category. For example, allocate employees' salaries on the basis of each employee's time. For some shared

expenses such as occupancy, supplies, and depreciation of office equipment, use an appropriate basis for each kind of cost. However, the organization should report some other shared expenses in column (C) only. The column instructions below discuss allocating expenses.

Column (A)—Total

For column (A), total each line item of columns (B), (C), and (D) in Part II. Except for expenses the organization reports on lines 6b, 8b, 9b, 10b, or 16 of Part I, the organization should use column (A) to report all expenses the organization paid or incurred.

Column (B)—Program Services

Program services are mainly those activities that the reporting organization was created to conduct and which, along with any activities commenced subsequently, form the basis of the organization's current exemption from tax. They may be self-funded or funded out of contributions, accumulated income, investment income, or any other source. Fundraising expenses should not be reported as program-related expenses even though one of the functions of the organization is to solicit contributions for other organizations.

Program services can also include the organization's unrelated trade or business activities. For example, publishing a magazine is a program service even though the magazine contains both editorials and articles that further the organization's exempt purpose and advertising, the income from which is taxable as unrelated business income.

If an organization receives a grant to do research, produce an item, or perform a service, either to meet the grantor's specific needs or to benefit the public directly, the costs incurred represent program service expenses. Do not treat these costs as fundraising expenses, even if the organization reports the grant on line 1 as a contribution.

Column (C)— Management and General

Use column (C) to report the organization's expenses for overall function and management, rather than for its direct conduct of fundraising activities or program services. Overall management usually includes the salaries and expenses of the chief officer of the organization and that officer's staff. If part of their time is spent directly supervising program services and fundraising activities, their salaries and expenses should be allocated among those functions.

Other expenses to report in column (C) include those for meetings of the board of directors or similar group; committee and staff meetings (unless held in connection with specific program services or fundraising activities); general legal services; accounting (including patient accounting and billing); general liability insurance; office management; auditing, personnel, and other centralized services; preparation, publication, and distribution of an annual report; and investment expenses (however, report rental income expenses on line 6b and program-related income expenses in column (B)).

The organization should report only general expenses in column (C). Do not use this column to report costs of special meetings or other activities that relate to fundraising or specific program services.

Column (D)— Fundraising

Fundraising expenses are the total expenses incurred in soliciting contributions, gifts, grants, etc. Report as fundraising expenses all expenses, including allocable overhead costs, incurred in: (a) publicizing and conducting fundraising campaigns; (b) soliciting bequests and grants from foundations or other organizations, or government grants reportable on line 1d; (c) participating in federated fundraising campaigns; (d) preparing and distributing fundraising manuals, instructions, and other materials; and (e) conducting special events that generate contributions reportable on line 1b, in addition to revenue reportable in the right-hand column on line 9a. However, report any expenses that are directly attributable to revenue shown on line 9a (for example, the direct expenses incurred in furnishing the goods or services sold) on line 9b.

Allocating Indirect Expenses

Colleges, universities, hospitals, and other organizations that accumulate indirect expenses in various cost centers (such as the expenses of operating and maintaining the physical plant) that are reallocated to the program services and other functional areas of the organization in single or multiple steps may find it easier to report these expenses in the following optional manner:

First, report the expenses of these indirect cost centers on lines 25 through 43 of column (C), *Management and general*, along with the expenses properly reportable in that column.

Second, allocate the total expenses for each cost center to columns (B), (C), and (D) (*Program services, Management and general,* and *Fundraising*) as a separate item entry on line 43, *Other Expenses*. Enter the name of the cost center on line 43. If any of the cost center's expenses are to be allocated to the expenses listed in Part I (such as the expenses attributable to special events and activities), enter these expenses as a negative figure in columns (A) and (C). This prevents reporting the same expense in both Parts I and II. If part of the total cost center expenses are to be allocated to columns (B), *Program services*, and (D), *Fundraising*, enter these expenses as positive amounts in these columns and as single negative amounts in column (C), *Management and general*. Do not make any entries in column (A), *Total*, for these offsetting entries.

Example. An organization reports in column (C) $50,000 of its actual management and general expenses and $100,000 of expenses of an indirect cost center that are allocable in part to other functions. The total of lines 25 through 43 of column (C) would be $150,000 before the indirect cost center allocations were made. Assume that $10,000 (of the $100,000 total expenses of the cost center) was allocable to fundraising; $70,000 to various program services; $15,000 to management and general functions; and $5,000 to special events and activities. To report this in Part II under this optional method:

1. Indicate the cost center, the expenses of which are being allocated, on line 43, as Allocation of (specify) expenses;

2. Enter a decrease of $5,000 on the same line in the column (A), *Total*, representing the special event expenses that were already reported on line 9b in Part I;

3. Enter $70,000 on the same line in column (B), *Program services*;

4. Enter $10,000 on the same line in column (D), *Fundraising*; and

5. Enter a decrease of $85,000 on the same line in column (C), *Management and general*, to represent the allocations to functional areas other than management and general.

Line	(A)	(B)	(C)	(D)
25–43a	$150,000	$ —	$150,000	$ —
43b Allocation of the $100,000 indirect cost center expenses reported in (C)	(5,000)	70,000	(85,000)	10,000
44	$145,000	$ 70,000	$ 65,000	$ 10,000

After making these allocations, the column (C) total (line 44, column (C)) would be $65,000, consisting of the $50,000 actual management and general expense amount and the $15,000 allocation of the aggregate

Specific Instructions for Form 990

cost center expenses to management and general.

The above is an example of a one-step allocation that shows how to report the allocation in Part II. This reporting method would actually be needed more for multiple step allocations involving two or more cost centers. The total expenses of the first would be allocated to the other functions, including an allocation of part of these expenses to the second cost center. The expenses of the second cost center would then be allocated to other functions and any remaining cost centers to be allocated, and so on. The greater the number of these cost centers that are allocated out, the more difficult it is to preserve the object classification identity of the expenses of each cost center (for example, salaries, interest, supplies, etc.). Using the reporting method described above avoids this problem.

 The intent of the above instructions is only to facilitate reporting indirect expenses by both object classification and function. These instructions do not permit the allocation to other functions of expenses that should be reported as management and general expenses.

Line 22. Grants and Allocations

The following instructions apply to lines 22a and 22b.

Report voluntary awards and grants to affiliated organizations for specific (restricted) purposes or projects also on line 22, but not required payments to affiliates reportable on line 16.

Report scholarship, fellowship, and research grants to individuals on line 22. Certain other payments to, or for the benefit of, individuals may be reportable on line 23 instead. See the instructions for line 23 for details.

Report only the amount of actual grants and awards on line 22. Report expenses incurred in selecting recipients, or monitoring compliance with the terms of a grant or award, on lines 25 through 43.

In the spaces provided, give separate totals for cash and noncash grants and allocations made. Cash grants include only grants and allocations paid by cash, checks, money orders, wire transfers, and other charges against funds on deposit at a financial institution.

Reporting for line 22, in accordance with SFAS 116, is acceptable for Form 990 purposes, but not required by IRS. However, see *General Instruction E*.

An organization that makes a grant to be paid in future years should, according to SFAS 116, report the grant's present value on line 22.

Accruals of present value increments to the unpaid grant should also be reported on line 22 in future years.

Line 22a. Grants Paid From Donor Advised Funds

Enter the amount of awards and grants to individuals and organizations paid from donor advised funds on line 22a. See the line 1a instructions for the definition of a donor advised fund. See the line 22 instructions, above, for general information on the reporting of grants and allocations paid. See the instructions for line 22b for information about the required schedule.

Line 22b. Other Grants and Allocations

 Do not include on line 22b amounts paid from a donor advised fund.

Enter the amount of other awards and grants (not included on line 22a) to individuals and organizations selected by the filing organization. United Way and similar fundraising organizations should include allocations to member agencies.

Attached schedule. Attach a schedule of amounts reported on line 22a and a separate schedule for line 22b as applicable. Any grants or allocations reported on line 22b that were approved during the year, but not paid by the due date for filing Form 990 (including extensions), must be identified and listed separately in the schedule for line 22b. On the applicable schedule show: (a) each class of activity; (b) grantee's name, address, and the amount given; and (c) (in the case of grants to individuals) relationship of grantee if related by blood, marriage, adoption, or employment (including employees' children) to any person or corporation with an interest in the organization, such as a creator, donor, director, trustee, officer, etc.

On the applicable schedule, classify activities in more detail than in such broad terms as charitable, educational, religious, or scientific. For example, identify payments for nursing services, laboratory construction, or fellowships.

If property other than cash is given, also show on the applicable schedule: (a) a description of the property; (b) its book value and how the book value was determined; (c) its fair market value and how the fair market value was determined; (d) the date of the gift. If the fair market value of the property when the organization gave it is the measure of the award or grant, record any difference between fair market value and book value in the organization's books of account and on line 20.

Colleges, universities, and primary and secondary schools are not required to list the names of individuals who were provided scholarships or other financial assistance whether they are the recipients of federal grant money or not. Instead, these organizations must (a) group each type of financial aid provided; (b) indicate the number of individuals who received the aid; and (c) specify the aggregate dollar amount.

Line 23. Specific Assistance to Individuals

Enter the amount of payments to, or for the benefit of, particular clients or patients, including assistance rendered by others at the expense of the filing organization. Do not include grants to other organizations that select the person(s) to receive the assistance available through the use of the grant funds. For example, report a payment to a hospital to cover the medical expenses of a particular individual on line 23, but do not report a contribution to a hospital to provide some service to the general public or to unspecified charity patients on this line. Also, do not include scholarship, fellowship, or research grants to individuals even though selected by the grantor organization. Report these grants on line 22b, or line 22a, if applicable.

Attached schedule. Attach a schedule showing the total payments for each particular class of activity, such as food, shelter, and clothing for indigents or disaster victims; medical, dental, and hospital fees and charges; and direct cash assistance to indigents. For payments to indigent families, do not identify the individuals.

Line 24. Benefits Paid to or for Members

For an organization that provides benefits to members or dependents (such as organizations exempt under section 501(c)(8), (9), or (17)), attach a schedule. Show amounts of: (a) death, sickness, hospitalization, or disability benefits; (b) unemployment compensation benefits; and (c) other benefits (state their nature). Do not report the cost of employment-related benefits the organization provides its officers and employees on this line. Report those expenses on lines 27 and 28.

Line 25. Compensation of Current and Former Officers, Directors and Certain Disqualified and Other Persons

Compensation. *Compensation* includes all forms of income earned or received for services provided.

In Part V-A, give the name and compensation (if any) of each current officer, director, trustee, and key employee, along with the other information requested. In Part V-B, give the name and compensation (if any) of each former officer, director, trustee, and key employee, along with the other information requested. See the Part V-A instructions for a definition of key employee.

Form 941 must be filed to report income tax withholding and social security and Medicare taxes. The organization must also file Form 940 to report federal unemployment taxes unless the organization is not subject to these taxes. See Pub.15 (Circular E) for details. See also the discussion of the *Trust Fund Recovery Penalty* given in *General Instruction D.*

Lines 25a and 25b

Enter on line 25a the total compensation for the tax year for the current officers, directors, trustees, and key employees listed in Part V-A. Enter on line 25b the total compensation for the tax year for the former officers, directors, trustees, and key employees listed in Part V-B.

Section 501(c)(3) and (c)(4) organizations and section 4947(a)(1) non-exempt charitable trusts must allocate the total compensation in column (A) for lines 25a and lines 25b by functional expense in columns (B), (C), and (D).

Example. Allocate the total compensation figure of line 25a, column (A), by functional expenses represented by line 25a, columns (B), (C), and (D). For instance, if key employee A spent 90% of her time running a program which constitutes the basis of the organization's exempt purpose and 10% in general management of the organization itself, key employee A's compensation should be allocated 90% to column (B), program services, and 10% to column (C), management and general. Conversely, if Director B is not paid as a member of the board, but is employed by the organization as a part-time fundraiser, all of Director B's compensation should be allocated to column (D), fundraising.

Line 25c. Compensation and Other Distributions to Disqualified Persons

Enter the total compensation or other distributions provided to disqualified persons (as defined under section 4958(f)(1)) and persons described in section 4958(c)(3) for the year. For a definition of compensation, see the instructions for line 25. Distributions include anything of value provided to a disqualified person that constitutes an

expense of the organization (such as interest on loans owed to the disqualified person), but not business expenses paid under an accountable plan or *de minimis* fringe benefits. Do not include on line 25c, amounts previously included on lines 25a or 25b.

For a definition of disqualified persons, see *Disqualified Persons* under *General Instruction P*, earlier.

Line 26. Salaries and Wages of Employees Not Included on Lines 25a, b, and c

Enter the total amount of employees' salaries and wages, fees, bonuses, severance payments, and payments of compensation deferred in a prior year to all employees not reported on lines 25a, b, or c.

Line 27. Pension Plan Contributions Not Included on Lines 25a, b, and c

Enter the employer's share of contributions to qualified and nonqualified pension plans for the year. Do not include contributions to qualified pension plans under section 401(a) for current or former officers, directors, trustees, or key employees, that were reported on lines 25a, b, or c.

Complete Form 5500 for the organization's plan and file it as a separate return. If the organization has more than one plan, complete a Form 5500 for each plan. File the form by the last day of the 7th month after the plan year ends. See *General Instruction D* for a discussion of Form 5500.

Line 28. Employee Benefits Not Included on Lines 25a–27

Enter the organization's contributions to employee benefit programs (such as insurance, health, and welfare programs) that are not an incidental part of a pension plan included on line 27.

Do not include contributions on behalf of current or former officers, directors, trustees, and key employees, that were included on lines 25a, b, or c. Report expenses for employee events such as a picnic or holiday party on line 28.

Line 29. Payroll Taxes

Enter the amount of federal, state, and local payroll taxes for the year but only those taxes that are imposed on the organization as an employer. This includes the employer's share of social security and Medicare taxes, the Federal unemployment tax (FUTA), state unemployment compensation taxes, and other state and local payroll taxes. Do not include taxes withheld from employees' salaries and paid to the various governmental units such as federal and state income taxes and the employees' shares of social security and Medicare taxes.

Line 30. Professional Fundraising Fees

Enter on line 30 fundraising fees paid to independent contractors and outside vendors and suppliers in carrying out fundraising activities. Include on line 30 fundraising expenses such as printing, paper, envelopes, postage, mailing list rental, and equipment rental, incurred in a fundraising activity conducted by an independent contractor. Fundraising expenses also include amounts the organization reimburses to a fundraiser.

For purposes of line 30, fundraising activities include gaming, vehicle and other property donation programs, and special events. Fees and expenses incurred by the organization, whether by payment to independent contractors, vendors, or suppliers, or by deduction from proceeds received by the organization, are included on line 30.

Do not include on line 30 salaries of employees who undertake fundraising as part of their employment duties. Compensation related to fundraising paid to non-key employees is allocated to line 26, Column (D). Compensation related to fundraising paid to officers, directors, trustees, and key employees is allocated to line 25, Column (D).

In addition to completing line 30, the organization should keep for its permanent records a list of fees and expenses for each fundraising activity. Do not include this list with the organization Form 990.

Line 31. Accounting Fees

Enter the total accounting and auditing fees charged by outside firms and individuals who are not employees of the reporting organization.

Line 32. Legal Fees

Enter the total legal fees charged by outside firms and individuals who are not employees of the reporting organization. Do not include any penalties, fines, or judgments imposed against the organization as a result of legal proceedings. Report those expenses on line 43, *Other expenses*.

Line 33. Supplies

Enter the total for office, classroom, medical, and other supplies used during the year, as determined by the organization's normal method of accounting for supplies.

Line 34. Telephone

Enter the total telephone, telegram, and similar expenses for the year.

Line 35. Postage and Shipping

Enter the total amount of postage, parcel delivery, trucking, and other delivery expenses, including the cost of shipping materials. Include the costs of outside mailing services on this line.

Line 36. Occupancy

Enter the total amount paid or incurred for the use of office space or other facilities, heat, light, power, and other utilities (other than telephone expenses reported on line 34), outside janitorial services, mortgage interest, property insurance, real estate taxes, and similar expenses.

Occupancy expenses paid or incurred for program-related income, reportable on line 2, are included on line 36. Do not subtract rental income received from renting or subletting rented space from the amount reported for occupancy expense on line 36. If the activities of the organization's tenant are related to the reporting organization's exempt purpose, report rental income as program-service revenue and allocable occupancy expenses on line 36. However, if the tenant's activities are not program-related, report such rental income on line 6a and related rental expenses on line 6b.

Do not include, as an occupancy expense, depreciation (reportable on line 42) or any salaries of the reporting organization's own employees (reportable on line 26).

Line 37. Equipment Rental and Maintenance

Enter the cost of renting and maintaining office equipment and other equipment, except for automobile and truck expenses reportable on lines 35 and 39.

Line 38. Printing and Publications

Enter the printing and related costs of producing the reporting organization's own newsletters, leaflets, films, and other informational materials on this line. Also include the cost of any purchased publications. However, do not include any expenses, such as salaries or postage, for which a separate line is provided in Part II.

Line 39. Travel

Enter the total travel expenses, including transportation costs (fares, mileage allowances, and automobile expenses), meals and lodging, and *per diem* payments.

Line 40. Conferences, Conventions, and Meetings

Enter the total expenses incurred by the organization in conducting meetings related to its activities. Include such

expenses as the rental of facilities, speakers' fees and expenses, and printed materials. Include the registration fees (but not travel expenses) paid for sending any of the organization's staff to conferences, meetings, or conventions conducted by other organizations. However, do not include on this line the salaries and travel expenses of the reporting organization's own officers, directors, trustees, and employees who participate.

Line 41. Interest

Enter the total interest expense for the year. Do not include any interest attributable to rental property (reportable on line 6b) or any mortgage interest treated as occupancy expense on line 36.

Line 42. Depreciation, Depletion, etc.

If the organization records depreciation, depletion, and similar expenses, enter the total for the year. Include any depreciation (amortization) of leasehold improvements. The organization is not required to use the Modified Accelerated Cost Recovery System (MACRS) to compute the depreciation reported on Form 990 or Form 990-EZ. If the organization records depreciation using MACRS, attach Form 4562, or a schedule showing the same information required by Form 4562. If the organization does not use MACRS, attach a schedule showing how depreciation was computed.

For an explanation of acceptable methods for computing depreciation, see Pub. 946.

If the organization claims a deduction for depletion, attach a schedule explaining the deduction.

Line 43. Other Expenses

Show the type and amount of each functional expense for which a separate line is not provided. The organization may report minor miscellaneous expenses as a single total. The total of minor miscellaneous expenses grouped together on line 43 cannot exceed 5% of the total of all functional expenses on line 44.

The following expenses must be categorized and reported separately on line 43:

1. For health care organizations, payments to heath care professionals who are not employees of the health care organization.

2. Investment counseling and other professional fees. (Do not include professional fundraising fees, accounting fees, or legal fees on line 43; these are reportable on lines 30 through 32.)

3. Penalties, fines, and judgments.

4. Unrelated business income taxes.

5. Insurance and real estate taxes not attributable to rental property or reported as occupancy expenses.

6. Other expenses the organization tracks, not included on other lines of Part II.

7. Payments of travel or entertainment expenses (including reimbursements for such costs) for any federal, state or local government officials (as determined under section 4946(c)) and their family members (as determined under section 4946(d)). The reported total amount should include:

a. Each separate expenditure relating to a government official or family member of such official that exceeds $200, and

b. Aggregate expenditures relating to a government official or family member of such official that exceed $1,000 for the year.

*Do not double count expenditures that are described in both **a** and **b** above. For expenditures that are not specifically identifiable to a particular individual, the organization may use any reasonable allocation method to estimate the cost of the expenditure to an individual. Amounts not described in **a** and **b** above may be included in this amount or, provided that such amounts do not exceed 5% of total functional expenses, may be grouped with other minor miscellaneous expenses. The organization is responsible for keeping records for all travel and entertainment expenses related to a government official regardless of whether reported in this amount or as other minor miscellaneous expenses.*

State reporting—miscellaneous expenses. Some states that accept Form 990, or Form 990-EZ, in satisfaction of their filing requirements may require that certain types of miscellaneous expenses be itemized regardless of amount. See *General Instruction E.*

Line 44. Total Functional Expenses

Add lines 22a through 43g and enter the totals on line 44 in columns (A), (B), (C), and (D). Report the total amounts for columns (B), (C), and (D) in Part I, lines 13 through 15.

Reporting of Joint Costs

Organizations that included in program service expenses (column (B) of Part II) any joint costs from a combined educational campaign and fundraising solicitation must disclose how the total joint costs of all such combined activities were reported in Part II.

Organizations answering "Yes" to the joint-cost question following line 44 must furnish the relevant financial data in the spaces provided.

An organization conducts a combined educational campaign and fundraising solicitation when it solicits contributions (by mail, telephone, broadcast media, or any other means) and includes, with the solicitation, educational material or other information that furthers a bona fide nonfundraising exempt purpose of the organization.

Expenses attributable to providing information regarding the organization itself, its use of past contributions, or its planned use of contributions received are not program service expenses and should not be included in column (B). This is true whether or not the organization accounts for joint costs in accordance with the AICPA's Statement of Position 98-2, *Accounting for Costs of Materials and Activities of Not-for-Profit Organizations and State and Local Government Entities that Include Fund Raising.* Any method of allocating joint costs to program service expenses must be reasonable under the facts and circumstances of each case. Most states with reporting requirements for charitable and other organizations that solicit contributions either require or allow the reporting of joint costs according to Statement of Position 98-2 standards.

Part III—Statement of Program Service Accomplishments

A program service is a major (usually ongoing) objective of an organization, such as adoptions, recreation for the elderly, rehabilitation, or publication of journals or newsletters.

Step	Action
1	State the organization's primary exempt purpose.
2	All organizations must describe their exempt purpose achievements for each of their four largest program services (as measured by total expenses incurred). If there were four or fewer of such activities, describe each program service activity. • Describe program service accomplishments through measurements such as clients served, days of care, therapy sessions, or publications issued. • Describe the activity's objective, for both this time period and the longer-term goal, if the output is intangible, such as in a research activity.

• Give reasonable estimates for any statistical information if exact figures are not readily available. Indicate that this information is estimated.

• Be clear, concise, and complete in the description. Avoid adding an attachment.

3 If part of the total expenses of any program service consists of grants and allocations reported on line 22a or 22b, enter the amount of grants and allocations in the space provided and include the grants and allocations in the *Expenses* column. If the amount of grants and allocations entered includes foreign grants, check the box to the left of the entry space for *Program services expenses.*

• Section 501(c)(3) and (4) organizations, and section 4947(a)(1) nonexempt charitable trusts, must show the amount of grants and allocations to others and must enter the total expenses for each program service reported.

• For all other organizations, completing the *Program Services Expenses* column (and the *Grants and allocations* entry) in Part III is optional.

4 Attach a schedule that lists the organization's other program services.

• The detailed information required for the four largest services is not necessary for this schedule.

• Section 501(c)(3) and (4) organizations, and section 4947(a)(1) nonexempt charitable trusts, however, must show the expenses attributable to their program services.

5 The organization may show the amount of any donated services, or use of materials, equipment, or facilities it received or utilized in connection with a specific program service.

• Disclose the applicable amounts of any donated services, etc., on the lines for the narrative description of the appropriate program service.

• Do not include these amounts in the expense column in Part III.

• See the instructions for line 82.

Part IV—Balance Sheets

All organizations, except those that meet one of the exceptions in *General Instruction F,* must complete all of Part IV and may not submit a substitute balance sheet. Failure to complete Part IV may result in penalties for filing an incomplete return. See *General Instruction K.* If there is no amount to report in column (A), *Beginning of year,* place a zero in that column.

See *General Instruction E* for details on completing a Form 990, or Form 990-EZ, to be filed with any state or local governmental agency.

Specific Instructions for Form 990

When a schedule is required to be attached for any line item in Part IV, it is only for the end-of-year balance sheet figure reported in column (B). Give the end-of-year figures for any receivables or depreciable assets and the related allowances for doubtful accounts or accumulated depreciation reported within the description column.

Line 45. Cash— Non-Interest-Bearing

Enter the total of non-interest-bearing checking accounts, deposits in transit, change funds, petty cash funds, or any other non-interest-bearing account. Do not include advances to employees or officers or refundable deposits paid to suppliers or others.

Line 46. Savings and Temporary Cash Investments

Enter the total of interest-bearing checking accounts, savings and temporary cash investments, such as money market funds, commercial paper, certificates of deposit, and U.S. Treasury bills or other governmental obligations that mature in less than 1 year. Report the income from these investments on line 4.

Line 47. Accounts Receivable

Enter the total accounts receivable (reduced by the allowance for doubtful accounts) from the sale of goods and/or the performance of services. Report claims against vendors or refundable deposits with suppliers or others here, if not significant in amount. Otherwise, report them on line 58, *Other assets*. Report any receivables due from officers, directors, trustees, or key employees on line 50. Report receivables (including loans and advances) due from other employees on line 51a.

Line 48a. Pledges Receivable

Enter the total pledges receivable recorded as of the beginning and end of the year. Do not include the amount of pledges estimated to be uncollectible.

Line 49. Grants Receivable

Enter the total grants receivable from governmental agencies, foundations, and other organizations as of the beginning and end of the year. Organizations that follow SFAS 116 may report the present value of the grants receivable as of each balance sheet date.

Line 50a. Receivables From Current and Former Officers, Directors, Trustees, and Key Employees

Report all receivables due from current and former officers, directors, trustees, and key employees, and all secured and unsecured loans to such persons, on line 50a and in an attached schedule discussed below. Report interest from such receivables on line 11. For a definition of key employee, see the instructions in Part V-A.

In the required schedule, report each receivable separately even if more than one loan was made to the same person or the same terms apply to all loans. Report salary advances, and other advances for the personal use and benefit of the recipient, and receivables subject to special terms, or arising from nontypical transactions, as separate loans for each current and former officer, director, trustee, and key employee. For credit unions, report only loans, or receivables that are not made on the same terms as all other members of the organization.

Schedule format. For each outstanding loan, or other receivable that must be reported separately, the attached schedule should show the following information (preferably in columnar form):

1. Borrower's name and title,
2. Original amount,
3. Balance due,
4. Date of note,
5. Maturity date,
6. Repayment terms,
7. Interest rate,
8. Security provided by the borrower,
9. Purpose of the loan, and
10. Description and fair market value of the consideration furnished by the lender (for example, cash—$1,000; or 100 shares of XYZ, Inc., common stock—$9,000).

Line 50b. Receivables From Other Disqualified Persons

Report all receivables due from disqualified persons (as defined under section 4958(f)(1)) and persons described in section 4958(c)(3)(B) for the year on line 50b and in a required attached schedule. Do not include on line 50b, amounts reported on line 50a.

For a definition of disqualified persons, see *Disqualified Person* under *General Instruction P*, earlier.

Report each receivable separately even if more than one loan was made to the same person or the same terms apply to all loans. Report advances for the personal use and benefit of the recipient, and receivables subject to special terms, or arising from nontypical transactions, as separate loans for each disqualified person that is not a current or former officer, director, trustee, or key employee. For credit unions, report only loans, or receivables that are not made on the same terms

as all other members of the organization.

Schedule format. For each outstanding loan, or other receivable that must be reported separately, the attached schedule should show the following information (preferably in columnar form):

1. Borrower's name and title,
2. Original amount,
3. Balance due,
4. Date of note,
5. Maturity date,
6. Repayment terms,
7. Interest rate,
8. Security provided by the borrower,
9. Purpose of the loan, and
10. Description and fair market value of the consideration furnished by the lender (for example, cash—$1,000; or 100 shares of XYZ, Inc., common stock—$9,000).

Line 51. Other Notes and Loans Receivable

Line 51a. Enter on line 51a the combined total of receivables (both notes and loans) to non-key employees. Do not include the following on line 51a.

• Receivables reported on line 50.
• Program-related investments. (Report program-related investments on line 58.)
• Notes receivable acquired as investments (report receivables acquired as investments on line 56).

For notes and loans that represent program-related investments (defined in the line 2 instructions), report the interest income on line 2. For all other notes and loans receivable included on line 51, report the income on line 11.

Line 51b. Enter on line 51b the total amount of doubtful accounts.

Notes receivable. Enter the amount of all notes receivable not listed on line 50 and not acquired as investments. Attach a schedule similar to that requested in the instructions for line 50. The schedule should also describe the family or business relationship of the borrower to any officer, director, trustee, key employee, or substantial contributor of the organization.

Notes receivable from loans by a credit union to its members and scholarship loans by a section 501(c)(3) organization do not have to be itemized. However, identify these loans as such on a schedule and indicate the total amount of such loans that are outstanding.

For a note receivable from another organization exempt under the same paragraph of section 501(c) as the filing organization, list only the name of the borrower and the balance due. For example, a section 501(c)(3) organization would have to provide the full details of a loan to a section 501(c)(4) organization but would have to provide only the name of the borrower and the balance due on a note from a loan to another section 501(c)(3) organization.

Loans receivable. Enter the gross amount of loans receivable, less the allowance for doubtful accounts, from the normal activities of the filing organization such as loans by a credit union to its members or scholarship loans by a section 501(c)(3) organization. A schedule of these loans is not required.

Report loans to current and former officers, directors, trustees, and key employees on line 50. Report loans to non-key employees, vendors, suppliers, and independent contractors on line 51. Attach a schedule similar to that called for in the instructions for line 50. The schedule should also describe the family or business relationship, if any, between the borrower and any officer, director, trustee, key employee, or *substantial contributor* of the organization as defined in section 507(d)(2)(A).

Family relationships include an individual's spouse, ancestors, children, grandchildren, great-grandchildren, siblings (whether by whole or half blood), and the spouses of children, grandchildren, great-grandchildren, and siblings.

Business relationships are employment and contractual relationships, and common ownership of a business where any officers, directors, or trustees, individually or together, possess more than a 35% ownership interest in common. *Ownership* is voting power in a corporation, profits interest in a partnership, or beneficial interest in a trust. Employment and contractual relationships include relationships through a sole proprietorship or partnership (for example, a borrower is employed by a partnership in which one of the organization's directors is a partner) but not through a corporation (for example, a borrower is employed by a corporation in which one of the organization's directors is a shareholder, director, or officer).

See *General Instruction X* regarding due diligence requirements to determine business relationships.

 TIP *Report program-related investments on line 58.*

Line 52. Inventories For Sale Or Use

Enter the amount of materials, goods, and supplies purchased, manufactured by the organization, or donated and held for future sale or use.

Line 53. Prepaid Expenses and Deferred Charges

Enter the amount of short-term and long-term prepayments of expenses attributable to one or more future accounting periods. Examples include prepayments of rent, insurance, and pension costs, and expenses incurred for a solicitation campaign of a future accounting period.

Line 54a. Investments—Publicly Traded Securities

Enter the book value, which may be market value, of securities held as investments. Check the appropriate box to indicate whether the securities are reported at cost or fair market value. Publicly traded securities include common and preferred stocks, bonds (including governmental obligations such as bonds and Treasury bills), and mutual fund shares that are listed and regularly traded in an over-the-counter market or on an established exchange and for which market quotations are published or otherwise readily available.

Do not report stock holdings that represent 5% or more of the outstanding shares of stock of the same class. Instead, report them on line 54b. Report dividends and interest from these securities on line 5 of Part I, Revenue.

Line 54b. Investments—Other Securities

Enter the book value, which may be market value, of securities held as investments that are not publicly traded or that represent 5% or more of the outstanding shares of the same class. Check the appropriate box to indicate whether the securities are reported at cost or fair market value. When valuing securities at fair market value, use commonly accepted valuation methods. (See Regulations section 20.2031-2.)

Attach a schedule that lists the securities held at the end of the year. Indicate whether the securities are listed at cost (including the value recorded at the time of receipt in the case of donated securities) or end-of-year market value. Do not include amounts reported on line 46.

Securities not publicly traded. Securities that are not publicly traded include investments such as stock in a closely held company whose stock is not available for sale to the general public or which is not widely traded.

Attached schedule. On the attached schedule, give the following information for each security held at the end of the organization's tax year.
• A description of the security, including the value recorded at the time of receipt in the case of donated securities,
• The book value of the security, and
• The valuation method that was used (cost or the total book value of all securities listed on the attachment must agree with the amount entered on line 54b, column (B)).

Line 55. Investments—Land, Buildings, and Equipment

Enter the book value (cost or other basis less accumulated depreciation) of all land, buildings, and equipment held for investment purposes, such as rental properties. Attach a schedule listing these fixed assets held as investments at the end of the year. Show for each item or category listed, the cost or other basis, accumulated depreciation, and book value. Report the income from these assets on line 6a.

Line 56. Investments—Other

Enter the amount of all other investment holdings not reported on line 54a, 54b, or 55. Attach a schedule, listing and describing each of these investments held at the end of the year. Show the book value for each and indicate whether the investment is listed at cost or end-of-year market value. Report the income from these assets on line 7. Do not include program-related investments. See the instructions for line 58.

Line 57. Land, Buildings, and Equipment

Enter the book value (cost or other basis less accumulated depreciation) of all land, buildings, and equipment owned by the organization and not held for investment. This includes any property, plant, and equipment owned and used by the organization in conducting its exempt activities. Attach a schedule listing these fixed assets held at the end of the year and showing, for each item or category listed, the cost or other basis, accumulated depreciation, and book value.

Line 58. Other Assets, Including Program-Related Investments

List and show the book value of each category of assets not reportable on lines 45 through 57. If more space is needed, attach a schedule (see *Attachment* under *General Instruction X*) and enter the total book value of all categories of other assets on line 58. For interest earned on notes and loans

Specific Instructions for Form 990

that represent program-related investments, report income on line 2.

One type of asset reportable on line 58 is program-related investments. These are investments made primarily to accomplish an exempt purpose of the filing organization rather than to produce income.

Line 59. Total Assets

Enter the total of lines 45 through 58. The amounts on line 59 must equal the amounts on line 74 for both the beginning and end of the year.

Line 60. Accounts Payable and Accrued Expenses

Enter the total of accounts payable to suppliers and others and accrued expenses, such as salaries payable, accrued payroll taxes, and interest payable.

Line 61. Grants Payable

Enter the unpaid portion of grants and awards that the organization has made a commitment to pay other organizations or individuals, whether or not the commitments have been communicated to the grantees.

Line 62. Deferred Revenue

Include revenue that the organization has received but not yet earned as of the balance sheet date under its method of accounting.

Line 63. Loans From Officers, Directors, Trustees, and Key Employees

Enter the unpaid balance of loans received from current and former officers, directors, trustees, and key employees. See the instructions for Part V-A for the definition of key employee. For loans outstanding at the end of the year, attach a schedule that shows, for each loan, the name and title of the lender and the information specified in items 2 through 10 of the instructions for line 50a.

Line 64a. Tax-Exempt Bond Liabilities

Enter the amount of tax-exempt bonds (or other obligations) issued by the organization on behalf of a state or local governmental unit, or by a state or local governmental unit on behalf of the organization, and for which the organization has a direct or indirect liability. Tax-exempt bonds include state or local bonds and any obligations, including direct borrowing from a lender, or certificates of participation, the interest on which is excluded from the income of the recipient for federal income tax purposes under section 103.

If the tax-exempt bond or obligation is in the form of a mortgage, include the

amount of the mortgage on line 64a, and not on line 64b. For such mortgage, include in the above listing, the maturity date of the debt, repayment terms, interest rate, and any security provided by the organization.

Line 64a does not, however, refer to situations where the organization only has a contingent liability, as it would if it were a guarantor of tax-exempt bonds issued by a related entity. Contingent liabilities, such as those that arise from guarantees, must be included as an entry in the separately attached schedule required for line 64a.

Attachment. For all such bonds and obligations outstanding at any time during the year, attach a schedule showing for each separate issue:
• The purpose of the issue,
• The amount of the issue outstanding, and
• The unexpended bond proceeds, if any.

Also, show if any portion of any bond financed facility was used by a third party (other than a governmental unit or a Section 501(c)(3) organization). If so, list the percentage of space used by the third party.

Line 64b. Mortgages and Other Notes Payable

Enter the amount of mortgages and other notes payable at the beginning and end of the year. Attach a schedule showing, as of the end of the year, the total amount of all mortgages payable and, for each nonmortgage note payable, the name of the lender and the other information specified in items 2 through 10 of the instructions for line 50a. The schedule should also identify the relationship of the lender to any officer, director, trustee, or key employee of the organization.

Line 65. Other Liabilities

List and show the amount of each liability not reportable on lines 60 through 65. Attach a separate schedule if more space is needed.

Lines 67 through 69. Net Assets

The Financial Accounting Standards Board issued Financial Statements of Not-for-Profit Organizations (SFAS 117). SFAS 117 provides standards for external financial statements certified by an independent accountant for certain types of nonprofit organizations. SFAS 117 does not apply to credit unions, voluntary employees' beneficiary associations, supplemental unemployment benefit trusts, section 501(c)(12) cooperatives, and other member benefit or mutual benefit organizations.

While some states may require reporting in accordance with SFAS 117,

the IRS does not (see *General Instruction E*). However, a Form 990, or Form 990-EZ, return prepared in accordance with SFAS 117 will be acceptable to the IRS.

Organizations that follow SFAS 117. If the organization follows SFAS 117, check the box above line 67. Classify and report net assets in three groups—unrestricted, temporarily restricted, and permanently restricted—based on the existence or absence of donor-imposed restrictions and the nature of those restrictions. Show the sum of the three classes of net assets on line 73. On line 74, add the amounts on lines 66 and 73 to show total liabilities and net assets. This figure should be the same as the figure for *Total assets* on line 59.

Line 67. Unrestricted

Enter the balances per books of the unrestricted class of net assets. Unrestricted net assets are neither permanently restricted nor temporarily restricted by donor-imposed stipulations. All funds without donor-imposed restrictions must be classified as unrestricted, regardless of the existence of any board designations or appropriations.

Line 68. Temporarily Restricted

Enter the balance per books for the temporarily restricted class of net assets. Donors' temporary restrictions may require that resources be used in a later period or after a specified date (time restrictions), or that resources be used for a specified purpose (purpose restrictions), or both.

Line 69. Permanently Restricted

Enter the total of the balances for the permanently restricted class of net assets. Permanently restricted net assets are (a) assets, such as land or works of art, donated with stipulations that they be used for a specified purpose, be preserved, and not be sold or (b) assets donated with stipulations that they be invested to provide a permanent source of income. The latter result from gifts and bequests that create permanent endowment funds.

Organizations that do not follow SFAS 117. If the organization does not follow SFAS 117, check the box above line 70 and report account balances on lines 70 through 72. Report net assets or fund balances on line 73. Complete line 74 to report the sum of the total liabilities and net assets.

Some states that accept Form 990, or Form 990-EZ, as their basic reporting form may require a separate statement of changes in net assets/fund balances. See *General Instruction E*.

Line 70. Capital Stock, Trust Principal, or Current Funds

For corporations, enter the balance per books for capital stock accounts. Show par or stated value (or for stock with no par or stated value, total amount received upon issuance) of all classes of stock issued and, as yet, uncancelled. For trusts, enter the amount in the trust principal or corpus account. For organizations continuing to use the fund method of accounting, enter the fund balances for the organization's current restricted and unrestricted funds.

Line 71. Paid-In or Capital Surplus, or Land, Bldg., and Equipment Fund

Enter the balance per books for all paid-in capital in excess of par or stated value for all stock issued and uncancelled. If stockholders or others gave donations that the organization records as paid-in capital, include them here. Report any current-year donations the organization included on line 71 in Part I, line 1. Enter the fund balance for the land, building, and equipment fund on this line.

Line 72. Retained Earnings or Accumulated Income, Endowment, or Other Funds

For corporations, enter the balance in the retained earnings, or similar account, minus the cost of any corporate treasury stock. For trusts, enter the balance per books in the accumulated income or similar account. For those organizations using fund accounting, enter the total of the fund balances for the permanent and term endowment funds as well as balances of any other funds not reported on lines 70 and 71.

Line 73. Total Net Assets or Fund Balances

For organizations that follow SFAS 117, enter the total of lines 67 through 69. For all other organizations, enter the total of lines 70 through 72. Enter the beginning-of-the-year figure on line 73, column (A), in Part I, line 19. The end-of-the-year figure on line 73, column (B) must agree with the figure on line 21 of Part I.

Line 74. Total Liabilities and Net Assets/Fund Balances

Enter the total of lines 66 and 73. This amount must equal the amount for total assets reported on line 59 for both the beginning and end of the year.

Parts IV-A and IV-B— Reconciliation Statements

Use these reconciliation statements to reconcile the differences between the revenue and expenses shown on the organization's audited financial statements prepared in accordance with SFAS 117 and the revenue and expenses shown on the organization's Form 990.

If the organization did not receive an audited financial statement for 2007 (or the fiscal year for which it is completing this Form 990) and prepared the return in accordance with SFAS 117, it does not need to complete Parts IV-A or IV-B and should instead enter "N/A" on line **a** of each Part.

These two Parts do not have to be completed on group returns.

On line **d1** of Parts IV-A and IV-B, include only those investment expenses netted against investment income in the revenue portion of the organization's audited financial statements. Do not include program-related investment expenses or other expenses reported as program service expenses in the audited statement of activities.

Part V-A — Current Officers, Directors, Trustees, and Key Employees

List each person who was a current officer, director, trustee, or key employee (defined below) of the organization or disregarded entity described in Regulations sections 301.7701-1 through 301.7701-3 at any time during the year even if they did not receive any compensation from the organization. If person is listed in Part V-A, then list all of that person's compensation from the organization in Part V-A, whether received as a current officer, as a former officer, or in another capacity (for example, independent contractor).

For purposes of reporting all amounts in columns (B) through (E) in Part V-A, either use the organizations tax year, or the calendar year ending within such tax year.

Enter a zero in columns (B), (C), (D), or (E) if no hours were entered in column (B) and no compensation, contributions, expenses, and other allowances were paid during the reporting period, or deferred for payment to a future reporting period.

Aid in the processing of the organization's return by grouping together, preferably at the end of its list, those who received no compensation. Be careful not to repeat names.

Give the preferred address at which officers, directors, etc., want the Internal Revenue Service to contact them.

Use an attachment if there are more persons to list in Part V-A.

Show all forms of cash and noncash compensation received by each listed officer, director, etc., whether paid currently or deferred.

If the organization pays any other person, such as a management services company, for the services provided by any of its officers, directors, trustees, or key employees, report the compensation and other items in Part V-A as if the organization had paid the officers, directors, etc., directly. Also see Ann. 2001-33, 2001-17 I.R.B. 1137.

A failure to fully complete Part V-A can subject both the organization and the individuals responsible for such failure to penalties for filing an incomplete return. See *General Instruction K.* In particular, entering the phrase on Part V-A, "Information available upon request," or a similar phrase, is not acceptable.

The organization may also provide an attachment to explain the entire 2007 compensation package for any person listed in Part V-A.

Each person listed in Part V-A should report the listed compensation on his or her income tax return unless the Code specifically excludes any of the payments from income tax. See Pub. 525 for details.

Key employee. A *key employee* is any person having responsibilities, powers, or influence similar to those of officers, directors, or trustees. The term includes the chief management and administrative officials of an organization (such as an executive director or chancellor).

A chief financial officer and the officer in charge of the administration or program operations are both key employees if they have the authority to control the organization's activities, its finances, or both.

Column (A)

Report the name and address of each person who was a current officer, director, trustee, or key employee (defined above), during the tax year or, if using the calendar year, at any time during the calendar year or tax year.

Column (B)

In column (B), a numerical estimate of the average hours per week devoted to the position is required for a complete answer. Statements such as "as needed," "as required," or "40+" are unacceptable.

-40-

Column (C)

For each person listed, report salary, fees, bonuses, and severance payments paid. Include current-year payments of amounts reported or reportable as deferred compensation in any prior reporting period.

Column (D)

Include in this column all forms of deferred compensation and future severance payments (whether or not funded; whether or not vested; and whether or not the deferred compensation plan is a qualified plan under section 401(a)). Include also payments to welfare benefit plans on behalf of the officers, directors, etc. Such plans provide benefits such as medical, dental, life insurance, severance pay, disability, etc. Reasonable estimates may be used if precise cost figures are not readily available.

Unless the amounts were reported in column (C), report, as deferred compensation in column (D), salaries and other compensation earned during the reporting period, but not yet paid by the date the organization files its return.

Column (E)

Enter both taxable and nontaxable fringe benefits (other than *de minimis* fringe benefits described in section 132(e)). Include expense allowances or reimbursements that the recipients must report as income on their separate income tax returns. Examples include amounts for which the recipient did not account to the organization or allowances that were more than the payee spent on serving the organization. Include payments made under indemnification arrangements, the value of the personal use of housing, automobiles, or other assets owned or leased by the organization (or provided for the organization's use without charge), as well as any other taxable and nontaxable fringe benefits. See Pub. 525 for more information.

Line 75b. Business Relationships

For a definition of *family and business relationships*, see *Family relationships* and *Business relationships* on line 51 of these instructions.

Line 75c. Compensation from Related Organizations

Answer "Yes," to this question if any of the organization's listed officers, directors, trustees, key employees, highest compensated employees, or highest compensated professional or other independent contractors received aggregate compensation amounts of $50,000 or more from the organization and all related organizations (as

defined below). For this purpose, compensation includes any amount that would be reportable in columns (C), (D), and (E) of Form 990, Part V-A, if provided by the organization. See *General Instruction X* regarding due diligence requirements to determine business relationships.

Required attachment. If the organization answered "Yes," it must attach a schedule that lists, for each officer, director, trustee, key employee, highest compensated employee, or highest compensated professional or other independent contractor, the information requested in 1 and 2, below.

1. For *Relationships* 1 through 5, provide:

a. The name of the officer, director, etc., receiving compensation from a related organization or organizations;

b. The name and EIN of each related organization that provided the compensation;

c. A description of the relationship between the organization and the related organization(s); and

d. The amount of compensation each related organization provided. Use the same format as required by columns (C) through (E) of Part V-A.

2. If the organizations are related only by *Relationship 6* or if the *Volunteer exception* to *Relationship 2* applies, report the following information, but do not report compensation paid by the related organization(s).

a. The name of the officer, director, etc., receiving compensation from a related organization(s);

b. The name and EIN of each related organization that provided such compensation; and

c. A description of the relationship between the organization and the related organization(s).

Reporting compensation. Report compensation paid by a related organization for only that time period during which a relationship existed between the organization and the related organization. Report compensation paid by a related organization in the same period (either calendar or fiscal year) as the organization reports compensation it paid.

Definition of related organization. Organizations may be related in several ways; the relationships are not mutually exclusive. *Related organizations* are tax-exempt or taxable organizations related to the tax-exempt organization in one or more of the following ways.

• *Relationship 1.* One organization owns or controls the other organization.

• *Relationship 2.* The same person(s) owns or controls both organizations.

• *Relationship 3.* The organizations have a relationship as supporting and supported organizations under section 509(a)(3) (see *Example 1*, later).

• *Relationship 4.* The organizations use a common paymaster. For a definition of common paymaster and illustrated examples, see Regulations section 31.3121(s)-1(b).

• *Relationship 5.* The other organization pays part of the compensation that the organization would otherwise be contractually obligated to pay (see *Example 2*, later).

• *Relationship 6.* The organizations conduct joint programs or share facilities or employees.

Ownership. The term ownership is holding (directly or indirectly) 50% or more of the voting power in a corporation, profits interest in a partnership, or beneficial interest in a trust.

Control. The term control is having 50% or more of the voting power in a governing body, or the power to appoint 50% or more of an organization's governing body, or the power to approve an organization's budgets or expenditures (an effective veto power over the organization's budgets and expenditures). Also, control can be indirect by owning or controlling another organization with such power.

The term governing body is defined by the relevant state law. Generally, the governing body of a corporation is its board of directors and the governing body of a trust is its board of trustees.

Reporting exceptions. The following exceptions apply:

• *Bank or financial institution trustee exception.* If the organization and the other organization are related only because they are both controlled by a common trustee that is a bank or financial institution, the organization does not need to report either the relationship or the trustee's compensation from the related organization.

• *Common independent contractor exception.* If an independent contractor listed in Schedule A, Part II-A or II-B does not exercise substantial influence, as defined in section 4958(f)(1) and Regulations section 53.4958-3 (treating the organization as though it were an applicable tax-exempt organization under section 4958(e)), over either the organization or the related organization, the organization does not need to report either the relationship or the independent contractor's compensation from the related organization. However, this exception does not apply to a management services company that performs for the organization functions similar to those of president, chief executive officer, chief operating officer, treasurer, or chief financial officer. Compensation paid by a related organization to such a management company must be reported by the organization unless another exception applies. See *Examples 4* and *5* later.

• **Volunteer exception.** If *Relationship 2* is met only because the same individuals control both the tax-exempt organization and a for-profit organization that is not owned or controlled directly or indirectly by one or more tax-exempt organizations, and none of the *Relationships* described in 1 or 3 through 5 are met, then the tax-exempt organization does not have to report the compensation from the for-profit organization of any persons serving the tax-exempt organization as a volunteer without compensation other than reimbursement of expenses under an accountable plan (treating the volunteer as an employee for this purpose). See *Example 3* later).

TIP *Providing information on compensation received from related organizations does not violate the disclosure provisions of section 7216(a). See also section 6033(a)(1).*

Examples illustrating relationships.

Example 1. X, a hospital auxiliary, raises funds for Hospital Y. Z, another hospital auxiliary, coordinates the efforts of Hospital Y's volunteer staff. Both X and Z are supporting organizations of Hospital Y and are considered related organizations to Hospital Y. Hospital Y is also considered a supported organization of the auxiliaries.

Hospital Y must report (in an attachment to line 75c) the compensation, if any, paid by each of the auxiliaries to the officers, directors, trustees, or key employees listed in the hospital's Form 990, Part V-A, or highest-compensated employees listed in the hospital's Schedule A, Part I, or highest-compensated professional or other independent contractors listed in the hospital's Schedule A, Part II-A or II-B. Both X and Z must report (in an attachment to line 75c) the compensation, if any, paid by Hospital Y to an officer, director, etc., of the auxiliary.

Example 2. Bob, a key employee of Organization B, a 501(c)(4) social welfare organization, conducts fundraising among Organization B's members, with the proceeds going to Organization A, a 501(c)(3) public charity, to carry out disaster relief. The Chief Executive Officers (CEOs) of Organizations A and B agree that Organization A will pay a portion of Bob's salary for a period of time in recognition of Bob's role in the fundraising assistance of Organization

B. Because Organization A is paying to Bob a portion of Bob's compensation that Organization B would otherwise be contractually committed to pay, Organizations A and B are related organizations for Form 990 reporting purposes. Organization B must report the payment from Organization A to Bob in an attachment to line 75c. If, instead, Organization B reimbursed Organization A for a portion of Bob's compensation and all of Bob's compensation was reported as paid by Organization A, then *Relationship 5* would not apply.

Example 3. Tom is the sole trustee of Organization A, a tax-exempt organization, and Organization B, a for-profit taxable organization wholly owned by Tom. So, Organizations A and B are related under *Relationship 2* because they are controlled by the same person. In this situation, Tom's compensation from Organization B (as well as the name and EIN of Organization B, and a description of the relationship between the two organizations) is reported in an attachment to line 75c of Organization A's Form 990.

However, if Tom serves Organization A without compensation and none of the other relationships described in 1 or 3 through 5 are met, then because of the *Volunteer exception*, Tom's compensation from Organization B is not reported by Organization A. However, the relationship between Organization A and Organization B must be reported.

Example 4. Organization A is filing its Form 990. Organization B is a taxable subsidiary of Organization A; so, Organizations A and B are related under *Relationship 1* because A controls B.

Organization A contracts with Company Y for janitorial services. Company Y is listed as one of Organization A's highest-compensated independent contractors. Organization B also contracts with Company Y for janitorial services. Company Y is not a 35% controlled entity of a disqualified person for organization A or Organization B. So, Company Y is listed in Organization A's Schedule A, Part II-B, and Company Y also receives compensation from Organization B, which is related to Organization A.

However, Company Y meets the requirements of the *Common independent contractor exception*, earlier. Company Y is not considered to exercise substantial influence over either Organization A or Organization B if they were applicable tax-exempt organizations within the meaning of section 4958(e). Because of the *Common independent contractor*

exception earlier, the relationship between Company Y and Organization B, and Company Y's compensation from Organization B for such janitorial services is not reported by Organization A.

None of Organization A's officers, directors, etc., receive compensation from Organization B. In conclusion, Organization A does not report its relationship with Organization B in an attachment to line 75c, and Organization A answers "No" on line 75c.

Example 5. The facts are the same as in *Example 4*, except that one of Organization A's officers, Sue, receives compensation from Organization B. Organization A must report in an attachment to line 75c its relationship with Organization B, and Sue's compensation from Organization B for services provided to Organization B. Even though Organization A must report Sue's compensation from Organization B, Organization A does not report Company Y's compensation from Organization B because of the *Common independent contractor exception.*

Part V-B. Former Officers, Directors, Trustees, and Key Employees That Received Compensation or Other Benefits

List each former officer, director, trustee, and key employee (as defined in Part V-A) of the organization or disregarded entity described in Regulations sections 301.7701-1 through 301.7701-3 that received compensation or other benefits during the reporting year. A reasonable effort should be made to determine whether any persons that were paid compensation or held loans are former officers, etc. Do not list persons in Part V-B that are listed in Part V-A, even if they were former officers, etc. for part of the year.

For purposes of reporting all amounts in columns (B) through (E) in Part V-B, either use the organization's tax year, or the calendar year ending within such tax year.

Give the preferred address at which these former officers, directors, etc., want the Internal Revenue Service to contact them.

Use an attachment if there are more persons to list in Part V-B.

Show all forms of cash and noncash compensation or benefits received by each listed former officer, director, etc., whether paid currently or deferred.

If the organization pays any other person, such as a management services company, for the services provided by any of its former officers, directors, trustees, or key employees, report the compensation and other items in Part V-B as if the organization had paid the former officers, directors, etc., directly.

A failure to fully complete Part V-B can subject both the organization and the individuals responsible for such failure to penalties for filing an incomplete return. See *General Instruction K.* In particular, entering the phrase on Part V-B, "Information available upon request," or a similar phrase, is not acceptable.

The organization may also provide an attachment to explain the entire 2007 compensation package for any person listed in Part V-B.

Each person listed in Part V-B should report the listed compensation on his or her income tax return unless the Code specifically excludes any of the payments from income tax. See Pub. 525 for details.

Column (A)

Report the name and address of each person who was a former officer, director, trustee, or key employee (defined in *Part V-A*) at any time during the calendar year.

Column (B)

In column (B), report all secured and unsecured loans and salary advances to former officers, directors, trustees, and key employees. For credit unions, report only loans not made on the same terms as for all other members.

Column (C)

For each person listed, report salary, fees, bonuses, and severance payments paid. Include current-year payments of amounts reported or reportable as deferred compensation in any prior year.

Column (D)

Include in this column all forms of deferred compensation and future severance payments (whether or not funded; whether or not vested; and whether or not the deferred compensation plan is a qualified plan under section 401(a)). Include also payments to welfare benefit plans on behalf of the officers, directors, etc. Such plans provide benefits such as medical, dental, life insurance, severance pay, disability, etc. Reasonable estimates may be used if precise cost figures are not readily available.

Unless the amounts were reported in column (C), report, as deferred compensation in column (D), salaries

and other compensation earned during the period covered by the return, but not yet paid by the date the organization files its return.

Column (E)

Enter both taxable and nontaxable fringe benefits (other than *de minimis* fringe benefits described in section 132(e)). Include expense allowances or reimbursements that the recipients must report as income on their separate income tax returns. Examples include amounts for which the recipient did not account to the organization or allowances that were more than the payee spent on serving the organization. Include payments made under indemnification arrangements, the value of the personal use of housing, automobiles, or other assets owned or leased by the organization (or provided for the organization's use without charge), as well as any other taxable and nontaxable fringe benefits. See Pub. 525 for more information.

Part VI—Other Information

• Section 501(c)(3) organizations and section 4947(a)(1) nonexempt charitable trusts must also complete and attach a Schedule A (Form 990 or 990-EZ) to their Form 990 or Form 990-EZ. See *General Instruction D* for information on Schedule A (Form 990 or 990-EZ).

• Answer "Yes," or "No," to each applicable question.

Line 76. Change in Activities

Attach a statement to explain any changes during the past 3 years in the activities the organization conducts to further its exempt purpose, or in the methods of conducting these activities. However, if a change has been reported to the IRS on a previously filed attachment, do not report the change again. An activity previously listed as current or planned in the organization's application for recognition of exemption does not have to be reported unless the method of conducting such activity has changed. Also, include any major program activities that are being discontinued.

Line 77. Changes In Organizing or Governing Documents

Attach a conformed copy of any changes to the articles of incorporation, or association, constitution, trust instrument, or other organizing document, or to the bylaws or other governing document.

A *conformed copy* is one that agrees with the original document and all amendments to it. If the copies are not signed, they must be accompanied by a written declaration signed by an officer

authorized to sign for the organization, certifying that they are complete and accurate copies of the original documents.

Photocopies of articles of incorporation showing the certification of an appropriate state official do not have to be accompanied by such a declaration. See Rev. Proc. 68-14, 1968-1 C.B. 768, for details. When a number of changes are made, attach a copy of the entire revised organizing instrument or governing document.

However, if the exempt organization changes its legal structure, such as from a trust to a corporation, it must file a new exemption application to establish that the new legal entity qualifies for exemption.

Line 78. Unrelated Business Income

Political organizations described in section 527 are not required to answer this question.

Check "Yes" on line 78a if the organization's total gross income from all of its unrelated trades and businesses is $1,000 or more for the year. Gross income is the amount of gross receipts less the cost of goods sold. See Pub. 598 for a description of unrelated business income and the Form 990-T filing requirements for section 501(c), (e), (f), (k), and (n) organizations having such income.

Form 990-T is not a substitute for Form 990. Report on Form 990, or Form 990-EZ, items of income and expense that are also reported on Form 990-T when the organization is required to file both forms.

 All tax-exempt organizations must pay estimated taxes for their unrelated business income if they expect their tax liability to be $500 or more. Use Form 990-W to compute this tax.

Line 79. Liquidation, Dissolution, Termination, or Substantial Contraction

For a complete liquidation of a corporation or termination of a trust, check the *Termination* box in the heading on page 1 of the form. If there was a liquidation, dissolution, termination, or substantial contraction, attach a statement explaining what took place.

On the attached statement, show whether the assets have been distributed and the date of distribution. Also attach a certified copy of any resolution, or plan of liquidation or termination, etc., with all amendments or supplements not already filed. In addition, attach a schedule listing the names and addresses of all persons who received the assets distributed in liquidation or termination, the kinds of assets distributed to each one, and each asset's fair market value.

A *substantial contraction* is a partial liquidation or other major disposition of assets except transfers for full consideration or distributions from current income.

A *major disposition of assets* is any disposition for the tax year that is:

1. At least 25% of the fair market value of the organization's net assets at the beginning of the tax year; or

2. One of a series of related dispositions begun in earlier years that add up to at least 25% of the net assets the organization had at the beginning of the tax year when the first disposition in the series was made. Whether a major disposition of assets took place through a series of related dispositions depends on the facts in each case.

See Regulations section 1.6043-3 for special rules and exceptions.

Line 80. Relation To Other Organizations

Answer "Yes" if most (more than 50%) of the organization's governing body, officers, directors, trustees, or membership are also officers, directors, trustees, or members of any other organization.

Disregard any coincidental overlap of membership with another organization; that is, when membership in one organization is not a condition of membership in another organization. For example, assume that a majority of the members of a section 501(c)(4) civic organization also belong to a local chamber of commerce described in section 501(c)(6). The civic organization should answer "No" on line 80a if it does not require its members to belong to the chamber of commerce.

Also, disregard affiliation with any statewide or nationwide organization. Thus, the civic organization in the above example would still answer "No" on line 80a even if it belonged to a state or national federation of similar organizations. A local labor union whose members are also members of a national labor organization would answer "No" on line 80a.

Line 81. Expenditures For Political Purposes

 Political organizations described in section 527 are not required to answer this question.

A *political expenditure* is one intended to influence the selection, nomination, election, or appointment of anyone to a federal, state, or local public office, or office in a political

organization, or the election of Presidential or Vice Presidential electors. It does not matter whether the attempt succeeds.

An expenditure includes a payment, distribution, loan, advance, deposit, or gift of money, or anything of value. It also includes a contract, promise, or agreement to make an expenditure, whether or not legally enforceable.

All section 501(c) organizations. An exempt organization that is not a political organization must file Form 1120-POL if it is treated as having political organization taxable income under section 527(f)(1).

If a section 501(c) organization establishes and maintains a section 527(f)(3) separate segregated fund, it is the fund's responsibility to file its own Form 1120-POL if the fund meets the Form 1120-POL filing requirements. Do not include the segregated fund's receipts, expenditures, and balance sheet items on the Form 990, or Form 990-EZ, of the section 501(c) organization that establishes and maintains the fund. When answering questions 81a and 81b on its Form 990, this section 501(c) organization should disregard the political expenses and Form 1120-POL filing requirement of the segregated fund.

However, when a section 501(c) organization transfers its own funds, to a separate segregated section 527(f)(3) fund for use as political expenses, the 501(c) organization must report the transferred funds as its own political expenses on its Form 990 or Form 990-EZ.

Section 501(c)(3) organizations. A section 501(c)(3) organization will lose its tax-exempt status if it engages in political activity.

A section 501(c)(3) organization must pay a section 4955 excise tax for any amount paid or incurred on behalf of, or in opposition to, any candidate for public office. The organization must pay an additional excise tax if it fails to correct the expenditure timely.

A manager of a section 501(c)(3) organization who knowingly agrees to a political expenditure must pay a section 4955 excise tax, unless the agreement is not willful and there is reasonable cause. A manager who does not agree to a correction of the political expenditure may have to pay an additional excise tax.

When a section 501(c)(3) organization promotes a candidate for public office (or is used or controlled by a candidate or prospective candidate), amounts paid or incurred for the following purposes are political expenditures:

- Remuneration to such individual (a candidate or prospective candidate) for speeches or other services;
- Travel expenses of such individual;
- Expenses of conducting polls, surveys, or other studies, or preparing papers or other material for use by such individual;
- Expenses of advertising, publicity, and fundraising for such individual; and
- Any other expense that has the primary effect of promoting public recognition or otherwise primarily accruing to the benefit of such individual.

An organization is effectively controlled by a candidate or prospective candidate only if such individual has a continuing, substantial involvement in the day-to-day operations or management of the organization.

A determination of whether the primary purpose of an organization is promoting the candidacy or prospective candidacy of an individual for public office is made on the basis of all the facts and circumstances. See section 4955 and Regulations section 53.4955.

Use Form 4720 to figure and report the excise taxes.

Line 82. Donated Services or Facilities

Because Form 990, or Form 990-EZ, is open to public inspection, the organization may want the return to show contributions the organization received in the form of donated services or the use of materials, equipment, or facilities at less than fair rental value. If so, and if the organization's records either show the amount and value of such items or give a clearly objective basis for an estimate, the organization may choose to enter this optional information on line 82b. The IRS does not require any organization to keep such records. However, do not include the value of such items in Part I or II, or in the expense column in Part III. The organization may indicate the value of donated services or use of materials, equipment, or facilities in Part III in the narrative description of program services rendered. See the instructions for Part III.

Line 83a. Public Inspection Requirements

Answer "Yes" only if the organization complied with its public inspection obligations described in *General Instruction M.*

Line 83b. Disclosure Requirements For *Quid Pro Quo* Contributions

See *General Instruction L.*

Line 84a. Solicitations of Contributions

All organizations that qualify under section 170(c) to receive contributions that are deductible as charitable contributions for federal income tax purposes, enter "N/A." See *General Instruction L.*

Line 85. Section 501(c)(4), (5), or (6) Organizations

Reporting membership dues, lobbying, and political expenses under section 6033(e). Only certain organizations that are tax-exempt under:

- Section 501(c)(4) (social welfare organizations),
- Section 501(c)(5) (agricultural and horticultural organizations), or
- Section 501(c)(6) (business leagues) are subject to (a) the section 6033(e) notice and reporting requirements, and (b) a potential proxy tax. These organizations must report their total lobbying expenses, political expenses, and membership dues, or similar amounts, on line 85 of Form 990.

Section 6033(e) notice and reporting requirements and proxy tax. Section 6033(e) requires certain section 501(c)(4), (5), and (6) organizations to tell their members what portion of their membership dues were allocable to the political or lobbying activities of the organization. If an organization does not give its members this information, then the organization is subject to a proxy tax. The tax is reported on Form 990-T.

However, if the organization meets *Exception 1* or *2*, it is excluded from the notice, reporting, and proxy tax requirements of section 6033(e). See also Rev. Proc. 98-19, 1998-1 C.B. 547.

Exception 1. Section 6033(e)(3) exception for organizations whose dues are nondeductible. *(Check "Yes" for line 85a.)*

1. All organizations exempt from tax under section 501(a), other than section 501(c)(4), (5), and (6) organizations.

2. Local associations of employees' and veterans' organizations described in section 501(c)(4), but not section 501(c)(4) social welfare organizations.

3. Labor unions and other labor organizations described in section 501(c)(5), but not section 501(c)(5) agricultural and horticultural organizations.

4. Section 501(c)(4), (5), and (6) organizations that receive more than 90% of their dues from:
    a. Section 501(c)(3) organizations,
    b. State or local governments,
    c. Entities whose income is exempt from tax under section 115, or

d. Organizations described in 1 through 3, above.

5. Section 501(c)(4) and (5) organizations that receive more than 90% of their annual dues from:
    a. Persons,
    b. Families, or
    c. Entities who each paid annual dues of $95 or less in 2007 (adjusted annually for inflation). See Rev. Proc. 2006-53 which is on page 996 of the Internal Revenue Bulletin 2006-48 at *www.irs.gov/pub/irs-irbs/irb06-48.pdf*

6. Any organization that receives a private letter ruling from the IRS stating that the organization satisfies the section 6033(e)(3) exception.

7. Any organization that keeps records to substantiate that 90% or more of its members cannot deduct their dues (or similar amounts) as business expenses whether or not any part of their dues are used for lobbying purposes.

8. Any organization that is not a membership organization.

 Special rules treat affiliated social welfare organizations, agricultural and horticultural organizations, and business leagues as parts of a single organization for purposes of meeting the nondeductible dues exception. See Rev. Proc. 98-19.

Exception 2. Section 6033(e)(1) $2,000 in-house lobbying exception. *(Check "Yes" for line 85b.)* An organization satisfies the $2,000 in-house lobbying exception if it:

1. Did not receive a waiver for proxy tax owed for the prior year,

2. Did not make any political expenditures or foreign lobbying expenditures during the 2007 reporting year, and

3. Made lobbying expenses during the 2007 reporting year consisting only of in-house direct lobbying expenses totaling $2,000 or less, but excluding:
    a. Any allocable overhead expenses, and
    b. All direct lobbying expenses of any local council regarding legislation of direct interest to the organization or its members.

Dues notices. An organization that checked "No" for both lines 85a and 85b, and is thus responsible for reporting on line 85c through 85h, must send dues notices to its members at the time of assessment or payment of dues, unless the organization chooses to pay the proxy tax instead of informing its members of the nondeductible portion of its dues. These dues notices must reasonably estimate the dues allocable to the nondeductible lobbying and political expenditures reported on line 85d.

IF . . .	THEN . . .
The organization's lobbying and political expenses are more than its membership dues for the year,	The organization must: (a) Allocate all membership dues to its lobbying and political activities, and (b) Carry forward any excess lobbying and political expenses to the next tax year.
The organization: (a) Had only *de minimis* in-house expenses ($2,000 or less) and no other nondeductible lobbying or political expenses; or (b) Paid a proxy tax, instead of notifying its members on the allocation of dues to lobbying and political expenses*; or (c) Established that substantially all of its membership dues, etc., are not deductible by members.	The organization need not disclose to its members the allocation of dues, etc., to its lobbying and political activities.

*Such as political campaign or grassroots lobbying expenses.

Members of the organization cannot take a trade or business expense deduction on their tax returns for the portion of their dues, etc., allocable to the organization's lobbying and political activities.

Proxy tax.

IF . . .	THEN . . .
The organization's actual lobbying and political expenses are more than it estimated in its dues notices,	The organization is liable for a proxy tax on the excess and reports it on Form 990-T.
The organization: (a) Elects to pay the proxy tax, and (b) Chooses not to give its members a notice allocating dues to lobbying and political activities,	All the members' dues remain eligible for a section 162 trade or business expense deduction.
The organization: (a) Makes a reasonable estimate of dues allocable to nondeductible lobbying and political activities, and (b) Agrees to adjust its estimate in the following year*.	The IRS may permit a waiver of the proxy tax.

*A facts and circumstances test determines whether or not a reasonable estimate was made in good faith.

Allocation of costs to lobbying activities and influencing legislation. An organization that is subject to the lobbying disclosure rules of section 6033(e) must use a reasonable allocation method to determine its total costs of its direct lobbying activities; that is, costs to influence:

- Legislation, and
- The actions of a covered executive branch official through direct communication (for example, President, Vice President, or cabinet-level officials, and their immediate deputies) (sections 162(e)(1)(A) and (D)).

Reasonable methods of allocating costs to direct lobbying activities include, but are not limited to:

- The ratio method,
- The gross-up and alternative gross-up methods, and
- A method applying the principles of section 263A.

See Regulations sections 1.162-28 and 1.162-29 and the special rules and definitions for these allocation methods given below.

An organization that is subject to the lobbying disclosure rules of section 6033(e) must also determine its total costs of:

- *De minimis* in-house lobbying,
- Grassroots lobbying, and
- Political activities.

There are no special rules related to determining these costs.

All methods. For all the allocation methods, include labor hours and costs of personnel whose activities involve significant judgment with respect to lobbying activities (lobbying personnel).

Special rules and definitions.

Ratio and gross-up methods.

1. May use even if volunteers conduct activities.

2. May disregard labor hours and costs of clerical or support personnel (other than lobbying personnel) under the ratio method.

Alternative gross-up method.

- Disregard labor hours, and
- Costs of clerical or support personnel (other than lobbying personnel).

Third-party costs are those paid to:

- Outside parties for conducting lobbying activities,
- Dues paid to another membership organization that were declared to be nondeductible lobbying expenses, and
- Travel and entertainment costs for lobbying activities.

Direct contact lobbying is a:

- Meeting,
- Telephone conversation,
- Letter, or
- Similar means of communication that is with a:

1. Legislator (other than a local legislator), or

2. Covered executive branch official

and that otherwise qualifies as a lobbying activity.

Treat all hours spent by a person in connection with direct contact lobbying as labor hours allocable to lobbying activities.

Do not treat the hours spent by a person who engages in research and other background activities related to direct contact lobbying, but who makes no direct contact with a legislator, or covered executive branch official, as direct contact lobbying.

De minimis rule. If less than 5% of a person's time is spent on lobbying activities, and there is no direct contact lobbying, an organization may treat that person's time spent on lobbying activities as zero.

Influencing legislation is:

- Any attempt to influence legislation through a lobbying communication; and
- All activities, such as research and coordination for the purpose of making or supporting a lobbying communication, even if not yet made.

A *lobbying communication* is any communication with any member or employee of a legislative body, or any other government official participating in the formulation of the legislation that:

- Refers to specific legislation and reflects a view on that legislation, or
- Provides support for views in a prior lobbying communication.

Purpose for engaging in an activity is based on all the facts and circumstances. If an organization's lobbying communication was for a lobbying and a nonlobbying purpose, the organization must make a reasonable allocation of costs to influencing legislation.

Correction of prior year lobbying costs. If in a prior year, an organization treated costs incurred for a future lobbying communication as a lobbying cost to influence legislation, but after the organization filed a timely return, it appears the lobbying communication will not be made under any foreseeable circumstance, the organization may apply these costs to reduce its current year's lobbying costs, but not below zero. The organization may carry forward any amount of the costs not used to reduce its current year's lobbying costs to subsequent years.

Example: Ratio method. X Organization incurred:

1. 6,000 labor hours for all activities,
2. 3,000 labor hours for lobbying activities (three employees),
3. $300,000 for operational costs, and
4. No third-party lobbying costs.

X Organization allocated its lobbying costs as follows:

$$\underset{\substack{\text{Lobbying} \\ \text{labor hrs.}}}{\frac{3,000}{6,000}} \times \underset{\substack{\text{Total} \\ \text{costs of} \\ \text{operations}}}{\$300,000} + \underset{\substack{\text{Allocable} \\ \text{third-party} \\ \text{costs}}}{0} = \underset{\substack{\text{Costs} \\ \text{allocable to} \\ \text{lobbying} \\ \text{activities}}}{\$150,000}$$

Total labor hrs.

Examples: Gross-up method and Alternative gross-up method.

A and B are employees of Y Organization.

1. A's activities involve significant judgment with respect to lobbying activities.

2. A's basic lobbying labor costs (excluding employee benefits) are $50,000.

3. B performs clerical and support activities for A.

4. B's labor costs (excluding employee benefits) in support of A's activities are $15,000.

5. Allocable third-party costs are $100,000.

If Y Organization uses the gross-up method to allocate its lobbying costs, Y multiplies 175% times its basic labor costs (excluding employee benefits) for all of the lobbying of its personnel and adds its allocable third-party lobbying costs as follows:

$$\underset{\substack{\text{Basic lobbying labor} \\ \text{costs of A + B}}}{175\% \times \$65,000} + \underset{\substack{\text{Allocable} \\ \text{third-party costs}}}{\$100,000} = \underset{\substack{\text{Costs allocable} \\ \text{to lobbying} \\ \text{activities}}}{\$213,750}$$

If Y Organization uses the alternative gross-up method to allocate its lobbying costs, Y multiplies 225% times its basic labor costs (excluding employee benefits) for all of the lobbying hours of its lobbying personnel and adds its third-party lobbying costs as follows:

$$\underset{\substack{\text{Basic lobbying labor} \\ \text{costs of A}}}{225\% \times \$50,000} + \underset{\substack{\text{Allocable} \\ \text{third-party costs}}}{\$100,000} = \underset{\substack{\text{Costs allocable} \\ \text{to lobbying} \\ \text{activities}}}{\$212,500}$$

Section 263A cost allocation method. The examples that demonstrate this method are found in Regulations section 1.162-28(f).

Line 85a. Section 6033(e)(3) Exception For Nondeductible Dues

If the organization meets any of the criteria of *Exception 1* in the line 85 instructions, answer "Yes" to question 85a. By doing so, the organization is declaring that substantially all of its membership dues were nondeductible. Skip lines 85b through 85h.

Line 85b. In-House Lobbying Expenditures

An organization is exempt from the notice, reporting, and proxy tax liability

Specific Instructions for Form 990

rules of section 6033(e) if it meets *Exception 2*, the $2,000 in-house lobbying exception. Both exceptions are discussed in the instructions for line 85.

An organization should answer "Yes" to question 85b if it met all of the requirements of *Exception 2*. Skip lines 85c through 85h.

If the organization's in-house direct lobbying expenditures during the 2007 reporting year were $2,000 or less, but the organization also paid or incurred other lobbying or political expenditures during the 2007 reporting year, or received a waiver for proxy tax owed for the prior year, it should answer "No" to question 85b and complete lines 85c through 85h. However, the $2,000 or less of in-house direct lobbying expenditures should not be included in the total on line 85d.

Definitions.

Grassroots lobbying refers to attempts to influence any segment of the general public regarding legislative matters or referendums.

Direct lobbying includes attempting to influence:
• Legislation through communication with legislators and other government officials, and
• The official actions or positions of covered executive branch officials through direct communication.

Direct lobbying does not include attempting to influence:
• Any local council on legislation of direct interest to the organization or its members, and
• The general public regarding legislative matters (grassroots lobbying).

Other lobbying includes:
• Grassroots lobbying,
• Foreign lobbying,
• Third-party lobbying, and
• Dues paid to another organization that were used to lobby.

In-house expenditures include:
• Salaries, and
• Other expenses of the organization's officials and staff (including amounts paid or incurred for the planning of legislative activities).

In-house expenditures do not include:
• Any payments to other taxpayers engaged in lobbying or political activities as a trade or business.
• Any dues paid to another organization that are allocable to lobbying or political activities.

Line 85c. Dues, Assessments, and Similar Amounts Received

Enter the total dues, assessments, and similar amounts allocable to the 2007 reporting year.

The term *dues* is the amount the organization requires a member to pay in order to be recognized as a member.

Payments that are similar to dues include:
1. Members' voluntary payments,
2. Assessments to cover basic operating costs, and
3. Special assessments to conduct lobbying and political activities.

Line 85d. Lobbying and Political Expenditures

Include on line 85d the total amount of expenses paid or incurred during the 2007 reporting year in connection with:
1. Influencing legislation;
2. Participating or intervening in any political campaign on behalf of (or in opposition to) any candidate for any public office;
3. Attempting to influence any segment of the general public with respect to elections, legislative matters, or referendums; or
4. Communicating directly with a covered executive branch official in an attempt to influence the official actions or positions of such official.

Also include on line 85d:
1. Excess lobbying and political expenditures carried over from the preceding tax year.
2. An amount equal to the taxable lobbying and political expenditures reported on line 85f for the preceding tax year, if the organization received a waiver of the proxy tax imposed on that amount.

Do not include:
1. Any direct lobbying of any local council or similar governing body with respect to legislation of direct interest to the organization or its members.
2. In-house direct lobbying expenditures, if the total of such expenditures is $2,000 or less (excluding allocable overhead).
3. Political expenditures for which the section 527 tax has been paid (on Form 1120-POL).

• Reduce the current year's lobbying expenditures, but not below zero, by costs previously allocated in a prior year to lobbying activities that were cancelled after a return reporting those costs was filed.
• Carry forward any amounts not used as a reduction to subsequent years.

Line 85e. Dues Declared Nondeductible In Notices To Members

Enter the total amount of dues, etc., allocable to the 2007 reporting year that members were notified were nondeductible under section 162(e).

Example:
• Membership dues: $100,000 for the 2007 reporting year,
• Organization's timely notices to members—25% of membership dues nondeductible, and
• Line 85e entry—$25,000.

Line 85f. Taxable Lobbying and Political Expenditures

The taxable amount reportable on line 85f is the amount of dues, etc.:
1. Allocable to the 2007 reporting year, and
2. Attributable to lobbying and political expenditures that the organization did not timely notify its members were nondeductible.

If the amount on line 85c (dues, etc.) is greater than the amount on line 85d (lobbying & political expenses), then:

Line 85d (lobbying & political expenses)
Less

Line 85e (dues shown in notices)
Equals

Line 85f (taxable lobbying & political expenses)

If the amount on line 85c (dues, etc.) is less than the amount on line 85d (lobbying & political expenses), then:

Line 85c (dues, etc.)
Less

Line 85e (dues shown in notices)
Equals

Line 85f (taxable lobbying & political expenses), and

Line 85d (lobbying & political expenses)
Less

Line 85c (dues, etc.)
Equals

The excess amount to be carried over to the following tax year and reported on line 85d (lobbying & political expenses), or its equivalent, on the year 2008 Form 990.

See *Examples* given below.

Lines 85g and 85h. Proxy Tax and Waivers

An organization must pay the section 6033(e) proxy tax on the amount reported on line 85f unless it has the option to check "Yes" on line 85h.

If the amount on line 85f is zero, or less than zero, enter on:

Line 85g	N/A
Line 85h	N/A

If the organization sent dues notices to its members at the time of assessment or payment of dues that reasonably estimated the dues allocable to the nondeductible lobbying and political expenditures reported on line 85d, enter on:

| Line 85g | No |
| Line 85h | Yes |

Include the amount from the 2007 Form 990, line 85f, on the year 2008 Form 990, line 85d, or its equivalent.

If the organization did not send these dues notices, enter on:

| Line 85g | Yes |
| Line 85h | No |

Report the proxy tax on Form 990-T.

Underreporting of lobbying expenses.
An organization is subject to the proxy tax for the 2007 reporting year for underreported lobbying and political expenses only to the extent that these expenses (if actually reported) would have resulted in a proxy tax liability for that year. A waiver of proxy tax for the tax year only applies to reported expenditures.

An organization that underreports its lobbying and political expenses is also subject to the section 6652(c) daily penalty for filing an incomplete or inaccurate return.

Examples

Organizations A and B:

1. Reported on the calendar year basis.
2. Incurred only grassroots lobbying expenses (did not qualify for the under $2,000 in-house lobbying exception (*de minimis* rule)).
3. Allocated dues to the tax year in which received.

For Organization A— Dues, assessments, and similar amounts received in 2007 were greater than its lobbying expenses for 2007.

Workpapers (for 2007 Form 990)—
Organization A

1. Total dues, assessments, etc., received		$800
2. Lobbying expenses paid or incurred		$600
3. Less: Total nondeductible amount of dues notices	100	100
4. (Subtract line 3 from both lines 1 and 2)	$700	$500
5. Taxable amount of lobbying expenses (smaller of the two amounts on line 4)		$500

 The amounts on lines 1, 2, 3, and 5 of the workpapers were entered on lines 85c through 85f of the 2007 Form 990.

Because dues, etc., received were greater than lobbying expenses, there is no carryover of excess lobbying expenses to line 85d of the year 2008 Form 990.

See the instructions for lines 85g and 85h for the treatment of the $500.

For Organization B— Dues, assessments, and similar amounts

received in 2007 were less than its lobbying expenses for 2007.

Workpapers (for 2007 Form 990)—
Organization B

1. Total dues, assessments, etc., received		$400
2. Lobbying expenses paid or incurred		$600
3. Less: Total nondeductible amount of dues notices	100	100
4. (Subtract line 3 from both lines 1 and 2)	$300	$500
5. Taxable amount of lobbying expenses (smaller of the two amounts on line 4)	$300	

 The amounts on lines 1, 2, 3, and 5 of the workpapers were entered on lines 85c through 85f of the 2007 Form 990.

Because dues, etc., received were less than lobbying expenses, excess lobbying expenses of $200 must be carried forward to line 85d of the year 2008 Form 990 (excess of $600 of lobbying expenses over $400 dues, etc., received). The $200 will be included along with the other lobbying and political expenses paid or incurred in the 2008 reporting year and reportable on line 85d (or the equivalent line) of the year 2008 Form 990.

See the instructions for lines 85g and 85h for the treatment of the $300.

Line 86. Section 501(c)(7) Organizations

Gross receipts test. A section 501(c)(7) organization may receive up to 35% of its gross receipts, including investment income, from sources outside its membership and remain tax-exempt. Part of the 35% (up to 15% of gross receipts) may be from public use of a social club's facilities.

Gross receipts are the club's income from its usual activities and include:
● Charges,
● Admissions,
● Membership fees,
● Dues,
● Assessments, and
● Investment income (such as dividends, rents, and similar receipts), and normal recurring capital gains on investments.

Gross receipts do not include:
● Capital contributions (see Regulations section 1.118-1),
● Initiation fees, or
● Unusual amounts of income (such as the sale of the clubhouse).

 College fraternities or sororities or other organizations that charge membership initiation fees, but not annual dues, do include initiation fees in their gross receipts.

If the 35% and 15% limits do not affect the club's exempt status, include

the income shown on line 86b on the club's Form 990-T.

Investment income earned by a section 501(c)(7) organization is not tax-exempt income unless it is set aside for:
● Religious,
● Charitable,
● Scientific,
● Literary,
● Educational purposes, or
● Prevention of cruelty to children or animals.

If the combined amount of an organization's gross investment income (that is not set aside for charitable purposes) and other unrelated business income exceeds $1,000, it must report the investment income and other unrelated business income on Form 990-T.

Nondiscrimination policy. A section 501(c)(7) organization is not exempt from income tax if any written policy statement, including the governing instrument and bylaws, allows discrimination on the basis of race, color, or religion.

However, section 501(i) allows social clubs to retain their exemption under section 501(c)(7) even though their membership is limited (in writing) to members of a particular religion, if the social club:

1. Is an auxiliary of a fraternal beneficiary society exempt under section 501(c)(8), and
2. Limits its membership to the members of a particular religion; or the membership limitation is:

a. A good-faith attempt to further the teachings or principles of that religion, and

b. Not intended to exclude individuals of a particular race or color.

Line 87. Section 501(c)(12) Organizations

One of the requirements that an organization must meet to qualify under section 501(c)(12) is that at least 85% of its gross income consists of amounts collected from members for the sole purpose of meeting losses and expenses. For purposes of section 501(c)(12), the term *gross income* is gross receipts without reduction for any cost of goods sold.

Gross income for mutual or cooperative electric companies is figured by excluding any income received or accrued from:

1. Qualified pole rentals,
2. Any provision or sale of electric energy transmission services or ancillary service if the services are provided on a nondiscriminatory open access basis under an open access transmission tariff; approved or

Specific Instructions for Form 990

accepted by the Federal Energy Regulatory Commission (FERC) or under an independent transmission provider agreement approved or accepted by FERC (other than income received or accrued directly or indirectly from a member),

3. The provision or sale of electric energy distribution services or ancillary services if the services are provided on a nondiscriminatory, open-access basis to distribute electric energy not owned by the mutual or electric cooperative company:

a. To end-users who are served by distribution facilities not owned by the company or any of its members (other than income received or accrued directly or indirectly from a member), or

b. Generated by a generation facility not owned or leased by the company or any of its members and which is directly connected to distribution facilities owned by such company or any of its members (other than income received or accrued directly or indirectly from a member).

4. From any nuclear decommissioning transaction, or

5. From any asset exchange or conversion transaction.

For a mutual or cooperative telephone company, *gross income* also does not include amounts received or accrued either from another telephone company for completing long distance calls to or from or between the telephone company's members, or from the sale of display listings in a directory furnished to the telephone company's members. Also, gross income does not include amounts received or accrued as qualified pole rentals.

Line 88a.

Answer "Yes" to this question if at any time during the tax year, the organization owned a 50% or greater interest in a taxable corporation or partnership or an entity disregarded as separate from the organization under Regulations sections 301.7701-2 and 301.7701-3. If an organization answers "Yes" on line 88a, complete *Part IX, Information Regarding Taxable Subsidiaries and Disregarded Entities.*

Line 88b.

Answer "Yes" if at any time during the tax year, the organization owned more than 50% of the:
● Stock (by vote or value) in a corporation,
● Interest (either profit or capital) in a partnership, or
● Beneficial interest in any other entity.

The organization must apply section 318 in determining its ownership of stock in a corporation and use similar

principles in determining its ownership interests in other entities.

If the organization answered "Yes," to line 88b, complete *Part XI, Information Regarding Transfers To and From Controlled Entities.*

Line 89a. Section 501(c)(3) Organizations: Disclosure of Excise Taxes Imposed Under Section 4911, 4912, or 4955

Section 501(c)(3) organizations must disclose any excise tax imposed during the year under section 4911 (excess lobbying expenditures), 4912 (disqualifying lobbying expenditures), or, unless abated, 4955 (political expenditures). See sections 4962 and 6033(b).

Line 89b. Section 501(c)(3) and 501(c)(4) Organizations: Disclosure of Section 4958 Excess Benefit Transactions and Excise Taxes

Sections 6033(b) and 6033(f) require section 501(c)(3) and (4) organizations to report the amount of taxes imposed under section 4958 (excess benefit transactions) involving the organization, unless abated, as well as any other information the Secretary may require concerning those transactions. See *General Instruction P* for a discussion of excess benefit transactions.

Attach a statement describing any excess benefit transaction, the disqualified person or persons involved, and whether or not the excess benefit transaction was corrected.

Line 89c. Taxes Imposed on Organization Managers or Disqualified Persons

For line 89c, enter the amount of taxes imposed on organization managers or disqualified persons under sections 4912, 4955, and 4958, unless abated.

Line 89d. Taxes Reimbursed by the Organization

For line 89d, enter the amount of tax on line 89c that was reimbursed by the organization. Any reimbursement of the excise tax liability of a disqualified person or organization manager will be treated as an excess benefit unless (1) the organization treats the reimbursement as compensation during the year the reimbursement is made, and (2) the total compensation to that person, including the reimbursement, is reasonable.

Line 89e. Prohibited Tax Shelter Transactions

Answer "Yes" if the organization was a party to a prohibited tax shelter transaction as described in section 4965(e) at any time during the tax year.

See *General Instruction W* for information about prohibited tax shelter transactions.

If the organization answered "Yes," it must complete Form 8886-T.

Line 89f. Applicable Insurance Contract Interest

Answer "Yes" if after August 17, 2006, but before August 17, 2008, the organization directly or indirectly acquired an applicable insurance contract which is a part of a structured transaction involving a pool of such contracts. If the organization answered "Yes," it also must complete Form 8921.

An *applicable insurance contract* is any life insurance, annuity, or endowment contract to which an applicable exempt organization and a person other than an applicable exempt organization have directly or indirectly held an interest in the contract (whether or not at the same time). However, an applicable insurance contract does not include any life insurance, annuity, or endowment contract if:

1. All persons directly or indirectly holding any interest in the contract (other than applicable exempt organizations) have an insurable interest in the insured under the contract independent of any interest of an applicable exempt organization in the contract, or

2. The sole interest in the contract of an applicable exempt organization or each person other than an applicable exempt organization is as a named beneficiary, or

3. The sole interest in the contract of each person other than an applicable exempt organization is:

a. As a beneficiary of a trust holding an interest in the contract, but only if the person's designation as the beneficiary was made without consideration and solely on a purely gratuitous basis, or

b. As a trustee who holds an interest in the contract in a fiduciary capacity solely for the benefit of applicable exempt organizations or persons described above in 1, 2, or 3a.

An *applicable exempt organization* is any organization to which contributions received are deductible for income tax purposes, estate and gift tax purposes, and Indian tribal governments.

Line 89g. Disclosure of Excess Business Holdings

Answer "Yes" if the organization is a supporting organization or a donor advised fund maintained by a sponsoring organization; had excess business holdings during its tax year; and began its tax year after August 17,

2006. See the Instructions for Form 4720, *Schedule C*, to determine if the organization is subject to the excess business holdings tax under section 4943. If the organization answered "Yes" to line 89g, it must also complete Form 4720.

Donor advised funds. For purposes of the excise tax on excess business holdings under section 4943, a donor advised fund will be treated as a private foundation. For a definition of donor advised funds, and a sponsoring organization, see the instructions for *Line 1a. Contributions to Donor Advised Funds.* Also see, *Donor advised funds* under *Excess Benefit Transaction*, in *General Instruction P*, to determine who is considered a disqualified person for purposes of determining the excise tax on excess business holdings for a donor advised fund.

Supporting organizations. Only certain supporting organizations are subject to the excess business holdings tax under section 4943. These include:
• Type III supporting organizations that are not functionally integrated; and
• Type II supporting organizations that accept any gift or contribution from a person who, by himself or in connection with a related party, controls the supported organization of such Type II supporting organization.

To determine if the organization is a supporting organization and if so, what type of supporting organization it is, see the Instructions for Schedule A, *Line 13. Supporting Organizations.*

Also see, *Supporting organizations* under *Excess Benefit Transaction*, in *General Instruction P*, to determine who is considered a disqualified person for purposes of determining the excise tax on excess business holdings for a supporting organization.

Line 90a. List of States
List each state with which the organization is filing a copy of this return in full or partial satisfaction of state filing requirements.

Line 90b. Number of Employees
Enter the number of employees on the organization's payroll during the pay period including March 12, 2007, as shown on its Form 941 or Form 943 (January-March calendar quarter return only). Do not include household employees, persons who received no pay during the pay period, pensioners, or members of the Armed Forces.

Line 91b. Foreign Accounts
Check the "Yes" box if either 1 or 2 below applies:
1. At any time during the calendar year, the organization had an interest in or signature or other authority over a

financial account in a foreign country (such as a bank account, securities account, or other financial account); and
a. The combined value of the accounts was more than $10,000 at any time during the calendar year; and
b. The accounts were not with a U.S. military banking facility operated by a U.S. financial institution.
2. The organization owns more than 50% of the stock in any corporation that would answer "Yes" to item 1 above.

If the "Yes" box is checked, enter the name of the foreign country or countries. Attach a separate sheet if more space is needed. File Form TD F 90-22.1 by June 30, 2008, with the Department of the Treasury at the address shown on the form.

Form TD F 90-22.1 is available by calling 1-800-TAX-FORM (1-800-829-3676) or by downloading it from the IRS website at *www.irs.gov*. Do not file Form TD F 90-22.1 with the IRS or attach it to Form 990.

Line 92. Section 4947(a)(1) Nonexempt Charitable Trusts
Section 4947(a)(1) nonexempt charitable trusts that file Form 990 instead of Form 1041 and have no taxable income under Subtitle A may use Form 990 to meet its Section 6012 filing requirement by checking the box on line 92. Also, enter on line 92 the total of exempt-interest dividends received from a mutual fund or other regulated investment company as well as tax-exempt interest received directly.

Part VII—Analysis of Income-Producing Activities
Political organizations described in section 527 are not required to complete this Part.

An organization is exempt from income taxes only if its primary purpose is to engage in the type of activity for which it claims exemption.

An exempt organization is subject to a tax on unrelated business taxable income if such income is from a trade or business that is regularly carried on by the organization and is not substantially related to the organization's performance of its exempt purpose or function. Generally, a tax-exempt organization with gross income of $1,000 or more for the year from an unrelated trade or business must file Form 990-T and pay any tax due.

In Part VII, show whether revenue, also reportable on lines 2 through 11 of Part I, was received from activities related to the organization's purpose or activities unrelated to its exempt

purpose. Enter gross amounts unless indicated otherwise. Show also any revenue excludable from the definition of unrelated business taxable income.

The sum of amounts entered in columns (B), (D), and (E) for lines 93 through 103 of Part VII should match amounts entered for correlating lines 2 through 11 of Part I. Use the following table to verify the relationship of Part VII with Part I.

 Contributions that are reportable on lines 1a through 1e of Part I are not reportable in Part VII.

Amounts in Part VII on Line:	Correspond to Amounts in Part I on Line:
93(a) through (g)	2
94	3
95	4
96	5
97 and 98	6c
99	7
100	8d
101	9c
102	10c
103(a) through (e)	11
105 (plus line 1e, Part I)	12

Completing Part VII

Column (A)
In column (A), identify any unrelated business income reportable in column (B) by selecting a business code from the *Codes for Unrelated Business Activity* in the 2007 Instructions for Form 990-T.

Use the current codes listed in the 2007 Instructions for Form 990-T.

Column (B)
In column (B), enter any revenue received from activities unrelated to the exempt purpose of the organization. See the Instructions for Form 990-T and Pub. 598 for a discussion of what is unrelated business income. If the organization enters an amount in column (B), then it must enter a business code in column (A).

Column (C)
In column (C), enter an exclusion code from the *Exclusion Codes* list on the last page of the *Specific Instructions* for Form 990 to identify any revenue excludable from unrelated business income. If more than one exclusion code applies to a particular revenue item, use the lowest numbered exclusion code that applies. If nontaxable revenues from several sources are reportable on the same line in column (D), use the exclusion code that applies to the largest revenue source. If the list of exclusion codes does not include an item of revenue

Specific Instructions for Form 990

that is excludable from unrelated business income, enter that item in column (E) and see the instructions for column (E).

Column (D)

For column (D), identify any revenue received that is excludable from unrelated business income. If the organization enters an amount in column (D), it must enter an exclusion code in column (C).

Column (E)

For column (E), report any revenue from activities related to the organization's exempt purpose; for example, income received from activities that form the basis of the organization's exemption from taxation. Also report here any revenue that is excludable from gross income other than by section 512, 513, or 514, such as interest on state and local bonds that is excluded from tax by section 103. Explain in Part VIII how any amount reported in column (E) relates to the accomplishment of the organization's exempt purposes.

Lines 93(a) through (g). Program Service Revenue

List the organization's revenue-producing program service activities on these lines. Program service activities are primarily those that form the basis of an organization's exemption from tax. Enter in the appropriate columns, gross revenue from each program service activity and the business and exclusion codes that identify this revenue. See the explanation of program service revenue in the instructions for Part I, line 2. For 501(c)(15) reporting of insurance premiums received, refer to instructions for Part I, line 2.

Line 93(f). Medicare and Medicaid Payments

Enter the revenue received from Medicare and Medicaid payments. See the *Example* of program service revenue in the instructions for Part I, line 2.

Line 93(g). Fees and Contracts From Government Agencies

In the appropriate columns, enter gross revenue earned from fees and contract payments by government agencies for a service, facility, or product that benefited the government agency primarily, either economically or physically. Do not include government grants that enabled the organization to benefit the public directly and primarily. See Part I, line 1d instructions for the distinction between government grants that represent contributions and payments from government agencies for a service, product, or facility that

primarily benefited the government agencies.

Report on line 2 of Part I (program service revenue) the sum of the entries in columns (B), (D), and (E) for lines 93(a) through (g).

Lines 94 through 96. Dues, Assessments, Interest, and Dividends

In the appropriate columns, report the revenue received for these line items. General instructions for lines 94 through 96 are given in the instructions for Part I, lines 3 through 5.

Lines 97 and 98. Rental Income (Loss)

Report net rental income from investment property on these lines. Also report here rental income from unaffiliated exempt organizations. Report rental income, however, from an exempt function (program service) on line 93. Refer to the instructions for Part I, line 6. A more detailed discussion of rental income is given in the Instructions for Form 990-T and Pub. 598.

Rents from real property are usually excluded in computing unrelated business taxable income, as are incidental amounts (10% or less) of rental income from personal property leased with real property (mixed lease). In a mixed lease where the rent attributable to personal property is more than 50% of the total rent, neither rent from real or personal property is excluded from unrelated business taxable income. The exclusion also does not apply when the real or personal property rentals depend wholly or partly on the income or profits from leased property, other than an amount based on a fixed percentage or percentage of gross receipts or sales.

The rental exclusion from unrelated business taxable income does not apply to debt-financed real property. In general, debt-financed property is any property that the organization finances by debt and holds to produce income instead of for exempt purposes. An exempt organization's income from debt-financed property is treated as unrelated business taxable income and is subject to tax in the same proportion as the property remains financed by the debt. If substantially all (85% or more) of any property is used for an organization's exempt purposes, the property is not treated as debt-financed property. The rules for debt-financed property do not apply to rents from personal property.

Lines 99 through 102

In the appropriate columns, report the revenue received for these line items.

General instructions for lines 99 through 102 are given in the instructions for Part I, lines 7 through 10.

Lines 103(a) through (e). Other Revenue

List any *Other revenue* activity on these lines. These activities are discussed in the instructions for line 11, Part I. In the appropriate columns, enter the revenue received from these activities. Select applicable business and exclusion codes. Report as *Other revenue,* on line 11 of Part I, the total revenue entered in columns (B), (D), and (E) for lines 103(a) through (e).

Line 105. Total

Enter the total revenue reported on line 104 for columns (B), (D), and (E). The amount reported on line 105, plus the amount on line 1e of Part I, should equal the amount entered for *Total revenue* on line 12 of Part I.

Part VIII—Relationship of Activities to the Accomplishment of Exempt Purposes

To explain how an amount entered in Part VII, column (E), was related or exempt function income, show the line number of the amount in column (E) and give a brief description of how the activity reported in column (E) specifically contributed to the accomplishment of the organization's exempt purposes (other than by providing funds for such purposes). Activities that generate exempt-function income are activities that form the basis of the organization's exemption from tax.

Also give the line number and an explanation for any income entered in column (E) that is specifically excluded from gross income other than by sections 512, 513, or 514. If no amount is entered in column (E), do not complete Part VIII.

Example. M, an organization described in section 501(c)(3), operates a school for the performing arts. Admission is charged at student performances. M reported admission income in column (E) of Part VII and explained in Part VIII that performances before an audience were an essential part of the students' training and related to the exempt purpose of the organization.

Because M also reported interest from state bonds in column (E) of Part VII, M explained in Part VIII that such interest was excluded from gross income by section 103.

If additional space is needed, see *Attachments* in *General Instruction X*.

Part IX—Information Regarding Taxable Subsidiaries and Disregarded Entities

Column (A). Enter the name, address, and EIN of each taxable corporation or partnership and each disregarded entity in which the organization held a 50% or greater interest at any time during the year. If a disregarded entity does not have its own EIN, state that it uses the organization's EIN.

Columns (D) and (E). Enter the corporation's or partnership's total income and end-of-year total assets as reported on each entity's federal tax return for the year ending within the year covered by the parent organization's Form 990. Since the financial information of a disregarded entity is reported on its parent organization's return, enter in column (D) the amount on line 12, *Total revenue*, that is attributable to the disregarded entity. Enter in column (E) the amount on line 59, *Total assets*, column (B), that is attributable to the disregarded entity.

Part X—Information Regarding Transfers Associated With Personal Benefit Contracts

See *General Instruction V* which also discusses the reporting requirements for this Part.

If, in connection with any transfer of funds to a charitable organization, the organization directly or indirectly pays premiums on any personal benefit contract, or there is an understanding or expectation that any person will directly or indirectly pay such premiums, the organization must report the premiums it paid and the premiums paid by others, but treated as paid by the organization, on Form 8870. The organization must report and pay an excise tax, equal to premiums paid, on Form 4720.

Part XI — Information Regarding Transfers To and From Controlled Entities

Line 106. Answer "Yes" and complete the schedule if at any time during the tax year the organization made any loans or transfers to a corporation, partnership, or other entity, which it controlled within the meaning of section 512(b)(13). In column (c), describe each loan or transfer (including but not limited to interest, annuities, royalties, or rents). In column (d) enter the amount for each loan or transfer to each controlled entity. Report only the total of all payments for a specific transfer transaction. For example, for a loan, report only the total of all payments rather than each individual

payment for that loan. If additional space is needed, attach a statement. See *Attachments* in *General Instruction X*.

Line 107. Answer "Yes" and complete the schedule if at any time during the tax year, the organization received any transfers of funds or payments from a controlled entity within the meaning of section 512(b)(13).

In column (c), describe each transfer. Indicate in the description if such transfer is a qualifying specified payment (described in line 108) and indicate the type of transfer such as interest, annuities, royalties, rents, dividends, fees or other payments for services, or contributions to capital, and loans.

In column (d), enter the amount received for each type of payment. If additional space is needed, attach a statement. See *Attachments* in *General Instruction X*.

Line 108. Answer "Yes" if the organization had a contract covering payments from a controlled entity of interest, annuities, royalties, or rents, but only if the contract was in writing, legally enforceable, and in effect on August 17, 2006. Also, answer "Yes" if the contract described above had been renewed with substantially similar terms.

Exclusion Codes

General Exceptions

01— Income from an activity that is not regularly carried on (section 512(a)(1))

02— Income from an activity in which labor is a material income-producing factor and substantially all (at least 85%) of the work is performed with unpaid labor (section 513(a)(1))

03— Section 501(c)(3) organization—Income from an activity carried on primarily for the convenience of the organization's members, students, patients, visitors, officers, or employees (hospital parking lot or museum cafeteria, for example) (section 513(a)(2))

04— Section 501(c)(4) local association of employees organized before 5/27/69— Income from the sale of work-related clothes or equipment and items normally sold through vending machines; food dispensing facilities; or snack bars for the convenience of association members at their usual places of employment (section 513(a)(2))

05— Income from the sale of merchandise, substantially all of which (at least 85%) was donated to the organization (section 513(a)(3))

Specific Exceptions

06— Section 501(c)(3), (4), or (5) organization conducting an agricultural or educational fair or exposition—Qualified public entertainment activity income (section 513(d)(2))

07— Section 501(c)(3), (4), (5), or (6) organization—Qualified convention and trade show activity income (section 513(d)(3))

08— Income from hospital services described in section 513(e)

09— Income from noncommercial bingo games that do not violate state or local law (section 513(f))

10— Income from games of chance conducted by an organization in North Dakota (section 311 of the Deficit Reduction Act of 1984, as amended)

11— Section 501(c)(12) organization—Qualified pole rental income (section 513(g)) and/or member income (described in section 501(c)(12)(H))

12— Income from the distribution of low-cost articles in connection with the solicitation of charitable contributions (section 513(h))

13— Income from the exchange or rental of membership or donor list with an organization eligible to receive charitable contributions by a section 501(c)(3) organization; by a war veterans' organization; or an auxiliary unit or society of, or trust or foundation for, a war veterans' post or organization (section 513(h))

Modifications and Exclusions

14— Dividends, interest, payments with respect to securities loans, annuities, income from notional principal contracts, loan commitment fees, and other substantially similar income from ordinary and routine investments excluded by section 512(b)(1)

15— Royalty income excluded by section 512(b)(2)

16— Real property rental income that does not depend on the income or profits derived by the person leasing the property and is excluded by section 512(b)(3)

17— Rent from personal property leased with real property and incidental (10% or less) in relation to the combined income from the real and personal property (section 512(b)(3))

18— Gain (or loss, to the extent allowed) from the sale of investments and other non-inventory property and from certain property acquired from financial institutions that are in conservatorship or receivership (sections 512(b)(5) and 512(b)(16)(A))

19— Income or loss from the lapse or termination of options to buy or sell securities, or real property, and from the forfeiture of good-faith deposits for the purchase, sale, or lease of investment real property (section 512(b)(5))

20— Income from research for the United States; its agencies or instrumentalities; or any state or political subdivision (section 512(b)(7))

21— Income from research conducted by a college, university, or hospital (section 512(b)(8))

22— Income from research conducted by an organization whose primary activity is conducting fundamental research, the results of which are freely available to the general public (section 512(b)(9))

23— Income from services provided under license issued by a Federal regulatory agency and conducted by a religious order or school operated by a religious order, but only if the trade or business has been carried on by the organization since before May 27, 1959 (section 512(b)(15))

Foreign Organizations

24— Foreign organizations only—Income from a trade or business NOT conducted in the United States and NOT derived from United States sources (patrons) (section 512(a)(2))

Social Clubs and VEBAs

25— Section 501(c)(7), (9), or (17) organization— Non-exempt function income set aside for a charitable, etc., purpose specified in section 170(c)(4) (section 512(a)(3)(B)(i))

26— Section 501(c)(7), (9), or (17) organization— Proceeds from the sale of exempt function property that was or will be timely reinvested in similar property (section 512(a)(3)(D))

27— Section 501(c)(9), or (17) organization— Non-exempt function income set aside for the payment of life, sick, accident, or other benefits (section 512(a)(3)(B)(ii))

Veterans' Organizations

28— Section 501(c)(19) organization—Payments for life, sick, accident, or health insurance for members or their dependents that are set aside for the payment of such insurance benefits or for a charitable, etc., purpose specified in section 170(c)(4) (section 512(a)(4))

29— Section 501(c)(19) organization—Income from an insurance set-aside (see code 28 above) that is set aside for payment of insurance benefits or for a charitable, etc., purpose specified in section 170(c)(4) (Regulations section 1.512(a)–4(b)(2))

Debt-financed Income

30— Income exempt from debt-financed (section 514) provisions because at least 85% of the use of the property is for the organization's exempt purposes (**Note:** *This code is only for income from the 15% or less non-exempt purpose use.*) *(section 514(b)(1)(A))*

31— Gross income from mortgaged property used in research activities described in section 512(b)(7), (8), or (9) (section 514(b)(1)(C))

32— Gross income from mortgaged property used in any activity described in section 513(a)(1), (2), or (3) (section 514(b)(1)(D))

33— Income from mortgaged property (neighborhood land) acquired for exempt purpose use within 10 years (section 514(b)(3))

34— Income from mortgaged property acquired by bequest or devise (applies to income received within 10 years from the date of acquisition) (section 514(c)(2)(B))

35— Income from mortgaged property acquired by gift where the mortgage was placed on the property more than 5 years previously and the property was held by the donor for more than 5 years (applies to income received within 10 years from the date of gift) (section 514(c)(2)(B))

36— Income from property received in return for the obligation to pay an annuity described in section 514(c)(5)

37— Income from mortgaged property that provides housing to low and moderate income persons to the extent the mortgage is insured by the Federal Housing Administration (section 514(c)(6)) (**Note:** *In many cases, this would be exempt function income reportable in column (E). It would not be so in the case of a section 501(c)(5) or (6) organization, for example, that acquired the housing as an investment or as a charitable activity.*)

38— Income from mortgaged real property owned by: a school described in section 170(b)(1)(A)(ii); a section 509(a)(3) affiliated support organization of such a school; a section 501(c)(25) organization, or by a partnership in which any of the above organizations owns an interest if the requirements of section 514(c)(9)(B)(vi) are met (section 514(c)(9))

Special Rules

39— Section 501(c)(5) organization—Farm income used to finance the operation and maintenance of a retirement home, hospital, or similar facility operated by the organization for its members on property adjacent to the farm land (section 1951(b)(8)(B) of Public Law 94-455)

40— Annual dues not exceeding $136 (subject to inflation) paid to a section 501(c)(5) agricultural or horticultural organization (section 512(d))

Trade or Business

41— Gross income from an unrelated activity that is regularly carried on but, in light of continuous losses sustained over a number of tax periods, cannot be regarded as being conducted with the motive to make a profit (not a trade or business)

Other

42— Receipt of qualified sponsorship payments described in section 513(i)

43— Exclusion of any gain or loss from the qualified sale, exchange, or other disposition of any qualifying brownfield property (section 512(b)(19))

Specific Instructions for Form 990-EZ

See also the *General Instructions* that apply to both Form 990 and Form 990-EZ.

Contents	Page

Completing the Heading of Form 990-EZ

The instructions that follow are keyed to items in the heading for Form 990-EZ.

Item A—Accounting Period

File the 2007 return for calendar year 2007 and fiscal years that begin in 2007 and end in 2008. For a fiscal year return, fill in the tax year space at the top of page 1.

Item B—Checkboxes

Address change, name change, and initial return. Check the appropriate box if the organization changed its address since it filed its previous return, or if this is the first time the organization is filing either a Form 990 or a Form 990-EZ.

If the tax-exempt organization has changed its name, attach the following documents:

IF the organization is .	THEN attach . . .
A corporation	An amendment to the articles of incorporation with proof of filing with the state of incorporation.
A trust	An amendment to the trust agreement signed by the trustee.
An association	An amendment to the articles of association, constitution, bylaws, or other organizing document, along with signatures of at least two officers/members.

Final return and amended return. Organizations should file final returns when they cease to be section 501(a) organizations or section 527 organizations; for example, when they cease operations and dissolve. See the instructions for line 36 that discuss

liquidations, dissolutions, terminations, or substantial contractions.

If the return is an amended return, check the box. There are amended return requirements when filing with a state. See *General Instructions E* and *J.*

Application pending. If the organization's application for exemption is pending, check this box and complete the return.

Item C—Name and Address

If the organization operates under a name different from its legal name, give the legal name of the organization but identify its alternate name, after the legal name, by writing "aka" (also known as) and the alternate name of the organization. However, if the organization has changed its name, follow the instructions for *Name change* in *Item B—Checkboxes.*

Include the suite, room, or other unit number after the street address. If the Post Office does not deliver mail to the street address and the organization has a P.O. box, show the box number instead of the street address.

If the organization receives its mail in care of a third party (such as an accountant or an attorney), enter on the street address line C/O followed by the third party's name and street address or P.O. box.

For foreign addresses, enter information in the following order: City, province or state, and the name of the country. Follow the foreign country's practice in placing the postal code in the address. Please do not abbreviate the country name.

If a change of address occurs after the return is filed, use Form 8822 to notify the IRS of the new address.

Item D—Employer Identification Number

The organization should have only one federal employer identification number (EIN). If the organization has more than one EIN and has not been advised which to use, notify the Internal Revenue Service Center, Ogden, UT 84201-0027. State what numbers the organization has, and the name and address to which each number was assigned, and the address of its principal office. The IRS will advise the organization which number to use.

 A section 501(c)(9) voluntary employees' beneficiary association must use its own EIN and not the EIN of its sponsor.

Item E—Telephone Number

Enter a telephone number of the organization that members of the public

and government regulators may use during normal business hours to obtain information about the organization's finances and activities. If the organization does not have a telephone number, enter the telephone number of an organization official who can provide such information.

Item F—Group Exemption Number

The group exemption number (GEN) is a number assigned by the IRS to the central/parent organization of a group that has a group ruling.

If the organization is covered by a group exemption letter, enter the four-digit group exemption number. Contact the central/parent organization if the organization is unsure of the GEN assigned.

Item G—Accounting Method

Indicate the method of accounting used in preparing this return. See *General Instruction G.*

Item H—Schedule B (Form 990, 990-EZ, or 990-PF)

Whether or not the organization enters any amount on line 1 of Form 990-EZ, the organization must either check the box in item H or attach Schedule B (Form 990, 990-EZ, or 990-PF). Failure to either check the box in item H or file Schedule B (Form 990, 990-EZ, or 990-PF) will result in a determination that the return is incomplete. See the Instructions for Schedule B (Form 990, 990-EZ, or 990-PF), for more information.

 Contributor *includes individuals, fiduciaries, partnerships, corporations, associations, trusts, and exempt organizations.*

Guidelines for Meeting the Requirements of Schedule B (Form 990, 990-EZ, or 990-PF)

Section 501(c)(3) Org. Meeting the 1/3 Support Test of 170(b)(1)(A)

If	A section 501(c)(3) organization that met the 1/3 support test of the regulations under 509(a)(1)/ 170(b)(1)(A) did not receive a contribution of the greater of $5,000 or 2% of the amount on line 1 of Form 990-EZ, from any one contributor,*
Then	The organization should check the box in item H to certify that it is not required to attach Schedule B (Form 990, 990-EZ, or 990-PF).
Otherwise	Complete and attach Schedule B (Form 990, 990-EZ, or 990-PF).

Section 501(c)(7), (8), or (10) Organizations

Specific Instructions for Form 990-EZ

If . . . . . . A section 501(c)(7), (8), or (10) organization did not receive *any* contribution or bequest for use *exclusively* for religious, charitable, scientific, literary, or educational purposes, or the prevention of cruelty to children or animals (and did not receive any noncharitable contributions of $5,000 or more as described below under **general rule**),

Then . . . . The organization should check the box in item H to certify that it is not required to attach Schedule B (Form 990, 990-EZ, or 990-PF).

Otherwise   Complete and attach Schedule B (Form 990, 990-EZ, or 990-PF).

All Other Form 990 or Form 990-EZ Organizations (General rule)

If . . . . . . The organization did not show as part of line 1 of the Form 990-EZ, a contribution of $5,000 or more from any one contributor,*

Then . . . . The organization should check the box in item H to certify that it is not required to attach Schedule B (Form 990, 990-EZ, or 990-PF).

Otherwise   Complete and attach Schedule B (Form 990, 990-EZ, or 990-PF).

* Total a contributor's gifts of $1,000 or more to determine if a contributor gave $5,000 or more. Do not include smaller gifts.

Item I—Website

Show the organization's website address if a website is available. Otherwise, write "N/A" (not applicable). Consider adding the organization's email address to its website.

Item J— Organization Type

If the organization is exempt under section 501(c), check the applicable box and insert, within the parentheses, the number that identifies the type of section 501(c) organization the filer is. See the chart in *General Instruction C.* The term section 501(c)(3) includes organizations exempt under sections 501(e), (f), (k), and (n). Check the box if the organization is a section 527 political organization. See *General Instruction U.*

If the organization is a section 4947(a)(1) nonexempt charitable trust, check the applicable box. Note also the discussion regarding Schedule A (Form 990 or 990-EZ) and Form 1041 in *General Instruction D* and the instructions for line 43.

Item K—Gross Receipts of $25,000 or Less

Check this box if the organization is not a section 509(a)(3) supporting organization and its gross receipts are normally not more than $25,000 but the organization chooses to file Form 990-EZ. If the organization chooses to file Form 990-EZ, be sure to file a complete return. See *General Instruction B* for a discussion on gross

Specific Instructions for Form 990-EZ

receipts and *General Instruction X* for a discussion on a complete return.

 To figure if a section 501(c)(15) organization qualifies for tax-exemption for the year, see the definition of gross receipts for section 501(c)(15) purposes under Section 501(c)(15) Organizations *in* General Instruction A. *Do not use the section 501(c)(15) definition of gross receipts to figure if the organization's gross receipts are normally $25,000 or less.*

Item L—Figuring Gross Receipts

Only those organizations with gross receipts of less than $100,000 and total assets of less than $250,000 at the end of the year can use the Form 990-EZ. If the organization does not meet these requirements, it must file Form 990. The organization's gross receipts are the total amount it received from all sources during its annual accounting period, without subtracting any costs or expenses. See the gross receipts discussion in *General Instruction B.*

 To figure if a section 501(c)(15) organization qualifies for tax-exemption for the year, see the definition of gross receipts for section 501(c)(15) purposes under Section 501(c)(15) Organizations *in* General Instruction A. *Do not use the section 501(c)(15) definition of gross receipts to figure the amount to enter here.*

Part I—Revenue, Expenses, and Changes in Net Assets or Fund Balances

All organizations filing Form 990-EZ with the IRS or any state must complete Part I. Some states that accept Form 990-EZ in place of their own forms may require additional information. See *General Instruction E.*

Line 1. Contributions, Gifts, Grants, and Similar Amounts Received

A. What is included on line 1

• Report amounts received as voluntary contributions; for example, payments, or the part of any payment, for which the payer (donor) does not receive full retail value (fair market value) from the recipient (donee) organization.
• Enter the gross amounts of contributions, gifts, grants, and bequests that the organization received from individuals, trusts, corporations, estates, affiliates, foundations, public charities, and other exempt

-55-

organizations, or raised by an outside professional fundraiser.
• Report the value of noncash contributions at the time of the donation. For example, report the gross value of a donated car as of the time the car was received as a donation.
• Report all related expenses on lines 12 through 16. The organization must show on line 13 professional fundraising fees relating to the gross amounts of contributions collected in the charity's name by fundraisers.

Reporting for line 1, in accordance with SFAS 116, Accounting for Contributions Received and Contributions Made, is acceptable for Form 990-EZ, or Form 990, purposes, but not required by the IRS. However, see *General Instruction E.*

An organization that receives a grant to be paid in future years should, according to SFAS 116, report the grant's present value on line 1. Accruals of present value increments to the unpaid grant should also be reported on line 1 in future years.

1. Contributions can arise from special events when an excess payment is received for items offered. Fundraising activities relate to soliciting and receiving contributions. However, special fundraising activities such as dinners, door-to-door sales of merchandise, carnivals, and bingo games can produce both contributions and revenue. Report as a contribution, both on line 1 and on line 6a (within the parentheses), any amount received through such a special event that is greater than the fair market value (retail value) of the merchandise or services furnished by the organization to the contributor.

This situation usually occurs when organizations seek support from the public through solicitation programs that are in part special events or activities and are in part solicitations for contributions. The primary purpose of such solicitations is to receive contributions and not to sell the merchandise at its retail value even though this might produce a profit.

Example. An organization announces that anyone who contributes at least $40 to the organization can choose to receive a book worth $16 retail value. A person who gives $40, and who chooses the book, is really purchasing the book for $16 and also making a contribution of $24. The contribution of $24, which is the difference between the buyer's payment and the $16 retail value of the book, would be reported on line 1 and again on line 6a (within the parentheses). The revenue received ($16 retail value of the book) would be reported in the right-hand column on line 6a. Any expenses directly relating to the sale of the book would be reported on line 6b. Any fundraising expenses relating to the contribution of $24 would be reported on lines 12 through 16.

If a contributor gives more than $40, that person would be making a larger contribution, the difference between the book's retail value of $16 and the amount actually given. See also the instructions for line 6 and Pub. 526.

 At the time of any solicitation or payment, organizations that are eligible to receive tax-deductible contributions should advise patrons of the amount deductible for federal tax purposes. See General Instruction L.

2. Contributions can arise from special events when items of only nominal value are given or offered. If an organization offers goods or services of only nominal value through a special event, or distributes free, unordered, low-cost items to patrons, report the entire amount received for such benefits as a contribution on line 1. Report all related expenses on lines 12 through 16.

See *General Instruction L* for a definition of benefits that have a nominal or insubstantial value.

3. Section 501(c)(3) organizations. These organizations must compute the amounts of revenue and contributions received from special events according to the above instructions when preparing their *Support Schedule* in Part IV-A of Schedule A (Form 990 or 990-EZ).

4. Grants equivalent to contributions. Grants made to encourage an organization receiving the grant to carry on programs or activities that further the grant recipient's exempt purposes are grants that are equivalent to contributions. Report them on line 1. The grantor may specify which of the recipient's activities the grant may be used for, such as an adoption program or a disaster relief project.

A grant is still equivalent to a contribution if the grant recipient performs a service, or produces a work product, that benefits the grantor incidentally (but see line 1, instruction B1, below).

5. Contributions received through other fundraising organizations. Contributions received indirectly from the public through solicitation campaigns conducted by federated fundraising agencies (such as United Way) are included on line 1.

6. Contributions received from associated organizations. Include on line 1 amounts contributed by other organizations closely associated with

the reporting organization. This includes contributions received from a parent organization, subordinate, or another organization having the same parent.

7. Contributions from a commercial co-venture. Include amounts contributed by a commercial co-venture on line 1. These contributions are amounts received by the organization for allowing an outside organization (donor) or individual to use the recipient organization's name in a sales promotion campaign.

8. Contributions or grants from governmental units. A grant, or other payment from a governmental unit, is treated as a grant equivalent to a contribution if its primary purpose is to enable the recipient to provide a service to, or maintain a facility for, the direct benefit of the public rather than to serve the direct and immediate needs of the grantor (even if the public pays part of the expense of providing the service or facility). (See also line 1, instruction B1, below.)

9. Contributions in the form of membership dues. Include on line 1 membership dues and assessments to the extent they are contributions and not payments for benefits received. (See line 3, instruction C1.)

B. What is not included on line 1

1. Grants that are payments for services are not contributions. A grant is a payment for services, and not a contribution, when the terms of the grant provide the grantor with a specific service, facility, or product, rather than providing a benefit to the general public or that part of the public served by the grant recipient. The recipient organization would report such a grant as income on line 2 (program service revenue).

2. Donations of services. Do not include the value of services donated to the organization, or items such as the free use of materials, equipment, or facilities, as contributions on line 1. However, for the optional reporting of such amounts, see the instruction for donated services in Part III.

Any unreimbursed expenses of officers, employees, or volunteers do not belong on the Form 990 or Form 990-EZ. See the instructions for charitable contributions and employee business expenses in Pub. 526 and 463, respectively.

3. Section 501(c)(9), (17), and (18) organizations. These organizations provide participants with life, sickness, accident, welfare and unemployment insurance, pension(s), or similar benefits, or a combination of these

benefits. When such an organization receives payments from participants, or their employers, to provide these benefits, report the payments on line 2 as program service revenue, rather than on line 1 as contributions.

C. How to value noncash contributions

See *General Instruction L* and Schedule B (Form 990, 990-EZ, or 990-PF).

D. Schedule of contributors

Attach Schedule B (Form 990, 990-EZ, or 990-PF). See *General Instruction L* and the *Specific Instructions for Completing the Heading of Form 990-EZ,* Item H.

Line 2—Program Service Revenue Including Medicare, Medicaid Payments, and Government Fees and Contracts

Enter the total program service revenue (exempt function income). Program services are primarily those that form the basis of an organization's exemption from tax.

1. Examples. A clinic would include on line 2 all of its charges for medical services (whether to be paid directly by the patients or through Medicare, Medicaid, or other third-party reimbursement), laboratory fees, and related charges for services.

Program service revenue also includes tuition received by a school; revenue from admissions to a concert or other performing arts event or to a museum; royalties received as author of an educational publication distributed by a commercial publisher; payments received by a section 501(c)(9) organization from participants or employers of participants for health and welfare benefits coverage; and registration fees received in connection with a meeting or convention.

2. Program-related investment income. Program service revenue also includes income from program-related investments. These investments are made primarily to accomplish an exempt purpose of the investing organization rather than to produce income. Examples are scholarship loans and low-interest loans to charitable organizations, indigents, or victims of a disaster. Rental income received from an exempt function is another example of program-related investment income. See also the instructions for line 4.

3. Unrelated trade or business activities. Unrelated trade or business activities (not including any special events or activities) that generate fees for services may also be program

Specific Instructions for Form 990-EZ

service activities. A social club, for example, should report as program service revenue the fees it charges both members and nonmembers for the use of its tennis courts and golf course.

4. Government fees and contracts. Program service revenue includes income earned by the organization for providing a government agency with a service, facility, or product that benefited that government agency directly rather than benefiting the public as a whole. See line 1, instruction A8, for reporting guidelines when payments are received from a government agency for providing a service, facility, or product for the primary benefit of the general public.

Line 3—Membership Dues and Assessments

Enter members' and affiliates' dues and assessments that are not contributions. See also *General Instruction L.*

A. What is included on line 3

1. Dues and assessments received that compare reasonably with the benefits of membership. When the organization receives dues and assessments that compare reasonably with membership benefits, report such dues and assessments on line 3.

2. Organizations that generally match dues and benefits. Organizations described in section 501(c)(5), (6), or (7) generally provide benefits with a reasonable relationship to dues, although benefits to members may be indirect.

B. Examples of membership benefits

These include subscriptions to publications; newsletters (other than one about the organization's activities only); free or reduced-rate admissions to events the organization sponsors; use of its facilities; and discounts on articles or services that both members and nonmembers can buy. In figuring the value of membership benefits, disregard such intangible benefits as the right to attend meetings, vote, or hold office in the organization, and the distinction of being a member of the organization.

C. What is not included on line 3

1. Dues or assessments received that exceed the value of available membership benefits. Whether or not membership benefits are used, dues received by an organization, to the extent they exceed the monetary value of the membership benefits available to the dues payer, are a contribution that should be reported on line 1.

2. Dues received primarily for the organization's support. If a member pays dues primarily to support the organization's activities, and not to obtain benefits of more than nominal monetary value, those dues are a contribution to the organization includible on line 1.

Line 4—Investment Income

A. What is included on line 4

1. Interest on savings and temporary cash investments. Include the amount of interest received from interest-bearing checking accounts, savings, and temporary cash investments, such as money market funds, commercial paper, certificates of deposit, and U.S. Treasury bills or other governmental obligations that mature in less than 1 year. So-called dividends or earnings received from mutual savings banks, money market funds, etc., are actually interest and should be included on this line.

2. Dividends and interest from securities. Include the amount of dividend and interest income from equity and debt securities (stocks and bonds) on this line. Include amounts received from payments on securities loans, as defined in section 512(a)(5).

3. Gross rents. Include gross rental income received during the year from investment property.

4. Other investment income. Include, for example, royalty income from mineral interests owned by the organization.

B. What is not included on line 4

1. Capital gains dividends and unrealized gains and losses. Do not include on this line any capital gains dividends. They are reported on line 5. Also do not include unrealized gains and losses on investments carried at market value. See the instructions for line 20.

2. Exempt function revenue (program service). Do not include on line 4 amounts that represent income from an exempt function (program service). Report these amounts on line 2 as program service revenue. Report expenses related to this income on lines 12 through 16.

An organization whose exempt purpose is to provide low-rental housing to persons with low income receives exempt function income from such rentals. An organization receives exempt function income if it rents or sublets rental space to a tenant whose activities are related to the reporting organization's exempt purpose. Exempt function income also arises when an

organization rents to an unaffiliated exempt organization at less than fair rental value for the purpose of helping that unaffiliated organization carry out its exempt purpose. Report rental income received in these instances on line 2 and not on line 4.

Only for purposes of completing this return, treat income from renting property to affiliated exempt organizations as exempt function income and include such income on line 2 as program service revenue.

Lines 5a through 5c—Gains (or Losses) From Sale of Assets Other Than Inventory

A. What is included on line 5

Report on line 5a all sales of securities and sales of all other types of investments (such as real estate, royalty interests, or partnership interests) as well as sales of all other noninventory assets (such as program-related investments and fixed assets used by the organization in its related and unrelated activities).

Total the cost or other basis (less depreciation) and selling expenses and enter the result on line 5b. On line 5c, enter the net gain or loss. Report capital gains dividends, the organization's share of capital gains and losses from a partnership, and capital gains distributions from trusts on lines 5a and 5c. Indicate the source on the schedule described below.

For this return, the organization may use the more convenient way to figure the organization's gain or loss from sales of securities by comparing the sales price with the average-cost basis of the particular security sold. However, generally the average-cost basis is not used to figure the gain or loss from sales of securities reportable on Form 990-T.

B. What is not included on line 5

Do not include on line 5 any unrealized gains or losses on securities that are carried in the books of account at market value. See the instructions for line 20.

C. Attached schedule

1. Nonpublicly traded securities and noninventory items. Attach a schedule to show the sale or exchange of nonpublicly traded securities and the sale or exchange of other assets that are not inventory items. The schedule should show security transactions separately from the sale of other assets. Show for these assets:
● Date acquired and how acquired,
● Date sold and to whom sold,
● Gross sales price,

- Cost, other basis, or if donated, value at time acquired (state which),
- Expense of sale and cost of improvements made after acquisition, and
- Depreciation since acquisition, if depreciable property.

2. Publicly traded securities. For sales of publicly traded securities through a broker, the organization may total the gross sales price, the cost or other basis, and the expenses of sale, and report lump-sum figures in place of providing the detailed reporting required in the above paragraph.

Publicly traded securities include common and preferred stocks, bonds (including governmental obligations), and mutual fund shares that are listed and regularly traded in an over-the-counter market or on an established exchange and for which market quotations are published or otherwise readily available.

Lines 6a through 6c—Special Events and Activities

On the appropriate line, enter the gross revenue, expenses, and net income (or loss) from all special events and activities, such as dinners, dances, carnivals, raffles, bingo games, other gaming activities, and door-to-door sales of merchandise.

These activities only incidentally accomplish an exempt purpose. Their sole or primary purpose is to raise funds that are other than contributions to finance the organization's exempt activities.

This is done by offering goods or services that have more than a nominal value (compared to the price charged) for a payment that is more than the direct cost of those goods or services. See line 1 instructions A1 and A2 for a discussion on contributions reportable on line 1 and revenue reportable on line 6. See also *General Instruction L.*

Calling any required payment a donation or contribution on tickets, advertising, or solicitation materials does not change how these payments should be reported on Form 990-EZ.

The gross revenue from gaming activities and other special events must be reported in the right-hand column on line 6a without reduction for cash or noncash prizes, cost of goods sold, compensation, fees, or other expenses. Be sure to check the box for gaming if the organization conducted directly, or through the promoter, any amount of gaming during the year.

Gaming includes, but is not limited to: bingo, pull tabs, instant bingo raffles, scratch-offs, charitable gaming tickets, break-opens, hard cards, banded tickets, jar tickets, pickle cards, Lucky Seven cards, Nevada Club tickets, casino nights, Las Vegas nights, and coin-operated gambling devices. Coin-operated gambling devices include slot machines, electronic video slot or line games, video poker, video blackjack, video keno, video bingo, video pull tab games, etc.

A. What is included on line 6

1. Gross revenue/contributions. When an organization receives payments for goods or services offered through a special event, enter:

1. As gross revenue, on line 6a (in the right-hand column), the retail value of the goods or services,

2. As a contribution, on both line 1 and line 6a (within the parentheses), any amount received that exceeds the retail value of the goods or services given.

Example. At a special event, an organization received $100 in gross receipts for goods valued at $40. The organization entered gross revenue of $40 on line 6a and entered a contribution of $60 on both line 1 and within the parentheses on line 6a. The contribution was the difference between the gross revenue of $40 and the gross receipts of $100.

2. Raffles or lotteries. Report as revenue, on line 6a, any amount received from raffles or lotteries that require payment of a specified minimum amount for each entry, unless the prizes awarded have only nominal value. See line 6, instruction B1 and B2, below.

3. Direct expenses. Report on line 6b only the direct expenses attributable to the goods or services the buyer receives from a special event. If the organization includes an expense on line 6b, do not report it again on line 7b. Report cost of goods related to the sale of inventory on line 7b. Fundraising expenses attributable to contributions reported on line 6a (within the parentheses), and also on line 1, are reportable on lines 12 through 16.

B. What is not included on line 6

1. Sales or gifts of goods or services of only nominal value. If the goods or services offered at the special event have only nominal value, include all of the receipts as contributions on line 1 and all of the related expenses on lines 12 through 16. See *General Instruction L* for a description of nominal or insubstantial benefits.

2. Sweepstakes, raffles, and lotteries. Report as a contribution, on line 1, the proceeds of solicitation campaigns in which the names of contributors and other respondents are entered in a drawing for prizes.

When a minimum payment is required for each raffle or lottery entry and prizes of only nominal value are awarded, report any amount received as a contribution. Report the related expenses on lines 12 through 16.

3. Activities that generate only contributions are not special events. An activity that generates only contributions, such as a solicitation campaign by mail, is not a special event. Any amount received should be included on line 1 as a contribution. Related expenses are reportable on lines 12 through 16.

C. Attached schedule

Attach a schedule listing the three largest fundraising events, as measured by gross receipts. If gaming is conducted, treat different types of gaming separately to determine the three largest events. For example, treat bingo and pull tabs as separate fundraising events. Describe each of these events by listing the type of event and the number of occasions that the event occurred and show (for each event):

1. Gross receipts,

2. Contributions included in gross receipts (see line 6, instruction A1, above),

3. Gross revenue (gross receipts less contributions),

4. Direct expenses, and

5. Net income or (loss) (gross revenue less direct expenses).

For gaming, direct expenses include: cash and noncash prizes, compensation to bingo callers and workers, rental of gaming equipment, cost of bingo supplies such as pull tab deals, etc.

Furnish the same information, in total figures, for all other special events held that are not among the largest three. Indicate the type and number of the events not listed individually (for example, three dances and two raffles).

An example of this schedule of special events might appear in columnar form as follows:

Special Events (and the number of occasions that the event occurred):	(A) #	(B) #	(C) #	All Other	Total
Gross Receipts	$xx	$xx	$xx	$xx	$xx
Less: Contributions	xx	xx	xx	xx	xx
Gross Revenue	xx	xx	xx	xx	xx
Less: Direct Expenses	xx	xx	xx	xx	xx
Net Income or (loss)	$xx	$xx	$xx	$xx	$xx

If the organization uses this format, report the total for Contributions on line 1 of Form 990-EZ and on line 6a (within the parentheses). Report the totals for *Gross Revenue*, in the right-hand column, on line 6a; *Direct Expenses* on line 6b; and *Net Income or (loss)* on line 6c.

Lines 7a through 7c—Gross Sales of Inventory

1. Sales of inventory. Include on line 7a the gross sales (less returns and allowances) of inventory items, whether the sales activity is an exempt function or an unrelated trade or business. Include all inventory sales except sales of goods at special events, which are reportable on line 6.

2. Cost of goods sold. On line 7b, report the cost of goods sold related to sales of such inventory. The usual items included in cost of goods sold are direct and indirect labor, materials and supplies consumed, freight-in, and a proportion of overhead expenses. Marketing and distribution expenses are not includible in cost of goods sold. Include those expenses on lines 12 through 16.

3. Investments. Do not include on line 7 sales of investments on which the organization expected to profit by appreciation and sale. Report sales of these investments on line 5.

Line 8—Other Revenue

Enter the total income from all sources not covered by lines 1 through 7. Examples of types of income includible on line 8 are interest on notes receivable not held as investments or as program-related investments (defined in the line 2 instructions); interest on loans to officers, directors, trustees, key employees, and other employees; and royalties that are not investment income or program service revenue.

Line 10—Grants and Similar Amounts Paid

Reporting for line 10 in accordance with SFAS 116 is acceptable for Form 990-EZ purposes, but not required by IRS. However, see *General Instruction E.*

An organization that makes a grant to be paid in future years should, according to SFAS 116, report the grant's present value on line 10. Accruals of present value increments to the unpaid grant should also be reported on line 10 in future years.

A. What is included on line 10

Enter the amount of actual grants and similar amounts paid to individuals and organizations selected by the filing organization. Include scholarship, fellowship, and research grants to individuals.

1. Specific assistance to individuals. Include on this line the amount of payments to, or for the benefit of, particular clients or patients, including

assistance by others at the expense of the filing organization.

2. Payments, voluntary awards, or grants to affiliates. Include on line 10 certain types of payments to organizations affiliated with (closely related to) the reporting organization. These payments include predetermined quota support and dues payments by local organizations to their state or national organizations.

 If the organization uses Form 990-EZ for state reporting purposes, be sure to distinguish between payments to affiliates and awards and grants. See General Instruction E.

B. What is not included on line 10

1. Administrative expenses. Do not include on this line expenses made in selecting recipients or monitoring compliance with the terms of a grant or award. Enter those expenses on lines 12 through 16.

2. Purchases of goods or services from affiliates. Do not report the cost of goods or services purchased from affiliates on line 10. Report these as expenses on lines 12 through 16.

3. Membership dues paid to another organization. Report membership dues that the organization pays to another organization for general membership benefits, such as regular services, publications, and materials on line 16, as *Other expenses.*

C. Attached schedule

Attach a schedule to explain the amounts reported on line 10. Show on this schedule:
- Each class of activity,
- The grantee's name and address,
- The amount given, and
- The relationship of the grantee (in the case of grants to individuals) if the relationship is by blood, marriage, adoption, or employment (including employees' children) to any person or corporation with an interest in the organization, such as a creator, donor, director, trustee, officer, etc.

Any grants reported on line 10 that were approved during the year, but not paid by the due date for filing Form 990-EZ (including extensions), must be identified and listed separately in the line 10 schedule.

Give the name and address of each affiliate that received any payment reported on line 10. Specify both the amount and purpose of these payments.

Classify activities on this schedule in more detail than by using such broad terms as charitable, educational, religious, or scientific. For example,

identify payments to affiliates; payments for nursing services; fellowships; or payments for food, shelter, or medical services for indigents or disaster victims. For payments to indigent families, do not identify the individuals.

If an organization gives property other than cash and makes an award or grant by the property's fair market value, also show on this schedule:
- A description of the property,
- The book value of the property,
- How the organization determined the book value,
- How the organization determined the fair market value, and
- The date of the gift.

Any difference between a property's fair market value and book value should be recorded in the organization's books of account and on line 20.

Colleges, universities, and primary and secondary schools are not required to list the names of individuals who were provided scholarships or other financial assistance whether they are the recipients of Federal grant money or not. Instead, these organizations must (a) group each type of financial aid provided; (b) indicate the number of individuals who received the aid; and (c) specify the aggregate dollar amount.

Line 11—Benefits Paid To or For Members

For an organization that gives benefits to members or dependents (such as organizations exempt under section 501(c)(8), (9), or (17)), enter the amounts paid for: (a) death, sickness, hospitalization, or disability benefits; (b) unemployment compensation benefits; and (c) other benefits. Do not include, on this line, the cost of employment-related benefits the organization gives its officers and employees. Report them on line 12.

Line 12—Salaries, Other Compensation, and Employee Benefits

Enter the total salaries and wages paid to all employees and the fees paid to officers, directors, and trustees. Include the total of the employer's share of the contributions the organization paid to qualified and nonqualified pension plans and the employer's share of contributions to employee benefit programs (such as insurance, health, and welfare programs) that are not an incidental part of a pension plan. Complete the Form 5500 return if the organization is required to file it.

Also include in the total the amount of federal, state, and local payroll taxes for the year that are imposed on the organization as an employer. This includes the employer's share of social security and Medicare taxes, Federal unemployment tax (FUTA), state unemployment compensation tax, and other state and local payroll taxes. Taxes withheld from employees' salaries and paid over to the various governmental units (such as Federal and state income taxes and the employees' share of social security and Medicare taxes) are part of the employees' salaries included on line 12. Report expenses paid or incurred for employee events such as a picnic or holiday party on this line.

Line 13—Professional Fees and Other Payments to Independent Contractors

Enter the total amount of legal, accounting, auditing, other professional fees (such as fees for fundraising or investment services) and related expenses charged by outside firms and individuals who are not employees of the organization. Do not include any penalties, fines, or judgments imposed against the organization as a result of legal proceedings. Report and identify those expenses on line 16. Report fees paid to directors and trustees on line 12.

Line 14—Occupancy, Rent, Utilities, and Maintenance

Enter the total amount paid or incurred for the use of office space or other facilities, heat, light, power, and other utilities, outside janitorial services, mortgage interest, real estate taxes and property insurance attributable to rental property, and similar expenses. Do not subtract from rental expenses reported on line 14 any rental income received from renting or subletting rented space. See the instructions for lines 2 and 4 to determine whether such income is reportable as exempt function income or investment income. However, report on line 14 any rental expenses for rental income reported on lines 2 and 4. If the organization records depreciation on property it occupies, enter the total for the year.

For an explanation of acceptable methods for computing depreciation, see Pub. 946.

Line 15—Printing, Publications, Postage, and Shipping

Enter the printing and related costs of producing the reporting organization's own newsletters, leaflets, films, and other informational materials on this line. Include the costs of outside mailing services on this line. Also include the cost of any purchased publications as well as postage and shipping costs not reportable on lines

5b, 6b, or 7b. Do not include any expenses, such as salaries, for which a separate line is provided.

Line 16—Other Expenses

Include here such expenses as penalties, fines, and judgments; unrelated business income taxes; insurance and real estate taxes not attributable to rental property or reported as occupancy expenses; depreciation on investment property; travel and transportation costs; interest expense; and expenses for conferences, conventions, and meetings.

Some states that accept Form 990-EZ in satisfaction of their filing requirements may require that certain types of miscellaneous expenses be itemized. See *General Instruction E.*

Line 18—Excess or (Deficit) for the Year

Enter the difference between lines 9 and 17. If line 17 is more than line 9, enter the difference in parentheses.

Line 19—Net Assets or Fund Balances at Beginning of Year

Enter the amount from the prior year's balance sheet or from Form 5500 or an approved DOL form if *General Instruction F* applies.

Line 20—Other Changes in Net Assets or Fund Balances

Attach a statement explaining any changes in net assets or fund balances between the beginning and end of the year that are not accounted for by the amount on line 18. Amounts to report here include adjustments of earlier years' activity; unrealized gains and losses on investments carried at market value; and any difference between fair market value and book value of property given as an award or grant. See *General Instruction G* regarding the reporting of a section 481(a) adjustment to conform to SFAS 116.

Part II—Balance Sheets

All organizations, except those that meet one of the exceptions in *General Instruction F*, must complete columns (A) and (B) of Part II of the return and may not submit a substitute balance sheet. Failure to complete Part II may result in penalties for filing an incomplete return. If there is no amount to report in column (A), *Beginning of year*, put a zero in that column. See *General Instruction K.*

Some states require more information. See *General Instruction E* for more information about completing a Form 990-EZ to be filed with any state or local government agency.

-60-

Line 22—Cash, Savings, and Investments

Include all interest and non-interest bearing accounts such as petty cash funds, checking accounts, savings accounts, money market funds, commercial paper, certificates of deposit, U.S. Treasury bills, and other government obligations. Also include the book value of securities held as investments, and all other investment holdings including land and buildings held for investment. Report the income from these investments on line 4.

Line 23—Land and Buildings

Enter the book value (cost or other basis less accumulated depreciation) of all land and buildings owned by the organization and not held for investment.

Line 24—Other Assets

Enter the total of other assets along with a description of those assets. Amounts to include here are (among others) receivable accounts, inventories, and prepaid expenses.

Line 25—Total Assets

Enter the amount of total assets. If the end-of-year total assets entered in column (B) are $250,000 or more, Form 990 must be filed instead of Form 990-EZ.

Line 27—Net Assets or Fund Balances

Subtract line 26 (total liabilities) from line 25 (total assets) to determine net assets. Enter this net asset amount on line 27. The amount entered in column (B) should agree with the net asset or fund balance amount on line 21.

States that accept Form 990-EZ as their basic report form may require a separate statement of changes in net assets. See *General Instruction E.*

Part III—Statement of Program Service Accomplishments

A program service is a major (usually ongoing) objective of an organization, such as adoptions, recreation for the elderly, rehabilitation, or publication of journals or newsletters.

Step	Action
1	State the organization's primary exempt purpose.
2	All organizations must describe their exempt purpose achievements for each of their four largest program services (as measured by total expenses incurred). If there were four or fewer of such activities, describe each program service activity.

Specific Instructions for Form 990-EZ

• Describe program service accomplishments through measurements such as clients served, days of care, therapy sessions, or publications issued.

• Describe the activity's objective, for both this time period and the longer-term goal, if the output is intangible, such as in a research activity.

• Give reasonable estimates for any statistical information if exact figures are not readily available. Indicate that this information is estimated.

• Be clear, concise, and complete in the description. Avoid adding an attachment.

3 If part of the total expenses of any program service consists of grants reported on line 10, enter the amount of grants in the space provided and include the grants in the *Expenses* column. If the amount of grants entered includes foreign grants, check the box to the left of the entry space for *Program Services Expenses*.

• Section 501(c)(3) and (4) organizations, and section 4947(a)(1) nonexempt charitable trusts, must show the amount of grants and allocations to others and must enter the total expenses for each program service reported.

• For all other organizations, completing the *Program Services Expenses* column (and the *Grants* entry) in Part III is optional.

4 Attach a schedule that lists the organization's other program services.

• The detailed information required for the four largest services is not necessary for this schedule.

• However, section 501(c)(3) and (4) organizations, and section 4947(a)(1) nonexempt charitable trusts must show the expenses attributable to their program services.

5 The organization may show the amount of any donated services, or use of materials, equipment, or facilities it received or utilized in connection with a specific program service.

• Disclose the applicable amounts of any donated services, etc., on the lines for the narrative description of the appropriate program service.

• Do not include these amounts in the expense column in Part III.

• See the instructions for line 1, B2.

Part IV—List of Officers, Directors, Trustees, and Key Employees

List each person who was an officer, director, trustee, or key employee (defined below) of the organization at any time during the year even if they did not receive any compensation from the organization.

For purposes of reporting all amounts in columns (B) through (E) in Part IV, either use the organization's tax year, or the calendar year ending within such tax year.

Enter a zero in columns (B), (C), (D), or (E) if no hours were entered in column (B) and no compensation, contributions, expenses, and other allowances were paid during the reporting year, or deferred for payment to a future accounting period.

Aid in the processing of the organization's return by grouping together, preferably at the end of the list, those who received no compensation. Be careful not to repeat names.

Give the preferred address at which officers, directors, etc., want the Internal Revenue Service to contact them.

Use an attachment if there are more than four persons to list in Part IV.

Show all forms of cash and noncash compensation received by each listed officer, director, etc., whether paid currently or deferred.

If the organization pays any other person, such as a management services company, for the services provided by any of its officers, directors, trustees, or key employees, report the compensation and other items in Part IV as if the organization had paid the officers, directors, etc., directly. Also, see Ann. 2001-33, 2001-17 I.R.B. 1137.

A failure to fully complete Part IV can subject both the organization and the individuals responsible for such failure to penalties for filing an incomplete return. See *General Instruction K*. In particular, entering the phrase on Part IV, "Information available upon request," or a similar phrase, is not acceptable.

The organization may also provide an attachment to explain the entire 2007 compensation package for any person listed in Part IV.

Key employee. A *key employee* is any person having responsibilities or powers similar to those of officers, directors, or trustees. The term includes the chief management and administrative officials of an organization (such as an executive director or chancellor).

A chief financial officer and the officer in charge of the administration or program operations are both key employees if they have the authority to control the organization's activities, its finances, or both.

Column (A)

Report the name and address of each person who was a current officer,

-61-

director, trustee, or key employee (defined above), during the tax year or, if using the calendar year, at any time during the calendar year or tax year.

Column (B)

In column (B), a numerical estimate of the average hours per week devoted to the position is required for a complete answer. Statements such as "as needed" or "as required," or "40+" are unacceptable.

Column (C)

For each person listed, report salary, fees, bonuses, and severance payments paid. Include current-year payments of amounts reported or reportable as deferred compensation in any prior year.

Column (D)

Include in this column all forms of deferred compensation and future severance payments (whether or not funded; whether or not vested; and whether or not the deferred compensation plan is a qualified plan under section 401(a)). Include also payments to welfare benefit plans on behalf of the officers, etc. Such plans provide benefits such as medical, dental, life insurance, severance pay, disability, etc. Reasonable estimates may be used if precise cost figures are not readily available.

Unless the amounts were reported in column (C), report, as deferred compensation in column (D), salaries and other compensation earned during the period covered by the return, but not yet paid by the date the organization files its return.

Column (E)

Enter both taxable and nontaxable fringe benefits (other than *de minimis* fringe benefits described in section 132(e)). Include amounts that the recipients must report as income on their separate income tax returns. Examples include amounts for which the recipient did not account to the organization or allowances that were more than the payee spent on serving the organization. Include payments made under indemnification arrangements, the value of the personal use of housing, automobiles, or other assets owned or leased by the organization (or provided for the organization's use without charge), as well as any other taxable and nontaxable fringe benefits. See Pub. 525 for more information.

Form 941 must be filed to report income tax withholding and social security and Medicare taxes. The organization must also file Form 940 to report Federal unemployment tax, unless the organization is not subject to these taxes. See Pub. 15 (Circular E) for more information. See also the *Trust Fund Recovery Penalty* discussion in *General Instruction D.*

Part V—Other Information
• Section 501(c)(3) organizations and section 4947(a)(1) nonexempt charitable trusts must also complete and attach a Schedule A (Form 990 or 990-EZ) to their Form 990-EZ. See *General Instruction D* for information on Schedule A (Form 990 or 990-EZ).
• Answer "Yes," "No," or "N/A" to each question.
• The organization must attach a statement regarding personal benefit contracts. See *General Instruction V.*

Line 33—Change in Activities
Attach a statement to explain any changes during the past 3 years in the activities the organization conducts to further its exempt purpose, or in the methods of conducting these activities. However, if a change has been reported to the IRS on a previously filed attachment, do not report the change again. An activity previously listed as current or planned in the organization's application for recognition of exemption does not have to be reported unless the method of conducting such activity has changed. Also, include any major program activities that are being discontinued.

Line 34—Changes in Organizing or Governing Documents
Attach a conformed copy of any changes to the articles of incorporation, or association, constitution, trust instrument, or other organizing document, or to the bylaws or other governing document.

A *conformed copy* is one that agrees with the original document and all amendments to it. If the copies are not signed, they must be accompanied by a written declaration signed by an officer authorized to sign for the organization, certifying that they are complete and accurate copies of the original documents.

Photocopies of articles of incorporation showing the certification of an appropriate state official need not be accompanied by such a declaration. See Rev. Proc. 68-14, 1968-1 C.B. 768, for details. When a number of changes are made, attach a copy of the entire revised organizing instrument or governing document.

However, if the exempt organization changes its legal structure, such as from a trust to a corporation, it must file a new exemption application to establish that the new legal entity qualifies for exemption.

Line 35—Unrelated Business Income and Lobbying Proxy Tax

Unrelated Business Income
Political organizations described in section 527 are not required to answer this question.

Check "Yes" on line 35a if the organization's total gross income from all of its unrelated trades and businesses is $1,000 or more for the year. Gross income is gross receipts less the cost of goods sold. See Pub. 598 for a description of unrelated business income and the 2007 Instructions for Form 990-T for the Form 990-T filing requirements. Form 990-T is not a substitute for Form 990-EZ. Items of income and expense reported on Form 990-T must also be reported on Form 990-EZ when the organization is required to file both forms.

 All tax-exempt organizations must pay estimated taxes with respect to their unrelated business income if they expect their tax liability to be $500 or more. Use Form 990-W to compute this tax.

Section 6033(e) tax for lobbying expenditures
If the organization checks "No" to line 35a, it is certifying that the organization was not subject to the notice and reporting requirements of section 6033(e) and that the organization had no lobbying and political expenditures potentially subject to the proxy tax.

Section 6033(e) notice and reporting requirements and proxy tax. Section 6033(e) requires certain section 501(c)(4), (5), and (6) organizations to tell their members the portion of their membership dues that were allocable to the political or lobbying activities of the organization. If an organization does not give its members this information, then the organization is subject to a proxy tax. The tax is reported on Form 990-T.

If the organization checks "Yes" on line 35a to declare that it had reportable section 6033(e) lobbying and political expenses in the 2007 reporting year (and potential liability for the proxy tax):
1. Complete lines 85a-h, page 7, of Form 990 (note instructions), and
2. Attach page 7 to Form 990-EZ.

Only certain organizations that are tax exempt under sections:
• 501(c)(4) (social welfare organizations),
• 501(c)(5) (agricultural and horticultural organizations), or
• 501(c)(6) (business leagues) are subject to (a) the section 6033(e) notice and reporting requirements, and (b) a potential proxy tax.

If the organization is not tax-exempt under sections 501(c)(4), (5), or (6), check "No" on line 35a, unless there was unrelated business income.

If the organization meets *Exception 1* or *2* below, it is excluded from the notice, reporting, and proxy tax requirements of section 6033(e), and it should check "No" to line 35a, unless the organization had $1,000 or more of unrelated business income. See also Rev. Proc. 98-19, 1998-1 C.B. 547.

Exception 1. Section 6033(e)(3) exception for nondeductible dues.
1. All organizations exempt from tax under section 501(a), other than section 501(c)(4), (5), and (6) organizations.
2. Local associations of employees' and veterans' organizations described in section 501(c)(4), but not section 501(c)(4) social welfare organizations.
3. Labor unions and other labor organizations described in section 501(c)(5), but not section 501(c)(5) agricultural and horticultural organizations.
4. Section 501(c)(4), (5), and (6) organizations that receive more than 90% of their dues from:
   a. Section 501(c)(3) organizations,
   b. State or local governments,
   c. Entities whose income is exempt from tax under section 115, or
   d. Organizations described in 1 through 3, above.
5. Section 501(c)(4) and (5) organizations that receive more than 90% of their annual dues from:
   a. Persons,
   b. Families, or
   c. Entities who each paid annual dues of $95 or less in 2007 (adjusted annually for inflation). See Rev. Proc. 2006-53 which is on page 996 of the Internal Revenue Bulletin at *www.irs.gov/pub/irs-irbs/irb06-48.pdf.*
6. Any organization that receives a private letter ruling from the IRS stating that the organization satisfies the section 6033(e)(3) exception.
7. Any organization that keeps records to substantiate that 90% or more of its members cannot deduct their dues (or similar amounts) as business expenses whether or not any part of their dues are used for lobbying purposes.
8. Any organization that is not a membership organization.

Specific Instructions for Form 990-EZ

Special rules treat affiliated social welfare organizations, agricultural and horticultural organizations, and business leagues as parts of a single organization for purposes of meeting the nondeductible dues exception. See Rev. Proc. 98-19.

Exception 2. Section 6033(e)(1) $2,000 in-house lobbying exception. An organization satisfies the $2,000 in-house lobbying exception if it:

1. Did not receive a waiver for proxy tax owed for the prior year,
2. Did not make any political expenditures or foreign lobbying expenditures during the 2007 reporting year,
3. Incurred lobbying expenses during the 2007 reporting year consisting only of in-house direct lobbying expenses totaling $2,000 or less, but excluding:
   a. Any allocable overhead expenses, and
   b. All direct lobbying expenses of any local council regarding legislation of direct interest to the organization or its members.

Definitions.

Grassroots lobbying refers to attempts to influence any segment of the general public regarding legislative matters or referendums.

Direct lobbying includes attempting to influence:
- Legislation through communication with legislators and other government officials, and
- The official actions or positions of covered executive branch officials through direct communication.

Direct lobbying does not include attempting to influence:
- Any local council on legislation of direct interest to the organization or its members, and
- The general public regarding legislative matters (grassroots lobbying).

Other lobbying includes:
- Grassroots lobbying,
- Foreign lobbying,
- Third-party lobbying, and
- Dues paid to another organization that were used to lobby.

In-house expenditures include:
- Salaries, and
- Other expenses of the organization's officials and staff (including amounts paid or incurred for the planning of legislative activities).

In-house expenditures do not include:
- Any payments to other taxpayers engaged in lobbying or political activities as a trade or business.

Specific Instructions for Form 990-EZ

- Any dues paid to another organization that are allocable to lobbying or political activities.

Line 36—Liquidation, Dissolution, Termination, or Substantial Contraction

If there was a liquidation, dissolution, termination, or substantial contraction, attach a statement explaining what took place.

For a complete liquidation of a corporation or termination of a trust, check the *Termination* box in the heading of the return. On the attached statement, show whether the assets have been distributed and the date. Also attach a certified copy of any resolution, or plan of liquidation or termination, etc., with all amendments or supplements not already filed. In addition, attach a schedule listing the names and addresses of all persons who received the assets distributed in liquidation or termination; the kinds of assets distributed to each one; and each asset's fair market value.

A *substantial contraction* is a partial liquidation or other major disposition of assets except transfers for full consideration or distributions from current income.

A *major disposition of assets* is any disposition for the tax year that is:

1. At least 25% of the fair market value of the organization's net assets at the beginning of the tax year; or
2. One of a series of related dispositions begun in earlier years that add up to at least 25% of the net assets the organization had at the beginning of the tax year when the first disposition in the series was made. Whether a major disposition of assets took place through a series of related dispositions depends on the facts in each case.

See Regulations section 1.6043-3 for special rules and exceptions.

Line 37—Expenditures for Political Purposes

Political organizations described in section 527 are not required to answer this question.

A political expenditure is one intended to influence the selection, nomination, election, or appointment of anyone to a federal, state, or local public office, or office in a political organization, or the election of Presidential or Vice Presidential electors. It does not matter whether the attempt succeeds.

An expenditure includes a payment, distribution, loan, advance, deposit, or gift of money, or anything of value. It also includes a contract, promise, or agreement to make an expenditure, whether or not legally enforceable.

All section 501(c) organizations. An exempt organization that is not a political organization must file Form 1120-POL if it is treated as having political organization taxable income under section 527(f)(1).

If a section 501(c) organization establishes and maintains a section 527(f)(3) separate segregated fund, see the specific instructions for line 81, Form 990.

Section 501(c)(3) organizations. A section 501(c)(3) organization will lose its tax-exempt status if it engages in political activity.

A section 501(c)(3) organization must pay a section 4955 excise tax for any amount paid or incurred on behalf of, or in opposition to, any candidate for public office. The organization must pay an additional excise tax if it fails to correct the expenditure timely.

A manager of a section 501(c)(3) organization who knowingly agrees to a political expenditure must pay a section 4955 excise tax, unless the agreement is not willful and there is reasonable cause. A manager who does not agree to a correction of the political expenditure may have to pay an additional excise tax.

When an organization promotes a candidate for public office (or is used or controlled by a candidate or prospective candidate), amounts paid or incurred for the following purposes are political expenditures:
- Remuneration to such individual (a candidate or prospective candidate) for speeches or other services;
- Travel expenses of such individual;
- Expenses of conducting polls, surveys, or other studies, or preparing papers or other material for use by such individual;
- Expenses of advertising, publicity, and fundraising for such individual; and
- Any other expense that has the primary effect of promoting public recognition or otherwise primarily accruing to the benefit of such individual.

An organization is effectively controlled by a candidate or prospective candidate only if such individual has a continuing, substantial involvement in the day-to-day operations or management of the organization.

A determination of whether the primary purpose of an organization is promoting the candidacy or prospective candidacy of an individual for public office is made on the basis of all the facts and circumstances. See section 4955 and Regulations section 53.4955.

Use Form 4720 to figure and report these excise taxes.

Line 38—Loans To or From Officers, Directors, Trustees, and Key Employees

Enter the end-of-year unpaid balance of secured and unsecured loans made to or received from officers, directors, trustees, and key employees. For example, if the organization borrowed $1,000 from one officer and loaned $500 to another, none of which has been repaid, report $1,500 on line 38b.

For loans outstanding at the end of the year, attach a schedule as described below. Report any interest expense on line 16 and any interest income on line 2, 4, or 8, depending on the nature of the receivable that created the interest income.

When loans should be reported separately. In the required schedule, report each loan separately, even if more than one loan was made to or received from the same person, or the same terms apply to all loans made. Salary advances and other advances for the personal use and benefit of the recipient, and receivables subject to special terms or arising from nontypical transactions, must be reported as separate loans for each officer, director, trustee, and key employee.

When loans should be reported as a single total. In the required schedule, report receivables that are subject to the same terms and conditions (including credit limits and rate of interest) as receivables due from the general public (occurring in the normal course of the organization's operations) as a single total for all the officers, directors, trustees, and key employees. Report travel advances for official business of the organization as a single total.

Schedule format. For each outstanding loan or other receivable that must be reported separately, the attached schedule should show the following information (preferably in columnar form):
• Borrower's name and title,
• Original amount,
• Balance due,
• Date of note,
• Maturity date,
• Repayment terms,
• Interest rate,
• Security provided by the borrower,
• Purpose of the loan, and
• Description and fair market value of the consideration furnished by the lender (for example, cash—$1,000; or 100 shares of XYZ, Inc., common stock—$9,000).

The above detail is not required for receivables or travel advances that may be reported as a single total. However, report and identify those totals separately in the attachment.

Line 39—Section 501(c)(7) Organizations

Gross receipts test. A section 501(c)(7) organization may receive up to 35% of its gross receipts, including investment income, from sources outside its membership and remain tax-exempt. Part of the 35% (up to 15% of gross receipts) may be from public use of a social club's facilities.

Gross receipts are the club's income from its usual activities and include:
• Charges,
• Admissions,
• Membership fees,
• Dues,
• Assessments, and
• Investment income (such as dividends, rents, and similar receipts), and normal recurring capital gains on investments.

Gross receipts do not include:
• Capital contributions (see Regulations section 1.118-1),
• Initiation fees, or
• Unusual amounts of income (such as the sale of the clubhouse).

 College fraternities or sororities or other organizations that charge membership initiation fees, but not annual dues, do include initiation fees in their gross receipts.

If the 35% and 15% limits do not affect the club's exempt status, include the income shown on line 39b on the club's Form 990-T.

Investment income earned by a section 501(c)(7) organization is not tax-exempt income unless it is set aside for:
• Religious,
• Charitable,
• Scientific,
• Literary,
• Educational purposes, or
• Prevention of cruelty to children or animals.

If the combined amount of an organization's gross investment income and other unrelated business income exceeds $1,000, it must report the investment income and other unrelated business income on Form 990-T.

Nondiscrimination policy. A section 501(c)(7) organization is not exempt from income tax if any written policy statement, including the governing instrument and bylaws, allows discrimination on the basis of race, color, or religion.

However, section 501(i) allows social clubs to retain their exemption under section 501(c)(7) even though their membership is limited (in writing) to members of a particular religion, if the social club:

1. Is an auxiliary of a fraternal beneficiary society exempt under section 501(c)(8), and
2. Limits its membership to the members of a particular religion; or the membership limitation is:
   a. A good-faith attempt to further the teachings or principles of that religion, and
   b. Not intended to exclude individuals of a particular race or color.

Line 40a—Section 501(c)(3) Organizations: Disclosure of Excise Taxes Imposed Under Section 4911, 4912, or 4955

Section 501(c)(3) organizations must disclose any excise tax imposed during the year under section 4911 (excess lobbying expenditures), 4912 (disqualifying lobbying expenditures), or, unless abated, 4955 (political expenditures). See sections 4962 and 6033(b).

Line 40b—Section 501(c)(3) and 501(c)(4) organizations: Disclosure of Section 4958 Excess Benefit Transactions and Excise Taxes

Sections 6033(b) and 6033(f) require section 501(c)(3) and (4) organizations to report the amount of taxes imposed under section 4958 (excess benefit transactions) involving the organization, unless abated, as well as any other information the Secretary may require concerning those transactions. See *General Instruction P* for a discussion of excess benefit transactions.

Attach a statement describing any excess benefit transaction, the disqualified person or persons involved, and whether or not the excess benefit transaction was corrected.

Line 40c—Taxes Imposed on Organization Managers or Disqualified Persons

For line 40c, enter the amount of taxes imposed on organization managers or disqualified persons under sections 4912, 4955, and 4958, unless abated.

Line 40d—Taxes Reimbursed By the Organization

For line 40d, enter the amount of tax on line 40c that was reimbursed by the organization. Any reimbursement of the excise tax liability of a disqualified person or organization manager will be treated as an excess benefit unless (1) the organization treats the reimbursement as compensation during the year the reimbursement is made, and (2) the total compensation to that person, including the reimbursement, is reasonable.

Specific Instructions for Form 990-EZ

Line 40e—Tax on Prohibited Tax Shelter Transactions

Answer "Yes" if the organization was a party to a prohibited tax shelter transaction as described in section 4965(e) at any time during the tax year. See *General Instruction W* for information about prohibited tax shelter transactions.

If the organization answered "Yes," it must complete Form 8886-T.

Line 41—List of States

List each state with which the organization is filing a copy of this return in full or partial satisfaction of state filing requirements.

Line 42b—Foreign Financial Accounts

Check the "Yes" box if either 1 or 2 below applies:

1. At any time during the calendar year, the organization had an interest in or signature or other authority over a financial account in a foreign country (such as a bank account, securities account, or other financial account); and

a. The combined value of the accounts was more than $10,000 at any time during the calendar year; and

b. The accounts were not with a U.S. military banking facility operated by a U.S. financial institution.

2. The organization "Yes" to item 1 above.

If the "Yes" box is checked, enter the name of the foreign country or countries. Attach a separate sheet if more space is needed. File Form TD F 90-22.1 by June 30, 2008, with the Department of the Treasury at the address shown on the form.

Form TD F 90-22.1 is available by calling 1-800-TAX-FORM (1-800-829-3676) or by downloading it from the IRS website at *www.irs.gov*. Do not file it with the IRS or attach it to Form 990-EZ.

Line 43—Section 4947(a)(1) Nonexempt Charitable Trusts

Section 4947(a)(1) nonexempt charitable trusts that file Form 990-EZ instead of Form 1041 and have no taxable income under Subtitle A may use Form 990-EZ to meet its Section 6012 filing requirement by checking the box on line 43. Also, enter on line 43 the total of exempt-interest dividends received from a mutual fund or other regulated investment company as well as tax-exempt interest received directly.

Privacy Act and Paperwork Reduction Act Notice. We ask for the information on this form to carry out the Internal Revenue laws of the United States. You are required to give us the information. We need it to ensure that you are complying with these laws. Section 6109 requires return preparers to provide their identifying numbers on the return.

The organization is not required to provide the information requested on a form that is subject to the Paperwork Reduction Act unless the form displays a valid OMB control number. Books or records relating to a form or its instructions must be retained as long as their contents may become material in the administration of any Internal Revenue law. The rules governing the confidentiality of the Form 990, and Form 990-EZ, are covered in Code section 6104.

The time needed to complete and file this form and related schedules will vary depending on individual circumstances. The estimated average times are:

Form	Recordkeeping	Learning about the law or the form	Preparing the form	Copying, assembling, and sending the form to the IRS
990	112 hr., 52 min.	16 hr., 4 min.	22 hr., 20 min.	1 hr., 4 min.
990-EZ	29 hr., 10 min.	11 hr., 33 min.	14 hr., 24 min.	32 min.
Schedule A (Form 990 or 990-EZ)	75 hr., 19 min.	11 hr., 37 min.	13 hr., 21 min.	-0-
Schedule B (Form 990, 990-EZ, or 990-PF)	4 hr., 46 min.	1 hr., 23 min.	1 hr., 31 min.	-0-

We welcome comments on forms. If you have comments concerning the accuracy of these time estimates or suggestions for making these forms simpler, we would be happy to hear from you. You can write to the Internal Revenue Service, Tax Products Coordinating Committee, SE:W:CAR:MP:T:T:SP, 1111 Constitution Ave. NW, IR-6526, Washington, DC 20224.

Do not send the form to this address. Instead, see *When, Where, and How To File* in *General Instruction H.*

Index

Frequently Asked Questions Regarding the Annual Form Filing Requirements for Section 527 Organizations

QUESTIONS ABOUT FORM 1120-POL

1. What is Form 1120-POL?
Form 1120-POL is the annual income tax return for political organizations.

2. Who has to file Form 1120-POL?
A political organization with taxable income after taking the $100 specific deduction for the taxable year must file Form 1120-POL.

3. When is Form 1120-POL due?
Form 1120-POL is due on the fifteenth day of the third month following the end of the political organization's taxable year. For organizations on a calendar year, Form 1120-POL is due on March 15 of the following year.

4. May a political organization request an extension of time for filing Form 1120-POL?
Yes, the organization may request an automatic six-month extension by filing Form 7004, Application for Automatic Extension of Time to File Corporate Income Tax Return, by the due date for Form 1120-POL.

5. Does a political organization report the contributions it receives on Form 1120-POL?
A tax-exempt political organization does not report its contributions or any other exempt function income on Form 1120-POL. Only taxable income (generally the investment income of the political organization) is reported on the Form 1120-POL (see Question 7 for what nonexempt political organizations report on Form 1120-POL).

6. May a political organization deduct the salaries, rents, and other expenses it incurs for its political campaign activity on Form 1120-POL?
No, the political organization may deduct only those expenses that are directly related to earning taxable income. For example, the organization may not deduct the salary ofits campaign director. However, if the political organization hires a broker to manage its stock portfolio, it can deduct that expense from the taxable dividend and capital gain income derived.

7. What does a political organization that is not exempt because it did not file Form 8871 report on Form 1120-POL?

In addition to reporting its investment income as discussed in Question 5, the political organization reports its exempt function income (contributions, etc.) as other income (line 7 on the 2005 form). It may deduct the expenses directly related to earning that income (such as fundraising expenses), but may not deduct its political campaign expenses.

8. What if the political organization fails to file Form 1120-POL?

A political organization that fails to file in a timely manner a required Form 1120-POL must pay an additional amount equal to 5 percent of the tax due for each month (or partial month) the return is late, up to a maximum of 25 percent of the tax due, unless the organization shows that the failure was due to reasonable cause.

9. What if a political organization fails to pay the tax shown on Form 1120-POL?

A political organization that fails to pay in a timely manner the tax shown or required to be shown on Form 1120-POL must pay an additional amount equal to 0.5 percent of the unpaid tax for each month (or partial month) the tax is not paid, up to a maximum of 25 percent of the unpaid tax, unless the organization shows that the failure was due to reasonable cause.

10. Are Forms 1120-POL filed by political organizations publicly available?

No, Forms 1120-POL filed by political organizations are not required to be made available for public inspection by either the IRS or the organization.

QUESTIONS ABOUT FORMS 990 AND 990-EZ

1. What is Form 990?

Form 990, Return of Organization Exempt from Income Tax, is the annual information return for tax-exempt organizations, including political organizations.

2. What is Form 990-EZ?

Form 990-EZ is the short form of the annual information return for exempt organizations, including political organizations. A political organization required to file Form 990 that has received less than $100,000 in total gross receipts and has total assets of less than $250,000 at the end of the year may file Form 990-EZ instead of the Form 990.

3. Who has to file Form 990?

Tax-exempt political organizations whose annual gross receipts are $25,000 or more must file Form 990, unless excepted. Any organization excepted from the requirements to file a Form 8871, and any political organization that is a caucus or association or a state or local official are excepted from the Form 990 filing requirement. Qualified state or local political organizations are required to file Form 990 only if they have annual gross receipts of $100,000 or more.

4. Does a tax-exempt political organization whose annual gross receipts are normally $25,000 or more have to file a Form 990 for any year in which its annual gross receipts are less than $25,000?

No. Unlike other exempt organizations, a tax-exempt political organization does not use the three-year averaging test to determine whether it meets the $25,000 threshold.

However, it may wish to file a Form 990 with box K checked, because the *~ions*
wise correspond with the organization regarding the filing of Form 990. If tu. *~*
tion does file the Form 990 with box K checked, it will not automatically receive
990 package in subsequent years. Note that the $25,000 filing threshold is increase
$100,000 for qualified state or local political organizations.

5. When is Form 990 due?

Form 990 is due on the fifteenth day of the fifth month following the end of the political
organization's taxable year. For organizations on a calendar year, the Form 990 is due
on May 15 of the following year.

6. May a political organization request an extension of the due date for filing Form 990?

Yes, the organization may request an automatic three-month extension, without showing
cause, by filing Form 8868, Application for Extension of Time to File an Exempt Organization Return, by the due date for Form 990. A second three-month extension, with
cause, may also be requested using Form 8868.

7. How does a political organization report its income in Part I of Form 990?

That an item of income is treated as a contribution for purposes of election law reporting does not necessarily mean it is reported as a contribution on Form 990. Instead, the
political organization must determine the various types of income it has, and report each
type on the appropriate line in Part I of Form 990. For example, membership dues and
assessments are reported on line 3 of the 2007 return, whereas political fundraising or
entertainment event income is generally be reported as special event income on line 9 of
the return. Unlike Form 1120-POL, all income of the political organization is reported
on the Form 990—including contributions (line 1), taxable income such as interest (line
4 of the 2007 form), and dividends (line 5).

8. Does a political organization need to identify contributions as direct public support, indirect public support, and government grants (see lines 1a through 1c of the 2005 return)?

No, a political organization may report all of its contributions on the total line (1e of the
2007 Form 990) without breaking out direct, indirect, and government support. It does
need to identify contributions as cash or noncash.

9. Does a political organization report as a contribution in Part I of Form 990 the value of the use of materials, equipment, or facilities provided by a connected organization that is not required to be reported as a contribution under federal election law?

No. However, the political organization may—but is not required to—disclose the value
of those contributions in Part VI (line 82 of the 2007 form).

10. How does a political organization report a loan?

A political organization reports a loan with repayment obligations in Part IV of Form 990 as
an account payable (line 60 on the 2007 form) or as a loan from an officer, etc. (line 63).

11. How does a political organization report its expenses in Part II of Form 990?

A political organization reports all its expenses—including its political campaign
expenses—in Part II, Column A of Form 990. It does not need to allocate these expenses

...een program services, management and general, and fundraising costs by completing columns B, C, or D.

12. How does a political organization that makes contributions to candidates or other political organizations report them in Part II of Form 990?

Contributions to candidates or other political organizations are reported as grants (line 22b of the 2007 form).

13. Does a political organization need to report joint costs in Part II of Form 990?

No, a political organization does not need to report joint costs in Part II of Form 990 because it is not required to allocate expenses between program services, management and general, and fundraising costs.

14. How should a political organization describe its exempt purpose in Part III of Form 990?

The exempt purpose of a political organization is to engage in political campaign activity. An organization may want to be more specific in describing its purpose. For example, a candidate committee may describe its purpose as "To elect X to Congress" while an environmental PAC may describe its purpose as "To elect candidates who support environmental issues."

15. How would a political organization describe its program service accomplishments in Part III of Form 990?

Part III of Form 990 provides an opportunity for a political organization to describe its activities and how they further its exempt purpose. In some cases, this will be fairly straightforward. For example, a candidate committee's program service accomplishment would be conducting the campaign to elect X to Congress. In other cases, particularly for those organizations that engage in indirect as well as direct political campaign activities, a political organization may use this section to describe how various activities are intended to influence elections.

16. What does a political organization report in Part IV of Form 990?

Part IV of Form 990 is the basic balance sheet of the political organization at the beginning and the end of the year. The political organization reports its cash (lines 45 and 46 on the 2007 form) and other assets, any liabilities—such as loans—and its retained earnings (line 72).

17. What does a political organization report in Part V of Form 990?

Internal Revenue Code section 527 does not require political organizations to be organized with boards of directors, officers, and trustees, but if the political organization is organized in this way, it must provide the names, addresses, title, average hours worked, and compensation of those officers, directors, and trustees, as well as its key employees.

18. Does a political organization have to report the compensation of one of its officers, directors, trustees, or key employees that is paid by a related organization?

If the total compensation paid to the officer, director, trustee, or key employee by the political organization and all related organizations is more than $100,000, and more than $10,000 of that was paid by the related organization, then the political organization must disclose the compensation paid by the related organization in Part V, Form 990.

19. What is a related organization for purposes of reporting compensation paid by related organizations in Part V of Form 990?

A related organization is any organization that meets one of the following tests:

- Fifty percent or more of the political organization's officers, directors, trustees, or key employees are also officers, directors, trustees, or key employees of the other organization.
- The political organization appoints 50 percent or more of the other organization's officers, directors, trustees, or key employees.
- Fifty percent or more of the political organization's officers, directors, trustees, or key employees are appointed by the other organization.

20. Does a political organization have to answer all of the questions in Part VI of Form 990?

No, the political organization does not have to answer any of the questions that are specifically designated for other types of exempt organizations (for example, section 501(c)(3) organizations).

21. Does a political organization need to complete Parts VII and VIII of Form 990?

No, because the political organization is subject to tax under Internal Revenue Code section 527 rather than under the unrelated business income tax provisions of sections 511 to 514.

22. What does a political organization report in Part IX of Form 990?

If the political organization owned 50 percent or more of any taxable subsidiary or disregarded entity—such as a partnership or limited liability company, it must report the name, address, employer identification number, activities, and income and assets of the entity, along with the percentage the political organization owns of the entity.

23. Does a political organization complete Part X of Form 990?

No, a political organization does not complete Part X of Form 990 because this part is for charitable organizations that engaged in activities involving personal benefit contracts.

24. Does a political organization need to complete Schedule A of Form 990?

No.

25. Does a political organization complete Schedule B of Form 990?

Yes, if the political organization received contributions from any one person aggregating $5,000 or more for the year.

26. If a political organization that files Form 8872 chooses not to disclose a contributor on that form, is it required to disclose the contributor on Schedule B of Form 990?

A political organization that files Form 8872 is not required to disclose on Schedule B of Form 990 the name and address of any contributor that it did not disclose on Form 8872.

It must disclose the amount of the contribution and that it paid the amount specified under section 527(j)(1) for that contribution.

27. What if the political organization fails to file Form 990?

A political organization that fails to file a required Form 990 or fails to include required information on those returns is subject to a penalty of $20 per day for every day such failure continues. The maximum penalty imposed regarding any one return is the lesser of $10,000 or 5 percent of the gross receipts of the organization for the year. In the case of an organization having gross receipts exceeding $1,000,000 for any year, the penalty is increased to $100 per day with a maximum penalty of $50,000.

28. Are Forms 990 filed by tax-exempt political organizations publicly available?

Yes, Forms 990 filed for taxable years beginning after June 30, 2000, including contributor information reported on Schedule B, will be made available for public inspection by the IRS. In addition, each political organization must make a copy of these returns, including contributor information reported on Schedule B, available for public inspection during regular business hours at its principal office (and any regional or district offices having at least three paid employees) in the same manner as Internal Revenue Code section 501(c) organizations provide copies of their annual returns.

29. What if the tax-exempt political organization does not make its Forms 990 publicly available?

A penalty of $20 per day may be imposed on any person with a duty to comply with the public inspection requirements for each day a failure to comply continues. The maximum penalty that may be incurred for any failure to disclose any one return is $10,000.

Revenue Ruling 2004-6
Section 527—Political Organizations

Part I

Section 527.—Political Organizations

26 CFR 1.527-2: Definitions.

(Also § 501.)

Rev. Rul. 2004-6

Organizations that are exempt from federal income tax under § 501(a) as organizations described in § 501(c)(4), § 501(c)(5), or § 501(c)(6) may, consistent with their exempt purpose, publicly advocate positions on public policy issues. This advocacy may include lobbying for legislation consistent with these positions. Because public policy advocacy may involve discussion of the positions of public officials who are also candidates for public office, a public policy advocacy communication may constitute an exempt function within the meaning of § 527(e)(2). If so, the organization would be subject to tax under § 527(f).

ISSUE

In each of the six situations described below, has the organization exempt from federal income tax under § 501(a) as an organization described in § 501(c)(4), § 501(c)(5), or § 501(c)(6) that engages in public policy advocacy expended funds for an exempt function as described in § 527(e)(2)?

LAW

Section 501(c)(4) provides exemption from taxation for civic leagues or organizations not organized for profit, but operated exclusively for the promotion of social welfare.

Section 1.501(c)(4)-1 of the Income Tax Regulations states an organization is operated exclusively for the promotion of social welfare if it is primarily engaged in promoting in some way the common good and general welfare of the people of the community.

Section 501(c)(5) provides exemption from taxation for labor, agricultural, or horticultural organizations.

Section 1.501(c)(5)-1 requires that labor, agricultural, or horticultural organizations have as their objects the betterment of the conditions of those engaged in such pursuits, the improvement of the grade of their products, and the development of a higher degree of efficiency in their respective occupations.

Section 501(c)(6) provides exemption from taxation for business leagues, not organized for profit and no part of the net earnings of which inures to the benefit of any private shareholder or individual.

Section 1.501(c)(6)-1 provides that a business league is an association of persons having some common business interest, the purpose of which is to promote such common interest and not to engage in a regular business of a kind ordinarily carried on for profit. A business league's activities should be directed to the improvement of business conditions of one or more lines of business as distinguished from the performance of particular services for individual persons.

Section 527 generally provides that political organizations that collect and expend monies for exempt function purposes as described in § 527(e)(2) are exempt from Federal income tax except on their investment income.

Section 527(e)(1) defines a political organization as a party, committee, association, fund or other organization (whether or not incorporated), organized and operated primarily for the purpose of accepting contributions or making expenditures, or both, for an exempt function.

Section 527(e)(2) provides that the term "exempt function" for purposes of § 527 means the function of influencing or attempting to influence the selection, nomination, election, or appointment of any individual to any Federal, State, or local public office or office in a political organization, or the election of Presidential or Vice-Presidential electors, whether or not such individual or electors are selected, nominated, elected, or appointed. By its terms, § 527(e)(2) includes all attempts to influence the selection, nomination, election, or appointment of the described officials.

Section 527(f)(1) provides that an organization described in § 501(c) and exempt from tax under § 501(a) is subject to tax on any amount expended for an exempt function described in § 527(e)(2) at the highest tax rate specified in § 11(b). The tax is imposed on the lesser of the net investment income of the organization for the taxable year or the amount expended on an exempt function during the taxable year. A § 501(c) organization is taxed under § 527(f)(1) only if the expenditure is from its general treasury rather than from a separate segregated fund described in § 527(f)(3).

Section 527(f)(3) provides that if an organization described in § 501(c) and exempt from tax under § 501(a) sets up a separate segregated fund (which segregates monies for § 527(e)(2) exempt function purposes) that fund will be treated as a separate political organization described in § 527 and, therefore, be subject to tax as a political organization under § 527.

Section 527(i) provides that, in order to be tax-exempt, a political organization is required to give notice that it is a political organization described in § 527, unless excepted. An organization described in § 501(c) that does not set up a separate segregated fund, but makes exempt function expenditures subject to tax under § 527(f) is not subject to this requirement. § 527(i)(5)(A).

Section 527(j) provides that, unless excepted, a tax-exempt political organization that has given notice under § 527(i) and does not timely make periodic reports of contributions and expenditures, or that fails to include the information required, must pay an amount calculated by multiplying the amount of contributions and expenditures that are not disclosed by the highest corporate tax rate. An organization described in § 501(c) that does not set up a separate segregated fund, but makes exempt function expenditures subject to tax under § 527(f), is not subject to the reporting requirements under § 527(j)..

Section 1.527-2(c)(1) provides that the term "exempt function" includes all activities that are directly related to and support the process of influencing or attempting to influence the selection, nomination, election, or appointment of any individual to public office or office in a political organization. Whether an expenditure is for an exempt function depends on all the facts and circumstances.

Section 1.527-6(f) provides that an organization described in § 501(c) that is exempt under § 501(a) may, if it is consistent with its exempt status, establish and maintain a separate segregated fund to receive contributions and make expenditures in a political campaign.

Rev. Rul. 2003-49, 2003-20 I.R.B. (May 19, 2003), discusses the reporting and disclosure requirements for political organizations in question and answer format. In Q&A-6, the ruling holds that while a § 501(c) organization that makes an expenditure for an exempt function under § 527(e)(2) is not required to file the notice required under § 527(i), if the § 501(c) organization establishes a separate segregated fund under § 527(f)(3), that fund is required to file the notice in order to be tax-exempt unless it meets one of the other exceptions to filing.

Certain broadcast, cable, or satellite communications that meet the definition of "electioneering communications" are regulated by the Bipartisan Campaign Reform Act of 2002 (BCRA), 116 Stat. 81. An exempt organization that violates the regulatory requirements of BCRA may well jeopardize its exemption or be subject to other tax consequences.

ANALYSIS OF FACTUAL SITUATIONS

An organization exempt from federal income tax under § 501(a) as an organization described in § 501(c) that, consistent with its tax-exempt status, wishes to engage in an exempt function within the meaning of § 527(e)(2) may do so with its own funds or by setting up a separate segregated fund under § 527(f)(3). If the organization chooses to establish a separate segregated fund, that fund, unless excepted, must give notice under § 527(i) in order to be tax-exempt. A separate segregated fund that has given notice under § 527(i) is then subject to the reporting requirements under § 527(j). See Rev. Rul. 2003-49. If the organization chooses to use its own funds, the organization is not subject to the notice requirements under § 527(i) and the reporting requirements under § 527(j), but is subject to tax under § 527(f)(1) on the lesser of its investment income or the amount of the exempt function expenditure.

All the facts and circumstances must be considered to determine whether an expenditure for an advocacy communication relating to a public policy issue is for an exempt function under § 527(e)(2). When an advocacy communication explicitly advocates the election or defeat of an individual to public office, the expenditure clearly is for an exempt function under § 527(e)(2). However, when an advocacy communication relating to a public policy issue does not explicitly advocate the election or defeat of a candidate, all the facts and circumstances need to be considered to determine whether the expenditure is for an exempt function under § 527(e)(2).

In facts and circumstances such as those described in the six situations, factors that tend to show that an advocacy communication on a public policy issue is for an exempt function under § 527(e)(2) include, but are not limited to, the following:

a) The communication identifies a candidate for public office;
b) The timing of the communication coincides with an electoral campaign;
c) The communication targets voters in a particular election;
d) The communication identifies that candidate's position on the public policy issue that is the subject of the communication;
e) The position of the candidate on the public policy issue has been raised as distinguishing the candidate from others in the campaign, either in the communication itself or in other public communications; and
f) The communication is not part of an ongoing series of substantially similar advocacy communications by the organization on the same issue.

In facts and circumstances such as those described in the six situations, factors that tend to show that an advocacy communication on a public policy issue is not for an exempt function under § 527(e)(2) include, but are not limited to, the following:

a) The absence of any one or more of the factors listed in a) through f) above;
b) The communication identifies specific legislation, or a specific event outside the control of the organization, that the organization hopes to influence;
c) The timing of the communication coincides with a specific event outside the control of the organization that the organization hopes to influence, such as a legislative vote or other major legislative action (for example, a hearing before a legislative committee on the issue that is the subject of the communication);
d) The communication identifies the candidate solely as a government official who is in a position to act on the public policy issue in connection with the specific event (such as a legislator who is eligible to vote on the legislation); and
e) The communication identifies the candidate solely in the list of key or principal sponsors of the legislation that is the subject of the communication.

In all of the situations, the advocacy communication identifies a candidate in an election, appears shortly before that election, and targets the voters in that election. Even though these factors are present, the remaining facts and circumstances must be analyzed in each situation to determine whether the advocacy communication is for an exempt function under § 527(e)(2).

Each of the situations assumes that:

1. All payments for the described activity are from the general treasury of the organization rather than from a separate segregated fund under § 527(f)(3);
2. The organization would continue to be exempt under § 501(a), even if the described activity is not a § 501(c) exempt activity, because the organization's primary activities are described in the appropriate subparagraph of § 501(c); and
3. All advocacy communications described also include a solicitation of contributions to the organization.

Situation 1. N, a labor organization recognized as tax exempt under § 501(c)(5), advocates for the betterment of conditions of law enforcement personnel. Senator A and Senator

B represent State U in the United States Senate. In year 200x, N prepares and finances full-page newspaper advertisements supporting increased spending on law enforcement, which would require a legislative appropriation. These advertisements are published in several large circulation newspapers in State U on a regular basis during year 200x. One of these full-page advertisements is published shortly before an election in which Senator A (but not Senator B) is a candidate for re-election. The advertisement published shortly before the election stresses the importance of increased federal funding of local law enforcement and refers to numerous statistics indicating the high crime rate in State U. The advertisement does not mention Senator A's or Senator B's position on law enforcement issues. The advertisement ends with the statement "Call or write Senator A and Senator B to ask them to support increased federal funding for local law enforcement." Law enforcement has not been raised as an issue distinguishing Senator A from any opponent. At the time this advertisement is published, no legislative vote or other major legislative activity is scheduled in the United States Senate on increased federal funding for local law enforcement.

Under the facts and circumstances in Situation 1, the advertisement is not for an exempt function under § 527(e)(2). Although N's advertisement identifies Senator A, appears shortly before an election in which Senator A is a candidate, and targets voters in that election, it is part of an ongoing series of substantially similar advocacy communications by N on the same issue during year 200x. The advertisement identifies both Senator A and Senator B, who is not a candidate for re-election, as the representatives who would vote on this issue. Furthermore, N's advertisement does not identify Senator A's position on the issue, and law enforcement has not been raised as an issue distinguishing Senator A from any opponent. Therefore, there is nothing to indicate that Senator A's candidacy should be supported or opposed based on this issue. Based on these facts and circumstances, the amount expended by N on the advertisement is not an exempt function expenditure under § 527(e)(2) and, therefore, is not subject to tax under § 527(f)(1).

Situation 2. O, a trade association recognized as tax exempt under § 501(c)(6), advocates for increased international trade. Senator C represents State V in the United States Senate. O prepares and finances a full-page newspaper advertisement that is published in several large circulation newspapers in State V shortly before an election in which Senator C is a candidate for nomination in a party primary. The advertisement states that increased international trade is important to a major industry in State V. The advertisement states that S. 24, a pending bill in the United States Senate, would provide manufacturing subsidies to certain industries to encourage export of their products. The advertisement also states that several manufacturers in State V would benefit from the subsidies, but Senator C has opposed similar measures supporting increased international trade in the past. The advertisement ends with the statement "Call or write Senator C to tell him to vote for S. 24." International trade concerns have not been raised as an issue distinguishing Senator C from any opponent. S. 24 is scheduled for a vote in the United States Senate before the election, soon after the date that the advertisement is published in the newspapers.

Under the facts and circumstances in Situation 2, the advertisement is not for an exempt function under § 527(e)(2). O's advertisement identifies Senator C, appears shortly before an election in which Senator C is a candidate, and targets voters in that election. Although international trade issues have not been raised as an issue distinguishing Senator C from any opponent, the advertisement identifies Senator C's position on the issue as contrary to O's position. However, the advertisement specifically identifies the legislation O is supporting and appears immediately before the United States Senate is scheduled to vote on that particular legislation. The candidate identified, Senator C, is a government official who is in a position to take action on the public policy issue in connection with the specific event. Based on these facts and circumstances, the amount expended by O on the advertisement is not an exempt function expenditure under § 527(e)(2) and, therefore, is not subject to tax under § 527(f)(1).

Situation 3. P, an entity recognized as tax exempt under § 501(c)(4), advocates for better health care. Senator D represents State W in the United States Senate. P prepares and finances a full-page newspaper advertisement that is published repeatedly in several large circulation newspapers in State W beginning shortly before an election in which Senator D is a candidate for re-election. The advertisement is not part of an ongoing series of substantially similar advocacy communications by P on the same issue. The advertisement states that a public hospital is needed in a major city in State W but that the public hospital cannot be built without federal assistance. The advertisement further states that Senator D has voted in the past year for two bills that would have provided the federal funding necessary for the hospital. The advertisement then ends with the statement "Let Senator D know you agree about the need for federal funding for hospitals." Federal funding for hospitals has not been raised as an issue distinguishing Senator D from any opponent. At the time the advertisement is published, a bill providing federal funding for hospitals has been introduced in the United States Senate, but no legislative vote or other major legislative activity on that bill is scheduled in the Senate.

Under the facts and circumstances in Situation 3, the advertisement is for an exempt function under § 527(e)(2). P's advertisement identifies Senator D, appears shortly before an election in which Senator D is a candidate, and targets voters in that election. Although federal funding of hospitals has not been raised as an issue distinguishing Senator D from any opponent, the advertisement identifies Senator D's position on the hospital funding issue as agreeing with P's position, and is not part of an ongoing series of substantially similar advocacy communications by P on the same issue. Moreover, the advertisement does not identify any specific legislation and is not timed to coincide with a legislative vote or other major legislative action on the hospital funding issue. Based on these facts and circumstances, the amount expended by P on the advertisement is an exempt function expenditure under § 527(e)(2) and, therefore, is subject to tax under § 527(f)(1).

Situation 4. R, an entity recognized as tax exempt under § 501(c)(4), advocates for improved public education. Governor E is the governor of State X. R prepares and finances a radio advertisement urging an increase in state funding for public education in State X, which requires a legislative appropriation. The radio advertisement is first broadcast on several radio stations in State X beginning shortly before an election in which Governor E is a candidate for re-election. The advertisement is not part of an ongoing series of substantially similar advocacy communications by R on the same issue. The advertisement cites numerous statistics indicating that public education in State X is under-funded. While the advertisement does not say anything about Governor E's position on funding for public education, it ends with "Tell Governor E what you think about our underfunded schools." In public appearances and campaign literature, Governor E's opponent has made funding of public education an issue in the campaign by focusing on Governor E's veto of an income tax increase the previous year to increase funding of public education. At the time the advertisement is broadcast, no legislative vote or other major legislative activity is scheduled in the State X legislature on state funding of public education.

Under the facts and circumstances in Situation 4, the advertisement is for an exempt function under § 527(e)(2). R's advertisement identifies Governor E, appears shortly before an election in which Governor E is a candidate, and targets voters in that election. Although the advertisement does not explicitly identify Governor E's position on the funding of public schools issue, that issue has been raised as an issue in the campaign by Governor E's opponent. The advertisement does not identify any specific legislation, is not part of an ongoing series of substantially similar advocacy communications by R on the same issue, and is not timed to coincide with a legislative vote or other major legislative action on that issue. Based on these facts and circumstances, the amount expended by R on the advertisement is an exempt function expenditure under § 527(e)(2) and, therefore, is subject to tax under § 527(f)(1).

Situation 5. S, an entity recognized as tax exempt under § 501(c)(4), advocates to abolish the death penalty in State Y. Governor F is the governor of State Y. S regularly prepares and finances television advertisements opposing the death penalty. These advertisements appear on several television stations in State Y shortly before each scheduled execution in State Y. One such advertisement opposing the death penalty appears on State Y television stations shortly before the scheduled execution of G and shortly before an election in which Governor F is a candidate for re-election. The advertisement broadcast shortly before the election provides statistics regarding developed countries that have abolished the death penalty and refers to studies indicating inequities related to the types of persons executed in the United States. Like the advertisements appearing shortly before other scheduled executions in State Y, the advertisement notes that Governor F has supported the death penalty in the past and ends with the statement "Call or write Governor F to demand that he stop the upcoming execution of G."

Under the facts and circumstances in Situation 5, the advertisement is not for an exempt function under § 527(e)(2). S's advertisement identifies Governor F, appears shortly before an election in which Governor F is a candidate, targets voters in that election, and identifies Governor F's position as contrary to S's position. However, the advertisement is part of an ongoing series of substantially similar advocacy communications by S on the same issue and the advertisement identifies an event outside the control of the organization (the scheduled execution) that the organization hopes to influence. Further, the timing of the advertisement coincides with this specific event that the organization hopes to influence. The candidate identified is a government official who is in a position to take action on the public policy issue in connection with the specific event. Based on these facts and circumstances, the amount expended by S on the advertisements is not an exempt function expenditure under § 527(e)(2) and, therefore, is not subject to tax under § 527(f)(1).

Situation 6. T, an entity recognized as tax exempt under § 501(c)(4), advocates to abolish the death penalty in State Z. Governor H is the governor of State Z. Beginning shortly before an election in which Governor H is a candidate for re-election, T prepares and finances a television advertisement broadcast on several television stations in State Z. The advertisement is not part of an ongoing series of substantially similar advocacy communications by T on the same issue. The advertisement provides statistics regarding developed countries that have abolished the death penalty, and refers to studies indicating inequities related to the types of persons executed in the United States. The advertisement calls for the abolishment of the death penalty. The advertisement notes that Governor H has supported the death penalty in the past. The advertisement identifies several individuals previously executed in State Z, stating that Governor H could have saved their lives by stopping their executions. No executions are scheduled in State Z in the near future. The advertisement concludes with the statement "Call or write Governor H to demand a moratorium on the death penalty in State Z."

Under the facts and circumstances in Situation 6, the advertisement is for an exempt function under § 527(e)(2). T's advertisement identifies Governor H, appears shortly before an election in which Governor H is a candidate, targets the voters in that election, and identifies Governor H's position as contrary to T's position. The advertisement is not part of an ongoing series of substantially similar advocacy communications by T on the same issue. In addition, the advertisement does not identify and is not timed to coincide with a specific event outside the control of the organization that it hopes to influence. Based on these facts and circumstances, the amount expended by T on the advertisement is an exempt function expenditure under § 527(e)(2) and, therefore, is subject to tax under § 527(f)(1).

HOLDINGS

In Situations 1, 2, and 5, the amounts expended by N, O, and S are not exempt function expenditures under § 527(e)(2) and, therefore, are not subject to tax under § 527(f)(1). In Situations 3, 4, and 6, the amounts expended by P, R and T are exempt function expenditures under § 527(e)(2) and, therefore, are subject to tax under § 527(f)(1).

DRAFTING INFORMATION

The principal author of this revenue ruling is Judith E. Kindell of Exempt Organizations, Tax Exempt and Government Entities Division. For further information regarding this revenue ruling contact Judith E. Kindell on (202) 283-8964 (not a toll-free call).

Appendix I

FEC Notices and Guidance Regarding PAC Administration

16695

Rules and Regulations

Federal Register

Vol. 72, No. 65

Thursday, April 5, 2007

This section of the FEDERAL REGISTER contains regulatory documents having general applicability and legal effect, most of which are keyed to and codified in the Code of Federal Regulations, which is published under 50 titles pursuant to 44 U.S.C. 1510.

The Code of Federal Regulations is sold by the Superintendent of Documents. Prices of new books are listed in the first FEDERAL REGISTER issue of each week.

FEDERAL ELECTION COMMISSION

11 CFR Part 104

[NOTICE 2007–9]

Statement of Policy; Safe Harbor for Misreporting Due to Embezzlement

AGENCY: Federal Election Commission.

ACTION: Statement of policy.

SUMMARY: The Commission is issuing a Statement of Policy to announce that it is creating a safe harbor for the benefit of political committees that have certain internal controls in place to prevent misappropriations and associated misreporting. Specifically, the Commission does not intend to seek civil penalties against a political committee for filing incorrect reports due to the misappropriation of committee funds if the committee has the specified safeguards in place.

EFFECTIVE DATE: April 5, 2007.

FOR FURTHER INFORMATION CONTACT: Mr. Joseph Stoltz, Assistant Staff Director, Audit Division, 999 E Street, NW., Washington, DC 20463, (202) 694–1200.

SUPPLEMENTARY INFORMATION: The Commission has encountered a dramatic increase in the number of cases where political committee staff misappropriates committee funds. Misappropriations are often accompanied by the filing of inaccurate disclosure reports with the FEC, leaving committees vulnerable to a FEC enforcement action and potential liability for those reporting errors. In response to the rise in this activity, the Commission has concluded that the following internal controls are minimal safeguards a committee should implement to prevent misappropriations and associated misreporting.

This policy does not impose new legal requirements on political committees; rather it creates a safe harbor. If the following internal controls are in place

at the time of a misappropriation, and the post-discovery steps described below are followed by the committee, the FEC will not seek a monetary penalty on the political committee for filing incorrect reports due to the misappropriation of committee funds.[1] The Commission will also consider the presence of some, but not all, of these practices, or of comparable safeguards, as a mitigating factor in considering any monetary liability resulting from a misappropriation.[2]

A. Internal Controls

☐ All bank accounts are opened in the name of the committee, never an individual, using the committee's Employer Identification Number, not an individual's Social Security Number.

☐ Bank statements are reviewed for unauthorized transactions and reconciled to the accounting records each month. Further, bank records are reconciled to disclosure reports prior to filing. The reconciliations are done by someone other than a check signer or an individual responsible for handling the committee's accounting.

☐ Checks in excess of $1000 are authorized in writing and/or signed by two individuals. Further, all wire transfers are authorized in writing by two individuals. The individuals who may authorize disbursements or sign checks should be identified in writing in the committee's internal policies.

☐ An individual who does not handle the committee's accounting or have banking authority receives incoming checks and monitors all other incoming receipts. This individual makes a list of all committee receipts and places a restrictive endorsement, such as: For Deposit Only to the Account of the Payee" on all checks.

☐ If the committee has a petty cash fund, an imprest system[3] is used,

---

[1] The internal controls set forth here represent the minimum efforts a committee must take to qualify for this safe harbor. The FEC provides additional guidance on internal controls best practices at http://www.fec.gov/law/policy.shtml#guidance.

[2] This policy does not absolve or mitigate FEC liability for individuals responsible or complicit in the misappropriations.

[3] An imprest fund is one in which the sum of the disbursements recorded in the petty cash log since

and the value of the petty cash fund should be no more than $500.

B. Post-Discovery of Misappropriation Activity

As soon as a misappropriation is discovered, the political committee:

☐ Notifies relevant law enforcement of the misappropriation.

☐ Notifies the FEC of the misappropriation.

☐ Voluntarily files amended reports to correct any reporting errors due to the misappropriation, as required by the FEC.

This notice represents a general statement of policy announcing the general course of action that the Commission intends to follow. This policy statement does not constitute an agency regulation requiring notice of proposed rulemaking, opportunities for public participation, prior publication, and delay in effective date under 5 U.S.C. 553 of the Administrative Procedures Act ("APA"). As such, it does not bind the Commission or any member of the general public. The provisions of the Regulatory Flexibility Act, 5 U.S.C. 605(b), which apply when notice and comment are required by the APA or another statute, are not applicable.

Dated: March 22, 2007.

Robert D. Lenhard,

Chairman, Federal Election Commission.

[FR Doc. E7–6299 Filed 4–4–07; 8:45 am]

BILLING CODE 6715–01–P

FEDERAL ELECTION COMMISSION

11 CFR Part 111

[Notice 2007–8]

Policy Regarding Self-Reporting of Campaign Finance Violations (Sua Sponte Submissions)

AGENCY: Federal Election Commission.

ACTION: Statement of Policy.

SUMMARY: In order to encourage the self-reporting of violations about which the Commission would not otherwise have learned, the Commission will generally

the last replenishment and the remaining cash always equals the stated amount of the fund. When the fund is replenished the amount of the replenishment equals the amounts recorded since the prior replenishment and should bring the cash balance back to the stated amount. Only one person should be in charge of the fund.

31438 Federal Register / Vol. 72, No. 109 / Thursday, June 7, 2007 / Rules and Regulations

Title—7 Agriculture

PART 24—[Removed and reserved]

■ 1. Remove and reserve part 24, consisting of §§ 24.1 through 24.21.

PART 400—GENERAL ADMINISTRATIVE REGULATIONS

■ 2. Revise the authority citation for part 400 to read as follows:

Authority: 40 U.S.C. 121, 41 U.S.C. 421.

■ 3. Amend § 400.169 by revising the last sentence of paragraph (c) and paragraph (d) to read as follows:

§ 400.169   Disputes.

*   *   *   *   *

(c) * * * Such determinations will not be appealable to the Civilian Board of Contract Appeals.

(d) Appealable final administrative determinations of the Corporation under paragraph (a) or (b) of this section may be appealed to the Civilian Board of Contract Appeals in accordance with 48 CFR part 6102.

Title 36—Parks, Forests, and Public Property

PART 223—SALE AND DISPOSAL OF NATIONAL FOREST SYSTEM TIMBER

■ 4. The authority citation for part 223 continues to read as follows:

Authority: 90 Stat. 2958, 16 U.S.C. 472a; 98 Stat. 2213, 16 U.S.C. 618, 104 Stat. 714–726, 16 U.S.C. 620–620j; unless otherwise noted.

■ 5. Amend § 223.138 by removing paragraph (b)(8) and revising paragraphs (b)(7)(i)(C) and (D) and by removing paragraph (b)(7)(i)(E) to read as follows:

§ 223.138   Procedures for Debarment.

*   *   *   *   *

(b) * * *

(7) * * *

(i) * * *

(C) State the period of debarment, including effective dates (see § 223.139); and

(D) Specify any limitations on the terms of the debarment.

*   *   *   *   *

Title 48—Federal Acquisition Regulations System, chapter 4, Department of Agriculture.

PART 409—CONTRACTOR QUALIFICATIONS

■ 6. Revise the authority citation for part 409 to read as follows:

Authority: 40 U.S.C. 121, 41 U.S.C. 421.

■ 7. Remove § 409.470.

PART 432—CONTRACT FINANCING

■ 8. Revise the authority citation for part 432 to read as follows:

Authority: 40 U.S.C. 121, 41 U.S.C. 421.

■ 9. Revise § 432.616 to read as follows:

§ 432.616   Compromise Actions.

Compromise of a debt within the proceedings under appeal to the Civilian Board of Contract Appeals is the responsibility of the contracting officer.

PART 433—PROTESTS, DISPUTES AND APPEALS

■ 10. Revise the authority citation for part 433 to read as follows:

Authority: 40 U.S.C. 121, 41 U.S.C. 421.

■ 11. Revise § 433.203–70 to read as follows:

§ 433.203–70   Civilian Board of Contract Appeals.

The organization, jurisdiction, and functions of the Civilian Board of Contract Appeals, together with its Rules of Procedure, are set out in 48 CFR part 6101.

Done in Washington, DC, this 25th day of May 2007.

Mike Johanns,

Secretary of Agriculture.

[FR Doc. 07–2702 Filed 6–6–07; 8:45 am]

BILLING CODE 3410–01–M

FEDERAL ELECTION COMMISSION

11 CFR Part 104

[Notice 2007–13]

Statement of Policy Regarding Treasurers' Best Efforts To Obtain, Maintain, and Submit Information as Required by the Federal Election Campaign Act

AGENCY: Federal Election Commission.

ACTION: Statement of Policy.

SUMMARY: The Federal Election Commission (the "Commission") is issuing a Policy Statement to clarify its enforcement policy with respect to the circumstances under which it intends to consider a political committee and its treasurer to be in compliance with the recordkeeping and reporting requirements of the Federal Election Campaign Act, as amended ("FECA"). Section 432(i) of FECA provides that when the treasurer of a political committee demonstrates that best efforts were used to obtain, maintain, and submit the information required by

FECA, any report or records of such committee shall be considered in compliance with FECA or the statutes governing the public financing of Presidential candidates. In the past, the Commission has interpreted this section to apply only to a treasurer's efforts to obtain required information from contributors to a political committee, and not to maintaining information or to submitting reports. However, the district court in *Lovely* v. *FEC*, 307 F. Supp. 2d 294 (D. Mass. 2004), held that the Commission should consider whether a treasurer used best efforts under FECA with regard to efforts made to submit a report in a timely manner. This Policy Statement makes clear that the Commission intends to apply FECA's best efforts provision to treasurers' and committees' efforts to obtain, maintain, and submit information and records to the Commission consistent with the holding of the Federal court in *Lovely*. Further information is provided in the supplementary information that follows.

DATES: *Effective Date:* June 7, 2007.

FOR FURTHER INFORMATION CONTACT: Mr. Ron B. Katwan, Assistant General Counsel, or Ms. Margaret G. Perl, Attorney, 999 E Street, NW., Washington, DC 20463, (202) 694–1650 or (800) 424–9530.

SUPPLEMENTARY INFORMATION:

I. Background

A. Statutory and Regulatory Provisions

FECA states the "best efforts defense" in 2 U.S.C. 432(i) as follows:

When the treasurer of a political committee shows that best efforts have been used to obtain, maintain, and submit the information required by this Act for the political committee, any report or any records of such committee shall be considered in compliance with this Act or chapter 95 or chapter 96 of title 26.

The Commission implemented this provision in 11 CFR 104.7(a) with regulatory language virtually identical to the statutory provision:

When the treasurer of a political committee shows that best efforts have been used to obtain, maintain and submit the information required by the Act for the political committee, any report of such committee shall be considered in compliance with the Act.

Paragraph (b) of 11 CFR 104.7 specifies the actions that treasurers of a political committee must take to demonstrate that they have exercised best efforts to obtain and report the "identification" of each person whose contribution(s) to the political committee and its affiliated political committees aggregate in excess of $200 in a calendar year (or in an election

Federal Register / Vol. 72, No. 109 / Thursday, June 7, 2007 / Rules and Regulations   **31439**

cycle in the case of an authorized committee).[1] "Identification" includes the person's full name, mailing address, occupation, and name of employer. *See* 11 CFR 100.12.

Both the language of FECA and the Commission's regulation at 11 CFR 104.7(a) apply the best efforts defense broadly to efforts by treasurers to "obtain, maintain and submit" the information required to be disclosed by FECA. In past enforcement actions, however, the Commission has interpreted this statutory and regulatory language to apply only to efforts to "obtain" contributor information.[2] This interpretation draws from an example contained in the provision's legislative history. *See* H.R. Rep. No. 96–422, at 14 (1979) ("One illustration of the application of this [best efforts] test is the current requirement for a committee to report the occupation and principal place of business of individual contributors who give in excess of $100").

B. The Lovely Decision

In *Lovely*, a political committee challenged an administrative fine the

---

[1] The U.S. Court of Appeals for the District of Columbia Circuit referred to 11 CFR 104.7(b) as a "Commission regulation interpreting what political committees must do under [FECA] to demonstrate that they have exercised their 'best efforts' to encourage donors to disclose certain personally identifying information." *Republican Nat'l Comm. v. FEC*, 76 F.3d 400, 403 (D.C. Cir. 1996).

[2] In 1980, the Commission explained that "[i]n determining whether or not a committee has exercised 'best efforts,' the Commission's primary focus will be on the system established by the committee for *obtaining* disclosure information." *Amendments to Federal Election Campaign Act of 1971; Regulations Transmitted to Congress*, 45 FR 15080, 15086 (Mar. 7, 1980) (emphasis added). In 1993, the Commission referred to "the requirement of [FECA] that treasurers of political committees exercise best efforts to obtain, maintain and report the complete identification of each contributor whose contributions aggregate more than $200 per calendar year." *Final Rule on Recordkeeping and Reporting by Political Committees: Best Efforts*, 58 FR 57725, 57725 (Oct. 27, 1993). And in 1997, the Commission stated that "[t]reasurers of political committees must be able to show they have exercised their best efforts to obtain, maintain and report [contributor identification information]." *Final Rule on Recordkeeping and Reporting by Political Committees: Best Efforts*, 62 FR 23335, 23335 (Apr. 30, 1997). In 2003, the Commission asserted in the *Lovely* litigation: "the Commission has long interpreted the best efforts provision as creating a limited safe harbor regarding committees' obligations to report substantive information that may be beyond their ability to obtain." FEC Supplemental Brief at 1, *Lovely* (Civil Action No. 02–12496–PBS). Furthermore, "when Congress originally enacted the 'best efforts' provision, it could not have been more clear that it was creating a limited defense regarding the inability to obtain specific information that was supposed to be disclosed, not the failure to file reports on time." *Id.* at 12–13. The *Lovely* court summarized the Commission's argument: "The FEC in its briefing claims that it limits the reach of the best efforts statute to best efforts to 'obtain' contributor information." *Lovely*, 307 F. Supp. 2d at 300.

Commission had assessed for failing to file timely a report. The committee argued that it had made best efforts to file the report and that this constituted a complete defense to the fine. The court concluded that the plain language of the Act requires the Commission to entertain a best efforts defense in the Administrative Fine Program ("AFP"), and that it was unclear from the record if the Commission had done so.

In so holding, the court drew on the legislative history of the best efforts provision, and specifically noted the 1979 amendments to FECA that made the best efforts defense "applicable to the entirety of FECA, rather than merely to one subsection." *Lovely*, 307 F. Supp. 2d at 299. The court quoted the provision's legislative history:

> The best efforts test is *specifically made applicable to recordkeeping and reporting requirements in both Title 2 and Title 26.* The test of whether a committee has complied with the statutory requirements is whether its treasurer has exercised his or her best efforts to obtain, maintain, and submit the information required by the Act. If the treasurer has exercised his or her best efforts, the committee is in compliance. Accordingly, *the application of the best efforts test is central to the enforcement of the recordkeeping and reporting provisions of the Act.* It is the opinion of the Committee that the Commission has not adequately incorporated the best efforts test into its administration procedures, such as the systematic review of reports.

Id. (emphasis added) (quoting H.R. Rep. No. 96–422, at 14 (1979), *reprinted in* 1979 U.S.C.C.A.N. 2860, 2873).

After remand of the *Lovely* case, the Commission acknowledged in its Statement of Reasons that "[t]he Court held that FECA's 'best efforts' provision . . . requires the Commission to consider whether a committee's treasurer exercised best efforts to submit timely disclosure reports." *Statement of Reasons in Administrative Fines Case #549* at 1 (Oct. 4, 2005), available at *http://www.fec.gov/law/ law_rulemakings.shtml* under the heading "Best Efforts in Administrative Fine Challenges." ("*Lovely Statement of Reasons*"). Upon further review, the Commission determined that the committee's treasurer had not made best efforts in filing the report in question and assessed a civil money penalty. *Id.* at 5.

C. Proposed Policy Statement

The Commission sought public comment on a Proposed Statement of Policy that would clarify the Commission's current enforcement practice to consider whether the treasurer and committee made best efforts to obtain, maintain or submit the

required information under 11 CFR 104.7(a). *See Proposed Statement of Policy Regarding Treasurer's Best Efforts to Obtain, Maintain, and Submit Information as Required by the Federal Election Campaign Act*, 71 FR 71084 (Dec. 8, 2006). The Commission received two comments, which are available at *http://www.fec.gov/law/ policy.shtml* under the heading "Best Efforts." One comment made several recommendations as to how the Commission could further clarify the best efforts defense by incorporating the business management concept of "best practices" regarding corporate operation, financial controls, risk prevention and risk assessment. The comment also suggested that the Policy Statement provide guidance to political committees and treasurers regarding what conduct would qualify under the best efforts defense, and not rely solely on examples of conduct that would not qualify under the defense. The other comment was not relevant to this Policy Statement.

II. Policy Regarding the Best Efforts Defense

Although the court decision in *Lovely* only concerned permissible defenses within the AFP, the Commission has decided to adopt the court's interpretation of the best efforts defense with regard to other enforcement matters. While the Commission's enforcement practices formerly reflected the view that the best efforts defense was limited to obtaining certain contributor identification information (*see* note 2 above) the Commission recognizes that this narrow application of the defense in previous enforcement matters derives from a single example of the defense's application in its 1979 legislative history.[3] In light of these considerations, the Commission hereby notifies the public and the regulated community through this Policy Statement that henceforth it intends to apply the best efforts defense of 2 U.S.C. 432(i), as promulgated at 11 CFR 104.7, not only to efforts made to obtain contributor information as currently set forth in section 104.7(b),[4] but also to

---

[3] A respondent's assertion in an enforcement matter that best efforts were made to maintain and/ or submit required information was formerly considered by the Commission to be a mitigating factor, but not an outright defense to an alleged violation of the recordkeeping and reporting requirements.

[4] As stated above, the standards for determining whether the best efforts defense is applicable in the context of obtaining specific contributor information are set forth at current 11 CFR 104.7(b). This Policy Statement does not affect or modify those standards.

efforts made to obtain other information, to maintain all information required by the statute, and to submit required information on disclosure reports.

This Policy Statement does not affect the Commission's AFP, but applies only to matters in the Commission's traditional enforcement and audit programs, and in the Alternative Dispute Resolution program ("ADR"). The Commission recently completed a rulemaking adding a best efforts defense to the enumerated defenses available in the AFP. *See Final Rules for Best Efforts in Administrative Fines Challenges,* 72 FR 14662 (Mar. 29, 2007). In that rulemaking, the Commission incorporated the statutory best efforts standard, while taking into account the unique streamlined nature of the AFP. *See id.* at 14666.

The Commission considers best efforts to be "a standard that has diligence as its essence." E. Allan Farnsworth, *On Trying to Keep One's Promises: The Duty of Best Efforts in Contract Law,* 46 U. Pitt. L. Rev. 1, 8 (1984). As the Commission explained in its *Lovely Statement of Reasons* at 2:

Section 432(i) creates a safe harbor for treasurers who "show[] that best efforts" have been made to report the information required to be reported by the Act. "Best" is an adjective of the superlative degree. "Best efforts" must therefore require more than "some" or "good" efforts. Congress's choice of a "best efforts" standard, rather than a "good faith" standard, suggests that a treasurer cannot rely upon his or her earnestness or state of mind to gain the shelter of Section 432(i)'s safe harbor. Rather, a treasurer has the burden of showing that the actions taken—the efforts he or she made to comply with applicable reporting deadlines—meet the statute's demanding benchmark.

With respect to 11 CFR 104.7(a), the Commission intends to consider a committee's affirmative steps to keep adequate records and make accurate reports, as well as the reasons for its failure to obtain, maintain, or submit information properly. The Commission generally intends to consider the following: (1) The actions taken, or systems implemented, by the committee to ensure that required information is obtained, maintained, and submitted; (2) the cause of the failure to obtain, maintain, or submit the information or reports at issue; and (3) the specific efforts of the committee to obtain, maintain, and submit the information or reports at issue. This general policy does not modify other guidance and policy standards issued by the Commission addressing specific circumstances, such as the *Internal Controls for Political Committees,* and *Policy Statement Regarding Safe Harbor*

for Misreporting Due to Embezzlement, 72 FR 16695 (Apr. 5, 2007), both available at *http://www.fec.gov/law/policy.shtml.*

The Commission will generally conclude that a committee has shown best efforts if the committee establishes the following:

• At the time of its failure, the committee took relevant precautions such as double checking recordkeeping entries, regular reconciliation of committee records with bank statements, and regular backup of all electronic files;

• The committee had trained staff responsible for obtaining, maintaining, and submitting campaign finance information in the requirements of the Act as well as the committee's procedures, recordkeeping systems, and filing systems;

• The failure was a result of reasonably unforeseen circumstances beyond the control of the committee, such as a failure of Commission computers or Commission-provided software; severe weather or other disaster-related incidents; a widespread disruption of information transmission over the Internet not caused by any failure of the committee's computer systems or Internet service provider; or delivery failures caused by mail/courier services such as U.S. Postal Service or Federal Express; and

• Upon discovering the failure, the committee promptly took all reasonable additional steps to expeditiously file any unfiled reports and correct any inaccurate reports.

In contrast, the Commission will generally conclude that a committee has not met the best efforts standard if the committee's failure to obtain, maintain, or submit information or reports is due to any of the following:

• Unavailability, inexperience, illness, negligence or error of committee staff, agents, counsel or connected organization(s);

• The failure of a committee's computer system;

• Delays caused by committee vendors or contractors;

• A committee's failure to know or understand the recordkeeping and filing requirements of the Act, or the Act's filing dates; or

• A committee's failure to use Commission-or vendor-provided software properly.

Under this policy, the Commission intends to consider the best efforts of a committee under section 432(i) when reviewing all violations of the recordkeeping and reporting requirements of FECA, whether arising in its traditional enforcement docket

(Matters Under Review), audits, or the ADR Program. The best efforts standard is an affirmative defense and the burden rests with the political committee and its treasurer to present evidence sufficient to demonstrate that best efforts were made. The Commission does not intend to consider the best efforts defense in any enforcement or ADR matter, or in an audit unless a respondent or audited committee asserts the facts that form the basis of that defense.

Effective as of this date, the Commission intends to apply the best efforts standard to all matters currently before the Commission in which a respondent has already asserted such a defense, and any matters in the future involving treasurers' and political committees' obligation to obtain, maintain, and submit information or reports. When treasurers make a sufficient showing of best efforts, the treasurers or committees shall be considered in compliance with FECA.

The above provides general guidance concerning the applicability of the Commission's best efforts defense and announces the general course of action that the Commission intends to follow. This Policy Statement sets forth the Commission's intentions concerning the exercise of its discretion in its enforcement and audit programs. However, the Commission retains that discretion and will exercise it as appropriate with respect to the facts and circumstances of each matter or audit it considers. Consequently, this Policy Statement does not bind the Commission or any member of the general public. As such, it does not constitute an agency regulation requiring notice of proposed rulemaking, opportunities for public participation, prior publication, and delay in effective date under 5 U.S.C. 553 of the Administrative Procedure Act ("APA"). The provisions of the Regulatory Flexibility Act, which apply when notice and comment are required by the APA or another statute, are not applicable.

Dated: June 1, 2007.

Robert D. Lenhard,

Chairman, Federal Election Commission.

FR Doc. E7–10997 Filed 6–6–07; 8:45 am]

BILLING CODE 6715-01-P

Internal Controls and Political Committees

Under the Federal Election Campaign Act (FECA) and the Commission's regulations all political committees are required to file accurate and complete disclosure reports. A system of internal controls can contribute to the accuracy of a committee's disclosure reports. While neither FECA nor the regulations require any particular set of internal controls, implementing effective internal controls plays an important role in meeting those requirements, since misappropriation of funds or unintentional error generally lead to the filing of inaccurate disclosure reports. Conversely, a lack of internal control and oversight can create an environment that contributes to misappropriation of funds, a lack of concern for the accuracy of committee accounting records, and misreporting to the Commission. With respect to misappropriations, in recent years the Commission has noticed an increasing number of instances where committee assets are misappropriated, generally by committee staff. In most of these cases, the staff person who engaged in the misappropriation was a trusted individual who was not properly supervised. There were often no systems of internal control in place that provided an independent check on the activity of those who process the committee's transactions. Absent some basic checks and balances, some people will inevitably give in to temptation. Finally, a system of internal controls, including policies, procedures and budgets, can contribute to the efficient and effective use of committee funds.

As a result, effective internal controls provide the triple benefit of assisting the committee in meeting its goals, protecting committee assets, and facilitating the filing of accurate disclosure reports. To that end, the Commission has prepared the following best practices recommendations. These are not mandatory requirements but are intended to assist committees in protecting their assets and complying with the requirements of the FECA.

We have noted that when the issue of internal control is raised with political committees, often their representatives' respond that they are small operations staffed by volunteers and can't afford elaborate systems of controls. It is, however, in the interest of both the committee and its staff, volunteer or paid, to establish a system of internal controls that will prevent or quickly detect any misappropriation while getting the maximum benefit from the funds that are available. The amount of money involved in the political process has grown rapidly over the past election cycles and it appears that trend will continue. This trend suggests that. as with any business, as the volume of activity grows, the risks and the need to control those risks grow with it.

The responsibility of establishing the necessary control procedures falls to a political committee's treasurer. Internal controls need not be elaborate or expensive to provide reasonable assurance that funds will not be misappropriated. Most importantly, costs associated with recovery from misappropriations, both monetary and non-monetary, are likely to be greater than the cost of prevention. The cost of inefficient use of committee resources may not be recoverable.

This guide should not be the only resource that is consulted. In addition to accounting professionals, there are numerous resources that can be found on the Internet. For example the Small Business Administration offers an internal control check list that can be used as a starting point. A copy can be located at http://www.prescott.edu/faculty_staff/faculty/scorey/documents/sba_2004a.pdf. The Government Accountability Office has published a guide for Government Agencies titled Standards for Internal Control in the Federal Government that explains the components and principles of internal control (http://www.gao.gov/special.pubs/ai00021p.pdf). There are also many other organizations that have posted their control procedures on the Web ranging from State and local government agencies, to educational institutions, to religious organizations. For example, the Comptroller of the State of Connecticut (http://www.osc.state.ct.us/manuals/AcctDirect/contents.htm) has an Accountability Directive that, in Appendix B, **SECTIONS APPLICABLE TO ALL AGENCY PROGRAMS,** includes not only internal control checklists, but flow charts. Much has been written on internal control by experts in the field, the material in this document borrows from a number of those sources.

Naturally, no one set of controls will be right for all political committees. Small organizations that have only a few people involved will have very different needs and resources than a large corporate or union Separate Segregated Fund that has a significant staff and access to the internal auditing resources of the connected organization. This document is aimed at the smaller organizations. Of course, effective internal control depends heavily on the separation of key functions among more than one person .

What are Internal Controls?

Internal control is a *process* designed to ensure that an organization's goals are met with respect to:

- Effective and efficient operations
- Reliable financial reporting,
- Compliance with laws and regulations, and
- Protection of the organization's assets

The best internal control system can provide only *reasonable*, not absolute, assurance that these goals are met. Any system may be defeated either by accident or intentionally through collusion. However, a well-designed system will reduce the risk that errors or intentional acts will occur or go undetected.

The internal control process typically includes the following elements:

- Control Environment
- Risk Assessment
- Control Activities

- Information and Communication
- Monitoring

Although this may sound complicated, in a small organization it is actually very simple. The following describes each of the elements:

Control Environment. At the core of any organization are its people with their individual attributes such as integrity and competence, and the environment in which they operate. There are three key aspects to controlling the environment: 1) Limiting the number of people who have access to any accounting function, assets or records system, 2) Maintaining a separation of functions so that no single individual has complete control over financial transactions, and 3) Providing proper instruction and guidance to relevant staff. Ideally, a committee should utilize the smallest number of individuals needed to accomplish the work and still maintain a separation of duties. These individuals should have an understanding of the importance of control procedures and the role they play in ensuring accurate reporting of all financial activities.

Risk Assessment. The committee must be aware of, and deal with, the risks it faces both monetary and non-monetary. Naturally some assets, such as cash, are more easily diverted than others and the control procedures should take into account the risk that each type of asset presents. Then the committee can establish cost effective ways of managing the related risks.

Control Activities. Control policies and procedures must be established to ensure that risks are minimized. Depending on the size of the organization these procedures may be simple and limited , or complex and more extensive. A simple example would be to assign one person to record transactions and file disclosure reports, while another to review and reconcile them to reports and accounting records.

Information and Communication. Information and communication systems surround all of these activities. They enable people to gather and share the information needed to conduct, manage, and control operations.

Monitoring. The entire process must be monitored, and modifications must be made as necessary. In this way, the system can react dynamically, changing as conditions warrant. In many political committees this is a critical part of the equation. Staff and structures change often and sometimes radically. Therefore it is necessary to reconsider the procedures in place to assure they are still effective and appropriate to the current circumstances.

Follow-up. Once a deficiency in internal control is identified, it is incumbent upon committee management to take steps to minimize the risk. After identifying a potential problem, it is expected that action will be taken to reasonably assure that the committee's affairs will be conducted in a manner that meets the internal control and organizational goals discussed above.

Selected Procedures for Internal Controls

As alluded to earlier, separation of duties is the key ingredient in any internal control system. Without that separation, it is virtually impossible to be reasonably assured that the organization's internal control goals are met. In a small organization there may be as few as two or three individuals involved in the processing, recording and reporting of transactions. With careful planning and assigning of duties it is possible to establish an elementary internal control system with very few people. If the committee staff is very small maintaining some level of separation of duties and independent review is of prime importance. The Treasurer can provide independent review so long as he or she does not process transactions on a day to day basis or prepare disclosure reports .

The controls discussed below include those over cash and non-cash assets that are readily convertible into cash (e.g., liabilities whose liquidation will require the use of cash, such as accounts payable and notes payable). The areas discussed below represent particular vulnerabilities the Commission has identified based on its regulatory experience. They do not represent an exhaustive list of assets to be safeguarded.

Bank Accounts

A. Limit the number of bank accounts to those absolutely required to manage the committee's business. It may, for example, be more convenient to have separate accounts for the primary and general elections and/or receipts and disbursements. Obviously, the fewer the accounts, the greater the control and the smaller the opportunity for errors or wrongdoing.

B. A political committee should obtain from the Internal Revenue Service an employer identification number ("EIN") in the name of the committee and all committee bank accounts should be in the name of the committee and utilize the committee EIN. Never approve the opening of an account in the name of an individual or using an individuals Social Security Number. The mailing address should be a committee address and the statements should be delivered unopened to a person not charged with processing transactions. Only the treasurer or his designee should be permitted to open and close bank accounts. Those with such authority should be specifically named in writing.

C. Limit the number of persons authorized to sign checks. In addition, checks in excess of a certain dollar amount should require the signature of two responsible individuals. The recommended threshold is $1,000. Facsimile signatures should be prohibited unless controlled by a check-signing machine with a numerical sequence counter. No signature stamps should be allowed.

D. Debit and credit cards must be carefully controlled since they represent easy access to committee assets. The committee's bank or credit card issuer may be helpful in this regard. It may be possible to place dollar restrictions on cards, both on a per transaction basis and a cumulative limit. Once expenditures are approved, the limit can be re-established. Limits or prohibitions can also be placed on cash withdrawals.

E. Review the transactions on bank statements and reconcile the statements to the accounting records each month in a timely manner. Many committees find that the use of one of the commercially available small business accounting software packages is useful in this process. They often include a simplified pre-programmed process for reconciling the accounts and locating differences. The review and reconciliation are essential to determining if any errors occurred, unauthorized checks were issued or receipts were stolen. Someone should reconcile the bank statement other than the check signers and those controlling the checking account and processing transactions. The individual responsible for reconciling the account should receive the bank statement unopened. This one step of segregating the processing of transactions and the reconciliation of accounts would have prevented or quickly revealed a number of the misappropriations and the associated false reporting that the Commission has observed in recent years. It is also an excellent technique for discovering errors and omissions that occur accidentally.

F. Prior to filing each report, a reconciliation between bank and accounting records and the disclosure reports should be undertaken. The use of electronic banking can contribute to the timely reconciliation process and allow reconciliations to be easily done when reports do not coincide with bank statement dates. Access to the electronic banking system should be limited.

G. Require all wire transfers to be pre-authorized by two responsible individuals and immediately recorded in the accounting records. A committee sequential identification number (similar to a check number) is often helpful in recording and controlling wire transfers. A gap in the sequence number indicates a wire transfer that was not recorded. The Commission has encountered situations where the failure to record wire transfers has resulted in substantial misstatements in disclosure reports. Naturally, the reconciliation of the checking accounts to the accounting records and the disclosure reports will help prevent the filing of erroneous reports.

H. Finally, investigate other control related services that the committee's bank may be able to provide. With electronic banking, information is available instantly that can contribute to a more secure control environment. Also banks may be able to screen checks that are drawn on committee accounts during their processing for compliance with agreed upon criteria.

Receipts

A. Make a list of receipts when the mail is opened. Ideally, the person opening the mail and preparing the list should be independent of the accounting function. A responsible official should periodically (during the monthly bank reconciliation if not more often) compare the list with the recorded amount for the deposit and the deposit amount on the bank statement. Some committee's have found using a lockbox service (to independently open mail, record the contributions, and make bank deposits) to perform this part of receipt processing beneficial. Such services may be available through the bank.

B. The employee responsible for opening the mail should complete to following:
    — Place restrictive endorsements, such as For Deposit Only to the Account of the Payee, on all checks received. Account number can be added but that addition may cause a security concern by providing each contributor the committee's account number..

— Prepare a list of the money, checks, and other receipts.
— Forward all receipts to the person responsible for preparing and making the daily bank deposits. Cash and check receipts should be deposited intact daily.

C. If the committee receives contributions via debit and credit card, the same type of information described above for checks and cash should be assembled for those contributions[1]. The same verification to bank deposits should also be performed. The procedure will depend on the system that the credit card processor has in place. These control issues should be taken into account before selecting a firm to process the committee's credit card contributions. Commission Advisory Opinion 1999-9 (available on the Commission's Web Site) provides guidance concerning the solicitation and receipt of credit card contributions. Although the Opinion was issued in the context of the Presidential Primary Matching Fund program, it is useful guidance for credit card contributions in non-pubicliy funded campaigns as well.

D. Prohibit delivery of unopened business mail to employees having access to the accounting records.

E. Contributions that are received by committee personnel at events and in person should be subject to the same procedures as those received via mail. Lists should be made and the checks submitted to the person(s) doing other contribution processing.

F. Secure undeposited receipts in a locked cabinet at all times.

G. Cash refunds should require approval.

H. Locations where the physical handling of cash takes place should be reasonably safeguarded.

Disbursements

A. Generally, disbursements should be made with pre-numbered checks, with the exception of petty cash. Using checks for all major cash payments ensures that there is a permanent record of the disbursement. The check should be pre-numbered so that it is accounted for properly. This procedure helps to prevent the issuance of a check that is not recorded in the cash disbursement records. As noted above, it is good practice to require checks in amounts greater than a specified amount to require two signatures. Additionally, pre-signed checks should not be allowed. The use of credit and debit cards should be very carefully controlled and detailed records of the transactions should be required of all users. Avoid using credit and debit cards to withdraw cash. Wire transfers should require dual authorization and each wire should be assigned a sequential number to help assure that all such payments have been recorded. Wire transfers should be recorded in the accounting records immediately.

B. If a mistake is made when preparing a check, void the check before preparing a new one. The voided check should then be altered to prevent its use, retained to make sure all pre-numbered checks are accounted for, and filed with other checks

---

[1] Be aware that credit card processing fees may be netted against the contribution amounts when deposited into the committee's accounts. If so, the gross amount of the contributions must be recorded with the processing fees shown as an expense.

for a permanent record. The stock of unused checks should be safeguarded and regularly inventoried.

C. If possible, check signing should be the responsibility of individuals having no access to the accounting records.

D. Draw checks according to procedures prescribing adequate supporting documentation and authorization. It is in a committee's best interest to ensure that invoices that have been properly authorized support disbursements. This documentation should include (1) a proper original invoice; (2) evidence that the goods or services were received; and (3) evidence that the purchase transaction was properly authorized. Some committees find the use of a check authorization form to be useful. The signatures required for such authorizations can vary based on the size and nature of the transaction.

E. All supporting documents should be canceled or marked "paid" once a disbursement is made to avoid double payments. In the past the Commission has observed instances where failure to take these steps has resulted in many costly duplicate payments. Payments should not be made on statements or balance-due billings unless underlying invoices are included.

F. Mail all checks promptly and directly to the payee or if they are to be delivered by committee staff, require that the person taking control of the checks signs for them. The person mailing the check should be independent of those requesting, writing, and signing it.

Petty Cash

Use an imprest petty cash fund with one custodian. The imprest fund involves replenishing petty cash only when properly approved vouchers and/or petty cash log entries are presented justifying all expenditures. The amount of the replenishment is equal to the difference between the stated amount of the fund and the remaining balance. For accountability, only one person should be in charge of the fund. The amount to be placed in the petty cash fund will need to be determined by the committee based on its operating needs, but should be kept to the minimum amount needed to make small disbursements. A petty cash fund of not more than $500 should be adequate in most cases. If that proves not to be the case, the committee should review its policies concerning which disbursements may be paid from petty cash. No cash disbursement in excess of $100 is permitted.

Payroll

Many committees use a payroll service for much of the payroll function. Where there are more than a few employees; a service can be a very effective way of handling payroll and maintaining a separation of duties within the payroll operation. As an additional benefit, the service will often take care of the preparation and filing of the necessary tax returns, and thereby help avoid errors and associated penalties.

If the committee chooses to handle payroll in-house, the signing and distribution of the checks must be properly handled to prevent their theft. The controls should include limiting the authorization for signing the checks to a responsible person who does not have access to timekeeping or the preparation of the payroll, the distribution of the payroll by someone who is not involved in the other payroll functions, and the immediate return of unclaimed checks for redeposit.

If the committee has more than a few employees, it is advisable that it use an imprest payroll account to help prevent the payment of unrecorded payroll transactions. An imprest payroll account is a separate checking account in which a small balance is maintained. A check for the exact amount of each net payroll is transferred from the general account to the payroll checking account immediately prior to the distribution of the payroll. The advantages of an imprest account are that it limits the organization's exposure to payroll fraud, allows the delegation of payroll check-signing duties, separates routine payroll expenditures from other expenditures, and facilitates cash management.

Payables

The accounts payable/notes payable procedures are clearly related to the procedures for cash disbursements and payroll. The control concern is to make certain that all liabilities are properly recorded and ultimately paid. There should be a proper segregation of duties over the performance of the functions of comparing receiving reports, purchase orders and invoices and the handling of the actual disbursement functions. As noted previously, invoices should be stamped "paid" and payments should not be made from statements of account unless accompanied by the related bills and invoices. These procedures prevent accidentally paying the same charges more than once. For disbursements that are not normally accompanied by an invoice (e.g., payment on a note or office rent), the authorization should come from a responsible official.

Computerized Systems

Most political committees are required to file their reports electronically and therefore many of their accounting records are automated. All of the same control considerations that apply to a manual transaction system apply to an automated system. In particular, separating functions so that data files are reconciled to other records by someone independent of the transaction processing and reporting functions is critical. In addition, in electronic systems the selection of software, the training of staff in the use of that software, limiting access to the system, and security of the data are important considerations.

In many cases, the electronic filing software is separate from accounting software. If this is the situation, determine if data can be exported from the accounting software to the filing software. Not only is it more efficient than entering the data twice, it reduces the opportunity for error.

There is an additional safeguard that is important and sometimes overlooked. The electronic data must be regularly backed up to avoid a loss of data that can interfere with a committee's ability to file timely and accurate disclosure reports. Regardless of whether such a data loss stems from a hardware failure, a software failure, human error, or a disaster such as a fire or flood, the result is the same. There are several ways to accomplish a data back up. In some instances the software supplier will "host" the data meaning that it resides on the supplier's server and is backed up by the supplier. If back up is to be done locally, it can be accomplished by copying the data to a tape or CD and storing the back up off site. Ideally the back up should be done daily.

Conclusion

While no system of internal controls can ever be foolproof and one set of controls is not a good fit for all types of committees, the elements identified above can significantly reduce the opportunity for intentional misappropriation of funds and any related false reporting. Furthermore, many of these internal controls can also reduce the likelihood of inadvertent errors that can result in reporting problems. This discussion of internal controls is not intended to be exhaustive or to prescribe any one set of controls. It is up to each political committee to carefully consider what internal controls are valuable and feasible.

Index

427

About the Author

Since leaving the Federal Election Commission in 1979, Jan Witold Baran has practiced law in Washington, D.C. He is a senior partner at Wiley Rein LLP, and has represented clients in election law and First Amendment cases before the Supreme Court of the United States, lower courts, the Federal Election Commission, state agencies, and the ethics committees of Congress. He served as a member of the Joint Commission to Review the ABA Model Code of Judicial Conduct, and was Special Advisor to the ABA Standing Committee on Judicial Independence. He is past chair of the ABA Standing Committee on Election Law and its Advisory Commission, and was a member of the ABA Commission on Public Financing of Judicial Campaigns.

Jan Baran also served on the President's Commission on Federal Ethics Law Reform and as U.S. Ambassador to an international communications conference. In addition to *The Election Law Primer for Corporations*, he is the author of numerous articles on the subject of law and politics. He is a regular commentator on news and public affairs programs. During the 2000 Florida presidential vote recount, he was a legal analyst for ABC News and ABCNews.com.